Published by
Rajneesh Foundation International
Rajneeshpuram, Oregon 97741, U.S.A.

KRISHNA
The Man and His Philosophy

BHAGWAN SHREE
RAJNEESH

Editors:	Sambuddha Swami Anand Maitreya, M.M., D.Phil.M. (RIMU), Acharya. Former member of the Parliament of India
	Ma Deva Sarito
Design:	Ma Deva Sandipa
Direction:	Sambodhi Ma Yoga Pratima, M.M., D.Phil.M. (RIMU), Arihanta
Copyright:	© 1985 Rajneesh Foundation International
Published by:	Bodhisattvaa Ma Anand Sheela, M.M., D.Phil.M., D.Litt.M. (RIMU), Acharya Rajneesh Foundation International P.O. Box 9, Rajneeshpuram Oregon 97741, U.S.A.
1st Edition:	July 1985 - 10,000 copies

Printed in the U.S.A.
ISBN: 0-88050-713-6
Library of Congress Catalog Card Number: 85-43055

CONTENTS

INTRODUCTION

The words of a Master have a quality that speaks to something deep within us, sometimes whispering, sometimes shouting, "This is it; this is what I have been searching for." And so it is with the message of truth given to us by the living Master, Bhagwan Shree Rajneesh.

These discourses were given fifteen years ago to small groups of seekers during a meditation camp at Manali, India, near the foot of the Himalayas. They are just as fresh, as full of meaning and relevance to our lives today as when Bhagwan gave them years ago.

When Bhagwan speaks of Krishna, He speaks not only of Himself but of the potential, the possibility that exists for each of us to become a dancing, celebrating Krishna—free to be strong, full of fire yet loving and compassionate; free to live life now, today, enjoying and accepting life's contradictions.

"In the whole galaxy of religious luminaries, Krishna is the sole exception who fully accepts the whole of life on this earth. He does not believe in living here for the sake of another world and another life. He believes in living this very life, here on this very earth. . . . Krishna's freedom is here and now."

And when Bhagwan decides, during the Manali meditation camp, to initiate His first neo-sannyasins, He leaves behind the negative sannyas of renunciation to give birth to a new sannyas of life-affirmative joy, freedom and celebration. He brings the spirit of Krishna and his dancing flute into the twenty-first century.

"Sannyas has to be invested with a new meaning, a new concept. Sannyas has to live; it is the most, the most precious treasure that mankind has. But how to save it, preserve it, is the question. I would like to share with you my vision."

Bodhisattva Swami Anand Madyapa, M.Ed., M.M., D.Phil.M.(RIMU), Acharya

KRISHNA
The Man and His Philosophy

BHAGWAN SHREE
RAJNEESH

Discourses from Bombay,
July 20, 1970
and
Kulu-Manali,
September 26 - October 5, 1970

FIRST DISCOURSE
JULY 20, 1970
CCI CHAMBERS, BOMBAY

THE FUTURE BELONGS TO KRISHNA

Questioner: What are the distinguishing virtues of Krishna that make him relevant to our time? What is his significance for us? Please explain.

rishna is utterly incomparable, he is so unique. Firstly, his uniqueness lies in the fact that although Krishna happened in the ancient past he belongs to the future, is really of the future. Man has yet to grow to that height where he can be a contemporary of Krishna's. He is still beyond man's understanding; he continues to puzzle and battle us. Only in some future time will we be able to understand him and appreciate his virtues. And there are good reasons for it.

The most important reason is that Krishna is the sole great man in our whole history who reached the absolute height and depth of religion, and yet he is not at all serious and sad, not in tears. By and large, the chief characteristic of a religious person has been that he is somber, serious and sad-looking—like one vanquished in the battle of life, like a renegade from life. In the long line of such sages it is Krishna alone who comes dancing, singing and laughing.

Religions of the past were all life-denying and masochistic, extolling sorrow and suffering as great virtues. If you set aside Krishna's vision of religion, then every religion of the past presented a sad and sorrowful face. A laughing religion, a religion that accepts life in its totality is yet to be born. And it is good that the old religions are dead, along with them, that the old God, the God of our old concepts is dead too.

It is said of Jesus that he never laughed. It was perhaps his sad look and the picture of his physical form on the cross that became the focal point of attraction for people, most of whom are themselves unhappy and miserable. In a deep sense Mahavira and Buddha are against life too. They are in favor of some other life in some other world; they support a kind of liberation from this life.

Every religion, up to now, has divided life into two parts, and while they accept one part they deny the other, Krishna alone accepts the whole of life. Acceptance of life in its totality has attained full fruition in Krishna. That is why India held him to be a perfect incarnation of God, while all other incarnations were assessed as imperfect and incomplete. Even Rama is described as an incomplete incarnation of God. But Krishna is the whole of God.

And there is a reason for saying so. The reason is that Krishna has accepted and absorbed everything that life is.

Albert Schweitzer made a significant remark in criticism of the Indian religion. He said that the religion of this country is life-negative. This remark is correct to a large extent, if Krishna is left out. But it is utterly wrong in the context of Krishna. If Schweitzer had tried to understand Krishna he would never have said so.

But it was unfortunate that we did not allow Krishna to influence our life in a broad way. He remains a lonely dancing island in the vast ocean of sorrow and misery that is our life. Or, we can say he is a small oasis of joyous dancing and celebration in the huge desert of sadness and negativity, of suppression and condemnation that we really are. Krishna could not influence the whole spectrum of our life, and for this we are alone to blame. Krishna is not in the least responsible for it. We were not that worthy, that deserving, to have him, to imbibe him, to absorb him.

Up to now, man's mind has thought of and looked at life in fragments—and thought dialectically. The religious man denies the body and accepts the soul. And what is worse, he creates a conflict, a dichotomy between the body and spirit. He denies this world, he accepts the other world, and thus creates a state of hostility between the two. Naturally our life is going to be sad and miserable if we deny the body, because all our life's juice—its health and vitality, its sensitivities and beauty, all its music—has its source in the body. So a religion that denies and denounces the body is bound to be anemic and ill, it has to be lackluster. Such a religion is going to be as pale and lifeless as a dry leaf fallen from a tree. And the people who follow such a religion, who allow themselves to be influenced and conditioned by it, will be as anemic and prone to death as these leaves are.

Krishna alone accepts the body in its totality. And he accepts it not in any selected dimension but in all its dimensions. Apart from Krishna, Zarathustra is another. About him it is said he was born laughing. Every child enters this world crying. Only one child in all of history laughed at the time of his birth, and that was Zarathustra. And this is an index—an index of the fact that a happy and laughing humanity is yet to be born. And only a joyful and laughing humanity can accept Krishna.

Krishna has a great future. After Freud the world of religion is not going to be the same as it was before him. Freud stands as a watershed between the religions of the past and the religion of the future. With Freud a great revolution has taken place and man's consciousness has achieved a breakthrough. We shall never be the same again after Freud. A new peak of consciousness has been touched and a new understanding, an altogether new perspective, a new vision of life has come into being. And it is essential to understand it rightly.

The old religions taught suppression as the way to God. Man was asked to suppress everything— his sex, his anger, his greed, his attachments—and then alone would he find his soul, would he attain to God. This war of man against himself has continued long enough. And in the history of thousands of years of this war, barely a handful of people, whose names can be counted on one's fingers, can be said to have found God. So in a sense we lost this war, because down the centuries billions of people died without finding their souls, without meeting God.

Undoubtedly there must be some basic flaw, some fundamental mistake in the very foundation of these religions.

It is as if a gardener has planted fifty thousand trees and out of them only one tree flowers—and yet we accept his scripture on gardening on the plea that at least one tree has blossomed. But we fail to take into consideration that this single tree might have been an exception to the rule, that it might have blossomed not because of the gardener, but in spite of him. The rest of the fifty thousand trees, those that remained stunted and barren, are enough proof the gardener was not worth his salt.

If a Buddha, a Mahavira or a Christ attains to God in spite of these fragmentary and conflict-ridden religions, it is no testimony to the success of these religions as such. The success of religion, or let us say the success of the gardener, should be acclaimed only when all fifty thousand trees of his garden, with the exception of one or two, achieve flowering. Then the blame could be laid at the foot of the one tree for its failure to bloom. Then it could be said that this tree remained stunted and barren in spite of the gardener.

With Freud a new kind of awareness has dawned on man: that suppression is wrong, that suppression brings with it nothing but self-pity and anguish. If a man fights with himself he can only ruin and destroy himself. If I make my left hand fight with my right hand, neither is going to win, but in the end the contest will certainly destroy me. While my two hands fight with themselves, I and I alone will be destroyed in the process. That is how, through denial and suppression of his natural instincts and emotions, man became suicidal and killed himself.

Krishna alone seems to be relevant to the new awareness, to the new understanding that came to man in the wake of Freud and his findings. It is so because in the whole history of the old humanity Krishna alone is against repression.

He accepts life in all its facets, in all its climates and colors. He alone does not choose; he accepts life unconditionally. He does not shun love; being a man he does not run away from women. As one who has known and experienced God, he alone does not turn his face from war. He is full of love and compassion, and yet he has the courage to accept and fight a war. His heart is utterly non-violent, yet he plunges into the fire and fury of violence when it becomes unavoidable. He accepts the nectar, and yet he is not afraid of poison.

In fact, one who knows the deathless should be free of the fear of death. And of what worth is that nectar which is afraid of death? One who knows the secret of non-violence should cease to fear violence.

What kind of non-violence is it that is scared of violence? And how can the spirit, the soul, fear the body and run away from it? And what is the meaning of God if he cannot take the whole of this world in his embrace?

Krishna accepts the duality, the dialectics of life altogether and therefore transcends duality. What we call transcendence is not possible so long as you are in conflict, so long as you choose one part and reject the other. Transcendence is only possible when you choicelessly accept both parts together, when you accept the whole.

That is why Krishna has great significance for the future. And his significance will continue to grow with the passage of time. When the glow and the glamor of all other godmen and messiahs has dimmed, when the suppressive religions of the world have been consigned to the wastebasket of history, Krishna's flame will be heading towards its peak, moving towards the pinnacle of its brilliance. It will be so because, for the first time, man will be able to comprehend him, to understand him and to imbibe him. And it will be so because, for the first time, man will really deserve him and his blessings.

It is really arduous to understand Krishna. It is easy to understand that a man should run away from the world if he wants to find peace, but it is really difficult to accept that one can find peace in the thick of the marketplace. It is understandable that a man can attain to purity of mind if he breaks away from his attachments, but it is really difficult to realize that one can remain unattached and innocent in the very midst of relationships and attachments, that one can remain calm and still live at the very center of the cyclone. There is no difficulty in accepting that the flame of a candle will remain steady and still in a place well secluded from winds and storms, but how can you believe that a candle can keep burning steadily even in the midst of raging storms and hurricanes?

So it is difficult even for those who are close to Krishna to understand him.

For the first time in his long history man has attempted a great and bold experiment through Krishna. For the first time, through Krishna, man has tested, and tested fully his own strength and intelligence. It has been tested and found that man can remain, like a lotus in water, untouched and unattached while living in the throes of relationship. It has been discovered that man can hold to his love and compassion even on the battlefield, that he can continue to love with his whole being while wielding a sword in his hand.

It is this paradox that makes Krishna difficult to understand. Therefore, people who have loved and worshipped him have done so by dividing him into parts, and they have worshipped his different fragments, those of their liking. No one has accepted and worshipped the whole of Krishna, no one has embraced him in his entirety. Poet Surdas sings superb hymns of praise to the Krishna of his childhood, Balkrishna. Surdas' Krishna never grows up, because there is a danger with a grown-up Krishna which Surdas cannot take. There is not much trouble with a boy Krishna flirting with the young women of his village, but it will be too much if a grown-up Krishna does the same. Then it will be difficult to understand him.

After all, we can understand something on our own plane, on our own level. There is no way to understand something on a plane other than ours.

So for their adoration of Krishna, different people have chosen different facets of his life. Those who love the *Geeta* will simply ignore the *Bhagwad*, because the Krishna of the *Geeta* is so different from the Krishna of the *Bhagwad*. Similarly, those who love the *Bhagwad* will avoid getting involved with the *Geeta*. While the Krishna of the *Geeta* stands on a battlefield surrounded by violence and war, the

Krishna of the *Bhagwad* is dancing, singing and celebrating. There is seemingly no meeting-point whatsoever between the two.

There is perhaps no one like Krishna, no one who can accept and absorb in himself all the contradictions of life, all the seemingly great contradictions of life. Day and night, summer and winter, peace and war, love and violence, life and death—all walk hand in hand with him. That is why everyone who loves him has chosen a particular aspect of Krishna's life that appealed to him and quietly dropped the rest.

Gandhi calls the *Geeta* his mother, and yet he cannot absorb it, because his creed of non-violence conflicts with the grim inevitability of war as seen in the *Geeta*. So Gandhi finds ways to rationalize the violence of the *Geeta*: he says the war of Mahabharat is only a metaphor, that it did not actually happen. This war, Gandhi says over and over again, represents the inner war between good and evil that goes on inside a man. The Kurushetra of the *Geeta*, according to Gandhi, is not a real battlefield located somewhere on this earth, nor is the Mahabharat an actual war. It is not that Krishna incites Arjuna to fight a real Mahabharat, Mahabharat only symbolizes the inner conflict and war of man, and so it is just a parable.

Gandhi has his own difficulty. The way Gandhi's mind is, Arjuna will be much more in accord with him than Krishna. A great upsurge of non-violence has arisen in the mind of Arjuna, and he seems to be strongly protesting against war. He is prepared to run away from the battlefield and his arguments seem to be compelling and logical. He says it is no use fighting and killing one's own family and relatives. For him, wealth, power and fame, won through so much violence and bloodshed, have no value whatsoever. He would rather be a beggar than a king, if kingship costs so much blood and tears. He calls war an evil and violence a sin and wants to shun it at all costs. Naturally Arjuna has a great appeal for Gandhi. How can he then understand Krishna?

Krishna very strongly urges Arjuna to drop his cowardice and fight like a true warrior. And his arguments in support of war are beautiful, rare and unique. Never before in history have such unique and superb arguments been advanced in favor of fighting, in support of war. Only a man of supreme non-violence could give such support to war.

Krishna tells Arjuna, "So long as you believe you can kill someone, you are not a man with a soul, you are not a religious man. So long as you think that one dies, you don't know that which is within us, that which has never died and will never die. If you think you can kill someone you are under a great illusion, you are betraying your ignorance. The concept of killing and dying is materialistic; only a materialist can believe so. There is no dying, no death for one who really knows." So Krishna exhorts Arjuna over and over again in the *Geeta*, "This is all play-acting; killing or dying is only a drama."

In this context it is necessary to understand why we call the life of Rama a characterization, a story, a biography, and not a play, a *leela*. It is because Rama is very serious. But we describe the life of Krishna as his *leela*, his play-acting, because Krishna is not serious at all. Rama is bounded, he is limited. He is bound, limited by his ideals and principles. Scriptures call him the greatest idealist: he is circumscribed by the rules of conduct and character. He will never step out of his limits; he will sacrifice everything for his principles, for his character.

Krishna's life, on the other hand, accepts no limitations. It is not bound by any rules of conduct, it is unlimited and vast. Krishna is free, limitlessly free. There is no ground he cannot tread; no point where his steps can fear and falter, no limits he cannot transcend. And this freedom, this vastness of Krishna, stems from his experience of self-knowledge. It is the ultimate fruit of his enlightenment.

For this reason the question of violence has become meaningless in Krishna's life. Now, violence is just not possible. And where violence is meaningless, non-violence loses its relevance too. Non-violence has meaning only in relation to violence. The moment you accept that violence is possible, non-violence becomes relevant at once. In fact, both violence and non-violence are two sides of the same coin. And it is a materialistic coin. It is materialistic to think that one is violent or non-violent. He is a materialist who believes he can kill someone, and he too is a materialist who thinks he is not going to kill anyone. One thing is common to them: they believe someone can be really killed. Spirituality rejects both violence and non-violence, it accepts the immortality of the soul. And such spirituality turns even war into play.

Spirituality or religion accepts, and unreservedly accepts, all the dimensions of life. It accepts sex and attachment together, relationship and indulgence, love and devotion, yoga and meditation, and everything there is to life.

And the possibility of the understanding and acceptance of this philosophy of totality is growing every day—because now we have come to know a few truths we never knew in the past. Krishna, however, has undoubtedly known them.

For instance, we now know that the body and soul are not separate, that they are two poles of the same phenomenon. The visible part of the soul is known as the body, and the invisible part of the body is called the soul. God and the world are not two separate entities; there is absolutely no conflict between God and nature. Nature is the visible, the gross aspect of God, and God is the invisible, the subtle aspect of nature. There is no such point in the cosmos where nature ends and God begins. It is nature itself that, through a subtle process of its dissolution, turns into God, and it is God himself who, through a subtle process of his manifestation, turns into nature. Nature is manifest God, and God is unmanifest nature. And that is what *adwait* means, what the principle of one without the other means.

We can understand Krishna only if we clearly understand this concept of *adwait*, that only one is— one without the other. You can call him God or *Brahman* or what you like.

We also have to understand why Krishna is going to be increasingly significant for the future and how he is going to become closer and closer to man. It will be so, because the days when suppression and repression ruled the roost are gone. After a lengthy struggle and a long spell of inquiry and investigation we have learned that the forces we have been fighting are our own forces. In reality we are those forces, and it is utter madness to fight them. We have also learned we become prisoners of the forces we oppose and fight, and then it becomes impossible to free ourselves from them. And now we also know that we can never transform them if we treat them as inimical forces, if we resist and repress them.

For instance, if someone fights with sex, he will never attain to *brahmacharya*, to celibacy in his life. There is only one way to celibacy and that is through the transformation of the sex energy itself. So we don't have to fight with the energy of sex; on the contrary, we should understand it and cooperate with it. We need to make friends with sex rather than make an enemy of it, as we have been doing for so long. The truth is, we can only change our friends; the question of changing those we treat as enemies simply does not arise. There is no way to even understand our enemies; it is just impossible. To understand something it is essential to be friendly with it.

Let us clearly understand that what we think to be the lowest is the other pole of the highest. The peak of a mountain and the valley around its base are not two separate things, they are part and parcel of the same phenomenon. The deep valley has been caused by the rising mountain, and in the same way the mountain has been possible because of the valley. One cannot be without the other. Or can it? Linguistically the mountain and the valley are two, but existentially they are two poles of the same thing.

Nietzsche has a very significant maxim. He says a tree that longs to reach the heights of heaven must sink its roots to the bottom of the earth. A tree that is afraid to do so should abandon its longing to reach the heavens. Really, the higher a tree the deeper its roots go. If you want to ascend to the skies you will have to descend into the abyss as well. Height and depth are not different things, they are two dimensions of the same thing. And their proportions are always the same.

Man's mind has always wanted to choose between the seeming opposites. He wants to preserve heaven and do away with hell. He wants to have peace and escape tension. He desires to protect good and destroy evil. He longs to accept light and deny darkness. He craves to cling to pleasure and to shun pain. His mind has always divided existence into two parts and chosen one part against the other. And from choice arises duality, which brings conflict and pain.

Krishna symbolizes acceptance of the opposites together. And he alone can be whole who accepts the contradictions together. One who chooses will always be incomplete, less than the whole, because the part he chooses will continue to delude him and the part he denies will continue to pursue and haunt him. He can never be rid of what he rejects and represses. The mind of the man who rejects and represses sex becomes increasingly sexual. So a culture, a religion that teaches suppression of sex ends up creating nothing but sexuality; it becomes obsessed with sex.

Up to now we have stubbornly denied the Krishna who accepts sex; we accept him only in fragments. But now it will be quite possible to accept him totally, because we are beginning to understand that it is the energy of sex itself that is transformed into the highest kind of celibacy, into *brahmacharya*— through the process of its upward journey to the *sahasrar*, to the ultimate center in the head. We are beginning to learn that nothing in life has to be denied its place and given up, that we have to accept and live life in its totality. And he who lives wholly attains to life's wholeness. And he alone is holy who is whole.

Therefore I say that Krishna has immense significance for our future. And that future, when Krishna's image will shine in all its brilliance, is increasingly close. And whenever a laughing, singing and dancing religion comes into being it will certainly have Krishna's stone in its foundation.

> *Questioner: Krishna played a great role in the war of the Mahabharat. It means he could have prevented it if he had wanted. But the war took place, bringing horrendous death and destruction in its wake. Naturally the responsibility should lie with him. Do you justify him or is he to be blamed?*

It is the same with war and peace. Here too, we choose. We want to keep peace and eliminate conflict and struggle. It seems we cannot act without choosing. But the world is a unity of contradictions and dialectics. The world is an orchestra of opposite notes; it cannot be a solo.

I have heard that once someone was playing a musical instrument. He played a single note on a single string at a single point, and he played it for hours on end. Not only his family, even the neighborhood felt disturbed by it. Finally a group of people came and said to him, "We have heard any number of musicians and they all play a number of different notes. How come you are stuck with a single note?" The man answered, "I have found the right note; others are still searching for it. That is why I stick to the right spot. I need not search any more."

Our minds would like to choose a single note of life and deny all others. But only in death can one find a single note. As far as life is concerned, it is composed of different and contradictory notes. If you have seen an arched door in some old building, you might have noticed that, to construct it, opposite kinds of bricks are laid side by side. And it is the opposite kinds of bricks, placed together, that hold the heavy burden of the house on their shoulders. Can you conceive of using the same kinds of bricks in the construction of an archway? Then the house cannot be constructed; it will collapse then and there.

The entire structure of our life is held together by the tension of its opposites—and war is a part of the tension that is life. And those who think that war is totally harmful and destructive are wrong; their vision is fragmentary, myopic. If we try to understand the course of development that man and his civilization have followed, we will realize that war plays the largest share in its growth. Whatever man has today—all the good things of life—were found primarily through the medium of war. If we find today that the whole earth is covered with roads and highways, the credit should go to war and to preparations for war. These roads and highways were first constructed for the sake of waging war, for the purpose of dispatching armies to distant lands. They did not come into being for the sake of two friends meeting or for a man and a woman belonging to two distant towns to marry. The fact is, they came into being for the encounter of two enemies, for the purpose of war.

We see big buildings all over. They all came in the wake of castles. And castles were the products of war. The first high walls on this earth were built with a view to keep out the enemies, and then other high walls and buildings followed. And now we have skyscrapers in all the big cities of the world. But it is difficult to think that these highrises are the progenies of war.

All of man's modern affluence, backed by scientific inventions and high technology—indeed all his achievements—basically owe their existence to war.

In fact, war creates such a state of tension in the mind of man and presents such challenges, that our dormant energies are shaken to their roots and, as a result, they awaken and act. We can afford to be lazy and lethargic in times of peace, but moments of war are quite different. War provokes our dynamism. Confronted with extraordinary challenges, our sleeping energies have to awaken and assert themselves. That is why, during a war, we function as extraordinary people; we simply cease to be the ordinary people that we are. Confronted with the challenge of war, man's brain begins to function at its highest level and capacity. In times of war man's intelligence takes a great leap forward, one it would ordinarily take centuries to make.

Many people think that if Krishna had prevented the war of Mahabharat, India would have attained to great affluence, she would have touched high peaks of growth and greatness. But the truth is just the opposite. If we had had a few more people of Krishna's caliber and had fought more wars like the Mahabharat, we would have been at the pinnacle of our growth today. About five thousand years have passed since the Mahabharat, and for these five thousand years we have not fought a single major war. The wars we have had since then were baby wars in comparison with that epic war of the Kurukshetra.

They have been quite petty and insignificant. Indeed it would be wrong to even call them wars, they were petty fights and skirmishes. Had we only fought some major wars we would be the richest and most advanced country on this planet today. But our present state of affairs is just the opposite: we are at the bottom of the ladder.

The countries that fought great wars are at the pinnacle of development and prosperity today. At the end of the First World War people thought Germany was destroyed, debilitated for good. But in just twenty years, in the Second World War, Germany emerged as an infinitely more powerful country than the Germany of the First World War. No one could have even dreamed this country could fight another war after she was so badly beaten in the first. Seemingly, there was no possibility for Germany to go to war for hundreds of years. But just in twenty years time the miracle happened, and Germany emerged as a giant world power. Why?—because with will and vigor this country utilized the energies released by the First World War.

With the conclusion of the Second World War it seemed that there might be no more wars in the world. But, so soon, the powers that fought it are ready for a much deadlier and dreadful war than the last. And the two countries—Germany and Japan—that suffered the worst destruction and defeat in the last war have emerged, amazingly, as two of the most affluent countries in the world. Who can say, after visiting today's Japan, that only twenty years ago atom bombs fell on this country? Of course, after visiting present-day India, one could say that this country has been subjected to recurring atomic bombardments. One look at our wretched state can make one think that, down the ages, we have been through unending destruction brought about by war after war.

The Mahabharat is not responsible for India's degradation and misery. The long line of teachers that came in the shadow of that war were all against war, and they used the Mahabharat to further their anti-war stance. Pointing to that great war they said, "What a terrible war! What appalling violence! No, no more of such wars! No more of such bloodshed!" It was unfortunate we failed to produce a line of people of the caliber of Krishna and also failed to fight more Mahabharats. Had it been so, we would have reached, in every succeeding war, a peak of consciousness much higher than the one reached during the Mahabharat. And, undoubtedly, today we would be the most prosperous and developed society on this earth.

There is another side of war which deserves consideration. A war like the Mahabharat does not happen in a poor and backward society; it needs riches to wage a great war. At the same time war is needed to create wealth and prosperity, because war is a time of great challenges. If only we had many more wars like the one Krishna led!

Let us look at this thing from another angle. Today the West has achieved the same height of growth that India had achieved at the time of the Mahabharat. Almost all the highly sophisticated weapons of war that we now possess were used in the Mahabharat in some form or other. It was a highly developed, intelligent and scientific peak that India had scaled at the time of that historic war. And it was not the war that harmed us. Something else harmed us. What really harmed us was the fit of frustration that came over us in the wake of the war, and its exploitation by the teachers of those times. The same fit of frustration has now seized the West, and the West is frightened. And if the West falls, the pacifists will be held responsible for it. And its fall is certain if the West follows the pacifists. Then the West will be in the same mess that India found herself in after the Mahabharat.

India listened to her pacifists and had to suffer for it for five thousand years. So this matter needs to be considered fully.

Krishna is not a hawk, not a supporter of war for war's sake. He, however, treats war as part of life's game. But he is not a warmonger. He has no desire whatsoever to destroy anyone; he does not want to hurt anyone. He has made every effort to avoid war, but he is certainly not prepared to escape war at any cost—at the cost of life and truth and religion itself. After all, there should be a limit to our efforts to avoid war, or anything else for that matter. We want to avoid war just for so it does not hurt and harm life. But what if life itself is hurt and harmed by preventing war? Then its prevention has no meaning. Even the pacifist wants to prevent war so that peace is preserved. But what sense is there in preventing a war if peace suffers because of it? In that case, we certainly need to have the strength and ability to wage a clear war, a decisive war.

Krishna is not a hawk, but he is not a frightened escapist either. He says it is good to avoid war, but if it becomes unavoidable it is better to accept it bravely and joyfully than to run away from it. Running away would be really cowardly and sinful. If a moment comes when, for the good of mankind, war becomes necessary—and such moments do come—then it should be accepted gracefully and happily. Then it is really bad to be dragged into it and to fight it with a reluctant and heavy heart. Those who go to war with dragging feet, just to defend themselves, court defeat and disaster. A defensive mind, a mind that is always on the defensive, cannot gather that strength and enthusiasm necessary to win a war. Such a mind will always be on the defensive, and will go on shrinking in every way. Therefore Krishna tells you to turn even fighting into a joyful, blissful affair.

It is not a question of hurting others. In life

there is always a choice of proportions, a choice between the proportion of good and of evil. And it is not necessary that war bring only evil. Sometimes the avoidance of war can result in evil. Our country was enslaved for a full thousand years just because of our incapacity to fight a war. Similarly, our five-thousand-year-old poverty and degradation is nothing but the result of a lack of courage and fearlessness in our lives, a lack of expansiveness in our hearts and minds.

We suffered not because of Krishna. On the contrary, we suffered because we failed to continue the line of Krishna, because we ceased to produce more Krishnas after him. Of course, it was natural that after Krishna's war a note of pessimism, of defeatism, became prominent in our life—it always happens in the wake of wars—and that a row of defeatist teachers successfully used this opportunity to tell us that war is an unmitigated evil to be shunned at all costs. And this defeatist teaching took root, deep in our minds. So for five thousand years we have been a frightened people, frightened for our lives. And a community that is afraid of death, afraid of war, eventually begins, deep down in its being, to be afraid of life itself. And we are that community—afraid of living. We are really trembling with fear. We are neither alive nor dead, we are just in limbo.

In my view, mankind will suffer if they accept what Bertrand Russell and Gandhi say. There is no need to be afraid of war.

It is true, however, that our earth is now too small for a modern war. A war, in fact, needs space too. Our instruments of war are now so gigantic that, obviously, war on this planet is simply not possible. But it is so, not because what the pacifists say is right and has to be accepted out of fear, but because the earth is now too small for the huge means of war science and technology have put into our hands. So war on this planet has become meaningless. Now the shape of war is going to change and its scope, escalate. New wars will be fought on the moon and Mars, on other planets and satellites.

Scientists say there are at least fifty thousand planets in the universe where life exists. And if we accept the counsel of despair, if we listen to those who are frightened of nuclear weaponry, we will prevent the great adventure which man is now going to make into the vast infinity of space. But it is true we have reached a point where war on this earth has become meaningless. But why it is so has to be clearly understood.

War has become meaningless not because what the pacifists say has struck home with us, war has lost its meaning because the science of war has attained perfection, because now a total war can be a reality. And to fight a total war on this earth will be a self-defeating exercise. War is meaningful so long as one side wins and another loses, but in a nuclear war, if and when it takes place, there will be no victor and no vanquished—both will simply disappear from the earth. So war on this earth has become irrelevant.

And for this reason I can see the whole world coming together as one world. Now the world will be no more than a global village.

The earth has become as small as a village— even smaller than a village. It now takes less time to go around the world than it took to go from one village to another in the past. So this world has become too small for a total kind of war; it would be sheer stupidity to wage a war here. This does not mean there should be no wars, nor does it mean there will be no wars in the future. War will continue to take place, but now it will take place on newer grounds, on other planets. Now man will go on newer adventures, newer incursions and greater campaigns. In spite of what the pacifists said and did war could not be abolished. It cannot be abolished because it is a part of life.

It makes an interesting story if we assess the gains we have had from war. A careful observation will reveal that all our cooperative efforts and institutions are the products of war. It is called cooperation for conflict: we cooperate to fight. And with the disappearance of war, cooperation will disappear.

So it is extremely important to understand Krishna. Krishna is neither a pacifist nor a hawk. He has nothing to do with any "ism". In fact, an "ism" means choice, that we choose one of the opposites. Krishna is "non-ism". He says that if good comes through peace, we should welcome peace, and that if good flows from war then war is equally welcome. Do you understand what I mean? Krishna says, and I say the same, that whatever brings bliss and benediction and helps the growth of religion is welcome. We should welcome it.

We would not have been that impotent if our country had understood Krishna rightly. But we have covered all our ugliness with beautiful words. Our cowardice is hiding behind our talk of non-violence; our fear of death is disguised by our opposition to war. But war is not going to end because we refuse to go to war. Our refusal will simply become an invitation to others to wage war on us. War will not disappear just because we refuse to fight: our refusal will only result in our slavery. And this is what has actually happened.

It is so ironic that, despite our opposition to war, we have been dragged into war over and over again. First we refused to fight, then some external power attacked and occupied our country and made us into slaves, and then we were made to join our masters' armies and fight in our masters' wars. Wars were continuously waged, and we were continuously dragged into them. Sometimes we fought as soldiers of the Huns, then as soldiers of the Turks and the Moghals and finally as soldiers of the British. Instead of fighting for our own life and liberty we fought for the sake of our alien rulers and oppressors. We really fought for the sake of our slavery; we fought to prolong our enslavement. We spilled our blood and gave our lives only to defend our bondage, to continue to live in servitude. This has been the painful consequence of all our opposition to violence and war.

But the Mahabharat is not responsible for it, nor is Krishna responsible. Our lack of courage to fight another Mahabharat is at the root of all our misfortunes.

Therefore I say it is really difficult to understand Krishna. It is very easy to understand a pacifist, because he has clearly chosen one side of the coin of truth. It is also easy to understand warmongers like Genghis, Tamburlaine, Hitler and Mussolini, because they believe in war as the only way of life. Pacifists like Gandhi and Russell believe that peace alone is the right way. Both doves and hawks are simplistic in their approach to life and living. Krishna is altogether different from both of them, and that is what makes him so difficult to understand. He says that life passes through both doors, through the door of peace and also through the door of war. And he says that if man wants to maintain peace, he needs to have the strength and ability to fight a war and win it. And he asserts that in order to fight a war well, it is necessary, simultaneously, to make due preparations for peace.

War and peace are twin limbs of life, and we cannot do without either of them. We will simply be lame and crippled if we try to manage with only one of our two legs. So hawks like Hitler and Mussolini and doves like Gandhi and Russell are equally crippled, lopsided, useless. How can a man walk on one leg alone? No progress is possible.

When we have men like Hitler and Gandhi, each with one leg, we find them taking turns, just like passing fashions. For a while Hitler is stage-center, and then Gandhi appears and dominates the stage. For a while we take one step with Hitler's leg and then another step with Gandhi's leg. So in a way they again make for a pair of legs. After Genghis, Hitler and Stalin are finished with their war and bloodshed, Gandhi and Russell begin to impress us with their talk of peace and non-violence. The pacifists dominate the scene for ten to fifteen years—enough time to tire their single leg, and necessitate the use of another. Then again a hawk like Mao comes with a Stein gun in his hands. And thus the drama is kept on going.

Krishna has his two legs intact; he is not lame. And I maintain that everyone should have both legs intact—one for peace and another for war. A person who cannot fight is certainly lacking in something. And a person who cannot fight is incapable of being rightly peaceful. And one who is incapable of being peaceful is also crippled, and will soon lose his sanity. And a restless mind is incapable of fighting, because even when one has to fight a kind of peace is needed. So even from this point of view Krishna is going to be significant for our future.

In regard to our future we need to have a very clear and decisive mind. Do we want a pacifist world in the future? If so, it will be a lifeless and lackluster world, which is neither desirable nor possible. And no one will accept it either. In fact, life goes its own way. While the doves fly in the sky, the hawks continue to prepare for war. And in the way of fashions, the pacifists will be popular for a while and then the warmongers will take their turn, becoming popular with the people. Really, the two work like partners in a common enterprise.

Krishna stands for an integrated life, a total life; his vision is wholly whole. And if we rightly understand this vision, we need not give up either. Of course, the levels of war will change. They always change. Krishna is not a Genghis; he is not fond of destroying others, of hurting others. So the levels of war will certainly change. And we can see historically how the levels of war change from time to time.

When men don't have to fight among themselves, they gather together and begin to fight with nature. It is remarkable that the communities that developed science and technology are the same that are given to fighting wars. It is so because they possess the fighting potential. So when they don't fight among themselves, they turn their energies towards fighting with nature.

After the Mahabharat, India ceased to fight with nature simply because she turned her back on fighting. We did nothing to control floods and droughts or to tame our rivers and mountains, and consequently we failed, utterly, to develop science and technology. We can develop science only if we fight nature. And if man continues to fight he will first discover the secrets of this earth by fighting its nature. And then he will discover the secrets of space and other planets by fighting their nature. His adventure, his campaign will never stop.

Remember, the society that fought and won a war was the first to land its men on the moon. We could not do it; the pacifists could not do it. And the moon is going to exert tremendous significance on war in the future. Those who own the moon will own this earth, because in the coming war they will set up their missiles on the moon and conquer this earth for themselves. This earth will cease to be the locale for war. The so-called wars that are currently being fought between Vietnam and Cambodia, between

India and Pakistan, are nothing more than play-fights
to keep the fools busy here. Real war has begun on
another plane.

The present race for the moon has a deeper
significance. Its objective is other than what it seems
to be. The power that will control the moon tomorrow will become invulnerable on this earth; there will
be no way to challenge it. They will no longer need
to send their planes to different countries to bomb
them; this job will be done more easily and quickly
from the moon. They will set up their missiles on the
moon, warheads directed toward the earth—rotating
a full circle in its orbit each twenty-four hours. And
that is how each country on this earth will be available, every day, to be bombed from the moon.

This is the secret of the great competition
between the world powers to reach the moon first.
And that is why the world powers are spending
enormous amounts of money on the exploration of
space. America spent about two billion dollars just to
land one man on the moon. This was done not for
the fun of it; there was a great objective behind this
effort. The real question was, who reaches the moon
first?

This contest for space is similar to another
historical contest that happened about three hundred
years ago when the countries of Europe were rushing
towards Asia. Merchant ships of Portugal, Spain,
Holland, France and Britain were all sailing towards
the countries of Asia—because occupation of Asia
had become immensely important for the expansionist
powers of Europe. But now it has no importance whatsoever, and so, soon after the Second World War,
they left Asia. The people of Asia believe they won
their freedom through their nationalist struggles, but
it is only a half-truth. The other half of the truth is
quite different.

In the context of the modern technology of warfare, the occupation of Asia in the old way has become meaningless; that chapter is closed forever. Now a new struggle for the conquest of lands altogether different and distant from this earth has begun. Man has raised his sights to the distant stars, to the moon and Mars and even beyond. Now wars will be fought in the vastness of space.

Life is an adventure, an adventure of energy. And people who lag behind in this adventure, for lack of energy and courage, eventually have to die and disappear from the scene. Perhaps we are such a dead people.

In this context also, Krishna's message has assumed special significance. And it is significant not only for us, but for the whole world. In my view, the West has reached a point where it will, once again, have to wage a decisive war, which of course will not take place on the planet Earth. Even if the contestants belong to this earth, the actual operation of the war will take place elsewhere, either on the moon or on Mars. Now there is no sense fighting a war on the earth. If it takes place here it will result in the total destruction of both the aggressor and the aggressed. So a great war in the future will be fought and decided somewhere far away from here. And what would be the result?

In a way, the world is facing nearly the same situation India faced during the Mahabharat war. There were two camps, or two classes, at the time of the Mahabharat. One of them was out-and-out materialist; they did not accept anything beyond the body or matter. They did not know anything except the indulgence of their senses; they did not have any idea of yoga or of spiritual discipline. For them the existence of the soul did not matter in the least; for them life was just a playground of stark indulgence, of exploitation and predatory wars. Life beyond the senses and their indulgence held no importance for them.

This was the class against which the war of Mahabharat was waged. And Krishna had to opt for this war and lead it, because it had become imperative. It had become imperative so that the forces of good and virtue could stand squarely against the forces of materialism and evil, so that they were not rendered weak and impotent.

Approximately the same situation has arisen on a worldwide scale, and in twenty years' time a full replica, a scenario of the Mahabharat will be upon us. On one side will be all the forces of materialism and on the other will be the weaker forces of good and righteousness.

Goodness suffers from a basic weakness: it wants to keep away from conflicts and wars. Arjuna of the Mahabharat is a good man. The word "arjuna" in Sanskrit means the simple, the straightforward, clean. Arjuna means that which is not crooked. Arjuna is a simple and good man, a man with a clean mind and a kind heart. He does not want to get involved in any conflict and strife; he wants to withdraw. Krishna is still more simple and good; his simplicity, his goodness knows no limits. But his simplicity, his goodness does not admit to any weakness and escape from reality. His feet are set firmly on the ground; he is a realist, and he is not going to allow Arjuna to run away from the battlefield.

Perhaps the world is once again being divided into two classes, into two camps. It happens often enough when a decisive moment comes and war becomes inevitable. Men like Gandhi and Russell will be of no use in this eventuality. In a sense they are all Arjunas. They will again say that war should be shunned at all costs, that it is better to be killed than to kill others. A Krishna will again be needed, one who can clearly say that the forces of good must fight, that they must have the courage to handle a gun and fight a war. And when goodness fights only goodness flows from it. It is incapable of harming anyone. Even when it fights a war it becomes, in its hands, a holy war. Goodness does not fight for the sake of fighting, it fights simply to prevent evil from winning.

By and by the world will soon be divided into two camps. One camp will stand for materialism and all that it means, and the other camp will stand for freedom and democracy, for the sovereignty of the individual and other higher values of life. But is it possible that this camp representing good will find a Krishna to again lead it?

It is quite possible. When man's state of affairs, when his destiny comes to a point where a decisive event becomes imminent, the same destiny summons and sends forth the intelligence, the genius that is supremely needed to lead the event. And a right person, a Krishna appears on the scene. The decisive event brings with it the decisive man too.

It is for this also that I say Krishna has great significance for the future.

There are times when the voices of those who are good, simple and gentle cease to be effective, because people inclined to evil don't hear them, don't fear them, blindly go their own way. In fact, as good people shrink back just out of goodness, in the same measure the mischief-makers become bold, feel like having a field day. India had many such good people after the Mahabharat, like Buddha and Mahavira. Nothing was lacking in their goodness; their goodness was infinite. In fact, it was too much—so much that the country's mind shrank under the weight of this goodness. The result was that the aggressors of the whole world set loose their hordes on India.

It is not only that some people invade others, there are people who invite invasion on themselves. You are not only responsible when you hit others, you are also responsible when others hit you. If you slap someone's face, your responsibility for this act is only fifty percent, the other fifty percent of the responsibility should go to the person who invited and attracted your slap, who took it passively, without resistance. Know well that when someone slaps you, half the responsibility rests with you, because your being weak and passive becomes an invitation for him to hurt you.

A long succession of good people, of absolutely good people, was responsible for constricting and enfeebling the mind of India, for making it weak and passive. And this became a kind of invitation to aggressors around the world. And, responding to this invitation, they came, almost with walking sticks in their hands, and subjugated us, enslaved us. For long spells of time they ruled over us and oppressed us. And when they left, they did so on their own; we did not throw them out.

What is unfortunate is that we continue to be a shrunken people, suppressed and enfeebled in our minds and hearts. And we can again invite some aggressor to enslave us. If tomorrow Mao overruns this country, he alone will not be responsible. Years back, Lenin predicted that communism's road to London lay through Peking and Calcutta. His prediction seems to be correct. Communism has already arrived in Peking, and the noise of its footsteps are being heard in Calcutta. And so London is not far off. It will not be difficult for communism to reach Calcutta, because India's mind is still shrunken, still suppressed and stricken with fear. Communism will come, and by accepting it, this country will go down the drain.

That is why I say that India should do some serious rethinking about Krishna.

Questioner: If Krishna were present today, which of the two sides would he choose?

Whenever there is a crisis like this, one finds it difficult to decide which side in the conflict is right and which is wrong. This was not easy even on the eve of the Mahabharat. Not all the people on the side of the Kauravas were bad; a great soul like Bhishma was with them. Similarly, not all those who were on the side of the Pandavas, who were being guided by Krishna, were good; there were bad people as well. So, in a matter like this, there is always some difficulty in coming to a decision.

But some values clinch the issue. Why was Duryodhana fighting? What was his motive in forcing such a great war? It was not that important whether the people on his side were bad or not, the important thing was his intention, his objective, the values for which he forced the war. And what were the values for which Krishna inspired Arjuna to fight bravely?

The most important and decisive value at stake in the Mahabharat was *justice*. The war had to decide what was just and what justice was.

Again today we have to decide what is just, what justice is. In my vision, freedom is justice and bondage is injustice. The group or class that is bent on forcing any kind of bondage on mankind is on the side of injustice. Maybe there are some good people on their side, but all good people do not necessarily have clarity and farsight. Often they are confused people, people who don't know that what they are doing is going to serve the side of injustice.

Freedom is of the highest; it is the most significant, most decisive issue today. We need a society, a world where man's freedom can grow and blossom. And we don't want a society, a world that will destroy man's freedom and put him in shackles. This has to be clearly understood.

It is natural that people wanting to impose bondage on others would not say so, would not use the word "bondage". The word has a bad odor; it is hateful and repelling. They will find a word or a slogan that will put people into bondage without letting them know it. "Equality" is such a new slogan, and it is full of cunning and deceit. Thus they sidetrack the issue of freedom and shout, instead, for equality. They say they stand for equality between man and man. They argue that equality is basic, and that freedom is not possible without equality. And this argument is appealing to many who are led to think that as long as people are not equal they cannot be free. And then they consent to forego freedom for the sake of equality.

Now it is very strange logic that equality has to be had for freedom to come, and that freedom has to be sacrificed for equality to come. The truth is, once freedom is lost it will be impossible to restore it. Who will restore it?

You all are here listening to me. I tell you that in order to make you all equal it is necessary to put you in shackles first. I tell you that without putting you in fetters it will not be possible to equalize you. Maybe someone has a bigger head than others, another has larger arms and a third one has longer legs—they all will have to be cut to equal size. And this painful operation will not be possible without first depriving you of your freedom. And it sounds very logical.

But people forget that the person who will make them all equal will himself remain free and unequal; he will remain outside them all. He will have no fetters on his feet and, besides, he will have a gun in his hand. Now you can well envision a situation, a society where most people are in shackles, maimed and crippled, and a handful of people are free and powerful with all the modern instruments of suppression and oppression at their disposal. What can you do in a situation like this?

Marx held the view that in order to achieve equality in society it would, in the first place, be necessary to suppress political freedom, destroy individual liberty and establish a dictatorship. And he thought that after the achievement of equality, freedom would be restored to the people. But do you think people with such enormous power in their hands that they can equalize everyone will ever give you back your freedom? We don't see any sign of it in the countries where such experiments have been conducted. In fact, as the power of the rulers grows, and as the people, the ruled, are systematically suppressed and debilitated, the hope for freedom becomes increasingly dim. Then it is difficult even to raise the question of freedom. Nobody dares ask a question, speak his thoughts, much less dissent and rebel against the established tyranny.

In the name of equality, and under the cover of equality, freedom is going to be destroyed. And once it is destroyed it will be nearly impossible to win it back—because those who destroy freedom will see to it that the chances of its being revived in the future are also destroyed.

Secondly, you should know that while freedom is an absolutely natural phenomenon, which everyone must have as his right, equality is not. Equality is neither natural nor possible. The concept of equality is unpsychological; all people cannot be equal. They are not equal; they are basically unequal. But freedom is a must. Everyone should be free to be what he is and what he can be. Everyone should have full freedom and opportunity to be himself.

In my view, Krishna is on the side of freedom; he cannot be on the side of equality. If there is freedom it is possible that inequality will diminish. I don't say equality will come with freedom, I only say inequality will gradually be reduced. But if equality is forced on people then their freedom is bound to diminish and disappear. Anything imposed with force is synonymous with slavery.

So basically it is a choice of values. And in my vision the individual is the highest value. So freedom of the individual is of the highest.

The camp of evil has always been against the individual and in favor of the group, the collective. The individual has no value whatsoever in the eyes of evil, and there is good reason for it. The individual is rebellious; he is the seed of rebellion. You will be surprised to know that if you want some evil act to be done you will find it easier through a group than through an individual.

It is very difficult for an individual Hindu to set fire to a mosque, but a crowd of Hindus can do it for fun. An individual Mohammedan will find it hard to stick a knife into the chest of a Hindu child, but a horde of Mohammedans can do it without a qualm of conscience. In fact, the bigger a crowd the less soul it has. But it is the sense of responsibility that forms the kernel of the soul. When I go to push a knife in somebody's chest my conscience bites at me. It says, "What are you doing?" But my soul does not feel disturbed when I am with a crowd, killing people recklessly and burning their property. Then I say it is not me but the people, the Hindus or Muslims, who are doing it, and I am just keeping company with them— and tomorrow I will not be held individually responsible for it.

The side of evil always wants to attract the crowd; it depends on the crowd. Evil wants to destroy the individual whom it feels is a thorn in its flesh. It wants the crowd, the mass to live and grow. Good, on the contrary, accepts the individual and wants him to grow to his supreme fulfillment and, at the same time, it wants the crowd to disappear gradually from the scene. Good stands for a society of individuals, free individuals. Individuals will, of course, have relationships, but then it will be a society and not a herd, not a crowd.

This needs to be rightly understood. Only free individuals make a society, and where the sovereignty of the individual is denied, society turns into a herd, a mob. This is the difference between a society and a crowd. Society is another name for the inter-relation-ship of individuals, a cooperative of individuals—but the individual has to be there, he is the basic unit of society.

When an individual freely enters into rela-tionship with another individual, it makes for society. So there cannot be a society inside a prison; a prison can only have a crowd, a collection of faceless indi-viduals. Prisoners also relate with each other, ex-changing greetings and gifts among themselves, but they are definitely not a society. They have just been gathered together and forced to live within the four walls of a prison; it is not their free choice.

Therefore I say that Krishna will choose the side where freedom and the sovereignty of the indi-vidual, where religion and the possibility to seek the unseen and the unknown will be available in predomi-nance. I say "in predominance" because it never hap-pens that one side has all these values and the other side is wholly devoid of them. The division between good and evil is never so clear-cut, even in a battle between Rama and Ravana. Even in Ravana there is a little of Rama, and there is a little of Ravana in Rama too. The Kauravas share a few of the virtues of the Pandavas, and the latter a few of the vices of the former. Even the best man on this earth has some-thing of the worst in him. And the meanest of us all carries a bit of goodness in him. So it is always a question of proportion and predominance of one or the other.

So freedom and the individual and the soul and religion are the values with which the intelli-gence of good will side.

SECOND DISCOURSE
MORNING, SEPTEMBER 26, 1970
MANALI, INDIA

KRISHNA IS COMPLETE AND WHOLE

Questioner: Why did you choose to speak on Krishna? And what is the central theme of this discussion?

f a man has to think, understand, and say something, for him there can be no more meaningful a topic than Krishna. He is the most significant person in all of history. It is not that other significant people did not happen in the past—and it would be wrong to say that significant people will not happen in the future; in fact, any number of remarkable people have walked this earth—but Krishna's significance is quite different. He is more significant for the future than for the past.

The truth is, Krishna was born much ahead of his time. All great persons are born ahead of their time, and all insignificant people are born after their time. It is only mediocre people who are born in their time.

All significant people come ahead of their time, but Krishna came too far ahead. Perhaps only in some future period will we be able to understand him; the past could not do so.

And remember, we begin to worship those we fail to understand in their lifetimes. We worship those who perplex and defeat our ability to understand them. We either praise or slander them, but both praise and slander are kinds of worship. We worship friends with praise and we worship enemies with slander. It is all the same. One who defies our judgment, we call him a god or God-incarnate. It is really difficult to accept one's ignorance; it is easier to call him a god or God-incarnate. But these are the two sides of the same coin. Such a person is God-like in the sense that we don't understand him, just as we don't understand God. This person is as unknowable and as mysterious as God himself. Despite our best efforts he, like God, ever remains to be known. And all such people become objects of worship.

It is precisely for this reason that I chose Krishna for discussion. He is, in my view, the most relevant, the most significant person in the context of the future. And in this regard, I would like to go into a few things.

With the exception of Krishna, all the remarkable people of the world, the salt of the earth like Mahavira, Buddha, and Christ, stood for some other world, for a life in some other world. They set distant things like the attainment of heaven and liberation as goals for man's life on this earth. In their day, life on this earth was so miserable and painful it was nearly impossible to live. Man's whole past was so full of want and hardship, of struggle and suffering, that it was hard to accept life happily. Therefore all the religions in the past denied and denounced life on this earth.

In the whole galaxy of religious luminaries Krishna is the sole exception who fully accepts the whole of life on this earth. He does not believe in living here for the sake of another world and another life. He believes in living this very life, here on this very earth. Where *moksha*, the freedom of Buddha and Mahavira, lies somewhere beyond this world and this time—there and then—Krishna's freedom is here and now. Life as we know it never received such deep and unconditional acceptance at the hands of any other enlightened soul.

In times to come there is going to be a considerable reduction in the hardship and misery of life in this world and a corresponding increase in its comfort and happiness. And so, for the first time, the world will refuse to follow those who renounced life. It is always an unhappy society that applauds the creed of renunciation; a happy society will refuse to do so. Renunciation and escape from life can have meaning in a society steeped in poverty and misery, but they hold no appeal for an affluent and happy society. A man can very well tell an unhappy society that since there is nothing here except suffering and pain, he is going to leave it—but he cannot tell the same thing to an affluent society; there, it will make no sense.

Religions believing in renunciation will have no relevance in the future. Science will eliminate all those hardships that make for life's sufferings. Buddha says that life from birth to death is a suffering. Now pain can be banished. In the future, birth will cease to be painful both for the mother and for the child. Life will cease to be painful; disease can be removed. Even a cure for old age can be found, and the span of life considerably lengthened. The life span will be so long that dying will cease to be a problem; instead people will ask, "Why live this long?"

All these things are going to happen in the near future. Then Buddha's maxim about life being an unending chain of suffering will be hard to understand. And then Krishna's flute will become significant and his song and dance will become alive. Then life will become a celebration of happiness and joy. Then life will be a blossoming and a beauty.

In the midst of this blossoming the image of a naked Mahavira will lose its relevance. In the midst of this celebration the philosophy of renunciation will lose its luster. In the midst of this festivity that life will be, dancers and musicians will be on center-stage. In the future world there will be less and less misery and more and more happiness. That is how I see Krishna's importance ever on the ascent.

Up to now it was difficult to think that a man of religion carried a flute and played it. We could not imagine that a religious man wore a crown of peacock feathers and danced with young women. It was unthinkable that a religious man loved somebody and sang a song. A religious man, of our old concept, was one who had renounced life and fled the world. How could he sing and dance in a miserable world? He could only cry and weep. He could not play a flute; it was impossible to imagine that he danced.

It was for this reason that Krishna could not be understood in the past; it was simply impossible to understand him. He looked so irrelevant, so inconsistent and absurd in the context of our whole past.

But in the context of times to come, Krishna will be increasingly relevant and meaningful. And soon such a religion will come into being that will sing and dance and be happy. The religions of the past were all life-negative, defeatist, masochistic and escapist. The religion of the future will be life-affirming. It will accept and live the joys that life brings and will laugh and dance and celebrate in sheer gratitude.

In view of this immense possibility for a good life in the future I have chosen to talk about Krishna. Of course it will be difficult for you to understand Krishna, because you are also conditioned, heavily conditioned by the misery of life in the past. You have, up to now, associated religion with tears and not with flutes.

Rarely have you come across a person who took to sannyas out of life's joys. Normally, when a man's wife died and his life became miserable, he turned to sannyas as an escape from his misery. If someone lost his wealth, went bankrupt and could not bear it, he took to sannyas in sheer despair. An unhappy person, a person ridden with sorrow and pain, escaped into sannyas. Sannyas stemmed from unhappiness and not from happiness. No one comes to sannyas with a song in his heart.

Krishna is an exception to the rule. To me he is that rare sannyasin whose sannyas is born out of joy and bliss. And one who chooses sannyas for the joy of it must be basically different from the general breed of sannyasins who come to it in misery and frustration.

As I say that the religion of the future will stem from bliss, so I also say that the sannyas of the future will flow from the joy and ecstasy of life. And one who chooses sannyas for the joy of it must be basically different from the old kind of sannyasin who left the world simply out of despair. He will take sannyas not because his family tortures him, but because his family is now too small for his expanding bliss—and so he adopts the whole world as his new family. He will accept sannyas not because his love turns sour, but because one person is now too small to contain his overflowing love—and he has to choose the whole earth as the object of his love.

And they alone can understand Krishna who understands this kind of sannyas that flows from the acceptance of life, from the juice and bliss of life.

If someone in the future says he took sannyas because he was unhappy we will ask him, "How can sannyas come from unhappiness?" The sannyas that is born out of unhappiness cannot lead to happiness and bliss. The sannyas that arises from pain and suffering can at best lessen your suffering, but it cannot bring you joy and bliss. You can, of course, reduce your suffering by moving away from the situation, but you cannot achieve joy and bliss through it. Only the sannyas, the Ganges of sannyas that is born out of bliss, can reach the ocean of bliss—because then all the efforts of the sannyasin will be directed towards enhancing his bliss.

Spiritual pursuit in the past was meant to mitigate suffering, it did not aim at bliss. And, of course, a traveler on this path does succeed, but it is a negative kind of success. What he achieves is a kind of indifference to life, which is only unhappiness reduced to its minimum. That is why our old sannyasins seem to be sad and dull, as if they have lost the battle of life and run away from it. Their sannyas is not alive and happy, dancing and celebrating.

To me, Krishna is a sannyasin of bliss. And because of the great possibility and potential of the sannyas of bliss opening up before us, I have deliberately chosen to discuss Krishna. It is not that Krishna has not been discussed before. But those who discussed him were sannyasins of sorrow, and therefore they could not do justice to him. On the contrary, they have been very unjust to him. And it had to be so.

If Shankara interprets Krishna, he is bound to misinterpret him; he is the antithesis of Krishna. His interpretation can never be right and just. Krishna could not be rightly interpreted in the past, because all the interpreters who wrote about him came from the world of sorrow. They said that the world is unreal and false, that it is an illusion, but Krishna says this world is not only real, it is divine. He accepts this world. He accepts everything; he denies nothing. He is for total acceptance—acceptance of the whole. Such a man had never trod this earth before.

As we discuss him here from day to day, many things, many facets of him, will unfold themselves. For me, the very word "Krishna" is significant. It is a finger pointing to the moon of the future.

Questioner: You once said that Buddha and Mahavira were masochistic sannyasins. But in fact they came to sannyas from very affluent families; their sannyas was a followup to their affluence. So how can you associate them with the sannyas of sorrow?

No, I did not say that Mahavira and Buddha were masochistic sannyasins. What I said was that sannyas in the past was masochistic. If you look at the lives of Mahavira and Buddha, you will see that they are for renunciation of life. I did not call them masochistic. I know they achieved the highest in life, and their unhappiness is very different. Their unhappiness is a kind of boredom arising from happiness; their unhappiness is not the absence of happiness. No one can say they turned to sannyas for want of happiness in life; it was not so. But the irony is that when there is too much happiness it becomes meaningless. So they renounced happiness. So while happiness became meaningless for them, its renunciation had meaning. They put a pronounced stress on renunciation. They stood by renunciation.

For Krishna, not only is happiness meaningless, its renunciation is also meaningless. Krishna's understanding of meaninglessness is much deeper. Try to understand it.

If I cling to a thing, it means it has meaning for me. And if I renounce it, then also, in a negative sense, it has meaning for me, because I think I will suffer if I don't give it up. I don't say that the sannyas of Mahavira and Buddha arose from suffering. I don't say so at all. Their sannyas flowed from a condition of happiness. They left this happiness in search of some higher kind of happiness. So in this matter there is a difference between them and Krishna.

Krishna does not renounce this happiness for the sake of some greater happiness; rather, he uses it as a stepping-stone to reach the other happiness we call bliss. He does not see any contradiction between the two kinds of happiness: the higher happiness is only the extension of the lower. Bliss, according to Krishna, is not opposed to the happiness of this world: it is the highest rhythm of the same music, the same dance. For Krishna, happiness contains some rudiments of bliss: one can have a little glimpse of bliss even in happiness. Happiness is the beginning of bliss; bliss is the climax of happiness.

It is from a situation of happiness that Buddha and Mahavira came to sannyas, it is true, but renunciation remains their stance: they renounce the world; they leave it. Renunciation has a place in their gestalt, and this gestalt assumes a good deal of importance in the eyes of masochistic people. Where Buddha and Mahavira left the world out of boredom, the masochists thought they had done so because of suffering and pain. Interpretations of Buddha and Mahavira were done by the masochists as well. Not only Krishna, even Mahavira and Buddha had to suffer at the hands of the masochists. Injustice—of course, in smaller measure—was done to these two luminaries in the same way it was done to Krishna.

We are unhappy, we are in misery. When we leave the world we do so because of our unhappiness. Buddha and Mahavira, however, left the world because of happiness. So there is a difference between us, on the one hand, and Mahavira and Buddha on the other, because the reasons for our renunciation are different.

Buddha and Mahavira are sannyasins of affluence; nonetheless there is a clear-cut difference between Buddha and Mahavira, on the one hand, and Krishna on the other. The difference is that where Buddha and Mahavira renounce happiness, Krishna does not renounce it. Krishna accepts that which is.

He does not find happiness even worth renouncing, let alone indulging. He does not find happiness even worth renouncing. He has no desire whatsoever to make even a slight change in life as it is; he accepts it totally.

A fakir has said in his prayer, "O Lord, I accept you, but not your world." In fact, every fakir says, "O Lord, I accept you, but not your world." This is opposite to the position taken by an atheist. The atheist says, "I accept your world, not you." Thus theists and atheists are two sides of the same coin.

Krishna's theism is quite unique. In fact, only Krishna is a theist: he accepts what is. He says to God, "I accept you and your world too," and this acceptance is so complete, so profound that it is difficult to know where the world ends and God begins. The world is really the extended hand of God, and God is the innermost being hidden in the world. The difference between the world and God is no more than this.

Krishna accepts the whole. It is important to understand that Krishna does not give up anything, neither pain nor happiness. He does not renounce that which is. With him the question of renunciation does not arise.

If we understand rightly we will see that the individual, the ego, the *I* begins with giving up, with renunciation. As soon as we renounce something *I*-ness comes into being. There is no way for *me*, for the ego to be if we don't give up anything.

It is difficult to find a more egoless person than Krishna. He is utterly egoless. And because he has no ego whatsoever, he can, with utmost ease, say things that sound egoistic. He tells Arjuna, "Give up everything and surrender to me, come to my feet." This seems to be a statement of great egoism. What greater egoistic statement can there be than to say, "Give up everything and come to my feet"? It is ironic that this statement, which seems so obviously egoistic even to ordinary minds like ours, does not seem so to Krishna himself. He has at least as much intelligence as we have; he should know it is an egoistic declaration. But he makes it with amazing ease and innocence and spontaneity. Really, only a person who is not in the least aware of his *me* and *mine* can make such a declaration.

What does Krishna really tell Arjuna? When he says, "Leave everything and come to my feet," he means to say that Arjuna should set aside everything and go to the feet of life itself, should accept life as it is.

It is amusing that Krishna exhorts Arjuna to fight. If we look at the dialogue between the two, Arjuna appears to be more religious, and what Krishna says is not that religious. Krishna provokes him to fight, and Arjuna refuses to do so. He says, "It is painful to kill my own people. I won't kill them even for the sake of a kingdom and a king's throne. I would rather go begging in the streets, rather commit suicide rather than kill my relatives, friends and teachers who are on the other side."

What religious person can say that Arjuna is wrong? Every religious person will say that Arjuna is absolutely right, that he is filled with a sense of righteousness, that he is on the path of religion. He will say he is a sage, a man of wisdom. But Krishna tells him, "You are deluded and you have gone off track. Your sense of religion has utterly left you."

And then he tells Arjuna, "You are mad if you think you can kill someone. No one ever dies. And you are mistaken to think you can save those standing before you. Who has ever saved anyone? And you cannot escape war, nor can you be non-violent, because as long as the *I* exists—and it is this *I* that is anxious to save itself and its family and relatives—non-violence is next to impossible. No, be rid of this nonsense and face reality. Set aside your sense of *I* and fight. Accept what is facing you. And what is facing you is not a temple where prayers are made, it is war. It is war you are facing. And you have to plunge into it. And so drop your *I*. Who are you?"

In the course of his exhortation Krishna makes a very interesting and significant remark. He tells Arjuna, "All those you think you have to kill are already dead. They are just awaiting death; at the most you can serve as a medium for hastening it. But if you think you will kill them, then you will cease to be a medium, you will become a doer. And don't think you will be their savior if you run away from the battlefield. That would be another illusion. You can neither kill them nor save them. You have only to play a role; it is nothing more than play-acting. Therefore go into it totally, and do your part unwaveringly. And you can be totally in anything only if you put aside your mind, drop your ego and cease looking at things from the angle of *I* or *me* and *mine*."

What does it all mean? Do you understand what Krishna means to say? It is of tremendous significance to understand it.

It means that if someone drops the viewpoint of the ego, he will cease to be a doer, and then he can only be a player, an actor. If I am Rama and my Seeta is kidnapped, I will cry for her. But the way I cry for her will be quite different if I am acting his part in a drama on his life. Then I will also cry, and maybe my crying is going to be more real than that of the actual Rama. Indeed, it is going to be a better performance, because the real Rama does not have the opportunity to rehearse his role. Seeta is lost to him only once and he comes to know of it only after she has been kidnapped. He is not prepared for it. And as a doer, he is lost in the act of crying. He cries, screams, and suffers for Seeta.

That is why India does not accept Rama as a perfect incarnation of God. He cannot be a perfect actor; he is more a doer than an actor. He tries and fails again and again. He remains a doer. So we describe his life as that of an ideal character. He is not an actor, a player.

An actor does not have a character, he has just a role to play. So we describe Krishna's life as a real play, a performance. Krishna's life is a *leela*; he just plays his part and plays it perfectly. Rama's life has a character, it is idealistic; Krishna's life is a free play, a *leela*.

Character is a serious thing. A man of character has to approximate his conduct to a set of ideas, rules and regulations. He has to pick and choose; he has to choose between good and evil, between shoulds and should-nots. Arjuna is trying to be a man of character; Krishna is trying to make an actor of him. Arjuna wants to know what he should do and what he should not do. Krishna asks him to accept that which is, that which comes his way, and not to choose, not to bring his mind, his ego into it. This is absolute acceptance—where you have nothing to deny.

But it is arduous, really arduous to accept the whole of existence without choosing. Total acceptance means there is no good and bad, no virtue and vice, no pain and pleasure. Total acceptance means one drops for good the old ways of dialectical thinking, of thinking by splitting everything into two, into its opposites. Krishna tells Arjuna there is really no birth and death, that no one is ever born and no one ever dies, that no one kills and no one gets killed, so Arjuna can plunge into war without fear and with abandon, so he can play freely with war.

Everything on this earth is divine; everything in existence is godly, so the question of right and wrong does not arise. Of course, it is really arduous to understand it and live it.

The vision of Krishna is extremely difficult for a moralistic mind to decipher. A moralist finds it easier to understand an immoral person than Krishna. He can brush an immoral man aside by calling him a sinner. But in regard to Krishna he finds himself in a quandary. How to place him? He cannot say that Krishna is a bad man, because he does not seem to be so. And he also cannot gather the courage to say that Krishna is good, because he is goading Arjuna into things that are obviously bad, very bad.

Gandhi found himself in such a dilemma when he wanted to discuss Krishna. In fact, he was more in agreement with Arjuna than with Krishna. How can Gandhi accept it when Krishna goads Arjuna into war? He could be rid of Krishna if he were clearly bad, but his badness is not that clear, because Krishna accepts both good and bad. He is good, utterly good, and he is also utterly bad—and paradoxically, he is both together, and simultaneously. His goodness is crystal-clear, but his badness is also there. And it is difficult for Gandhi to accept him as bad.

Under the circumstances there was no other course for Gandhi but to say that the war of Mahabharat was a parable, a myth, that it did not happen in reality. He cannot acknowledge the reality of the Mahabharat, because war is violence, war is evil to him. So he calls it an allegorical war between good and evil. Here Gandhi takes shelter behind the same dialectics Krishna emphatically rejects. Krishna says a dialectical division of life is utterly wrong, that life is one and indivisible. And Gandhi depicts the Mahabharat as a mythical war between good and evil where the Pandavas represent good and the Kaurawas represent evil, and Krishna urges Arjuna to fight on behalf of good. Gandhi has to find this way out. He says the whole thing is just allegorical, poetic.

There is a gap of five thousand years between Krishna and Gandhi, and so it was easy for Gandhi to describe a five-thousand-year-old event as a myth. But the Jainas did not have this advantage, so they could not escape like Gandhi by calling the whole Mahabharat a metaphor. For them it had really happened. Jaina thinking is as old as the *Vedas*.

Hindus and Jainas share the same antiquity. So the Jainas could not say like Gandhi—who was a Jaina in mind and a Hindu in body—that the war did not really take place or that Krishna did not lead it. They were contemporaries of Krishna, so they could not find any excuse. They sent Krishna straight to hell; they could not do otherwise. They wrote in their scriptures that Krishna has been put in hell for his responsibility for the terrible violence of the Mahabharat. If one responsible for such large scale killing is not committed to hell, what will happen to those who scrupulously avoid even killing a fly as the Jainas do? So the Jainas had to put Krishna in hell.

But this is how his contemporaries thought. Krishna's goodness was so outstanding and vast that even his contemporary Jainas were faced with this difficulty, so they had to invent another story about him. Krishna was a rare and unique man in his own right. It is true he was responsible for a war like the Mahabharat. It is also true he had danced with women, had disrobed them and climbed up a tree with their clothes. Such a good man behaving in such a bad way! So after dumping him into hell they felt disturbed: if such good people as Krishna are hurled into hell then goodness itself will become suspect. So the Jainas said that Krishna would be the first Jaina *tirthankara* in the next *kalpa*, in the next cycle of creation. They put him in hell, and at the same time gave him the position of their *tirthankara* in the coming *kalpa*.

It was a way of balancing their treatment of Krishna, he was so paradoxical. From a moralistic viewpoint he was obviously a wrong kind of man, but otherwise he was an extraordinary man, worthy of being a *tirthankara*. Therefore they found a middle way: they put him in hell for the time being and they assigned him the hallowed position of their own future *tirthankara*. They said that when the current *kalpa*, one cycle of creation, would end and the next begin,

Krishna would be their first *tirthankara*. This is a compensation Krishna really had nothing to do with. Since they sent him to hell, the Jainas had to compensate. They compensated themselves psychologically.

Gandhi has an advantage: he is far removed from Krishna in time, so he settles the question with great ease. He does not have to send Krishna to hell, nor to make him a *tirthankara*. He solves his problem by calling the Mahabharat a parable. He says the war did not really take place, that it is just an allegory to convey a truth about life, that it is an allegorical war between good and evil. Gandhi's problem is the same one that faced the Jainas of his time. Non-violence is the problem. He cannot accept that violence can have a place in life. It is the same with good. Good cannot admit that bad has a place in life.

But Krishna says that the world is a unity of opposites. Violence and non-violence always go together, hand-in-hand. There was never a time when violence did not happen, nor was there a time when non-violence did not exist. So those who choose only one of the opposites choose a fragment, and they can never be fulfilled. There was never a time when there was only light or when there was only darkness, nor will it ever be so. Those who choose a part and deny another are bound to be in tension, because in spite of denying it, the other part will always continue to be. And the irony is, the part we choose is dependent for its existence on the part we deny.

Non-violence is dependent on violence; they are really dependent on each other. Light owes its existence to darkness. Good grows in the soil of what we call bad, and draws its sustenance from it. At the other pole of his existence the saint is ultimately connected with the sinner. All polarities are irrevocably bound up with each other: up with down, heaven with hell, good with bad. They are polarities of one and the same truth.

Krishna says, "Accept both the polarities, because both are there together. Go with them, because they are. Don't choose!" It can be said that Krishna is the first person to talk of choicelessness. He says, "Don't choose at all. Choose and you err, choose and you are off track, choose and you are fragmented. Choice also means denial of the other half of truth, which also is. And it is not in our hands to wipe it away. There is nothing in our hands. What is, is. It was, when we did not exist. It will be when we will be no more."

But the moralistic mind, the mind that has so far been taken for the religious mind, has its difficulty. It lives in conflict; it divides everything into good and bad. A moralist takes great pleasure in condemning evil; then he feels great and good. His interest in goodness is negative; it comes from his condemnation of evil. The saint derives all his pleasure from his condemnation of sinners; otherwise he has no way to please himself.

The whole joy of going to heaven depends on the suffering and misery of those who are sent to hell. If those in heaven come to know there is nothing like hell, all their joy will suddenly disappear; they will be as miserable as anything. All their labor will go down the drain if they know no hell exists. If there is no hell, every criminal, every sinner will be in heaven. Where then will the saint go? The happiness of the virtuous is really dependent on the misery of the sinners. The happiness of the rich really stems from the misery of the poor; it does not lie in richness itself. The happiness of a good man is really derived from those condemned as sinners, it is not derived from goodness itself. The saint will lose all his glamor and cheer the moment everyone becomes good; he will instantly become insignificant. Maybe, he will try to pursuade a few ex-sinners to return to their old jobs.

The whole significance of the cosmos comes from its opposites, which are really complementaries.

And one who observes it wholly will find that what we call bad is the extreme point of good and, similarly, good is the omega point of bad.

Krishna is choiceless, he is total, he is integrated, and therefore he is whole and complete. We have not accepted any other incarnation except Krishna's as whole and complete, and it is not without reason. How can Rama be complete? He is bound to be incomplete, because he chooses only half the truth. He alone can be whole who does not choose— but simply because of not choosing he will come up against difficulties. His life will be an interplay of light and shade. Now it will be illumined; now, shaded. It can never be a monotone; it cannot be flat and simple.

The life of one who chooses will be all gray, flat and simple, because he has cleaned and polished a corner of his life. But what will he do with the rest of it, which he has rejected and left uncared for? His living room is bright and elegant, well-furnished and decorated, spick-and-span—but what about the rest of the house with all the rubbish and refuse pushed under the carpet? The rubbish will gather and stink under the carpet.

But what about one who accepts the whole house with its neatness and its rubbish, with its lighted parts and its dark corners? Such a person cannot be categorized. We will see him in our own light, in the light of our choices and preferences, of our likes and dislikes. If one wants to see good in him one will find it there. And if a man wants to see only evil in him, he too, will not be disappointed, because in his life, both good and evil are present together. In fact only linguistically, are they two. Existentially they are different aspects of the same thing. They are really one.

Therefore I maintain that Buddha and Mahavira have their choices, are not choiceless. They are good, absolutely good, and for this very reason they are not whole. To be whole, good and bad have to go together. If all the three—Buddha, Mahavira and Krishna—stand in a row, Buddha and Mahavira will obviously shine brighter and attract us more than Krishna. Buddha and Mahavira look spotlessly clean; there is no stain whatsoever on their mantles.

If we have to choose between Mahavira and Krishna we will choose Mahavira. Krishna will leave us in some doubt. Krishna has always done so, because he carries with him all the seeming opposites. He is as good as Mahavira is, but in another respect Mahavira cannot be his equal, because Krishna has the courage to be as bad as Genghis and Hitler are. If we can pursuade Mahavira to stand on a battlefield with a sword in his hand—which we cannot—then he will look like a picture of Krishna. Or if we make Genghis shed his violence and give up everything and stand naked like Mahavira, pure and peaceful like Mahavira—which is not possible—then he too will resemble Krishna.

It is next to impossible to judge and evaluate Krishna; he defeats all evaluation, all judgment. With respect to Krishna we have to be non-judgmental. Only those who don't judge can go with him. A judging mind will soon be in difficulty with him and will run away from him. He will touch his feet when he sees his good side, but what will he do when he comes across the other side of the shield?

Because of this paradox, each of Krishna's lovers divided him into parts and chose for himself only that part which accorded with him. No one had the courage to accept the whole of Krishna. If Surdas sings hymns of praise to Krishna, he keeps himself confined to the time of his childhood. He leaves the rest of his life; he does not have the courage to take him wholly. Surdas seems to be a cowardly person: he put his own eyes out with needles—he blinded himself—for fear of a beautiful woman. Think of the man who chooses to go without eyes lest those eyes arouse his lust for a woman, lest he falls in love with her. Can such a man accept Krishna totally? It is true Surdas loves Krishna as few people do. He cannot do without him, so he clings to his childhood and ignores his youth. The youthful Krishna is beyond him.

Surdas could have accepted him if, in his youth, Krishna had gone blind like him. Krishna's eyes must have had rare beauty and power; they attracted and enchanted so many women, as few pairs of eyes have done. In history it is rare that a single person's eyes were the center of attraction for thousands of women. They must have been extraordinarily captivating, enchanting. They were really magnetic eyes. Surely Surdas did not have eyes like his; his eyes were very ordinary. It is true that women attracted him, but I don't know if he also attracted women. So Surdas had to remain content with the childish pranks of Krishna. He ignored the rest of him.

That is how all the scriptures about Krishna are—fragmentary. As Surdas chooses his childhood, another poet, Keshavadas, opts for a different Krishna, the youthful Krishna. Keshava is not in the least interested in the child Krishna, he is in love with the youthful energy of Krishna, singing and dancing with his village girls. Keshava's mind is youthful and vigorous and hedonistic; he delights in the indulgence and exuberance of youth. He would never go blind; if he could, he would even keep his eyes open in the dark.

So Keshava does not talk of Krishna's childhood; he has nothing to do with it. He chooses for himself the dancing Krishna. It is not that he understands Krishna's dance, he chooses it because he has a sensuous mind, a dancing mind. He eulogizes the Krishna who disrobes young women and climbs up a tree with their clothes. Not that Keshava understands the deeper meaning of Krishna's pranks, he does so because he derives vicarious pleasure from Krishna disrobing the women of his village. So he too, like Surdas, has chosen a fragment of Krishna, a truncated Krishna.

That is why the *Geeta* talks of a Krishna who is utterly different from the Krishna of the *Bhagwad*. It is so because of the differing choices and preferences of his devotees and lovers. Krishna himself is choiceless and whole, but we are not. And only a man who is himself choiceless and whole can accept and assimilate the whole of Krishna. Those of us who are fragmented and incomplete will first divide him into parts and then choose what we like. And when you choose a part, at the same time you deny the rest of him. But you will say that the remaining Krishna is a myth, an allegory. You will say that the rest of Krishna will suffer in hell till the end of creation. You will say you don't need the whole of Krishna, that a fragment is enough for you. So there are many Krishnas, as many as his lovers and devotees.

Krishna is like a vast ocean on whose endless shore we have made small pools of water we call our own. But these pools don't even cover a small fraction of the immensity that is Krishna. You cannot know the ocean from these petty pools. The pools represent Krishna's lovers and their very limited understanding of him. Don't take the pools for the ocean.

So I am going to discuss the whole of Krishna, the complete Krishna. Because of this, many times in the course of these talks, you will find it difficult to understand me. Many things will defy your mind and intellect, and a few things will even go beyond you. I would like you to rise to the height of the occasion and in spite of your mind's conditioning, prepare yourself to go along with me. If you remain bogged down and cling to the Krishna of your concepts, you will, as you have done so far, again miss the complete Krishna. And I say that only an integrated Krishna, a whole Krishna can be of use to you, not the truncated one you have known so long.

Not only Krishna, even an ordinary person is useful only if he is integrated and whole. Dissect him and you have only his dead limbs in your hands; the live man is no more. So those who divided Krishna into fragments did a great disservice to him and to themselves. They have only his dead limbs with them, while his whole live being is missing. The real Krishna is missing.

There is only one way to have the whole of Krishna, and that is to understand him choicelessly. And understanding him so will be a blissful journey, because in the process you will be integrated and made whole. In the very process of understanding him, you will begin to be whole and holy. If you consent to drop your choices and preferences, and understand Krishna in his totality, you will find, by and by, that your inner contradictions and conflicts have diminished and disappeared, and that all your fragments have come together into an integrated whole. Then you will attain to what is called yoga or unity. For Krishna, yoga has only one meaning; to be united, to be integrated, to be whole.

The vision of yoga is total. Yoga means the total. That is why Krishna is called a *mahayogi*, one who has attained to the highest yoga. There are any number of people who claim to be yogis, but they are not really yogis because they all have their choices, they all lack unity and integration. Choicelessness is yoga.

These talks on an undivided and whole Krishna are going to be difficult for you, because intellect has its own categories, its own ways of thinking in fragments. Intellect has its own ways of measuring men, events and things. These measures are all petty and fragmentary. It does not make much difference whether one's measure is new or old, modern or medieval, metric or otherwise. It does not make any difference whether the intellect is old or new, ancient or modern, classical or scientific. There is one characteristic common to all intellect: it divides things into good and bad, right and wrong. Intellect always divides and chooses.

If you want to understand Krishna then for these ten days drop your judgment altogether, give up dividing and choosing. Only listen and understand without judging, without evaluating anything. And whenever you come to a point where your understanding, your intellect begins to falter and fail, don't stop there, don't retreat from there, but boldly enter the world which is beyond rational understanding, or what you call the irrational world. Often we will come across the irrational, because Krishna cannot be confined to the rational; he is much more than that. In him, Krishna includes both the rational and the irrational, and goes beyond both. In him, Krishna also includes that which transcends understanding, which is beyond understanding.

It is impossible to fit Krishna into logical molds and patterns, because he does not accept your logic, he does not recognize any divisions of life as you are used to doing. He steers clear of every kind of fragmentation without accepting or denying it. Although he touches all the pools of your beliefs and dogmas and superstitions, he himself remains untouched by them; he always remains the vast ocean that he is. Evidently he is going to create difficulties for you. And the greatest difficulty you will face is when your own tiny pools dry up and die, and Krishna's ocean lives and goes on and on and on. He is beyond and ever beyond.

Krishna's ocean is really all over; he is all-pervasive. He is in good and he is in bad too. His peace is limitless, yet he takes his stand on a battlefield with his favorite weapon, the *sudarshan chakra* in his hand. His love is infinite, yet he will not hesitate to kill if it becomes necessary. He is an out-and-out sannyasin, yet he does not run away from home and hearth. He loves God tremendously, yet he loves the world in the same measure. Neither can he abandon the world for God nor can he abandon God for the world. He is committed to the whole. He *is* whole.

Krishna has yet to find a devotee who will be totally committed to him. Even Arjuna was not such a complete devotee; otherwise Krishna would not have had to work so hard with him. It is evident from the *Geeta*, from the lengthy statement made on the battleground, how doubting and skeptical and argumentative Arjuna is. Two warring armies are facing each other on the grounds of the Kurukshetra, the bells of war are tolling, and Arjuna is stubbornly refusing to take up arms and fight. Against Krishna's exhortations he is raising question after question— which run through eighteen chapters of the *Geeta*. Again and again he gently protests Krishna's seemingly bipolar vision. He says that Krishna is paradoxical, that he says things that contradict each other.

The questions he has raised in the *Geeta* are consistent and logical. He feels baffled and confused and asks Krishna to explain the same thing over and over again. But Krishna fails to explain and convince Arjuna; even a total person like Krishna fails. And then he takes recourse in another method: he unfolds himself, his reality before Arjuna.

Krishna knows Arjuna is right logically: he is confused and demands consistency. Krishna really confuses him. On the one hand he talks of the significance of love and compassion and, on the other, urges him to boldly take up arms and fight his enemies. So Krishna is tired of talking, because it is a moment of war. Trumpets have sounded, and this man Arjuna, who is the kingpin of the whole drama, is still hesitating, wavering. If he runs away, the whole game will fall to pieces. So when arguments fail, Krishna unfolds his whole being, his immensity before him, and Arjuna is greatly disturbed to see it. Anyone would be disturbed to see it, because Krishna's real being, his universal being, comprises all the contradictions of

existence. One sees that life and death are there together. But one cannot accept them together.

In our ordinary life, birth and death are dis-
tanced by a span of time—say seventy years. We are
born seventy years before our death; we die seventy
years after our birth. This distance between birth and
death makes us think that life and death are separate
things. But when Krishna confronts him with his immense body, his universal being, Arjuna sees life and
death together in him. He sees both the creation and
destruction of worlds taking place simultaneously. He
sees the sprouting seed and the dying tree together.
And he panics, seeing the immensity and paradox of
Krishna's totality. In the midst of it he entreats
Krishna to stop; he cannot bear it any longer. But
after seeing this he stops raising questions, because
now he knows that what we see as inconsistencies
and contradictions in life are nothing but integral
parts of the same truth—which is one. And he quietly
joins the war.

But it does not mean that Arjuna is fully convinced. Although he has had a glimpse of reality, his
mind, his intellect, yet continues to doubt. Doubt is
the way of the mind.

Whatever questions you may have, you can
direct them to me, but please don't raise questions
about Krishna while understanding Krishna. Use all
your intellect with me, but understand Krishna without questions. You are going to have very trying times
with him, because many times he will leave the world
of the rational and enter the irrational, which is really
the space beyond the rational. You may call it the
super-rational. There you will need patience and great
courage—maybe the greatest courage possible. Be
prepared to walk with me into that unfamiliar unknown territory where your little lighted world will
come to an end, where you will enter a sort of altogether dark space. In that unlit space you will find
no pathways, neither doors nor openings. You will

find nothing there that will resemble the forms and faces you have been familiar with in the past. All old forms will dissolve and disappear, and all consistencies and contradictions will simply cease to be. And it is only then that you can come close to that which is immense, to that which is infinite, to that which is immeasurable—the eternal.

You can have that rare opportunity if you are prepared, with courage and patience, to go the whole length with me. It is not that Arjuna has some special ability to see the immense, everyone has that ability. Everyone can raise the questions he raises. So if you are prepared to journey into the mysterious, into that which transcends the rational, the known, you will be equally entitled to confront the immense, the eternal. That immensity is awaiting you.

All my efforts here, during these discussions, will be directed towards bringing that immensity to you. A personalized name for that immensity is Krishna. We don't have really much to do with Krishna, he is just the symbolic name for the immense, the total. So don't be disturbed if at times we digress from him. My efforts will always be directed towards the one goal, towards the immense, the infinite, the eternal. And it can happen to you too, if only you are prepared for it. It is not that it can happen at Kurukshetra only, it can happen right here at Manali.

Questioner: Before you go ahead with the discussion, I would request that you explain something we seem to have missed so far. If Buddha's concept of unhappiness is a fact of life, then how is it wrong to bring it into focus? Isn't life, as it is, full of pain and misery?

Misery is a fact of life, but it is not the only fact—happiness is equally a fact of life. And happiness is as big a fact of life as misery is. And when we take misery to be the only fact of life, we turn it into a non-fact, into a fiction. Then what will you do with happiness, which is very much there? If life were only suffering, Buddha had no reason to take pains to explain the significance of suffering; there was no point to it. And Buddha explains at great length the meaning of suffering, yet nobody runs away from life because it is a suffering. We are all miserable, but we don't stop living for that reason.

There must be something other than suffering, different from suffering, which makes us hold on to life, cling to it in spite of its many hurts and pains. For instance, someone is miserable because he is in love. Love has its own problems and complexities. But if there were no happiness in love, who would consent to go through so much suffering for its sake? And if, for the sake of an ounce of happiness, one goes through tons of suffering, it means that the intensity, the flavor of an ounce of happiness outweighs all the sufferings of life. Happiness is equally true.

Because all the advocates of renunciation lay all their emphasis on suffering, they turn suffering into a fiction. In the same way the hedonists turn happiness into a fiction by laying all their stress on it. The materialists give too much importance to happiness, and they deny suffering altogether. But that is not true. Remember, a half-truth is a lie: truth can only be whole; it cannot be fragmentary. If someone says that life is, he tells a lie, because death is inseparably linked with life. Similarly it is a lie to say that only death is, because life is irrevocably joined to death.

It is not a fact that life is unmitigated suffering. What *is* a fact then? That life is both happiness and sorrow is a fact. If you observe it carefully and closely and deeply, you will find that every happiness is blended with pain and every pain is mixed with happiness. And if you go still deeper into it, it will be difficult to know when pain turns into pleasure and when pleasure turns into pain. They are really convertible: one changes into the other. And it happens in our everyday life. Really, the difference between them is one of emphasis. What felt like happiness yesterday feels like suffering today, and what seems to be suffering today will turn into happiness tomorrow.

If I take you in my embrace you will feel happy about it, but if I continue to hug you for a few minutes you will begin to find the same hug becoming painful. And if I continue to hold you in my grip for half an hour, you will feel restless and think of shouting for help; you may even call the police. So one who knows, releases you from his embrace before you would like to be released. And one who is unaware of this law soon turns his happiness into suffering. So when you take someone's hand in your hand, take care that you release it sooner than later, otherwise the pleasure will very soon change into pain. We are all wont to reduce our happiness into pain and suffering. Since we don't want to part with happiness, we cling to it, and it is clinging that turns it into suffering.

We very much desire to be rid of pain and suffering, and for this very reason our suffering deepens. But if we accept suffering and stay with it for a while, it will be transformed into happiness. The feeling of suffering stems from its being unfamiliar, but it will not take you long to become familiar with it. The same is the case with happiness. Familiarity changes everything.

I have heard that a person came to visit a new village where he asked someone for a loan. The other person said, "It is strange that you ask me for a loan when I don't know you at all. You are a complete stranger to me." The visitor answered, "It is strange that you should talk like this. I left my own village and came to yours because my co-villagers refused to give me a loan on the grounds they knew me well. And now you say that because you don't know me you will not give me a loan. Where can I go now?"

All our troubles begin when we break life up into segments and see things fragmentarily. No, all places are alike. There is no such place in life where only happiness abides. And similarly there is no such place where you meet with suffering and only suffering. Therefore, our heaven and hell are just our imagination. Because we have gotten into the habit of looking at things fragmentarily, we have imagined one place with abounding happiness and another with unmitigated sorrow and suffering—and we call them heaven and hell. No, wherever life is there is happiness and suffering together. They go together. You have happy moments or relaxation in hell and painful spells of boredom in heaven.

Bertrand Russell has said he would not like to go to heaven, where only happiness abounds. How can you know happiness without knowing suffering? How can you know health without knowing sickness? Where you have everything just by wishing for it, there cannot be any joy in having it.

The joy of having something comes from the length of time you have been wanting it, expecting it. Happiness really lies in the expectation. So once you achieve it, it loses its charm for you. Every happiness is imaginary: so long as you don't possess it, it seems to be abounding happiness. But as soon as it is actualized, it ceases to be happiness; our hands are as empty as before. And then we seek some other object for our desire, and we begin to expect it again. We feel so unhappy without it and imagine that happiness will come with it.

Rothschild was one of America's multi-millionaires. There is a story about him, and I don't know if it is true or not. He was on his deathbed, and he said to his son, "You have seen from my life that I made billions and they didn't make me really happy, they didn't bring happiness with them. Do you see that wealth is not happiness?"

His son said, "It is true, as I learned from your life, that wealth is not happiness, but I also learned from your life that if one has wealth, one can have the suffering of his choice; one can choose between one suffering and another. And this freedom of choice is beautiful. I know that you were never happy, but you always chose your own kind of suffering. A poor man does not have this freedom, this choice; his suffering is determined by circumstances. Except this, there is no difference between a rich man and a poor man in the matter of suffering. A poor man has to suffer with a woman who comes his way as his wife, but the rich man can afford women with whom he wants to suffer. And this choice is not an insignificant happiness."

If you examine it deeply, you will find that happiness and suffering are two aspects of the same thing, two sides of the same coin, or, perhaps, they are different densities of the same phenomenon.

Besides, what is happiness for me may be a matter of suffering for you. If I own ten million and I lose five, I will be miserable in spite of the fact that I still own five million. But if you have nothing and you come across five million, you will be mad with joy and happiness. Although both of us will be in the same situation financially—we have five million each—I will be beating my head against the wall and you will be dancing and celebrating. But also remember, your celebration will not last long, because someone who comes to own five million will also be faced with the fear of losing it. In the same way, my sufferings will soon wither away, because one who loses five million soon becomes engaged in recovering that loss—which is quite possible for him.

Strange are the ways of life. My happiness cannot be your happiness, nor can my suffering become your suffering. Even my happiness of today can not be my happiness for tomorrow. I cannot say if my happiness in this moment will continue to be my happiness in the next. Happiness and suffering are like clouds passing through the sky. They come and go.

Both happiness and suffering are there, and they are facts of life. In fact, it is wrong to call them two, but we have to, because all our languages divide things into two. Really it is one truth, sometimes seen as happiness and other times as suffering. In reality, pleasure and pain are just our interpretations, psychological interpretations. They are not real situations, they are largely interpretations of them. And it depends on us how we interpret something. And there may be a thousand interpretations of the same thing. It all depends on us.

If you know that both happiness and sorrow are true and are together, then you will also know that Buddha's statement that life is all suffering is fragmentary, and that it suffers from over-emphasis. This statement, however, is going to work; it will appeal to people. Buddha can have tens of thousands of followers, but not Krishna. Charwaka will attract millions to his fold, but Krishna cannot have that appeal.

Buddha and Charwaka have made choices, and they have both chosen one of the two polarities of truth. One says life is all suffering and the other says life is indulgence. And they make their statements clearly and emphatically. And whenever you find your own situation conforming with their statements you say Buddha is right or Charwaka is right. You will not agree with Buddha in every state of your life, you will only agree with him when you are in suffering. When you are not in any pain you will not say Buddha is right. A happy person, one who thinks himself to be happy, will ignore Buddha, but the moment he is in pain again, Buddha will become significant for him. It is, however, a case of your own situation occasionally approximating the statement of Buddha; it does not testify to its significance, to its meaningfulness.

But Krishna will always remain incomprehensible. Whether you are in pain or you are happy, it does not make any difference. You can only understand Krishna when you accept both happiness and misery together and at the same level. Not before. And do you know the state you will be in when you say an unconditional yes to both, when you know pain as the precursor of pleasure and pleasure as the precursor of pain, when you receive them without being agitated in any way, with equal equanimity, when you refuse to interpret them, even to name them? It will be a state of bliss. Then you will be neither happy nor unhappy, because you will have stopped interpreting and labeling things. The person who accepts things without judging them, without naming them, immediately enters the state of bliss. And one who is in bliss can understand Krishna. Only he can understand him.

One's being in a state of bliss does not mean that one will not be visited by suffering now. Suffering will of course visit you, but now you will not interpret it in a way that makes it really suffering. Bliss does not mean only happiness will visit you now. No, bliss only means that now you will not interpret happiness in a way that makes you cling to it and desire it more and more. Now things are as they are; what is, is. If it is sunny, it is sunny; if it is dark, it is dark. And as life is, it is going to be, by turn both sunny and dark. But you are not going to be affected by either, because now you know that things come and go but you remain the same. Pain and pleasure, happiness and sorrow, are like clouds moving in the sky but the sky remains untouched, the same. And that which remains the same, untrammeled and unchanging, is your consciousness. This is Krishna-consciousness. This Krishna-consciousness is just a witnessing: whatever happens to you, pain or pleasure, you simply watch it without any comment, without any judgment. And to be in Krishna-consciousness is to be in bliss.

For Krishna, there is only one meaningful word in life, and that is bliss. Happiness and unhappiness are not meaningful; they have been created by dividing bliss into two. The part that is in accord with you, that you accept, is called happiness, and the part that is discordant to you, that you deny, is called unhappiness. They are our interpretations of bliss, divided—and as long as it agrees with you it is happiness and when it begins to disagree with you it is called unhappiness. Bliss is truth, the whole truth.

It is significant that the word bliss, is *anand* in Sanskrit, is without an opposite. Happiness has its opposite in unhappiness, love has its opposite in hate, heaven in hell, but bliss has no such opposite. It is so because there is no state opposed to bliss. If there is any such state, it is that of happiness and of misery both. Similarly, the Sanskrit word *moksha*, which means freedom or liberation, has no opposite. *Moksha* is the state of bliss. *Moksha* means that happiness and misery are equally acceptable.

> Questioner: *What are the reasons for calling Krishna a complete incarnation of God? Kindly shed more light on this matter. Please explain in detail what is meant by saying that Krishna possessed all the sixty-four arts that comprise a complete incarnation.*

There is no other reason but one, and that is total emptiness. Whosoever is empty is whole. Emptiness is the foundation of wholeness. Rightly said, emptiness alone is whole. Can you draw a half emptiness? Even geometry cannot draw a half zero; there is no such thing as a half zero. Zero or emptiness is always complete, whole. Part-emptiness has no meaning whatsoever. How can you divide emptiness? And how can it be called emptiness if it is divided into parts? Emptiness is irreducible, indivisible. And where division begins, numbers begin; therefore, number one follows zero. One, two and three belong to the world of numbers. And all numbers arise from zero and end in zero. Zero or emptiness alone is whole.

He is whole who is empty. And it is significant that Krishna is called whole, because this man is absolutely empty. And only he who is choiceless can be empty. One who chooses becomes something: he accepts being somebody, he accepts "somebodiness". If he says he is a thief, he will become somebody; his emptiness will be no more. If he says he is a saint, then also is his emptiness destroyed. This person has accepted to be something, to be somebody. Now "somebodiness" has entered and "nothingness" is lost.

If someone asks Krishna who he is, he cannot answer the question meaningfully. Whatever answer he gives will bring choice in, and it will make something or somebody of him. If one really wants to be all, he must be prepared to be nothing.

Zen monks have a code, a maxim among themselves. They say, "One who longs to be everywhere must not be anywhere." One who wants to be all cannot afford to be anything. How can he be something? There is no congruity between all and something; they don't go together. Choicelessness brings you to emptiness, to nothingness. Then you are what you are, but you cannot say who you are, what you are.

It is for this reason that, when Arjuna asks Krishna who he is, instead of answering his question, he reveals himself, his real being to him. In that revelation he is all and everything. The deepest significance of his being whole lies in his utter emptiness.

One who is something or somebody will be in difficulty. His very being something will become his bondage. Life is mysterious; it has its own laws. If I choose to be something, this "something" will become my prison.

There is a beautiful anecdote from the life of Kabir. Every day a number of people gather at Kabir's place to listen to his words of wisdom. At the end of the *satsang*, Kabir always requested them to dine with him before going home.

One day the matter came to a head. Kabir's son Kamal came to him and said, "It is now becoming too much. We can no longer bear the burden of feeding so many people every day. We have to buy everything on credit, and we are now heavily in debt." Kabir said, "Why don't you borrow more?"

"But who is going to repay it?" Kamal asked.

Then his father said, "One who gives will repay it. Why should we worry about it?"

Kamal could not understand what his father meant. He was a worldly man. He said, "This answer won't do; it's not a spiritual matter. Those who lend us money ask for repayment, and if we fail to repay them we will prove to be dishonest."

To this Kabir simply said, "Then prove to be so. What is wrong with it? What if people call us dishonest?"

Kamal could not take it. And he said, "It is too much. I can't put up with it. You just stop inviting people to dinner, that's all."

Kabir then said, "If it comes to this, so be it."

The next day people came to *satsang* again, and as usual Kabir invited them to eat with him. His son reminded him of his unfulfilled promise to stop feeding the visitors. Kabir said, "I can't give you my word, because I don't want to bind myself to anything. I live in the moment. I let what happens in the moment, happen. If some day I don't ask them to stay to dinner, it will be so. But as long as I happen to invite them, I will invite them."

Kamal then said in desperation, "It means that I will now have to resort to stealing, because nobody is prepared to give us credit any more. What else can I do?"

Kabir said grinning, "You fool, why didn't you think of this before? It would have saved us the trouble of borrowing."

Kamal was simply amazed to hear his father say this. He was known as a wise man, a sage, who always gave people profound advice. "What is the matter with him?" he wondered. Then he thought that maybe his father was just playing a joke, so he decided to put it to a test.

Late in the night when the whole village was asleep, Kamal awakened his father and said, "I am going to steal. Will you accompany me?"

Kabir said, "Now that you have awakened me, I should go with you." Kamal was startled once again; he could not believe his father would agree to steal. But he was Kabir's son, and he did not like beating a hasty retreat, so he decided to see the whole of this joke, or whatever it was, through to the end.

Kamal walked to the back of a farmer's house, his father following him, and he began to break through the wall of the house. Kabir was standing silently near him. Kamal still expected his father to call off the whole thing as a joke. And at the same time he was afraid. Kabir said, "Why are you afraid, Kamal?"

"What else can I be when I am going to commit theft?" he retorted. "Isn't it ironical to suggest I should not be afraid while stealing?"

Kabir said, "It is fear that makes you feel guilty, that makes you think you are stealing; otherwise there is no reason to think that you are a thief. Don't fear, do your job rightly; otherwise you will needlessly disturb the sleep of the entire family."

Somehow Kamal drilled a hole in the wall, still hoping his father would call it quits. Then he said, "Now let's enter the house." And Kabir readily joined him and went inside the house. They had not gone there to steal money, they only wanted grain, and so they picked up a bag of wheat and left the house.

When they were out again, Kabir said to his son, "Now that dawn is at hand, it would be good if you went and informed the family that we are taking a bag of wheat away with us."

This startled Kamal once again and he exclaimed, "What are you saying? We are here as thieves, not as merchants."

But Kabir said, "Why make them worry unnecessarily about this missing bag of wheat? Let them know where it is going."

Followers of Kabir have completely ignored this odd episode. They never mention it because it is so inscrutable. In the light of this event it would be difficult to decide whether Kabir was a sage or a thief. Undoubtedly a theft has been committed, hence he is indictable as a thief. But his being wise is equally indisputable, because first he asks Kamal not to fear and then to inform the family about it so they are not put to unnecessary trouble.

Kamal had then warned Kabir, "But if I inform the family, we will be known as thieves."

And Kabir had very innocently said, "Since theft has happened, we are thieves. They will not be wrong to think of us as thieves."

Kamal had again warned, "Not only the family concerned, but the whole village will come to know that you are a thief! Your reputation will be in the mud. No one will come to visit you again."

And Kabir had said, "Then your troubles will be over. If they don't come, I will not have to ask them to eat with us."

Kamal could not understand it; the whole episode was so paradoxical.

Krishna is complete in another sense: his life encompasses all there is to life. It seems impossible how a single life could contain so much—all of life. Krishna has assimilated all that is contradictory, utterly contradictory in life. He has absorbed all the contradictions of life. You cannot find a life more inconsistent than Krishna's. There is a consistency running through the life of Jesus. So is Mahavira's life consistent. There is a logic, a rhythm, a harmonic system in the life of Buddha. If you can know a part of Buddha you will know all of him.

Ramakrishna has said, "Know one sage and all sages are known." But this rule does not apply to Krishna. Ramakrishna has said, "Know a drop of sea water and all the sea is known." But you can't say it about Krishna. The taste of sea water is the same all over—it is salty. But the waters of Krishna's life are not all salty; at places they can be sugary. And, maybe, a single drop contains more than one flavor. Really, Krishna comprises all the flavors of life.

In the same way, Krishna's life represents all the arts of existence. Krishna is not an artist, because an artist is one who knows only one art, or a few. Krishna is art itself. That completes him from every side and in every way.

That is why those who knew him had to take recourse in all kinds of exaggeration to describe him. With others we can escape exaggeration, or we have to exaggerate a particular facet of their lives, but we find ourselves in real difficulty when we come to say something about Krishna. Even exaggeration doesn't say much about him. We can portray him only in superlatives; we cannot do without superlatives. And our difficulty is greater when we find the superlative antonyms too, because he is cold and hot together.

In fact, water is hot and cold together. The difficulty arises when we impose our interpretation on it: then we separate hot from cold. If we ask water itself whether it is hot or cold, it will simply say, "To know me you only have to put your hand in me, because it is not a question of whether I am hot or cold, it is really a question of whether you are hot or cold." If you are warm, the water will seem to be cold, and if you are cold the water will seem to be hot. Its hotness or coldness is relative to you.

You can conduct an experiment. Warm one of your hands by exposing it to a fire, and cool your other hand on a piece of ice, and then put both hands together into a bucket of water. What will you find? Where your one hand will say the water is cold, the other will say the contrary. And it will be so difficult for you to decide if the water, the same water, is hot or cold.

You come upon the same kind of difficulty when you try to understand Krishna. It depends on you, and not on Krishna, how you see him. If you ask a Radha, who is in deep love with him, she will say something which will be entirely her own vision of Krishna. Maybe she does not call him a complete god, or maybe she does, but whatever she says depends on her, not on Krishna. So it will be a relative judgment. If sometimes Radha comes across Krishna dancing with another woman she will find it hard to accept him as a god. Then Krishna's water will feel cold to her. Maybe she does not feel any water at all. But when Krishna is dancing with Radha, he dances so totally with her that she feels he is wholly hers. Then she can say that he is God himself. Every Radha, when her lover is wholly with her, feels so in her bones. But the same person can look like a devil if she finds him flirting with another woman. These

statements are relative; they cannot be absolute. For
Arjuna and the Pandavas, Krishna is all-god, but the
Kauravas will vehemently contest this claim. For
them Krishna is worse than a devil. He is the person
who is responsible for their defeat and destruction.

There can be a thousand statements about
who Krishna is. But there cannot be a thousand statements about who Buddha is. Buddha has extricated
himself from all relative relationships, from all in-
volvements, and so he is unchanging, a monotone.
Taste him from anywhere, his flavor is the same.
Therefore, Buddha is not that controversial; he is like
flat land. We can clearly know him as such-and-such,
and our statements about him will always have a consistent meaning. But Krishna belies all our statements. And I call him complete and whole because
he has disaffirmed all our pronouncements on him.
No statement, howsoever astute, can wholly encom-
pass Krishna; he always remains unsaid. So one has
to cover the remaining side of his life with contrary
statements. All these statements together can wholly
cover him, but then they themselves seem paradoxical.

Krishna's wholeness lies in the fact that he
has no personality of his own, that he is not a person,
an individual—he is existence itself. He is just existence; he is just emptiness. You can say he is like a
mirror; he just mirrors everything that comes before
him. He just mirrors. And when you see yourself mir-
rored in him, you think Krishna is like you. But the
moment you move away from him, he is empty again.
And whosoever comes to him, whosoever is reflected
in his mirror thinks the same way and says Krishna is
like him.

For this very reason there are a thousand commentaries on the *Geeta*. Every one of the commentators saw himself reflected in the *Geeta*. There are
not many commentaries on the sayings of Buddha,
and there is a reason for this. There are still fewer on
the teachings of Jesus, and they are not much different

from each other. In fact, a thousand meanings can only be implanted on Krishna, not on Buddha. What Buddha says is definite and unequivocal; his statements are complete, clear-cut and logical. There may be some differences in their meaning according to the minds of different commentators, but this difference cannot be great.

The dispute over Mahavira was so small it only led to two factions among his followers. The dispute between the Shwetambaras and the Digambaras is confined to petty things like Mahavira lived naked or did not live naked. They don't quarrel over the teachings of Mahavira, which are very clear. It would be difficult to create differing sects around the Jaina *tirthankara*.

It is strange that it is as difficult to create sects around Krishna as it is around Mahavira. And it is so for very contrary reasons. If people try to create sects around Krishna, the number will run into the tens of thousands, and even then Krishna will remain inexhaustible. Therefore in the place of sects, around Krishna thousands of interpretations arose. In this respect too, Krishna is rare in that sects could not be built around him. Around Christ two to three major factions arose, but none around Krishna. But there are a thousand commentaries on the *Geeta* alone. And it is significant that no two commentaries tally: one commentary can be diametrically opposed to another, so much so they look like enemies. Ramanuja and Shankara have no meeting point. One can say to the other, "You are just an ignoramus!" And what is amazing is that in their own way both can be right; there is no difficulty in it. Why is it so?

It is so because Krishna is not definite, conclusive. He does not have a system, a structure, a form, an outline. Krishna is formless, incorporeal. He is limitless. You cannot define him; he is simply indefinable. In this sense too, Krishna is complete and whole, because only the whole can be formless, indefinable.

No interpretations of the *Geeta* interpret Krishna, they only interpret the interpreters. Shankara finds corroboration of his own views from the *Geeta*: he finds that the world is an illusion. From the same book Ramanuja discovers that devotion is the path to God. Tilak finds something else: for him the *Geeta* stands for the discipline of action. And curiously enough, from this sermon on the battlefield, Gandhi unearths that non-violence is the way. Nobody has any difficulty finding in the *Geeta* what he wants to find. Krishna does not come in their way; everyone is welcome there. He is an empty mirror. You see your image, move away, and the mirror is as empty as ever. It has no fixed image of its own; it is mere emptiness.

Krishna is not like a film. The film also works as a mirror, but only once: your reflection stays with it. So one can say that a particular photo is of so-and-so. You cannot say the same about a mirror; it morrors you only as long as you are with it. What does it do after you move away from it? Then it just mirrors emptiness. It mirrors whatsoever faces it, exactly as it is. Krishna is that mirror. And therefore I say he is complete, whole.

Krishna is whole in many other ways too, and we will come to understand this as we go on with this discussion. Someone can be whole only if he is whole in every way. A person is not whole if his wholeness is confined to a particular dimension of life. In their own dimensions Mahavira and Jesus are whole. In itself the life of Jesus is whole, and it lacks nothing as such. He is whole, as a rose is whole as a rose and a marigold is whole as a marigold. But a rose cannot be whole as a marigold, only a marigold is whole as a marigold. Similarly, a marigold cannot be whole as a rose. So Buddha, Mahavira and Jesus are whole in their own dimensions; in themselves they lack nothing.

But the wholeness of Krishna is utterly different. He is not one-dimensional, he is really multidimensional. He enters and pervades every walk of life, every dimension of life. If he is a thief he is a whole thief, and if he is a sage he is a whole sage. When he remembers something he remembers it totally, and when he forgets it he forgets it totally. That is why, when he left Mathura, he left it completely. Now the inhabitants of that place cry and wail for him and say that Krishna is very hard-hearted, which is not true. Or if he is hard-hearted, he is totally so.

In fact, one who remembers totally also forgets totally. When a mirror mirrors you it does so fully, and when it is empty it is fully empty. When Krishna's mirror moves to Dwarka it now reflects Dwarka as fully as it reflected Mathura when it was there. He is now totally at Dwarka, where he lives totally, loves totally and even fights totally.

Krishna's wholeness is multidimensional, which is rare indeed. It is arduous to be whole even in one dimension; it is not that easy. So it would be wrong to say that to be multidimensionally whole is arduous, it is simply impossible. But sometimes even the impossible happens, and when it happens it is a miracle. Krishna's life is that miracle, an absolute miracle.

We can find a comparison for every kind of person, but not for Krishna. The lives of Buddha and Mahavira are very similar; they look like close neighbors. There is little difference between them. Even if there is any difference, it is on the outside; their inside, their innermost beings are identical. But it is utterly improbable to find a comparison for Krishna on this planet. As a man he symbolizes the impossible.

It is natural that a person who is whole in every dimension will have disadvantages and advantages both. He will not compare well with one who has achieved wholeness in a particular dimension, in so far as that particular dimension is concerned. Mahavira has exerted all his energy in one dimension, so in his own field he will excel Krishna, who has diversified his energy in all dimensions. Christ will also excel him in his own field. But on the whole, Krishna is superb. Mahavira, Buddha and Christ cannot compare with him; he is utterly incomparable.

The significance of Krishna lies in his being multidimensional. Let us for a moment imagine a flower which from time to time becomes a marigold, a jasmine, a rose, a lotus and a celestial flower too—and every time we go to it we find it an altogether different flower. This flower cannot compare well with a rose which, through and through, has been only a rose. Where the rose has, with singlemindedness, spent all its energy being a rose, this imaginary flower has diversified its energy in many directions. The life of this imaginary flower is so pervasive, so extensive that it cannot possibly have the density there is in the life of a rose. Krishna is that imaginary flower: his being has vastness, but it lacks density. His vastness is simply endless, immense.

So Krishna's wholeness represents infinity. He is infinite. Mahavira's wholeness means he has achieved everything there is to achieve in his one dimension, that he has left nothing to be achieved as far as this dimension is concerned. Now, no seeker will ever achieve anything more than Mahavira achieved in his own field; he can never excel Mahavira. Therefore, Krishna is whole in the sense that he is multidimensional, expansive, vast and infinite.

A person who is whole in one dimension is going to be a total stranger in so far as other dimensions are concerned. Where Krishna can even steal skillfully, Mahavira will be a complete failure as a thief. If Mahavira tries his hand at it there is every chance of his landing in a prison. Krishna will succeed even as a thief. Where Krishna will shine on the battlefield as an accomplished warrior, Buddha will cut a sorry figure if he takes his stand there. We cannot imagine Christ playing a flute, but we can easily think of Krishna going to the gallows. Krishna will feel no difficulty on the cross. Intrinsically, he is as capable of facing crucifixion as of playing a flute. But it will be a hard task for Christ if he is handed a flute to play. We cannot think of Christ in the image of Krishna.

Christians say Jesus never laughed. Playing a flute will be a far cry for one who never laughed. If Jesus is asked to stand like Krishna, with one leg on the other, a crown of peacock feathers on his head and a flute on his lips, Jesus will immediately say, "I prefer the cross to this flute." He is at ease with the cross; he never felt so happy as on the cross. From the cross alone could he say, "Father, forgive them for they don't know what they are doing." He meets his death most peacefully on the cross, because it is his dimension. He finds no difficulty whatsoever in fulfilling his destiny. What was destined to happen is now happening. His journey's direction is now reaching its culminating point.

Jesus is rebellious, a rebel, a revolutionary, so the cross is his most natural destination. A Jesus can predict he is going to be crucified. If he is not crucified it will look like failure. In his case crucifixion is inevitable.

Krishna's case is very different and difficult. In his case no prediction is possible; he is simply unpredictable. Whether he will die on the gallows or amid adulation and worship, nobody can say. Nobody could predict the way he really died. He was lying restfully under a tree; it was really not an occasion for death. Someone, a hunter, saw him from a distance, thought a deer was lying there and hit him with his arrow. His death was so accidental, so out of place; it is rare in its own way. Everybody's death has an element of predetermination about it; Krishna's death seems to be totally undetermined. He dies in a manner as if his death has no utility whatsoever. His life was wholly non-utilitarian; so is his death.

The death of Jesus proved to be very purposeful. The truth is, Christianity wouldn't have come into existence had Jesus not been crucified. Christianity owes its existence to the cross, not to Jesus. Jesus was an unknown entity before his crucifixion. Therefore, crucifixion became significant and the cross became the symbol of Christianity. The crucifixion turned into Christianity's birth. Even Jesus is known to the world because of it.

But Krishna's death seems to be strange and insignificant. Is this a way to die? Does any one die like this? Is this the way to choose one's death, where someone hits you with an arrow, without your knowing, without any reason? Krishna's death does not make for an historical event; it is as ordinary as a flower blooming, withering and dying. Nobody knows when an evening gust of wind comes and hurls the flower to the ground. Krishna's death is such a non-event. It is so because he is multidimensional. Nothing can be said about his goings-on; none can know how his life is going to shape itself.

Lastly, let us look at it in another way. If Mahavira has to live another fifty years it can certainly be said how his life will shape up. Similarly, if Jesus is given an extra span of fifty years, we can easily outline on paper how he is going to spend it. It is predictable; it is within the grasp of astrologers. If Mahavira is given only ten years, the story of how he will live them can be written down here and now. It can be said precisely when he will leave his bed in the morning and when he will go to bed at night. Even the daily menus for his breakfast, lunch and dinner can be laid out. One can reduce to writing what he is going to say in his discourses. What he will do in ten years will be just a repetition of what he did in the preceding decade.

But in the case of Krishna, not only ten years, but even ten days will be as unpredictable. No one can say what will happen in the world in that ten days' time; no repetition whatsoever is possible in his case. This man does not live according to a plan, a schedule, a program; he lives without any planning, without any programming. He lives in the moment. What will happen will happen. In this sense too, Krishna is an infinity. He does not seem to end anywhere.

Now I will give you the ultimate meaning of Krishna as a complete incarnation. It is that he alone is complete who does not seem to be completing, to be concluding. What completes itself comes to its end, is finished. This will seem to be paradoxical to you. Ordinarily we believe that to be perfect means to reach the point of culmination beyond which nothing remains to be done, where one is finished with oneself. If you think so, this is really the idea of one-dimensional perfection. Krishna's wholeness is not like that which concludes itself, comes to an end and finishes itself, his completeness means that no matter how long he lives and journeys through life he is never going to come to a finish, he is going to go on and on and on.

The Upanishads' definition of wholeness is, therefore, right. It says, "From wholeness emerges wholeness, and if you take away wholeness from wholeness, wholeness still remains." If we take away thousands of Krishnas from Krishna, this man will still remain; more and more Krishnas can still be taken from him. There is no difficulty. Krishna will have no trouble whatsoever, because he can be anything.

Mahavira cannot be born today. It will be utterly impossible for him to be born at the present time, because Mahavira reached wholeness in a particular situation, in a particular time. That dimension could be perfected only in that particular situation. In the same way Jesus cannot be born today. If today he comes at all, in the first place nobody will crucify him. No matter how much noise he makes, people will say, "Just ignore him." Jews have learned their lesson from their first mistake, which gave rise to Christianity. There are a billion Christians all over the earth today. Jews will not commit the same mistake again. They will say, "Don't get involved with this man again, leave him alone. Let him say and do what he likes."

In his lifetime Jesus could not get many people to become interested in him; after his death millions became interested. Out of the hundred thousand people who had gathered to watch him being crucified, hardly eight were those who loved him. Eight in a hundred thousand! Even that handful of his lovers were not courageous enough to say "Yes" if they were confronted with the question as to whether they were Jesus' friends. They would have said, "We don't know him." The woman who brought the dead body of Jesus down from the cross had not come from a respectable Jerusalem family, because it was difficult for Jesus to reach the aristocracy and influence them. She who could gather courage to bring Jesus down from the cross was a prostitute. As a prostitute she was already at the lowest rung of the social ladder, what worse could society do to her? So it was a prostitute, not a woman of the aristocracy, who brought his dead body down. In my view, even today, no woman from a respectable family will agree to do so if Jesus comes and happens to be crucified a second time.

Jesus can be neglected, because his statements are so innocent.

There is another danger, in case people of today don't neglect him: they will take him for a madman. What was the bone of contention which led to his crucifixion? Jesus had said, "I am God; I and my father in heaven are one." Today we would say, "Let him say it. What does it matter?"

For Jesus to be born again it is necessary for the same situation to exist that was present in his time. That is why Jesus is an historical person. Please remember it is only the followers of Jesus who began writing the history of religion. No other people had done it. History begins with Jesus. It is not accidental that an era begins with Jesus. Jesus is an historical event, and he can happen only in a particular historical moment.

We did not write Krishna's history. The dates of his birth and death are not definitely known. And it is useless to know them: any dates would do. Particular dates and times are irrelevant in relation to Krishna: he can happen at any date and time; he will be relevant to any time and situation. He will have no difficulty whatsoever in being what he is; he will be the same in all times. He does not insist on being like this or that. If you have any conditions, you will need a corresponding situation for it, but if you say that anything will do, you can be at ease in every situation. Mahavira will insist on being naked, but Krishna will even put on peg-legged pants, he will have no difficulty. He will even say that had you made him this outfit earlier, he would gladly have worn it.

To live so choicelessly is to live in infinity. No time, no place, no situation can be a problem for him. He will be one with any age, with any period of human history. His flower will bloom wherever and whenever he is.

Therefore I say that where Mahavira, Buddha and Jesus are historical persons, Krishna is not. This does not mean that Krishna did not happen. He very much happened, but he does not belong to any particular time and space, and it is in this sense that he is not historical. He is a mythical and legendary figure. He is an actor, a performer really. He can happen any time. And he is not attached to a character, to an idealized lifestyle. He will not ask for a particular Radha, any Radha will be okay for him. He will not insist on a particular age, a special period of time; any age will suit him. It is not necessary that he only play a flute, any musical instrument of any age will do for him.

Krishna is whole in the sense that no matter how much you take away from him, he still remains complete and whole. He can happen over and over again.

We will have another question-and-answer discussion this afternoon. You can send in writing whatever questions arise in your mind.

THIRD DISCOURSE
EVENING, SEPTEMBER 26, 1970
MANALI, INDIA

WHERE BUDDHA ENDS KRISHNA BEGINS

Questioner: Throughout the Geeta Krishna appears to be utterly egoistic, but this morning you said it was because of his egolessness that Krishna asked Arjuna to surrender to him, giving up everything else. But Buddha and Mahavira don't say this to their disciples. So is there a difference between their kinds of egolessness? If so, what is the basic difference between them?

here are two ways to achieve egolessness. One way is through negation. One goes on negating his ego, negating himself, gradually eliminating himself until a moment comes when nothing remains to be eliminated. But the state of egolessness achieved like this is a negative one, because deep down one is still left with a very subtle form of ego which says, "I have made short work of my ego."

The other is the way of expansion. The seeker goes on expanding himself, his self, so much that all of existence is included in him. The egolessness that comes through this way is total, so total that nothing remains outside of him—not even this much, that he can say, "I am now egoless."

A seeker who follows the technique of negation attains to the soul, to the *atman*, which means that the last vestige of his ego remains in the form of "I am." Everything of his ego has disappeared, but the pure "I" remains. Such a seeker will never attain to God, to the supreme. And the seeker who follows the way of expansion, who expands himself to the extent that he embraces the whole, knows God straightaway. He does not have to know the soul.

Krishna's life is positive, it is not negative. He does not negate anything there is in life, not even the ego. He tells you to enlarge your ego so much that the whole is included in its embrace. And when nothing remains outside you as "thou" then there is no way to say "I am." I can call myself "I" only so long as there is a "thou" separate from me. The moment "thou" disappears "I" also ceases to be real. So the egoless "I" has to be vast, infinitely immense.

It is in the context of this immensity of the "I" that the rishi, the seer of the Upanishad exclaimed, "*Aham brahmasmi,*" "I am God, I am the supreme." It does not mean to say that you are not God, it only means that since there is no "thou" only "I" remains. It is I who am passing through the tree as a breeze. It is I who am waving as waves in the ocean. I am the one who is born, and I am also the one who will die. I am the earth, and I am also the sky. There is nothing whatsoever other than me; therefore, there is now no way even for this "I" to exist. If I am everything and everywhere, who am I going to tell that "I am"? In relation to what?

The whole of Krishna is co-extensive, co-expansive with the immense, the infinite; he is one with the whole. That is why he can say, "I am the supreme, the *Brahman*." There is nothing egoistic about it. It is just a linguistic way of saying it: "I" is just a word here; there is no I-ness to it. Krishna's "I" has ceased to be.

As I said, the other way is negative. A seeker on the path of negation goes on negating, renouncing, bit by bit, everything that constitutes the ego and strengthens it. If wealth is one of the factors of ego, he renounces wealth. But it would be wrong to think that only a rich person has an ego, and that only a poor man is egoless. A poor person has a poor ego, but ego is there. And don't think only the householder is egoistic, and not the sannyasin. Even a sannyasin has his ego. However, if I give up everything that makes up and strengthens the ego; if I give up money, family, relationships; if I renounce all the props of my ego, my ego will be left without any support. But even then the "I" will not disappear; it will now cling to itself, to its own pure I-ness.

This is the most subtle form of "I", the one that comes through the process of negation. And many people get stuck there and remain hung up on it, because this "I" is subtle, invisible. A rich person's ego is gross and loud: he says he owns so much money. The ego of a sannyasin, a renunciate, is subtle, invisible, but it is there: he says he has renounced so much money.

A householder's ego is obvious: he has a house, a family, possessions. These are the ingredients of his ego and its signposts too. But even a monk has his monastery, his ashram, his family of disciples. And besides, he is either a Hindu monk or a Christian monk or a Mohammedan monk. A monk has his own things that bind him and feed his ego; he too is stuck somewhere. But his ego is subtle, invisible: he does not even use the word "I"; he has dropped it. But it does not make a difference.

One has to go beyond the subtlest form of I-ness, and it is so arduous. Mahavira and Buddha transcend it: it needs very hard work; it calls for tremendous austerity. Even if I have renounced all my possessions, all that I called mine, the pure "I" remains. How can I go beyond it? One in a thousand attains to egolessness through the path of negation; nine hundred and ninety-nine will be stuck with the subtle "I". While Mahavira transcends the subtlest of egos, those following him become stuck, because it is really difficult, very difficult to achieve egolessness the negative way. It is easy to drop the various props that strengthen the "I", but it is nearly impossible to drop the last vestige of the "I", the pure "I".

It is at the last stage of his journey that a seeker on the path of negation encounters his major hurdle, but a seeker on the path of affirmation comes upon it right at the first stage. Right at the start of his journey a life-affirming seeker finds it very difficult to deny the "thou", because it is there, it is so obvious. The spiritual discipline of Krishna is most difficult in the beginning, but once you get over that, there is smooth sailing to the end. But in the discipline of Mahavira and Buddha the beginning is easy enough. The real difficulty is at the end when, bereft of all its props, the ego remains in its purified form. How to get rid of this very subtle ego is the real problem.

What a seeker on the positive path does at the beginning, the seeker on the negative path does at the end. What does an affirmative seeker do? He tries to discover his "I" in "thou". And the other kind of seeker, seeking through negation, tries to find the "thou" in his "I". But his task is so difficult. It is much easier to see the "I" in "thou" than to see the "thou" in "I". And it is still more difficult to see it when it comes to the point of pure "I", because now it is just a feeling of I-ness, which is so very fine and subtle. So the last part of the journey on the path of Buddha and Mahavira is decisive. Hence it is just possible that a seeker may give up his pursuit and retreat even before he comes to it. He has struggled all his life to save his "I" and now he is called upon to sacrifice it. It is extremely difficult.

But even this pure "I" can be dropped. It can be dropped if the seeker comes to see the "thou" included in his "I". Therefore the last stage of the discipline of Mahavira and Buddha is called *Kevala Jnan* or "only knowing". *Kevala Jnan* means that when the knower is no more, when only knowing remains, unity, ultimate unity can be found. The ultimate freedom is freedom from the "I". It is not freedom of the "I", but freedom *from* the "I" itself.

But one who comes after Buddha or Mahavira as his follower, comes with the wishful question, "How will I achieve *moksha*, freedom?" And this is his difficulty. No "I" has ever achieved freedom; freedom *from* "I" and "me" is what the case really is.

It is for this reason that seekers in the tradition of Mahavira easily fall prey to egoism. It is not surprising they turn into great egoists. Renunciation, austerity and asceticism, practiced for long, go to strengthen and harden their egos. In the end they get rid of everything, and yet a hard core of ego which they find extremely difficult to dissolve—you may call it a holy ego—remains with them. But it can be dissolved; it has been dropped by men like Buddha and Mahavira. And there are separate techniques to dissolve it.

On the path of Krishna this hard core of ego has to be dropped in the first instance. Is it any good to carry on with a disease you have to drop ultimately? The longer you live with it the worse and worse it will become: it will turn into a chronic and communicable disease. Therefore, where Mahavira's *Kevala Jnan* or "only knowing" comes last, Krishna's *sakshi* or "witnessing" comes first. Right from the beginning I have to know this truth, that I am not separate from the whole.

But if I am not separate, the question of renunciation becomes meaningless. What is there to renounce if I am all? I am that which is being renounced. Who will renounce whom? And where can I go if I am everything and everywhere?

In one of his poems Rabindranath Tagore has made a beautiful joke about Buddha's renunciation. When Buddha returns to his home after his enlightenment; his wife Yashodhara tells him, "For a long time I have had only one question to ask of you. And now that you are here again I want to know if what you achieved in the jungle was not available right here?" Buddha finds it very difficult to answer her. If he says it was available in his home—and it is true, what is available in the vastness of a forest can also be available in one's home— Yashodhara will remind him that she had told him so. And Yashodhara really had said it. It was for this reason that Buddha had left his house in the dead of night without informing her. If he accepts that truth is everywhere, Yashodhara will immediately say there was no point in renunciation, that it was sheer madness on his part. And it would be a falsehood to say that truth is not to be found in the home, that it is only to be found in the forest, because Buddha now knows for himself that what he found in the wilderness is available right in his own home, it is available all over.

Krishna is not for renunciation: he does not run away from anywhere; he does not give up anything. What Buddha comes to see at the last hour, Krishna sees at the very first. What is it that Buddha comes to know at the end of a long and arduous search? It is that only truth is, and that truth is everywhere. Krishna knows it from the beginning, that only truth is, and that it is everywhere.

I have heard about a fakir who spent his lifetime living on the outskirts of a town. Whenever someone asked him why he did not do some *sadhana* or spiritual practice to achieve the supreme he always said, "What is there to achieve? It is already achieved." If someone asked him why he did not go on a pilgrimage, he said, "Where to go? I have already arrived." And when someone asked if he did not have something to seek, he said, "What one seeks is already found." Now this fakir does not need *sadhana*, spiritual discipline.

Hence no *sadhana*, no spiritual discipline could grow in the tradition of Krishna. You will not come across anyone who can be called a *sadhaka* or seeker on the path of Krishna. What is there to seek? You seek that which you don't have, and you can have it only if you make efforts for it. Effort is needed to achieve something which you have not yet achieved. *Sadhana* means the search for the probable. No effort is needed to achieve what is already achieved. We strive for what should be, not for what is. There is no point in achieving the achieved.

When at long last Gautam Siddhartha attained to enlightenment, when he became the Buddha, the awakened one, someone asked him, "What is it that you have achieved?"

Buddha is reported to have said, "I achieved nothing. I only came to know what was already the case. I discovered what I already had with me. Earlier I did not know that it had been with me forever and ever; now I know it. It is nothing new that I have come upon, it has always been there. Even when I was unaware of it, it was very much there, not an iota less than it is now."

What Buddha says in the last moment, Krishna will say at the very first. Krishna will tell you, "What is the point of going anywhere? You are already where you want to go. What you think to be a stopover on your journey is actually your destination—where you happen to be right now. Why run in any direction? You are already in that place you want to reach to after you have done your running. You have already arrived."

So there is a period of effort, of *sadhana* in the lives of Buddha and Mahavira, followed by a state of fulfillment, attainment. Krishna is ever a *siddha*, a fulfilled one; there is no such thing as a period of *sadhana* in his whole life. Have you ever heard that Krishna went through any sort of spiritual discipline? Did he ever meditate? Did he practice yoga? Did he ever fast and undergo other austerities? Did he retire to a jungle to practice asceticism? There is nothing, absolutely nothing like a *sadhana* in his whole life.

What Buddha and Mahavira attain after heroic efforts Krishna already has, without any effort whatsoever. He seems to be eternally enlightened. Then why a *sadhana*? For what? This is the fundamental difference between Krishna and others. So there is no way for the ego to affect Krishna's vision in the least, because there is no "thou" for him, no one is the other for him.

I was talking about Kabir only this morning. There is another anecdote, which is as beautiful, in the life of Kabir and his son Kamal. One morning Kabir sends Kamal to the forest to bring green grass for the cattle. Kamal goes to the forest with a sickle in his hands. Plants are dancing in the wind, as they are dancing right here before us. Morning turns into midday and midday passes into evening, and yet Kamal does not return home from the forest. Kabir is worried, because he was expected to be back home for his midday meal. Kabir makes inquiries and then goes to the forest with a few friends in search of his son. On reaching the forest, he finds Kamal standing in the thick of grass tall enough to reach his shoulders. It is wrong to say that he is standing, he is actually dancing with the dancing plants. The wind is dancing, the plants are dancing and Kamal is dancing with them. His eyes are closed and he is wholly absorbed in the dance. Kabir finds that he has not chopped a single blade of grass for the cattle. So he gently puts his hands on his shoulders and asks, "What have you been doing, my son?"

Kamal opens his eyes and looks around. He tells his father, "You did well to remind me," and then picks up his sickle with a view to his assigned task. But he finds it is already dark and not possible to cut any grass.

The people with Kabir asked him, "But what have you been doing for the rest of the day?"

Kamal says, "I became just like a grass plant; I forgot I was a man or anything. I also forgot this was grass I came to chop and take home to my cattle. The morning was so beautiful and blissful, it was so festive and dancing with the wind and the trees and the grass, it would have been sheer stupidity on my part not to have joined the celebration. I began dancing, forgetting everything else. I did not even remember I was Kamal who had come here to collect food for my animals. I am aware of it again only now that you come to remind me."

Krishna, like Kamal, is engrossed in a dance, the cosmic dance. Kabir's son dances with a few plants in a small forest, but Krishna dances with the whole universe: he dances with its stars, with its men and women, with its trees and flowers and even its thistles. And he is so one with the cosmic dance there is no way for "I" and "thou" to exist in that space. The state of egolessness Krishna achieves in this moment of dance is the same that Buddha and Mahavira achieve at the end of a long and arduous journey, a journey of hard work, austerity and asceticism. Where Krishna begins his journey, after completing a marathon race Mahavira and Buddha arrive.

Krishna is not a seeker. It would be wrong to call him a seeker. He is a *siddha*, an adept, an accomplished performer of all life's arts. And what he says in this *siddha* state, in this ultimate state of mind, may seem to you to be egoistic, but it is not. The difficulty is that Krishna has to use the same linguistic

"I" as you do, but there is a tremendous difference in connotation between his "I" and yours. When you say "I" it means the one imprisoned inside your body, but when Krishna says it he means that which permeates the whole cosmos. Hence he has the courage to tell Arjuna, "Give up everything else and come to my feet." If it were the same "I" as yours—a prisoner of the body—it would be impossible for him to say a thing like this. And Arjuna would have been hurt if Krishna's "I" were as petty as yours. Arjuna would have immediately retorted, "What are you saying? Why on earth should I surrender to you?" Arjuna would have really been hurt, but he was not.

Whenever someone speaks to another in the language of the ego, it creates an instant reaction in the ego of the other. When you say something in the words of the "I" of the ego, the other immediately begins to speak the same language. We are skilled in knowing the undertones of each other's words, and we react sharply.

But Krishna's "I" is absolutely free of all traces of egoism, and for this reason he could call upon Arjuna to make a clean surrender to him. Here, "Surrender to me" really means "Surrender to the whole. Surrender to the primordial and mysterious energy that permeates the cosmos."

Egolessness comes to Buddha and Mahavira too, but it comes to them after long, hard struggle and toil. But it may not come to most of their followers, because on their paths it is the very last thing to come. So the followers may come to it or they may not. But egolessness comes first with Krishna; he begins where Buddha and Mahavira end. So one who chooses to go with Krishna has to have it at the very beginning. If he fails, there is no question of his going with Krishna.

You can walk a long way in the company of Mahavira with your "I" intact, but with Krishna you have to drop your "I" with the first step; otherwise you are not going to go with him. Your "I" can find some accommodation with Mahavira, but none with Krishna. For Krishna the first step is the last; for Mahavira and Buddha the last step is the first. And it is important for you to bear this difference in mind, because it is a big difference, and a basic difference at that.

What *sadhana* can you do with Krishna? You can dance with him, you can sing with him, you can celebrate with him, and you can merge with him. Or if you call this *sadhana*, then it is a different matter. Therefore Krishna has no expectations from you. What is there to expect when the journey begins with egolessness? If you go to Buddha or Mahavira to say you are an egoist and want to be free of it, he will give you some method, he will tell you to first give up this and give up that and then the problem of the ego will be taken care of. But if you go to Krishna with the same question, he will not prescribe any methods, he will say the ego has to go in the first instance, that you have to begin with its cessation. Krishna will say that methods and techniques are ways of postponement. That is why no community of seekers could grow around him; it was not in the very nature of things.

As far as a seeker is concerned, he very much likes to play with methods. He will say it is very difficult to part with the ego, but he can part with his money if it is going to help. But Krishna is not going to oblige you. He will say parting with money won't do, because your disease will continue to afflict you even if you give up all your wealth. If a man suffering from cancer says he cannot give up his cancer, but he can get his head shaved, what will you say? Shaving his head will make no difference whatsoever to his disease, the cancer will continue to torment him. There is no connection between cancer and shaving; cancer will continue to be a problem even if you shave your head a hundred times. If the seeker says to begin with, he is prepared to give up his clothes, Krishna will say clothes have nothing to do with cancer.

But Mahavira and Buddha will not say this. Mahavira will say, "Okay, begin with shaving your head. Then we will see." Everybody can have access to Mahavira and Buddha. They will say, "Do whatever you can do; we will take care of the ultimate thing at the end."

Krishna deals straightaway with the ultimate question; he does not like any dilly-dallyings. He says if someone is prepared for the ultimate matter, then he alone will have entry into his house. It is for this reason that his house remains nearly empty. Entry into his house is not easy. And so Krishna could not create any order of disciples and followers. Mahavira has fifty thousand disciples; it is simply natural. With Krishna it is nearly impossible. Where can you find fifty thousand egoless people right at the beginning?

If we say it rightly, Buddha and Mahavira stand for gradual enlightenment, for gradual growth towards enlightenment. And we understand the language of gradualism. We can understand that a rupee can grow into two rupees and two rupees into three, and so on and so forth. But that a poor person can become rich at once is something we don't understand. What Krishna stands for is sudden enlightenment. He says, "Why go through a long and needless process? You are poor if you have one rupee, and you remain poor even if you own ten rupees; now you will be called ten-rupee-poor. You will remain poor even if you possess a million rupees, because there are people who own billions. So be rid of this poor man's arithmetic. I am going to make you a king all at once."

What Krishna means to say is that it is not a matter of becoming a king, it is just a matter of remembering that you are a king. You are already a king, but you have forgotten. Therefore, while *sadhana* is the way of Mahavira and Buddha, remembering, just remembering is the way of Krishna. Just remember, recall who you are, and the journey is complete in a single sweep.

Just remembering is enough; it is Krishna's keyword. I will tell you a story.

I have heard that a king expelled his son from his kingdom. He was angry with his son, a spoiled son, and so in a moment of rage he threw him out. The son did not have any skills or vocation. What can a king's son know? He was not even educated, so he could do nothing to make a decent living. However he had, by way of a hobby, learned a little singing and dancing in his childhood. So he took to singing and dancing on the streets of a town belonging to a hot and arid neighboring country where he found refuge.

For ten years the king's son lived the life of a homeless beggar in tattered and dirty clothes. So he completely forgot that he was ever a prince. And curiously enough, in these ten years, he was increasingly maturing towards kingship, since he was the only son of a king who was growing older and older. But, at present, he was a faceless person moving from door to door with a begging bowl in his hands.

When the king became very old he grew worried about the future of his throne. Who was going to succeed him and manage his kingdom after his death? So he asked his prime minister to search for his only son, whom he had expelled years ago, and bring him back so he could take over the reins of his kingdom from him. Even if he was stupid he had to be recalled, the king thought. There was no other alternative.

The prime minister went out in search of his king's son. After a great deal of inquiry and effort he reached the town where his future master was living as a nobody. His chariot halted in front of a hotel, where he found him under a scorching midday sun, a young man begging a little money from the hotel manager to buy himself a pair of sandals. He was pointing to his bare and bleeding feet, lacerated with wounds. The prime minister stepped down from the chariot and approached the young beggar. He took no time to recognize him—he was the king's son—although he was in rags, his body emaciated, his face shriveled and sunburned. He bowed to him and said, "The king has pardoned you and asks you to return to your kingdom."

In a second, a split-second, the young man's face was transformed and he threw away his beggar's bowl. In no time at all he ceased to be a beggar and became a king. And he told the prime minister, "Go to the market and bring me a pair of good shoes and good clothes, and in the meantime make arrangements for my bath." And with the stride of a prince he walked to the chariot and stepped aboard.

In and around the hotel, everybody, who a little while ago had given him alms or denied them, came rushing, crowding around his chariot. And they found he was a different man altogether, he was not even looking at them now. They asked him, "How is it you forget us in a moment?" The prince said, "I remembered you as long as I had forgotten who I was. Just now I have remembered who I am, so forget I am a beggar." When the crowd reminded him of what he had been only a moment ago, he said, "Now I remember. Now I know I am a king. I have always been a king."

Krishna's way is just to remind man who he is. This is not something to practice, this is just a remembering. And within a moment of this remembering everything is transformed; the beggar's bowl is thrown away. In one moment one ceases to be a beggar and becomes a king.

But this becoming a king is a sudden event. And remember, it is only suddenly that someone becomes a king. Someone can be a beggar gradually, step by step, but not a king. It is wrong to think there are steps leading to kingship. There are steps to being a beggar. If you climb those steps and stand at the top, you will become at best a better beggar, a moneyed beggar, and nothing else. It will make no significant difference. If you still want to be a king you will have to leap from the top you have reached step by step. This moment comes to Buddha and Mahavira, but it comes in the last hour. To Krishna it comes right in the beginning. Krishna will tell you, "First take a jump, and then we will take care of the next thing." And after you have taken a jump this "next thing" is not necessary at all.

Throughout the *Geeta*, Krishna does nothing but remind Arjuna who he is. He does not give a sermon, he only hits him on the head again and again so that he remembers who he is. He is not there to teach, but to awaken him. He shakes Arjuna to wake up and know his self-nature, his innate nature. He tells him, "You are engrossed in very petty matters like people will die at your hands if you fight. Wake up and see for yourself if anyone has ever been dead. You are eternally alive." But Arjuna is asleep, he is dreaming, and so every now and then he asks why he should kill his own kinsmen. Krishna does not explain anything, he gives him shock treatment so he wakes up and sees the reality for himself. It is an illusion to think that one is related with one and not related with another, the truth is he is either related with all or with none. Similarly, either everybody dies or nobody dies. Ultimately it is the truth that counts.

Remembering is the essence of Krishna's philosophy of life. Therefore it is not any kind of spiritual discipline, it is a direct leap into awakening, into enlightenment. But we don't have the courage to take such a leap and so we say it is not our cup of tea. We want to move cautiously and slowly, step by step. But remember, if you move in this manner, you will save your ego at every step. It is really to save your ego that you refuse to take a jump. A jump is certainly dangerous for the ego; your ego cannot survive after a jump. You go slow just to save yourself, but what is being saved at every step will remain safe even at the last step of the journey. And then your ego will tell you to somehow enter *moksha* or liberation keeping yourself intact. But it is simply impossible to save yourself and enter *moksha*. It has never happened. Entry into *moksha* is possible only after the ego has been completely annihilated. The death of the ego is the price of freedom.

This is the problem you are going to encounter at the end, howsoever you avoid it. It is inescapable. Therefore I say it is far better to invite the problem and face it at the very beginning rather than postpone it until the end. Why waste so much time and energy?

What Buddha and Mahavira come upon in the last moment is nothing other than remembering; it is not the result of any *sadhana*. But since we see any number of people engaged in *sadhana*, we think that *sadhana* works. A person makes twenty rounds of his village and then remembers who he is. Another person remembers who he is after making only one round. And someone else can know himself without making a single round. But a spectator can conclude that twenty rounds are necessary to come upon this remembering. But the fact is, there is no cause-and-effect relationship between remembering and making rounds of a village. And this needs to be understood clearly.

There is no causal link between what Mahavira did and what he came upon. You cannot say that Vardhman became Mahavira because he went through a specific course of spiritual discipline. If it is so, then Jesus cannot become Christ because he does nothing like Mahavira did. Then Buddha cannot happen, because Gautam Siddhartha does not follow Mahavira's *sadhana*, his course of spiritual discipline.

If water is heated to the boiling point it turns into vapor, so there is a causal connection between vapor and heating. But the spiritual life is not subject to the law of cause and effect. And that is why spiritual life can be absolutely free. Freedom is not possible within the chain of cause and effect. The law of cause and effect is a kind of bondage: every effect is tied in with its cause. Cause and effect are dependent on each other; one cannot be without the other. And as a cause turns into an effect, so an effect turns into a cause for some other effect. So everything is bound up with everything else, and there is no end to it. It is a kind of cause-and-effect continuum. When water turns into vapor it becomes subject to the law of vapor as it was subject to the law of water a little while ago. And in the same way, when it turns into ice it becomes subject to the law of ice. So it is bounded at both ends; it is in bondage.

What we call *moksha* or freedom is non-causal. Freedom is not subject to the law of cause and effect. It is not caused; it cannot be. Freedom is causeless. You cannot say that someone attained to freedom because of this or that reason—because he fasted for so many days. If it is so then anybody can become a Mahavira if he fasts. But it is not so. Every kind of water, from a well or from the sea, heated to the boiling point, turns into vapor—but every person will not be freed by fasting. Mahavira had fasted and he became free, but it does not mean his freedom was the result of fasting. Mahavira lived naked, so everybody who goes naked should be free. Any number of poor people are going without clothes, but they are not going to be free. Freedom has nothing to do with nakedness.

The truth is that freedom means going beyond the chain of cause and effect. The transcendence of the law of cause and effect is freedom. Really, whatever is subject to the law of cause and effect is called matter, and what goes beyond the frontiers of this law is known as God.

But where is the frontier, the limit that you are going to cross and go beyond? We are used to connecting everything with the law of cause and effect.

I was telling a story a little while ago. A villager boards a railway train for the first time in his life. He has reached the age of seventy-five and his co-villagers have celebrated his anniversary and want to give him a birthday gift. So they hit upon a novel idea. Only recently their village has been connected to the railroad and trains have been passing through it. And up to now no one among them has gone on a railway journey. So they decide to give the old man the opportunity to be the first among them to enjoy such a trip. This will be their birthday gift to him. So they buy the old man a ticket and put him on the train. A friend of his also goes with him for company and comfort. The two board the train and are exceedingly happy.

When the train moves out of the village a vendor of soft drinks enters their compartment with a tray of sodas and begins selling them. The old man and his friend have never tasted soda before, so they look around to see if anyone is drinking it. When they see some people buying it and drinking it they buy themselves a bottle and agree to share it between them, half-and-half. One of them drinks it first and likes it. But when he has consumed his share of the drink, his friend becomes impatient for his share and snatches the bottle from his hands. Exactly at this moment the train enters a tunnel and suddenly the whole train is plunged into darkness. And the man who has already tasted the drink shouts at his friend, "Don't touch that stuff! I have been struck blind! It seems to be something very dangerous!"

The man had no idea of the train entering a dark tunnel, and he thinks the drink has made him blind. A causal link is established between the drink and darkness, which is absolutely absurd. But this is how we think and look at life. And this leads us into all kinds of illusions.

The experiencing of freedom is beyond the world of cause and effect. Buddha attained to *nirvana* not because of the efforts he made for it, but in spite of those efforts. Mahavira achieved *moksha* not because of the severe *sadhana* he is said to have followed, but in spite of it all. If someone imitates Mahavira totally from A to Z, he is not going to achieve liberation. Nothing will happen to him even if, by way of a *sadhana*, he does everything as perfectly as Mahavira did.

Freedom is a kind of explosion totally outside the chain of cause and effect. There is absolutely no connection between the two.

Krishna says that if you only understand it for yourself, you can be free here and now. Whether one deserves it or does not deserve it is not the question. It is not a matter of worthiness or otherwise. It is also not a question of any *sadhana*. But we are in the habit of making detours. If we have to reach our own homes, we go on a tour of the whole village to do so. Even if we have to come to ourselves, we do so via the other. It has become our lifestyle; we cannot do without it. Besides, everybody has his own *karmas* to fulfill, and they will go through them. But the difficulty is that you not only fulfill your own portion of *karmas*, you want to do everything that others have done. And then you are in a mess. Maybe someone came to himself in a particular way, but you are not that person, you are a different person altogether. You cannot come to yourself by imitating him.

When the Upanishads were translated into the western languages for the first time, people were amazed to see they did not prescribe any sadhana, any spiritual discipline in the form of "do's and don'ts"; they did not lay down any moral code. What kind of a religious scripture are they? The Bible has laid down everything so clearly; it has its Ten Commandments, all its "do's and don'ts". The Upanishads did not deal with the matter of morality.

It is difficult to understand that the moral code prescribed in the Bible or elsewhere has nothing to do with religion. Unfortunately, morality has become synonymous with religion. The Upanishads are truly books of religion; they don't deal with the problems of ethics. The central theme of the Upanishads is remembering, and it is remembering that religion is all about. They say that man has only to remember what he has forgotten, has to remember who he really is, who he is right now. He does not have to do a thing except recollect what he has forgotten.

In Krishna's vision, man does not have to recover a lost treasure that he once had—it is still with him, but he has forgotten that he has it. So it is only a matter of recalling, of remembering what is hidden in the basement of his consciousness. It is nothing more than that. Therefore Krishna tells you to go straight to remembering it.

And this remembering is sudden; it is not a gradual process. Krishna does not prescribe any discipline, any moral codes, any rituals that religions in general do. Krishna asks you just to wake up and open your eyes and see, and your ego will disappear in an instant. Krishna's ego ceases to be in the very first instant. And whoever will see with open eyes will see his ego disappear in no time. Because we live with our eyes shut, our egos go on and on. Open your eyes, and you will not have to say that what happened to Krishna did not happen to you.

You live with your eyes closed, and this is the first thing to see. Have you ever pondered over, considered your life? How did you come into the world? Who created you? Did you create yourself? At least this much is certain: you did not create yourself. It may not be certain who created you, but this much is certain: you did not create yourself. This much is definite: as you are, it is not your handiwork. But even in a matter like this we delude ourselves. There are people who claim to be "self-made". They don't give God this trouble, they take the job of making themselves upon themselves. This is stupid. But we are so blind we fail to see such a simple truth that our own being is not in our hands.

Have you ever contemplated the fundamental question of being and living? Have you ever asked yourself, "I am, but how am I responsible for my being? Where would I have gone to complain if I did not happen to be? Where are they who are not, going to complain? If I am, I am; if I am not, I am not. It is okay as I am, but what would I do if I am not as I am?"

If we only take a hard look at the facts of life, we will know that, really, nothing is in our hands— not even our hands are in our hands. Just try to hold your hand with your hand and you will know the reality. Really, nothing is in our power. Then what is the meaning of saying "I" and "me" and "mine"? Here everything is happening, and happening together. It is an organic arrangement, an organic whole. Here everything is a member of everything else. Who can say that I would have been here if the flowers that bloomed in my garden this morning had not bloomed? Ordinarily we can say there is no connection between my being here and the blooming of a few flowers in my garden; I could have been here even if those flowers had not bloomed. But really, the two events are intimately connected. The presence of that blooming flower in the garden and my presence here are two poles of the same event.

Now if the sun becomes extinct tonight, all life on this earth will be extinct immediately. There will be no morning tomorrow. So we are dependent for our life on the sun, which is a billion miles away from us. And the sun is dependent on some bigger suns, and in their turn those bigger suns are dependent on some still bigger suns that exist in the galaxy.

Here everything is dependent on everything else. All life is really inter-dependent. We are not separate from one another; we are not islands. We are a vast continent, an endless continent. Here everything is united and one.

If you only see this fact with your eyes open then it will not be necessary to remind you that "I" and "thou" are mere inventions of man, and utterly wrong inventions at that. And when you perceive it, you also know that which is, you know the truth. Unless you see it with clarity, you cannot know who you are and what reality is. And as long as you don't know it, you will continue to cling to the concepts of "I" and "thou", you will continue to live in a myth, a dream.

Krishna tells you to remember in the very first step, and do nothing else. And your whole journey is complete with one single step. Remember who you are, what you are, where you are, because with this remembering everything is revealed and known. This remembering is benediction.

> Questioner: I have a question in regard to wholeness. You say that emptiness is the basic characteristic of wholeness. Buddha had attained to absolute emptiness. Should he not be called whole? And why is emptiness not multidimensional in itself?

A few things have to be understood in this connection. As I was saying earlier, Buddha attained to emptiness, so emptiness is his achievement. And the emptiness that is achieved has to be necessarily one-dimensional, and it becomes dependent on the one who achieves it.

Try to understand it in another way. If I empty out my inside, if I negate something in me, it will cease to be, and I will achieve a kind of emptiness. But this emptiness will be just the absence of something that I have negated. But there is a different kind of emptiness which is not of our making: this emptiness is born out of our awareness of our being. We are empty; we are emptiness itself, so we don't have to become it. Emptiness is our very nature; we are it. And when we come to it, it is not the result of some *sadhana*, some discipline or effort. And this emptiness is multidimensional. We have not emptied out something to become empty, we have only recollected that we are empty, void; we are emptiness itself.

The emptiness of Buddha, which is seen by us, is one that has been achieved. And only that emptiness which has been achieved can be seen. We never see any emptiness in Krishna; on the contrary, one can say that he is fulfilled, that he is occupied and active. Krishna's presence is felt, not his absence. We can know that there is something tangible in Krishna, but we cannot know that he is empty. We can, however, know that Buddha is empty. The reason is that we are all filled with something that Buddha has negated. We are full of anger, and Buddha has thrown out his anger. We are full of violence, and Buddha has dropped his violence. We are full of clinging and attachments, and Buddha has given them up. We are full of illusions, and Buddha has renounced his illusions. Buddha has emptied himself of all the crap we are stuffed with, and so we can recognize his emptiness. There is no difficulty to it.

But we cannot know Krishna's emptiness. He is free of greed, and yet he can gamble. He is free of anger, and yet he takes up arms and steps onto a battlefield. He is non-violent, and yet he incites Arjuna to fight and kill his enemies. He is without attachments, and yet he loves. We find in Krishna all that we find in ourselves, and so his emptiness is beyond our grasp.

Buddha's emptiness is really the absence of something we all have, and so we come to know it. Buddha is empty of all that we know as man's maladies. As far as human ailments are concerned, he is free of them. None of our weaknesses and diseases afflict him. And we can see Buddha's emptiness to this extent. But he takes another jump from that space, yet we cannot see it. From the emptiness that we can see, he leaps into the supreme emptiness which we cannot see.

Buddha is on his deathbed and, even in this moment of departure, his disciples ask him, "Where will you go after death? Where will you be? Will you be in *moksha* or *nirvana* or where? And how will you be there?"

Buddha says, "I will be nowhere. In fact, I will not be." This the disciples fail to grasp, because they think one who has renounced everything like greed and attachment should be somewhere in heaven, in *moksha*; he has to be somewhere. Buddha again says, "I will be nowhere; I will disappear like a line drawn on the surface of water. Can you say where a line drawn on the water's surface goes after it ceases to be? Where does it live forever after? It lives nowhere; it is nowhere; it is not. In the same way I will be nowhere, I will not be." His disciples still fail to understand what Buddha means to say.

Krishna lives all his life like a line drawn on the surface of water, and so he does not find a disciple and is beyond anyone's grasp.

Buddha and Mahavira, in their last moments, make that great forward leap—from one-dimensional emptiness to the supreme emptiness—but we cannot see it, we cannot grasp it. It is beyond understanding and beyond words. Our difficulty with Krishna is greater because he lives in that supreme emptiness, he lives that emptiness. It is not that Krishna's lines

on water take time to disappear, he draws them every
moment and every moment they disappear. Not only
does he draw those lines that live and die in the moment, he also draws their contrary lines on the same
water. There are lines and lines all over, simultaneously appearing and disappearing all at once.

One fine morning Buddha attains to emptiness; Krishna is emptiness itself. Because of this,
Krishna's emptiness is beyond comprehension.

The day Buddha becomes empty, the consciousness, the being that lay imprisoned inside him
becomes free, becomes one with the immense, the
infinite. And the same day Buddha too ceases to be;
he now has nothing to do with Gautam Siddhartha
who once was born and who died under the bodhi
tree. What was emptiness of being inside him, is now
released to become one with the immense, the infinite. That is why there is no story whatsoever which
can say anything about that emptiness, about that
becoming one with the immense existence.

But the way Krishna lives his whole life from
pole to pole makes for a story of that emptiness, and
we have that story to tell us how it would be if Buddha
continued to live on this earth after attaining to supreme emptiness. This does not happen, and we don't
have the opportunity to witness it. That rarest of
opportunities comes our way with Krishna.

Where Buddha's attainment of absolute emptiness and his end happen together, Krishna's absolute
emptiness and his being walk together. If Buddha returns from his total *nirvana* or *mahaparinirvana*, as it
is called, he will be very much like Krishna. Then he
will not choose, he will not say this is bad and that
is good. Then he will not choose this and discard
that. Then he will do nothing, he will only live and
live totally. Krishna always lives that way. What is
Buddha's supreme achievement is just the natural
lifestyle of Krishna, his ordinary way of life. Therefore, about himself he puts us into great difficulty.

Those who attain to the supreme emptiness soon disappear from this earth. They disappear in the very process of attainment, and so they don't trouble us in the way Krishna does. As long as they live, our ideas of morality and ethics seem to derive support from them. But Krishna is living emptiness. He does not seem to support any of our moral beliefs. On the contrary, he disturbs and disarranges the whole thing. This man leaves us in utter confusion, where we don't know what to do and what not to do.

From Buddha and Mahavira comes the law of action; from Krishna the law of being. We learn from Buddha and Mahavira the way of action, from Krishna the way of being. Krishna is just is-ness.

A man visited a Zen Master and said he wanted to learn meditation. The Master said, "You just watch me and learn meditation if you can."

The man was puzzled, because the Master was busy digging a hole in the garden. He watched him a little while and then said, "I have seen enough digging, and I have done quite a lot of digging myself. I am here to learn meditation."

The Master said, "If you cannot learn meditation watching me, how else can you learn it? I am meditation itself. Whatever I do here is meditation. Observe rightly how I dig."

Then the visitor said, "Those who told me to come to you said you are a man of great knowledge, but it seems I have come to the wrong person. If I had to watch digging I could have done it anywhere." The Master then asked him to stay with him a few days. And the man stayed on at the Zen monastery.

In the meantime the Master went his own way. He bathed himself in the morning, dug holes in the garden and watered the plants, ate his meals and went to bed at night. In two days' time the visitor was annoyed and again he said, "I am here to learn meditation. I have nothing to do with what you do from morning to night."

The Master smiled and said, "I don't teach doing, I teach being. If you see me digging holes, then know it is how meditation digs. When you see me eating, then know it is how meditation eats. I don't do meditation, I am meditation itself."

Now the visitor became worried and said, "It seems I came to a madman. I was always told that meditation is doing, I had never heard someone can be meditation itself."

To this the Master simply said, "It is difficult to decide who is mad, you or me. But we cannot settle it between ourselves."

All of us have loved, but no one has ever been love itself. Now if someone comes along who is love itself, he will certainly nonplus us. Because love always comes to us as an act of behavior, we never know it as being. We love this person and that person; we sometimes love and sometimes don't: it is always a form of activity for us. So someone who is love itself will be an enigma to us. His very being is love: whatsoever he does is love, and whatsoever he does not do, that too is love. If he hugs someone it is love, and it is love when he fights with someone. It is really difficult to understand such a person; he baffles us. If we say to him, "My good man, why don't you love us?" he will say, "How can I love? I am love. Love is not an act for me, it is an act for those who are not love."

This is our difficulty with Krishna. Krishna's whole existence is empty, void. It is not that he has become empty, or that he has emptied some space by removing its contents. He accepts that which is, and his emptiness stems from this total acceptance. There is a difference between this emptiness and the emptiness of Buddha or Mahavira, and this difference continues to be there until they make their last leap into the space of supreme emptiness. Until then, something of Buddha and Mahavira remains; they become nothing only after the last jump has been taken. But

Krishna is that nothingness, all his life, and his emptiness is the living nothingness Buddha and Mahavira lack until they make the ultimate leap. To the last moment of their lives they are filled with the kind of emptiness we can know, because it has been created by removing contents. When they take the last jump they reach the emptiness that is Krishna's emptiness, his nothingness.

It is for this reason both Buddha and Mahavira assert that this supreme emptiness is the point of no return, that one cannot come back from there again. But Krishna says to Radha, "We have been here and danced together many times in the past and we are going to be here and dance together many more times in the future." For Buddha and Mahavira, the emptiness that comes with death is the ultimate death where one is lost forever and ever. There is no return from that void, from that beyond. This is absolute cessation of the chain of births and deaths, of arrivals and departures. But Krishna can say he is not afraid of the chain of births and deaths, because he is already empty—he does not expect anything more in *moksha* or ultimate freedom. He says wherever he is, he is in *moksha*, and he has no difficulty whatsoever in coming here again and again.

Krishna makes an extraordinary statement on the battlefield of Kurukshetra, one no other man of enlightenment has ever made. He tells Arjuna, "I will continue to come whenever the world is in trouble. I will continue to come whenever religion declines and disintegrates."

Buddha and Mahavira cannot say this. There is no statement of theirs on record that they will come back again when the earth is beset by darkness and disease, by irreligion and profanity. Rather, they will say, "How can we come again? We are now liberated, we have attained to *mahanirvana*." But Krishna says, "Don't worry, I can come back whenever this earth is in distress."

When Krishna says he can come again, he only means he has no difficulty whatsoever in coming and going. It makes no difference for him. His emptiness is so total that nothing can affect it.

There is a difference between emptiness and emptiness.

Mahavira and Buddha can take emptiness only in the sense of release, of liberation, *moksha*, because they have longed for and labored all their lives for this liberation. So when they come to this emptiness they feel free and relaxed. It is the point of no return for them; the question of going back does not arise. For them, going back will mean going back to the same old world of greed and anger, of craving and attachment, of hate and hostility, of sorrow and suffering. Why go back to the rotten world of senseless strife and war and misery? Therefore when they come to emptiness they just become dissolved into it, they just disappear into the infinite. They will not talk of returning to the same corruption and horror they have left behind.

But going back to the world does not make any difference to Krishna: he can easily go back if it becomes necessary. He will remain himself in every situation—in love and attachment, in anger and hostility. Nothing will disturb his emptiness, his calm. He will find no difficulty whatsoever is coming and going. His emptiness is positive and complete, alive and dynamic.

But so far as experiencing it is concerned, it is the same whether you come to Buddha's emptiness or Krishna's. Both will take you into bliss. But where Buddha's emptiness will bring you relaxation and rest, maybe Krishna's emptiness will lead you to immense action. If we can coin a phrase like "active void", it will appropriately describe Krishna's emptiness. And the emptiness of Buddha and Mahavira should be called "passive void". Bliss is common to both but with one difference: the bliss of the active void will be creative and the other kind of bliss will dissolve itself in the great void.

You can ask one more question, after which we will sit for meditation.

> Questioner: How is it that Buddha
> lives for forty years after attaining to
> nirvana or the great emptiness?

It is true Buddha lives for forty to forty-two years after he becomes Buddha. Mahavira also lives about the same period of time. But Buddha makes a difference between *nirvana* and *nirvana*. Just before leaving his body he says that what he had attained under the bodhi tree was just *nirvana*, emptiness, and what he is now going to attain will be *mahanirvana* or supreme emptiness. In his first *nirvana* Buddha achieves the emptiness we can see, but his second emptiness, his *mahanirvana*, is such that we cannot see it. Of course men like Krishna and Buddha can see it.

It is true that Buddha lives for forty years after his first *nirvana*, but this is not a period of supreme emptiness. Buddha finds a little difficulty, a little obstruction in living after *nirvana*, and it is one of being, still there in its subtlest form. So if Buddha moves from town to town, he does so out of compassion and not out of bliss. It is his compassion that takes him to people to tell them that they too can long for, strive for and attain what he himself has attained.

But when Krishna goes to the people he does so out of his bliss and not out of compassion. Compassion is not his forte.

Compassion is the ruling theme in the life of Buddha. It is out of sheer compassion that he moves from place to place for forty years. But he awaits the moment when this movement will come to an end and he will be free of it all. That is why he says that there are two kinds of *nirvana*, one which comes with *samadhi* and the other with the death of the body. With *nirvana* the mind ceases to be, and with *mahanirvana* the body too ceases to be. This he calls sovereign *nirvana*, that which brings supreme emptiness with it.

It is not so with Krishna. With him, *nirvana* and *mahanirvana* go hand in hand.

FOURTH DISCOURSE
MORNING, SEPTEMBER 27, 1970
MANALI, INDIA

RELIGION HAS NO HISTORY,

IT IS ETERNAL

Questioner: What is the time of Krishna's birth? What investigations have been made up to now? And what is your own view on this matter? Do you think an enlightened person cannot rightly answer such a question?

o record has been kept about the time of Krishna's birth and death. And there is a good reason for it.

We did not think it wise to keep a chronological record of those who, in our view, are not subject to birth and death, who are beyond both. A record is kept in the case of people who are born and who die, who are subject to the law of birth and death. There is no sense in writing the biography of those who transcend the limits of birth and death, of arrival and departure. Not that we were not capable of writing their biography—there was no difficulty to it—but such an attempt would go against the very spirit of Krishna's life. That is why we did not do it.

Countries in the East did not write the stories of their great men and women as is done in the West. The West has been very particular about writing them, and there is a reason for this too. However, in this matter, the East has now been imitating the West, ever since it came under the latter's influence. And that, too, is not without reason.

Religions of the Judaic tradition, both Christianity and Mohammedanism, believe there is only one life, one incarnation given to us on this earth. All of life is confined to one birth and one death; it begins with birth and totally ends with death. There is no other life either before or after this one. It is therefore not accidental that people who think that life completes its entire tenure in the brief interval between one birth and death should insist on keeping a record of it all. It is simply natural.

But those who have known that life recurs again and again, that one is born and then dies countless numbers of times, that the chain of arrivals and departures is almost endless, see no point in writing its history. It is rather impossible to write about an event which extends from eternity to eternity. And moreover it would deny our own understanding of it. For this reason history was never written in the East. And it was a very deliberate omission, an omission that came with our understanding of reality. It is not that we lacked the ability to write history or that we did not possess a calendar. The oldest calendar of the world was produced here. So it is obvious we refrained from writing history knowingly.

You also want to know why an enlightened person cannot rightly say when Krishna was born.

An unenlightened person may tell you when Krishna was born, but an enlightened person cannot, because there is no connection whatsoever between enlightenment and time. Enlightenment begins where time ends. Enlightenment is non-temporal; it has nothing to do with time. It is timeless. Enlightenment means going beyond time to where the count of hours and minutes comes to an end, to where the world of changes ceases to be, to where only that is which is eternal, to where there is no past and no future, to where an eternal present abides.

Samadhi or enlightenment does not happen in the moment, it happens when the moment ceases to be.

Let alone telling Krishna's story, an enlightened person cannot even tell his own. He cannot say when he was born and when he is going to die, he can only say, "What is this question of birth and death? I was never born and I will never die." If you ask an awakened one what it is we call the river of time that comes and goes, that constantly moves from the past to the future, making a brief present, he will say, "Really, nothing comes and goes. What is, is. It is immovable and unchanging."

Time is a concept of an unenlightened mind. Time as such is a product of the mind, and time ceases with the cessation of the mind.

Let us understand it from a few different angles. For various reasons we say time is the handiwork of the mind. Firstly, when you are happy time moves fast for you, and when you are unhappy it slows down. When you are with someone you love time seems to be on wings, and when you are with your enemy the clock seems to move at a snail's pace. So far as the clock is concerned it goes its own way whether you are happy or miserable, but the mind takes it differently in different situations. If someone in your family is on his deathbed the night seems to be too long, almost unending, as if another morning is not going to come. But the same night, in the company of a loved one, would pass so quickly, as if it were running a race. The clock remains the same in both situations. Chronological time is always the same, but psychological time is very different, and its measure depends on the changing states of the mind. But the movement of the clock indicating chronological time is unconcerned with you.

When someone asks Einstein to explain his theory of relativity, he is reported to have said, "It is very difficult to explain. There are hardly a dozen persons on this earth at the moment with whom I can discuss this theory, yet I will try to explain it to you through an illustration." By way of illustration Einstein always explained that time is a concept of the mind. He said if someone were made to sit by the side of a burning stove, time would pass for him in a different way than it would if he were sitting by the side of his beloved. Our pleasure and pain determine the measure of time.

Samadhi is beyond pleasure and pain. It is a state of bliss, and there is no time in bliss, neither long nor short. So no one who has achieved *samadhi* can say when Krishna was born and when he departed. All that one in the state of *samadhi* can say is that Krishna is, that his being is everlasting, eternal.

Not only Krishna's being, everybody's being is everlasting, eternal. All being is eternal.

Asleep in the night, you all dream, but you may not have observed that the state of time in a dream undergoes a radical change from what it is in your waking hours. A person dozes for only a minute and in that brief minute he dreams about something that would ordinarily take years to happen in the waking world. He dreams he has married a woman, that his wife has borne him children, that he is now busy with the marriages of his sons and daughters. Events that would take years are compressed into a tiny minute. When he tells us his whole dream after waking up, we refuse to believe how it could happen. But he says it is a hard fact. The mind undergoes a change in the dreaming state, and with it the concept of time changes.

And time stops altogether in the state of deep sleep, which is called the state of *sushupti* in Sanskrit. When you wake up in the morning and report you had a deep sleep last night, this knowledge is not derived from the state of sleep itself, but from your awareness of the time of your going to bed in the night and of leaving it in the morning. But in case you are not aware of it, you cannot say how long you slept.

Recently I visited a woman who has been in a coma for the last nine months, and her physicians say that she will remain in the coma for three years and will also die in the coma. There is hardly any possibility of her regaining consciousness. But if by some chance she regains her consciousness after three long years, will she be able to say how long she has been in the coma? She will never know it on her own.

In deep sleep the mind goes to sleep, and so it has no awareness of time. And in *samadhi* the mind ceases to be. *Samadhi* is a state of no-mind.

So one cannot know through *samadhi* when Krishna was born and when he died.

Rinzai was a famous Zen monk. One fine morning, in the course of his lecture, he said that Buddha never happened. His listeners were stunned. They thought perhaps Rinzai had gone out of his mind, because he had been living in a Buddhist temple where he worshipped Buddha's idol and was a lover of Buddha. Sometimes he was even seen dancing before the statue of the Sakyamuni, and now the same person was saying, "Who says Buddha ever happened?"

His audience said, "Have you gone mad?"

Then Rinzai said, "Yes, I was mad for so long, because I believed that Buddha happened." One who happens in time will someday cease to happen. So there is no sense in saying about the eternal that it happens. That is why I say Buddha never happened, and all stories about him are lies."

But the listeners said, "How can you say that when the scriptures say that Buddha happened, that he walked on this earth, and that there are eyewitnesses to this event?"

But Rinzai insisted that Buddha never happened. "Maybe his shadow arose and walked. But Buddha? Never."

That which is now born and then dies, which now appears and then disappears, is nothing more than our shadow; we are not it. So, deliberately, no chronological records of Krishna's life were maintained.

Religion has no history. That which appears and disappears, comes and goes, begins and ends, has history; religion is eternal, without beginning and without end. Eternal means that which is everlasting, timeless. So religion cannot have a history, a record of events and dates. And no enlightened person can say when Krishna happened or did not happen. It is not at all necessary, nor has it any relevance. If someone says it has, he only betrays his ignorance.

We were never born, nor are we ever going to die. We have been here since eternity. Only eternity is.

But we all keep track of time continuously, from morning to morning. And we measure everything with the yardstick of time, which is natural and yet not true. It is an index of our poor understanding, and we cannot do better than our understanding. In this context I am reminded of a fable.

A frog from the ocean visited his friend living in a small well. The well-frog wanted to know what the ocean was like. The visiting frog said it was much too big to be known from such a small space as a well. The well-frog jumped halfway across the well and said, "Is your ocean this big?"

The other frog said, "Excuse me, it is impossible to measure the vastness of the ocean by the tiny yardstick of a well."

Then the well-frog took a bigger jump, jumping from one end of the well to the other, and said, "This large?" But when the visiting frog shook his head his friend grew angry and said, "You seem to be crazy. No place on the whole earth can be bigger than my well. Yet I will try another way to know how large your ocean is." And then he made a round of the whole well and said, "It cannot be more than this."

But he still failed to convince the visitor who said again, "In comparison with the ocean this well is nowhere; it is too small to be a measure of the ocean."

The well-frog lost his temper and said to his visitor, "Get out of here! I cannot stand this nonsense. Have you ever seen anything bigger than this well? Even the sky, which is said to be the largest space, is only as big as this well, no bigger. I have always watched it from here; it is no more than the well."

We all live in the well of time. Here everything appears and disappears, comes and goes. Here everything is fragmented something has become the past, something is future, and in between the past and future there is a tiny movement known as the present, which goes as soon as it comes. And we want to know who happened in what moment. In some moment we experience ourselves imprisoned in some well and we want to know that moment and that well.

No, Jesus, Buddha, Mahavira and Krishna cannot be imprisoned in a moment. We do try to imprison them so, because we are attached to our limitations, to our fragments. The day people in the West grow in understanding, they will forget all about the time of Christ's birth and death. In this matter the understanding of the people of the East is much deeper. And it has given rise to a lot of misunderstanding in the West in regard to us. The way we look at things, the way we think and say things is such that the world cannot understand. When someone from the West wants to know about the lives of the *tirthankaras* he is astounded to hear that some of them lived for millions of years. How can he accept it? It seems to be impossible. How can he believe that some of the *tirthankaras* were as high as the skies? It cannot be so.

It is not a matter of believing, it is a matter of understanding. If a well-frog wants to be bold enough to describe the measurement of an ocean, what will it say? It will say it is equal to hundreds of millions of wells combined. The well has to be its yardstick and there has to be a figure. So we represent the age of the eternal with a figure of a thousand million years. And to describe the magnitude of the infinite we say that while its feet are firmly rooted in the earth its head reaches the sky—even the sky is not the limit.

That is why those who knew decided to drop all measurements and did not write the history of religion.

Krishna is immeasurable, eternal. And he is inexpressible, beyond words.

> *Questioner: If a record of Christ's life could be maintained, we know he was born nineteen hundred and seventy years ago. How is it that a similar record of Krishna is not available?*

It was possible to keep such a record and it depended on the people who lived with Krishna. The people living with Jesus kept a record of his life, Jesus himself did not do it. If you look at a saying of Jesus' you will understand what I mean.

When someone asked Jesus if Abraham happened before him, he said, "No, before Abraham was, I am." What does it mean? By saying it, Jesus denied time altogether. Abraham had happened thousands of years before Jesus, but Jesus says, "Before Abraham was, I am." The people who lived with Jesus had a concept of time, were time-oriented. They had not seen an ocean, they had only seen wells. So they thought Jesus was saying something mysterious, they failed to understand that Jesus denied time itself.

Someone asks Jesus, "What will be the special thing in your kingdom of God?" Jesus says, "There shall be time no longer." But again his disciples failed to understand him. Neither Jesus nor Krishna kept a record of their lives, it is the people around them who did it. Jesus did not have disciples like those who lived with Krishna. In this respect too, Krishna was remarkably fortunate. The disciples of Jesus were much too ordinary; they could not understand Jesus. That is why Jesus was crucified: he became so inscrutable, so incomprehensible. We did not crucify Krishna or Buddha or Mahavira not because these people were less dangerous than Jesus. The only reason we did not kill them is that India has traveled a long way, in the course of which she has had to put up with any number of such dangerous people.

This country has been witness to a long line of extraordinary and unearthly people, many-splendored and divine. So gradually we learned to live with them. And consequently we came to have an understanding of the way they lived and functioned. The people of the time of Jesus and Mohammed did not have this understanding. Mohammed did not have disciples of the caliber of the disciples of Mahavira. The people who lived with Jesus did not have the insight of those who lived with Krishna. That is what made the difference, and a big difference at that.

It should be clearly understood that neither Krishna nor Christ wrote anything. Whatever passed for their utterances was all recorded by those who heard them.

Christ comes to a village and a group of people gather around him. While he is talking to them someone from the rear of the crowd shouts, "His mother has arrived. Give her passage."

Jesus laughs and says, "Who is my mother? I was never born." But the historian appointed a date and wrote that Jesus was born on this date. Now this man says, "I was never born. How can I have a mother? I am eternal." But the historians who recorded this saying of his also recorded that he was born on such and such a date.

Those who wrote about Krishna were men of profound insight. They thought it would be doing injustice to Krishna, who says again and again that he is eternal and who tells Arjuna, "What I say to you has been said to many others in past millennia. And don't think that this is the last of it, I will continue to come and say it again and again. And you are mistaken to think that those before you here will die at your hands. They have been born and died countless times in the past and they will be here again and again in the future." It was for this reason a biography of Krishna was not recorded.

It would be hard for history to research and recover the lost records of Krishna's life, because they were deliberately allowed to be lost. Every effort has been made to suppress the chronological account of Krishna and persons like him. Nobody knows who wrote the Upanishads and who wrote the Vedas; their authors are all anonymous. Why? Their anonymity says it is God who is speaking through them and so they need not be mentioned.

But in the West they kept records, although time and again Jesus says, "Not I, but my father in heaven says it." But the chronicler writes that Jesus says it.

Therefore it is not a failing on the part of this country if it does not have a sense of history. It is so not for lack of an awareness of history, but because of a still higher awareness that we have, an awareness of the eternal. A higher awareness, by its very nature, denies the lower. We don't attach so much value to an event as to the spirit running through the event, to the soul of the event. So we did not care to notice what Krishna ate and drank, but we did take every care to notice the witness inside Krishna who was simply aware when Krishna ate and drank. We did not care to remember when Krishna was born, but we certainly remembered the spirit, the soul that came with his birth and departed with his death. We were much more concerned with the innermost spirit, with the soul, than with its material frame.

And as far as the soul is concerned, dates and years are not significant.

> Questioner: It is true that the innermost spirit of men like Krishna and Christ is eternal, but their temporal bodies also come and go, and we here are interested in the time-sequence of their temporal bodies. Gross events like Krishna-leela and Mahabharat are worth knowing and we want to be enlightened about them.

Those who attach importance to the gross body also attach importance to gross events. But it has no importance for those who know the body to be just a shadow. Krishna does not accept that he is his body that is visible to the eyes. Nor does Jesus accept it as himself. They deny they are bodies, so any account of their bodies will not comprise an account of them.

No statues of Buddha were made for a full five hundred years after his death, because Buddha had forbidden his disciples to do so. He had clearly said no statues of his physical body should be made. So his followers had no way to create idols of Buddha. For five hundred years they had to reconcile themselves with the bare picture of the bodhi tree under which their Bhagwan had attained to enlightenment. They did not even show Buddha sitting under the tree; just the empty space occupied by him was shown.

The physical body is nothing more than a shadow, so it is not necessary to keep its record. Those who kept such records did so because they had no idea of the subtle, of the unseen. The gross, the physical, the outer becomes meaningless for those who know the subtle, the inner, the soul. Do you keep any record of your dreams? Do you remember when you dreamed and what you dreamed about? You dream every day and forget them. Why?—because you know they are dreams.

The life of Krishna that is apparent to us, is nothing more than a shadow, a dream. Do we have a record of the dreams Jesus had? No, we don't. Maybe a day will come when people will ask for an account of Krishna's dreams. They will say if he ever happened to be on this earth, he must have dreamed, and if he did not, then the fact of his existence will be in doubt. If it happens in some future time that dreams become important to some community and they keep a record of their dreams, then those who have no such records will not be believed to have existed at all.

What we know as our gross life is nothing more than a dream in the eyes of Krishna, Christ and Mahavira. And if people living with them also understand it in the same way, then there is no need whatsoever to keep a record of such dreams. And it is for this reason we don't have a biography of Krishna.

This absence of a biography speaks for itself: it says his time rightly understood Krishna.

I was saying that for five hundred years no statue, no picture of Buddha was made. If someone wanted to paint his picture, he painted a picture of the bodhi tree with Buddha's place under it left empty. Buddha was truly an empty space. His statues and pictures came into being after five hundred years, because by then all those people who had understood rightly that Buddha's gross life was nothing more than a dream had disappeared from the earth. And the people who came after them thought it necessary to create a biography of Buddha, detailing when he was born, when he died, what he did, what he looked like and how he spoke. These records of Buddha were created much later.

Those who knew did not keep a record, ignorant admirers of Buddha did it. Such data are the products of ignorant minds.

Moreover, what difference would it make if Krishna had not happened? It would make no difference. What difference would it make in your life if he had really existed? None. But you will say it would really make a difference for you if he had not happened. But I say it would make no difference whatsoever. Whether Krishna existed or not is not the question. The real question is whether the innermost being, the spirit and soul that Krishna symbolizes, is possible or not possible. What we are really concerned with is whether a person like Krishna is possible or not. It is not important if Krishna actually happened or did not happen. What is significant is that a man like him is possible. In case it is possible, then it does not matter if Krishna did not actually happen. And if it is settled that a man like him is not possible, then it won't have any meaning if he, in fact, had happened.

An enlightened person is not concerned with the question of Krishna's being historical or otherwise. If someone comes and tells me he is not an historical figure, I will say, "Then take it to be so; there's no harm in accepting this." It is an irrelevant question. What is relevant and significant is the inquiry whether a Krishna is possible or not possible, because if you come to realize he is possible your life will be transformed.

On the other hand, if you are a skeptic you will not believe it even if, some day, all records of the life of Krishna, written on ancient stones, are made available to you. In spite of these records you will say such a man is not possible, that you don't believe them.

I say such a man *is* possible. And because such a man is possible, I say that Krishna happened, that he can happen and that he is there. But it is his innermost being, his spirit, his soul that is supremely important.

We see only the body; we don't see the inner, that which lives inside the body. Hence we become deeply involved with the outer, with the body. Buddha is dying, and somebody asks him where he will be after his death. Buddha says, "I will be nowhere, because I have never been anywhere. I am not what you see me to be, I am what I see me to be." So the outer life is nothing more than a myth, a drama; it has no significance. And saying loudly and effectively that the outer has no significance whatsoever, we refused to write its history. And we are not going to write such a history in the future either.

But later on, this country's mind became weak and afraid. It became afraid that in contrast with Christ, who seems to be an historical figure, Krishna looked legendary and mythical. While there is pretty good evidence in support of Christ's being an historical figure, there is none in the case of Krishna. So this country has been demoralized. And our minds have now been influenced by the same considerations which guided the followers of Christ to preserve his history—so we are raising such meaningless questions. It would be better if someday we again gathered courage to be able to tell the Christians it was very unfortunate that when a man like Christ happened among them, they busied themselves with collecting and recording the times of his birth and death. It was a sheer waste of time. It was not necessary to preserve such insignificant information about such a significant person.

Therefore I tell you not to be concerned about such small matters. This concern only shows the way your mind works: it shows that you give value to the physical body, to its birth and death, to its external incidents. But the body is just the periphery of life, the external. What is really significant is that which lies at its center—alone, untouched, free of all associations and attachments. The witnessing soul at the center is what is really, really significant.

When, at the moment of your death, you look back on your life you will see it is no different from dreams. If, even today, you look back on the life you have lived, you will wonder whether it was real or the stuff of dreams. How will you know if you have really lived it or just dreamed about it?

Chuang Tzu has made a profound joke about life as we know it. One fine morning he left his bed and called his disciples to him, saying he was faced with an intricate problem and wanted them to help solve it. All his monastery gathered round him and they were puzzled that their Master, who always helped solve problems for them, was now asking them to do the same for him. They had never thought Chuang Tzu could have a problem of his own. So they said, "How come you have a problem? We always thought you had gone beyond all life's problems and difficulties."

Chuang Tzu said, "The problem is such that it can well be called a problem of the beyond. Last night I dreamed I am a butterfly sipping at flowers in the garden."

The disciples said, "What is the problem in this dream? Everybody dreams about something or the other."

Chuang Tzu said, "The problem does not end with the dream. When I woke up this morning I found that I am again Chuang Tzu. Now the question is, is the butterfly now dreaming it has become Chuang Tzu? If a man can dream he is a butterfly, there should be no difficulty in a butterfly dreaming it is a man. Now I want to know the reality, whether I dreamed last night or the butterfly is dreaming right now?"

Chuang Tzu's disciples said, "It is beyond our capacity to answer you. You have put us in a difficult situation. Up to now we have been certain that what we see in sleep is a dream and what we see while awake is reality. But now you have confused us totally."

Then Chuang Tzu said, "Don't you see that when you are dreaming in the night you forget all about what you have seen in the day, as you forget the dreams of the night when you go through the chores of the day? And it is interesting to note that while you can remember something of your dreams during your waking hours, you cannot, while dreaming, remember anything of what you see or do in the daytime. If memory is the decisive factor, then the dreams of the night should be more real than the dreams of the day. If a man sleeps, and sleeps everlastingly, how can he ever know what he is dreaming is not real? Every dream appears to be so real while you are dreaming—not one dream appears to be unreal in a dream."

For men like Krishna, what we know as our life, what we know as our gross life, is nothing more than a bundle of dreams. And when those who lived with him came to understand Krishna rightly, they decided not to record the events of his outer life. And this decision was made with full awareness; there was nothing accidental or unconscious about it. And it is significant. Besides, it has a message for you: completely avoid becoming involved with history. If you get involved with history you will miss that which is beyond all records, all history. You will miss the truth.

> Questioner: We fully agree with you that we need not concern ourselves with the records of Krishna's gross life, like the dates of his birth and death. But we should certainly want to know the way Krishna lived his life, the message he had for us, the significance of his life's story. You said a little while ago that religion cannot have a history because it is eternal. But what does Krishna mean by dharma or religion when he says in the Geeta that one's own dharma, even if it is qualitatively inferior, is preferable to an alien dharma, that it is better to die in one's own dharma than to live with an alien dharma? He says that every alien dharma is perilous, and should be shunned at all costs. If dharma is one and eternal, why should Krishna think it necessary to divide it into good and bad, into personal and alien?

It was very necessary for Krishna to say it. The Sanskrit text of his saying is, Swadharme nidhanam shreyah, pardharmo bhayawaha. And we need to understand it from various angles.

Here Krishna does not use the word *dharma* to mean the traditional religions like those of the Hindus, Christians and Mohammedans. The Sanskrit word *dharma* really means self-nature, one's innate nature, one's essential nature, and it is in this sense that Krishna divides it into the primal nature or the self-nature, and the alien nature, the nature other than one's own. It is a question of one's own individuality, one's own subjectivity being quite different from the individuality of others. It is a question of your being truly yourself and not imitating another, not trying to be like another person, whoever he may be. Krishna here says, "Be immaculately yourself. Follow your own true nature and don't follow and imitate any other." He says, "Don't follow a guru or guide. Be your own guide. Don't allow your individuality, your subjectivity to be dominated, dictated and smothered by anybody else. In short, don't follow, don't imitate any other person."

Maybe the other person is going somewhere wherein lies his own individual, subjective destiny—which is his freedom—but it may turn out to be your bondage if you follow him. It is bound to turn into a bondage for you.

Mahavira's individuality is his own; it cannot be the individuality of any other person. The path of Christ cannot be a path for another. Why?

Wherever I go I can only go as myself; I can go the way I am. It is true that on reaching the destination my self, the "I" will disappear. But the day the "I" disappears, the other, the "he", will also disappear. And the state of nature or being that I will then attain is everlasting, eternal. This transcendent nature is impersonal and oceanic. But right now we are not like the ocean, we are like a river. And every river has to find its own way to the ocean. On reaching the ocean, of course, both the river and its path will disappear into the ocean.

Here Krishna is talking to a river and not to the ocean itself. Arjuna is still a river seeking a path to reach the ocean. And Krishna tells the river to go its own way and not to try to follow and imitate the ways of any other river. The other river has its own route, its own direction and its own movement. And it will reach the ocean on its own, by its own path. In the same way you have to build your own path, your own direction and your own movement, and then you will certainly reach the ocean. If there is a river it will undoubtedly reach the ocean.

Remember that a river never moves on a ready-made path, it always creates its own path to the ocean. Life, too, does not follow a ready-made path; it cannot. Life is like a river, not like a railroad.

Of course, when you follow another, imitate another, there is always someone ready to supply you with a road map, a chart, which has to be phony and false. And the moment you take this journey you embark on a journey to suicide. Then you begin to destroy yourself and to impose an alien personality on yourself. If someone follows me he will have to destroy himself first. He will have to constantly keep me in his mind: he will do as I do, he will walk as I walk, he will live as I live. Then he will obliterate himself and try to become like me. But despite his best efforts to imitate me he can never become me; I will serve only as a facade, a mask for him. Deep down he will remain what he is: he will remain the one who imitates, he can never be the one he imitates. Whatever he does, the masquerader cannot become the masqueraded.

Krishna says it is better to die in one's own nature than to live in any other's nature, that imitation is destructive, suicidal. To live the way another lives is worse than death, it is a living death. And if one dies the way one is, it means one has found a new life for himself, new and sublime. If I can die the way I am, retaining my individuality, then my death becomes authentic, then it is my death.

But we all live borrowed lives. Even our own lives are not our own, real and authentic. We are all second hand and false people. Krishna stands for an authentic life, a life that is our own. To be authentic means to be an individual, to retain one's individuality. The word "individual" is significant. It means indivisible, united and one.

There are people all around who are out to destroy your individuality, who are trying to enslave you and turn you into their camp-followers. It is their ego-trip; it gratifies their ego to know so many people follow them. The larger the number of followers, the greater is their ego. Then they feel they are somebodies people have to follow. And then they try to enslave those who follow them, and enslave them in every way. They impose their will, even their whims on them, in the name of discipline. They take away their freedom and virtually reduce them to their serfs. Because their freedom poses a challenge to their egos, they do everything to destroy their freedom. All gurus, all Masters do it.

This statement of Krishna is extraordinary, rare, and it has tremendous significance. No guru, no Master can have the courage to say what Krishna says to Arjuna, "Be immaculately yourself." Only a friend, a comrade can say it. And remember, Krishna is not a guru to Arjuna, he is his friend. He is with him as a friend and not as a Master. No Master could agree to be his disciple's charioteer as Krishna does with Arjuna in the war of the Mahabharat. Rather, a Master would have his disciple as his charioteer; he would even use him for a horse for his chariot.

It is a rare event that Krishna worked as Arjuna's charioteer on the battlefield of Kurukshetra. This event says it is a relationship of equal friends, and in friendship there is no one above you or below you. And Krishna tells Arjuna to find his self-nature, his intrinsic individuality, his primal being, his authentic face—and to be it. He tells him not to deviate from his authenticity, not to be in any way different from what he is. Why did he have to say this?

The entire being of Arjuna is that of a warrior, a *kshatriya*. Every fiber of his being is that of a fighter; he is a soldier. And he is speaking the language of a sannyasin, a renunciate. He is talking like a renegade, not like a warrior, which he really is. If he takes sannyas and runs away to a forest, and if he meets a lion there he will not pray, he will simply fight with the lion. He is not a *brahmin*, not a member of the intelligentsia. He is not a *vaishya*, not a businessman. He is not even a *shudra*, a workman. He cannot be happy with an intellectual pursuit, nor with earning money.

He can find his joy only in adventure, in meeting challenges, in fighting. He can find himself only through an act of adventure. But he is speaking of something which is not his forte, and therefore he is going off track, deviating from his self-nature, from his innate being. And so Krishna tells him, "I knew you to be a warrior, not a renegade, an escapist. But you are talking like an escapist. You say that war is bad, fighting is bad, killing is bad. A warrior never speaks this language. Have you borrowed it from others? It is definitely not the language of a warrior. You are deviating from your path if you are trying to imitate somebody. Then you are wasting yourself. So find yourself and be yourself, authentically yourself."

If Arjuna had really been a *brahmin*, Krishna would never have asked him to fight, he would very gladly have let him go. He would have blessed his going the way of a *brahmin*. He is not a *brahmin*, but he does not have the courage to say so. He is a swordsman; in his makeup he has the sharpness and thrust of the sword. He can shine only if he has a sword in his hand. He can find his soul and its fulfillment only in the depths of courage and valor, of battle and war. He cannot be fulfilled in any other manner. That is why Krishna tells him, "It is better to die upholding one's true nature than to live a borrowed life, which is nothing less than a horror. You die as a warrior, rather than live as a renegade. Then you will live a dead life. And a living death is better than a dead life."

Here Krishna does not use *dharma* in the sense of religions like Hinduism, Christianity or Mohammedanism. By *dharma* he means one's individuality. India has made four broad divisions or categories on the basis of individuality. What is popularly known as *varna* is nothing but broad categorizations of human beings on the basis of their own individualities. These categories are not specific and exclusive. Not that two *brahmins* or intellectuals are the same; they are not. Not even two *kshatriyas* or warriors are the same. But there is certainly a similarity betwen those known as *kshatriyas*. These categorizations were made after in-depth study of man's nature.

There is someone who derives his life's joy only through work—he is a workman, a *shudra*. Not that he is a lowly being because of his being a *shudra*—it is grievously wrong to think so—but unfortunately this mistaken interpretation did receive wide acceptance, for which the wise people who originally conceived it are not responsible. The responsibility should lie with those ignorant people who imposed their wrong interpretations of *varna* on society. The wise ones said only this much, that there are people who can find their joy only through work, through service. If they are deprived of their work they will be unhappy, they will lose their souls.

Now a woman comes and wants to massage my legs. She does it for her own joy. Neither have I asked for it nor is she going to gain anything from me. And yet, because service is her forte, she feels rewarded. She regains her individuality; she gains her soul.

Someone gives up wealth for the sake of knowledge. He leaves his family, goes begging in the streets, even starves for the sake of knowledge. We wonder if he has gone out of his mind. A scientist puts a grain of deadly poison on the tip of his tongue just to know how it tastes and how it kills. He will die, but he is a *brahmin*, he is in search of knowledge. He will die, but he will discover the secret of that particular poison. Maybe he does or does not live to tell the world about his findings. There are poisons that kill instantly, but a daring scientist can take a particular poison, because through his death he will tell the world what it is. That will be enough fulfillment for him.

We can say he was simply crazy to give up a thousand pleasures of the world and die to test a kind of poison. There were many other things he could have chosen for a scientific test. But this person has the mind of a knower, a *brahmin*; he will not derive any joy through service.

There is someone whose genius shines brightest in the moments of war, war of any kind, who attains the height of his potentials in fighting. When he reaches a point where he can stake his all he feels fulfilled. He is a gambler; he cannot live without risking. And he is not content with staking petty things like money, he will stake his whole life, where every moment hangs between life and death. Then alone, he can come to his full flowering. Such a man is a *kshatriya*, a samurai, a warrior.

Someone like Rockefeller or Morgan finds his fulfillment by creating wealth. There is an interesting anecdote in the biography of Morgan. One day his secretary told him jokingly, "Sir, before I saw you I nursed a dream that I would someday become a Morgan, but now that I have seen you at close quarters in the capacity of your personal secretary, my dream has vanished. If I had a choice I would say to God to make me anything but a Morgan. It is much better to be Morgan's secretary than Morgan himself."

Morgan was a little startled and asked, "What is wrong with me that makes you say this?" The secretary said, "I have been wondering at the way you function. Office boys come here at 9 am, the clerks reach the office at ten, the managers at eleven, and the directors at twelve. The directors leave the office at 3 pm, the managers leave at four, the clerks at five and the office boys at six. But so far as you are concerned, you arrive every day at seven in the morning and leave for home at seven in the evening. It is enough for me that I am your secretary. How do you manage, sir?"

This man cannot understand Morgan, who has the mind of a *vaishya*, a businessman. He is seeking his happiness, his soul, by creating and owning wealth. Morgan laughed and told his secretary, "It is true I come here even before the office boys, but the office boys cannot have the joy I have by coming here at the earliest hour as the owner of the establishment. Granted, the directors leave the office at three, but they are only directors. I am the owner." A man like Morgan is fulfilled only when he creates and owns wealth.

After studying millions of human beings over a long stretch of time we decided to divide mankind into four broad categories. There was nothing hierarchical about this division; no category was higher or lower than the other. But the foolish *pundits*, the foolish scholars, took no time in reducing it into a hierarchy, which created all the mischief. The categorization of four *varnas* is, in itself, very scientific, but to turn it into a hierarchy was unfortunate and unhealthy. It was not necessary at all.

The division of mankind into *varnas* represents an insight, and a deep insight at that. Therefore Krishna tells Arjuna, "Know rightly who you are. It is better to die upholding your self-nature than to live as a second-hand man. That is sheer madness."

In fact, *varna* does not characterize the self-nature adequately; it is, after all, only a broad and rough categorization. Really, every person is unique and different; not even two are alike. God is a creator, not a technician, and he only creates original things, first-hand things. He never repeats what he once creates. Not even poets and painters do it. If someone asks Rabindranath Tagore to compose a poem like one he composed earlier, he will protest, "Do you think I am a spent bullet? Do you think I am dead? If I repeat a piece of poetry it will mean that the poet, the creator in me is dead. Now I can only write another original piece." No painter worth his salt repeats his paintings.

Once a very amusing incident took place in the life of Picasso. Someone bought a painting of his for a hundred thousand dollars and then brought it to him to confirm it was an original and not an imitation. The great painter said, "It is a downright imitation; you just wasted your money."

The man was startled and said, "What are you saying? Your wife confirmed it was your original painting."

As he said this, Picasso's wife came in and said to Picasso, "You are quite wrong to say it is not your painting; it is very much yours. I saw you doing it. You even signed it; it is your signature. How can you say it is a copy?"

Picasso then said, "I did not say I did not paint it. But it is a remake. I made a copy of one of my own old paintings, and so it is not authentic, original. It has nothing to do with Picasso the creator. It was the imitator in me who made it. Any other painter could have done it. So I cannot say it is my authentic painting, it is an imitation of my own painting. The first one was authentic because I had created it. This one is just an imitation."

God creates; he is creativity itself. So his every act of creativity is original and unique and authentic. Let alone two human beings, not even two rose flowers are alike, not even two leaves on a tree are alike. Pick up a rock by the roadside and go round the earth to see if there is another piece like it. It is impossible. And God has not yet exhausted himself. When he is spent he will, of course, repeat and begin to make inauthentic human beings.

He created Krishna only once, and although five thousand years have since passed, he has not made another Krishna. Nor is he going to, ever. He created Mahavira only once, the first and last Mahavira. Two thousand years have passed, but he has not repeated Jesus Christ. Likewise, each one of you is a unique creation of his—and he is not going to repeat you either. And this is your glory and grandeur. There has never been another person like you in the whole past, nor will there be in any future.

So don't lose yourself, your individuality, that which you are. God did not create you in the image of any other person, a carbon copy of another, he made you altogether genuine and new. So don't turn it into a counterfeit: it would be a betrayal of his trust. That is why Krishna says, "Rather die in your own nature than live in an alien nature." It is simply suicidal. Beware of it. Do not, even by mistake, follow any other, or become like another. To be oneself is the only virtue and to be like another the only sin."

But don't forget that this teaching is relevant to you as a river, not as an ocean. For the ocean you have yet to be, there is nothing like oneself or the other. The ocean is the destination, it is not where you begin your journey as a river. And you have to begin your journey as an individual, as a somebody. And when you arrive where neither "I" nor the other exists, you will cease to be an individual, you will be just nobody. But remember, you will reach there only as yourself, not as somebody else. It is in this context that Krishna said, *Swadharme nidhanam shreyah par-dharmo bhayavahah.*

> *Questioner: It seems that Krishna is trying to suppress Arjuna when he says, "It is better to die in one's own nature than to live in an alien one." Perhaps Arjuna is trying to transcend his warrior's nature and become a brahmin. When he is overwhelmed with grief and compassion, he is just trying to achieve his self-nature, his true nature, but Krishna pulls him back.*
>
> *Secondly, you say that Krishna does not dominate Arjuna; on the contrary, he frees him. But as the Geeta begins Arjuna tells Krishna, "I am your disciple and I surrender to you," and when it ends Arjuna says again, "I will do your bidding." Does it not suggest that Krishna has been trying to impose himself on Arjuna as his Master?*

In this context a few things should be rightly understood. If one knows Arjuna, even in passing, he cannot say he is not a warrior. He is indeed a warrior; it is his distinct individuality—and his sadness, his grief is a momentary thing. He is not sad because he is going to kill some people, he is sad because he is going to have to kill his own family and relatives. If they were not his own people, Arjuna would have killed them like flies. He grieves not because of war, not because of violence, but because of his attachments to those on the opposite side. He does not think killing is bad, although he says so. It is just a rationalization. His basic grief is that he has to fight with those who are so closely related to him. Most of them are his relatives.

The eldest of Arjuna's family, Bhisma, and his teacher Dronacharya are on the other side of the battlefield. The Kauravas are cousins, with whom he has grown up since childhood. Never did he imagine he would have to kill them. Violence is not the real cause of his resistance to war; he has been indulging in violence, in lots of violence, for a long time. This is not his first contact with war and violence. He is not a man to be scared of killing. He is, however, scared of killing his own people. And he is scared because of the bonds of his attachment to them.

It is wrong to say Arjuna is trying to become a *brahmin*, because to be a *brahmin* means to be non-attached. In fact, it is Krishna who is telling him to shed his attachments. If Arjuna had said straightaway that he is against violence, Krishna would not have tried to persuade him to fight. He would not try to persuade Mahavira, who is also a *kshatriya*, a warrior. He would not try to change Buddha, who is a warrior too. It is amazing that all the twenty-four *tirthankaras* of the Jainas are *kshatriyas*. Not one of them thought of being born in any other *varna* than that of the *kshatriyas*. What is really amazing is that the philosophy of non-violence is the *kshatriya's* gift to the world. And there is a reason for it.

The idea of non-violence could only take root in a soil deeply steeped in violence. People who had lived with violence for generations were the right vehicles for non-violence, and the *kshatriyas* became the vehicle.

Krishna could not have persuaded Mahavira to take to violence, because Mahavira did not say he would not kill his family and relatives, he was not grieving for them. In fact, he had renounced them, he had renounced the whole world of relationships.

His stand was altogether different: he had totally denied violence as inhuman and meaningless. He would have said, "Violence is irreligious." If Krishna had argued with him that, "It is better to die in one's own nature," he would simply have said, "Not to kill is my self-nature; I would die before killing." He would have told Krishna, "Don't tell me to kill. Killing is alien to me." If the Geeta had been preached to Mahavira, he would simply have stepped out of Krishna's chariot, said goodbye and retired to the forest. The Geeta would not have cut any ice with Mahavira.

But the Geeta had appeal for Arjuna; he was impressed and changed b, it. The Geeta appealed to him not because Krishna succeeded with him, it changed his mind because he was intrinsically a warrior, because fighting was in his blood and bones. And all his distractions from war and its attendant violence, and his grief and sorrow, were passing reactions caused by his deep clannish attachments.

So Krishna succeeded in dispelling those patches of clouds that had temporarily covered the sky of his mind. Those clouds did not represent his real mind, they did not make up his sky. If it were his real sky, Krishna would not have tried to change it. This would be out of the question. Then the Geeta would not have been delivered at all. Krishna would have known it was Arjuna's own sky, his own self-nature. But the sky does not come so suddenly.

Arjuna's entire life bears witness to the fact that his real sky is that of a warrior, and not of a brahmin. And his deviations are like transient clouds in the sky, which Krishna seeks to dispel. If it is his true nature there is no reason for Arjuna to move from it. This is precisely what Krishna tells him, "It is better to die in one's own nature than to live in any alien nature."

And had Arjuna this much to say, "This is my true nature, that it would be better to die than to kill others. Forgive me, I am walking out on the battle."

The story would have ended right there. Krishna does not ask him to take on an alien nature; on the contrary, he insists over and over again on his knowing his true nature and remaining steadfast in it. Krishna's entire effort, running through the whole of the *Geeta*, is directed towards making Arjuna realize his self-nature. He has no wish whatsoever to impose anything alien on him.

The other part of your question also deserves consideration.

Of course, I said that Krishna is not a Master, that he is a friend to Arjuna, but I did not say that Arjuna is not a disciple. I did not say that. Arjuna can well be a disciple, and this will be a relationship from Arjuna's side. He, on his side, can submit to being a disciple—which has nothing to do with Krishna who, nevertheless, remains a friend. And Arjuna is really a disciple; he wants to learn. To be a disciple means a readiness to learn. Therefore a disciple asks questions. Arjuna asks questions, inquires, because he wants to learn.

And there is a way of asking questions as a disciple; it has a discipline of its own. In order to inquire and learn, the disciple has to sit at the feet of the Master; that is a part of learning, of being a disciple. To inquire and learn, it is first necessary that the disciple be earnest enough to learn, that he has the humility to learn, to know. Not that Krishna wants him to be humble and to sit at his feet—from his side he remains a friend; he is not a Master. He answers his questions as a friend; it is a matter of friendship with him. And therefore he takes pains to explain things at great length.

Had he been a Master he would easily have been angered by Arjuna's long questioning, by his persistent doubting. He would have said, "Enough is enough. Drop your doubts and do what I say. It is not good to question, to doubt; you have to trust and obey your Master. You have to fight without raising a question when I ask you to fight. I need not explain." No, Krishna is always willing to answer and explain everything Arjuna would like to know.

Such a lengthy debate, such an elaborate exposition that the Geeta is, is enough evidence. Arjuna raises the same questions over and over again; he does not have any new questions, but Krishna does not object even once. Now Kriyanand is doing the same here. He has been putting the same questions over and over again. But that does not make any difference to me.

When you put the same question time and time again, it only shows you have yet to understand it. So I will continue to explain it over and over again; it is not a problem for me. It is in this spirit that the Geeta was delivered at such length. This Geeta is not Krishna's gift, it is Arjuna's, because he goes on raising one question after another. Krishna has to respond to his persistent inquiry. Arjuna has a mind that wants to learn, to know, and that is very significant.

After all is said and done on the battlefield of Kurukshetra, you tend to think Krishna imposed his will on Arjuna and almost forced him to fight. You may say that Arjuna is trying his best to escape, but Krishna, through his intelligent arguments, goads him to fight. But you are wrong to think so. The truth is, all the time Krishna is trying to liberate Arjuna, to lead him to his freedom. That is why he explains to him at length what he can be, what his potentiality is, what his intrinsic nature is. He exposes Arjuna to Arjuna; he unfolds Arjuna to Arjuna. And if, after listening to the whole of the Geeta, Arjuna had refused to fight and escaped, Krishna was not going to tell him, "Don't go." There was no one to prevent him from escaping.

It is significant that Krishna, on his own part, has decided not to take part in the war of Mahabharat. One who is not going to fight is trying to persuade another to fight. He keeps himself completely aloof from the war; he is not going to take up arms. It is extraordinarily amusing that Arjuna is persuaded to fight by one who is not going to fight himself. It is certainly a matter of tremendous significance. If Krishna had to impose himself on Arjuna, he should have asked him to follow him and not to fight. And only then could Arjuna have a grievance, that Krishna was imposing himself on him. Do you know one of the many names of Krishna is Ranchordas, which literally means one who is a renegade from war? Here a renegade is inciting Arjuna to fight as a brave man should fight. If Krishna wanted to impose himself on him he should have said, "Okay, now that you are my disciple, I ask you not to fight. Let us escape from the war together." No, it is not at all a matter of imposition.

All that Krishna tells Arjuna is this: "I know you to be a *kshatriya*, and I have known you very intimately as a warrior. And I know you better than you know yourself; your innate nature is that of a warrior. And so I am just reminding you of it. I tell you who you are. Know it rightly and then do what you choose to do."

The whole of the *Geeta* is an effort to remind you who you are.

Because Arjuna eventually agrees to fight after what Krishna has to say, you are inclined to think Krishna imposed his will on him. But this is a travesty of the truth. Krishna has no desires of his own; he is totally desireless. His desirelessness is superb and self-evident. It is total.

In the war of Mahabharat Krishna alone is on the side of the Pandavas, while his whole army is on the other side, on the enemy side. Is this the way to fight a war, where your own army is on the side of

those you are opposing? While Krishna is on the side
of the Pandavas, his own army, his entire army is
fighting from the side of the Kauravas.

It is a rare event in the entire history of war,
in the whole history of mankind. And if this is the
way a war should be fought then all other wars and
warriors are wrong. Can you imagine Hitler would
agree his army should fight on the side of the Allies,
his enemies? Impossible. Armies are meant to fight
for those who create and own them; there is no other
meaning of an army. A belligerent's mind does everything to see that all of his resources are used to help
him win the war.

The Mahabharat is a weird kind of war, where
Krishna is on one side and the whole of his own army
on the side of the enemy. Obviously this man does
not seem to relish fighting. He is certainly not a
hawk, not a warmonger. He has no stake in war, but
he is not an escapist either. Since a state of war is
there, he offers himself to the Pandavas and his army
to the Kauravas so that you don't blame him later. It
is an extraordinary situation in which Krishna puts
himself. Really, the structure of his whole makeup,
his individuality, is unique.

And the Mahabharat itself is an exceedingly
uncommon kind of war where, as fighting stops every
evening, people from both sides get together, exchange pleasantries, inquire about one another and
pay condolences to the bereaved. It does not seem to
be a war between enemies, it looks like a play that
has to be played, a drama that has to be enacted, an
inevitable destiny that has to be accepted happily.
Not a trace of enmity can be found after sunset when
the two enemies visit each other, chit-chat and play
together, and even drink and dine together.

Not only Krishna, there are many others who
find themselves in the same strange situation. Members of the same family have divided themselves and
joined the two warring camps; even intimate friends

find themselves on opposite sides of the battlefield. And what is most amazing is that, after the war ends, Krishna sends the Pandava brothers to Bhisma to take a lesson in peace from him—from Bhisma, who is the top general of the Kauravas' army, their commander-in-chief. They have to take a lesson in peace from the general of the enemy's forces, and they sit at his feet as his disciples. And Bhisma's message is known as the chapter on peace in the epic of the Mahabharat. It is amazing, it is miraculous that one goes to the enemy to learn about peace. An enemy is a lesson in war, not peace, and you need not go to him to take a lesson. But here Bhisma teaches them the secrets of peace and righteousness.

It is certainly not an ordinary war; it is extra-ordinarily extraordinary. And the soldiers of this war are not ordinary soldiers. That is why the Geeta calls it a *dharma-yuddha*, a righteous war, a religious war. And there is a very good reason to call it so.

Krishna does not deliver the Geeta with a view to persuading Arjuna to fight. No, he delivers it only to reveal to him his true nature, the nature of a warrior.

Here I am reminded of the story of a famous sculptor. He is busy carving a statue from a rock, when a visitor comes to watch him sculpting. The artist is working with a chisel and hammer in his hand. As he cuts away chips of rock with expert skill a statue begins to manifest itself. And then a statue of superb beauty appears before the visitor's eyes. The visitor is simply enchanted and he tells the sculptor, "Congratulations, you are a marvelous artist. I have never seen another sculptor creating such an exqui-sitely beautiful piece."

The artist cuts in, "You understand me wrongly. I don't create a statue, I only help manifest it. A little while ago, passing by on the street, I saw by the wayside a statue hidden in this rock. I brought the rock home and with my chisel and hammer removed the unnecessary chips from it and the unmanifest became manifest. I did not create it, I just uncovered it."

Krishna does not create Arjuna, he only uncovers him, only uncovers his self-nature. He makes him see what he is. Krishna's chisel cuts away the unnecessary and ugly parts of his personality and restores him to his pristine being and beauty. What emerges at the close of the Geeta is Arjuna's own being, his individuality. But it seems to us that Krishna has created a new statue of Arjuna. The sculptor's visitor said the same thing, that he had seen him create it with his own eyes. But this is not what a sculptor feels about his art. Many sculptors have confessed they had seen the statues inside the rocks first and only then uncovered them. Rocks speak out to sculptors that statues are hidden inside and call to be uncovered. Not all rocks are pregnant with statues; not all rocks are useful for sculpting. Sculptors know where a statue is hidden and they uncover it. This statue happens to be the being, the individuality of the rock that bears it.

The entire Geeta is just a process of uncovering. It reveals the pristine possibilities of Arjuna.

> Questioner: You said that Krishna
> happens to be Arjuna's friend, not
> his Master, and therefore he bears
> with him so patiently and clears his
> numerous doubts. But in the same
> Geeta Krishna says, "Sanshayatma
> vinashyati—A doubting mind per-
> ishes." He says so looking at the doubt-
> ing mind of Arjuna himself. But the
> irony is that Arjuna does not perish,
> the Kauravas perish instead. Please
> explain.

When Krishna says "*Sanshayatma vinashyati*," he is speaking a great truth. But most people make a mistake in translating the word *sanshaya*. The Sanskrit word *sanshaya* does not mean doubt, it means indecisiveness, a state of conflict and indecision.

Doubt is a state of decision, not of indecision. Doubt is decisive; trust is also decisive. While doubt is a negative decision, trust is a positive one. One person says, "God is. I trust in him." This is a decision on his part. And this is a positive decision. Another person says, "There is no God. I doubt his existence." This is also a decision, a negative one. A third person says, "Maybe God is, maybe God is not." This is a state of *sanshaya*, indecisiveness. And indecisiveness is destructive, because it leaves one hanging in the balance.

In the *Geeta* Krishna tells Arjuna, "Don't be uncertain, indecisive. Be certain and decisive. Use your decisive intelligence and know for certain who you are, what you are. Don't be indecisive as to whether you are a *kshatriya* or a *brahmin*, whether you are going to fight or you are going to renounce the world and take sannyas. You have to be clear and decisive about your basic role in life. Indecision splits one into fragments, and fragmentation leads to confusion and conflict, to grief and disintegration. Then you will disintegrate, you will perish."

The word *sanshaya* in the *Geeta* has been taken to mean doubt, and therein lies the whole confusion and mistake. I am in support of doubt, but I don't support indecision. I say it is good to doubt, that skepticism is necessary. And Krishna, too, would not deny skepticism. He stands by skepticism, and that is why he asks Arjuna to put his questions again and again. To raise a question means to raise one's doubts. But at the same time Krishna warns him against indecision. He tells Arjuna not to be indecisive, not to remain in conflict and confusion. He should not be incapable of deciding what he should do and what he should not do. He should not get bogged down in the quagmire of either-or, either to be or not to be.

Soren Kierkegaard was an important thinker of the last century. He wrote a book with the title, "Either-Or". Not only did he write a book with this title, his whole life was the embodiment of this phrase, either-or. People in Copenhagen, his birthplace, forgot his real name and called him only "Either-Or". When he passed through the streets of his town they said to one another, "Here goes Either-Or." He would stand a long while at a crossroad, thinking whether he should turn to the right or to the left. After inserting a key in the lock he took long to decide which way to turn it.

Soren Kierkegaard was in deep love with a woman named Regina. When Regina proposed to him, for his whole life he could not decide whether to marry her or not to marry her.

This is indecisiveness, not doubt.

Krishna admonishes Arjuna not to fall prey to indecisiveness, because it will destroy him. Whosoever becomes a prisoner of indecision inevitably falls to pieces, because indecision divides one into contradictory fragments, a sure way to disintegration and ruin. Integration is health, and it comes with decisiveness. If you have ever taken a clear decision in your life you must have immediately become integrated in that moment. The bigger the decision, the greater the integration. And if one comes to a total decision in life, he has a will of his own, he becomes one, he attains to a togetherness, to yoga, to *unio mystica*.

All of Krishna's effort is directed toward eradicating indecisiveness, it has nothing to do with doubt. He says, "Doubt fully, but never remain indecisive." I am fully in favor of doubt. Doubt you must. Go on using the chisel of doubt until the statue of trust becomes manifest. Keep chiseling from the rock, with the hammer of doubt, the foreign elements that have entered your nature, until you eliminate the last of them and nothing remains to be eliminated. Then the statue of trust will appear in its full splendor.

But remember, if you continue to use the hammer of doubt even after the statue has manifested, you will injure the statue, you will hurt your own being.

Trust is the ultimate product of doubt, and insanity is the ultimate result of indecision. An indecisive person will end up insane; he will disintegrate and perish.

If you understand it in this light, you will understand what Krishna means to say.

FIFTH DISCOURSE
EVENING, SEPTEMBER 27, 1970
MANALI, INDIA

FOLLOW
NO
ONE
BUT
YOURSELF

Questioner: What were the social, political and religious conditions of his times that made it necessary for a soul like Krishna's to take birth among us? Please explain.

ll times and all conditions are good enough for a consciousness like Krishna's to be born. In fact, to come to the world, a consciousness like his does not depend on any social and political conditions. Such a soul is not at all dependent on time. People who are asleep and unconscious depend on certain conditions for being born. No awakened person takes birth in a time which he may call his time; on the contrary, he molds time in his own way. Time follows him; he does not follow time. It is the unawakened ones, the unconscious people who come in the wake of time and go on trailing behind it.

But we always think Krishna was born to respond to the needs of the times, because the times were bad, because the times were terrible. But this kind of thinking is basically wrong: it means that even a man like Krishna comes as a link in the chain of cause and effect. And it shows that we reduce even the birth of Krishna into a utilitarian item. It means we see Krishna as serving our interests. We cannot see him in any other way.

It is as if a flower blooms by the wayside and a passerby thinks it has bloomed for his sake and that its fragrance is meant for him. Maybe he writes in his diary that wherever he goes flowers bloom to perfume his path. But flowers bloom even in secluded places where humans never go. Flowers bloom for the sheer joy of blooming; they don't bloom with the purpose of pleasing others. If someone happens to partake of their fragrance, it is quite a different matter.

People like Krishna take birth out of their own joy and bliss and for the love of it; they don't do so for the sake of others. It is different if others partake of his fragrance. And is there a time when people would not profit from the presence of a man like Krishna? Every age will need him, and every age will bask in his sunshine. Really, every age is unhappy; every age is steeped in suffering. So a man like Krishna is relevant and meaningful for all ages. Who is not fond of fragrance? Who is not going to enjoy it if he comes upon it? Wherever a flower blooms a passerby will certainly partake of its fragrance. What I want to tell you is that it is utterly wrong to think of Krishna in terms of utility.

But we have our own limitations. We are conditioned to see everything in terms of its utility for us. We don't attach any significance to that which is non-utilitarian, purposeless. When clouds gather in the sky, we think they are there to irrigate our fields and fill our tanks. If your wristwatch could think, it would think your wrist was made for its use and for no other reason. If your eyeglasses could think they would think your eyes were meant for them. Their difficulty is that they can't think.

Because man thinks and he is egocentric, he thinks that everything in the cosmos is meant to serve him and his ego. If the flowers bloom they bloom for him, and if the stars move they do so in his service. He thinks that the sun is there just to give him warmth and light. And if Krishna is born, he is born for his sake. But this kind of thinking is utterly egoistic and stupid.

To think in terms of utilitarianism is basically wrong. The whole movement of life is non-utilitarian; it is purposeless. Life is for its own sake, for the sake of being life. The flower blooms out of its own joy. The river flows for the joy of flowing. The clouds, the stars, the galaxies all move out of their own bliss. And what do you think you are for and why?

You too are here out of your own joy. And a person like Krishna lives totally out of his ecstacy. It is a different matter that we utilize the light of the sun in various ways, that we grow our food with the help of the rains and make garlands of flowers, but they are not there to serve these purposes. In the same way we take advantage of his presence when a Krishna or a Christ is among us.

But we are entrenched in the habit of looking at everything through the eyes of our petty egos. And so we always ask why was Mahavira born. We ask what the special social and political conditions were that made it necessary for Buddha to be born. Remember that this kind of thinking has another implication, which is dangerous. It means that human consciousness is the product of social conditions.

This is how Karl Marx thought. Marx says that consciousness is shaped by social conditions, not that social conditions are shaped by consciousness. But the irony is that even the non-communists think the same way. They may not be aware that when they say that Krishna was born because of certain social and political conditions that they are saying he was the product of those conditions.

No, social conditions are not responsible for Krishna's birth. No social condition is capable of producing a consciousness of the height of Krishna. When a person like Krishna visits the world he finds society far behind him. Such a backward society cannot create a Krishna. The truth is, it is Krishna who gives that society, without its being aware of it, a new image, a new direction and a new milieu of life.

In my vision, social conditions are not important; it is consciousness that has the highest value. And I tell you that life is not utilitarian: it serves no purpose, no end; life is like a play, a *leela*. Try to understand the difference between life with purpose and life as play. Someone walks a street in the morning in order to reach somewhere, say his office. And the same person walks the same street in the evening for a stroll; he does not have to reach anywhere. Though the person is the same and the street is the same, there is a great difference between the two walks. While going to the office is an effort, a drudgery, the evening stroll is a play, a joy. Walking to the office he feels heavy and dull; walking for walking's sake he feels delight.

People like Krishna don't live for a purpose; their life is like an evening stroll. Their life is just a play, a *leela*. Of course, if he finds a thistle lying on the path, he removes it, which is a different matter. This too is part of his joyful play; he does not do so with a motive to earning merit. He walks for the love of walking, but walking, he will lovingly help someone who has lost his way. The man should not go away with the impression that Krishna is a traffic policeman deputized especially to help him. People like Krishna don't do things with a purpose, with a motive. They do not conform to the law of cause and effect.

I do not think men like Krishna, Buddha, Christ and Mahavira are products and parts of our traditions; they are outside every tradition. They happen without a cause. Or you can say that the cause of their being is totally inner; it has nothing to do with any social or external conditions.

I have heard about a famous astrologer whose townsmen had become scared of him because whatever he predicted came true. So two young men of his town conspired to do something so that for once the astrologer would be proved false. As it was winter time, one of them put on an overcoat and hid a pigeon inside it. Together they went to the astrologer's house to test him. They told the astrologer that they had a pigeon hidden inside the overcoat and they wanted him to say if it was alive or dead. They had settled among themselves that if the astrologer said the pigeon was alive, the pigeon would be throttled and killed before being taken out, and in case he said it was dead the live pigeon would be taken out. The astrologer would have no way to be right, so the two friends thought.

But the answer of the astrologer was one they could not have conceived. He said, "It is in your hands." He said, "The pigeon is neither alive nor dead; it is in your hands. It depends on you." They were flabbergasted and they said, "You have defeated us, sir."

Our life is in our hands, and for people like Krishna it is utterly in their hands. They live the way they want to live. Society as such, its social and political conditions, or any kind of external pressures, do not make a difference to them; they go their own way. Their beings are exclusively their own. Of course, they do make some adjustments with the societies they live in, but they do so out of compassion for those societies. Such adjustments are made not for fear of punishment or for reward. And many things happen just because of their living in a particular time, things that would not take place without their presence. But these things are insignificant and irrelevant; they have nothing to do with their inner lives as such.

Please listen. Men like Krishna do not come to this world for the sake of a particular society or for the sake of some particular social and political condition. Nor do they come to protect some kind of special people. It is true some people receive guidance, and even protection at their hands, but it is a different matter altogether. Krishna flowers out of his own ecstasy and this happens without a cause. It is as causeless as the dance of the stars in the heavens and the blossoming of the flowers on the earth. It is as causeless as the passing of the breeze through the pine tree and the clouds raining in the monsoon.

But we are not so purposeless. All of us are tethered to some purpose in life, and therefore we are unable to understand Krishna. We live with a goal in life, with a purpose, a motive. Even if we love someone we do so with a purpose; we give our love with a condition, a string attached to it. We always want something in return. Even our love is not purposeless, unconditional, uncontaminated. We never do a thing without motive, just for the love of it. And remember, unless you begin to do something without a cause, without a reason, without a motive, you cannot be religious. The day something in your life happens causelessly, when your action has no motive or condition attached to it, when you do something just for the love and joy of doing it, you will know what religion is, what God is.

Questioner: You said that Krishna's birth is without a cause. But in the Geeta Krishna himself says that

"Whenever there is a decline in right-
eousness and rise in unrighteousness,
I incarnate myself." Please explain.

Yes, Krishna says that whenever there is a decline in religion, he has to come to the world. But what does he really mean to say?

Only a person who is absolutely free can make a statement like this. You cannot say you will come whenever you need to come. You cannot even say that you will not come if some conditions are not fulfilled. Your birth and death are subject to the law of cause and effect; you are fettered by a long chain of your past *karmas*. You cannot afford to give a promise like this. You dare not do so.

Krishna has the courage to make such a promise for the reason that he lives without cause, he lives with abandon, he lives just for the joy of living. And anything can spring out of this causeless bliss. Only a free consciousness is capable of giving such an assurance. And when Krishna comes, he comes, not because of a particular situation, but because of his freedom; he is free to come and go as he likes. He does not say that if certain conditions are there they will force him to incarnate himself. It is a promise. And who is capable of making such a promise?

I remember an extraordinary anecdote mentioned in the Mahabharat. It was a fine morning, and Yudhisthira, the eldest of the Pandavas, was sitting on the veranda of his house when a beggar came asking for alms. Yudhisthira told him that since he was busy the beggar should visit him the following day. And the beggar went away. Bhima, one of Yudhisthira's brothers, heard him say this. He quickly picked up a drum and ran shouting to the village. Yudhisthira was surprised to see him do this and asked, "What is the matter with you?"

Bhima said, "I am going to inform the village that my brother has conquered time, because he has made a promise for tomorrow. I really did not know you had become master of time, but your promise to the beggar tells me so. Are you sure you will live tomorrow? Are you sure this beggar will live tomorrow? Do you know for sure that tomorrow you will be in a charitable mood and give alms to the beggar? Is it certain that tomorrow this beggar will remain a beggar? And do you know that you and the beggar will see each other again tomorrow? It seems you have conquered time and I should tell the village about this great event. And I am in a hurry, I don't want to delay, because I am not sure that if I miss this hour I will have it again."

Yudhisthira then said to Bhima, "Wait a moment; I made a mistake. He alone can make such a promise who has attained to supreme freedom. Call the beggar back so I can give him something right now. Tomorrow is really unknown."

Krishna's promise is not confined to a day or two, it covers the whole of infinity. He says, "I will come whenever religion will decline." No prisoner can make such a promise. Put a person in a prison and then ask him to give you an assurance he will come to you tomorrow if the need be. He cannot give such an assurance. An assurance like this can be made only in a state of absolute freedom. Only freedom which is utterly uninhibited can do so.

So remember, Krishna's birth is not dependent on any conditions; it is an act of supreme intelligence, utterly uninhibited, free, sovereign. This difference needs to be clearly understood. It is evident from this promise that Krishna is not bound by time and its conditions. He is not subject to any laws, like the law of causation. He is free; he is freedom itself. And this promise is a promise of freedom.

But it is difficult to understand the language of freedom, because we don't know what freedom is. We are in bondage, we are inhibited and conditioned. So when Krishna says something it seems to be paradoxical, and we find ourselves in difficulty. We think that Krishna is bound by some laws, by rules and regulations, to visit us from time to time. Water is subject to the law that it has to turn into steam when heated to the boiling point. But if someday water says it can turn into heat even at a ninety-degree temperature, you can take it that it has become free, that now it is not subject to a law. The assurance that Krishna makes in the *Geeta* arises from an awareness of utter independence, where every vestige of dependence has been destroyed. Such a pledge is the flowering of freedom and ecstasy.

No, a man like Krishna does not come here because of you. He comes on his own. He is not bound like us. He is free. He is freedom itself.

> *Questioner: What does Krishna mean when he says in the* Geeta, *"I will come into being for the protection of the righteous and for the destruction of the wicked"?*

"Protection of the righteous and destruction of the wicked"—both these phrases mean the same. But it is necessary to understand how the wicked are destroyed. How are the wicked finished? Are they destroyed by killing?

Killing does not destroy the wicked. Krishna knows very well that nothing is killed by killing. The only way to finish a wicked person is to help transform him into a righteous person, into a sage. Killing will never finish him, it will only result in a change of body for him. Killing will not make a difference; he will continue to be wicked in his next life. The wicked can come to an end only if they are helped to become righteous. There is no other way.

Another amusing thing Krishna says is that he will come for the protection of the righteous, of the sage. A sage is in need of protection when he ceases to be a sage, when he is a phony sage, a fake one. How can a sage need protection? It will be a bad day when a righteous person, a sage, will be in need of protection. When Krishna says he will come for the protection of the righteous, he means to say that when the righteous turn unrighteous he will come. Only the unrighteous is in need of protection; the righteous man has no such need. Even if Krishna comes, the righteous man will tell him, "Why waste your effort? I am secure in my insecurity." A sage, a righteous person, is one who is secure in his insecurity, who lives dangerously, who is at ease with danger. A sage is one for whom there is nothing like insecurity. Why will he need a Krishna or anyone to protect him?

This promise of Krishna is very meaningful. He says he will come for the protection of the righteous. It means he will come when the righteous cease to be righteous and when the unrighteous masquerade as the righteous. And only then a need to transform the wicked will arise. A Krishna is not needed to punish the wicked; anybody can do it. We all do it. The law and the law courts do it; the magistrates and judges do it. But they only punish the guilty man— they do not change him; they do not make a good and righteous man out of him. But how will the unrighteous fare in a world where even the righteous turn into the unrighteous?

This saying of Krishna's has been widely misunderstood. The so-called righteous man thinks Krishna will come to protect him. But we forget that one who needs protection is not a sage. A sage is his own protection; unprotected he is protected. And the wicked man thinks that Krishna will come to destroy him. And he is right to think so. Since he is deeply interested in hurting others, in killing others, he is always in fear of being hurt and killed in retribution. But no one can really be killed; the wicked man will be reborn as a wicked man. So Krishna is not going to indulge in this kind of foolishness.

"For the destruction of the wicked . . ." The wicked can be eliminated only through righteousness, spirituality. "For the protection of the righteous . . ." The righteous needs to be protected when he is righteous only in name, when his inner spirit ceases to be righteous.

This saying is pregnant with deep meaning.

Monks living in temples and monasteries believe that Krishna has a special concern for them, that he will come to their aid whenever they are in trouble. And they derive a kind of gratification from thinking that those who hurt them in any way are wicked, evil. This is the monk's definition of a wicked person, which is wrong. A true sage is one who treats even his tormentor as a friend and not as an enemy. He is not a sage who thinks that his tormentor is wicked, that he is his enemy. He alone is a sage who has ceased to see anyone as his enemy, not even his persecutor. But the so-called righteous people, who are really unrighteous, gleefully think Krishna is pledged to destroy those who hurt and harass them. For this very reason this saying has received wide attention in this country: it is being chanted like a *mantra*; it has become a watchword.

But they are not aware that this statement of Krishna makes a great joke of the very monks who gloat over it. It is a satire on them. But the satire is so subtle they fail to see it. When people like Krishna make a joke it has to be very subtle and deep. It is not an ordinary kind of joke. Sometimes we take centuries to understand it.

They say that when a joke is told, it makes people laugh in three different ways. There are people who understand its subtlety, its punchline immediately and laugh. Then there are those who laugh in imitation of this laughter. And some people laugh lest they are discovered to be so dull they don't understand a joke.

It takes time even to understand an ordinary joke. And it takes much too long to understand a joke made by people like Krishna. This statement is a profound satire on the so-called sages: it says that a time will come when even sages will need to be protected.

> Questioner: We gather from mythological sources that Krishna incarnates himself as Rama, and Rama incarnates himself as Krishna. So it seems that both of them are the same entity. Please comment.

The process of the creation of the universe, according to those who study it in depth, is threefold. Investigation into the structure of matter, as done by science in recent times, also says that the atom has three components: it can be divided into electron, positron and neutron. Those who were endowed with deep insight in the world of religion discovered long ago that the process of creation can be divided into three parts: Brahma, the creator; Vishnu, the sustainer; Mahesh, the destroyer. There is birth at the beginning, there is death at the end, and in between them lies the small span of life. That which begins must come to its end, and between the two poles there is a brief stretch of the journey which we call life.

Vishnu is in the middle of the two, between Brahma and Mahesh or Shiva. Vishnu sustains life. He is the middle part of the process. Brahma is needed once, at the moment of creation, at birth. So also, Shiva is needed once, at the moment of destruction, at death. Vishnu comprises the span of life between birth and death. So between birth and death there is life. Brahma, Vishnu and Mahesh are not the names of persons, they are names of energies, forces.

As I said, in the course of the creation of the universe Brahma and Shiva are needed very briefly, but Vishnu, who sustains life, who is life-energy, or *élan vital* in the words of Bergson, has a large role to play. That is why every avatara or incarnation in this country is the incarnation of Vishnu. It has to be so. You too are an incarnation of Vishnu. Vishnu alone can incarnate because he is life.

But it is wrong to think that the person known as Rama is the same as Krishna. No, the energy, the *élan vital* that manifested itself in Rama is also manifesting in Krishna, and it is the same energy manifesting itself in you. And don't be under the illusion that what manifested itself in Rama is not manifested in Ravana, his opponent. It is really the same energy gone astray. Ravana is Vishnu deviated. There is no other difference between the two. In the case of Ravana the same energy has gone off track.

All of life is Vishnu. All of incarnation is Vishnu's.

It is erroneous to think of Vishnu as a person. Rama is a person; Vishnu is not. Krishna is a person; Vishnu is not. Vishnu is the name of energy, power. But there is a reason for the mistake of taking him to be a person. Every insight in the past was expressed in poetry, and poetry even turns energy into a person. Out of necessity it had to do so; we could not have expressed it otherwise. But then this way of expression resulted in creating any number of riddles in mythology.

I have heard . . . A man is lying on his deathbed. He is a Christian and the priest has come for the last rites. As is the custom, the priest asked the dying man, "Do you believe in God the father?" The man kept quiet. The priest again asked, "Do you believe in God the son?" The dying man remained silent.

Lastly the priest asked, "Do you believe in God the holy ghost?"

The dying man turned to his own people around him and said, "Look, here I am dying and this man is giving me puzzles to solve." Evidently they were like puzzles for the dying man.

Let alone for the dying, even for the living, life is the greatest of riddles. What is it we call our life? How does it come into being? How does it go on? How does it come to an end? What is that energy which makes it move, grow, ultimately shrink and disappear? In its own way, science calls it electron, positron and neutron, which make up a trinity like the religious trinity of Brahma, Vishnu and Shiva. And it is interesting to note that the meaning of both the trinities—one of science and the other of religion—is approximately the same. The positron is a positive energy which we can equate with Brahma. The neutron is negative electricity and can sit well with Shiva the destroyer. And in between the positron and the neutron is the electron, which may be called Vishnu. There seems to be just a linguistic difference. One thing is said in the language of science and the other in the language of religion.

The whole of life is Vishnu incarnated. When a flower blooms it is Vishnu blooming, when a river flows it is Vishnu flowing, when a tree grows it is Vishnu growing. And it is again Vishnu who takes birth, grows and lives as man or woman. And the moment of death, of annihilation, belongs to Shiva. At the moment of death Shiva takes over from Vishnu. He is the lord of destruction. And therefore mythology has it that no one will agree to marry his daughter to Shiva. How can one offer one's offspring to death? How can one give to Shiva a woman who is basically a source of creation?

The incarnation of Vishnu does not mean that some person named Vishnu incarnated in Rama, then in Krishna and yet again in someone else. It is the energy known as Vishnu that descends in Rama, Krishna and everybody else. It has ever been descending and it will continue to descend forever. And the energy known as Shiva or Shankar is that which terminates life. If you understand it in this perspective, everything will be clear to you. Then it is not a riddle, not a puzzle at all.

To create something the minimum number required is three; less than three won't do. Two are not enough, and one will make creation impossible. With one all diversity disappears and everything turns into a monotone. Even two won't work, because to unite any two, a third factor becomes essential. Otherwise the two will never unite, they will remain separate, apart. So the minimum number required is three. With three, creation and growth becomes possible. It may be more than three, but never less.

However, these three are not really three; they are different forms of one and the same energy, because reality is basically one. And because of this we created the statue of *trimurti*—one body with three faces. We did not create the statues of these gods separately, one apart from another; that would have been a mistake. They are not really separate, they are one. If they are separate entities they would need something else to join them together and that would lead to a process of infinite regression. Therefore we created the *trimurti*—three faces in one body, representing the one *élan vital* which gives birth to life, develops and sustains it and finally destroys it over and over again. This is just a formal division, a division of labor. It is all one life-force which divides itself into three parts to bring the world into being.

Questioner: Do you think Krishna's plays, his leelas are worth emulating, imitating? Or have these plays of his

*only to be considered? Will one not
degrade oneself if he follows Krishna?*

Timid people, people who are afraid, would do well
to keep away from Krishna. But your question is
relevant.

Not only Krishna, no one should be followed.
It is not that you will degrade yourself if you follow
Krishna, you will degrade yourself if you follow anybody. Every kind of following, imitation, is degrading
and destructive. But we raise this question of degradation especially in regard to Krishna. We don't raise
such a question with regard to Mahavira, Buddha and
Rama. No one will say that you will debase yourself
if you follow Rama. So why do they raise this question
only in regard to Krishna? We encourage our children
to follow Rama, but when it comes to following
Krishna we tell them to beware. Why?

We are afraid. We are a frightened people.
We are utterly lacking in courage. And hence this
question.

I say to you, all following is degrading; all
imitation is debasing. The moment you imitate someone, whosoever he is, you destroy yourself. Neither
Krishna nor anyone else is worth imitating. Certainly
people like Krishna, Buddha and Christ should be
considered, studied and rightly understood. All the
awakened people have to be considered.

When we come to consider Buddha it is not
that difficult. Nor do we find any difficulty in considering Christ. The real difficulty arises when we
come to consider Krishna. Why? It is so because the
life of Buddha or Mahavira or Christ is such that it
fits in with our philosophical matrices; Buddha, Mahavira and Christ can be accommodated in our systems
of thought. Discipline is their way of life; there are
certain norms, principles they don't transgress. On
the other hand, Krishna's life does not fit in with our
systems of thought, because it transcends every norm,

every limitation, every discipline, every constraint. Krishna's life is simply illimitable.

No matter how lofty it is, our every thought is limited, finite, so when we come to consider Krishna we soon reach the end of our tether, and Krishna remains unending and incomprehensible. We cannot transgress our limitations; we find it dangerous to do so—whereas Krishna knows no limits; he is infinite. So Krishna is always ahead of us, beyond and beyond.

But I say, we should consider Krishna all the more just because he is illimitable, because he is vast and immense. In my view he alone should be considered and thought over who can take you to a space where consideration comes to an end, where all thought ceases. One who can take you beyond thought and concept, beyond word and image, who can show you something which is without end, which is eternal, which is inexpressible, is alone worthy of consideration. If you walk with Krishna, you will have to walk endlessly. His journey has no destination, or should I say, for him journeying itself is his destination. But on your part you would like to reach somewhere and rest. But Krishna would say, "We have to go farther and still farther."

Thought, thinking, is not the ultimate, it is only the beginning. A moment should come in the life of each one of you when you can transcend thought, when you can go beyond words and images. But he alone can take you beyond thought who is capable of shaking and shocking your thought, your way of thinking. He alone can lead you into the beyond who refuses to be contained in your thought, who, in spite of your efforts, blows all of your thought systems, who transcends them.

Consider everybody, but follow no one—not even Krishna, Buddha and Christ. You have to follow only one person, and that is you. Understand everybody and follow yourself, follow your intrinsic nature.

If you want to imitate, imitate yourself and no one else.

Why is it that such a question is raised only in the context of Krishna? It is obviously out of fear: we are afraid of Krishna. But why? We are afraid, because we have all lived lives of utter suppression. It is not much of a life, it is a bundle of suppressions and repressions. There is no openness in our life; it is utterly inhibited and blocked. That is why we are afraid of Krishna. We are afraid that even if we think of him all that we have suppressed will begin to pop up and surface. We are afraid lest our suppressive logic, our philosophy of suppression is weakened and the wall that we have built around us, all our defenses, will begin to crumble and fall apart. We fear that if we come in contact with Krishna all our imprisoned feelings and emotions will cry for an outlet to express themselves.

The fear is inner; the anxiety is psychological. But Krishna cannot be held responsible for it; the responsibility is ours. We have utterly misbehaved with ourselves; we have mistreated ourselves all down the road of life. We have constantly suppressed ourselves, our lives. We have always lived tepid and fragmented lives. We have never tried to know and accept ourselves. We have hardly lived our lives.

Our life is like a sitting room, a drawing room in our house. We decorate our sitting room, furnish it, keep it clean, very spick and span, and leave the rest of the house in a mess. This sitting room is very different from the rest of the house. If you happen to visit someone's sitting room, don't take it for his house. He does not eat here or sleep here; here he only receives his guests. This room is made as a showpiece to create a good impression on others. His house is where he lives, eats, grumbles, quarrels and fights, where he is himself. The sitting room is just a cover, a mask to deceive others. It is not his house, his real life.

Every one of us is wearing a mask to hide what we really are and to show what we are not. That is not our real face; our real life is hidden, suppressed deep down in our unconscious, so much so that we are ourselves unaware of it. We have ceased to take care of it; we have forgotten it.

We are afraid of our suppressions and repressions hidden in the basement of our minds. We are afraid even to look at them. It means we are like one who has forgotten the rest of his house and is confined to his sitting room alone. The rest of the house is a heap of rubbish, and he is afraid to enter it. It is no wonder our lives have become shallow and superficial, shadowy and shady.

This is the reason for our fear of Krishna.

Krishna does not have a separate sitting room; he has turned his whole house into a sitting room and lives all over. He receives his guests in every corner of his house and takes them all over. Krishna's whole life is an open book; there is nothing he needs to cover and hide. Whatever is, is. He does not deny anything; he does not suppress anything: he does not fight with his life. He accepts his life totally.

So it is natural that we are afraid of Krishna, we who are so suppressive and secretive. We have rejected and repressed ninety-nine percent of our life and buried it deep in the darkness of the unconscious. We barely live one percent of what we call life. But the rejected and repressed part is always clamoring and knocking at the door and pushing to come out and live in the open. All that we have repressed is constantly struggling to express and assert itself; every day it expresses itself in our dreams and daydreams and in many other ways. We do everything to push it back, but the more we thwart it the more it asserts itself. All our life is spent in fighting with our own repressed emotions and desires and cravings. Man is against himself. He is wasting his life in fighting against himself, because he courts defeat after defeat and ultimately ends up in smoke.

For this very reason we are afraid of Krishna, who has no facades, who has no masks whatsoever, who is open-ended, who does not suppress anything, who has nothing to hide, who accepts life totally, who accepts its sunshine and its darkness together. We fear that, coming in contact with such a man, our repressed souls will rise in revolt against us and overwhelm us. We fear that, coming close to him, we will cease to be what we are—pseudo entities, false *homo sapiens*.

But even this fear deserves to be considered and understood rightly. This fear is there not because of Krishna, but because of us, because of the way we have lived up to now. A man who is open, simple and clean and who has lived a natural life will not be afraid of Krishna. If he has not suppressed anything in his life, he will never fear Krishna. Then there is no reason to fear him. So we have to understand our own fear and why we fear. If we have fears it simply means we are ill at ease with ourselves; it means we are diseased, we are neurotic. And we have to make efforts to change this condition, to be totally free of fear.

It is therefore essential that we come in contact with Krishna and know him intimately. We need him more than anyone else. But we say we are already in contact with lofty thoughts. We read the teachings of Buddha, who says, "Shun anger." We read the sayings of Christ, who says, "Love thine enemy." But remember, these lofty ideas and thoughts that we repeat every day do nothing but help us suppress ourselves, alienate ourselves from ourselves. But we are afraid of Krishna. Why?

If you are afraid of Krishna, so far so good. It means that Krishna is going to be of great help to you. He will help you to uncover, to expose yourselves, to understand yourselves and to make you once again natural and simple. Don't resist him; don't run away from him. Let him come into your life. Let him encounter you. In this encounter you have not to imitate him, you have only to understand him. And understanding him you will understand yourself. In the course of your encounter with Krishna you will come to encounter yourself, you will come to know who you are, what you are. Maybe you will come to know you are what Krishna is, what God is.

A friend came to me the other day and said, "Do you believe that Krishna had sixteen thousand wives?"

I told him, "Leave Krishna aside, think of yourself. Can you be satisfied with less than sixteen thousand women?"

He was a little startled and said, "What do you mean?"

I said, "Whether Krishna had sixteen thousand wives or not is not that important. What is important to know is that every man longs to have that large number of women, that less than that won't do. And if I come to know for sure that Krishna had sixteen thousand wives, the man in me will immediately assert himself and begin to demand them too. And we are afraid of that man inside us, imprisoned in us. But it is no good fearing him and running away from him. He has to be encountered. He has to be known and understood."

We will discuss it further tomorrow. Now prepare for meditation.

SIXTH DISCOURSE
MORNING, SEPTEMBER 28, 1970
MANALI, INDIA

NUDITY AND CLOTHING SHOULD GO TOGETHER

Questioner: Please explain the special circumstances in which Krishna was born. And is there some analogy between Krishna and Christ in regard to their births?

hether it is the birth of Krishna or Christ, or anybody else, it does not make a great difference. But we have always made a distinction between one birth and another, because of our failure to understand the meaning of some symbols of birth as given in mythology. So it is necessary to understand them.

It is said that Krishna was born on a dark night, on the night of the new moon. In fact, everything is born in the darkness of night, in the dark of the moon. The phenomenon of birth takes place in darkness: everything is born in darkness; nothing is born in daylight. Even as a seed opens and sprouts, it does so in the dark recesses of the earth. Although a flower blooms in light its birth takes place in the dark.

The process of birth is so mysterious it can only happen in darkness, it can only happen darkly. An idea, a poem, is first born in the dark recesses of the poet's mind, in the darkness of his unconscious. A painting takes root in the dark depths of the painter's mind. Similarly, meditation and ecstasy are born in the dark where the light of intellect cannot reach, where every process of mentation comes to a stop, where even knowledge ceases to be.

Legend has it that the night of Krishna's birth was one of total invisibility. But is there anything that is not born in the dark? It is the very ordinary process of birth. There is nothing extraordinary about it.

Another thing associated with Krishna's birth is that he was born in prison, in bondage. But who is not born in prison? Everyone is born in bondage. Maybe one is released from bondage before he dies, but it is not always necessary. By and large we are born in fetters and we die in fetters. The truth is that every birth binds us, limits us; entering a body is tantamount to entering a prison. It is a confinement. So whenever and wherever a soul comes to be born it is always born in jail.

It is unfortunate that this symbol has not been rightly understood. A highly poetic expression has been misinterpreted as an historical event. In fact, every birth takes place in prison; so also, every death—with a few exceptions—takes place in prison. Very few deaths happen in freedom; they are really rare. Mostly we are born in shackles and we also die in shackles. Birth is inescapably linked with bondage, but if one can become free before he dies he will be fulfilled, he will be blessed.

There is a third thing associated with the birth of Krishna, and it is fear of his death. There is a danger, a threat of his being killed. But does not everyone of us face the fear of death? With birth, death comes as the inevitable possibility. One can die just a moment after one is born. And one's every moment after birth is beset with the danger of death. One can die any moment, and this moment comes darkly, uninvited. Death has only one necessary condition attached to it, and that is the condition of birth. How can one die without being born? And a moment-old child is as eligible for death as a seventy year-old man. To die you don't need any other qualification than to be born.

Soon after his birth Krishna is confronted with the danger of death, with the fear of death. But this is precisely the case with each one of us. What do we do after being born? We begin to die and we continue to die. We die each day, each hour of our lives. What we know as life is nothing but a long and dreary journey towards death. It begins with birth and ends in death. That is all.

There is yet another thing associated with Krishna's birth which is very significant. It is that Krishna is confronted with any number of deadly dangers to his life, and he escapes them all. Whoever comes to kill him gets killed himself. We can say that death dies when it confronts Krishna. It uses every means to finish him and it fails utterly. This is very meaningful. It is not the same with all of us. Death can finish us in its very first attempt; we cannot escape its single onslaught. The truth is that we are as good as dead; a small stroke and we will be no more. We really don't know what life is; we don't know the life that defeats death.

Krishna's story is a story of life's victory over death. Death comes to him in countless forms and always goes back disappointed. We all know the many stories where death, in various guises, encircles Krishna and courts defeat after defeat at his hands. But we never care to go deeply into these stories and discover their truth. And there is a single truth underlying them all: it is that every day Krishna is triumphantly marching towards life and every day death is laying down its arms before him. Every conceivable means is used to destroy him and he frustrates them all and continues to live to the maximum. And then a day comes when death accepts defeat and surrenders to him. Krishna really represents life's triumph over death.

But this truth has not been said so plainly as I am now saying it to you. And there is a reason for it. People in past ages had no way to say it so plainly. And it would be good to understand this clearly.

The more we go back into olden times, the more we find that the way of thinking is pictorial, and not verbal. Even now when you dream, you may have noticed you use pictures and images instead of words. We still dream in pictures, because dreaming is our most primitive language. Our dreams have yet to be updated, modernized. With respect to dreams there is no difference whatsoever between modern man and the man who lived ten thousand years before him. Our dreams continue to be primitive; no one dreams in a modern way. Our dreams are as old as they were ten thousand years ago, even ten hundred thousand years ago. The way a man living in an air-conditioned house dreams today is the same as the caveman in times immemorial. In the manner of dreaming no difference whatsoever has occurred between a caveman living in the vastness of the forests and a man living in a skyscraper in New York.

One distinctive feature of dreams is that they express themselves wholly in pictures. How does an ambitious person dream to express his ambition? He creates a picture that suitably expresses his ambition. Maybe he grows wings and flies high in the sky. All ambitious people invariably fly in their dreams. They fly higher and higher, leaving below the trees, the mountains, even the stars. It means their ambition knows no limits, that even the sky is not its limit. But their dreams will never use the word "ambition"; the picture of flying will say it much better.

One of the reasons we find it hard to understand our dreams is their pictorial language, which is utterly different from the verbal language we use in our everyday life. We speak through words in the daytime, and we speak through pictures when we dream in the night. While our daytime language is modern and up-to-date, the language of our nocturnal dreams is the most primitive ever. There is a distance of millions of years between them. That is what makes it so hard to understand what a dream has to say.

Krishna is very old in the sense that his stories were written at a time when man thought about his life and his universe not so much in words as in symbols, in images and pictures. Therefore we now have to decode them to know what they want to convey. We have to translate them into our language of words.

It is significant that the life of Christ begins more or less in the same way as Krishna's; there is not much difference. For this reason a good many people had this illusion—a few still cling to it—that Christ never happened, that it is really the story of Krishna carried to Jerusalem.

There is great similarity between the stories of their births. Jesus too is born on a dark night; he too is born amid fear of death. Here King Kansa, his own uncle, is trying to kill Krishna; in Jerusalem King Herod is looking to kill Jesus. Kansa has a number of children killed in the fear that one of them will grow up and kill him. In Jerusalem Herod does the same: he has any number of newborn babes killed lest one of them later turns out to be his murderer.

But Christ is not Krishna. Jesus is a different person, and the rest of his story is quite different, his own. But the symbols and metaphors of their stories are very similar, because all primitive minds are very similar.

You will be amused to know that the language of dreams is the same all the world over. An Englishman, a Japanese and an Eskimo all dream alike. But the languages that we use in our daily life, for communication with one another, are quite different and diverse. And like the language of dreams, the language of the myths, mythologies and *puranas* is also the same all over the world. Therefore the symbols, pictures and parables describing the births of Krishna and Christ are approximately the same.

There is yet another reason for taking Krishna and Christ to be the same person. He was originally called Jesus and much later he became known as Christ, and there is much similarity between the two words, Krishna and Christ. So Christ came to be taken as a derivative of Krishna. I know a man whose name is Kristo Babu. When I asked him what his name meant, he said that originally his name was Krishna, which through long usage subsequently turned into Kristo. This is how words undergo metamorphosis. Then I told Kristo Babu why some people think that Christ is a derivative of Krishna.

Jesus is definitely a different person, but it is likely that the word Christ is a derivative of Krishna. After attaining enlightenment Jesus became known as Christ, as Gautam Siddhartha became known as Buddha and Vardhaman as Mahavira. It is just possible that Christ is a derivative of Krishna, and people of Jerusalem called Jesus after Krishna's name when he became a Master and a teacher in his own right.

Krishna and Christ are two different persons. There is similarity in the circumstances of their births, but this similarity is not because they are the same person, but because of the common symbols and metaphors used to describe their births.

Carl Gustav Jung has discovered a unique thing about man's mind which he calls the archetype. He says that in the depths of the mind of man there are some basic, primordial images that keep recurring, and they are the same all over the world. The same archetypical images have recurred in the stories of the births of Krishna and Christ. And as I said, if you rightly understand the phenomenon of birth you will know that the birth of every one of us is alike.

It is necessary to go into the meaning of the word Krishna. Krishna means the center, the center of gravitation, that which pulls, attracts everything towards itself. Krishna means the one who works as the center of a magnet, attracting everything to it.

In a sense every birth is the birth of Krishna, because the soul inside us is the center of gravitation that tends to draw bodies together. Our physical body is drawn and formed around this center. Family and society, even the world, are drawn and formed around it. Everything happens around that center of gravitation which we call Krishna. So whenever a person is born it is really Krishna born. First the soul, the center of attraction is born, and then everything else begins to be structured around it. Crystallization takes place around Krishna, which leads to the formation of the individual. Therefore the birth of Krishna is not only the birth of a single individual, it is also the birth of everybody else.

The darkness, prison and fear of death associated with Krishna's birth have their own significance. But the question is why we associate them with Krishna in particular. I don't mean to say that the story of his birth taking place inside a prison is not true. I don't mean to say that he was not born in bondage. I want to say only this: it is not that relevant whether or not he was born in a prison, in bondage, what is relevant is that when a person of the stature of Krishna is made available to us we do include in his story the whole archetype of man's birth.

Remember, the story of a great person runs counter to our own. The story of an ordinary person begins with his birth and ends with his death; it has a sequence of events running from birth to death. But the story of a great one is written retrospectively for the simple reason that his greatness comes to be recognized much later and then his story is written. It takes years, nearly forty to fifty years, to recognize the greatness of a person like Krishna. Then a legend, a story begins to be formed around this glorious and unique person. And then we choose relevant pieces from his story, his life, and reinterpret them. Therefore I tell you that the story of a great person can never be historical, it is always poetic, mythical, mythological. It is so because it is written retrospectively.

When we look back on an event, when something is seen in retrospect, it becomes symbolic and takes on another meaning it never had at the time of its birth. And then the story of a person like Krishna is not written once and for all; every age writes and rewrites it. Moreover, thousands of writers write about him, and hence a thousand and one interpretations of a single life follow. And by and by Krishna's story ceases to be the story of an individual, Krishna turns into an institution. Krishna becomes the quintessence of all births, and all lives. In fact, his biography becomes the biography of all mankind.

Therefore I don't attach any importance to it in the sense of its being the story of a person, of an individual. A man like Krishna ceases to be an individual, he becomes the symbol, the archetype of our collective mind.

Let us understand it by way of an anecdote.

A great painter has made a portrait of a woman, a very beautiful woman. When his friends want to know who this woman is, he tells them, "This is not a picture of any one woman; she is the quintessence of thousands of beautiful women I have seen in the course of my life. Her eyes belong to one and her nose belongs to another and her lips to a third. I have taken different things from different women. Go all over the world, nowhere you will find a woman like her." So I tell you, don't believe a painter's picture of a woman and go out in search of her. Go where you will, you will not find her, you will only find ordinary women.

For this reason we often get into trouble; we are in search of women that don't exist except in paintings and poetry. The woman in a painting represents the cumulative beauty, the essence of thousands of women that a painter comes across. She is really thousands of women rolled into one; you can't find her in flesh and blood. She is the keynote of the song of countless women the painter came across in the course of his search for beauty.

So when a person like Krishna happens to be among us, the substance, the essence of millions of men and women is incorporated in him. So don't take him to be a single individual, separate from the rest of mankind. If someone looks for him in history he will not find him there. He is the symbol of mankind—a particular segment of mankind born in this country. And all that this mankind has ever experienced has become part of Krishna.

In the same way the quintessence of another segment of humanity that lived in Jerusalem became part of Jesus. An ordinary individual comes and goes alone, but an archetype like Krishna continues to be supplemented ad infinitum. And this addictive process continues unimpeded. Every age will contribute its bit to his richness, to his affluence, in the form of its new experiences. The collective archetype will thus go on growing infinitely.

This is the significance of Krishna's birth as I see it. The events associated with his birth may or may not be historical; for me they have no importance whatsoever. For me, understanding Krishna in the light of these events is of the highest importance. And if you can see them in the right perspective you will also see that they are part and parcel of the stories of your own births too. And if you find an accord, a harmony between your birth and that of Krishna, you can, by the time you come to leave your body, also achieve an accord with Krishna's death, which is of the highest.

> *Questioner: You said yesterday that Krishna is making a joke when he says, "Surrender to me, abandoning all other duties," and that "I will come for the establishment of righteousness and for the protection of the righteous and for the destruction of the unrighteous."*
>
> *However, it seems to me that while the Krishna of the Geeta is not given to joking, perhaps the Krishna of the Bhagwad is. But because of our uncritical attitude we mix up the two Krishnas and take him for one, and then we tend to think that the Krishna of the Geeta is joking too. We have to be clear, when we talk about the Krishna of the Geeta, that he happened some two thousand years before the Krishna of the Bhagwad, and that they are clearly two different persons. And if we take them to be one and try to harmonize them we will only involve ourselves, at places, in obvious contradictions.*
>
> *The Geeta itself is such that Shankara interprets it in one way, Tilak in quite another way and you in a third way. In this context is it*

not necessary to consider if the Geeta *is an authentic anthology of Krishna's teachings?*

I did say yesterday that Krishna made a joke when he said, "I will come for the protection of the righteous and the destruction of the unrighteous," and I explained why I think so. But I never said Krishna was joking even when he said, "Abandoning all other religions, come to me alone for shelter." Let us be clear about it before we go into the rest of the question.

What does Krishna mean to say, "Abandoning all religions, come to me alone for shelter"? It is necessary here to take note of the phrase "abandoning all religions". In fact, there can be only one religion in the world, because truth is one. He who thinks that there are many religions is just in illusion. So Krishna means to say that every religion with an adjective like Hindu, Christian or Mohammedan, should be abandoned, because none of them is really religion. He says that giving up the many religions one should come to the true religion, which is one and only one.

The words Krishna uses in this connection are extraordinary, unique; he says *Mamekam sharanam vraja*, which means "Take shelter in me, which is the only shelter." Krishna does not speak here as an individual, as a person; he really speaks on behalf of religion itself. He is religion incarnate. And he says, "Giving up religions, come to religion, the religion; giving up the many come to the one." This is one thing.

Secondly, when he says, "Come to me, the only shelter," it has subtler meanings if you go into it. When I say "I" or "me", it is "I" or "me" for me, but for you it becomes "you"; it will cease to be "I" or "me". For you, your own "I" will be yours, not mine.

If Krishna means to say that you should surrender to him, to Krishna, it will mean you have to surrender to some "you", to the other, and not to your own "I", to yourself. When Krishna says that Arjuna should take refuge, he knows that he, Krishna, is not the "I" of Arjuna; Arjuna's own "I" is his "I". So Arjuna will seek shelter in his own "I", which means he will take refuge in his own *swadharma*, in his self-nature, in his own innate nature.

Krishna certainly did not say it as a joke. It is a rare statement, a statement of tremendous depth and significance. Perhaps no other statement in all the history of mankind has this depth: "Abandoning the many take refuge in the one; abandoning the 'thou' take shelter in the 'I'; abandoning religions with adjectives, traditional religions, take refuge in religion, which is one and only one."

But this statement has still deeper meanings. If Arjuna says that he will take shelter in himself, then also he fails to understand Krishna, because in order to find the shelter of religion one has to give up his ego, his "I" first. To surrender it is essential to renounce the ego. Surrender really means surrender of the "I", annihilation of the "I". If Arjuna says he will surrender to himself he has missed the whole point. Surrender is possible only after the complete cessation of the "I".

Now we are treading on a difficult and complex ground when we say, "Abandoning yourself, take shelter in yourself; renouncing religions take shelter in religion; giving up many take shelter in the one." But if you are left with one you are left with many, because we cannot think of one without many. Therefore to seek shelter in the one you have to give up the one too; you have to give up numbers altogether.

That is why, eventually, a new term had to be invented when it was realized that the word "one" was likely to create confusion. The new term is *adwaya*, meaning non-dual, not two. We did not go for monism, because the one presupposes the existence of two, something other than one. So we opted for non-duality, which is a negative term. It means not two, one without the second; it means beware of two. It is so because one is relative to two, one can be known only in the context of two. If I know that "I am" then I know it only in the context of "you", in relation to you. Without "you" where is "I" going to begin and end? What is its limit? Whoever knows that he is, knows it in contrast with the other. One cannot be without the other. If someone says truth is one, his very emphasis on its being one says that he is aware of the other which he is denying.

Therefore this statement of Krishna's is tremendously profound.

In this context, remember firstly that Arjuna is not being asked to surrender to Krishna, but to himself; he is being asked to be self-surrendered. The second thing to bear in mind is that when Arjuna is being asked to be self-surrendered, he is being asked to surrender not to his ego but to the egolessness innate nature that he is. And thirdly, remember that he is being asked to renounce all religions without the exception of any particular religion. All religions, without exceptions like the Hindu religion, have to be given up, because so long as one clings to any particular religion he cannot attain to religion, to true religion.

How can one attain to true religion, which is not bound by any adjectives whatsoever, as long as he owes allegiance to any particular religion, Hindu, Christian or Mohammedan? Religion is that which comes into being after a seeker like Arjuna gives up the particular religion he traditionally belongs to, after he gives up all religions that bear adjectival and divisive names like Hindu, Christian and Buddhist, after he gives up all adjectives and all numbers including one, after he even gives up Krishna and his "I", his ego.

This statement is not made in jest.

The questioner also wants to know if the Krishna of the *Geeta* and the Krishna of the *Bhagwad* are not two different persons. Since the friend who put this question joined the gathering later, he missed what I said earlier in this connection. So I am going to go over it again.

Our minds would very much like to make a distinction between the Krishna of the *Geeta* and the Krishna of the *Bhagwad*. It is very difficult for our intellects to harmonize the two Krishnas. The two seem to be so different, not only different but contradictory to each other. While the *Geeta's* Krishna is very serious and ponderous and grave, the Krishna of the *Bhagwad* is utterly non-serious. There seems to be no meeting ground between the two. And so we would like to separate them and treat them as two different persons.

Either we have to separate them or we have to take Krishna to be a split personality, a person suffering from schizophrenia. Schizophrenia is a mental disease which splits a single person into two disconnected and different personalities, behaving almost independently of each other. A schizophrenic person is a kind of madman who now says one thing and then another in utter contradiction of his own statement. He has cyclic periods of elation and depression, peace and disorder, sanity and insanity. He is one thing in the morning and quite another in the afternoon. So we may take Krishna for a schizophrenic case, a multipsychic person, insane. A Freud, a Freudian psychoanalyst, will surely declare Krishna to be a schizophrenic case, a split personality.

If you ask an historian to explain the paradox that Krishna is, the Krishna of the *Geeta* and that of the *Bhagwad*, he will say that he cannot be the same person; there are really two different Krishnas happening in two different times. This will be the interpretation of an historian, because he cannot comprehend that one person could behave like so many people so different from each other. So he will say that the Krishna of the *Bhagwad* is not the same as the Krishna of the *Geeta*, that they are really two persons happening in two different times. He can even go to the length of creating, out of the vast literature available, more than a dozen Krishnas, each different from the other.

But I tell you I am not going to accept the opinion of Freud and the Freudians; I cannot accept that Krishna is a schizophrenic person. I say so for the simple reason that a schizophrenic person, a person with a split, fragmented mind cannot attain to the bliss that Krishna has. A mentally sick person who is multipsychic cannot have that peace, that silence, that serenity that Krishna possesses in abundance. Nor am I going to agree with the historian, because his conclusion is based on the same reasons as the Freudian conclusion. He is not prepared to believe that a single person could play so many different roles diametrically opposed to each other. And so he concludes that quite a number of persons with the same name happened at different times, or maybe, even at the same time. What the psychoanalyst does by dividing a single mind into many minds, a multipsyche, the historian does by creating many people in the place of one.

My own view is that with all these contradictions there is only one Krishna, and that is his greatness and glory. Shorn of it he becomes meaningless, insignificant. His significance, his greatness lies in the fact that he is all things together, all things rolled into one, all contradictions living hand in hand, and there is a great harmony in all his contradictions. He can play the flute and he can dance, and with the same ease he can fight his enemy in the battlefield with his *chakra*, his wheel-like weapon. And there is no contradiction between the two roles. He can play pranks with the girls of his village, running away with their clothes when they are bathing in the river, and he can also make the most profound statements like in the *Geeta*. He can be a thief and a perfect yogi together. Krishna is one person in so many diverse roles—and that is his grandeur, his glory. And this is the uniqueness of Krishna, his individuality. You will not find it in Rama, Buddha, Mahavira or Jesus Christ.

Krishna is a blending of contradiction, a beautiful synthesis of all contradictions. I say so for the reason that I don't find these contradictions to be really contradictory. In fact all of life's truth is a blending, a synthesis of contradictions. The whole of life is based on contradictions, and there is no discordance in those contradictions; rather, there is full accord, absolute harmony among them.

A person who is a child today will grow into an old man—the same person, and there is no contradiction between the two stages. Can you say when you were a child and when you turned into a young man? You cannot. It would be difficult to draw a dividing line between youth and old age. In words, in language they seem to be opposites. But are they really contradictory? Can you name the date when youth comes to an end and old age begins? It would be so difficult for you to answer this question. There is no such date; every day youth is turning into old age. We can say that a young person is a would-be oldie, and that an oldie is one who has completed his youth. There is no other difference.

We think peace and disorder are two different things. But are they really different? Where does peace end and disturbance begin? In the dictionary, peace and disturbance, happiness and suffering, life and death, have opposite meanings, but in real life it is peace that turns into disturbance, happiness that turns into suffering, life that turns into death. Again, in real life, disorder turns into order, suffering into happiness and death into life. In real life light turns into darkness, morning turns into evening and day into night and vice versa. In real life plus and minus are not opposites. In real life all seeming opposites are complementaries, an interplay of one and the same energy.

If we can see through this eternal harmony of life, its supreme, sublime music, its significance, then alone can we understand Krishna. That is why we call him the complete incarnation of God. He is a complete symbolization of life; he represents life totally.

Buddha does not represent the whole of life. He represents only its sunny parts; he represents all that is good in life. He represents only the morning and the day of life. But what about the evening and the night of life? Buddha will take care of light, but what will happen to darkness? He will symbolize the nectar, but who will look after the poison? For this reason Buddha has a clear-cut image; there are no contradictions in him. No one can say that the Buddha of the *Dhammapada* is different from the Buddha of the *Tripitakas*. In every book of Buddhism, Buddha remains the same. And so no one can call Buddha a schizophrenic personality, no one can say that he is fragmented and contradictory. He is integrated and one. But we invariably raise the question of contradictions in the case of Krishna.

It would be better if, instead of looking at Krishna through the screen of our concepts and categories in order to reconcile him with our conditioned minds, we look at him directly and as a whole. To do so, it will be necessary to put aside all our concepts and categories and all our prejudices. I don't say that more than one Krishna is not possible; I am not concerned about it. Maybe, historians will prove there is a distance of two thousand years between the Krishnas of the *Geeta* and the *Bhagwad*. That is not going to deter me; I will say that for me there is no distance whatsoever between the two. For me Krishna has significance only if he is one; he is utterly meaningless if he is not one.

I am not concerned with Krishna's historicity; it does not matter whether he really happened or did not. In my view, whenever someone is fulfilled, after he attains to the full flowering of life and being, he will necessarily become multidimensional, he will be many persons rolled into one. Whenever someone attains to the totality of life, there will be a consistency in his inconsistencies, there will be a harmony in his contradictions. Whenever someone achieves the peak of life, the extremes of life will meet in him with perfect cohesion and unity. We may not see that unity because of our poor vision, but it is there.

It is as if I am climbing a staircase and while I see its lower and upper flights, I do not see the middle one. In that case, can I think the bottom flight and the top flight are joined together? Only when I see the middle flight too, will I agree they are together. The bottom and top flights are parts of the same staircase; you begin the journey at the bottom and end it at the top. They are extensions of the same thing.

The middle flight of Krishna's life is not visible to you, because your own middle flight is not visible to you. The link between the extremes is invisible to you. You have seen your peacefulness and you have seen your disquiet, but have you seen the moment of gap between peace and disquiet, which is very thin and subtle? You have not seen it. You know love and you know hate, but have you also known how love turns into hate and how hate turns into love? You have made enemies of friends and friends of enemies, but have you ever observed the subtle process, the alchemy which turns friendship into enmity and vice versa?

There have been alchemists who are said to have been trying to turn baser metals into gold—but they have been misunderstood. People thought they were really interested in turning iron into gold. All they wanted to ascertain was that there should be some link between the baser metals and the highest metal—the gold, which is not visible to us. It is impossible that there is no connection between iron and gold, that iron and gold are not joined together. It is impossible that the whole cosmos is not one, unified and together.

If there is a flower blooming in the garden over there, and I am sitting here, there must be some link between me and the flower. If I am happy here, the flower over there must have contributed to my happiness. Maybe we don't see the link, but it is there. Similarly, if the flower withers away and I am saddened, there is a connection between the two events which we don't see. Life is together; everything in life is together. Togetherness is life. Alchemists say that there must be some connection between the baser metals and gold, and they were striving to discover that link.

Alchemy is not just confined to metals, it says that in all of life the baser instinct must be connected with the higher, with the highest; it cannot be otherwise. Sex should be connected with God. The earth should be connected with the heavens. Similarly, life is connected with death and matter is connected with consciousness. Even a rock is associated with God in some intimate way. It cannot be otherwise.

Krishna is like a symbol of this sublime unity and harmony. And I say such a Krishna happened, really happened. Whatever arguments the historians may produce, I will throw them into the trash. Psychologists may come up with their jargon, but I will tell them, "You have gone mad; you cannot understand Krishna. You only know how to analyze and understand human mind in its fragments; you don't know how to integrate, to synthesize and know the togetherness, the integrity of mind."

It is true that Freud has investigated the mind of man, and very few people know as much about anger as Freud does. But if somebody treads on his toes, he will immediately lose his temper. He does not know when non-anger turns into anger, in spite of all his work on anger. Hardly anyone else knows as much about mental disorders, but there are streaks of insanity in his own personality. Its potential is there; he can go insane any moment. There have been moments in his life when he himself behaves like a mental case. So I don't attach any importance to what the psychologists say about Krishna, because Krishna has transcended the mind, gone beyond mind.

Krishna has transcended the mind; he has gone beyond mind. And he has attained to that integrity which is the integrity of the soul, which is altogether capable of being in every mind, in every kind of mind. Therefore I will talk about Krishna as one person, as a single individual.

Questioner: Do you take the Geeta *as the authentic voice of Krishna?*

You ask if I take the Geeta to be the authentic voice of Krishna. If a person like Krishna has happened then the Geeta has to be authentic. It is not relevant if Krishna said it or not, what is relevant is that if a person like Krishna says something, he will only say something like the Geeta. Even if the Geeta is taken to be written by Vyasa, and not delivered by Krishna, it does not make a difference. A Vyasa cannot write the Geeta without a Krishna being there. Even if it is taken to have been said by Vyasa and not by Krishna, it is the Geeta that he spoke, and it remains the same.

It is immaterial whether Krishna, Vyasa or some XYZ is the author of the Geeta. Authorship is not important, what is important is the Geeta itself.

It has not appeared from the blue; someone must have authored it. But to find his name is not important, because the Geeta is enough unto itself. Who wrote it makes no difference whatsoever.

I see it from the very opposite side. I wouldn't pose the question whether or not the Geeta is the authentic voice of Krishna, rather I would ask if the Geeta is authentic or not. And I say to you that the Geeta is, that it is authentic, and that it is enough evidence of Krishna's being there. I see the whole thing like this: the Geeta is, the Geeta is spoken, the Geeta is written, the Geeta is in existence, and that it cannot be in existence without a Krishna. Someone is needed to say it or write it; who he is is not that important. There must be a consciousness, an intelligence to have given birth to the Geeta, to have brought it into being.

The existence of the river Ganges is proof enough that its source, the Gangotri, has to be somewhere. The Gangotri is not the proof for the existence of the Ganges; rather, the Ganges is the proof for the existence of the Gangotri. If the Ganges is, we can say there must be a Gangotri, a mother to it. So if the Geeta is there, then there must be a Krishna to author it. So I would like to begin with the Geeta and move to Krishna from there; that is how it should be. I say so because the Geeta is still with us, it is in existence. If we begin with Krishna and go from him to the Geeta, we will be in unnecessary difficulty. Because then the question will arise if Krishna is real or not, and in case his existence becomes doubtful the Geeta becomes doubtful. But we always behave in a crazy manner.

Questioner: The Bhagwad mentions an anecdote from Krishna's adolescent life which is clearly erotic. It is said that while a group of young women known as gopis are bathing naked in the river Yamuna, Krishna runs away with their clothes and thus forces them to come out of the river nude. When the gopis emerge from the water bashfully hiding their sexual organs with their hands, Krishna tells them that since they have offended the water god by bathing naked, they should ask for his forgiveness with their hands raised in salutation to him, and then they can take back their clothes.

In this context the Bhagwad says that Krishna deceitfully made them expose their sexual organs to him, and that he was very pleased to see them in their virgin state.

And you seem to be a strong supporter of Krishna—the pioneer of nudism in human society. But is there a difference between your conception of nudism and that of the current nudist clubs in the western countries?

It is said that clothes represent civilization and skin represents culture. If we remove our clothes we will on one hand appear in our natural state, but on the other we will also look like barbarians. Would it not amount to a going back to the primitive way of life, a return to the jungle? And would you call this turning back of the hands of the clock a progressive step?

Here is a dialogue between a dancing girl and a monk.

A dancing girl said to a monk, "You have become a monk by heavily repressing your desire for dancing."

The monk said to the dancing girl, "You have become a dancing girl by heavily suppressing your desire to be a monk."

First things first. Freud's concept of the libido is very significant. The correct meaning of the word libido is sex energy. Sex energy permeates, and permeates profoundly, not only the life of man, but the life of the whole creation. The whole universe is saturated with sex energy. The Hindu mythology known as *puranas*, says that Brahma, the creator, being driven by sex, made the world. Without sex, creation, creativity is impossible. The entire creation stems from sex. Whatever there is in the universe, it is the ramification of sex. The whole of life's play, of life's manifestation, whether it is a flower blooming or a bird singing, is the play of sex energy. We can say there is an ocean of sex energy from which arise infinite waves of creativity in infinite forms.

In a deeper meaning God himself is the center of this sex energy.

There is a simple, natural and innocent acceptance of sex in the life of Krishna. The spontaneous, immaculate and easy nature of man has found its full expression in his life. Nothing is denied, nothing is suppressed, nothing whatsoever is repressed. Life as it is, is accepted and lived in its utter simplicity, naturalness. And it is lived with a sense of deep gratefulness to it, to existence.

So those who try to suppress, change and distort the events of Krishna's life only betray their own guilty minds, their repressed sex and mental sickness. Efforts are made to suggest that it is the child Krishna who steals the clothes of the *gopis* and plays pranks with their nude bodies. We feel relieved to think of them as the pranks of a child, because kids of both sexes are interested in seeing one another's nudity.

This curiosity of boys and girls is simply natural. As soon as a child, whether he is a boy or a girl, becomes aware of his body, he or she also becomes aware that there is someone around whose body is somewhat different from his or hers. A boy comes to notice that the body of his sister is different from his and similarly a girl comes to know that the body of her brother is different from hers. This awareness would not be a problem if the boys and girls were allowed to live naked for a length of time. But the elders of the family are so obsessed with sex that they force the kids to wear clothes at a very early age, which prevents the boys and girls from becoming naturally familiar with each other's bodies. So it is suggested that there is nothing unusual about Krishna in his childhood running away with the clothes of the *gopis* and prying into their nudity. Every boy is anxious to see a girl in the nude.

Now that civilization has deprived us of the company of trees and lakes and rivers, kids have to find new ways to pry into one another's bodies. Freud has mentioned a children's game in which a boy plays the doctor, puts the girl on the bed as a patient and examines her in her nudity. This is a very natural curiosity and there is nothing wrong in it. Boys and girls would like to be familiar with each other's bodies; this familiarity will prepare them for deeper familiarity with each other in adulthood.

It is possible that Krishna did all this when he was a child. But it is not impossible for a grown-up Krishna too. It may be impossible for us, but not for Krishna, because Krishna accepts life as it is and lives it naturally, without any affectations, without any pretentions. And the culture in which he was born must have been as natural and spontaneous and as life-affirmative as Krishna is. Had he been born in our society we would never have mentioned these events at all, we would simply have suppressed them, deleted them from our records of him, from our literature. But the *Bhagwad* and other kindred books mention them with an innocence and naturalness that shows that they did not see them as anything wrong and improper. These books have been in existence for thousands of years, and for these thousands of years nobody raised the question, "What kind of a man is this Krishna?" It is only now that this question has been raised; it is we who are raising it.

The culture in which these episodes of Krishna's life took place accepted them as nothing unnatural. This shows they were not exclusively Krishna's pastimes, but were common games of his times in which many other Krishnas, many other *gopis* participated. The times of Krishna must have been utterly different from ours. It was a highly life-affirmative, alive, natural and understanding culture. It was great.

And I cannot accept that the *gopis* mentioned in the *Bhagwad* were just kids. They must have been of the age when girls begin to be aware that they are girls, a different sex altogether, when they become shy and bashful, when they know that they have something to hide from others. This is exactly the time when boys become interested in them, in knowing and seeing their bodies. The two things happen together. Those *gopis*, his girlfriends, must have been about the same age as Krishna. That is why Krishna is interested in seeing them in the nude and they are trying to hide their nudity.

In this context it is necessary to understand that among the many differences there are between the male mind and the female mind, one prominent difference is this: while a man is interested in seeing a woman in the nude—he is a voyeur—the woman is not that interested in seeing a naked man. It is amusing that a man is deeply interested in the nude body of a woman. It is for this reason that there are so many statues of nude women all over the world.

Statues of male nudes are rare, and they are available only in cultures that accept homosexuality. For instance, such nude male statues were made in Greece in the times of Socrates and Plato when homosexual relationships were in vogue. So those statues of male nudes were also made by men and for men. Women are not in the least interested in nude males. So magazines for men come out with any number of pictures of naked women, but no magazine meant for women prints pictures of naked males. Women simply laugh at this craze of man's.

You may not have noticed but in deep moments of love it is the man who wants to disrobe his beloved; it is not so with the woman. While making love a man keeps his eyes open, but the woman invariably keeps hers closed. Even when she is being kissed by her lover, a woman usually shuts her eyes. She is not interested in seeing; she is interested in absorbing her lover, in being one with him. But a man is deeply interested in seeing his woman, and it is this male interest which gives rise to a desire in the woman to hide herself.

So women all the world over hide their bodies in many ways. But this desire to hide their bodies creates a problem for them, because they cease to be attractive if they hide too much. So they do two things together: they hide their bodies and at the same time they hide them in a manner that they are also exposed. They hide and expose their bodies together. The same clothes are used to hide them and also to expose them in a clever way. They hide because they are afraid of voyeurs in general, but they need to expose their bodies in order to attract men as well. So they are always in a conflict between hiding and exposing themselves at the same time; they have to find a balance between the two needs.

So it is natural that the *gopis* emerged from the river hiding their sexual organs with their hands. This episode is quite natural. And Krishna's asking them to salute the water god with folded hands is equally natural. There is nothing odd about it. This is how the male mind behaves. And Krishna has a very simple and natural male mind; one should say he has a perfect male mind. There are no distortions, no suppressions, no affectations so far as his mind is concerned. And the people who wrote those stories were also very simple and innocent people, without any pretensions. They wrote them exactly as they happened; they did not have any inhibitive principles, or sense of guilt about the matter.

It is significant that these stories, which you call erotic, are written into the *Bhagwad*, which hails Krishna as the perfect incarnation of God. The authors of the book did not think for a moment, as you do now, that these stories may make his being a god suspect. But I tell you God alone, and no man, can be as innocent, as simple, as natural, as unpretentious, and as spontaneous. No man can be as simple and spontaneous. He is very complex: he does everything according to concepts, ideas and ideals; he preplans everything he says and does. And I also say that Krishna did not pre-plan it; he did not have any idea how the *gopis* were going to behave and what he was going to do in response. Everything happened utterly spontaneously and naturally. And those people who portrayed it exactly as it happened were great indeed. Certainly they were simple and sincere people, unsophisticated, innocent people. They did not try to suppress and edit them as you would like them to have done.

It was much later that these episodes in the life of Krishna began to embarrass us and put us into difficulty. There are many such things from the past which eventually begin to disturb us, because of our changing ideas and ideals and new rules of morality. And we try to apply them retrospectively and judge things according to them. And that is what lands us in difficulty.

In my view, the sex energy has found its most natural and beautiful expression in the life of Krishna. He accepted sex without any reservations, without any pretentions. And he lived a most natural life. And what is significant is that the society he lived in accepted Krishna as naturally and as unreservedly.

The questioner also wants to know if I am a pioneer of nudism. In a sense, I am. Not that I am against clothes. Going against clothes would certainly amount to turning back the hands of the clock. Clothes have their utility; they are necessary, but they certainly don't have any moral values. They are utilitarian, but they have nothing to do with morality. In winter we need clothes to protect us from the cold; in summer different kinds of clothes are required. And you need clothes when you are in public, because you have no right to offend the sensibilities of those who don't want to see you in the nude. That would be a kind of trespass.

But this does not mean that because of them we are not even free to bare our bodies in our homes. No, clothes should be used as we use shoes; we are not in our shoes when we are in our homes. Reaching home we leave our shoes on the porch and walk barefoot from one room to another. And nobody asks us why our feet are naked, although our feet are really naked.

We should accept clothes naturally; there should be no harshness about it. And it is possible only if we accept nudity as naturally. Without accepting nudity as natural, you cannot accept clothes naturally. If you deny and condemn nudity, then clothes take on a moral value they don't have. In fact, man has now been wearing too many clothes, so much so that he has to find ways and means to expose himself through the same clothes. And this gives rise to immorality.

I think we should accept nudity as a natural thing. We are born naked and we remain naked even behind our clothes. God makes us all naked; he does not send us here in clothes. Nudity is simple and natural; there is an aura of innocence about it, but it does not mean that we should go naked.

We do make changes in the way God makes us. To protect ourselves from the hot sun, which is of God's making, we use umbrellas, and it does not mean any defiance of God. An umbrella shields us against the hot sun, and this is as much a part of the divine love as the hot sun is. There is no contradiction between light and shade; we are free to choose either for our convenience and enjoyment.

But if some day sitting in the shade is made into a virtue, and walking in sunshine a sin, then sitting in the shade will turn into a kind of punishment. And then people will begin to enjoy sunshine secretly and stealthily; such a simple and natural thing like enjoying sunshine will turn into a crime. This is how we give rise to lots of immorality and guilt and crime, utterly uncalled for and stupid. Much of the load of guilt that we have to carry and suffer is the outcome of our own stupid thinking.

I believe that nudity is a fact of life, and we should accept it simply as a natural phenomenon. There is no need whatsoever to run away from it. But we have made it a taboo, and because of it we are having to take recourse in any number of devious devices to circumvent this taboo. Nudist posters, porno and night clubs are the byproducts of this prohibition. They will disappear the day we accept nudity as a natural part of our life. I don't advocate a blanket ban on clothes—that would certainly be turning back the hands of the clock—but it would be good if sometimes members of a family would sit together without clothes. It would be wholesome if, on a winter's morning, we sat nude in the sun, and sometimes in summer bathed naked in the river. It would be good for our health, both our physical and mental health. If we accept clothes and nudity together as ways of life, we will have the benefits of clothes, which the naked primitive people were deprived of, and at the same time we will escape the inconveniences and incongruities that come with being too obsessed with clothes. And it is, therefore, a progressive proposition that I am making; it is a step forward for both the nudists and the people obsessed with clothes.

The nudist clubs are a kind of revolt, a reaction against those who have imposed too many clothes on society. I am not in support of the nudist clubs, nor am I in support of those who are obsessed with clothes. I offer you an alternative: do away with your obsession with clothes and the nudist clubs will disappear. The nudist clubs are supposed to be a step in the direction of remedying the ills of our obsession with clothes, but I say, do away with the illness and the remedies will disappear. Let the whole society be disease-free and healthy.

I tell you, if a father and his young son, a mother and her young son bathe together naked in their house, this son will never indulge in teasing girls and brushing against them in the marketplace; it will cease to have any meaning for him. If the distance existing between man and woman is considerably reduced, much of what are called youthful misdemeanors will be gone. When a young man brushes against a young woman he is really trying to reduce that distance. Because he has no way to touch her gently he does it the harsh way, the angry way. If I can take the hand of a woman I like in my hand and say "How lovely," and the society I live in is natural enough to accept it gracefully, then misbehavior with women will become rare. But such a society is yet a far cry off.

When we come across a beautiful blossom, we stop near it for a brief moment, take a look at it and then go our way. One never feels like brushing against the flower and hurting it. But if one day the flowers make a law and engage policemen to prevent people from looking at them, people will soon begin to commit excesses with flowers too. Then immorality will come into being. In fact, too much morality creates immorality. If you become too moralistic you are bound to become immoral before long. So if a society is obsessed with clothes, it will soon give rise to nudist clubs.

I am not in support of nudist clubs, because I am not in support of obsessions with clothes. I am in support of a life that is easy, natural and spontaneous. I am for accepting life as it is, without any distortions. And Krishna is a unique symbol of this acceptance, a natural acceptance of all that is natural.

> *Questioner: You said we need a society in which a man can freely take the hand of a woman he likes in his, without fear of being ostracized. Since it raises the question of immorality, we would like to know your view on immorality. What if someone, by way of taking a woman's hand in his, asks for more, asks to go to bed with her? Would it not create conflict in the lives of many men and women? Would it not put many husbands in trouble?*

Then there is another question similar to it:

> *Krishna represents two extremes of life. On the one hand he steals the clothes of the gopis and on the other he brings clothes to Draupadi when she is being publicly*

disrobed by the Kauravas. This aspect of his life is really unique, unearthly and divine. Or is it just an exceptional instance?

Then there are conflicting reports about his bodily color. While the color of Krishna, who provided Draupadi with abundant clothes, is said to be dark, the Bhagwad describes him in three shades: white, yellow and blue. And poets have eulogized his blue color in a fantastic manner. Please comment.

As far as naturalness is concerned there is no difference between one limb of the body and another—and if there is a difference it is manmade. The difference we see is our own creation; it is not real. All the limbs of the body are the same; there is no difference between a hand and a leg. But we have divided even the parts of our body and categorized them. There are parts that are like living rooms in a house to be shown to everybody, and some other parts of the same house, like lockers, to be kept hidden and secret. Even our physical body is fragmented, and a fragmented body is an unhealthy body. But in itself the body is an organic whole; it is indivisible. There is no division whatsoever between one limb and another. And the day man achieves his natural health these manmade divisions will disappear.

But you are right when you ask how far one can take liberties with the body of another in relating with him or her. It is okay to take someone's hand lovingly in yours, but in doing so you have also to take the other person's feelings into full consideration. In a natural society, with the possibilities of the natural life I am talking about, one will always take the other person into full consideration. Taking another's hand, you have to see that he or she is not unnecessarily hurt or inconvenienced. This consideration will be basic to that naturalness. Maybe holding hands is pleasurable to me, but it may be hurtful to the person whose hands I hold. He is as free to seek his happiness as I am to seek mine. He has as much right to his happiness as I have to mine. So in taking someone's hand I have not only to see that it is pleasurable to me, I also have to know how the other person is going to take it.

I am free. My freedom is complete, but it is confined to me. My freedom cannot impinge on the freedom of another person, because his freedom is as complete as mine. Where the other person begins, my freedom will be responsible for his freedom too. Otherwise freedom becomes a license, becomes meaningless, because freedom is indivisible. Freedom and responsibility go naturally together.

If you come and hug me, surely you will feel happy about it. But it is not necessary that I should also feel the same way. Maybe I am hurt and disturbed by your hug. So if you are entitled to seek your happiness, I am equally entitled to escape being hurt. This understanding is essential for a natural, sane and healthy society to come into being. And a natural society will not have laws to be enforced with the help of magistrates, police and prisons, it will only depend on the understanding and awareness of its caring membership.

You also want to know what morality is, according to me. To me, respect for another person is morality. I should respect the other person as much as I respect myself. This is the heart of morality, and under its wings it covers all other kinds of morality. Respect for the other, the same respect that I want for myself, is the cornerstone of morality. There is no morality higher than this. The day I put myself above another I become immoral. The day I consider myself to be the end and treat others as means, I turn utterly immoral. I am not moral until I truly know that each person is an end unto himself or herself.

And you say that a husband can be hurt if his wife allows another person to hold her hand or to hug her. It is just possible. In fact, the institution of the husband is itself a kind of immorality. Marriage is a declaration of the fact that he has turned the woman he has married into a means for the rest of her life. It says that a man has bought a woman to establish his ownership over her. But people cannot be owned, only things can be owned. And when you own a person you reduce him or her into a thing. And this ownership over people is the worst kind of immorality.

I say that marriage is immoral. While love is moral, marriage is utterly immoral. And there will be no marriages in a better world. In a better world a man and a woman will live as friends and partners for the whole of their lives, but there will be no element of a contract, a bargain, a binding, a compulsion involved in this relationship. This relationship will be wholly based on their love for each other; it will be a reflection of their love and nothing else.

The day love seeks the shelter of law, it courts death. Love dies the day it is turned into a contracted, legalized marriage. When I tell a woman I am entitled to receive her love because she is my wife, I am not really asking for her love, I am asserting my legal right of ownership over her. Maybe in that moment the wife is not in a loving mood, because there are moments of love and they are very few. Ordinary people cannot be in a loving state twenty-four hours a day; that is possible for rare persons who become love itself. Ordinary people cannot always be loving; they have to wait for their loving moments, which are few and far between. But the law will not wait for those moments: I can tell my wife that she should love me right now, because she is my wife—and she will have to yield. And love dies the moment you are forced to love someone. And if my wife tells me that she is not in a loving mood, that she does not love me right now, legal troubles will soon arise.

Most of our ethical concepts and moral laws are unnatural, arbitrary and impractical. In the name of morality we have imposed sheer impossibilities on ourselves. And it is because of them that immorality is rampant. It seems strange to say that our concept of morality itself is immoral—it is morality that breeds immorality—but it is a fact. If I love someone today, can I give him or her a promise that I will not love any other tomorrow? It is impossible to guarantee it. How can I speak for tomorrow, which has yet to come? And how can I speak for a person I have yet to know? And if I give such a promise, troubles are bound to arise tomorrow. Tomorrow, on the scene, that person can appear who is not aware of my pledge, of my promise. Tomorrow an altogether different state of my heart-mind can arise, which will be unaware of the promise I make today. And if I fall in love with another person tomorrow, this promise, this pledge will come in the way of that love.

If I fall in love with another person tomorrow—and it is not impossible—I will be faced with two alternatives. Then, on one hand, I will have to enter into a clandestine love affair, and on the other I will have to pretend to love the person I had promised to love forever. And that is what is happening all around. But isn't it an immoral and ugly society whose true love is forced to go underground and whose false love rules the roost?

So I consider marriage to be immoral. And I say it is the handiwork of an immoral society. And then marriage, in turn, gives rise to a thousand and one immoralities. Prostitution is one of them; it is a byproduct of marriage. Where people seek to make the institution of marriage strong and sacrosanct, the prostitute appears on the scene immediately.

The prostitute protects the chastity of wives, like Savitri of Indian myth. If you have to save the chastity of wives the prostitute is the answer. Even a wife would prefer her husband go to a prostitute rather than fall in love with his neighbor's wife—because love is an involvement, and so it is dangerous. A wife will be in danger if her husband falls in love with another woman, but there is no danger if he visits a brothel once in a while; her position remains safe. Prostitution does not demand involvement; you can buy it with money. Love demands deep involvement, and therefore wives consented to the institution of prostitution—but they cannot consent to love, to their husbands falling in love with another woman.

When I say it, when I say that sex or love is natural and should be accepted naturally, you object to it with the plea it will put a person conditioned by moralistic upbringing and ridden with taboos into difficulty. I tell you, that person is already in deep trouble and what I am saying here can help him free himself from his difficulty. He is already beset with enough troubles and problems. Where is that man who is not in deep waters? He is really drowning. But we don't see those troubles because they are so old and we are so used to them. If a disease is chronic we tend to forget it. What I say can create a new difficulty, not in the sense that it will really bring difficulty to you, but that it will call on you to give up your old habits, your old conditionings, which is really arduous.

But if someday mankind consents to accept life as it is, simple, natural and spontaneous; if people give up imposing unnatural and impossible moralities on themselves, which are anything but moral, then hundreds of thousands of Krishnas will walk this earth. Then the whole earth will be covered with Krishnas.

Lastly, you want to know why Krishna has been described in many colors. Really, he was a man of many colors. He was a colorful man. He cannot be presented in a single color; he was really multicolored. The color of his skin cannot be more than one, but his life, of course, has all the colors of the rainbow. And a lot depends on the quality of the eyes with which you see him. In fact, you see him in the color of your own perception.

A single person takes on different colors and also sees different colors in different states of mind, because a single person is not really the same in different states of his heart-mind. I take on a particular color when I am loving and a quite different color when I am angry. And you see me in one way when you are in love with me and quite differently when you hate me. And colors are changing every day, almost every hour of the day, every moment of the day. Here everything is in flux; nothing is permanent. The concept of permanence in this world is a lie. Everything is changing except the law of change.

It is true that Krishna's color has mostly been described as dark, and there are reasons for it. The dark color, it seems, is the symbol of his steadiness. It means that he is constantly changing, that changeability is the constant factor represented by varying shades of darkness. This country has some special liking for this color. In fact, white is never as beautiful as dark.

Generally, white skin is considered to be beautiful, because its gloss and glamor can hide many ugly features of the body, but dark skin never hides anything; it clearly shows every feature of the body as it is. That is why beauty is rare among dark-skinned people, while you can find any number of handsome faces among the white-skinned peoples. But whenever there is a really beautiful person with dark skin he puts even the most beautiful white person into the shade. Beauty in black is superb; it is a rarity. For this reason we have depicted Rama, Krishna and other beautiful people in dark colors. They are rare. It is an ordinary thing to look handsome with white skin; it is very rare with dark.

There are other reasons for our preference for this color. White lacks depth. It is of course expansive. A white face is usually flat; it is rarely deep. But the dark color has a depth and an intensity. Of course, it is not extensive. Have you noticed that wherever a river is deep its water looks dark and beautiful? The beauty of a dark face does not end with the skin; it is not skin-deep. It has many layers, layers of transparency. On the other hand a white face is flat; it ends with the skin. That is why when you meet a white person, you begin to feel bored with him after a little while. The dark color is enduring; it does not bore you. It has shade upon shade.

You will be surprised to know that currently all the glamorous women of the West are mad about suntans, tanning their skin by exposure to the sun. In scores you can see them lying on every beach under the scorching sun so their color gets dark. Why this craze for suntans? The fact is, whenever a culture reaches its peak, expansiveness ceases to have much significance for it, it begins to seek depth and intensity. We tend to think western people are more beautiful, but westerners are finished with appearances, they are now out to seek beauty in depth. Now the beautiful women in the West are trying to get darker and darker. White has the characteristic that many more people appear beautiful than in a dark color, but its beauty lacks depth and transparency; it is flat and dull.

That is why we opted for the dark color. I don't accept that Krishna was really black; it is not necessary. But we saw him in a dark color; we ascribed this color to him. He was such a lovely person that we could not think of his being white. Maybe he was really dark—which is not so important for me. For me the facticity of a thing is not that important; what is important is its poetic aspect, its poetry. Krishna was a multicolored person, and he had such depths of being that we could not conceive of his being a flat color like white. It was a real joy to go on looking into his face and penetrating its beauty and beatitude.

Therefore, although one saw Krishna in many colors, we assigned a single color, a dark color to him. And we called him Shyam, which means dark or deep blue. Krishna means dark too. Not only did we conceive him so, we even named him so. Whether you say Krishna or Shyam or Sawalia, it means the same.

You also want to know why on one hand Krishna disrobes the *gopis* and on the other rushes to provide clothes to Draupadi when she is being publicly disrobed by the Kauravas. The question is significant. In fact, a person who has never once really disrobed a woman will continue, in dreams and fantasies, to disrobe women all his life. But he who has known nudity can now well afford to cover it, to clothe it.

Then there is a significant difference between robing and disrobing a woman. In love, disrobing is allowed. If you are in love with a woman, she can happily consent to being disrobed by you. But Draupadi was being disrobed not out of love, she was being disrobed in utter hate and spite. The people who disrobed her had no love whatsoever for her. They were out to humiliate her, so it was an outrageous and barbaric act.

As I have said over and over again, I don't attach much importance to facts. I don't look at the story of Krishna providing clothes to Draupadi from a great distance by a miracle as an historical fact. This is just an allegory to say that Krishna, in a very effective manner, came in the way of her being made naked. I believe that he really prevented the Kauravas from dishonoring her. But when a poet describes this event, he turns it into a poem. And when we eventually look at the same poem of an event, it seems to be a miracle. Poetry itself is a miracle; there is no greater miracle than poetry. It only means to say that Krishna intervened and prevented it in his own way.

It is significant to know that one of the names of Draupadi is Krishnaa, the feminine form of Krishna. The truth is, in all human history, there has never been a man as many-splendored as Krishna and a woman as magnificent and glorious as Draupadi. Draupadi is simply incomparable. We have talked a lot about Sita and other women, but Draupadi was as great as any of them. But we have difficulty with Draupadi because she happened to be the wife of five men; in making a right appraisal of her life this fact often comes in our way. But remember how difficult it is to be a single husband's wife; only a woman of exceptional ability and accomplishments could be the wife of five men at the same time.

Krishna is in deep love with Krishnaa; she is one of his most intimate beloveds. And that love comes to her rescue in a moment she is being subjected to the worst humiliation. But that is a different topic which we will discuss when I speak on Draupadi.

> Questioner: You said in the course of a discussion of Krishna at Ahmedabad that the intercourse that Vasudeo had with his wife Devaki was not just sexual, but was a spiritual intercourse and that is why a person like Krishna was born. In view of it one wonders why the sons of Rama and Krishna were not as talented and brilliant as their parents. Can it be said that Rama and Krishna did not have spiritual intercourse with their wives?

In this connection, two things have to be understood.

When I talk of spiritual intercourse between two lovers it does not mean that I am condemning sexual intercourse. By spiritual intercourse I mean that when two persons, a man and a woman, make love, they meet not only on the physical plane but at the spiritual level too. A child born out of mere physical coitus cannot reach to that height of excellence one born out of spiritual intercourse can. I take Krishna to be a child of spiritual intercourse. That is why people who knew Jesus could say that his mother Mary remained virgin even after giving birth to Jesus. Though Mary and Joseph must have made love physically, it is true that the intercourse was much more spiritual than physical. Their desire for sex was not that strong. The physical part of it was like the shadow of the spiritual meeting. Evidently the responsibility for giving birth to Jesus does not lie with the shadow, with physical intercourse.

But the question is significant. Why were the sons of Krishna and Rama not as talented and brilliant? There are good reasons for it. Firstly, it is impossible to give birth to a son who can excel Krishna; Krishna is the apex any son can ever reach. Of course, Vasudeo, who is an ordinary person, can produce a son greater than himself, but Krishna cannot. A son of Krishna is bound to be forgotten by history, because Krishna will always tower above him. Even the highest peaks of the Vindhyachal mountain range will look like dwarfs before Everest. Everything is relative; everyone pales into insignificance before Krishna.

The offspring of people like Krishna, Buddha, Rama and Mahavira have to live under certain inherent disadvantages. Lava and Kusha, the sons of Rama, are great in their own right, yet they pale before their father's towering greatness. If they had been born of ordinary parents they would have made history; they were really extraordinary people. How could the sons of Rama be ordinary people? But in comparison with

Rama they had to take a back seat in history. Dashratha was a very ordinary person; he is known only because he was Rama's father. On his own he was insignificant, but he became great just because he was father of a great person. But even a great son of a great father cannot be that great; he will be smaller than his father by comparison.

The intercourse between Krishna and his wives was spiritual; his offspring were born of spiritual union. But when we come to evaluate them, it has necessarily to be relative, comparative; there is no other way to do it.

You are aware of an anecdote connected with the great Indian King Akbar. Once he was sitting with his court discussing some important matter of state. He rose from his seat and drew a line on a blackboard with white chalk and asked his courtiers to make the line smaller without touching it in any way. Nobody could think how to reduce it without touching it. Then the King's intimate friend Birbal, who was known for his great wit, rose from his seat and drew another line longer than the existing one, and the existing line became smaller without being reduced in size.

Lava and Kusha are indeed great, but they could not surpass their father, who was already at the height of greatness. So they were lost in the shadow of his greatness, which was immense. They would have shone if they had not been Rama's sons. Then history would certainly have remembered them.

> *Questioner: You talked about libido, sex energy and spiritual intercourse. In this context a delicate but clear question arises in regard to Krishna's relationship with Radha. It seems as if the flute belongs to Krishna, but the music emanating from it belongs*

to Radha. If Krishna sings a song, its poetic juice and beauty come from Radha. And when Krishna dances, Radha makes the clinking sound and its rhythm—so inextricably one they are. That is why Radhakrishna has become our watchword, our chant. Nobody says Rukmini-Krishna, although Rukmini was married to Krishna. If Radha is removed from the life of Krishna, he will look so fragmentary and pale. But the irony is that Radha is not even mentioned in the Bhagwad, in the basic scripture depicting the countless erotic plays of Krishna. Since you are so much like Krishna, you are the right person to shed light on this question. Would you please explain?

The people who delve into the scriptures are really amazed by the fact that the scriptures don't even mention Radha. It is because of it some people think no one like Radha ever existed. They say that she is an imaginary creation of the poets of later times. It is natural that people who rely on history and its facts should find themselves in great difficulty on this score. It is true that Radha does not find mention in the earliest scriptures on Krishna, it is only the later literature that talks about her.

My own standpoint on this issue is just the contrary. I believe that the reason for her not being mentioned is quite different. Radha dissolved herself so completely in the being of Krishna, she became so united and one with him, that a separate account of her in literature became unnecessary.

Those of her associates who maintained their separate identities have been mentioned very much, but the scriptures did not think it necessary to mention those who lost their separate identities, merged in Krishna and lived like Krishna's shadows. To mention someone it is necessary that he or she have an independent identity. Rukmini is separate; she has her identity intact, and she has been well recorded by the scriptures. She might have loved Krishna but she did not become one with him. She was related to Krishna, but she did not dissolve herself in him. To be related with someone means you are separate from him or her.

Radha is not in a kind of relationship with Krishna; she is Krishna himself. So in my view it is quite just that she has not been mentioned separately; it is as it should be.

So remember this first reason for Radha not being mentioned in the old scriptures: she is invisible, like a shadow of Krishna; she is not even separate enough that we could know her and recognize her. She is so inseparably one with him that one could not identify her and assign a name and place to her.

It is true that Krishna would be incomplete without Radha. I have said more than once that Krishna is a complete man, a perfect male. This thing has to be understood in depth. There are very few men on this earth who are complete men. Every man has his feminine part and, similarly, every woman has her masculine part. Psychologists say that every human being is bisexual, that there is a woman in every man and a man in every woman. The difference between a man and a woman is one of degrees: a man is sixty percent man and forty percent woman, and similarly, a woman is sixty percent woman and forty percent man. But there are men who seem to be feminine because their female component is predominant. Similarly, there are manly women because of the preponderance of the male element in them.

Krishna is an exception to this rule. I consider him to be a whole man; there is no feminine element whatsoever in him. In the same way I will call Meera a complete woman; she has no masculinity whatsoever in her.

There is another side to this matter of full manhood. If a person is a whole man, he will be incomplete in another sense, and he will need a whole woman to complete him. He cannot do without her. Of course, an incomplete man, who is partly man and partly woman, can do without a woman, because there is already an inbuilt woman in him. But for a whole man like Krishna, a Radha is a must, a whole woman like Radha is a must. He cannot do without a Radha.

Basically, aggressiveness is the way of a man, and surrender the way of a woman. But being incomplete men and women, as most of us are, no man is capable of being fully aggressive and no woman is capable of being fully surrendered. And that is why, when two incomplete men and women relate with each other, their relationship is plagued by constant conflict and strife. It has to be so. Since there is an element of agressiveness in every woman, she sometimes becomes aggressive—while the essential woman in her is ready to submit and surrender. So there are moments when she puts her head at the feet of her man and there are also moments when she would like to strangle him to death. These are the two sides of her personality. In the same way the man is so aggressive at times he would like to dominate his beloved wholly, to keep her under his thumb, and sometimes he is so submissive that he becomes the picture of a henpecked husband. He has his two sides too.

Rukmini cannot be in deep harmony with Krishna, because of the male component in her. Radha is a complete woman and therefore can dissolve herself in Krishna absolutely. Her surrender to him is total. Krishna cannot be in deep intimacy with a woman who has any measure of masculinity in her. To have intimacy with such a woman he needs to be partially feminine. But he is a whole man; there is not a trace of femininity in him. So he will demand complete surrender on the part of a woman if she wants to be intimate with him. Nothing short of total surrender will do; he will ask for the whole of her. This, however, does not mean that he will only take and not give of himself; he will give of himself totally in return.

For this reason Rukmini, who finds so much mention in the old scriptures, and who is the rightful claimant, goes out of the picture eventually, and Radha, an unknown entity, who cannot have any rightful claim on Krishna, comes to center stage. While Rukmini is his lawful wife, duly married to him, Radha is an outsider who is nobody to Krishna. While his relationship with Rukmini was institutional, socially recognized, his relationship with Radha was one of friendship, of love. Radha can have no legal claim on Krishna; no law court will ever decree that she has any lawful claim on Krishna. But the irony is that in the course of time Rukmini is forgotten, disappears from history, and this woman Radha becomes everything to Krishna—so much so that her name is attached to his for ever and ever.

And what is more significant in this connection is that Radha, who sacrifices everything for Krishna's love, who loses her own individual identity, who lives as Krishna's mere shadow, becomes the first part of their joint name. We call them Radhakrishna and not Krishnaradha. It means that one who surrenders totally gains totally, gains everything, that one who stands last in the line eventually comes out at the head of it.

No, we cannot think of Krishna without Radha. Radha constitutes the whole of Krishna's tenderness and refinement; whatever is delicate and fine in him comes from Radha. She is his song, his dance and all that is feminine in him. Alone, Krishna is out and out male, and therefore there is no meaning in mentioning his name alone. That is why they become united and one, they become Radhakrishna. Both the extremes of life meet and mingle in Radhakrishna. And this adds to Krishna's completeness.

You cannot think of Mahavira standing side by side with a woman; a woman has no relevance to him. He is very much himself without a woman. Mahavira was married to a woman and they gave birth to a child, but one of the sects of the Jainas, the Digambaras, do not accept this to be a fact. They say Mahavira had no wife and no child. But I think that while it is historically true that Mahavira was married, psychologically what the Digambaras say is right. Psychologically, there can be no connection between a man like Mahavira and a woman. It is utterly meaningless. Even if it were a fact we cannot accept it. How can Mahavira love a woman? Impossible. There is not even a trace of that love in the whole of Mahavira's life.

Buddha had a wife, but he left her when he renounced the world. Similarly, you cannot associate Christ with a woman; he is beautiful as a bachelor. And his bachelorhood is meaningful. And in this sense too, all of them, Mahavira, Buddha and Christ, are incomplete, fragmentary.

As in the great organization of the universe, the positive is incomplete without the negative, the positive electricity is incomplete without the negative, so in the makeup of human life, man is quite incomplete without the woman. Man and woman together, rather masculinity and femininity together, aggressiveness and surrender together, war and peace together, make for a perfect union, a complete life.

If we want an appropriate symbol to describe the union of Radhakrishna there is one, and only one, available in the Chinese language: it is called yin and yang. Chinese is a pictorial language with a picture for every thing and every word. It has a picture representing yin and yang, the Chinese symbol for the universe. This symbol is in the form of a circle whose circumference is made up of two fish, one white and the other dark. The tail of each fish is in the mouth of the other, and thus they make a complete circle, representing the universe. One half of the circle, made up of the white fish, is exhibited in darkness, and the other half made up of the dark fish, is exhibited in light. The white fish represents yang, the masculine active principle in nature, and the dark fish represents yin, the feminine passive principle in nature—and yang and yin combine with each other to produce all that comes to be.

Radha and Krishna make for a complete circle of life, whole and abundant. In this sense too, Krishna is complete, total. We cannot think of him in fragments and separate from Radha. If you tear him away from Radha, he will become lackluster, he will lose all his color. Radha serves as the most appropriate canvas for the portrait of Krishna to emerge and shine forth. We cannot think of bright stars without a dark night; the darker the night the brighter the stars. Stars are very much there even during the daytime; don't think they disappear from the firmament. Even now, as we are sitting here on a clear morning, the sky is studded with stars, but we cannot see them in the sunshine. If you enter a deep well—say three hundred feet deep—you can see the stars from there right now, because there is a deep layer of darkness covering the well. They shine forth in the night because of the background of darkness.

With the background of Radha, who surrounds him from all sides, the life of Krishna shines bright. In her company Krishna achieves his absolute flowering. If Krishna is the flower, Radha serves as its root. They are completely together; we cannot separate tnem. They really represent the togetherness of life.

Radhakrishna makes for a complete couple, a complete name. Krishna alone is an incomplete name.

SEVENTH DISCOURSE
EVENING, SEPTEMBER 28, 1970
MANALI, INDIA

MAKE
WORK
A
CELEBRATION

Questioner: You say that marriage is immoral. And here is Krishna who perhaps goes for the highest number of marriages in history. Is he guilty of encouraging the immorality which marriage is?

 say marriage is immoral, but I don't say marrying is immoral. A man and a woman in love with each other would like to live together, so a marriage stemming from love will not be immoral. But we are doing just the contrary; we are trying to squeeze love from marriage, which is not possible. Marriage is a bondage, and love is freedom. But a couple in love would like to live together, which is natural. This togetherness will flow from love. Marriage should be the shadow of love and not otherwise.

I don't say that after the abolition of marriage a man and a woman will not live together. The truth is, only then will they really live together. At the moment they only seem to be living together, they really don't live together. Mere physical togetherness is not togetherness. Living in close proximity in space is not living together. And just to be coupled in marriage is not really coupling, not true union.

It is the institution of marriage which I call immoral. The institution of marriage would like love to be banished from the world. As such, every institution is unnatural: it is against man's natural feelings and emotions; it cannot exist without suppressing them. When any two people fall in love with each other, their love is unique and incomparable; no other two people have ever loved each other the same way. But when two persons get married, that marriage is very ordinary, commonplace; millions of people have known marriage the same way. Love is an original and unique phenomenon, while marriage is just a tradition, a repetition. A marriage strangles and kills love. As the institution of marriage becomes dominant and powerful, it thwarts and throttles love to the same degree.

The day we accord love its priority in our lives; the day a man and a woman live together not by way of a contract and compromise but out of love and love alone, marriage as we know it will cease to exist. And with marriage will go today's system of divorce. Then a couple will live together for the sake of their love and happiness, and for no other consideration, and they will part company and separate when the love between them dries up and disappears. Society will not come in their way in any manner.

I repeat: marriage as an institution is immoral, and marriage that comes in the wake of love is quite natural. There is nothing immoral about it.

Questioner: What will be the position of children in a marriage which has love as its basis? Where will they belong? And will they not become a social problem? Please explain.

So many problems seem to loom up if love becomes the basis of marriage. But they loom up only because we see things through the screen of our old concepts and beliefs. The day we accord love its highest value, the idea that children belong to individuals, to parents, will become meaningless. Really, children don't belong to individuals; they really never belong to them. There was a time when the father was unknown, only the mother was known. That was the age of matriarchy, when the mother was the head of the family and descent was reckoned through the female line.

You will be surprised to know the word "father" is not that old; the word "uncle" is much older. "Mother" is an ancient word, while "father" is very new. The father really appeared on the scene when we institutionalized marriage; he was not known before. The whole male population of a tribe was father-like; only the mother of a child was known. The whole tribe was loving to its children, and since they belonged to none they belonged to all.

It is not right to say that ownership of children by individuals, by parents, has been good for children. True good will happen when children belong to a whole commune or society.

You ask what the position of children will be when we will make love the basis of marriage. Will not they become a social problem? No, they will not be a social problem then. They are a social problem right now, when we have left them at the mercy of a few individuals, be they parents or relations. And in view of the new vista of future possibilities opening up before us, it is certain that the old foundations of our society are not going to last any longer.

For instance, in the old world a father was a must for a child to be born; it will not be so in the future. In fact, he has already become redundant. Now my sperm can be preserved for thousands of years after my death, and it can give birth to a child even ten thousand years after me.

Then in the future, even the mother, who has so far been so indispensable, will not be needed for the birth of a child. Soon science is going to find ways and means—we are at the doorstep of its consummation—when a mother will not need to carry the burden of a baby in her womb for nine months. A machine, an instrument like the test tube will do the job better. All the facilities that are available to a baby in the mother's womb will be provided to him, and he will be better provided for in a test tube or whatever we will call it. And then it will be difficult to know the parentage of a child. Then the whole social structure will have to be changed. Then all women will play mothers and all men will play fathers to children who will grow up under the collective care of the community. For sure, everything is going to change.

What I am saying has become necessary because of the way science is currently developing throughout the world. But we don't understand it because we continue to think in our old ways, which are out of date. Now when a child is born to you, you consult the best possible physician about his health and upkeep; you don't think that, being his father or mother, you can treat your child medically too. In the same way you go to a good tailor to have clothes made for him; you don't sew them yourself because you happen to be his parent. Likewise, with the deepening of your understanding you will want your child to be born with the help of much healthier sperm than your own, so that he is not retarded physically or mentally, so that he is endowed with a healthy body and an intelligent mind. So you would want to secure the best sperm available for the birth of your child.

On her part, a would-be mother would not like to drag on for nine months with a baby in her womb when facilities will be made available to grow a child externally in a better and healthier manner. The function of parents, as it is today, will then cease to be necessary. And with the cessation of the function of parents, how will marriage itself exist? Then the very basis of marriage will disappear. Technology on one hand and the science of man's mind on the other, are heading towards a point when individual claim on children will come to an end.

This does not mean that all man's problems will end with this radical change in the social structure. Every new experiment, every change we make brings its own problems with it. It is not a great question that problems as such should cease to be—man will always have problems—the great question is that we should have newer and greater problems to deal with than what we now have. The real question is that our problems of today should be better than those we had yesterday.

It is not that with the abolition of marriage every conflict between man and man, between man and woman will disappear for good. But, for sure, the conflicts that arise from marriage—and they are more than enough—will go. However, newer conflicts and newer problems will arise and it will be a joy to deal with them. To live on this planet problems will always be needed, because it is through our struggle with problems that we grow and mature.

In this connection it is necessary to take notice of a particular problem which comes our way again and again. The problem is that we get used to putting up with the problems of the social system we are given to live in. And so we are afraid of facing those new and unfamiliar problems that are likely to come with a better and higher social system—even if such a system becomes necessary and feasible. And thus we get stuck with a decadent and dying system, and that is what makes for our real difficulty, our real problem. But it is the task of intelligence to understand that if newer and better problems are available, in the wake of change, it is right to go for the change and to grapple with those problems and solve them.

I hold that so long as love does not bloom fully in a man's life he will not attain to the glory and grandeur of life, he will remain lackluster. A life devoid of love is dull and dreary; it is a veritable desert. And I think that a life full of problems, full of energy and glow, is far more preferable to a life that is dull, dreary and dead. I would like to conclude this discussion with a small anecdote.

A little bunch of wildflowers lived sheltered in the crevices of an old city wall. Winds and storms failed to disturb them since they were well-protected by the high wall and its crevices. For the same reason, the sun's rays could not burn them nor could the rains ruin them.

There was a rosebush in the neighborhood of this little bunch of wildflowers. The presence of gorgeous roses made the wildflowers feel inferior and ashamed of their own existence. So one fine morning the wildflowers prayed to God, "So long we have lived as faceless flowers; now please turn us into roses."

God said in answer, "Why get into unnecessary troubles? The life of a rose is very hard. When there is a storm, it shakes it to its roots. And when it blooms, there is already someone around to pluck it. You live a well-protected life; don't forsake it."

But the wildflowers insisted, "We have long lived a sheltered life; we now want to live dangerously. Please make us roses for twenty-four hours."

Other wildflowers pleaded, "Don't be crazy. We have heard that a few of our ancestors had to suffer terribly because of this very craze to become a rose. Our racial experience says we are okay as we are, we should not try to be roses."

But the little plant again said, "I want to gossip with the stars; I want to fight with the storms; I want to bathe in the rains. I am determined to become a rose."

At long last God yielded and one fine morning the little bunch of wildflowers became a rose. And immediately its saga of trials and tribulations began. Storms came and shook its roots. Rains came and it was drowned in water. The midday sun burned its petals and made it suffer immeasurably. At all times it was exposed to dangers from all sides. Once again other elderly wildflowers gathered round the newborn rose and said, "We had told you so; you did not listen. Don't you see how secure you were in your old life? Granted it had its problems, but they were old and familiar problems, and we were used to them. It was okay. Do you see what a mess you have made of your life?"

To this the new rose said, "You are fools. I say that it is far better to be a rose just for twenty-four hours and live dangerously than to live in lifelong security as little wildflowers protected by a high wall. It was great to breathe with the storms and fight with the winds. I was in contact with the sun and I had a dialogue with the stars. I have achieved my soul and I am so fulfilled. I lived fully and I am going to die fully. As far as you are concerned you live a life of living death."

But going back to the world does not make any difference to Krishna: he can easily go back if it becomes necessary. He will remain himself in every situation—in love and attachment, in anger and hostility. Nothing will disturb his emptiness, his calm. He will find no difficulty whatsoever is coming and going. His emptiness is positive and complete, alive and dynamic.

But so far as experiencing it is concerned, it is the same whether you come to Buddha's emptiness or Krishna's. Both will take you into bliss. But where Buddha's emptiness will bring you relaxation and rest, maybe Krishna's emptiness will lead you to immense action. If we can coin a phrase like "active void", it will appropriately describe Krishna's emptiness. And the emptiness of Buddha and Mahavira should be called "passive void". Bliss is common to both but with one difference: the bliss of the active void will be creative and the other kind of bliss will dissolve itself in the great void.

You can ask one more question, after which we will sit for meditation.

> *Questioner: How is it that Buddha lives for forty years after attaining to nirvana or the great emptiness?*

It is true Buddha lives for forty to forty-two years after he becomes Buddha. Mahavira also lives about the same period of time. But Buddha makes a difference between *nirvana* and *nirvana*. Just before leaving his body he says that what he had attained under the bodhi tree was just *nirvana*, emptiness, and what he is now going to attain will be *mahanirvana* or supreme emptiness. In his first *nirvana* Buddha achieves the emptiness we can see, but his second emptiness, his *mahanirvana*, is such that we cannot see it. Of course men like Krishna and Buddha can see it.

It is true that Buddha lives for forty years after his first *nirvana*, but this is not a period of supreme emptiness. Buddha finds a little difficulty, a little obstruction in living after *nirvana*, and it is one of being, still there in its subtlest form. So if Buddha moves from town to town, he does so out of compassion and not out of bliss. It is his compassion that takes him to people to tell them that they too can long for, strive for and attain what he himself has attained.

But when Krishna goes to the people he does so out of his bliss and not out of compassion. Compassion is not his forte.

Compassion is the ruling theme in the life of Buddha. It is out of sheer compassion that he moves from place to place for forty years. But he awaits the moment when this movement will come to an end and he will be free of it all. That is why he says that there are two kinds of *nirvana*, one which comes with *samadhi* and the other with the death of the body. With *nirvana* the mind ceases to be, and with *mahanirvana* the body too ceases to be. This he calls sovereign *nirvana*, that which brings supreme emptiness with it.

It is not so with Krishna. With him, *nirvana* and *mahanirvana* go hand in hand.

If we want to be fully alive, if we want to live a rich and full life, we should be ready to invite and face any number of new and living problems. And we will live a morbid and dead life if we try to be finished with all our problems for good. Problems are necessary, but they must always be new and live problems, and man should have will, confidence and courage to meet them squarely and solve them. That is what makes for real life. And there is no reason why man should not solve them.

Our present social setup is based wholly on fear—fear of all kinds. There is fear in its very foundation; it is fear-oriented from A to Z. We are afraid of everything around us and this fear inhibits us, does not allow us to step out of our age-old limitations. And we never think of what a mess we have made of our life and living. Fear of what is going to happen prevents us from taking any new steps forward, and so we refuse to see the actual state of our affairs. Because if we see what really is, we will be compelled to change the old for the new; the old is so rotten. But our fear of the new fetters our feet and we go on dragging with the old.

I have had occasion to come into contact with hundreds of thousands of people and I observed them very closely; I really peeked into their hearts and minds. And I say I did not find a single person, man or woman, who is satisfied with his or her marriage and who is not steeped in misery on account of it. But if you point out their reality to them, they will immediately enumerate the various problems that will arise if they try to do something about it. The irony is that they are already ridden with problems, but they are not aware of them because they have become so used to them.

It is as if we ask a bird in a cage to fly into the open sky and it says that it is so secure in its cage, whereas the freedom of the sky will create so many problems for it. If you make a change, problems are bound to arise. And so far as the caged bird is concerned, its difficulties will be enormous, because it has no experience of flying in the vast sky. Yet a choice has to be made.

Granted that there is security in the cage, but what worth is this security in comparison with the freedom and ecstasy of flying in the open sky? If you think only of security then the grave is the most secure place on the earth.

Questioner: Swami Sahajanand accuses Krishna of corrupting people rather than liberating them through his path of sensuous enjoyment. And he offers two reasons in support of his accusation. Firstly, if one worships Krishna as a gopi-like devotee this worship is likely to degenerate into something like the Maharaj libel case of Gujarat. And secondly, if one turns life into a celebration in Krishna's way it will give impetus to man's desire for indulgence.

There is yet another question arising from the same source.

*Is not the way of Rama's devotee
superior to that of Krishna's? Virtues
like celibacy, detachment, dynamism
and wisdom associated with Hanumana—a chief devotee of Rama—
are lacking in the devotees of Krishna
like Meera, Narsi and Surdas, who
are all introverts disinterested in the
service of society.*

*And lastly I want to know why pain-
ters of their times did not show Rama,
Krishna, Mahavira and Buddha with
beards as they did in the case of Jesus
Christ.*

Firstly, let us find out whether life is a schedule of
duties and works to be performed, or it is a celebration. If life is work, a duty, then it is bound to turn
into a burden, a drag, and we will have to go through
it, as we do, with a heavy heart. Krishna does not
take life as work, as duty; he takes it as a celebration,
a festivity. Life is really a great feast, a blissful festivity. It is not homework, not a task that has to be
performed willy-nilly.

It is not that someone will cease to work if he
takes life as a celebration. He will certainly work, but
his work will be a part of the festivity, it will have
the flavor of celebration. Then work will happen in
the company of singing and dancing. It is true there
will not be too much work, it will be less in quantity,
but in quality it will be superb. Quantitatively the

work will be less, but qualitatively it is going to be immeasurable.

You must have noticed how people who are addicted to work, who turn everything into work, have filled life with tension and only tension. All anxieties of life are the handiwork of the workoholics; they have turned life into a workshop. Their slogan is, do or die. They say, "Do something as long as you are alive, or die if you cannot do anything." They have no other vision of life except work. And they don't have even a right perspective of work. Work for what? Why does man work?

Man works so he can live. And what does living mean? To live means to celebrate life. We work so that we can have a moment of dance in our lives. Really, work is just a means to celebrate life.

But the irony is that the way we live there is no leisure left to sing and dance and celebrate life. We turn means into an end; we make work the be-all and end-all of life. And then life is confined between two places, our home and the office. Home to office and back home is all we know of life. In fact, home ceases to be a home, we bring our office home with us after we leave it in the evening. Then psychologically we are in a mess; we live an entangled life, a confused and listless life. Then we keep running for the rest of our lives in the hope that someday we will have time to relax, rest and enjoy life. But that day really never comes; it will never come. Really, workoholics will never know that there is rest and joy and bliss in life.

Krishna takes life as festivity, as a play, fun. It is how flowers, birds and stars take life. Except man, the whole world takes life as play, fun. Ask a flower why it blooms. For what? It blooms without a purpose. A star moves across the sky without a purpose. And purposelessly the wind blows, and keeps blowing. Except man, everything under the sun is a play, a carnival. Only man works and toils and sheds copious tears. Except man, the whole cosmos is celebrating. Every moment of it is celebration.

Krishna brings this celebration into the life of man. He says, let man be one with this cosmic celebration.

It does not mean that there will be no work if we turn life into a celebration. It is not that the wind does not work; it is always moving, blowing. It is not that the stars are idle; they are constantly moving. It is not that flowers don't do anything when they bloom; really, they do a lot. But for them, doing it is not that important; what is important is being. Being is primary and doing is secondary for them. Celebration comes first and work takes a back seat in their lives. Work is preparatory to celebration.

If you go and watch the way the primitive tribes live, you will know what work is in relation to celebration. They work the whole day so they can sing and dance with abandon at night. But the civilized man works not only in the day, but also at night. He takes pride in working day and night. And if you ask him why he works, he will say that he works today so he can relax tomorrow. He postpones relaxation and continues to work in the hope that he will relax some day. But that day never comes for him.

I am in complete agreement with Krishna's vision of life, which is one of celebration. I am a celebrationist. May I ask what man has achieved by working day in and day out? It is different if he works for the love of work, but I would like to know what he has achieved so far by working meaninglessly?

There is the story of Sisyphus in Greek mythology. He was a king who was condemned by the gods to push a heavy stone uphill and, when it rolled down the hill, to begin again. Time and again Sisyphus had to carry the stone from the base of the hill to its top; this is what "an uphill task" means. A workoholic is a Sisyphus endlessly pushing a stone uphill and beginning again when it rolls down. He i‹

now engaged in pushing the stone uphill and then chasing it when it rolls down and then beginning to push it up again. And he never comes to know a moment of leisure and joy in all his life.

These workoholics have turned the whole world into a madhouse. Everyone is mad with running and reaching somewhere. And no man knows where this "somewhere" is. I have heard that a man got into a taxi and asked the driver to drive fast. And the taxi sped. After a little while the driver inquired where he had to go, and the man said, "That is not the question, I have to go fast."

Everyone in the world is running like him, everyone is hurrying through life. "Hurry up," has become our watchword. But no one asks, "Where are we going?" We work hard, but we don't know why we work so hard. One does not even have time to think why he is toiling day in and day out. He is running just because his neighbor is running, his friends are running, the whole world is running. Everyone is running for fear of being left behind the other runners.

His son said, "It is true, as I learned from your life, that wealth is not happiness, but I also learned from your life that if one has wealth, one can have the suffering of his choice; one can choose between one suffering and another. And this freedom of choice is beautiful. I know that you were never happy, but you always chose your own kind of suffering. A poor man does not have this freedom, this choice; his suffering is determined by circumstances. Except this, there is no difference between a rich man and a poor man in the matter of suffering. A poor man has to suffer with a woman who comes his way as his wife, but the rich man can afford women with whom he wants to suffer. And this choice is not an insignificant happiness."

If you examine it deeply, you will find that ~~piness~~ and suffering are two aspects of the same thing, two sides of the same coin, or, perhaps, they are different densities of the same phenomenon.

The workoholics have done immense harm to the world. And the greatest harm they have done is that they have deprived life of its moments of celebration and festivity. It is because of them that there is so little festivity in the world, and every day it is becoming more and more dull and dreary and miserable.

In fact, entertainment has taken the place of celebration in the present world. But entertainment is quite different from celebration; entertainment and celebration are never the same. In celebration you are a participant; in entertainment you are only a spectator. In entertainment you watch others playing for you. So while celebration is active, entertainment is passive. In celebration you dance, while in entertainment you watch someone dancing, for which you pay him. But there is a world of difference between dancing and watching a dance performed by a group of professionals who are paid for it. You work hard during the day, and when you are tired in the evening you go to a concert to watch others dancing. It is all you can do, but it is not even an apology for celebration.

Albert Camus has said that the time is very near when we will have servants to make love on our behalf, because we don't have time for love. We are so busy we don't have time for love; we will employ others to do this job for us. Love is a celebration, but for workoholics it has become a superfluous thing. It does not yield any profits; it does not add to their bank balances. Love is an end unto itself; it cannot be turned into a business. So those who are addicted to work think it a waste of time to indulge in love. A kind of secretary can be asked to deal with it and dispose of it.

Obsession with work has taken away the moments of celebration from our life, and we have been deprived of the excitement and thrill that comes celebration. That is why nobody is happy, nobody is cheerful, nobody is blossoming. That is why suffering has become the badge of mankind.

We had to find a substitute for celebration, and entertainment is that substitute, because we do need a few moments of relaxation, a brief spell of diversion. But entertainment is a very poor substitute, because others do it and we are only spectators. It is like the vicarious pleasure we derive from watching someone in love. This is precisely what you do when you watch a movie. You watch a man and woman loving each other and you enjoy it vicariously. It is a false substitute; it is utterly useless. It is not going to give you a taste of love; it is not going to satiate your thirst for love. On the other hand, your disaffection and torment will deepen and land you in still greater misery.

For God's sake, know love directly, enter into it, and only then you will be satiated and happy. Real love alone can make life festive; entertainment won't.

Krishna is all for celebration; he takes life as a great play, a mighty drama. The work-addicts have, instead of doing any good to the world, only created confusion and complication in the life of man. They have made life so complex that living has become extremely hard and painful.

It is true that devotees of Rama, like Hanumana, seem to be strong, active and sincere people; the devotees of Krishna are not so. Meera goes about dancing and singing, but she does not seem to be as dynamic as Hanumana. She cannot be. The reason is that while Rama takes life seriously, believes life is all work, Krishna is non-serious and takes life as a dance, a celebration. And life as celebration is a different thing altogether. Life as work pales in insig-ificance before it. If you are asked to spend twenty-hours in the company of Hanumana you will twice. You would want to run away from him ere made to live in the same room with him for a long while. But you can live with Meera joyfully for any length of time.

It is true that Krishna's lovers gradually withdrew themselves from the world of outer activity, from the world of extroversion. They dived deep into the interiority of life and drank at the fountain of its bliss. This is as it should be, because Krishna knows how, when you lose yourself in its outer activities, you are missing life itself.

It will be a peaceful and happy world that will abound with Meeras. And a world full of Hanumanas will be a restless and warring world, a sorry world. If it comes into being, wrestling rings will appear all over and society will be ridden with conflict and strife. We can accommodate one or two Hanumanas; more than that would be too much. But any number of Meeras will be welcome. Meera is in contact with life at its deeper levels; Hanumana lives at the surface. Hanumana is nothing more than a faithful servant, a volunteer; he is just serving his master. He is, of course, sincere, persevering and hard-working. Meera is a class by herself; she is rare. Her bliss, her ecstasy comes from being, not from doing. For her, just being is festive and joyous. Her song, her dance, is not a piece of work for her, it is an expression of her bliss, her ecstasy. She is so blissful that she is bursting into song and dance.

I would like this world to be more and more filled with song and dance, with music and festivity. And so far as the external world, the world of extroversion and action is concerned, we should go into it only to the extent needed for our inward journey. More than that is not necessary. We need bread, but bread is not everything. We need bread to live, but there are people who go on stockpiling bread and, in the meantime, forget all about eating and living. By the time they succeed in making a mountain of bread their appetite is gone and they don't know what to do with the huge stock.

When Alexander was leaving for India he went to see Diogenes, a great sage of the times. Diogenes asked Alexander, "Where are you going and for what?"

Alexander said, "I am going to conquer Asia Minor first."

Then Diogenes queried, "And what will you do after conquering Asia Minor?"

"I will then go to conquer India," said the would-be conqueror.

"And what then?" asked the sage.

And the answer was, "I have to conquer the whole world."

Diogenes was lying on the sandy bank of a river; he was completely naked and enjoying the morning sunshine. He asked again, "What will you do after you have conquered the world?"

Alexander said, "Then I will rest and relax."

This reply of Alexander's sent Diogenes into loud laughter, and he called his companion, his dog, who was sitting some distance from him. When the dog came to him Diogenes said, addressing the dog, "Listen to what this mad king is saying. This man says that he will rest after he conquers the world. And here we are resting right now without conquering a single place." And he said to Alexander, "If rest is your ultimate objective, why not join me and my dog right now on this beautiful river bank? There is enough space here for us all. I am already resting. Why are you going to create so much trouble and disturbance around the world just to rest at the end of it all? You can rest right here and now."

An embarrassed Alexander then said, "What you say seems to be very sensible, but I cannot rest right now. Let me first conquer the world."

And then the sage said, "There is no connection whatsoever between world conquest and rest. Here I am, resting well, without having to go in conquest of the world."

"There is meaning in what you say," said Alexander, and then he added, "but I am already on my way; I cannot turn back in the middle of my journey."

What Diogenes told Alexander at the end of their dialogue proved to be prophetic. He said, "You will in fact, turn back mid-journey. Who has ever returned after completing his journey?" On his way back from India the conqueror died; he could not reach Greece.

All Alexanders die, and die mid-journey. They gather wealth but don't have the time to enjoy it. They do everything to collect all the instruments of an orchestra, and when everything is ready they find to their despair that they have lost the capacity to play them. Their hands are empty and they can't do anything but weep. Alexander died empty-handed.

No, life is meant to be a celebration; celebration is its central note. If someone asks you, better ask this question of yourself: "Do I live to work or work to live?" Then the answer will become very clear to you, and you will move much closer to Krishna. You do everything so you live, and not so you live to work and work meaninglessly. And to live you don't need to do much; too much doing has no meaning.

If this attitude that we work to live gains ground, much of our trouble and misery will disappear. Most of our troubles arise from our madness to do too much, and if this madness goes, there will be much more peace and joy and cheer in the world than we have at the moment. With the disappearance of overdoing, many things will disappear—tension and anxiety will disappear, mental diseases and madhouses will disappear. This much harm it will do, if you take it as harm. It will be a sane world indeed.

Therefore I say that I am in complete accord with Krishna's festive vision of life.

You also want to know why all the *avataras* and *tirthankaras* of this country, like Rama, Krishna,

Mahavira and Buddha, have been portrayed without beards. What may the reasons be?

I don't think all of them were without beards; one or two might have been exceptions to the rule. It is not factual that they did not have beards, yet it is true that not one of them has been portrayed with a beard. There must be reasons for it.

Firstly, the time before one grows a beard is the freshest and finest time of his life. That is the peak moment of life's freshness; after that it begins to decline. But as far as men like Krishna are concerned we saw them as the very picture of that freshness, of that infinite freshness, and saw that they retained this freshness through their whole lives. There is never a point of decline in their freshness; they are always young and new. Not that they don't age and grow old. They all age, but as far as their consciousness is concerned it is always in the adolescent state. Their consciousness is eternally young, eternally new, eternally fresh.

These paintings and portraits of Rama, Krishna, Mahavira and Buddha that we see without beards, do not represent their persons; they represent their spirit, their soul, their consciousness. We saw a constant freshness, youthfulness, accompanying them through their childhood, their youth and old age, and we captured that freshness in our paintings and pictures of them.

We can never think of Krishna as an old man leaning on a cane. He must have grown to old age, for he lived long, but we fail to imagine how he looked as an old man. There is something in him which is eternally young and alive.

On the other hand there are children who seem to be born old. Recently I visited a town where a young girl met me—she was hardly thirteen or fourteen years old—and she said that she wanted *moksha*, liberation. Now this girl is already an old woman, and I told her so. She has yet to live life and she talks of liberation. She has yet to be in bondage and she wants to be free of it. She told me that she belongs to a family where everyone is religious. I even visited her family, which was really a religious family—sad, somber and dead. Everyone in that family was waiting for *moksha*; no one had time to live. Her father looked dead, her mother looked dead; even the youngsters of the family looked anemic and ill. It seemed to me they were living in the shadow of fasting and starvation; they were dissipated and dead.

Naturally this girl has grown old, and if an artist paints a picture of her he would not want to show her as a young woman. That would be an inauthentic picture. The artist will have to show her as a seventy or eighty year-old woman. That would be her correct mental age.

Buddha, Mahavira, Krishna and Rama are ever young, really adolescent. We could have painted them as twenty-five years old as well. That is the age of youth, but then they would have to be shown with beards. But we portrayed them as teenagers without beards and mustaches. Why? There is a reason for this too. It was not proper to portray them as twenty five year-olds with beards and mustaches, because that would have shown they were on their way to old age. Once a thing begins, it necessarily has to come to an end. You cannot portray the eternally young with beard and mustache; that would defeat the very purpose. So adolescence is the right age in which to show them, because it is the prime time of newness.

There is yet another reason why men like Krishna are shown without beards. Man's concept of beauty is feminine; it is derived from the beauty of women. For him, woman, and not man, is the image of beauty. And most of our painters and sculptors, our poets and our writers of scriptures have been men. Naturally if they have to depict someone as handsome, beautiful, they will do so in terms of feminine beauty. So if Krishna has to be portrayed as a beautiful person—and he is superb; who can be more beautiful than him?—he will certainly be shown in exquisite feminine beauty. That is why statues and portraits of Buddha, Krishna and others like him have feminine faces. Their images are distinctly feminine; they are far from masculine, because man's understanding of beauty comes from his appreciation of woman's beauty.

It is for this reason that with the growth of man's aesthetic sense, all the world over, he began to shave his beard and mustache. First, he removed them from the faces of Krishna and Buddha, and then from his own. Because he believes that woman's face is much more beautiful than his own, he has been trying to imitate her in various ways.

But woman's concept of beauty is quite different; her concept of beauty is masculine, is based on her appreciation of man's beauty. A woman is not attracted by another woman's beauty, she is always attracted by the beauty of man. Her image of beauty comes from the man's face. So I think if women had painted pictures of Krishna and Buddha they would definitely have shown them with beards and mustaches.

I don't think that even today women like men with shaved faces; they look feminine to them. The beard and mustache are symbols of masculinity for women. Just think how you would react to a woman who appears before you with a beard and mustache on her face; she will be repelling. In the same way a man without a beard and mustache should repel a woman. Whether she says so or not is another thing, because women don't have even this much freedom, that they can express their likes and dislikes. Even their ways of thinking are determined by men; they cannot assert their own preferences.

Remember, whenever and wherever masculine beauty manifests itself in its full grandeur, beards and mustaches return to men's faces. It has always been that masculine beauty gains its peak with the return of the beard and mustache. But when man begins to imitate women, he shaves his beard and thus loses a part of his masculinity.

It is ironic that women are out to imitate men on a very large scale. This craze has become almost worldwide. Women now want to dress in jeans like men, because their concept of beauty is based on their appreciation of the male look. They like to wear watches on their wrists exactly as men do. They are taking to men's professions for the same reason. They think that man is the picture of beauty and strength. Their whole lib movement is moving in the direction of imitating man. And if someday they win—there is every likelihood that they will win, because men have dominated long, and they must now quit so that women take center stage—it will not be surprising to see women wearing beards and mustaches. Today we cannot even think of it; it seems quite unthinkable. But they have already started wearing beards and mustaches in subtler ways; they are doing their very best to imitate men in every way. They want to look like men; they are out to become carbon copies.

But whether men imitate women or women imitate men, it is ugly and absurd. It is utterly stupid. Imitation itself is stupid.

Painters and sculptors who portrayed Krishna, Rama and Buddha, were men, admirers of feminine beauty, and for this very reason none of these portraits can be said to be authentic. If you see the statues of the twenty-four Jaina *tirthankaras* you will be surprised to find that they are all alike, that there is not the least difference between one and another. If you remove the different signs engraved at the bottom of their statues, you cannot tell one from the other; they are exactly the same. Similarly, there is no difference between the statues of Mahavira and Buddha other than of clothes. While Mahavira is naked, Buddha is in clothes. Do you think all of them really looked alike?

No, it is impossible they all looked alike. It rarely happens that two persons have exactly the same face, not even twins. But the painters and sculptors have achieved the miracle. How? The painter engaged in portraying Buddha is doing his best to make his portrait the most beautiful ever. The sculptor of Mahavira's statue works with the same objective in mind. And the net result of this effort of theirs to achieve perfection in beauty is that their images turn out alike.

> Questioner: You say that one should work only enough to live, not more than that. If this attitude towards work becomes prevalent, Meera will cease to have a tanpoora, an instrument in her hands and we will not be able to record your discourses. The tanpoora and the tape recorder are the fruits of human labor. So the question is: How will poverty go if man accepts celebration as the way of life?

It is worth considering whether Meera's tanpoora is the handiwork of work-addicts or of those who take celebration as a way of life. Work-addicts don't produce a tanpoora, they produce a spade. The tanpoora has no connection with work; the exponents of work produce a hammer, a hatchet and a sword. The tanpoora is the creation of those who take life as play, fun. Whatever is superb in human creation, be it a tanpoora or a Taj Mahal, is the gift of those whose way of life is celebration. These things of beauty arise from their dreams and fantasies.

It is natural that men and women who take life as celebration should accept the help of those who take life as work and toil. But the work-addicts can also take their work as a play, and then the quality of their work will be very different, and so will be the quality of their lives and ways of living. I think the laborers who put the marble of the Taj Mahal together never knew the joy that a mere look at this marvelous piece of architecture brings to you. For the laborers who built the Taj it was merely work, a means of livelihood. But was it not possible that the same marble could have been put together in a celebrative way?

I love to tell this story again and again. A temple is under construction on the outskirts of a town and a few laborers are busy cutting stones for it. A passerby stops to see what is being built. He goes to one of the laborers and asks, "What are you doing?"

The man was sad and serious, even looked angry with himself. Without raising his gaze to the visitor the laborer said, "Don't you see I am cutting stones?"

The visitor moved to another laborer, and put the same question to him, "What are you doing?"

This man looked sad too, but was not angry. He put down his hammer and chisel, raised his eyes to the visitor, said glumly, "I am earning my bread," and resumed his work.

The visitor moved to a third workman who was engaged in the same kind of work near the main gate of the temple. He was in a happy mood, singing. "What are you doing, my friend?" the passerby asked of him too.

And the man said in a very pleasant voice, "I am constructing a temple." And then he resumed his stone-cutting and his singing.

All three workmen are engaged in the same job, stone-cutting, but their attitude to work is quite different from one another. As far as the third workman is concerned he has turned work into a celebration; he can work and sing together.

I don't say don't abolish poverty, don't have technology and affluence. All I say is that you can create technology and wealth by way of celebration; it is not necessary to treat them as duty and work. The affluence that comes with celebration has a beauty of its own. You can abolish poverty through hard and painful work, but you will remain poor in spite of your wealth. Poverty of the spirit cannot go until you turn work into a celebration. Maybe the way of celebration will take more time, but it will abolish both kinds of poverty—material and spiritual.

It is really a question of our attitude towards what we do. And with the change of attitude, with work turning into a celebration, the whole milieu of life changes.

A gardener works in your garden; it is his livelihood. He does not take his work as celebration. But he can; no one can prevent him if he chooses to change his attitude. Granted that he has to earn his bread, that he must earn his bread, but at the same time he can enjoy his work, he can celebrate with the blossoming flowers, he can sway and sing with them. Who comes in his way except himself, except his attitude towards work? And curiously, he does not earn a lot by taking his work as a means to an end. But if he takes his work joyfully, if he rejoices with the blooming flowers, if celebration becomes primary and work secondary, he will attain to a richness of life he has never known. Then the same gardening will bring him a blissfulness he will never know otherwise.

Poverty should go, suffering should go, but they should go to enable man to take part in the celebration of life. As long as a man remains poor, it is hard for him to celebrate life, to participate in its festival. That is why I stand for the abolition of poverty. To me, elimination of poverty does not mean merely providing the poor with food, clothes and shelter. It is necessary, but it is not all. In my view, unless man's physical needs are fulfilled, he cannot raise his sights to the higher need of life, to the fulfillment of spirit, soul, call it what you may. Bread can only fill his belly; to fulfill his spirit he badly needs the milieu of joy and festivity in his life.

And if we direct our attention to the higher realms of life, to soul or spirit, then we can turn all work into celebration. Then we will plough a field and sing a song together; we will sow and dance together. Until recently, this was the way of life all over. The farmer worked on his farm and also sang a song. The worker in a modern factory has lost that magic, and consequently his work has ceased to be joyful, it is dull and listless. The factory is only a workshop; it knows nothing but seven hours of work for which the worker is paid adequately or inadequately. That is why, when a worker returns home in the evening after a day's toil, he is dead tired, broken and unhealed.

But I tell you, sooner or later song is going to enter the precincts of the factory. Great studies are underway in many advanced countries and this realization is dawning on them, that work should cease to be work alone, that it has to be pleasant and joyful. The day is not far off when factories will resound with music, because without it man will be more and more empty and unhappy. And the introduction of music in factories will not only bring some joy to their workmen, it will add to the quality of their work.

A housewife cooks in her home. She can cook in the way a cook in some hotel does. But then it will be work, dull and tiring. But she can also cook as a woman cooks for her lover who is to visit her. Then cooking is a celebration which never tires you. Really, such work is highly fulfilling. But mere work is going to tire you, exhaust you, leave you utterly empty.

It is really a matter of our attitude towards what we do.

Questioner: You said that Krishna had gone beyond mind, and you also said that, impelled by the natural instincts of the mind, he deprived the gopis of their clothes. How is it that a person who has transcended the mind acts through it? And if it is so, is it any different from the instinctual behavior of animals?

When I say Krishna has gone beyond mind it does not mean that he is not left with a mind. To go beyond the mind means that one has known that which is beyond mind. Mind remains even after you have transcended it, but it is a different mind altogether, it is a mind cleansed and stilled and saturated with the beyond. Krishna is larger than his mind, but the mind has a place in him.

Transcendence of mind can be attempted in two ways. If you try to transcend it through suppression, through fight, the mind will be divided and torn, it will degenerate into a schizophrenic mind. But if you transcend it in a friendly way, through love and understanding, the mind will be integrated and settled in wisdom.

When I say that I have transcended my body it does not mean that I am not my body, or that my body has ceased to be, it only means that I am now not only my body, but much more than it. I am body plus something; something has been added to it. Until yesterday I thought I was only the body, but now I know that I am something more than the body. I remain the body; that "something plus" has not eliminated it, rather it has highly enhanced and enriched it. Now I have also a soul; I am both body and soul.

In the same way, when I come to know God it does not mean that my soul or spirit has ceased to be, it only means that I am now body, spirit and God all together. Then mind and soul are absorbed in that which is immense, which is infinite. It is not a matter of losing something, it is gaining more and more all the way up.

So when I say that Krishna has gone beyond mind I mean to say that he has known that which is beyond the mind, he has known the immense, the eternal. But he continues to have a mind, a mind with heightened sensitivity and awareness. Krishna is not inimical to mind; he has not transcended it by way of fight and suppression, he has gone beyond it by living with it in a very friendly way. Therefore I say that whatever happens between him and his girlfriends is the spontaneous outpouring of his exceedingly innocent mind; he cannot but act naturally, innocently and spontaneously.

Mind is unnatural when it is in conflict, when it is fighting with itself. Mind is unnatural when one of its fragments says do this and another says don't do this. And when the whole mind is together, integrated and one, then everything it does becomes natural, then whatever happens or does not happen is natural and spontaneous. Then there is nothing unnatural about it. And what is natural is right. But you have rightly asked: If it is so what is the difference between man and animal?

In one respect there is no difference whatsoever between man and animal, and in another respect the difference is great. The animal is natural and innocent, but it is not aware of it. Krishna is natural and innocent, but he is also aware of it. In respect to their naturalness and innocence Krishna and the animal are very similar, but with regard to their consciousness there is a tremendous difference.

An animal moves and acts instinctively, spontaneously and naturally, lives in a state of let-go, but has no awareness of it, all its acts are mechanical. Krishna also lives in a state of let-go, allows his nature free and full play, but he is fully aware of it. His witnessing center is always alert and aware of everything that happens in and around him. The animal has no witnessing center.

While Krishna has gone beyond mind, the animal is below the level of mind. The animal does not have a mind, it has only a body and instincts and it functions mechanically. So there is a kind of similarity between one who is above mind and one who is below it.

There is an old saying prevalent among sages that when one attains to the highest wisdom he becomes like the most ignorant person on the earth. There is some truth in this saying.

One of the sages of ancient India is known as Jarbharat, which literally means Bharat the Ignorant. Really, he was one of the wisest sages of this country, but he was named Jarbharat, Bharat the Ignorant, because he looked like an extremely ignorant person. In a way perfect wisdom looks like perfect ignorance; at least in perfection they are similar. A man of wisdom is at rest, because he has known everything, nothing remains to be known. An ignorant person is also at rest, because he does not know a thing. To be restless it is necessary to know a little. An animal functions very unconsciously; Krishna functions with full awareness. Nothing happens to him in unawareness.

That is why we say when someone attains to the highest wisdom he becomes like a child. Somebody asks Jesus, "How is your kingdom of God? How is one who attains to God?"

Jesus says, "One who attains to God becomes like a child." But Jesus does not say that a child attains to God. If it were so all children would attain to God. He does not say that one who attains to God becomes a child, he says he becomes *like* a child. If he says that a sage becomes a child, it would mean that a child has perfect wisdom, which is not the case. If children were perfect we need not do anything with them. No, the child is below the level of the developed mind, while the sage has gone beyond. The child will have to pass through a phase of conflict, tension and struggle; the sage has outlived all conflicts and tensions. The child potentially carries with him all the sicknesses man is heir to; the wise man has outlived such sicknesses. In the course of evolution even the animal will have to pass through all the sicknesses of man. But here is Krishna who has outlived them, transcended them, gone beyond them.

The similarity and difference between man and animal are well-defined.

> Questioner: You talked about swadharma, self-nature, the innate individuality of man. The Geeta says that one's own nature, even if it be inferior in quality, is preferable to an alien nature of superior quality. Then the question is: How can self-nature, which is one's innate individuality, be inferior in quality?

Let it be the last question for this discourse, and then we will sit for meditation.

You ask how one's self-nature or the innate individuality can be inferior in quality. In this connection two things have to be considered.

The first. Everything in its origin is without any attribute, quality; it gathers attributes only after it takes a form and grows. There is a seed; it has no attributes whatsoever. The seed has just potentiality; it has no quality other than this. It can give birth to a flower which is not yet there. Tomorrow it will turn into a flower, and then this flower will have certain attributes, qualities. It will be red in color, it will be fragrant; then it will have an individuality of its own.

But right now, as a seed, there is nothing in it. It will take on attributes only after it comes to express itself, after it sprouts, grows and blossoms into a flower.

The world has many attributes; God has none. God is seed-like; he is unmanifest. When God manifests himself in the form of the world he acquires attributes, and these attributes disappear when he again becomes unmanifest. Someone is a saint and another person is a thief. As saint and thief they have certain attributes, but when they, the saint and the thief, go to sleep, they are without any attributes. Neither does the saint remain a saint nor the thief remain a thief. In sleep all attributes disappear; sleep is a state without attributes. Attributes appear with the waking state; with sleep they go to sleep too. When they wake up the saint will become a saint and the thief will become a thief again. In sleep we are very close to our individuality, our innate nature; rather, we are closest to it. And in *samadhi*, in ecstasy, we actually attain to our supreme nature, which is of the highest.

So the experiencing of the pristine nature has no attributes, no traits whatsoever. But when self-nature manifests itself it acquires attributes. Attribute and non-attribute are not two things; they are not contradictory. They are just the ways of the manifest and the unmanifest.

Self-nature, supreme nature, has two states. One is the unmanifest state when it is in seed form, asleep, absorbed in itself. And the other is the manifest state when it takes form and attributes. Really, no manifestation can be without form and attributes; it has to have a form, a shape, a color and a speciality.

A small story comes to mind, a Zen story. A Zen Master teaches his disciples how to paint. Painting is the medium through which he really leads his disciples into meditation. One can travel to meditation from anywhere and everywhere. There is no point in the world from where you cannot make a start for meditation. This Master has ten disciples who are gathered round him one morning. He tells them, "Go and make a picture whose broad outlines should be like this. There is a cow in a grassy land, and the cow is grazing. You have to paint it, but remember, the painting has to have no form, no attributes."

The disciples find themselves in great difficulty. It is the job of a Master to put his disciples in difficulty, in crisis, because only in crisis can they become aware of themselves. The disciples find it extremely hard to paint a picture without form and attributes; it seems an impossible task. They have to use lines and colors. They have to give the cow some form; they have to show the grass all over the field.

Nine of the ten disciples attempt to paint and the next day return with some sort of paintings which don't have any clearcut outlines, everything is hazy and unclear. But a sort of cow is there in each painting. In drawing the grass they certainly made use of abstract art so it is formless as much as possible. Nevertheless, they have to use colors of some sort.

Inspecting each other's paintings, a disciple asks one of his friends, "Where is the cow?"

The other says, "I had some idea of a cow when I was in the process of painting, but now I cannot say where the cow is."

And the Master rejects all nine pictures saying, "How can you have color and a cow in a painting that has to be without form and attributes?"

The tenth disciple has just a blank sheet of paper in his hand, and the Master says, "Yes, this is it."

The nine disciples who have attempted to paint feel disappointed and they protest, "Where is the cow?"

The Master says, "The cow went home after grazing."

"And where is the grass?" they protest further.

The Master says, "The cow ate it up. So things have gone back to their original places. Things have returned to their unmanifest state. This is really painting without form and attributes. It shows a cow who is finished grazing and a plot of grass the cow has eaten up. Empty space, just space is there."

At its deepest level self-nature is without any form, without any attributes; it is utter emptiness. It becomes manifest with the grass appearing and the cow coming to graze on it. Then the play of attributes happens. And it all becomes unmanifest once again after the cow has eaten up the grass.

This vast expanse of our world was born out of emptiness, which is without form, and it will return to the same emptiness. Everything appears and disappears, but the source is the same emptiness, the immense void. And the whole is hidden in that emptiness which by its nature cannot have a name, a shape and an adjective.

In this sense, self-nature, like everything else, has two states: the manifest and the unmanifest. While the manifest has a name and form, attributes, the unmanifest has none whatsoever.

In the same way we have to see Krishna from two sides, because he has two sides. His one side is visible and his other side is invisible. The skeptic will see only the visible, the manifest form of Krishna, but one who has faith, who is trusting will see the other side too, the invisible, the unmanifest. Thought, contemplation and logic cannot go beyond the form, the manifest; but trust, prayer and meditation can enter the reality, the unseen, the unmanifest. But one who fails to grasp even the form, the manifest, the gross, can hardly be expected to reach the formless, the unmanifest, the subtle.

But thought and logic, rightly used, can take you to the point where the seen, the manifest ends and the unseen, the unmanifest begins. Beyond it thought is absolutely useless; beyond it a jump, a leap is a must. Beyond it you have to get out of your intellect, your mind; you have to go beyond your own mind, beyond self. Actually you have to transcend yourself.

But this transcendence of the mind does not mean that one will cease to know everything that he has known before. Now all that he has known before will be absorbed and assimilated in the newly acquired knowledge of the beyond. The day the manifest and the unmanifest meet and merge into each other, the ultimate truth comes into being.

EIGHTH DISCOURSE
MORNING, SEPTEMBER 29, 1970
MANALI, INDIA

HE ALONE WINS WHO DOES NOT WANT TO WIN

Questioner: Krishna's life, particularly his childhood, is full of stories of his extraordinary heroism. He killed the tyrant king Kansa and destroyed demons like Kirti, Agha, Baka and Ghotaka; in a duel he defeated powerful wrestlers like Chanoor and Mustika. He subdued a very venomous snake known as Kalia, and put out a whole forest fire single-handed. Do you think these are true stories or mythical ones? And what do they suggest and symbolize?

In this context I would like to recall your words, "When Krishna says that he is here to destroy the wicked, he actually means to change them, to reform them." But these stories clearly say he really destroyed them. Please explain.

n this connection it is necessary to understand one thing which has always puzzled people who wanted to understand Krishna. How is it that Krishna, in his teens, fights and defeats such powerful persons as those you mention? And people had only one way to solve this puzzle, and that was to accept Krishna as an incarnation of God—omnipotent, all powerful, capable of doing anything he wants to do. But in its depths it means the same thing, that the strong defeats the weak, that a great power wins over a small power. They say that though Krishna is young in age, he is so powerful that even demons are no match for him. But in my view such interpretations do scant justice to Krishna's life. Basically these interpretations stem from confused and wrong thinking. They stem from the general belief that the strong wins over the weak.

I have something entirely different to say here, and it is necessary to understand it. In my view, he alone wins who does not desire to win, and he who wants to win loses. All these stories, as I understand them, say the same thing; one with no desire to win is going to win and one desiring to win is going to lose. In fact, defeat is hiding itself in the very desire to win, in the depths of this desire. And absence of this desire to win means the person concerned has already won, that he does not need it anymore.

You can understand it in a different way. If someone is desiring and striving to win in life, it means that deep down he is lacking something, that he is suffering from an inferiority complex. Deep down, such a person is aware of the inferiority he is trying to cover through winning. And if, on the other hand, someone is not out to win it means he is already established in his eminence; there is not even a shade of inferiority in him to disprove by resorting to winning.

It will be easy to understand if we look at it from the Taoist viewpoint. One day Lao Tzu told his friends, "No one could defeat me all my life."

One of his friends rose from his seat and said, "Please tell us the secret which made you invincible, because each one of us wants to win and no one wants to be defeated in life."

Lao Tzu began to laugh, and he said, "Then you will not be able to understand the secret, because you don't have the patience to hear the whole thing. You interrupted me when I had not completed my statement. Let me complete it. I say, no one could defeat me because I was already defeated. It was difficult to defeat me because I never wanted to win." Then Lao Tzu told them they were mistaken if they thought they could understand his secret.

Your very desire to win is going to turn into your defeat. It is the craving for success that ultimately turns into failure. Your excessive desire to live lands you in the grave. Your obsession for health is bound to turn into sickness. Life is very strange. Here we miss the very thing that we crave for and cling to, and we find what we don't seek. If one does not seek anything, it means he does not lack it, he already has it.

I will not say that Krishna wins because he is very powerful. It would be the same old logic that the big fish devours the small fish. There is nothing extraordinary in it if Krishna won because of his strength. Then the demons would have won if they had been stronger than Krishna. It is the simple arithmetic of power. But up to now people have interpreted Krishna's victory in these very terms, because they did not have any other criteria.

Jesus says, "Blessed are the meek, because they shall inherit the earth." It is a very contradictory statement, that those who are humble will own the earth. But it is true. Krishna wins because he does not long to win. In fact, a child is not concerned about winning, he is only interested in playing the game. The desire to win, to conquer, is a later development in the life of man, when his mind is diseased. For Krishna everything is play. It is play for Krishna even when he is fighting powerful demons and others. On the other hand, the demons are anxious to win, and that too against an innocent and meek child who has no idea of victory or defeat, who takes everything as play. And the demons are defeated at his hands. That is as it should be.

In Japan there is an art of fighting which is called judo. There is another, similar, known as jujitsu. It is good to know and understand them. Judo is an art of wrestling, but it is a very strange and unique way of wrestling. Its rules are quite contrary to the ordinary rules of games with which we are familiar. If I have to fight you in a wrestling bout, I will strike you, attack you first and you will do everything to defend yourself. In the same way you will strike me and I will defend myself. This is the general rule of fighting all over. But judo has just the opposite rules.

The main rule of judo says: never attack; one who attacks will court defeat. Because it is believed that much energy is spent in attacking, it is always good that I provoke my opponent to attack me and I remain at ease, relaxed. I should do nothing on my part except provoke the contestant to attack me. While I should incite his anger, his hostility, I should take every care to keep my own peace in spite of my opponent's provocations. And another rule of judo says that I should not resist at all if my opponent attacks me, strikes me. On the contrary, my body should remain in such a relaxed state that it wholly takes in and absorbs the attack. It is strange, but true.

This is the secret of judo. Do not attack on your part, provoke your contestant to attack, and if attacked take in the attack with perfect ease and absorb it.

Do you know that if you travel with a drunkard in a bullock cart and the cart falls in a ditch, you will be hurt while the drunk will come out unhurt and unscathed? And do you know why it is so? Is it that the drunk is unhurt because he is the more powerful? And you are hurt because of being weak? No, it is not so. When the cart meets with an accident you are quite conscious, which makes you nervous about the hazards of the accident. You think you are going to be hurt, and therefore your whole body becomes tense and rigid with a view to saving itself from the impending hurt.

On the other hand, the drunkard has no idea the cart has fallen; for him it makes no difference if the cart is on the road or in the ditch. He does not make any effort to protect himself; on the contrary, he cooperates fully with the falling cart, with the whole accident. He does not resist in any way, and it is for this reason that he remains unhurt. When a drunkard falls, he falls like a bagful of cotton; he is not hurt.

Look at a child: he falls every day and does not break his bones. An old man falls and soon goes to the hospital. What is the matter? Is the child stronger than the grownup? No, the child remains unhurt for the simple reason that he does not resist, that he cooperates with the fall. He accepts it. It is this acceptability, and not strength, that helps him.

Judo says that if someone hits you, you should accept it without any resistance. Judo is difficult; it is arduous to learn this art. In a judo contest you have neither to be on the offensive nor on the defensive, because both ways energy is wasted. Rather than hitting your contestant you have to provoke him to attack you, to hit you, and be in complete readiness to receive and absorb it. In short, you have to fuse with it. If you do so, you not only go unhurt but you also gain the extra energy that comes with the opponent's attack. So it often happens in judo that a weak contestant wins and his very strong opponent loses.

I don't say that Krishna knew judo. But in fact, every child knows judo in a way; judo is his secret. If Krishna won against his powerful enemies, the reason was that for him fighting was a play, play-acting, fun. I don't say that all these stories about his heroism are historical; I am not concerned with their historicity. I am investigating their psychological truth.

It has to be remembered that Krishna is not aggressive; he is not on a mission of conquest. It is always others who attack him with a view to destroying him. And I can say that if a Muhammad Ali comes to fight with a child like Krishna he is bound to be defeated. His act shows he is intrinsically weak and afraid, that he utterly lacks self-confidence. He is already a vanquished man; he need not go after a fight. He should have accepted his defeat before the contest.

When one thinks of attacking and defeating another, it means one has already accepted one's inferiority before the other. One who is really strong and great cannot think of fighting and subduing anyone, because he does not find himself inferior to another in any manner. He does not need to defeat someone to buttress his self-confidence; he is sufficient unto himself. It is always the inner feeling of inferiority that makes one aggressive and violent.

The secret of Krishna's victory over his very powerful adversaries lies in his being a child, soft and weak. It lies in his not being fond of fighting and defeating anyone. It lies in his utter desirelessness. Whether these events are historical or not is not my concern, but I hold that the whole philosophy of judo, the active art of ju-jitsu, begins with Krishna's life.

I would say that Krishna is the first master of ju-jitsu. No one in India, China or Japan knows the secret of Krishna's amazing victory over his adversaries. That he does not want to win is his secret. He takes everything—even an enemy's attack—as a play, and he responds to it with utter playfulness. On the other hand, his attacker is tense and anxious, anxious to win, anxious for his life; he is divided and broken, and so he is bound to lose before Krishna. It all means that it is difficult to defeat a child.

> Questioner: Krishna is said to have shown Yashoda, his foster mother, the whole of the universe enclosed in his mouth. He is also said to have gifted his divine eye to Arjuna to enable him to see his universal form. It is also said that Krishna took back the divine eye from Arjuna after he had seen his universal form. Please explain the significance of these episodes.

We don't have the eyes to see it, but the universal form of the divine exists everywhere. If we had eyes we could see the universe all over. Krishna is just an instrument for Yashoda to see the whole of the universe in his mouth. By and large, every mother sees the vision of the universe epitomized in her son. Every mother has the vision of the supreme in her son. It is another thing that she loses this vision with the passage of time, but at some stage she has it for sure.

Yashoda could see the universe, the universal form of the divine and the divine itself in the mouth of Krishna; so does every mother, more or less. But Yashoda could see it fully because she is a perfect mother. And Krishna could be a right vehicle for it because he is a perfect son. There is nothing miraculous about it. If you can see me with very loving eyes you will see the divine in me too. All you need is to have eyes that see.

And secondly, a right medium is equally necessary. Then you can see the face of the whole universe enclosed in a small fruit or flower. Here, the whole, the immense, is hidden in every atom. The whole of the ocean is ensconced in a single drop of water. If you can look deeply and totally into a drop, you will see the whole ocean hidden in it.

Arjuna too, could see, because he is in such deep love with Krishna. It is a rare kind of friendship that exists between him and Krishna. It is no wonder that Arjuna, in a moment of deep intimacy with Krishna, sees the universal form of the divine in him.

It is not that such a thing has happened only once, it has happened thousands of times. It always happens. It is a different thing that all of the instances have not been recorded.

It is good to understand if the divine vision, once gifted, can be withdrawn. Divine vision, really, can neither be given as a gift nor withdrawn. It happens in some moments and it can be lost again. It is really a happening. In some moments you touch the peak of your consciousness where everything is seen so clearly. But it is very arduous to live on that peak; it takes millions of lives to deserve it, to earn this blessing. Ordinarily one has to come down from that peak again and again. It is as if you jump off the ground, and for a moment, like a bird on the wing, you are out of the gravitational pull of the earth—but only for a moment. With the passing of the moment you are back on the ground again. But you have known how it is to fly like a bird on the wing for a moment.

In the same way consciousness has its own field of gravitation, its magnetic pull which keeps it down. In a particular situation your consciousness is able to take such a high jump that, like a flash of lightning, you can have a glimpse of the immense, and then you return to the earth. For sure, now you are not the same person you were before you had the glimpse. You cannot be the same again, because even a momentary glimpse of the immense is enough to change you; you are now a different person. But the glimpse is again lost.

It is as though I am walking on a dark night and there is a sudden flash of lightning which enables me to see clearly the flowers and the hills before me. With the lightning gone, the flowers and the hills are again enveloped in darkness. But now I am not the same person I was before the lightning occurred, although I am back in the same darkness. It is even worse. Before the lightning, I was not aware that there are hills and flowers and trees, but now I am aware that they are there. Although the darkness is as deep as before, now it cannot deprive me of my awareness of the hills and trees and flowers; now they have become parts of my being. Whether I see them again or not, I know in the depths of my being that they are there, that they exist. Now the fragrance of the flowers will reach me even in the dark, and the winds will bring me a message from the hills. Darkness can hide them from me, but it cannot erase my awareness that they exist.

No one can give you the divine vision, but Krishna seems to be telling Arjuna that he will give it to him. This is what creates difficulty for you. Really, human language suffers from obscurity; it still lacks clarity of expression. We have to use words that don't have the vitality to convey what one really means to say. One often says, "I gave so and so my love." But love cannot be given, it is not a commodity. Love simply happens; it is neither given nor taken. But putting it into words, a mother says, "I give so much love to my son." It is a wrong statement. Love has just happened between the mother and her son.

It is the same linguistic clumsiness that has led to this question with regard to Krishna's statement about divine vision. It is nothing more than that. Like love, it happens; it cannot be given or taken. And like love, it can also be lost. Heights are attained and lost; it is difficult to stay at great heights. Hillary and Tensing climbed Everest, hoisted a flag there, and then returned to the plains. It is hard to live on Everest, or on any great height for that matter. It is possible, however, that some day we will manage to live on Everest for a long period. But to live at the peak of consciousness is still more difficult, tremendously difficult. But it is not impossible. People like Krishna live there. People like Arjuna once in a while leap to it, see it and drop back to the earth.

Divine vision happens; it is not a thing to be given or taken. But our language thinks in terms of give and take, and therefore this difficulty has arisen. It would be correct to say that divine vision happened between Krishna and Arjuna in that moment. Krishna was the instrument, the medium, and Arjuna was the one who took the jump. But in ordinary language we will say that Krishna gifted him with divine vision. As I said, if someone with open and loving eyes looks at me sitting here, something will happen to him. But when it happens he will say that it is a gift from me. But who am I to gift it?—although I will say it the same way if I have to say it in words. But in reality I cannot gift it.

Chemistry has a term known as catalytic agent, and it is significant. A catalytic agent is one whose very presence causes something to happen. It facilitates and accelerates the process of this happening, although it does not do anything in the matter and remains completely unaffected itself. For example, if we have to produce water by combining hydrogen and oxygen, then we will need the presence of electricity for this combination to take place. Without the presence of electricity hydrogen and oxygen will refuse to combine and turn into water.

It is because of lightning in the sky that the elements of hydrogen and oxygen in the clouds combine and produce water and rain. Without the aid of lightning, clouds would not turn into rain. But no one can say that electricity does anything to affect this change; it does nothing. On its part electricity remains absolutely inactive and unaffected by this process of hydrogen and oxygen combining and turning into water. Its presence is enough to do the miracle.

There are many catalytic agents like electricity known to the science of chemistry, and all investigations show that catalysts lose nothing in the process; neither do they lose or do anything.

Krishna is such a catalytic agent.

A Master, a guru, is an illusion. There are no Masters in the world, they are all just catalysts. In the presence of someone your consciousness can attain to a height which may not be possible without that presence. But Arjuna is bound to feel that Krishna favored him with divine vision. When something like this happens to Vivekananda in the presence of Ramakrishna, he is certainly going to say that it was Ramakrishna's gift. And if Ramakrishna does not want to get involved with linguistic nuances, he will okay it too. Except people like me, no one wants to get involved with linguistic finesse; the language of give and take is enough for them. That term "give and take" is not appropriate here, but we really don't have a suitable word to express such transcendental experiences.

Ask a painter like Van Gogh if he has painted a certain picture. He will say, "No, I did not paint it, it just happened through me." But you will say, "What difference does it make?" It really makes a great difference. Maybe Van Gogh, to escape the trouble of linguistic finesse, tells you that he painted the picture. In a way it is not wrong: he did paint it and people did see him paint it. But Van Gogh knows in his innermost being that he is really not the creator of this painting; he is just an instrument, a medium. It is a happening and not a doing. It emerged from his innermost being, from the unknown, and he only became its medium, its vehicle. Van Gogh will say, "I was just a witness to its manifestation."

This happening of divine vision between Krishna and Arjuna is not a solitary event; it has happened any number of times. This is what happened between Buddha and Moggalayan, between Buddha and Sariputta, between Mahavira and Gautama, between Jesus and Luke, between Ramakrishna and Vivekananda. It has happened thousands of times, and it is not a miracle. Miracles simply don't happen. It is our ignorance which takes something to be a miracle; otherwise, miracles have no place in existence. Whatever happens is a scientific phenomenon, a fact, a truth. Everything in existence is real and true, but we in our ignorance see it as something miraculous.

Questioner: Is divine vision really frightening? How is it that Arjuna was scared by it?

You want to know if divine vision is frightening, because Arjuna was scared. It can be so, if one is not prepared for it. Even happiness, if it comes to you unexpectedly, will suddenly frighten you. People who win lotteries should know this. Poverty does not kill somebody as much as wealth if it floods him all of a sudden.

I love to tell this story again and again. Someone won a lottery. His wife became very anxious, since it was far too much money for her poor husband. The lottery was worth one hundred thousand dollars. Even five dollars was a big sum for him, and here he was going to get one hundred thousand in a lump. But luckily the husband was not present in the house when the news arrived; he was in his office where he was a petty clerk. So she rushed to the local church and told the priest, "My husband has won a lottery worth one hundred thousand dollars. It is too much money for him. Soon he will return from his office, and I am afraid this happy news might kill him. Can you do anything about it?"

The priest said, "Don't worry, I will come to your house soon."

The priest came. The woman asked him what he was going to do. The priest said, "I have thought out the whole plan. He will receive his happiness in installments." When the old man came home, the priest told him, "You will be glad to know that you have won a lottery worth fifty thousand dollars."

The clerk said, "If it is true, I will donate twenty-five thousand to your church." Hearing this the priest died of heart failure. Twenty-five thousand proved too much for the poor priest.

What happened to Arjuna was very sudden. It was not so with Sariputta and Moggalayan; they had long prepared themselves for it. People on the path of meditation are never scared by experiencing the divine. But it is really shattering for those who have not been through meditation, because the experience in itself is so great, so sudden and so blissful, that it is very difficult to bear it. Its suddenness and the excessive joy it brings with it can choke your heart, can even kill you.

Suffering does not scare us so much, because we are so used to it. In a way we are always prepared for it; in fact, we go through it every day. We live in suffering from morning to night. We grow with suffering; we are brought up with suffering. Suffering has become the way of our lives. So we are capable of handling the greatest misfortunes and the sufferings they bring with them; it does not take more than a few days to adjust to them. But happiness is not the way of our life; even a small dose of happiness can make us restless. And it was not an ordinary happiness that dawned on Arjuna; it was an avalanche of bliss. And as it came very suddenly, it had great intensity. So he was scared and he almost shouted, "Stop it! Withdraw it! I can take no more!" It was natural, very natural. It is ironic, but it is so.

There are many strong people in the world who can cope with the greatest suffering, but there are not many who can cope with a great measure of happiness. Although we always pray for happiness, we will scream with terror if we come upon it suddenly. That is why God grants us happiness in installments, in small measures, in a very miserly manner. And whenever happiness comes suddenly and in large measure, it scares us.

> Questioner: The last part of the first question remains unanswered by you. According to you, when Krishna says he is here to destroy the wicked, he really means to change them, to transform them. But the

*many stories of his life clearly say he
actually destroyed the wicked.*

It would be good to understand this matter.

What seems to us as killing is not really killing
in the eyes of Krishna. Those who understand the
Geeta will understand. What we think of as killing is
not actually killing. To Krishna nobody is ever killed;
nobody can ever be killed. But then, what is it that
Krishna does? We find him killing any number of
demons and monsters in the stories of his life.

To understand it you will have to go with me
into the very depths of the matter; to understand it
we will have to go into a few things, a few *sutras* that
will even go beyond your understanding.

If you understand it rightly, in terms of the
science of religion, then it means only this much:
Krishna uprooted the physical organization of a particular demon or wicked person, destroyed the whole
system of his conditioning, his body and mind together, and released his inner soul from bondage. In
terms of religion it means only this much. If Krishna
sees that a particular person cannot be transformed
with his existing body-mind, then it is better to release him from its clutches and send him in search of
a new body which will be helpful in his future growth.
If the physical frame of a person is so dulled and
deadened that it rejects all change, then it is necessary
to help him find a new form for himself.

Let us try to understand it with the help of
an example. If we want to educate an old person who
is illiterate, from the beginning, from the very abc,
we will find it an impossible task. It is really a hard
job to educate a grownup. He is so heavily conditioned, his sensibilities are so dull and dead, his old
habits are so entrenched and strong that it is impossible to free him from his age-old conditioning and
habits. Even if the person concerned is willing to
learn, he cannot. But now science is going to create

conditions in which it will be possible to provide an old person with the body of a child, so that he can learn everything from the beginning. And it will be great. This is what Krishna is doing in the case of some hardened wicked people. He releases them from their old bodies so they can begin their life's journey anew.

It is strange but significant that Ravana feels grateful to Rama after being killed at his hands on the battlefield, and he thanks him profusely from his deathbed. Similarly, all those who were killed by Krishna felt grateful to him. This feeling of gratitude arose from the very depth of their souls, because they felt free of a prison whose walls were as strong as granite, and they also felt they could begin their journey afresh, from abc. But to us it appears that they are simply finished. If you want to know my view about it, I will say that Krishna gave them a fresh opportunity to begin their life anew, and live it in a right way. He gave them a clean slate to write on.

In Krishna's view, in my view, nobody dies; there is no way to die. Death is a lie. It does not mean that you should go on a killing spree and kill people with abandon. Of course, the day you come to know that no one dies, you will acquire the right to kill, because then killing will have altogether a different meaning. But then you, on your part, should have the readiness to die, because this readiness alone will prove that you really know that death is a misnomer and that nobody really dies.

Krishna has this readiness in full measure. Every now and then he enters the den of death with a smile on his face. That is the only test. He is yet a child, and he fights and wrestles with a terrible snake known as Kalia. As a child he fights with the most powerful demons. What does it all mean? It means that no one dies and that death is a lie, an illusion. It means that although death has an appearance, it has no reality. And if we know that death is a lie then we can realize the need to change our bodies.

Try to understand it in another way. If somebody's kidney fails to function, the surgeon transplants another kidney in its place, and we don't object to it. But in a way your body has been changed. Your lungs go out of order and are replaced by lungs of plastic; that too amounts to a partial change of the body. At the moment we change the body in parts, but very soon we will be able to change the whole of the body. There will be no difficulty. Up to now it has been the job of nature to change our bodies, but now science is taking over from nature. Science had not developed so much in the times of Krishna, so he had to kill a wicked person and ask nature to provide him with a new body so that he could begin his life afresh. In the future, however, it will be quite possible to change the whole body of a seasoned criminal who refuses to change his ways in any other way. We will not punish him, we will simply change his whole physical frame. It will be done in a laboratory for human beings. And then we will understand Krishna fully. At the moment we don't have the full facts in our hands.

Therefore, I do not accept the allegation that Krishna destroyed the wicked; he just transformed them. In other words, Krishna started them on a new journey of transformation. He sent them back to the workshop of nature with a request to remake them with new bodies, new eyes and new minds, so that they could begin life once again from the beginning.

Questioner: Do you think that the past conditioning of the subtle body and its mind changes with the change of the gross body?

They don't change on their own, but it makes a great difference if one has the rare opportunity of dying at the hands of a person like Krishna. And this opportunity comes once in a long while as a result of great meritorious *karmas*.

Ordinarily, after death, one's mind does not undergo a change, only the body changes. Except the body, nothing of one's subtle form changes with death. But a death at the hands of a person like Krishna is in itself a great phenomenon, because it happens in the presence of a catalytic agent. If you die in the presence of such a being, his vibes will go with your subtle body. And with the removal of the gross body, which was an impediment in the way of your meeting with Krishna, and with the assimilation of Krishna's vibes by your subtle body, your meeting with Krishna will be much facilitated. And that meeting will yield extraordinary results for you.

Such a meeting with Krishna is available to Arjuna in a very normal way, because Arjuna is quite capable of getting out of his body. In deep love everyone is capable of taking such a jump, but it is impossible if you are in a state of deep enmity. In a state of enmity your body becomes a strong prison for you; you can never walk out of it. This is the difference between love and hate. If you and I are in love with each other, we can walk out of our bodies and meet and mingle in a space where subtle bodies meet. But if we are enemies, we will be like prisoners in our bodies, we can never walk out of them and enter the space where two lovers meet. In the case of enmity we can meet each other only on the physical level and not beyond it. But in love we can transcend our bodies.

It is not necessary for Krishna to kill Arjuna with a view to transforming him, because Arjuna is full of love. But if someone is full of hate, it becomes necessary to give him a change of body so that he can be in a position to be transformed. His physical prison has to be demolished so that he comes out of it. Then he will be in the same space in which Arjuna is as a lover of Krishna. It is necessary in the case of the wicked, and it is an act of compassion on the part of Krishna. Krishna is equally compassionate with both the good and the wicked. Whether one is good or wicked does not make any difference in the compassion of Krishna.

But as I told you earlier, it is something that will go beyond your understanding. So don't try to understand it, just hear it and forget it.

Questioner: One of Marshal Mc-Luhan's maxims says: The medium is the message. Some critic substituted "the massage" for "the message" and thus gave an altogether new meaning to the maxim. In the same way can we call Krishna's flute a being's loving call to God? Then I want to know what is the meaning of Krishna blowing his conch, panchjanya, on the battlefield of Kurukshetra. And is it something symbolic that he carries his flute and a weapon like the sudarshanchakra together? There is a shloka, a stanza in the Bhagwad's chapter on Maharaas, which describes Krishna's play with the gopis in these words: Yatha abhraka swapratibimba Vibhramah—as if the child is playing with his own shadow. What is the underlying meaning of this metaphor? And a mystic has said that "living being's ego is God's food." Is this the reason that Krishna suddenly disappears from the midst of the dancing gopis in Maharaas?

Marshal McLuhan is a great thinker, and his statement that "The medium is the message" is highly significant. He came out with something which is quite new. Before McLuhan it was thought that the medium and his message were separate things. It was thought that although the message comes through the medium, still the message is not the medium, nor is the medium the message. The dualistic mind has always thought like this; it always divides everything in two. It says that the body and mind are two separate entities—the body being the medium and the mind its message. It says that movement and the mover, light and the lighter are different. In the same way the world and God are two. And this dualistic approach has dominated up to now, resulting in the belief that the message and the medium are separate.

I consider McLuhan to be a non-dualist, an *advaitwadin*. He himself might not be aware of it, but I call him so. For the first time he has brought the non-dualistic approach to the matter of the medium and the message. He means to say that what you say and the way you say it are the same, are not different.

To understand this maxim of McLuhan's we need to go into it in depth. For instance, when a sculptor sculpts a statue, he is separate from his creation. We can see it clearly. As the statue is complete it stands apart from the sculptor; they are two separate entities. And it needs a profound monist, an *advaitwadin*, to say that the sculptor and the sculpted, the statue, are one. It will be difficult for us to accept it. Our eyes, our intellect, our mind will refuse to accept that they are one. To say so seems to be utterly fantastic. Tomorrow the sculptor will die, but his statue will remain. It needs very penetrating eyes to see and to say that the sculptor will live as long as his handiwork lives. Even if the artist moves away from his art in space, he will remain one with it spiritually. There is an inner unity between the two which will last forever, which cannot perish.

The example of a dancer and his dance comes closer. It also comes very close to Krishna. And it is easier to understand. Are the dancer and his dance separate from each other? If you separate the dancer from his dance, the dance will immediately disappear. And in the same way if you detach the dance from the dancer, the dancer will be a dancer no more. So the dancer and the dance are one. The flute and the flute player are one. The singer and his song are one. Similarly, God and nature are one and the same.

The message and the medium are one. To know that the medium is the message, it is necessary to have a wide range of view. It is easy to understand that the dancer and his dance are one. But if one is a hard-headed dualist he will divide them into two; it is not difficult. He will argue that while the dance is an external act, the dancer is the inner being, who is not dancing, who stands still in the thick of the dance, which is happening on the outside. The dualist can say that the dancer, if he wants, can observe his own dance, can be a witness to it. In that case the dancer and the dance are separate from each other.

How you look, how you observe is the question. Seen with superficial eyes, even one will seem to be two, and seen with insight two will become one.

You are playing a flute. Can you tell where your lips separate from the flute? And if they are really separate, how can your lips play the flute? Then there is an unbridgeable gap between the two which will make flute playing impossible. After all, notes will come from you and they have to reach the flute. If you and the flute are really separate then you cannot play it. No, they only seem to be separate; really they are not. In fact, the flute is the extension of your lungs, throat and lips; it is their instrumental form.

Let us understand it in another way which will accord with McLuhan. We look at the stars with the help of a telescope, and the stars that were invisible to the naked eye become visible at once. Can you say that the telescope and the eyes are separate? No, the telescope is an extension of the eyes made possible by science. Now, with the help of the telescope your eyes can see much more than they saw before. Or, I touch you with my hands. Is it I who touch you or is it my hands that do so? Apparently my hands touch you, but is there a distance between me and my hands? Where do my hands separate from me? No, my hands are extensions of my being, they are not different from me.

Even if I touch you with the help of a stick, it is again I who touch you. The stick is just an extension of my hand. And when I speak with you through the telephone, the latter becomes my own extended form. It is the same as when I look at the stars with the help of the telescope—the latter is the extension of my eyes. Even the stars are not separate from me. Or are they? There must be some inner connection between the stars and my eyes; otherwise, how can I see them with my eyes? I cannot see them with my ears. For certain there is some intimate connection between my eyes and the stars. Therefore, not only the telescope, even the stars are extensions of my eyes. Or, seen conversely, my eyes are extensions of the stars.

This is the vision of the non-dual, the *advait*. Then all things are extensions of one and the same. And there is an inner harmony permeating them all. Then the medium is the message, and the message is the medium.

It is right to ask if Krishna's flute and its songs are prayers to God. I will not say it is a prayer, because a man like Krishna does not pray. To whom is he going to pray? Prayer creates a distance, a separation between the one who prays and the object of his prayer. Prayer is dualistic. And it would be good to understand this point clearly.

Prayer is dualistic; Krishna cannot pray. Playing the flute, Krishna is in meditation, because meditation is non-dualistic. There is a basic difference between prayer and meditation. Prayer is the discovery of the dualist who believes that he and God are separate, that God is somewhere far away in the distant heavens, and that he needs to pray for his mercy, for his grace, or whatever. Prayer is a kind of supplication. Meditation is a non-dualistic state: it says God is not somewhere else, away from me, nor am I here, separate from him; whatever is, is one whole. So Krishna's flute is not a prayer, it is the voice of meditation. It is not a supplication to some God; it is just a thanksgiving, directed not to God but to oneself. The musical notes of the flute are an expression of gratefulness, utter gratefulness.

It is only in gratefulness that one is free and expansive. In prayer you are inhibited and afraid, because prayer flows from some desire and desire creates fear. You are afraid if your prayer is going to be heard at all. You are also afraid if there is someone listening to your prayer or if it is being lost in the wilderness. In thanksgiving you are fearless and free, because you don't want anything in return. And you are not afraid about its acknowledgement; it is just an outpouring of your heart. It is not addressed to someone; it is unaddressed—or, it is directed to the whole. The winds will hear it and carry it on their wings. The skies will hear it, the clouds will hear it, the flowers will hear it. It is not a means to some end; it is an end unto itself. Prayer is enough unto itself. Playing the flute is all and everything.

It is for this reason that Krishna plays his flute with immense bliss. Meera could not dance with that abandon and blissfulness, because there is no meditation in her dance. Her dance is a kind of prayer, a prayer to her beloved Krishna, who, in spite of all her closeness, all her intimacy with him, is separate and distant from her. Meera's dance lacks that freedom there is in the dance of Krishna. There is an ache of separation in the songs of Meera; they are wet with her tears. Her songs are addressed to Krishna for whom she makes a beautiful bed and awaits with utter fondness. Her songs have a purpose, and therefore are tinged with her desire and fear. Krishna is utterly free from desire and fear. His songs are not addressed to any God, they are God's own songs. There is no cause behind Krishna's flute; it is causeless. He is utterly fulfilled, and he is celebrating this fulfillment with flute and dance.

Usually we associate the flute with a state of ease. We say in a Hindi proverb that "So-and-so is playing a flute of ease". It means that someone is at ease, and now he has nothing more to do except play his flute. It is an act without a purpose, and so it is an act of real thanksgiving.

> *Questioner: You often say that prayer is a state of consciousness. And you also say that prayer is a state of gratefulness. Then how is it that prayer is not non-dualistic?*

No, I never say that prayer is a state of mind, I say that prayerfulness is a state of mind. My word is not prayer, it is prayerfulness. And there is a great difference between prayer and prayerfulness.

Someone offers a prayer in the morning; it is a kind of ritual. Another person is prayerful even where he just rises from his seat and walks in the garden. He is prayerful, in a state of prayerfulness even as he ties the laces of his shoes. And when he takes off his shoes and puts them in their place, he does so as if he is handling an idol of God. This man is prayerful. When he stops by a flower on the roadside, he stands there as if he has come across God himself. This man is prayerful; he is not praying. He never prays, yet he is in prayer, in a state of prayer. I don't call prayer a state of consciousness; prayerfulness is that state. A prayerful heart is altogether different; such a heart is in meditation. To be prayerful and to be meditative are the same.

Only he who goes to prayer is not prayerful. How can a prayerful person pray? He lives in prayer; he is prayer itself, and he does not do anything except prayer. And one who prays does many other things at the same time. He runs a shop, he competes with others, he is jealous, he is angry, he hates, and he does a hundred and one things—one of which is prayer. Prayer is a small item in the long list of his activities.

Prayerful is he who is prayerful even when he is selling tea in a tea shop. Kabir is prayerful. He is a weaver by trade, and he has attained to the highest in life, he has found God. Yet he continues to weave and sell clothes. Someone asks him why he does so even after attaining to lofty sagehood. In answer Kabir tells him, "It is my prayer." Kabir says, "It is meditation when I walk, it is meditation when I eat, and it is meditation when I weave the cloth." He says, "O monk, the enlightenment that is natural, is of the highest. Whatever I do is meditation, prayer and worship." When Kabir goes to the market with a bundle of cloth to sell, he goes there dancing. He addresses his customer as Rama, his God, and tells him that he has woven this piece of cloth especially for him, that he has interlaced it with prayers. For him both the seller and buyer are God; it is God who sells and it is again God who buys.

This is what I call a state of prayerfulness, a state of consciousness. And this is what I call prayer.

No one ever sees Kabir praying. He never goes to a temple or a mosque, as others do to say their prayers. He says in one of his beautiful poems, "O priest, is your God deaf that you shout your prayer to him? I don't even say my prayer and he hears it; I don't even utter a word and he understands it. So why do you make so much noise about it?" Here Kabir is kidding those who have turned prayer and worship into a ritual. And he can well joke at their expense because he is really prayerful; otherwise, he cannot poke fun at them.

So I stand for prayerfulness, and not for prayer.

> Questioner: A part of the question
> still remains unanswered. It is about
> Krishna's conch, panchjanya, and
> his weapon, chakrasudarshan. And
> what about the Bhagwad's descrip-
> tion of Maharaas—the great dance—
> as a child's play with his shadows?

Everything associated with Krishna has a symbolic meaning. Man has five senses, five doors through which he expresses himself and relates with the rest of the world. These are eyes, ears, nose, mouth and skin. We know and experience everything through them, and it is through them we go out into the world and relate with it.

When the storyteller writes that Krishna blew his panchjanya on the battlefield of Mahabharat, it only means that he was totally present on the battlefield with all his five senses, nothing more. War is not an occupation for him; nothing is an occupation for him, so whatever he happens to be doing at the moment he does totally. As Kabir goes to the market with his total being to sell cloth, Krishna goes to the battlefield with his whole being. Through the *panchjanya* he announces his total presence on the battlefield. He is not there partially; in fact, he does nothing partially. Wherever he happens to be, he is there in his totality, with all his senses, with all his being.

Everyone taking part in the war of Mahabharat has his own conch, with a special name and quality of its own. It has its own special sound too. And every conch has a corresponding unity with the personality of the warrior who wears it. But Krishna's *panchjanya* is unique and incomparable. Except him, nobody is present there totally. And the irony is that he is the one person who is not going to take part in the fight. He is not committed to fight.

The truth is that only he who has no commitments can be total. If you are committed to anything, you are bound to be partial in your endeavor to fulfill it. You cannot stand totally behind your commitment; at least "you" will be left behind. Only the uncommitted can be total; he will be wholly in whatever he does. That is why Krishna alone is totally in the battlefield, although he is not going to take part in the fighting. And the *panchjanya* heralds his total presence there. He has really nothing to do with the war that is going to be fought on the Kurukshetra; he is neutral. He is not interested in victory or defeat; he has no vested interest in either of the two sides of the war. And yet a moment comes and he enters the war with his own weapon, the *sudarshan*.

This *sudarshan* too has a great meaning symbolically. The people who wrote the epic of the Mahabharat worked very hard with words. Really, it is the words that constitute the heart of a great poem, and so words are very important. There are words in this epic that have taken centuries of hard work to bring to perfection. The word *sudarshan* is one such word. *Sudarshan*, a Sanskrit word, means that which is good looking, beautiful.

It is amazing that a weapon of death and destruction can be beautiful. Death is not supposed to be beautiful, but it becomes beautiful in the hands of a man like Krishna. That is the meaning of Krishna's weapon; it lends beauty even to death. The *sudarshan* is a very lethal, very destructive weapon, as destructive as the atom bomb. But we cannot give this name *sudarshan* to the atom bomb. But Krishna does the miracle; he turns death into a blessing. Even death is beautiful if it is in the hands of a Krishna. And by the same logic a flower ceases to be beautiful if it is in the hands of a Hitler. Beauty depends on the quality of the person who holds it. That is how at the hands of Krishna even death is blissful. And people on both sides of the Mahabharat know it; that is why they called his weapon by this beautiful name.

A moment comes when Krishna plunges into battle with a weapon in his hands. This is an expression of his spontaneity. Such a person lives in the moment; he lives moment to moment. He is not tied to the past, not even to the minute that has just passed. And such a person does not promise anything.

Jaspers, a great thinker, has defined man as an animal who makes promises. Some others have defined man as a thinking animal. But Krishna does not fit with Jaspers' definition of man; he simply does not promise. Gandhi may be one of those who fulfill Jaspers' definition of man. Krishna is one who lives in the moment; he accepts what every new moment brings with it. If it brings war, Krishna will accept war and go into it.

Only he who lives in freedom lives in the moment. And one who makes promises is bound by the past, and this past begins to impinge on his freedom and goes on diminishing it. Really, the past hangs heavy on his future; he is fettered by the past.

That is why a moment comes in the war of the Mahabharat when Krishna actually takes up arms and fights, although he has no desire to take part in the war. Those who want to understand Krishna find this event coming in their way again and again. They wonder why he actually takes part in the war. The reason is that such a person cannot be relied upon; he is simply unpredictible. He will live the way a new situation demands; he responds to every situation afresh. And you cannot ask him why he is so different today from what he was yesterday. He will tell you, "Yesterday is no more. Much water has gone down the Ganges. Today's Ganges is quite different from what it was yesterday. Right now I am what I am, and I don't know what I am going to be like tomorrow. I too will know it only when tomorrow comes."

Prediction about men like Krishna is not possible. The astrologer will accept defeat before them. The astrologer is concerned with the future; he predicts your tomorrow on the basis of what you are today. He can say what you are going to do tomorrow on the basis of what you are doing today, because you are bound by time. But astrology will utterly fail in the case of Krishna, because his tomorrow will not flow from his today. Nobody can say what he will do tomorrow, because he lives in the moment. Tomorrow's Krishna may have nothing to do with today's. Tomorrow's Krishna will be born tomorrow. There is no linear connection between the Krishnas of today and tomorrow.

This matter of living has to be understood in some depth. There are two kinds of life. One kind of life is sequential, chain-like, each link is joined with another. It has a continuity. And the other is atomic, atom-like, every moment independent of another. It is not continuous. One who lives a life of continuity will find there is a link between his yesterday and his today; his today comes from his yesterday. His life is a continuation of his dead past; his today springs from the ashes of his yesterday. So his knowledge is the product of his memory; it is just a bundle of memories. To say it metaphorically, his life's rose grows on his grave.

The other kind of life is utterly different. It is not continuous; it is atomic. Its today does not come from its yesterday; it is absolutely independent of the past. It springs exclusively from that which is the whole of today's existence. It has nothing to do with the chain of my memories of my yesterdays and their conditionings; it is absolutely untouched by the past. My being today is entirely based in the great existence that is here today, right now; it is existential. It arises from the existing moment, and its next moment will arise from the next existing moment, and so on and so forth.

Of course, there is a sequence in such a life too, but it is never continuous, contiguous. It is each moment's moment. And such a person lives in the moment and dies to the passing moment. He lives today and dies to it as soon as it is gone. Before he goes to bed at night he will die to the bygone day; he does not carry even a bit of it over. And when he wakes up tomorrow, he will live in the moment that will exist then. That is how he is always new and young. He is never old; he is ever young and fresh. And because his being springs from the whole of existence, it is divine.

This is the meaning of Bhagwan, the blessed one, the divine one. His being is atomic, existential, comes from what is, from reality. He has no past and no future, he has only a living present. That is why we call Krishna Bhagwan, a divine consciousness. It does not mean that there is a God sitting in some faraway heaven who has incarnated in the form of Krishna. Bhagwan only means the divine, the whole, one whose being springs from the whole.

For this reason it is so difficult to find any consistency in a person who lives in the moment.

And if we try to force consistency on him, we will have to ignore so many episodes of his life, or we will have to establish some arbitrary uniformity among them, or we will have to say that it is all a play, a *leela*. When we fail to understand this inconsistency, we have to say it is all a play. But the difficulty really arises from our failure to know what it is to live in the moment, to live spontaneously.

> Questioner: It is said that Valmiki wrote the biography of Rama much before he happened, and Rama is also known as an incarnation of the divine. So how is it that there is a sequence, a chain-like continuity in his life?

It is a good question that you have raised: How is it that Valmiki wrote the life of Rama even before he happened?

It is possible, it is quite possible to write the life story of Rama, because he is a man of principles, ideals. There is a joke hidden in this anecdote of Valmiki writing the Ramayana long before Rama's existence. It means that Rama is a kind of man whose life story can be foretold. He is like a character in a drama: what he will do and what he will not do can be foreseen. Rama is an idealist, he lives according to some set rules and regulations of life, so in a way his life is pre-planned and pre-determined.

It is not that Valmiki had really written his biography before he happened; it is a very profound and subtle joke which this country alone is capable of making with respect to her great men. And it is so subtle that it is difficult to get it.

It says that Rama's life is so limited and confined, so confined to set ideas and ideals, so sequential that the poet Valmiki could have easily written his story, the *Ramayana*, even before Rama was born. It is like a drama or a movie which is enacted in strict adherence to a written script. So it can be foretold what Rama would do after his wife Sita is abducted by Ravana. It can be foretold that after her return from Ravana's city Rama would put her to some severe test like the fire-test. He will make her pass through fire before admitting her into his palace. Everything about Rama is certain, even this—though Sita comes out from the fire-test unscathed, Rama throws her out of his house just because a washerman makes a carping remark about her character.

But nothing can be said about Krishna.

> Questioner: Do you interpret
> Krishna in the terms of Martin
> Buber?

No, not so. Martin Buber is, after all, a dualist; he is not a monist, a non-dualist. In fact, the roots of Martin Buber lie in the Jewish tradition. He stands for perfect intimacy between "I" and "thou", but he is not prepared for the annihilation of the "I and thou". It is so because the tradition itself to which Buber belongs, cannot go beyond dualism. The Jews crucified Jesus because he said things which transgressed the concept of dualism. He said, "I and my father in heaven are one."

It proved to be dangerous. Jewish tradition failed to understand it, and the Jews said, "We cannot tolerate it. Whatever you say, you cannot be equal to God. He is far above you; your place is at his feet. You cannot say that you are God. This is blasphemy."

The same Judaic tradition of thinking is responsible for the persecution and killing of the Sufis by the muslims. When Mansoor said, "*Ana'l haq*—I am God", they could not take it. They said, "Howsoever high you rise, you cannot be God." And they crucified him, very brutally. Mohammedans could not give the status of God even to Mohammed; they called him the prophet, the messenger of God. They believe that man and God are two. While God is supreme, man can only have his place at his feet. His feet are the limit of man's greatest height.

> Questioner: What does it mean when someone says, "I am God"? Does he turn into a superman?

It is wrong to call him superman. When I say that the "I" turns into God, it means that the "I" has ceased to be. Not only "I", even the man has ceased to be. When "I" becomes God, then only God remains, the man ceases to be. It is sheer transcendence, after which nothing survives.

It is possible with regard to Rama; his story can be written before he happened. It is really a serious joke. But we are a serious people, and we fail to appreciate the joke. Particularly people interested in Rama are very serious, and therefore, instead of taking the joke as a joke they go on interpreting it seriously. The joke is: "Rama, you are such a person that a poet like Valmiki can write your story even before you appear on the scene. There is not much in your life."

> Questioner: What is the place of memory in what you call a sequential life and in a life of spontaneity?

While a life with sequence follows its memory like a slave, a spontaneous life uses it like a master. This is the difference. If you live a natural life, if you are renewed from moment to moment, it does not mean your memory is wiped out—it is rightly stored in your mind, and you can use it as you like. It is as if many things are stored in the basement of your house and you can take out anything you need from this store. That is why Buddha has called it an *agaar*, a storehouse of memories, of consciousness. One who lives spontaneously also needs his memory. If he is in town and wants to return to his house in the evening, it is his memory of the house and the way to it that will enable him to do so. And he will use it rightly.

> *Questioner: Do not old memories create a problem for Krishna when he is explaining the Geeta to Arjuna?*

It is a different matter, an altogether different matter. What I am explaining to you right now is that someone who lives spontaneously does not lose his memory; on the contrary, his memory will be fully alive and fresh. And his consciousness, which is being renewed every moment, will be the master of this memory and use it the way he needs it. On the other hand, one who lives a sequential life, a life of continuity with the dead past, will ever remain old and stale, will not know what renewal is, will remain a slave of his memories, which really rule over him and his activities.

> *Questioner: Does not Krishna, in his relationship with Arjuna, make use of his past memories? Is he always young and spontaneous?*

He is always spontaneous, but he does use his memory. I say again that only Krishna uses his memory as its master. So far as you are concerned, you are not the master of your memories; you are a slave in their hands and they use you as they like.

Someone is sitting with you in the bus, and you inquire about his caste. He tells you he is a Mohammedan. Your memory already has something regarding a Mohammedan, what he is, how he is, and you will immediately impose your memory, your idea of a Mohammedan on this man who may have nothing to do with this Mohammedan of your memory. Maybe the Mohammedan of your memory lives in your village, is a hoodlum, and burned your village's temple. Although this man sitting next to you has nothing to do with the hoodlum of your village, you will move away from him scornfully. Now you are a slave of your memory.

This is how Hindus kill Mohammedans in India and Mohammedans kill Hindus in Pakistan. This is memory's handiwork, and this is sheer madness. You live by your memory; you kill somebody in the place of somebody else. What is common betwen two Mohammedans? What is common between two Hindus? Everybody is his own man. But you will impose your memory, your idea of one Mohammedan on every Mohammedan. This is utterly wrong and stupid. You are being used by your memory; you are its slave.

If you are the master of your memory, you will say that although the man sitting next to you is a Mohammedan, he is different from the village hoodlum who burned your temple. Then you will not judge him, and you will not move away from him in scorn and anger. You will not be ruled by your prejudices; you will observe and understand this man anew and on his own.

While a person who lives a natural and spontaneous life is the master of his memory, the person who lives a sequential life is just a slave to his memory.

Questioner: You say that if someone dies at the hands of Krishna it means that he has earned it through meritorious karmas. To hear you say it gives rise to a blissful pain in my heart. So I venture to ask if all your play-acting is without cause?

It is utterly without cause. Yes, it is absolutely causeless. And you are right, it is all play-acting.

And when I talk about meritorious acts and their consequences, it means this: in the manifest world nothing happens without a cause. If in this world of cause and effect you happen to come across a person like Krishna, it is never accidental. Nothing in this wide world is accidental. Not even accidents take place accidentally, so how can a death at the hands of Krishna be accidental?

Really, nothing is accidental here. If I hug someone and quarrel with another, if I love someone and hate another, if I am a friend to someone and an enemy to another, each one of these acts has stemmed from my infinite past existence; there is nothing accidental about them. I repeat, nothing is accidental in this manifest world. And that is why, when something happens without reason, it seems to be a miracle, something coming from the other world, the unmanifest world.

The being of Krishna is absolutely causeless, but Arjuna's relationship with Krishna is not. As far as Arjuna is concerned, his relationship with Krishna cannot be without cause, without a reason, a purpose. This is rather difficult to understand, so I will go into it at some length.

Our relationship with a person like Krishna is like one-way traffic. You can love him, but it cannot be said that he will also love you. All that can be said about him is that he is loving, that he is love itself;

hence, when you go to him you will easily avail of his love. It may seem to you that he loves you, that he is related to you, but that is not a fact. He is simply loving; his love will shower on you when you are in his presence. It is as if you go out of your house on a cold morning and the light of the sun envelopes you, warms you and cheers you. From your side you can be in love with Krishna, but from his side Krishna is not going to be in a love relationship with you. It is always one-way traffic, although you can think that Krishna loves you. He *is* love and this love is available to everyone who seeks it.

If Krishna kills someone, he does it without cause. But you cannot say the same thing in regard to the person who has been killed by Krishna. His death, from his side, is not without cause. This man had been living a sequential life, a life connected with a long dead past; he was not living a spontaneous life. How can the life of a demon be spontaneous? And whoever is not spontaneous is no different from a demon. His life is inextricably bound up with his past; he lives through his dead past.

If such a person dies at the hands of Krishna it means that his death is a link, the latest link in the long chain of his past. His death flows from his past, although it is causeless for Krishna, from Krishna's side. Krishna would not have gone searching for this man in order to kill him; on the contrary, the man himself came to him to court death. This is altogether a different thing.

Similarly, whosoever goes to him, Krishna's love is spontaneously available. If he had not come, Krishna would not have gone searching for him. Even if no one goes to Krishna, and he is sitting alone in a forest, he will be loving, and the solitude of the forest, the emptiness around him, the entire void of the cosmos will be the recipient of his love. It will make no difference for him and his love if someone is near him or there is nothing or no one.

> Questioner: What you have been
> saying about Krishna and his myriad
> virtues has swept us off our feet, and
> we seem to have turned into his de-
> votees. Is it possible that there are no
> inadequacies in his life? Is it necessary
> that we justify his every action
> whether it is dancing with the gopis
> or his stealing their clothes or goading
> pious Yudhisthira to lie about the
> death of Ashwasthama? And can we
> call it a scientific approach?

Your question is right. It is good to know why we
don't find shortcomings in Krishna's life. But do you
think it is scientific to purposely go in search of
shortcomings? It would be unscientific if we decided
to find fault with him; it would be equally unscientific
if we decided not to find fault with him. Every approach with a pre-judgment or prejudice, whether for
or against, is wrong and unscientific.

Then what is a scientific approach? It is scientific to see Krishna as he is. And whatever I have
been saying about him here is exactly as I see him. It
would, of course, be unscientific if I asked you to see
him the way I see him. You are free to see him in
your own way. It is okay if you find fault with him,
and it is okay if you don't find fault with him. I have
no desire whatsoever for you to accept what I say
about Krishna. But I am free to see him the way I see
him. It would be unscientific if I tried to see him
differently.

It is good to know what a scientific approach
is. Is it necessary to apply what we call the scientific
approach to anything and everything in the world?
There are things in this world—are there not?—
which defy the scientific approach; it would be utterly

unscientific to apply this approach to them. And certainly, there are a few things that go beyond the scientific approach. For instance, we cannot think about love in a scientific manner; there is no way to do so. The very phenomenon of love seems to be unscientific. And if we try to examine love scientifically we will have to deny it altogether. We will then have to say that nothing like love exists in this world. The very existence of love is against science.

The difficulty is that either we approach love unscientifically—and that would be really scientific—or we deny love altogether. It would be scientific to see love as love is.

We can look at it from another angle. As I said earlier, eyes see and ears hear, and if we try to see with our ears and hear with our eyes it will be utter madness. It is madness to look at things we hear as though they have been seen. Eyes will just say that ears don't see. And it is true. And since eyes don't hear they cannot accept that ears hear. So the eyes can come to only two conclusions: one, that the ears don't see—and that would be right—and the other, that the ears don't hear—and that would be wrong.

The scientific process is such that it cannot grasp anything but matter. Science is confined to the understanding of matter; it cannot go beyond the material world. As eyes are confined to seeing light and ears to hearing sound, the methodology of science is such that it can only know matter and nothing else. Then there is only one possibility left: the scientist can say that there is nothing in the universe except matter. And some scientists have really said so.

But as scientific knowledge is growing, science finds itself in deep waters, because it has reached a point where matter has ceased to be matter. In the course of the last two decades, science has had to accept there is something beyond its grasp. If scientists don't accept this, then the very basis of all they have known becomes doubtful. If they deny the existence of the electron, which seems to be beyond their grasp, then the existence of the atom, which is within their grasp, becomes suspect, because the electron is the basis of the atom. Therefore, with humility, science now accepts that there is certainly something which is eluding its understanding, but it is not yet ready to accept that anything is unknowable. Science still believes that sooner or later it is going to know it, and it will continue to press its efforts in that direction.

Maybe science will know many more things; maybe it will know the secret of the electron, but it does not seem probable it will ever know love. It is impossible to find love in a scientific lab. If it goes in search of love, it will surely come across the lungs, but it will never find the heart. That is why it believes the lungs are all there is, and there is nothing like the heart the poets talk about. But the experiences of even an ordinary person say for sure that there is something like the heart. There are many moments in our lives when we live not by the lungs alone, but by something much more than the lungs, and that is our heart. And sometimes this heart becomes so important for us that we can sacrifice everything, including the lungs, for its sake.

Someone dies for love. He dies for the sake of the heart that does not exist in the eyes of the scientist. What will you say about this man? How can you deny the fact of his death? Someone, a Majnoo, is madly in love with a Laila. He is mad to win the heart of his beloved. You can say that this madness is wrong, but in spite of what you say, it is there; Majnoo exists.

He may be wrong; he may be mad, but he is what he is. He lives for Laila, he sings in her memory, he is poetic about her. An examination of his lungs will not reveal any of these things, neither the presence of a Laila or his love for her. An investigation of the lungs will only reveal the breath and blood that circulate through them, the oxygen and other substances, but it will miss the very thing for which Majnoo is ready to give up his breath and his blood, even his whole life.

So there are only two ways to solve this difficulty. Either we deny love or we refuse to look at it with the eyes of a scientist. But how can we deny the existence of love? It exists. But then we look at love in a way that is not scientific. So we accept that we cannot bring the scientific approach to bear on each and every thing in the world.

If we look at Krishna with the eyes of science, he will be nothing more than a great man with his black and his white shades. But remember, he will then completely cease to be Krishna. The Krishna that I am talking about here is not a great man; he is a phenomenon, an event. And we cannot understand this phenomenon scientifically. And you know well that I am not against science. On the contrary, I am all for science. I walk with science to the extent where it begins to falter and fall down. I drag it into spaces where even its breathing stops. I can be charged with being too much on the side of science; I will never be charged with being less on its side. I try my very best, but there is a limit beyond which science cannot go. Will it be right to stop with science, to give up my efforts and go no further?

But I see there is a vast space beyond science.

> Questioner: Is it possible that sometimes mind and heart, thought and feeling, meet and mingle with each other? Perhaps they do, and it is great. Please comment.

It is possible that once in a while mind and heart, thought and feeling, get together and become one. In their depths they are already one; they are separate only on the surface. It is like the branches of a tree are separate from one another, while their trunk is one and the same.

Similarly, our thoughts and feelings are like branches of our being, which is one. Mind and heart are separate only on the surface; in the depths they are united and one.

The day we know that mind and heart are one, we also know that science and religion are not separate. Then we know that science has a limit beyond which it cannot go, beyond which the world of transcendence begins, beyond which religion begins.

Krishna is a man of religion, and I am talking about Krishna—the man of religion. And I talk about him exactly the way I see him. But I have not the least desire that you should see him through my eyes. However, if on your own, you can see in him what I see, even fractionally, it will prove to be a transforming factor in your life.

NINTH DISCOURSE
EVENING, SEPTEMBER 29, 1970
MANALI, INDIA

THE COSMOS IS A DANCE OF OPPOSITES

Questioner: How is it that Krishna is called a celibate in spite of his being a man of joyous dance and sensuous celebration? What is the place and relevance of Raasleela—*the dance of celebration—in modern society?*

o understand *Raasleela*, the dance of celebration, what is first necessary to know is that the whole of life is a meeting of contradictory forces, and that all its happiness comes from this union of the opposites. The very mystery and ecstasy of life lies hidden in this *unio mystica*.

To begin with, it is good to understand the metaphysical meaning of the celebration that our universe is. And then, together, we will go into the life of Krishna, a complete miniature of this celebrating universe.

Raise your sights and look at whatever is happening all around in this vast universe of ours. Is it anything other than a dance, a celebration, an abounding carnival of joy? It is all celebration, whether it is clouds gliding in the heavens or rivers rushing to the seas or seeds on their way to becoming flowers and fruit, or bees humming or birds on the wing or love affairs between men and women. It is all a panorama of play and dance and celebration.

Raas has a universal meaning; it has a cosmic connotation and significance.

Firstly, the meeting of opposite energies is the cornerstone of all creation, of the universe. To construct a house with a door, we put an arch at the top of the door with the help of opposite shapes of bricks to support it. It is just this placing of opposite kinds of bricks in the arch that upholds not only the door but the whole building. If we use uniform kinds of bricks in the arch, it will be impossible to construct a house. In the same way, the whole play of creation, at every level of life, begins when energy becomes divided into two opposite parts. This division of energy is at the root of all creation, of all life in the universe, and with the cessation of this division all life's play comes to a full stop. When the same energy becomes one, when it returns to its primordial state, total destruction, the ending of the universe happens. And when the same energy again divides itself into two, creation begins anew.

Raas, the dance of celebration, is the most profound attribute of the mighty stream of creation. And creation in itself is the interplay of polar opposites—thesis and antithesis. When opposites collide with each other it results in conflict, hostility and war, and when they embrace each other there is love and friendship. Without the meeting of the two, creation is impossible. So we have to go into the significance of Krishna's *raas* in this context.

It is not all that we see when Krishna dances with the *gopis*, the milkmaids, but we can see only that much with our gross eyes. Krishna's *raas* with the milkmaids of his village is not an ordinary dance; on a small scale it really represents the universal dance of creation that, since eternity, goes on and on. It epitomizes the everlasting drama of the making and unmaking of the universe. It gives you a glimpse of that divine dance and that immense orchestra.

It is for this reason that Krishna's *maharaas* ceases to have a sexual connotation. Not that it prohibits any sexual interpretation, but for certain sex has been left far behind. In reality Krishna does not dance as a mere Krishna, he represents here the whole of the male element in creation, known in Sanskrit as *purusha*. And similarly the *gopis* represent the entire female element, *prakriti*. The *maharaas* represents the combined dance of *prakriti* and *purusha*.

People who take the *maharaas* as a sexual representation of life are mistaken; they really don't understand it. And I am afraid they will never understand it. To put it rightly, it is a dance of the meeting of the male and female energies, of *purusha* and *prakriti*. It has nothing to do with any individual man and woman; it represents the mighty cosmic dance.

It is because of this that a single Krishna dances with any number of *gopis*. Ordinarily it is not possible for a single man to dance with many women at a time. Ordinarily no man can be in love with many women together, but Krishna does it, and does it beautifully. It is amazing that every milkmaid, every *gopi* taking part in the *maharaas*, believes that Krishna is dancing with her, that he is hers. It seems Krishna has turned into a thousand Krishnas so that he pairs off with each of the thousand women present there.

It is utterly wrong to take the *maharaas*, the celebration dance of Krishna, as that of an individual person. Krishna is not a person here; he represents the great male energy, *purusha*. The *maharaas* is a representation in dance of the great meeting between male and female energies. But the question is: Why only dance is chosen as a medium for this representation?

As I said this morning, the medium of dance comes nearest to the mysterious, to the non-dual, and to celebration. Nothing can express it better than dance.

Let us look at it in another way. Dance is the most primitive form of human language, because when man had not yet learned to speak, he spoke through gestures. If one man had to communicate with another, he made gestures with his face, his eyes, his hands and feet. Even today a dumb person only expresses himself through gestures. Verbal language came much later. Birds don't know a language, but they know how to chirp and dance together. Gestures make up the whole language of nature. It is used and understood all over.

So there is a reason why dance came to center stage for the *raas*, the celebration.

Gesture is the most profound medium of expression because it touches the deepest parts of man's mind and heart. Dance reaches where words fail. The sound of the ankle bells of a dancer says a lot even where speech is ineffective. Dance is more articulate than anything else. A dancer can go from one end of the earth to another and will, more or less, make himself understood through his dance. No language will be needed to understand and appreciate him. No particular level of civilization and culture will be required to understand a dance. Dance is a kind of universal language; it is understood everywhere on this planet. Wherever a dancer goes he will be understood. Man's collective unconscious is well aware of this language.

To me, the great *raas* happening in infinite space, with millions of stars like the sun and moon dancing rhythmically, is not an ordinary dance. It is not meant for entertainment; it is not show business. In a sense it should be described as overflowing bliss. There is such an abundance of bliss in the heart of existence that it is flowing, overflowing. That is what we call the river of existence. The presence of the polar opposites in the universe facilitates its flow.

Man alone cannot flow; he needs the presence of woman. Without the woman man is inhibited and closed. In the same way, without man the woman is inhibited and closed. Their togetherness causes their energies to spring into the form of love. What we know as love between man and woman is nothing but the flowing of yin and yang together. And this love, if it is not personalized, can have great spiritual significance.

The attraction of man and woman for each other is what brings them together so that their latent energies flow into the stream of love and life. That is why a man feels relaxed with a woman and a woman feels at ease with a man. Separated and alone they feel tense and anxious; coming together they feel as light as feathers, weightless. Why? Because something in them, some subtle energy has become alive and moving, and as a result they feel at home and happy.

Unfortunately we have been trying to put man and woman in a cage, the cage of marriage. But as soon as we bind them with marriage and its institution, their energy ceases to flow, it stagnates. Life's play has nothing to do with institutions; it cannot be institutionalized. Krishna's *raas* does not have an order, a system; it is utterly free and spontaneous. You can say it is chaotic. It is chaos itself.

There is a significant saying of Nietzsche's. He says, "It is out of chaos that stars are born." Where there is no system, no order, only the interplay of energies remains. In this interplay of energies, which is *raas*, Krishna and his milkmaids cease to be individuals, they move as pure energies. And this dance of male and female energies together brings deep contentment and bliss; it turns into an outpouring of joy and bliss. Rising from Krishna's *raas* this bliss expands and permeates every fiber of the universe. Although Krishna and his girlfriends are no more with us as people, the moon and the stars under which they danced together are still with us, and so are the trees and the hills and the earth and the skies that were once so drunk with the bliss of the *raas*. So, although millenia have passed, the vibes of the *maharaas* are still with us.

Now scientists have come forward with a strange theory. They say although people come and go, the subtle vibes of their lives and their living remain suffused in existence forever. If someone goes to dance on the grounds where Krishna once danced with his *gopis* he can hear the echoes of the *maharaas* even today. If someone can play a flute near the hills that in the past echoed with the music of Krishna's flute, he can hear those hills still echoing it, everlastingly.

In my view, the *raas* symbolizes the overflowing, outpouring of the primeval energy as it is divided between man and woman. And if we accept this definition, the *raas* is as relevant today as it was in the times of Krishna. Then it is everlastingly relevant.

Lately I have received a suggestion from many friends that men and women should be segregated from each other when we go for meditation, because they think it will help their meditation. This suggestion is utterly stupid. They don't know that if men and women are segregated from each other, if they are put into separate blocks, it will make them two homogeneous groups cut off from each other, blocking the flow of energy between them. Friends who come up with such suggestions are ignorant of their implications. I hold just the contrary view on the matter. If men and women meditate together as a mixed gathering, it can be immensely helpful to their meditation. Then something can happen to both of them without their knowing it, and it will deepen their meditation. Your being here together without any reason—you are not here as husbands and wives—will help you in catharsis as nothing else can do. The very presence of the opposite sex will stir many deeply repressed emotions in both men and women, and it will then be so easy to cathart them.

The terrible mental tension through which mankind is passing at the moment is the result of this segregation, this apartheid of men and women. We have separate schools and colleges for boys and girls; men and women sit in separate groups in churches and temples. Everywhere the sexes are being made to keep a distance from each other. Much of our present-day trouble and misery stems from this unnatural and unhealthy practice, because it violates the basic laws of nature. In this world the entire structure of life is based on the togetherness of the opposite forces. The more natural and spontaneous this togetherness, the more beneficial it is.

The significance of *raas*, the dance of celebration, is everlasting; it issues from the fundamental principle of life. This fundamental principle says that men and women are incomplete in themselves, they are fragments of a single whole. And they become whole and healthy only in close togetherness, in union with each other. If this togetherness happens unconditionally, it will complete the two in an extraordinary and unearthly way. On the other hand, if the union is conditional, if it has a motive, it is bound to lead to enormous difficulty and trouble in the process of its completion. However, so long as men and women exist on this earth, the *raas* will continue to be in vogue in many shapes and sizes. Maybe it does not attain the height and depth it had with Krishna, but if we grow in understanding and wisdom it is not impossible.

More or less every primitive community is aware of the beauty and significance of the *raas*, of their own kind of *raas*. They work hard through the day, and in the night both men and women gather together under the open sky and dance with abandon for hours and hours. While dancing, they forget their family relationships and mix freely with each other as men and women, and dance madly, as if all of life is meant for dancing and celebrating. They go to sleep only when they are utterly tired, and so they enter into a sleep so deep it may cause the civilized societies envy. It is for this reason that the peace of mind and the joy of life these poor people enjoy is unknown to the most affluent people who, just by wishing, can have all the good things of life. The rich are missing some basic truths of life for certain, and somewhere they are erring very grievously.

> *Questioner: Legend has it that Ahilya, a woman turned into stone, had waited long enough for the coming of Rama to resurrect her, and that another ordinary woman, Kubja, persuaded Krishna to make love to her. Do these stories have some spiritual significance?*

Everything in existence happens in its own time, a time for which one has to wait with tremendous patience. Everything has its season; nothing happens out of season. Time and occasion have great importance in life. And it is necessary to go into it from different angles.

I don't believe that Ahilya had actually turned into stone; this is just a poetic way of saying that she lived a stony life, a dull and dreary life until she met Rama whose love transformed her life. It is possible a woman will come to her flowering only through a particular man like Rama, and that she will patiently wait for such a man to come into her life.

It is a poetic metaphor to say that Ahilya had turned into stone. It means to say that with the right opportunity, with real love, even stone comes alive. It also says that no one except Rama could have fulfilled her. The crux of the story is that everybody and everything has its own season, its own moment of fulfillment for which one must wait with patience. Until this moment comes, it is not going to happen. Only the touch of her lover, his warm hug can fulfill her.

Let us understand it in another way. Woman is passive; passive waiting is her way. She cannot be aggressive; she is receptive. She has not only a womb in her body, even her mind is like a womb. The English word woman, "wo-man", is very meaningful; it means a man with a womb. Woman's whole makeup is receptive, while man's makeup is active, aggressive. And although these two qualities, receptivity and aggressivity, seem to be contradictory, in reality they are complementary to each other. And as man and woman are complementary, so are their attributes. Man has what woman lacks and woman has what man lacks. That is how both together make a complete whole.

Woman's receptivity turns into waiting and man's aggressivity into search, into exploration. So while Ahilya will wait for Rama like a piece of stone, Rama will not do so. Instead, Rama will search many paths. It is interesting to note that a woman never takes the initiative in proposing love to a man, she always receives proposals from the man. She does not take the first step; it is man who takes it. Not that she does not begin loving someone, but her love is always a kind of waiting. Waiting is her way of love, and she can wait long—for lives.

In fact, when a woman becomes aggressive she immediately loses a part of her femininity, she loses her feminine attraction. Her beauty, her significance, her very soul lies in passive waiting, in infinite waiting. She can wait endlessly; she can never be aggressive. She will not go to a man and tell him, "I love you." She will not say it even to a man she loves with all her heart. She will, on the contrary, want the man she loves to come to her and say that he loves her. Another beauty of feminine love is that it never says a straightforward yes when the man a woman loves comes to propose his love to her. While verbally she says no—which means yes—she says yes with her silent gestures, with her whole being turned into love. It is always man who takes the initiative.

A woman can wait endlessly for Krishna; she can never be fulfilled without him.

It is in this context that, in the past, we had an extraordinary rule, and it is good to know it and understand it. Women did not ordinarily propose love to men, but if once in a long while a woman came forward to propose her love to a man, he had to accept her; it was utterly immoral to say no to her. Since it happened rarely, it was ruled that such a proposal could not be turned down. If ever a man said no, it was thought that he had failed in his manhood. It was thought to be an insult to womanhood, which was so much respected in this country in the past.

There is an anecdote in the life of Arjuna which is worth mentioning here. Arjuna is under a vow of celibacy for one year. A beautiful young woman falls in love with the ascetic-looking young man, and tells him, "I wish I had a son like you." It is significant that when a woman makes a request, a proposal, she does not propose to be a beloved or a wife, but a mother. Arjuna was put into a dilemma. He was under a vow of celibacy which could not be broken before its time. And it was equally wrong to violate the rule which said it was immoral to say no to a woman who came with a proposal of love. Arjuna did not want to be that immoral. A male energy ceases to be male if a man turns down the request of a woman—the receiving energy—to make love to her.

Arjuna's difficulty was real. So he told the young woman, "I am ready, but how is it certain that our son will be like me? It is therefore better that you accept me as your son. I will become your son; this fulfills your desire."

A similar anecdote is recorded in the life of George Bernard Shaw. A French actress, the most beautiful actress of the times, made a similar proposal to Shaw. In a letter she wrote that she wanted to marry him. Although the western woman has moved a long way from being a woman, yet this French actress expressed a womanly desire to be a mother. She said in her letter that she wanted to have a son by Bernard Shaw, because this son would be something marvelous, combining her beauty and Shaw's intelligence.

I say that this western woman could not suppress the inherent feminine desire to be a mother, because motherhood is a woman's highest fulfillment. A woman does not feel guilty in becoming a mother, she feels great. And when a woman expresses her desire to be a mother, she is not transgressing her modesty, she is not demeaning herself, she is not falling behind man. To become a mother she makes use of man in a very small way; she does the rest of it all herself. But to be a wife she needs the man the whole way.

Bernard Shaw was faced with the same difficulty as Arjuna, but Shaw could not answer the woman in the way Arjuna did. Since Arjuna belonged to the East, his answer was typically eastern. And Shaw's answer was clearly coarse and vulgar. Bernard Shaw wrote back asking the actress how she would feel if their son received his looks and her intelligence. No man in the East could say this; it is an insult to womanhood. Shaw not only turned down a woman's love, he did it in a very indecent manner.

Kubja has waited long for Krishna; she has waited for him for many lives. Krishna cannot say no to her, because no has no place in his life. Even if Kubja asks for love on the physical level, Krishna will not refuse her, because he is not opposed to the body. The body is as much accepted as anything else; it has its own place in life. The body is not everything, but it has its significance; it has its own juices and joys. The body has its own existence.

Krishna does not deny it. He accepts both body and soul; he embraces both matter and God. He cannot insult womanhood by refusing sex on the physical level; he can go to any length to respect womanhood. He is prepared to fulfill every wish of Kubja's, and he will not have to persuade himself, strain himself in the matter. He will not have to make any effort to oblige Kubja; he will naturally and happily accept that which is.

For us it is difficult to think that Krishna would go in for physical sex; it seems outrageous. It is so because we are divided, we are dualists; we believe that the body and soul are separate, and while the soul is great the body is something lowly. But I don't view—nor does Krishna—the body and soul, sex and superconsciousness, matter and God as separate entities. They are all one and the same. The body is that part of the soul which is within the grasp of our senses—like our eyes and hands—and the soul is that part of the body which is beyond the grasp of our senses and intellect. The body is the visible soul and the soul is the invisible body. They are united

and one; nowhere do they separate from each other
or contradict each other. What is sexual joy at the
physical level becomes ecstasy at the level of the soul.
To Krishna's mind there is no conflict between sex
and ecstasy. The joy of sex is nothing but a faint
reflection, a faint trace of ecstasy, and therefore sex
can become a door to ecstasy, to *samadhi*.

I cannot say what there is in the mind of
Kubja, but I can speak very well for Krishna. I don't
think Kubja has any readiness to use sex as a door to
samadhi. That is not even relevant here. What is relevant is that whatever Kubja desires, Krishna is ready
to fulfill it. He does not care if her desires are petty;
he does not tell her to ask for something great because
he has it and he can give it. Kubja approaches him
with a request for physical gratification; she does not
know what it is to be fulfilled spiritually. And Krishna
is not going to turn her down because of it. He meets
Kubja on Kubja's ground, and that is how a physical
union between the two could be possible.

> *Questioner: In the morning you com-
> pared Rama with Krishna and Meera
> with Hanumana. In our tradition all
> of them—Rama, Krishna, Meera
> and Hanumana—have equal status;
> no one is superior or inferior. Perhaps
> each one of them is living his own
> individual destiny. And it is possible
> that some of us find ourselves in ac-
> cord with Rama and Hanumana. In
> that case would it not be transgressing
> one's self-nature or swadharma if
> one follows Krishna and Meera be-
> cause they are superior?*

I did not say that they were either superior or inferior. All I said was that they were distinctly different from each other. I am not concerned with their status; I am only interested in the distinctive individuality of each one of them. And if someone finds himself in accord with Hanumana, he will not accept Hanumana as inferior because of me. As far as I am concerned Hanumana is not in accord with me. And I am not going to lie about my view of Hanumana because someone else is in accord with him. You put the question to me and I answered it the way I saw it. If I have to choose between them, I will choose Meera and Krishna, and I told you why. But I don't say that you should choose Krishna in preference to Rama. It is enough that you understand what I say, and then go wherever your individuality takes you.

In my view, Rama's personality is confined, confined to certain norms and ideals, and I think even Rama's followers will not deny it. In fact, they follow him because he lives within norms; Rama appeals to people who love to live within norms. But I say that to live within the confines of norms is to live a petty life, a limited, inhibited and narrow life. Life is not confined to norms; it goes far beyond norms and rules, ideas and concepts. Truth is unlimited and illimitable. The whole truth cannot be covered by any ideas and ideals, however great they may be. Truth can be at home only with the unlimited, the infinite. You limit it and it ceases to be truth. So truth is at home with Krishna, not with Rama, because Krishna too, like truth, is unlimited, infinite.

And it is wrong to say that your tradition does not make a distinction between Rama and Krishna. It does. It does not accept Rama as a complete incarnation of God; Krishna alone is accepted as such. Your tradition is very clear about it. I don't know if they have a comparative evaluation of Hanumana and Meera—perhaps not—but they have certainly evaluated Rama and Krishna, judging

Krishna to be the highest among all the Hindu *avataras*, all the Hindu incarnations.

It is obvious that followers of Rama do not accept Krishna; they don't even want to hear his name. In the same way devotees of Krishna are allergic to Rama—and it is natural. But I am a follower of no one; I follow neither Rama nor Krishna. I have nothing to do with them; therefore, I can see them exactly as they are, and I will say the truth.

To me, it seems that Rama's life is clear-cut and defined; there is nothing hazy about it. Krishna's life is not that neat and clear-cut; it cannot be. And that is why it has great depth. Rama has cut out a portion of a vast and wild jungle and turned it into a neat and clean garden by removing unwieldy bushes and shrubs. But this does not mean that the vast jungle has ceased to be; it is there, surrounding the little garden.

D.H. Lawrence often said he wanted to see man in his wild form, that modern man had turned into a garden and was diseased. While Rama is a small and enclosed garden, Krishna is the vast jungle itself, wild and rugged and chaotic. It lacks planning and organization, order; it has no roads, no pathways, no sidewalks, not even flowerbeds. It is full of wild animals like lions and tigers; it is infested with all kinds of snakes and reptiles and lizards. At places it is dark and awesome. Even fugitives from the civilized world, like robbers and thieves, take shelter here. It is packed with wilderness, with ruggedness, dangers.

Krishna's life is that gigantic jungle, while Rama's life is a kitchen garden in the backyard of your house, where everything is in order, where there is nothing to fear. I don't say to you, "Don't have a kitchen garden," what I say is that a garden is a garden and a jungle is a jungle.

When you are bored with your garden you think of the jungle, because it is nature's own creation; it is not of your making. There is a life, grandeur and beauty in the jungle which no garden can have.

Your tradition has made a comparison between Rama and Krishna, but not between Hanumana and Meera. It is not that necessary to evaluate Meera and Hanumana comparatively. Since you raised the question I have to say something about it. Where will you place Hanumana when his lord Rama himself is only a kitchen garden? At best he can be a flower pot; nothing more than that. And as a flower pot in the garden of Rama he is very neat and clean, at times more orderly than Rama himself.

> *Questioner: Does Hanumana take to dancing once in a while?*

It is possible. When a strong wind comes, the plants of a garden sway and dance, even the plant in a flower pot begins to sway. But the dance of a jungle is like Shiva's *tandava*, his dance of destruction. This dance is mighty. It is immense; it is awesome. This dance of the jungle is, as the jungle is, beyond our control, and it is frightening to us. The dance of a garden is small and manageable; we can manage it. Hanumana can dance, but he is subject to Rama's control. Meera is different. When she dances even Krishna cannot control her. Hanumana cannot disobey Rama; he is disciplined and obedient.

It is true that we need discipline in the world, but discipline is not everything. Everything that is profound, great and immense in life is free from discipline. Everything that is true, good and beautiful in life comes exploding; it follows no rules, no discipline.

However, this is how I see them, Meera and Hanumana. And I told you about my choice: I choose Meera. But it does not mean that you should do the same. And I don't think in terms of the superiority or inferiority of one; I am simply pointing out the difference that is there. Everyone has his own criteria of what is superior and what is inferior. If someone finds greatness in Hanumana, it only shows his way of evaluation. And if I find Meera to be great, it speaks for my meaning of greatness. In this evaluation Meera and Hanumana are not that important; they only reflect our preferences.

> *Questioner: What do you think about cow worship? As Darwin says that the monkey is man's predecessor in physical evolution, you say that the cow precedes man in the evolution of the soul. How is it that among all animals the cow comes so close to man spiritually? Or is it that we call the cow our mother because we are an agricultural community? And what is your view on the question of cow slaughter?*

When Charles Darwin first said, looking at man's physical frame, that it seems he has evolved from some species of monkeys, we were shocked and could not easily take it. How could man, who believed God was his father, suddenly come to replace God with the monkey? It came as a great blow to our egos, but there was no way out. Darwin backed his theory with powerful evidence, and the whole scientific discipline supported him. That is why, in spite of tremendous opposition, it had to be accepted. There was no way out.

There is so much similarity, both physical and mental, between man and monkey that it is difficult to deny Darwin. Even the ways of their being and living are so strikingly similar that we had to accept that man is very much linked with the monkey. Even today, when we walk our hands move rhythmically with our moving legs—the left hand with the right leg and vice versa—although it is not at all necessary for our hands to move. We can walk very well without moving our hands; those whose hands are amputated walk as easily. Evidently Darwin thinks that this movement of the hands is only a habit, a hangover from our old life as monkeys millions of years ago when we walked on all fours. Even the little opening where a monkey has its tail is discernible on man's body as a linkage. It indicates that man had a tail when he was a monkey.

In this context Hanumana is very significant. Had he known about Hanumana, Darwin would have been greatly pleased. Darwin was searching for the missing link between monkey and man; he believed that there must be some species in the evolution of man from monkey who was halfway between the two, neither a full monkey nor a complete man. Between the two there must be a transitory period which the monkey took to evolve into man; it is impossible that a monkey was all of a sudden transformed into a man. It should have been over millions of years when some monkeys became men and others remained monkeys.

Biologists and anthropologists are still wondering what happened to the missing link. A worldwide search is still underway to discover the skeleton of that intermediary between monkey and man. Hanumana seems to be, in many ways, related to that missing link, and it would be great if his skeleton were found. Darwin's theory met with stiff opposition, and it took a long time to be accepted. It was accepted because it was supported by proof.

I say yet another thing which is concerned with the evolution of man. I say that as man has evolved from the monkey at the level of his body, similarly, he evolved from the cow at the level of his soul. If the monkey is his predecessor on the physical side, the cow is his predecessor on the spiritual side.

While man's physical frame has evolved from the monkey's body, his soul has evolved from the soul of the cow. Of course, in support of this theory we can not advance proofs as direct and strong as Darwin's in support of his. But there are many other kinds of evidence in support of what I am saying: man as a soul has evolved from the cow.

It is not reason enough to call the cow our mother because we are an agricultural community and the cow has great use and importance for us. If it were so, we should have called the bull our father, which we did not. And we don't turn every utilitarian object into our mother. There is no reason to do so. The railway train has great utility for us and we cannot do without it, but we are not going to give it the status of a mother. No community calls the airplane mother, although it is so important to modern life. Never and nowhere has an object of utility been called mother, despite the fact that there are any number of things that have utility. And there is no relationship between motherhood and utility. There must be some other reasons for regarding the cow as our mother.

In my view, the cow is man's mother exactly in the same way as the monkey, according to Darwin, happens to be his father. And I have good reasons to say it. Further, most of these reasons are based on the findings of psychic research into man's memory of his past lives, called *jati-smaran* in Buddhist terminology. Thousands of yogis down the centuries have explored and recalled the memories of their past lives and have found retrospectively that as soon as the chain of their human lives comes to an end, the life of the cow begins. If you go back into your past lives—and there are tested methods to do it—you will find that for many lives you were a human being, but as soon as the series of human lives ends, you will enter the life of the cow that you were. Everyone who experimented with *jati-smaran* has come to the same conclusion: behind the layers of memory of human lives lies the layer belonging to the life of a cow. And it is on this basis that the cow has been described as man's mother.

Apart from this, there are other reasons to say so. If you explore the whole animal world you will note that no other animal has such a developed soul as the cow. Looking into the eyes of a cow you will find a kind of humanly quality, a humanness no other animal has. The innocence, the simplicity, the humility of a cow is rare. Spiritually, the cow is the most evolved being in the whole animal world; its high qualities of soul are evident. Its evolved state clearly indicates it is ready for a spiritual leap forward.

If you watch the physical restlessness in which a monkey lives, it will be obvious to you that it is not going to rest until it achieves a higher form of body. The monkey seems to be utterly dissatisfied with his body; in fact, he is dissatisfied with everything about it. It is so agile, speedy and restless all the time. Looking at a newborn child, you will find, while his body has the agility of a monkey, his eyes have the peace and serenity of a cow. Physically he reminds one of a monkey, and spiritually he resembles a cow.

The cow is held in deep respect in this country not because we are predominantly an agricultural society, it is so because after protracted investigations in the psychic world, it was learned that man has spiritually evolved from the cow. And as psychic knowledge grows—and it is growing—science will soon support this truth that India discovered long ago about the cow. There will be no difficulty in the matter.

You will understand it better if you look at the long chain of God's incarnations as conceived by the Hindus. It begins with the fish—the first incarnation of God is the fish—and goes up to Buddha. Until recently one wondered how God could incarnate as a fish; the whole thing seemed so ridiculous. But now the science of biology accepts that life on this earth began with the fish. Now it is difficult to mock the

Hindu concept of *matsyavatara*, God's first incarnation as a fish. Science has such a hold on our minds that we have to accept whatever it says. Science says that life on this earth has evolved from the fish. That is why this country said centuries ago that the fish was the first incarnation of God. The Sanskrit word for incarnation is *avatara*, which means descent of consciousness. Since life as consciousness first dawned in the fish, it is not wrong to call it the first incarnation. This is the language of religion. Science says the same thing: the first appearance of life on earth was in the shape of the fish.

We have yet another of God's incarnations which is still more puzzling and unique. It is called *narsinghavatara*, God's incarnation as half man and half animal. When Darwin says that the missing link between monkey and man should be half monkey and half man, we don't have any difficulty in accepting him. But we find it difficult to accept the concept of *narsinghavatara*. This is again the language of religion, and undoubtedly it carries with it a deep insight.

The cow is man's mother in the same way as the monkey is his father. Darwin was concerned with the evolution of the physical body; in fact, the whole of the West is concerned with the physical. But India has long been concerned with the spirit, the soul; it is not much concerned with the body. We have always wanted to explore the spirit and its ultimate source. For this reason we emphasized the soul much more than the body.

Secondly, you want to know my view on cow slaughter.

I am against all kinds of slaughter, so the question of my favoring cow slaughter does not arise. But whether I am for or against it, cow slaughter is not going to stop. The conditions of our life are such that the cow will continue to be killed. I am against meat-eating, but it is not going to make a difference. Under the present conditions meat-eating cannot go.

We are not yet in a position to provide the entire population of the world with an adequate amount of vegetarian food. Let alone the world, even a single country cannot afford to be vegetarian at the moment. It will simply die of starvation if it decides to go vegetarian. Unless we have enough food grains and vegetables and milk to feed the whole world, non-vegetarianism will continue to predominate. There is no way out at the moment. It is a necessary evil. So is cow slaughter.

It is ironic that people who are anxious to ban cow slaughter are doing nothing to create the necessary conditions to make the society vegetarian. So cow slaughter is not going to end because of these people. If it ends someday, it will end because of the efforts of those who are not at all anxious to do away with cow slaughter. Slogan-mongering and agitation are not going to end it, nor is it going to end through legislation. Though we have the largest number of cows, they are the most uncared for; they are as good as dead and useless. On the other hand, beef-eating countries have the best kinds of cows, healthy and strong. While a single cow in the West yields forty to fifty kilos of milk per day, it would be too much for an Indian cow to give half a kilo. We have only skeletons in the name of cows, and we make such a hullabaloo about them.

The production of vegetarian food, of nutritive and health-giving vegetarian food, is the first imperative if you want to abolish cow slaughter. Supporters of vegetarianism have yet to meet the argument of the non-vegetarians that the world is much too short of vegetarian food to provide nutrition and health to mankind. There is logic in their argument.

It is very interesting that both cow and monkey are vegetarians. Man inherits his body and soul from vegetarian sources. It is another thing that a monkey sometimes swallows a few ants, but by and large he is a vegetarian. The cow is wholly vegetarian;

it will eat meat only when it is forced to. Under the circumstances it is strange how man has turned non-vegetarian, because his whole physical and psychic system is derived from vegetarian sources. The structure of his stomach is such as only vegetarian animals have, and so is his mental makeup. Obviously man must have been forced by circumstances to become non-vegetarian. And even today he cannot do without animal food.

It seems to me that cow slaughter will continue in spite of all our good intentions to stop it. In my view, it will only stop when we make provisions for adequate synthetic food for all. And then people have to be persuaded to take to synthetic food on a large scale. Synthetic food is the only alternative to non-vegetarianism. The day man accepts living on scientific food, meat-eating will disappear, not before.

So I am not interested in the agitation for banning cow slaughter by law; it is absurd and stupid. It is a sheer waste of time and energy. I am interested in something else: I want science to put its energy into the creation of synthetic food so that man is freed from meat-eating. There is no other way except this. Food derived from the earth will not do; food will have to be produced in factories in the form of pills. The population of the world today ranges between three and a half to four billion, and this goes on increasing. In spite of what we do to control population, it is going to increase in an unprecedented manner.

The day is not far off when we will leave behind this agitation against cow slaughter and will instead be agitating for a large-scale slaughter of men. The day is not distant when man will eat man, because you cannot argue with hunger. As we now ask a dying man to donate his eyes or kidneys, we will soon ask him to donate his flesh for the hungry. And we will honor him who donates his flesh, as today we honor one who donates his heart or lungs. There is going to be such a population explosion on the earth.

Very soon we will begin to think it is unjust to cremate dead bodies, they should be saved for food—and it will not be something new and extraordinary; cannibalism has been known to man since ancient times. There have been tribes where man ate man to satiate his hunger. Once again we are coming close to that situation when cannibalism will be revived. In view of it, it is just stupid to agitate for a ban on cow slaughter. It is utterly unscientific to do so.

I don't suggest that cow slaughter should not and cannot go. It can go. Not only the killing of cows, all kinds of killing can go. But then we will have to take a revolutionary step in the direction of our food and food habits. I am not in favor of cow slaughter, but I am also not in favor of those who shout out against it. All their talk is sheer nonsense. They don't have a correct perspective and a right plan to stop cow slaughter. But it must stop; the cow should be the last animal to be killed. She is the highest in animal evolution; she is the connecting link between man and animal. She deserves all our care and compassion; we are connected with her in an innate and intimate manner. We have to take every care for her.

But remember, caring is possible only when you are in a position to take care. Without the facilities and the wherewithal, caring is impossible. We have to be pragmatic; it is no use being sentimental.

I should tell you an anecdote which I narrated to some friends the other day while we were on a walk.

A priest has to go to a church to give a Sunday sermon. The priest is an old man and his church is four miles away, and the road to it is difficult as it passes through a hilly area with many ups and downs. So the old priest hires a horse-driven coach for his journey. He sends for the owner of the coach and tells him that he will be well paid for his services. The coachman says, "That is okay, but my horse, Gaffar, is very old, and we will have to take care of him."

The priest says, "Don't worry, I will be as considerate of the horse as you are. He will be well cared for."

After only a half mile's drive the coach reaches a steep rise in the hills. So the coach stops and the coachman tells the priest, "Now please step out of the coach, because the uphill road begins and since Gaffar is very old we have to care for him." The old priest gets out and begins to walk alongside the coach. And when they reach the plain the priest is asked to board the coach again. This is how the whole journey is covered—the priest is made to walk when the road is uphill and rides in the carriage when it is on flat ground. On a four-mile journey he drives hardly a mile in the coach, and the rest he has to cover by walking. In fact, he has to walk where for his age it is necessary to ride, and he rides where he can well afford to walk.

When the coach reaches the church, the priest pays the coachman and tells him, "Here is your fare, but before you go I would like you to answer a question. I came here to give a sermon and you came here to earn money. It is okay, but why did you bring Gaffar? It would have been easier if only you and I had come. Why Gaffar?"

Life is lived according to its needs and exigencies, not according to ideas and theories. The cow cannot be saved when man himself is facing death. To save the cow it is necessary for man to become so affluent that he can afford it. Then, along with the cow, other animals will be saved too. The cow is, of course, nearest to us as an animal, but other animals are not that distant. Even the fish is our kin, although a distant kin. Life really began with the fish. So, as man grows affluent he will not only save the cow, he will save the fish too.

We have to be clear in our view that the cow and, for that matter, all other animals have to be saved. But it is sheer stupidity to insist on saving them even when the conditions necessary to do so are lacking.

Now we will sit for meditation.

TENTH DISCOURSE
MORNING, SEPTEMBER 30, 1970
MANALI, INDIA

SPIRITUALISM, RELIGION AND POLITICS

Questioner: Krishna was essentially a spiritual man, but he freely took part in politics. And as a politician he did not shrink from using the tricks of the trade. In the battle of the Mahabharat he got Bishma killed by deceit —a naked woman was made to stand before that venerated old sage, who was a vowed celibate. In the same way, deception was used to kill Dronacharya, Karna, and Duryodhana. The question arises: Should a spiritual man take part in politics, and if so, should he behave as ordinary politicians do? And, was Mahatma Gandhi wrong in laying stress on the purity of ends and means? Is not purity of means important to politics?

et us first understand the difference between religion and spiritualism; they are not the same thing. Religion is one avenue of life, like politics, art and science. Religion does not contain the whole of life; spiritualism does. Spiritualism is the whole of life. Spiritualism is not an avenue of life; it encompasses the whole of it. It is life.

A religious person may be afraid of taking part in politics, but a spiritual person is not afraid. A spiritual person can take part in politics without any fear. Politics is difficult for a religious person because he is tethered to certain ideas and ideals which come into conflict with politics. But a spiritual person is not bound by any ideas or concepts. He accepts life totally; he accepts life as it is. So he can easily participate in politics.

Krishna is a spiritual man, he is not religious. Mahavira is a religious man in this sense, and so is Buddha; they have opted for one particular avenue of life, which is religion. And for the sake of religion they have denied all other avenues of life. They have sacrificed the rest of life on the altar of a part. Krishna is a spiritual man; he accepts life in its totality. That is why he is not afraid of politics, he does not shrink from going headlong into it. For him, politics is part of life.

It is important to understand that people who have kept away from politics in the name of religion have only helped to make politics more irreligious; their non-cooperation has not made it any better.

I repeat: Krishna accepts life with all its flowers and thorns, its light and shade, sweet and sour. He accepts life choicelessly, unconditionally. He accepts life as it is. It is not that Krishna chooses only the flowers of life and shuns its thorns; he accepts both together, because he knows thorns are as necessary to life as the flowers. Ordinarily we think thorns are inimical to flowers. It is not true. Thorns are there for the protection of flowers; they are deeply connected with each other. They are united—members of each other. They share common roots, and they live for a common purpose. Many people would like to destroy the thorn and save the flower, but that is not possible. They are parts of each other, and both have to be saved.

So Krishna not only accepts politics, he lives in the thick of politics without the least difficulty.

The other part of your question is also significant. You say that in politics Krishna uses means that cannot be said to be right. To achieve his ends, he uses lies, deception and fraud—which cannot be justified in any way. In this connection one has to understand the realities of life. In life there is no choice between good and bad, except in theory. The choice between good and evil is all a matter of doctrine. In reality, one always has to choose between the greater evil and the lesser evil. Every choice in life is relative. It is not a question of whether what Krishna did was good or bad. The question is whether it would have resulted in good or bad had he not done what he did. The question would be much easier if it was a simple choice between good and bad, but this is not the case in reality. The realities of life are that it is always the choice between greater evils and lesser evils.

I have heard an anecdote:

A priest is passing a street when he hears a voice crying, "Save me, save me! I am dying!" It is dark and the street is narrow. The priest rushes to the place and finds that a big strong man has overpowered another man, who seems to be very poor and weak. The priest demands that the strong man release the poor man, but he refuses. The priest physically intervenes in the struggle and succeeds in releasing the victim from the strong man's grip, and the poor man takes to his heels.

The strong man says, "Do you know what you have done? That man had picked my pocket and you have helped him to run away with my purse."

The priest said, "Why didn't you say it before? I thought you were unnecessarily torturing a poor man. I am sorry; I made a mistake. I had thought I was doing something good, but it turned out to be evil." But the man had already disappeared with the purse.

Before we set out to do good, it is necessary to consider if it will result in evil. It is equally necessary to know that a bad action may ultimately result in good.

The choice before Krishna is between lesser evil and greater evil. It is not a simple choice between good and evil. The fighting tactics which Krishna uses are nothing compared to those used in the war of Mahabharat by the other side, who are capable of doing anything. The Kauravas are no ordinary evil-doers—they are extraordinarily evil. Gandhi would be no match for them; they could crush him in moments. Ordinary good cannot defeat an evil that is colossal. Gandhi would know what it is to fight with a colossus of evil if he had fought against a government run by Adolph Hitler. Fortunately for him, India was ruled by a very liberal community—the British—not by Hitler. Even among the British—if Churchill had been in power and Gandhi had to deal with him, it would have been very difficult to win India's independence. The coming of Attlee into power in Britain after the war made a big difference.

The question of right means, which Gandhi talks about so much, deserves careful consideration. It is fine to say that right ends cannot be achieved without right means. However, in this world, there is nothing like an absolutely right end or absolutely right means. It is not a question of right versus wrong; it is always a question of greater wrong versus lesser wrong. There is no one who is completely healthy or completely sick; it is always a matter of being more sick or less sick.

Life does not consist of two distinct colors— white and black; life is just gray, a mixture of white and black. In this context men like Gandhi are just utopians, dreamers, idealists who are completely divorced from reality. Krishna is in direct contact with life; he is not a utopian. For him life's work begins with accepting it as it is.

What Gandhi calls "pure means" are not really pure, cannot be. Maybe pure ends and pure means are available in what the Hindus call *moksha*, or the space of freedom. But in this mundane world everything is alloyed with dirt. Not even gold is unalloyed. What we call diamond is nothing but old, aged coal. Gandhi's purity of ends and means is sheer imagination.

For example, Gandhi thinks fasting is a kind of right means to a right end. And he resorts to fasting—fast unto death—every now and then. But I can never accept fasting as a right means, nor will Krishna agree with Gandhi. If a threat to kill another person is wrong, how can a threat to kill oneself be right? If it is wrong of me to make you accept what I say by pointing a gun at you, how can it become right if I make you accept the same thing by turning the gun to point it at myself? A wrong does not cease to be a wrong just by turning the point of a gun. In a sense it would be a greater wrong on my part if I ask you to accept my views with the threat that if you don't I am going to kill myself. If I threaten to kill you, you have an option, a moral opportunity to die and refuse to yield to my pressure. But if I threaten to kill myself, I make you very helpless, because you may not like to take the responsibility of my death on yourself.

Gandhi once undertook such a fast unto death to put pressure on Ambedkar, leader of the millions of India's untouchables. And Ambedkar had to yield, not because he agreed that the cause for which Gandhi fasted was right, but because he did not want to let Gandhi die for it. Ambedkar was not ready to do even this much violence to Gandhi. Ambedkar said later that Gandhi would be wrong to think that he had changed his heart. He still believed he was right and Gandhi was wrong, but he was not prepared to take the responsibility for the violence that Gandhi was insisting on doing to himself.

In this context it is necessary to ask if Ambedkar used the right means, or Gandhi? Of the two, who is really non-violent? In my view Gandhi's way was utterly violent, and Ambedkar proved to be non-violent. Gandhi was determined till the last moment to pressure Ambedkar with his threat to kill himself.

It makes no difference whether I threaten to kill you or to kill myself to make you accept my view. In either case, I am using pressure and violence. In fact, when I threaten to kill you I give you a choice to die with dignity, to tell me you would rather die than yield to my view which is wrong. But when I threaten you with my own death, then I deprive you of the option to die with dignity; I put you in a real dilemma. Either you have to yield and accept that you are in the wrong, or you take the responsibility of my death on you. You are going to suffer guilt in every way.

In spite of his insistence on right means for right ends, the means that Gandhi himself uses are never right. And I am bold enough to say that whatever Krishna did was right. In a relative sense, taking his opponents into consideration, Krishna could not have done otherwise.

Questioner: Could he not have killed them straightaway with weapons, instead of resorting to dubious means?

They are being killed with weapons. Don't forget that cunning and deceit are parts of the arsenal of war. And when your enemies are making full use of this arsenal, it is sheer stupidity to play into their hands and get defeated and killed.

Krishna does not use deception against a group of good and saintly people. They are an unsaintly and unscrupulous people. It has been proved a thousand times, and Krishna is having to deal with them. Before going to war Krishna has done everything to bring them round to some compromise so that war is avoided. But they force a war. They are not ready for anything short of war, and they are ready to use every foul means to destroy the Pandavas. And their whole past record is one of unabashed dishonesty and treachery. If Krishna had behaved with such people in a gentlemanly way, the Mahabharat would have ended very differently. Then the Pandavas would have lost the war and the Kauravas would be the victors. Then evil would be victorious over good.

We say that truth wins—*satyameva jayate*—but history says it differently. History always puts the victor on the side of truth. If the Kauravas had won, historians would have written their story, extolling them to the skies. Then the Pandavas would have been forgotten, and no one would have known Krishna. An altogether different story would have been written.

I think Krishna did the only right thing to do in the face of the realities of the situation, and all talk of purity of means is irrelevant. In the world we live in, every means has to be tainted more or less. If the means is absolutely pure, it will soon turn into an end; there will be no need to strive for the end. A wholly pure means ceases to be different from the end; then ends and means are one and the same. But ends and means are different from each other, as long as the means is tainted and the end is clean. While it is true that a clean end is never attained through unclean means, is a pure end ever achieved in this world? It is always there in our dreams and desires, but it is never really achieved.

Gandhi could not say at the time of his death that he had attained to his lofty ends of truth and non-violence and celibacy, for which he worked hard throughout his life. He died experimenting with them. If the means were right, then why did he not achieve his ends? What was the difficulty? If the means are right, there should be no difficulty in achieving the end.

No, means can never be wholly pure. It is like putting a straight rod of wood in the water—it becomes slightly crooked. There is no way to keep the rod straight in the water. Not that the rod actually becomes crooked in the water, it just appears so. The medium of water makes the rod crooked to look at. It is straight again when you take it out of the water.

In this vast world of relativity, everything is slightly crooked; it is in the very nature of things. So it is not a question of being straight and simple, it is just a question of being crooked and complex as little as possible. And to me, Krishna is the least crooked and complex person there is. It is ironic, however, that to the ordinary mind Krishna appears to be crooked and complex and Gandhi appears to be straight and simple.

To me, Gandhi seems to be a very crooked and complex personality. In comparison with him, Krishna is far more straight and simple. Gandhi has a knack of making a complexity of every simple thing. If he has to coerce someone else, he will begin by coercing himself. To hurt others he will hurt himself. His ways of coercion are indirect and devious. If Krishna has to punish someone he will do it straight, he will not take a devious course like Gandhi. But we are in the habit of looking at things very superficially, and we go by our superficial impressions.

Questioner: There was a king named Pondrak in the times of Krishna. This man had declared Krishna to be a fake and himself to be the real Krishna. Can you say if similar things have happened in the lives of Buddha, Mahavira and other enlightened beings?

Yes, they did happen. In the times of Mahavira, a man named Goshalak had declared that he, not Mahavira, was the real *tirthankara*.

The Jews crucified Jesus on the basis that a carpenter's son was falsely claiming to be a Messiah; he was not real. The real messiah was yet to come. The Jewish tradition believed that a messiah would come; many past prophets like Ezekiel and Isaiah had predicted it. Just before the birth of Jesus, John the Baptist had gone from village to village announcing that the messiah is on his way who will redeem all people. And then a young man named Jesus came on the scene declaring that he was the messiah. But the Jews refused to accept him; instead they crucified him, on the grounds that he was a fake, he was not the real messiah.

No other person except Jesus claimed to be the messiah, but any number of people claimed that Jesus was not the messiah. Why? They said that to be acknowledged as their messiah, a person would have to fulfill certain conditions. He would have to perform a few miracles. One of the miracles to be performed was that the messiah would come down from the cross alive. The Jews believed that descending alive from the cross would be enough of a miracle to make them accept him as their messiah.

Now Christians believe that the resurrection of Jesus happened on the third day after the crucifixion. They say that after three days, two women devotees of Jesus saw him alive. But his opponents don't accept it; they say these two women were so much in love with Jesus that they could see Jesus in fantasy; it could not be real. There is nothing on record in the whole of Jewish scriptures that Jesus came down from the cross alive, that he fulfilled that condition of being their messiah. Jews are still waiting for the coming of the messiah their prophets predicted.

But Goshalak made a clear and emphatic claim to be the real *tirthankara* in place of Mahavira. There were many people who accepted Goshalak as the *tirthankara*, and their number was not small, it was large. And the controversy lasted long, because Jaina tradition believed that the twenty-fourth *tirthankara*, who would be the last in a long line of *tirthankaras*, was coming. So Goshalak staked his claim and a large group of Jainas accepted him as such.

Apart from Goshalak, there were about six contemporaries of Mahavira who were believed by their followers to be the twenty-fourth *tirthankara*. They did not openly state their claim as Goshalak did, but their followers believed they were. Sanjay Vilethiputta and Ajit Keshkambal were among a half dozen people who were believed to be *tirthankaras*. Even Buddha's devotees thought that Buddha was the real *tirthankara*; they often scoffed at Mahavira.

It is always possible that when a person like Krishna is born, or is being awaited according to certain predictions made in the past, many people will claim that exalted position, there is no difficulty in it. But time is what finally decides who the rightful claimant is. The truth is that when one claims to be something, it shows clearly that he is not the right person. Only a wrong person claims to be something that he is not. Krishna does not need to claim to be Krishna, he *is* Krishna. The very fact that someone claims to be Krishna shows that he is a pretender, that his being is not enough. He has to claim it to be so.

Mahavira does not claim that he is a *tirthan-*

kara, he is it. But Goshalak has to lay claim to it, because he himself is in doubt. In fact, it is our feeling of inferiority that leads us to claim to be this or that. If someone claims to be a saint it clearly means that he is not a saint; he will be just the contrary to what he claims.

But it is just natural and human that such claims are made.

Questioner: Why did Jesus claim?

Jesus did not. He did not claim that he was the messiah. His claims were quite different. In fact, his claims don't come in the form of statements; he claimed through his being. People recognized that he was the messiah.

As I mentioned earlier, John the Baptist, a rare sage, had declared that the messiah was coming and he was his messenger. He also said that the day the messiah would arrive he, the messenger, would depart from the world. He lived on the banks of the River Jordan and initiated people in the water of that river. Thousands of people were initiated by him. Jesus too, had his initiation from John the Baptist. When Jesus was standing in water up to his neck, John initiated him and then said, "Now, you should begin your work and I go."

The news of this event in the River Jordan spread like wildfire all over the country, and people came to know that the messiah had arrived. And that very day John disappeared and nobody ever heard of him again. John's disappearance was the real declaration of the coming of the messiah, because he had gone to every village saying that the messiah was coming and the day he would come, John would disappear. He said that he was only the forerunner of the messiah; he was there only to prepare the way for his coming, and that he would leave the world when the messiah came. So John's disappearance announced that Christ, the messiah, had arrived. Now people began to ask Jesus if he was the messiah. And he could not have lied to them; he said that he was the one they were waiting for, he was the one who was there everlastingly, who was there even before their first messiah Abraham was.

When people inquired, he had to tell them this much.

> Questioner: The line of Hindu incarnations begins with the fish and continues through Rama, Krishna, and Buddha. Even the coming incarnation, to be known as Kalki, is included in this series. But how is it that in this long line of incarnations Krishna is said to be the complete incarnation of God, although Buddha happened long after him? Why was Buddha denied this honor? And what, from the viewpoint of evolution, is the secret of Krishna preceding Buddha? Is it so because the movement of time is circular?

Even a partial incarnation of God is as good as the complete one. It makes no difference as far as incarnation is concerned. An incarnation means that divine consciousness has become manifest. In how many dimensions it manifests itself is another matter. Krishna is a complete incarnation in the sense that divine energy has become manifest in all dimensions of his life. Buddha's incarnation is not that complete, nor is the coming incarnation of Kalki going to be. As far as the descent of divine energy is concerned, the process of descent is going to be complete in the case of every incarnation, but it may not touch every dimension of a man's life. And there are many reasons for it.

In the ordinary process of evolution, completion should happen at the end. But incarnation is outside this process of evolution. Incarnation means descent from the beyond; it is not a part of the evolutionary process, where something grows with evolution. Incarnation comes from some space that is beyond evolution. Try to understand it: We are all sitting here with closed eyes, and the sun has risen in the East. If someone opens his eyes partially he will see light partially. And another person will see light fully if he opens his eyes fully. The same person can go through both processes—now opening his eyes partially and then opening them fully. And he can do it any time he likes; there is no evolutionary process involved, no compulsion.

Krishna's life is open, fully open on all sides; he can take in the whole of the divine. Buddha's life is partially open; he can take in the divine only partially. If today someone exposes himself fully to the divine, he will have the whole of it. And if tomorrow someone closes himself, he will wholly miss the divine. No evolutionary process is involved. This process is applicable only in a general way; you cannot apply it to individual cases. Twenty-five hundred years have passed since Buddha, but a man of our times cannot say that he is more evolved than Buddha. Of course, we can say that our society is more evolved than Buddha's society.

In fact, evolution takes place at two levels— one at the level of groups and the other at the level of individuals. An individual can always overtake his society; he can move ahead of his time by his own effort. And those who do not try to grow on their own will drag their feet with the rest of their society. Also, all members of a group do not evolve uniformly;

each individual has his different way of growth. So many people are sitting here, but not everyone is on the same rung of the ladder of growth. Someone is on the first rung, another is on the tenth and a third can be at the top. General rules are applicable only to groups.

For example, we can say how many persons died annually in traffic accidents in Delhi during the last ten years. If fifty have died in the current year, forty-five died last year, and forty the year before last, we can predict that next year fifty-five people are going to die in traffic accidents. And this forecast will prove true to a large extent. But we cannot say who these fifty-five people will be individually. We cannot ferret them out and identify them. They are all unknown persons. And if the population of Delhi is two million, this figure of fifty-five will vary a little. But if the population is two hundred million, fifty-five will remain fifty-five; there will not be the least variation. The larger the group, the greater the chances of making correct statistical forecasts about them.

General rules are applicable only to groups, not to individuals. Evolution is a collective process, and an individual can always come ahead of this process.

A single bird's chirping can herald the coming of the spring, but it takes time before all the birds begin to sing. A single blossom can say that spring is on its way, but it takes time for all the flowers to bloom. Spring is really full only when all flowers have bloomed, but even a single blossom can say it is coming. Individual flowers can bloom both before and after the spring, but collective flowering happens only in the spring.

Krishna's becoming a complete incarnation even though he happened midway in the long line of incarnations, shows that his life was fully open from all sides; all its dimensions were available to divine consciousness. Buddha is not that open in all his dimensions. And remember, Buddha must have wanted it that way, it was his own choice. If somebody asks him to complete himself because he has the possibility to be a Krishna, he will refuse. Buddha has chosen not to be so; it is not that Buddha falls behind Krishna in any way. Buddha has decided to be the way he is, and so has Krishna. And in this respect they are their own men, masters of their own destinies. Buddha comes to his flowering the way he wants it. Krishna chooses to come to complete flowering, because it is his nature. And in its own dimension Buddha's flowering is as complete.

There is no sequence of evolution in the matter of incarnations. The law of evolution does not operate on individuals; it operates only on groups.

> Questioner: Krishna put up with nine hundred and ninety-nine invectives hurled on him by King Shishupal, but he killed him with his chakra—a wheel-like weapon—when the king fired his last invective. Does it not show that Krishna's tolerance is only skin deep, that deep down he was intolerant?

It can appear so, because we all have only skin deep tolerance. If I lose my temper on the fourth foul word hurled at me, it means I had lost it with the very first one, but somehow I put up with three of them, and appeared in my true colors as soon as the fourth one came. But the contrary can also happen, and Krishna is that contrary; he is not like us. There is every possibility that he was an exception to this generality.

It is not that Krishna's tolerance could take only nine hundred ninety-nine invectives. Do you think nine hundred ninety-nine are not enough? And that one who can bear this huge number of abuses cannot bear one more? It is really hard to believe. The real question before Krishna is not that his tolerance has run out, the real question is that the man confronting him has reached his limit. Not only has he reached his limit, he has really surpassed it. And to put up with any more would not exhaust Krishna's patience, but it would certainly amount to putting a premium on evil. To tolerate any more would go toward strengthening unrighteousness. It is obvious that nine hundred ninety-nine curses are more than enough.

Someone, a disciple, asks Jesus, "What should I do if someone slaps me once?"

Jesus says to him, "Bear it."

The disciple then asks, "And what if he slaps me seven times?"

To this Jesus says, "You should bear it not only for seven times but for seventy-seven times."

The disciple does not ask again what he should do if he is slapped for the seventy-eighth time, so we don't know what Jesus would say. But I believe that if the disciple raises this question Jesus would say, "Don't take it quietly after the seventy-seventh. Enough is enough, because you have not only to take care of your forbearance, you have also to see that unrighteousness does not go beserk."

I have heard a joke:

A follower of Jesus is passing through a village when some stranger slaps him on his cheek. He remembers this saying of Jesus, "If someone slaps you on the left cheek, turn your right cheek to him." And he turns his right cheek to the person, who inflicts a harsher slap on it. But the stranger has no idea of what the disciple is going to do next. There is no instruction from Jesus as to what one should do after he is slapped for the second time. The disciple thinks now he is free to decide on his own, and he smites the stranger with all his strength.

The stranger is flabbergasted! He protests, "What kind of a Jesus devotee are you? Don't you remember that he says, 'If someone slaps you on the left cheek turn the right one to him?' "

The disciple answers, "But I don't have a third cheek. I obeyed Jesus so far as his saying goes, and now I take leave of him, because I have already turned my two cheeks to you. Now your cheek should take a turn. That is why I slapped you."

Krishna kills Shishupal not because his patience has come to an end; his patience is unending. But we are apt to think otherwise, because our own tolerance is very brittle. Krishna does not lack tolerance, but he also knows that it is dangerous to put up with unrighteousness beyond a certain limit; it amounts to encouraging it. Tolerance is good just because intolerance is evil. There is no other reason for praising patience except that impatience is ugly. But does it mean that I should care for my own patience and let the impatience of another run riot and ruin him? This is not compassion; it is really cruelty to the other. A point comes when I have to stop evil from going too far. This is how I see it.

Looking at the whole life of Krishna, it does not seem that anything can exhaust his patience, but it is equally difficult for him to encourage evil. So he has to find a golden mean between the two extremes—his own patience and the impatience of another.

Questioner: Would you not call Krishna a kidnapping champion? He not only kidnaps Rukmini and marries her, but also induces Arjuna to kidnap her sister Subhadra. What do you say?

When social systems change, many things suddenly become absurd and obsolete. There was a time when if a woman was not kidnapped by some man it was thought no one loved her, that she was an ugly and unwanted woman. In those days kidnapping was a way of honoring women. Of course, that time is past, and we are in different times. But even today if inside a university campus a young woman is never brushed against by a young man while passing in the corridors, she feels rejected and miserable; there is no end to her unhappiness. And watch a woman carefully who complains that she is being jostled by men around her, and you will notice how really happy she feels about this business. A woman wants that some man should really think of kidnapping her, that he should love her so much he feels compelled to steal her instead of begging for her.

You will understand it only if you try to understand the times in which Krishna lived. And I believe that it was really a heroic age, when marriages were not made with the consent of lovers' parents and astrologers. Such a marriage is not worth a farthing. If Krishna encourages someone to kidnap his beloved, he is saying that love is such a valuable thing that even kidnapping is permissible. Everything can and should be staked for love. Love does not accept any law; it is a law unto itself. And Krishna's age was the age of love, when love held a supreme place in the life of man and his society. When love begins to be governed by conventions and laws, you will know love's power is fading; it has ceased to be a force, a challenge, a thing of value. So you have to consider the age in which Krishna was born. It had its own social order which was very different from ours. And it would not be right to measure that age with the yardstick of our times. If you do, Krishna's actions will look immoral.

To me, it is an heroic age, a brave world, when life, bursting with energy, full of fire and radiance, invites challenges and stakes everything to meet them. And it is a cowardly and dead society when life's light is dimmed; it loses zest and vitality. Like a weakling it runs away from challenges and dangers and plays safe. Such a society makes different kinds of laws and moral codes which are insipid and dead. I will say that it will be an insult to womanhood if Krishna does not kidnap a woman he loves but instead sends supplications to her parents and maneuvers for her hand in marriage. At least Krishna's age would never approve of it. And the woman concerned would say to Krishna, "If you don't have the courage to steal me it is better you had not thought of me."

Although times change and old systems die, making way for the new, something of the past remains with us. We forget that what we call a *baraat*—a wedding procession—today is nothing but a remnant of old times when armed troops were sent with the lover to forcibly bring his beloved from the house of her parents. Even today, the bridegroom with a sword in his hand is made to ride a horse when he leaves for the house of his bride. A horse and a sword don't fit with marriage today; they are just relics of ancient customs.

In olden times a lover had to go on horseback so that he could elope with his beloved. And for this very purpose he carried a sword, and a troop of armed men rode with him. And you know that even now when a wedding party arrives at the house of the bride's parents, the women of the family and neighborhood gather together and receive the guests with insults and invectives. Why this strange practice? In the days when brides were forcibly seized it was natural that the kidnappers were treated with abuse and curses. The practice is now meaningless, because marriages are arranged—but it continues. Even today the bride's father bows to the bridegroom's father; this too

is a residue from the same dead past, when in acknowledgement of his defeat the father of the bride bowed
to the victor's father.

> Questioner: Once when Krishna is
> on his way to Dwarka he meets
> Kunta who requests of him a gift of
> pain and suffering. But Krishna only
> laughs; he does not even say that such
> a request is not right. What does it
> mean?

When a devotee prays for pain it is very meaningful.
And there are reasons for it.

To pray for happiness seems to be somewhat
selfish. It is. When one prays to God for happiness,
he does not really pray to God, he only seeks happiness. His prayer has nothing to do with God, it is
only concerned with his happiness. If he can find
happiness without God, he will gladly give him up
and move directly toward happiness. He prays to God
only because he believes that happiness can be had
through him. So he uses God as a means; happiness
remains his end, his objective. Therefore a true devotee will not pray for happiness, because he would
not like to place anything, not even happiness, above
God.

When a devotee prays for unhappiness, he
simply means to say to God, "Even if you give me
unhappiness, it would be far better than happiness
coming from somewhere else." A devotee will prefer
unhappiness coming from God to happiness that
comes from the world. Now there is no way left for
this person to move away from God. Man is in the
habit of moving away from unhappiness and chasing
happiness. The devotee seeking happiness can part

with God, but one who asks for suffering cannot; he has now burned his bridges.

A prayer for unhappiness is immensely significant. It is asking for the very thing which people avoid at all costs. A true devotee asks for unhappiness.

There is yet another side to this prayer to God for unhappiness. You can easily risk this kind of prayer, because God can never inflict unhappiness on you. His gift is always happiness. In fact, whatever comes from God is happiness. And if happiness is the only gift that comes from God then why beg for it? There is some sense in seeking happiness from those who cannot give it. And it is safe to pray to God for unhappiness, because he is incapable of granting this prayer. He has only one gift to make, and that is happiness. This devotee is trying to be clever with God; he is playing a joke on him. Really he is telling him that he would not ask for happiness, because whatever God gives is happiness; he can easily ask for the opposite. He is putting God in an awkward position. It always happens in a love relationship—lovers have fun at each other's expense. In a way the devotee is kidding God, because he knows that although he is omnipotent God is nevertheless incapable of inflicting pain on his lovers.

There are other reasons too, which are psychological. Happiness is transient; it comes and goes. But suffering is lasting, once it visits you it will not leave you so soon. And happiness is not only fleeting, it is very shallow too. Happiness lacks depth. That is why happy people also lack depth; they have a superficiality about them. Suffering has great depth and it lends its depth to those who suffer.

There is a depth in the life of people who go through suffering; there is a depth in their eyes, in their look, in their whole demeanor. Suffering cleanses and chastens you, it gives you a sharpness. Suffering has great depth which is utterly lacking in happiness. Happiness is like Euclid's point which has neither breadth nor length; it is virtually non-existent. You cannot draw a point on paper; the moment you draw it there is a little length and breadth to it. So it is with happiness; it exists in your thoughts and dreams; it does not really exist. So there is no point in praying for happiness.

A devotee asks for something enduring, something lasting, that can broaden and deepen his being. By asking for suffering he is asking for all that is profound and everlasting in life.

And the last thing: There is a kind of joy even in the suffering that comes to you from the one you love. And even happiness that comes from an unloving quarter is devoid of this joy. Has it ever occurred to you that suffering has its own joy? This joy has nothing to do with the pleasure Masoch used to have in flogging himself.

A masochist is one who receives a kind of pleasure by inflicting pain on himself, by torturing himself. Gandhi was such a masochist. The suffering a devotee prays for is something entirely different from masochistic pleasure. He is talking of the joy that comes from love's suffering, which only lovers know. Love's suffering is profound. Ordinary pain is not so devastating as the pain of love. Love's pain wipes out the lover, while ordinary pain leaves your ego intact. Love is the death of the ego, which remains unaffected by ordinary suffering. So the devotee prays for a suffering that can efface him altogether. He prays for love's suffering.

That is why Krishna just laughs on hearing Kunta's prayer; he does not say a word. Sometimes a smile, a giggle can say more than words do; words are not that articulate. And if you use words where a smile is enough you will only spoil the game. That is why Krishna does not say a word beyond giggling, because he knows that the devotee is cleverly putting him in a corner, he is really asking for something that is good and great. There is nothing to explain.

Questioner: It all sounds paradoxical. You have said more than once that while Krishna's life is extraordinary and miraculous, like a flower in bloom, full of laughter and playfulness, the life of others like him is masochistic. For instance, nobody ever saw Jesus laugh. In this context how is it possible that a devotee praying for suffering can have a vision of the Krishna of your concept?

A devotee who prays for suffering is not masochistic. A masochist creates so much suffering on his own that he need not pray for it any more. He is so rich in suffering that you cannot add any more to it. He does not ask for suffering; he himself can create it.

A devotee asks for suffering because he has enough happiness and now he wants to have some taste of pain and suffering as well. He wants to know what it is really. He is never unhappy, and even if he sheds tears they are tears of bliss. A devotee cries a lot, but he does not cry out of despair. But we mistakenly think he is in misery because we are familiar only with the tears of misery; we do not know what it is to cry with joy. We think that tears are inescapably linked with misery. But really tears have nothing to do with pain and suffering; tears are an expression of excess emotion, an outpouring of emotion.

Whether it is a happy emotion or otherwise is immaterial. Any emotion, when it goes beyond a certain limit, expresses itself through tears. If you have an excess of misery you will cry, and you will cry if you have an excess of happiness. Even excessive anger bursts into tears. But we are familiar with only one kind of tears, tears of misery. So in our minds we have formed a connection between tears and misery which is not a fact. Tears are not exclusive to misery; they are an expression of every kind of abundance of emotion. If an emotion is too much, it overflows in the form of tears.

A devotee cries and a lover cries too, but they always shed tears of joy. This pain of love, devotion and bliss has nothing to do with masochism.

> Questioner: As you talk about God and his devotee, and you call Krishna "Bhagwan", the blessed one, a question arises in my mind if Krishna is a devotee. If so, who is the blessed one he is devoted to? And if he is not a devotee why does he sing hymns of praise to devotion?

We have already discussed this matter, but because you could not get it you raise it again and again. What I said about prayer is relevant to this question.

I said prayerfulness, not prayer is my word. Similarly, a devotional attitude, not devotion to some god or deity is my word. Devotion is a name for the feeling, the psychological climate, the heart of a devotee. God is not essential to it. Devotion can exist without God; there is no difficulty in it. The truth is that there is no God; it is because of devotion that he came into being. It is not that devotion is dependent on God; it is because of devotion that God came into being. For those whose hearts are filled with devotion the whole world turns into God. And people devoid of devotion ask, "Where is God?"—they are bound to raise this question. But no one can tell them where God is, because this very world seen through the eyes and heart of the devotee becomes God.

The world is not God, but a heart full of devotion sees the world as God. The world is not even a stone, but a stony heart sees it as stone. What we find in the world is just a projection; we see in the world that which we are. The world is just a mirror; it reflects us as we are. As the feeling of devotion deepens, the world itself turns into God. Not that God is sitting in a heaven or in a temple, no; devotion finds godliness in everything and everywhere.

Krishna is both God and devotee, and whoever begins as a devotee is going to reach his destination as God. When he finds God everywhere there is no reason he should not find God inside himself. A devotee begins as a devotee but he finds his fulfillment as God himself. His journey begins with looking at the world. He looks at what is there in the world with a prayerful heart, with a loving heart, the heart of a devotee; and by and by he comes to look at himself the same way. Ultimately he is bound to find himself to be the very image of God. He can find himself in the very state in which Ramakrishna found himself. There is a beautiful episode in his life:

Ramakrishna was appointed priest in the temple of Dakshineshwar in Calcutta. He was given a small salary of sixteen rupees every month, and assigned the job of doing *puja*, worshipping the idol of goddess Durga, every day. But just a few days after his appointment he found himself in trouble with the managing trustees of the temple. They came to know that the new priest's way of worship was all wrong! First he tasted the food himself and then made an offering of it to the goddess. He even smelled the flowers before they were offered to the deity. It was, they thought, very improper of him to pollute the purity of the offerings.

So they sent for Ramakrishna and asked for an explanation. Why did he not observe the correct standards of worship and devotion? Ramakrishna said, "I have not heard that there are any accepted standards for worship, that there is a discipline of devotion."

The trustees said, "We have heard that you first taste the food meant to be offered to the goddess. Isn't it highly improper?"

Ramakrishna answered, "Before my mother served me any food, she always tasted it to know if it was properly cooked, if it was tasteful. How can I serve any food to the goddess without knowing whether it is delicious or not? The offering must be worthy of the goddess. I cannot do it otherwise. It is up to you to have my services or to dispense with them."

Now a devotee like Ramakrishna cannot be content with an external God. He will soon find God is within him. So the journey which begins with the devotee completes itself with God. And God is not somewhere on the outside. After going round the whole world, we ultimately return to ourselves, we come home, and find that God is there. God has always been inside us.

Krishna is both God and devotee, and so are you. Everyone is God and devotee together. But you cannot begin as God; the beginning has to be made as a devotee. If you say, "I am God," you will be in trouble. In fact, many people who begin with saying they are God get into such troubles. They utterly lack the humility of a devotee, so when they proclaim they are God they become egocentric; they immediately become gurus initiating others as their devotees. Evidently their God needs devotees—but they fail to find God in others. They find God in themselves, and in others they find only devotees. And the world is full of such gurus.

You have to begin as a devotee; you have to begin from the beginning.

Krishna can very well be accepted as God, because this man is as much devoted to a horse as he is to God himself. Every evening, when the horses yoked to his chariot are weary after a hard day's work on the battlefield, Krishna personally takes them to the river and gives them a good bath and massage. This man possesses all the attributes of God, because he bathes horses with the same devotion as a devotee would give a bath to the idol of God himself. There is no risk in accepting him as God. If he was arrogant about being God he would not have agreed to be Arjuna's charioteer. Instead, he would have asked Arjuna to be his charioteer, because he was God and Arjuna was only a devotee. Ask any one of those who claim to be God to take a seat below you, and you will know their arrogance.

The journey should begin with being a devotee, and it will complete itself with God.

Questioner: What is the test of one's highest devotion to Krishna?

As I said, there is no discipline of devotion, and there is no test for love. Love is enough unto itself; why bother about testing it? You think of testing it only when love is not there. Care for love, not for its test. Why do you need a test? You think of testing only when there is no love.

So be concerned with love. Be loving. And when there is love, it is always true love. There is nothing like false love; it is a wrong term. Love is or it is not; the question of test does not arise. There is a test for gold because there is false gold too. Love is never false; it is or it is not. And when love is, you know it the way you know when the shoe pinches. It is painful when the shoe pinches; pain is the test of the pinch. There is no other test. Do you have a test for pain? Pain is its own test; you know when it hurts and when it does not. In the same way you know it when love happens and when it does not. Watch yourself and you will have no trouble knowing whether there is love or is not. What will a test do when there is no love? Love has nothing to do with a test. So care for love, your love.

But we are afraid to turn in and watch ourselves. We are afraid because we know there is no love in there. Instead we always look to others for love; we are anxious to know if they are loving toward us. Rarely one wants to know if he is loving toward others. Day in and day out couples have been quarreling over love. A wife is always complaining that her husband does not love her as much as she loves him. And a husband in his turn is complaining that his wife is not as loving to him. A son is full of resentment that his father does not love him. And a father in his turn grumbles equally. Everybody is complaining, but no one asks if he himself is loving or not.

We are not loving; we really don't have love. We don't feel any love for living human beings who surround us from everywhere. We don't love plants and flowers that are visible everywhere. We don't love the hills and mountains and stars who are all members of the visible world. And when we don't love the seen, the tangible, how can we love that which is unseen, invisible?

Let us begin with the visible world—the tangible. Love should begin at home. And you will find that one who loves the visible soon begins to feel the presence of the invisible that is hidden just behind. You love a rock and the rock turns into God. You love a flower, and you will come in contact with the *elan vital* that is throbbing inside the flower's heart. You love a person and soon the body disappears and the spirit becomes visible. Love is the alchemy which can turn the visible into the invisible, the subtle. Love is the door to the unknown, the unknowable. So just be concerned with love and don't worry about testing it.

And never ask what the highest state of love is. Love is always the highest state. When love comes, it comes at its pinnacle. There is no other state of love; it is always the highest.

There are no degrees of love—less and more. Let us go into it more deeply. I cannot say that I love you a little. Love is never less than the whole. A little love has no meaning. Either there is love or there is not. It is meaningless to say, "Right now I love you less than I loved you before." It does not happen like that. If I love you, I love you totally or I don't love you at all. For example, if someone steals two cents and another person steals two hundred thousand dollars, you cannot say that one committed a small theft and another a big one. Of course, people who worship money will say that a theft of two hundred thousand is big and that of two cents is petty. But in reality theft is theft, whether it involves two cents or two hundred thousand dollars. There are no degrees of theft, large and small. One is as much a thief when he pockets two cents as he is when he bags two hundred thousand dollars.

Love is neither small nor big; love is simply love. There is no such thing as the highest state of love; love is the highest state. Love is always the climax; there are no short climaxes and long ones. Water becomes steam at a hundred degrees. You cannot say that it will be less steam at ninety-five or ninety degrees. No, water changes into steam only at a hundred degrees, not before. So the hundredth degree is the first and the last point of that climax when water turns into steam. Similarly love is the first and the last; love is the climax. Its alpha and omega points are the same. The first and the last rungs of love's ladder are the same. Love's journey begins and ends with the first step; one step is enough.

Since we don't know love we raise strange questions about it. I have yet to come across a person who asks a right question about love. I am reminded of a story:

Morgan, a multi-millionaire, was having a discussion with another multi-millionaire who was his rival in business. Morgan said, "There are a thousand ways of earning money, but the way of earning it honestly is only one."

His rival asked with some amazement, "What is that one way?"

Morgan said, "I knew you would ask this question, because you don't know. I was certain about your raising the question because you don't know an honest way to make money."

It is the same with love. We cannot formulate a right question about love; we never ask a right question about it. Whatever questions we raise are irrelevant, beside the point, because we don't know a thing about love. Like Morgan, I knew you would ask this wrong question. We can only ask wrong questions about love. And the irony is that one who knows love is not going to ask a question, which would be the right question, about love. The question does not arise because he knows it.

> Questioner: Krishna inspires Arjuna to fight in the battle of the Mahabharat. But it is said that once it happens, Krishna himself prepares to fight with Arjuna. What is the matter?

The truth is that a person like Krishna never takes anything for granted; he is uncommitted. He is neither somebody's friend nor his enemy. Krishna has no fixed ideas about men or things. He knows a friend can turn into an enemy and an enemy into a friend; it all depends on circumstances.

But as far as we are concerned, we live differently; we take things for granted. We are friends with some and enemies to others. And so when circumstances change, we find ourselves in great difficulty. Then we try to carry on with our old relationships and suffer. Krishna does not. He allows life to go its way and he goes with life. Even if Arjuna comes to fight with him, he will not waver. He will not have any difficulty; Krishna can fight against Arjuna with the same enthusiasm with which he fights for him.

For Krishna, friendship and enmity are not something permanent, static; they are fluid. Life is a flux, and so it is difficult to ascertain who is a friend and who is an enemy. Today's friend can turn into an enemy tomorrow; today's enemy can turn into a friend tomorrow. So it is always good to deal with both friends and enemies with an eye on tomorrow. Tomorrow is unpredictable, even the next moment is unpredictable. Everything changes with the changing moment.

Life is always changing; change is its nature. Life is a play of light and shade. Now there is light here and shade there; the next moment this light and shade will be somewhere else. Observe this garden where we are meeting now, from morning through evening, and you will find everything constantly changing; morning turns into evening, day into night, and light into shade. The flower that blooms with the sunrise withers away by sunset.

It is difficult for you to think how Krishna and Arjuna can encounter each other in a fight, but it is just possible. Krishna can very well fight with a friend. In this respect, the Mahabharat is a unique war; it is amazing! Friends are arrayed against friends, relatives against relatives. Arjuna has been Dronacharya's student, and he now aims an arrow at his master. He received so much from Bishma, the eldest of the family, and he is ready to kill him. That way the Mahabharat is a rare war in all history. It says that in life nothing is permanent; everything is changing. Brother is fighting against brother, student is fighting against teacher.

Another remarkable thing about the Mahabharat is that when fighting ends in the evening enemies visit each other's camps, make inquiries about their well-being, exchange pleasantries and even eat together. It is an honest war; there is nothing underhand or dishonest about it. When they fight they fight as true enemies, and when they meet each other they meet without any reservations, without any bitterness in their hearts. There is nothing deceitful in the Mahabharat. The Pandavas don't hesitate to kill Bhishma in the battle, but in the evening they gather together to mourn his death, that they have lost such a valuable man. This is strange.

The Mahabharat proclaims that even enemies can fight in a friendly way. But it is just the opposite today: even as friends we are inimical to each other. There was a time when wars were made in a friendly way, and now even friendship is not friendship; it is just a kind of intimate enmity. Time was when even enemies were friends, and now even friends are enemies.

And this is very significant in the larger context of life. It is worth knowing that when my enemy dies, something in me dies with him. Not only my enemy dies, with his death I too die in some measure. My being has been bound with the being of my enemy, so with his death a part of me dies at the same time. Not only I lose something with the death of my friend, I also lose when my enemy dies. After all, even my enemy is as much part of my life as a friend is. So it is not good to be very inimical to our enemies, because in some deeper sense even enemies are friends. In the same way, friends are also enemies. Why is it so?

As I have been explaining to you these few days, the polarities into which we divide life are polarities only in appearance, only in words and concepts; in reality they are not. There is no polarity at the depth of life; there, all polarities are united, one. North and south, up and down are all united as one.

If we see the basic unity of life, the war between Krishna and Arjuna will be easy to understand. Otherwise it will be very difficult for us to accept. Even those who are thought to be authorities on Krishna have found it difficult to explain this episode. It is difficult because our concepts and beliefs immediately come in the way when we try to comprehend it. We believe that a friend should always remain a friend and an enemy should remain an enemy. We break life into fragments and put the fragments in fixed categories. But it is utterly wrong to do so. Life is fluid like a river, it is always moving. You look at a wave this moment and the next moment it has moved far away. A wave that was before your eyes in the morning will be hundreds of miles away by the evening of the same day.

On the road of life someone walks with you a few steps and then he parts company. All relationships are transient; you cannot say how long anyone is going to be for or against you. Friends turn into enemies and enemies into friends in a split second. So a person who lives his life like a river makes neither friends nor foes; he accepts whatever life brings. If someone comes to him as a friend, he is accepted as a friend, and if another person comes as a foe, he too is accepted. He chooses nothing; he rejects nothing.

To Krishna no one is his friend and no one is his enemy. Time decides; circumstances create both friends and foes. And Krishna has no grievance against anybody. It is amazing that while Krishna is on the side of the Pandavas, his whole army is on the other side—the side of the Kauravas. He divides and distributes himself between the two warring camps, because both of them accept Krishna as their friend.

The chiefs of both camps arrive at Krishna's place at the same time to ask for his support and cooperation in the war that is imminent, and Krishna gives each of them a choice. He tells them, "Since both of you are my friends—and fortunately you come to me at the same time—I offer that I will personally be on one side and my forces will be on the other side. You can choose." It is something incredible.

> Questioner: Krishna could also say that since both of them are his friends he is not going to fight on any side.

He could not say so, because the war of the Mahabharat is going to be such a great and decisive event that Krishna's participation in it is essential. Perhaps the Mahabharat would not be possible without Krishna. Secondly, it would be dishonest of him to tell friends that he would be neutral in the way India is currently neutral, non-aligned in international affairs.

Neutrality has no place in life; it may be an inner feeling, but in day-to-day life neutrality is meaningless. One has to take sides—either this side or that. Of course, one can pretend to be neutral, but pretention is pretention. Krishna could pretend to be neutral, but it would be meaningless. Friends have come to ask for his help, not his neutrality. And Krishna has to say yes or no to their request; neutrality is not an answer. If he says he is neutral, it only means that he is not their friend, that he has nothing to do with them. Neutrality means indifference; neutrality means that one is not concerned with the fate of the war.

Krishna cannot say that he is not concerned with the war; he is really concerned. Although he is a friend to both, he clearly wants the Pandavas to win, because he knows the Pandavas are fighting for righteousness and the Kauravas are against it. But he is friendly to both of them; even the Kauravas look to him as their friend, they have no enmity with him. They respect him, they love him.

By and large, these people are very simple, and their behavior is frank and open. Even their differences and divisions are clear-cut; they don't hide their likes and dislikes. In a domestic war, they divide themselves clearly between the two camps. Issues are well-defined, so they don't take long to decide.

Krishna is not indifferent, apathetic. He is aware that great issues are at stake; he cannot be neutral. He is also aware that both sides look to him as their friend, and he is prepared to give each its share. But he does not treat them equally, because he knows who is just and who is not. And he also knows that the way he will divide his help and cooperation between the two warring camps is going to be a decisive factor in the impending conflict.

So the way he divides himself is extraordinary; it is of immense significance. He tells them that they have two options: he and his army; they can choose either him or his whole army. This division makes things still clearer as far as which side stands for righteousness. It is obvious that no one anxious for victory would choose Krishna without his army. Only he who cares for values and not for victory, who trusts the spiritual force much more than the material one, will choose Krishna alone.

The way the choice is made is also significant. Representatives of the two sides arrive at Krishna's place at the same time to ask for his help in the war. Krishna is lying on his bed. The representative of the Pandavas comes first and takes his place at the foot of his bed. Next comes the representative of the Kauravas, who sits at the head of his bed. Krishna is asleep, but he wakes up with their arrival. The way the two emissaries take their seats is meaningful. Only a man of humility can sit at the feet of the sleeping

Krishna; an arrogant person will sit near his head. Even such small things speak for themselves. Our every act, even a twitch of the nose, reveals us. Actually we do that which we are. It is not accidental that the Kaurava representative sits near his head, and the Pandava sits near his feet. And when Krishna awakens, his eyes fall first on the Pandava and not on his rival. Of course he gives the Pandavas first choice.

This is how humility wins. Jesus has said, "Blessed are the meek, for they shall inherit the earth."

The Pandavas have the first choice. This makes the Kaurava representative anxious, lest his rival get away with the best prize. The army, and not Krishna, is the best prize in the eyes of the Kaurava who believes in physical force. He knows Krishna's army is vast and thinks that whoever has it is going to win the war. Krishna alone will be of no use in a matter like war. But he is immensely pleased when the Pandava representative opts for Krishna and leaves his whole army to be taken by the Kauravas. He thinks the Pandavas' envoy has acted foolishly and their defeat in the war is guaranteed.

Really this choice decides the fate of the war. The Pandavas' choice of Krishna says clearly that they stand for righteousness and religion. Krishna's personal support of the Pandavas becomes the decisive factor in the war of Mahabharat.

As I said, the sitting of the Pandava at Krishna's feet makes the whole difference. I am reminded of a small anecdote in the life of Vivekananda.

Vivekananda is leaving India for America. He goes to Mother Sharada, the wife of his Master, Ramakrishna, for her blessing. Ramakrishna had died, leaving Sharada behind him. So Vivekananda goes to her and says, "I am leaving for America, and I seek your blessing."

Sharada queries, "What are you going to do in America?"

Vivekananda says, "I will spread the message of *dharma* in that country."

Sharada, who is in her kitchen, directs the young monk to pass her a knife meant for cutting vegetables. Vivekananda hands the knife to her. Then Sharada says, "You have my blessings." But Vivekananda wants to know if there was any connection between her asking for the knife and her blessings to him. Sharada says, "I wanted to know the way you handle the knife while passing it to me."

Ordinarily, anyone would do it indifferently, without awareness. He will hold the handle of the knife in his hand and pass it with the blade directed toward the one who asks for it. But Vivekananda has the blade of the knife in his hand and its handle is directed toward his master's wife. Sharada says to Vivekananda, "Now I think you are worthy of carrying the message of *dharma* to America."

If you were in Vivekananda's place, you would have taken the handle in your hand, because that is the usual way. Ordinarily, no one would do it any differently, but Vivekananda does it very differently. And it is not accidental. Vivekananda is not expected to be prepared for it. It is not written in any book that, "When Vivekananda will go to Sharada for her blessings she will ask him to pass her a knife." No scripture can say it, and a person like Sharada is unpredictable. Who could know that she was going to test Vivekananda's awareness in this way? Is this a way of knowing a person's religiousness? But Sharada says, "I bless you, Vivekananda, because you have a religious mind."

In the same way the Pandavas, by sitting at the feet of Krishna, proclaim that righteousness is on their side. They have the courage to sit at Krishna's feet. And by choosing Krishna they further proclaim that they would rather risk defeat than give up righteousness, they would prefer defeat to victory rather than go with unrighteousness. And he alone can go with righteousness who has the courage to risk defeat.

As I said earlier, only one who is ready to go through pain and suffering can go with God. Similarly one who is ready to go down fighting is worthy of religion. One who wants victory at any cost is bound to land in irreligion. Irreligion is forever in search of the easy way, the shortcut, while the road to religion is long and hard. Unrighteous ways bring easy success; this is the reason most people adopt them. The ways of righteousness are long and arduous. Going with righteousness can lead to defeat; walking with religion can even lead to disaster.

It is significant that one who is prepared to go with religion even at the cost of defeat and disaster, can never be defeated. But the readiness for defeat is necessary. The road to irreligion is tempting, because it gives you an assurance of cheap success. Its attraction lies in its promises, and because of it people take up corrupt ways. Evil is a cunning persuader; it says, "If you want success, never take the path of righteousness; it is an impossible path. My path guarantees effortless, easy success. You begin and you win." But the irony is that nobody ever wins through evil; evil ultimately leads to utter ruin. On the contrary, righteousness is a challenge; you have to be prepared for defeat. But its glory is that if you choose it with this awareness, you will never be defeated.

This is the paradox of life. It is truth that wins—*Satyameva Jayate.*

> *Questioner: You explained to us this saying of Jesus: "Blessed are the meek, for they shall inherit the earth." There is another saying of Jesus: "Blessed are the pure in heart, for theirs is the kingdom of heaven." Can you say somethng about it?*

Yes, there is another saying of Jesus: "Blessed are the pure in heart, for theirs is the kingdom of heaven." But there is a small difference between the two sayings: "Blessed are the meek for they shall inherit the earth," and "Blessed are the pure for theirs is the kingdom of heaven." In fact, humility is the beginning and purity is the end, the attainment.

To be humble is to be on the first leg of the journey to purity. The humble has yet to be on the first leg of the journey to purity. The humble has yet to be pure; he is on his way to it. One cannot be pure without being humble, because there is no greater impurity than ego. One who is full of ego can never be pure, but one who drops his ego, who is humble, who is surrendered, is on the path that leads to purity. So humility is not enough; it only sets you on the road to purity that is innocence.

For example, a man is standing on the bank of a river. Say he is standing in the water on the river and a huge expanse of water is flowing before him, and he is thirsty. But unless he bends and reaches for the water his thirst cannot be quenched. If he is not ready to bend he will remain thirsty, though he is surrounded on all sides by water.

Then it is not the river but his ego that is responsible for his misery. If he only bends, all the water will be his.

So humility comes first; it is the beginning of innocence; it is the door. Humility purifies, because it negates everything that creates impurity. A humble person cannot have ego, he cannot be greedy, he cannot be angry, he cannot be sexual. To be greedy, sexual and angry, one needs to be aggressive; aggression is the prerequisite. So a humble person will be forgiving and generous; he will share his happiness, everything with others. He cannot be ambitious and dominating; he cannot be acquisitive, he cannot hoard. And a humble man will give up all self-aggrandizement, instead, he will sink into anonymity.

And when humility comes to completion, innocence is complete. It is this state that Jesus is talking about when he says, "Blessed are the pure in heart, for they shall inherit the kingdom of God."

There is yet another statement of Jesus which is similar. He says, "Blessed are the poor in spirit." It is a strange saying: "poor in spirit", but it includes both humility and purity. One is so poor, so empty within that there is no space left for any impurity to exist. To be arrogant, to be egoistic, one needs to have something—money, power, prestige. And to be impure one needs things like avarice, anger, hate, and violence. It is significant that while anger is something, non-anger is just the absence of anger. Violence is something; non-violence is just its absence. If a person is utterly empty of everything—greed, hate, violence, money, and fame—he is really poor in spirit, and only such a person is really rich and affluent. And he will, as Jesus says, "inherit the kingdom of heaven". The poorest is the richest; he has everything worth having.

In this context there is yet another very significant saying of Jesus. He says, "Seek ye first the kingdom of God, and all else shall be added unto you." But when someone asks him how he can find the kingdom of God Jesus says, "Be humble and pure, poor and empty, and the kingdom of God is yours. After realizing the kingdom of God all else shall be added unto you." A strange condition: if you lose everything, you will gain everything. And if you save anything, you will lose everything. Those who are ready to lose themselves will gain everything, and those who will save themselves will lose everything.

This, according to me, is the meaning of sannyas: one who is ready to lose everything becomes heir to everything that is worth gaining.

Questioner: Why should one think of gaining after losing everything?

It is not a question of your thinking; it is so. If you think of losing, you cannot lose. If you try to be humble in order to gain the kingdom of God, you cannot be humble.

What Jesus says is not a guarantee to you, it is just a statement of what happens. If someone says that he is ready to give up everything so that he gains everything, he cannot give up really. The last part of the statement is not an assurance, it is a consequence that follows renunciation. It has been found that those who give up everything become their own masters, and that is everything there is to gain. And it is also true that those who desire to gain everything cannot give up a thing.

> *Questioner: What you say is possible only in a state of enlightenment, and we find everything of that enlightenment in you. You are utterly humble, but when you come out as a relentless critic, we are assailed by doubt and confusion*

I am not going to do anything to destroy your doubt and confusion. A person who imposes humility on himself, who cultivates and practices humility, will always seem to be humble. But the humility that comes naturally, that is not imposed, cultivated, can be bold enough to be impolite if need be. Only a humble person can have the courage to be utterly impolite; only a man of love can afford to be hard-hitting if need be.

It is always possible that I will appear to be contradictory in many ways. That is what I have been telling you about Krishna—that he is a bundle of contradictions. There are any number of contradictions in me, and you will encounter them often. I accept the whole of life, and that is my humility. If sometimes I feel like being harsh, I don't suppress it, I become harsh. I am not; there is no one to suppress anything. Similarly when I am humble, I am just humble. I don't come in the way of anything. I allow whatever is there to be and to express itself as it is. There is no effort on my part to become anything— humble or arrogant. Therefore you will continue to be in confusion regarding me; it is not going to end.

Who, as you conceive it, is enlightened? Will you not accept Krishna as enlightened? But Krishna confuses you as much as I do. At times he seems to be departing from his enlightenment. When he takes up arms to fight in the battle of Kurkshetra, it seems he has lost his steadiness, his wisdom. But what is our concept of enlightenment, of wisdom that is unshake-able? Does it mean that an enlightened person acts the way we think to be the right way? Does it mean that his wisdom has been steadied in the way we think it should be?

No, steadfast wisdom does not mean wisdom that is inert and dead. It only means that one who has become enlightened, who has attained to the highest intelligence and wisdom allows this wisdom to act as it chooses. He is just a vehicle; he does not do a thing on his own. Such a person owns nothing, neither merit or demerit, neither virtue nor vice, neither respect nor disrespect. He does not say that what he does is right or wrong; he neither brags nor repents; now he does not look back on the past. He dies to every passing moment, and he lives in the moment at hand. He is not a doer; he just allows that which is, to happen. There is no one about him to oversee his spontaneity, to come in its way or decide for it. Now he is utterly choiceless.

So it is possible that sometimes I may appear to you to be harsh; I cannot help it. When I am harsh I am harsh, and when I am soft I am so. I have al-together ceased to be anything on my own; I don't insist any more that I should be this, that I should not be that.

This is what I call steady wisdom.

ELEVENTH DISCOURSE
EVENING, SEPTEMBER 30, 1970
MANALI, INDIA

DRAUPADI: A RARE WOMAN

Questioner: Draupadi, who is also known as Krishnaa, has been subjected to harsh criticism and detraction, but Krishna loves her tremendously. Please say something about her in the context of our own time.

s among men Krishna baffles our understanding, so does Draupadi among women. And how the critics look at Draupadi says more about the critics themselves than about Draupadi. What we see in others is only a reflection; others only serve as mirrors to us. We see in others only that which we want to see; in fact, we see what we are. We do nothing but project ourselves on the world.

It is difficult to understand Draupadi. But our difficulty does not come from this great woman, it really emanates from us. Our ideas and beliefs, our desires and hopes come in our way of understanding Draupadi.

To love five men together, to play wife to them at the same time is a great and arduous task. This needs to be understood rightly. Love does not have much to do with persons; it is a state of mind. And love that is confined to a single person is a poor love. Let us go into this question of love in depth.

We all insist that one's love should be confined to a single person—a man or a woman. If someone loves you, you want that he should love you and you alone, that he not share his love with another person. You would like to possess that person, to monopolize him or her. We not only want to possess things, we also want to possess men and women. And if we had our way we would possess even the sun and the moon and the stars. So we crave to monopolize love. Because we do not know what love is, we are prone to think that if it is shared with many it will disperse and dwindle and die. But the truth is that the more love is shared, the more it grows. And when we try to restrict it, to control it—which is utterly unnatural and arbitrary—it dries up and eventually dies.

I am reminded of a beautiful story.

A Buddhist nun had a statue of Buddha made of sandalwood. She loved the statue and always kept it with her. Being a nun she traveled from place to place, where she mostly stayed in Buddhist temples and monasteries. And wherever she lived she worshipped her own statue of Buddha.

Once she happened to be a guest at the famous temple of a thousand Buddhas. This temple was known for its thousand statues of Buddha; it was filled with statues and statues. The nun, as usual, sat for her evening worship, and she burned incense before her statue of Buddha. But with the passing breeze the perfume of the incense strayed to other statues of Buddhas which filled that temple.

The nun was distressed to see that while her own Buddha was deprived of the perfume, others had it in plenty. So she devised a funnel through which the smoke would ascend to her statue only. But this device, although successful, blackened the face of her

Buddha and made it especially ugly. Of course the nun was exceedingly miserable, because it was a rare statue of sandalwood, and she loved it. She went to the chief priest of the temple and said, "My statue of Buddha has been ruined. What am I to do?"

The priest said, "Such an accident, such an ugliness is bound to happen whenever someone tries to block the movement of truth and possess it for oneself. Truth by its nature has to be everywhere, it cannot be personalized and possessed."

Up to now, mankind has thought of love in terms of petty relationship—relationship between two persons. We have yet to know love that is a state of mind, and not just relationship. And this is what comes in our way of understanding Draupadi.

If I am loving, if love is the state of my being, then it is not possible to confine my love to a single person, or even a few persons. When love enters my life and becomes my nature, then I am capable of loving any number of people. Then it is not even a question of one or many; then I am loving, and my love reaches everywhere. If I am loving to one and unloving to all others, even my love for the one will wither away. It is impossible to be loving to one and unloving to the rest. If someone is loving just for an hour every day and remains unloving for the rest of the time, his lovelessness will eventually smother his small love and turn his life into a wasteland of hate and hostility.

It is unfortunate that people all around the world are trying to capture love and keep it caged in their relationships. But it is not possible to make a captive of love; the moment you try to capture it, it ceases to be love. Love is like air; you cannot hold it in your fist. It is possible to have a little air on your open palm, but if you try to enclose it in your fist, the air escapes. It is a paradox of life that when you try to imprison love, to put it in bondage, love degenerates and dies. And we have all killed love in our foolish attempts to possess it. Really we don't know what love is.

We find it hard to understand how Draupadi could love five persons together. Not only we, even the five Pandava brothers had difficulty in understanding Draupadi. The trouble is understandable; even the Pandavas thought that Draupadi was more loving to one of them. Four of them believed that she favored Arjuna in particular, and they felt envious of him. So they had a kind of division of her time and attention. When one of the Pandava brothers was with her, others were debarred from visiting her.

Like us, they believed that it is impossible for someone to love more than one person at a time. We cannot think of love as anything different from a relationship between two persons—a man and a woman. We cannot conceive that love is a state of being; it is not directed to individuals. Love, like air, sunshine and rain, is available to all without any distinctions.

We have our own ideas of what love is and should be, and that is why we misunderstand Draupadi. Despite our best efforts to understand her rightly, there is a lurking suspicion in our minds that there is an element of prostitution in Draupadi: our very definition of a *sati*, a faithful and loyal wife, turns Draupadi into a prostitute.

It is amazing that the tradition of this country respects Draupadi as one of the five most virtuous women of the past. The people who included her among the five great women of history must have been extraordinarily intelligent. The fact that she was the common wife of five Pandavas was known to them, and that is what makes their evaluation of Draupadi tremendously significant. For them it did not matter whether love was confined to one or many; the real question was whether or not one had love. They knew that if really there was love, it could flow endlessly in any number of channels; it could not be controlled and manipulated. It was symbolic to say that Draupadi had five husbands; it meant that one could love five, fifty, five hundred thousand people at the same time. There is no end to love's power and capacity.

The day really loving people will walk on this earth, the personal ownership of love rampant today in the form of marriages, families and groups, will disappear. It will not mean that the love relationship between two human beings will be prohibited and declared to be sinful—that would be going to the other extreme of stupidity. No, everybody will be free to be himself, and to function within his limits and no one will impose his will and ideas on others. Love and freedom will go together.

Draupadi's love is riverlike, overflowing. She does not deny her love even for a moment. Her marriage to the Pandava brothers is an extraordinary event—it came about almost playfully. The Pandavas came home with Draupadi, who they had won in a contest. They told their mother they had brought a very precious thing with them. Kunti, their mother, without asking what the precious object was, said, "If it is precious then share it together."

The Pandava brothers had no idea that their mother would say this; they just wanted to tease her. But now they had to do their mother's bidding; they made Draupadi their common wife. And she accepted it without complaint. It was possible because of her infinite love. She had so much that she loved all her husbands profoundly, yet never felt any shortage of love in her heart. She had no difficulty whatsoever in playing her role as their common beloved, and she never discriminated between them.

Draupadi is certainly a unique woman. Women, in general, are very jealous; they really live in jealousy. If one wants to characterize man and woman, he can say that while ego is the chief characteristic of man, jealousy is the chief characteristic of woman. Man lives by ego and woman by jealousy. Really jealousy is the passive form of ego, and ego is the active form of jealousy. But here is a woman who rose above jealousy and pettiness; she loved the Pandavas without any reservations. In many ways Draupadi towered over her husbands who were very jealous of one another on account of her love. They remained in constant psychological conflict with each other, while Draupadi went through this complex relationship with perfect ease and equanimity.

We are to blame for our failure to understand Draupadi. We think that love is a relationship between two persons, which it is not. And because of this misconception we have to go through all kinds of torment and misery in life. Love is a flower which once in a while blooms without any cause or purpose. It can happen to anyone who is open. And love accepts no bonds, no constraints on its freedom. But because society has fettered love in many ways we do everything to smother it, to escape it. Thus love has become so scarce, and we have to go without it. We live a loveless life.

We are a strange people; we can go without love, but we cannot love someone without possessing him or her. We can very well starve ourselves of love, but we cannot tolerate that the person I love should share his or her love with anybody else. To deprive others of love we can easily give up our own share of it. We don't know how terribly we suffer because of our ego and jealousy.

It is good to know that Draupadi is not a solitary case of this kind; she may be the last in a long line. The society that preceded Draupadi was matriarchal; perhaps Draupadi is the last vestige of that disintegrating social order. In a matriarchial society the mother was the head of the family and descent was reckoned through the female line. In a matriarchy a woman did not belong to any man; no man could possess her. A kind of polyandry was in vogue for a long time, and Draupadi seems to be the last of it. Today there are only a few primitive tribes who practice polyandry. That is why the society of her times accepted Draupadi and her marriage and did not raise any objections. If it was wrong, Kunti would have changed her instructions to her sons, but she did not. If there was anything immoral in polyandry even the Pandava brothers would have asked their mother to change her order. But nothing of the kind happened, because it was acceptable to the existing society.

It happens that a custom that is perfectly moral in one society appears completely immoral to another. Mohammed had nine wives, and his Koran allows every Mohammedan man to have four wives. In the context of modern societies, polygamy and polyandry are considered highly immoral. And the prophet of Islam had nine wives. When he had his first marriage he was twenty-four years old, while his wife was forty.

But the society in which Mohammed was born was very different from ours and its circumstances were such that polygamy became both necessary and moral. They were warring tribes who constantly fought among themselves. Consequently they were always short of male members—many of whom were killed in fighting—while the number of their women went on growing. Out of four persons, three were women. So Mohammed ordained that each man should have four wives. If it was not done, then three out of four women would have been forced to live a loveless life or take to prostitution. That would have been really immoral.

So polygamy became a necessity and it had a moral aura about it. And to set a bold example, Mohammed himself took nine women as his wives, and permitted each of his male followers to have four. No one in Arabia objected to it; there was nothing immoral about it.

The society in which the Mahabharat happened was in the last stages of matriarchy, and therefore polyandry was accepted. But that society is long dead and with it polygamy and polyandry are now things of the past. They have no relevance in a society where the numbers of men and women are in equal proportion. When this balance is disturbed for some reason, customs like polygamy and polyandry appear on the scene. So there was nothing immoral about Draupadi.

Even today I say that Draupadi was not an ordinary woman; she was unique and rare. The woman who loved five men together and loved them equally and who lived on their love could not be an ordinary woman. She was tremendously loving and it was indeed a great thing. We fail to understand her because of our narrow idea of love.

> Questioner: You say that persons like Krishna don't make friends nor do they make foes. Then how is it that he as a king comes running down to the gate of his palace to receive Sudama, his poor old friend of childhood days and gives him all the wealth of the world in return for a handful of rice that his poor friend has brought as his present to him? Please shed some light on this special friendship between Krishna and Sudama.

It is not a special kind of friendship, it is just a friendship. Here too, our ideas come in the way of our understanding. It seems to us that giving away all the wealth of the world in return for a handful of rice is too much. We fail to see that it is more difficult for poor Sudama to bring a handful of rice as a present for his friend, than it is for Krishna to give all the wealth of the world to Sudama. Sudama is so utterly poor, a beggar, that even a handful of rice is too much. Therefore his gift is more important than Krishna's; he is the real giver, not Krishna.

But we see it differently; we look at the quantity and not the quality of the gift. We are not aware how difficult it was for a beggar like Sudama to collect a handful of rice; it is not that difficult for Krishna to give away lots of wealth, he is a king. He does not do a special favor to Sudama, he only responds to his friend's gift; and I think Krishna is not satisfied with his own gift to Sudama. Sudama's gift is rare; he is destitute. In my eyes Sudama shines as a greater friend than Krishna.

I did say that Krishna does not make friends or foes, but it does not mean that he is against friendship. If someone advances the hand of friendship to him, he responds to it with greater love and friendship. He is like a valley which echoes your one call seven times. A valley is not waiting for your call, nor is it committed to respond to you, but it is its nature to return your call seven times. What Krishna does stems from his nature; he is just responding to Sudama's love, which is extraordinary.

It is significant that Sudama comes to Krishna not for any favor, but just to express his friendship, his love to him, and even as a poor man he brings a gift for his old friend. Usually a poor person wants to receive something, he rarely gives anything. Here Sudama comes with a gift and not for a gift; he does not go to Krishna's palace as a beggar. And when a poor man gives his gift, his affluence of heart is incomparable. In the same way, a rich man is expected to give something to charity. But when the contrary happens, when the rich man chooses to beg, as it happened with Buddha—a king turned beggar is again something extraordinary.

If you consider Buddha and Sudama together you will know the significance. Sudama has nothing, and yet he gives; Buddha has everything, and yet he begs. These two events are extraordinary, unearthly. Ordinarily a poor man begs and a rich man gives; there is nothing special about it. But when they reverse their roles, it has immense significance. Sudama is as extraordinary as Buddha; both are rare persons. Poor Sudama bringing a gift to Krishna, who is a king, is what makes the event great. But this is love's way; it does not bother whether you have too much or too little, it goes on giving. Love will never accept that you have too much.

Let us understand this aspect of love, which does not accept the idea that anyone has so much he does not need more. Love goes on giving and it will never say it has given you enough. There is no end to love's bounty. Love goes on pouring its gifts and yet it feels shy that it is insufficient. If you tell a woman that she has done a lot for her child, if she is a nurse, she will thankfully acknowledge your compliments. But if she is a mother she will protest saying, "I could do only a little; a lot remains to be done." A nurse is aware of what she has done; a mother is aware of what she has yet to do. And if a mother brags about her sacrifices for her child, she is a nurse and not a mother. Love is always aware that a lot more remains to be done.

Sudama knows that Krishna lacks nothing; he is a king. Yet he is anxious to bring a gift to him. When he was leaving his home, his wife said, "Your friend happens to be a king, don't forget to bring a substantial gift from him." But he comes with a gift, and does not ask for anything.

When Sudama meets Krishna he feels very hesitant about his gift; he hides the packet of a handful of rice from his friend. That is the way of love; even if it gives a lot it never thinks it is enough. Love does not give with fanfare as ordinary donors do; it likes to give anonymously. So Sudama hesitates, he hides his gift from Krishna. He is hesitant not just because it is a poor gift of rice; he would have hesitated even if he had rare diamonds. Love does not proclaim its gift; proclamation is the way of the ego.

So Sudama is hesitant and afraid; it is something rare. And what is more amusing is that immediately on seeing him Krishna begins to inquire what gift he has brought. Krishna knows that love always comes to give and not to take. And he also is aware that the ways of love are shy and secretive; he asks for his presents over and over again. And ultimately he succeeds in snatching his gift from his old friend. And what is more amazing, Krishna immediately begins to eat the raw rice that he finds in the packet.

There is nothing special about it; it is love's way. It is because love has become so scarce for us that we are so surprised about it.

> Questioner: It is said that Krishna gave Sudama so much that it wiped out his life-long poverty. But the same Krishna does nothing to wipe out the poverty of the society in which he lives. It is understandable if Mahavira and Buddha don't pay any attention to this problem, which is thought to be a mundane problem, but how is it that a man of such broad vision as Krishna ignores it? It is ironic that religious people don't give a thought to the problem of the poor. Karl Marx, who thought a lot about it, is not a religious person. You are essentially a man of spiritualism and

*religion. We would like to know if
you are going to do something about
it?*

This question has been raised often enough. Buddha,
Krishna, Mahavira, Jesus, Mohammed, all can be accused of ignoring the problem of poverty which is so
widespread. But there are reasons for it. It was not
possible for them to think of this problem, because
the social conditions in which they lived did not war-
rant such thinking. We think as conditions demand.
Marx thought of it because an industrial revolution
had taken place in the West. Before the industrial
revolution nothing could have been done to change
the economic conditions of society, even to make a
dent on its poverty. It is important to understand.

In the world preceding the industrial revolution, the only instrument of production in the hands
of man was his manual labor. And what he produced
with his hands was hardly enough to provide him
with a decent meal; he could just somehow manage
to keep his body together. Such a society was doomed
to remain poor; there was no way to eliminate poverty. And the question of equitable distribution of
production did arise; they had nothing much in the
form of wealth to distribute among themselves. So
along with poverty, inequality was inevitable. And I
am going to go into it.

Firstly, it was not possible in the feudal society existing before the coming of industrialization to
wipe out poverty, because it did not have the necessary wealth. It was possible of course to eliminate a
handful of people who were rich; they could have
been brought down to the same level as the poor. If
there was one rich person out of a thousand people,
that person could have been reduced to the ranks of
the poor, but it would not have made any difference

whatsoever to the state of their poverty. Human labor alone could never produce so much that it could raise society above the poverty line. One could think of ending poverty only after machines took the place of human labor in producing wealth. Now a single machine could produce in a day as much as a hundred thousand men could produce with their hands. Only then production of wealth on a large scale became possible and we could conceive that the poor need not remain poor any longer. Now there was no historic need for poverty to exist.

So it was only after the Industrial Revolution that Marx came on the scene. The industrialization of society enabled him to conceive of equality. And if there was a Krishna in the place of Marx he would have thought with greater clarity than Marx did. But Krishna happened long before the Industrial Revolution. One can even ask Marx why he did not come before industrialization.

It is not that in the past man lacked the capacity to think, or that he had no idea of ending poverty. Buddha had it; Mahavira had it. They had their own way of dealing with the problem of poverty. Both Mahavira and Buddha were kings and they voluntarily became poor. They voluntarily renounced their wealth and joined the huge ranks of the poor. Mahavira distributed all his wealth among the poor before he took up sannyas. But poverty remained, it could not be eliminated; their renunciation was nothing more than a moral support to the poor. Mahavira's own psychological pain was gone, but the poverty of the masses continued.

It is for this reason that all the thinkers of the past put so much emphasis on non-acquisition, non-possession. They repeatedly said, "Don't hoard wealth." They could not have asked people not to be poor—that was just unthinkable given the social conditions of their days, but they did ask people not to amass wealth, not to be rich. They could not have done anything more to console the poor than ask the rich not to hoard and flaunt their wealth. All the religions of the past stood for renunciation and non-possession of wealth. They stood for sharing all one had with the less fortunate members of society.

But Krishna, Mahavira and Buddha also knew that non-acquisition and charity were not going to remove poverty from the society. It is like trying to sweeten the water of the ocean with a spoonful of sugar. A Mahavira or a Buddha can give away all they have, but it will not be more than a spoonful of sugar in the vast ocean of poverty. It does not make any difference.

Sages of the past did not think of eradicating poverty because it was not possible under the given conditions.

You also want to know why men like Krishna did not do anything to remove inequality. If it was not possible to abolish poverty, at least inequality should have been abolished. Why did not they give a thought to this problem?

There are reasons why no thought was given to the problem of inequality in society. We have to understand it carefully. The thought of removing inequality arises only when a measure of equality begins to surface in a given society. That there is inequality in the society, this awareness comes only when the society ceases to remain divided between distinct classes and instead is divided into different strata of property-holders. For instance, the wife of a poor scavenger will not feel any envy if she comes across a queen wearing a necklace of precious diamonds; the distance between the two is so vast that the poor woman cannot ever dream of competing with the queen. But the same woman will burn with envy if another woman of her own community visits her with a necklace of ordinary stones. Why? Because she belongs to the same class; the disparity between them is very small and there is a possibility to compete with the other.

As long as society was divided into two distinct classes—one consisting of the huge masses of the poor and the other of a handful of super-rich, and the gap between the two was unimaginably vast—there was no way to think of bringing about equality between the rich and the poor. It was just unthinkable that the gap could ever be bridged. So the status quo had to be accepted.

But with the advent of the industrial revolution, gaps began to be bridged and in the place of classes various strata began to be formed. Between the rich at the top and the poor at the bottom, middle strata of income groups came into existence. Between a Rockefeller at the top and a manual laborer at the bottom, there is now a whole army of middle-class people like managers and supervisors with varying scales of income. Society now is not divided into two clearcut classes of the rich and the poor, but into many strata of income groups. The industrial society is not like a two-storied house, it is like a long ladder with many rungs all joined with one another. And because of it every member of society can think of being equal with the one above him.

The idea of equality comes into being when a society is divided not into two classes but into various income groups, all joined with one another like the rungs of a ladder. Unless this happens, the thought of equality cannot arise.

This does not mean that Mahavira, Buddha and Krishna did not talk of equality. They did. They talked of the kind of equality that was possible in their times. It was spiritual equality that they preached throughout their lives. They said that the soul, the spirit of every human being was the same; spiritually all human beings were equal. They could not have said that with respect to external conditions of life like property, houses and clothes, all human beings were equal. Such equality was impossible then. Of course it is quite possible in our time.

But there are things which we cannot think of even today, and the coming generations will surely accuse us for our failure to do so. I will explain it to you with the help of an illustration:

Today a person has to work seven hours each day in a field or factory or office so that he can earn his bread. And we think this is how it should be. But the coming generations will wonder why no one amongst us considered that it is immoral to compel a person to work for a piece of bread. The time is not far away when all production will happen through automation and man will be freed from the drudgery of labor. Then it will not be at all necessary to work to earn one's bread. Human labor will cease to have the value which it has had down the ages. The necessities of life will be available to all without having to work for them. How to spend one's leisure time will be a problem then, not employment. Perhaps those who will demand work will be entitled to less amenities of life than those who agree to go without work. It will look odd if someone insists on having both—work and the good things of life together.

Already economists of America are grappling with a kind of futurist problem, when complete automation of production will make human labor superfluous and unnecessary. Just twenty-five to thirty years from now a situation will arise when people not doing any work will be paid more than those who work. After automation, a single person will operate a huge automobile factory, which today needs a hundred thousand people to operate it. Then people will begin to ask for work because to live without work will be harder than hard work itself. Besides, people will have to be paid by the powers-that-be so that they are enabled to buy cars and other things produced by automatic factories. These are the futurist problems that the economists are grappling with right today.

For sure, someone in the future is going to ask why men like Krishna, Buddha and Karl Marx did not say it is immoral and inhuman to compel people to work for the basic necessities of life. If people were hungry they should have been provided with adequate food and not made to work seven hours every day. But right now it is difficult to conceive it as a moral or social problem. Today sometimes even people with employment have to go without bread, so the question of getting bread without work does not arise.

Ideas and thoughts are intimately connected with the realities of time and space. The pain of inequality was never felt in the times of Krishna. Even the ache of poverty was not felt the way it is felt today. That is why the slogan of equality is not heard in the days of Krishna. It is interesting to know that a thinker like Plato, who was a pioneer of equality, could not think that slavery should be abolished. He believed that slavery was going to live, because slavery was so common in Greece in those days. Plato thought equality could not exist without the slaves.

Questioner: Does it mean that an elite class will always be there?

An elite group has always been there, and it is going to be forever there. Forms change, but it makes no difference. The elite will always dominate the society. Sometimes it dominates in the form of emperors and kings, sometimes as messiahs and saints, and then as pioneers and leaders. I don't foresee a future when elites will disappear. In fact, so long as a few elites are there amongst us they will continue to be dominant over the rest of the society. The difference is that in the past we called them kings and emperors and now we call them presidents and prime ministers. In the past they came as incarnations and prophets and now they appear as mahatmas and leaders. Names don't matter, but elitism is going to live with us.

As long as human society does not evolve so that everyone attains to the same level of growth in every direction of life, there is no escape from elitism. And I don't think such a development is ever going to happen. And it will be a stupid and lackluster society where everyone is at the same level of growth physically and mentally. It will be terribly boring. A chosen few will always be there. A skilled sitar player will outshine one less skilled than he; there is no way to prevent it. An accomplished dancer will dominate the less accomplished ones. It can't be helped. An Einstein is bound to overshadow all those who cannot even put two and two together. In any given situation someone or other is bound to become elite, predominant.

It is true that from time to time we get bored with the old elites and replace them with new ones. It is just natural. Elites of a particular kind also cease to be relevant in a changing world, and they have to be replaced by another variety. Russia made such a change through a bloody revolution; it liquidated all its old elitist classes. But soon a new class came into being in Russia and it is as dominant as the previous one. The truth is that the new class in Russia is much more domineering than any in the past. And the same story is being repeated in China.

So long as the disparity in intelligence, talent and ability remains between man and man, it is impossible to get rid of domination by the chosen few. And it is also impossible that there will not be those who want to be dominated by them: there will always be people wanting to be dominated by the elites. The elite and non-elite will continue to need each other. That is how the story goes on: one kind of elitism is replaced by another, and because we accept the new one the things of the past seem to be stupid.

In the time of Krishna, coexistence of poverty and richness was acceptable. The poor were content with being poor, and therefore the rich did not feel guilty about their richness. The feeling of guilt can arise only if the poor protest against the existence of the rich. In the absence of such a protest the rich is at ease with his riches; he suffers no qualms of conscience. And for this reason no one thinks of changing the status quo. Now we say there should be equality between rich and poor, but we say so not because we are intellectually ahead of Krishna's time, but because social conditions have undergone a great change.

But even today no one says there should be equality of intelligence: the less intelligent does not demand equality with the more intelligent person. But fifty years from now a slogan like that will be heard, because in fifty years' time science will be able to effectively manipulate man's intelligence. Then every child will say that he is not going to remain stupid, he is as much entitled to have enough intelligence as everyone else. But he cannot say so right now, because the possibility is not yet there.

Now science has penetrated into the genes of man, the basic unit of heredity which carries with it a complete program for man's physical and mental growth from A to Z. Science has gone a long way in exploring the possibilities of the gene and already it is on the threshhold of a breakthrough. The science of genetics can tell the IQ of a child from the sperm and egg of his parents that go into his making. Not only that, soon genes will be manipulated in a manner that children will be assured of a good standard of physical and mental health and longevity even before they are born. Now you go to the market and buy flower seeds in beautiful packages that carry on their covers pictures of the complete flowers those seeds will produce in your garden. Similarly within fifty years human seeds will be available in packages that picture the children who may be born from those seeds. The packages will furnish detailed information about the form and color, height and health, IQ and longevity of each future child. These things will be guaranteed in a way. These things are now quite possible; they were unthinkable only a few decades ago.

When the genetic revolution unfolds itself fully, we will again ask why Krishna did not think of equality of intelligence. It was not possible; there was no way to think of it then.

> Questioner: I have again a small question in regard to Sudama. When Sudama came to Krishna, he was given all the wealth of the world as a gift. How is it that Krishna did not think of helping his indigent friend earlier?

In this world you have to search for and find everything you need; nothing is given gratis. God is everywhere, and it is not that he is not aware of your sufferings. But you have turned your back on him— and you are free to do so. This much freedom you have that you can choose him or deny him. Now if you turn your face to God and find him, can you complain why he did not seek you before you sought and found him? If you complain, God will say that it would be a trespass on your freedom if he forced himself on you without your asking.

Freedom means that I am entitled to find what I seek and not that which I don't seek. And remember, nothing in this world is had without seeking. Seeking is a must, and it is part of your freedom.

Sudama's difficult material condition is not the question; his freedom is the real question. Sudama could refuse Krishna's generosity. And I believe Sudama would have refused if Krishna had offered to help him on his own. It is not necessary that Sudama should accept. And there is also the question of Sudama's preparations to deserve it.

All these events have deep psychological meanings. We can find what we seek only after we have done everything to search for it. Without seeking and searching you cannot find even something that is lying at arm's length. Seeking is the door to finding. The mere poverty of Sudama won't do; he is not alone, there are many who are as poor. And it makes no difference to Krishna whether Sudama is poor or someone else is poor; what makes a difference is that Sudama, in spite of his poverty, came to him to give and not to take. This man deserves to be rich. It is his capacity to give that brings about the transformation in his fortune.

Everyone is responsible for what he is. And everyone has to begin his journey of transformation as an individual, on his own. No one else can walk for him. And once he is started on his journey, all the forces in existence come rushing to his aid. If a person chooses to be poor, he will receive every help from existence; he will find around him everything that is necessary to make him poor. If another person chooses to be ignorant, existence will cooperate fully with him, so that he remains ignorant. And if somebody else decides for knowledge, all the avenues of knowledge will become available to him.

In this world we only find that which we seek. Our own desires and longing and prayers come back to us, just like our own sounds are echoed back by the hills and valleys. If you explore the whole psyche of a poor man, you will be surprised to find he has done everything necessary to remain poor; poverty is his choice. Outwardly he may complain against his condition of poverty, but inwardly he is not only reconciled to it, he is at ease with it. If by chance his poverty disappears he will begin to miss it. Similarly an ignoramus is content with his ignorance, and he does everything to protect it. If you try to remove his ignorance he will not only resent it, he will defend it with all his strength.

No, we find what we seek. Sudama finds Krishna because he goes seeking him. It is not proper that Krishna should go to him unasked; Krishna of course will wait for him. Waiting on the part of Krishna is essential. It is not that God is not coming to you because he is unhappy with you, but it is necessary that you should go to him. And the day you go to him and meet him, you will know he was waiting long for you to come, he was standing at his gate to receive you, but it was you who were not willing to see him.

> Questioner: In an earlier question on Draupadi it was said that Krishna had great love for her. Please say something about Krishna's love for Draupadi.

Draupadi fully deserves Krishna's love. Krishna's love is available to all, but Draupadi deserves it in a special way. The truth is that you come to have what you deserve. If you go to the ocean for water, it will give you only as much as your container can hold. The ocean is vast, but how much water you have depends on the size of your container. And the ocean does not refuse; everyone can take according to his capacity.

Draupadi's capacity to receive love is tremendous, and she received abundant love from Krishna. And the love between them was so profound, so platonic that it could exist without any longing for physical intimacy. That is why Krishna's love and help has always been at the disposal of this extraordinary woman. Krishna does much more for her than he does for anyone else. I told you earlier

that when she was being disrobed by the Kauravas,
Krishna came rushing to her rescue.

There is a kind of love that is articulate,
vocal, and there is another kind of love that is in-
articulate, silent. And remember, the love that is
vocal is never deep; it is superficial, shallow. Words
don't have much depth; silence is most profound. So
is silent love. And Draupadi's love is silent and profound. It is discernible on many occasions, but it is
never open and aggressive. It is true that silent love
makes a much deeper impression on the lovers than
does any other kind of love.

Although Krishna's love is always available
to Draupadi in the hours of her distress, it does not
show itself often in physical intimacy. In fact, when
love fails to achieve intimacy at the subtler levels, it
craves physical intimacy. Love can be so silent and
subtle that physical distances in time and space don't
matter for it; it remains even in aloneness. Love can
be so deeply silent that it need never express itself in
words. And a man like Krishna can very well know
this silent love, others cannot.

It is lack of love that gives rise to extrava-
gance of words about love. What we don't have we
compensate with words, because words can be easily
understood. Now any number of books are being written on love. Psychologists are producing great volumes on love in which they stress that even if one
does not feel love in his heart, he should not shrink
from declaring it to the loved ones. When a husband
returns home from the office in the evening, he
should hug his wife and kiss her, even if it amounts
to play-acting. He should not shy away from saying
some words of love which we call sweet nothings.
And when he leaves for his office the next morning,
he must say he will miss her the whole day, although
in his heart of hearts he is happy to be leaving.

And the psychologists are right; they are right
because we live on words and we know nothing of

real love. Love has disappeared from our lives; we live on words of love.

We have turned love into a ritual. Really we have turned everything into a ritual. Someone does you a good turn and you say, "Hearty thanks" to him without meaning it. And the other person is pleased to receive it even though you don't feel any thankfulness to him inside your heart. And he will be miserable if you don't say your thanks even though you feel in your heart really thankful for his favor.

Since we don't understand silence, we have to make do with words. Words are so important to us because we live on words.

But remember, when we really love someone, when we are overwhelmed with love for someone, words become futile. You may or may not have noticed it, but it is a fact that in moments of overwhelming love we suddenly find there is nothing to be said in words. Lovers prepare themselves mentally, rehearse for long, every word of a dialogue that they would like to have when they meet each other, but on actual meeting they find to their amazement that they have forgotten every word they had so meticulously rehearsed—the whole dialogue has suddenly evaporated and they are left utterly speechless, silent.

Draupadi's love for Krishna is utterly silent; it is not vocal, but it is deeply felt by Krishna nonetheless. That is why he helps Draupadi more than anybody else. Throughout the story of the Mahabharat we find Krishna standing by the side of Draupadi as her shadow, protecting her against every danger. This extraordinary relationship is too fine to be grossly visible; it does not manifest itself so often like ordinary relationships. It is ethereal, subtle; it is silently intimate.

Questioner: Krishna is said to have left Mathura and settled in distant

> *Dwarka so that the western coast*
> *could be defended against external ag-*
> *gression. It is also said that the people*
> *of Mathura believed that Krishna was*
> *the cause of their troubles because it*
> *is on his account that kings like*
> *Jarasandh recurringly waged war on*
> *Mathura. It is also believed that*
> *Krishna suffered defeat at the hands*
> *of King Jarasandh, which shows up*
> *his human aspect. Please comment.*

Victory and defeat in life are like the warp and woof with which a piece of cloth is woven. Victory alone cannot make a life, as warp alone cannot create a piece of cloth. Nor can defeat alone make a life. To weave the cloth of life, the warp and woof of victory and defeat, success and failure, gain and loss, right and wrong, are essential. Life is made of these opposites; the opposites are like two sides of a coin.

The real question is not whether Krishna wins a battle or loses it; the real question is whether the totality of one's life results in victory or defeat. And it applies to everyone's life. It is immaterial whether one wins a battle here and loses a battle there. It is possible that a defeat becomes a stepping stone to victory. It is also possible that a victory may serve as a jumping board to fall into abysmal defeat. The warp and woof of life are so vast and complex, every defeat does not mean defeat and every victory does not mean victory. It is okay if one loses a battle or two and wins the war. The ultimate judgment on one's life depends not on a count of wins and losses, but on the final summation of one's whole life story.

It is natural that Krishna had moments of defeat in his life. It is inevitable with life. If God has to live in the world he will have to live as humans do; he will have to accept everything that life brings with it. Success and failure, happiness and pain, light and shade, will walk hand-in-hand together. In fact, one who is not ready to face defeats in life should give up all thought of victory.

Krishna's life contains both victory and defeat; that is why it is so human. But this humanness does not detract from the grandeur and glory of his life, really it adds much to it. It means that Krishna is so unique that he can take defeat too. He is not set on winning, not an egoist who is sworn to win and who is not going to accept a defeat. Krishna is prepared for everything that life brings with it. He is prepared to lose a war, even to run away from it, to escape it from any point. He accepts the ups and downs of life unconditionally; he is really choiceless. He does not say that he will go this far and no further. This is what makes Krishna tremendously human, and at times because of his humanness he looks small in comparison to the divinity of Buddha and Mahavira. Both Buddha and Mahavira look absolutely divine; they do not look human at all. But remember, too much divinity is likely to turn harsh and inhuman; it loses that beautiful quality called human tenderness.

Krishna is not going to be harsh, so he accepts all that we call human weakness. A proverb says, "To err is human," but there is no corresponding proverb that says, "Not to err is inhuman." There should be one; it is utterly inhuman if one does not ever err. And Krishna does not take a mistake as mistake; he takes it in stride, as something coming with life.

And it is true that Krishna had to leave Mathura. A man like Krishna might have to leave many places; he might prove to be troublesome at many places. Any number of places may find it increasingly difficult to bear him; they can ask to be excused for their inability to go with him. To understand him and to go with him is really arduous. So Krishna moves away without difficulty; he is not set on staying in a particular place. He moves from one place to another with the ease you move from one room of your house to another. And he leaves a place so utterly that he does not once turn his head to look back at it again. While his lovers feel disturbed about it, and implore him again and again to come back, they want to know if he still remembers them or not, on his part he has left them completely and finally. Now he is mindful of the other place to which he has moved; he forgets Mathura altogether. Wherever Krishna is, he is there totally. And because of it he sometimes seems to be harsh and hard-hearted.

Krishna's life is a flux; he moves with the winds. He goes eastward with the east wind; he goes westward with the westerly. He has no choice of his own to be here or there or anywhere; he goes with life totally. There is a saying of Lao Tzu: Be like the winds; move with the winds; go wherever they take you. And don't choose.

I am reminded of a small Zen parable:

There is a river which is flooded. It is rushing toward the ocean with tremendous speed and force, and two small stalks of some plant are also flowing with its currents. One of the stalks has placed itself crosswise against the currents; it is tense and anxious, tries to fight against them . . . it makes no difference for the currents which are too powerful to be resisted. The currents are not even aware that a little straw is in their way, trying to resist their triumphant advance. But as far as the little stalk is concerned, it is fighting for its life and wasting all its energy for nothing.

The other stalk has left itself lengthwise in the currents, which are taking it with them effortlessly. This stalk is relaxed and joyous and festive. It is dancing with the ripples of the river; it has a feeling of sharing and celebrating with the great river. The ways of the stalks make not the least difference to the river, but make all the difference to themselves.

Like the two straws there are two kinds of people in the world. One is demanding, aggressive and resistant like the first stalk which places itself against the river and fights with it and suffers at every step. And there are people—the other kind of people—who say "Yes" to life, who cooperate with it like the other stalk, which places itself in the currents lengthwise and moves effortlessly and happily with them. These people have a sense of deep kinship with existence; they move with it, with a song in their hearts.

There is a flute in Krishna's hands because he has left himself completely in the hands of existence; he flows effortlessly with its currents. He does not come in the way of life, he does not fight with it. That is how he sings and dances and plays the flute and goes blissfully through life. You cannot put a flute in the hands of Mahavira; he cannot play it. It is unthinkable.

Only Krishna can afford a flute, because he is totally with life, not against it. He is ready to go wherever the river of life takes him. He is as happy in Dwarka as he was in Mathura or anywhere else. And wherever he is, he is dancing and celebrating. That is the way of a choiceless person. And choicelessness is the door to bliss, ecstasy.

> Questioner: A legend says that Kalayavan believes that Krishna is running away, while in fact Krishna is driving Kalayavan into a cave where Muchkund is asleep. The legend also says that as Muchkund wakes up he looks at Kalayavan and kills him with his look. Please explain the significance of the legend.

These names are symbolic and they are parts of Krishna's story. They are part metaphor, part events and part metaphysics. That Krishna is driving someone into a cave is how it seems to us. Even the person concerned can think so, but I understand it differently. A person like Krishna does not drive anyone, although someone can be driven to a point on his own. And it is possible that Krishna follows him. The situation is rather complex.

I have heard that a cowherd is taking his cow from one place to another. A rope is fastened around the neck of the cow and the cowherd has the other end of the rope in his hands. On his way, he meets with a group of traveling Sufis. The head of the group, the Master, halts the cowherd with his cow and asks his disciples to stand around them. This is how a Sufi Master teaches his disciples. He asks of the cowherd, "Is it you who is tied to the cow, or the cow who is tied to you?"

The man promptly says, "The cow is tied to me. Why should I be tied to the cow?" The Master then removes the rope from the cow's neck and leaves the cow free, and the cow immediately takes off. The cowherd is perplexed, but loses no time in running after the cow.

Then the Master says to his disciples, "Although the cowherd thinks the cow is in his hands, in reality he is in the hands of the cow."

In fact, every bondage is twofold: the driver is bound with the driven. Sometimes it is difficult to say what is what. Maybe Kalayavan is fleeing and Krishna is forced to run after him. This much is true, however, that a flight is taking place in which one is the driver and the other is the driven. Maybe both of them are being driven. As we know him, Krishna can accept any situation in life. If he has to struggle with something, his struggle too is a part of his great cooperation with existence. Here also he goes with the river.

The legend says that Kalayavan is reduced to ashes by the sight, the look of an awakened Muchkund. This is a metaphor to say that *kaal*, or time, ceases to exist for one who is awake. Time is perhaps the greatest tension and trouble of our life. Time is the conflict, anxiety, and anguish of man. To live in time means to live stretched between its two poles— the past and the future—and that is what tension is, what stress and anxiety are. Time is the only enemy which we have to fight constantly, and it is time that devours us. Only rarely does someone defeat time and is finished with it. Only rarely does someone transcend time and go beyond it. Only rarely time is burned and destroyed.

But who is it that burns time? You say that Krishna is running ahead of Kalayavan—that is time. And he alone can destroy time who goes ahead of it, who transcends it. One who goes behind time cannot destroy it; he will live as time's camp-follower, its slave. But for one who goes ahead of time, time becomes his shadow, his slave. Here Muchkund's look after he wakes up, burns time.

As I said, this is a parable. Time exists for one who has his eyes closed, who is asleep. And it ceases the moment one opens his eyes and wakes up. Time always exists in exact proportion to our unconsciousness, to our psychological sleep. And when we are fully awake, aware, time ceases to be. The fire of awareness burns time altogether.

We are all like people sleeping in the caves of their unconsciousness. Krishna's presence can be instrumental in opening our eyes, in awakening us. And time trailing behind Krishna can be burned with his look. I believe time does not exist for Krishna; it exists for Muchkund, and Krishna can free Muchkund too from the grip of time.

If we apply these symbols to the realities of our lives and explore them, they can bring us astonishing experiences and rare insights. It is unfortunate that

we take them as just stories and parables and repeat
them meaninglessly over and over again. We treat
them as historic episodes and relay them from generation to generation. They are really more psychological than historical; they are stories of our
psychological potentialities. They are parts of the
great psychological drama that man is. But we have
never tried carefully to look at them with this perspective, and so a great treasure is being lost. It is for this
reason that a rare person like Krishna is gradually
reduced into a myth. There is so much in his life that
it becomes difficult to know that it is real.

It is necessary to explore the lives of men like
Krishna from the perspective of psychology; they are
entitled to extensive psychological commentaries.

And lastly I want to say that in the past there
was no other way except to express even the great
psychological truths of life through symbols, metaphors and parables. They not only served as good
vehicles of expression for these truths, they were also
safe vaults for keeping treasures of such immense
value. These stories have precious gems of wisdom
hidden in them. The ancients had no other way than
this to preserve them for posterity. But now we have
to uncover them and interpret them rightly. Jesus has
said somewhere that he speaks in a language which
will be understood by those who can understand it,
and those who cannot will not be harmed in any way.
He spoke so that those who understood him could
gain, and those who could not understand him had
the joy of listening to a story.

For thousands of years we have had the joy of
listening to these stories which are now with us as
nothing more than mere stories. In the course of time,
we have lost the keys with which we could unlock
these treasures and decode their hidden meanings.
These discussions I am having with you are meant to
make available to you some of the lost keys, so that
you decode the real meanings of these metaphors and

symbols, myths and parables, and they are transformed into the realities of your lives. Whether or not these are their real meanings is not my concern, but if they help you uncover your minds and discover your reality, they will have served their purpose. Then they will prove to be a benediction, a bliss to you.

TWELFTH DISCOURSE
MORNING, SEPTEMBER 30, 1970
MANALI, INDIA

DISCIPLINE, DEVOTION AND KRISHNA

Questioner: We have had the rare opportunity of listening to you speak on Krishna's multi-splendored life—his raas, his flute, his Radha and his unique weapon, the sudarshan. We would like to hear from you today something about his philosophy, the spiritual discipline and the way of worship that he taught to dispel the delusion of a single person, Arjuna. Here you have before you so many of us who are all deluded and confused. Happily for us you are the most competent authority to remove our delusion.

Another questioner: In the course of the past five days you have presented Krishna, who is known as a butter-thief and performer of raas, as a perfect embodiment of the fullness of life and of yoga. If we understand you rightly we can say that Krishna's raas

*is the true portrayal of existence and
his Geeta the quintessence of life itself. You have said that the Geeta,
and not the raas, is a testimony to
Krishna. You have also said that
Mahavira and Buddha were incomplete because they were one-dimensional. And elsewhere you have said
about Mahavira that he had transcended even the sixth and seventh
bodies and attained to the fullness of
yoga. In this context, we should like
to know whether it was the Geeta or
frivolities like the raas that made
Krishna a complete incarnation. We
would also like to know if, like
Mahavira, all other Jaina tirthankaras were unaware of multidimensional life. And lastly explain: What
is samyama (discipline of balance
in life) without repression? And
what would be its place in spiritual
discipline?*

et us first understand what I mean by
completeness, wholeness.

Wholeness can be both one-
dimensional and multidimensional.
A painter can be complete as a
painter, but it does not mean that he
is also complete as a scientist. A scientist can be
whole as a scientist, but that does not make him
whole as a musician. So there is a one-dimensional
completeness. I say Mahavira, Buddha and Jesus were
complete in a particular dimension. But Krishna was
complete in a multidimensional way.

It is quite possible that one chooses a particular dimension of life to the exclusion of the rest, and attains to its wholeness. This wholeness too can lead to the supreme truth. The river that flows in a single stream is as much entitled to reach the ocean as one flowing in many streams. With respect to reaching the ocean, there is no difference between the two. Mahavira and Buddha and Krishna all reach to the ocean of truth, but while Mahavira does it as a one-dimensional man, Krishna does it as one who is multidimensional. Krishna's completeness is multidimensional, while Mahavira's is one-dimensional. So don't think that Mahavira does not attain to wholeness; he transcends the seventh body and attains to wholeness as much as Krishna does.

Krishna reaches the same goal from many, many directions, and that is significant.

Another significant thing about Krishna is that unlike Mahavira and Buddha, he does not deny life, he is not life-negative. There is an unavoidable element of negation in the lives of Mahavira and Buddha which is completely absent in Krishna's life. There is not a trace of negativity in this man with the flute. Mahavira attains through renunciation of life; Krishna attains through total acceptance of it. That is why I differentiate Krishna's wholeness from that of others. But let no one think that Mahavira is incomplete. All one can say is that while his wholeness is one-dimensional, Krishna's wholeness is multidimensional.

One-dimensional wholeness is not going to have much meaning in the future. For the man of the future, multidimensional wholeness will have tremendous significance. And there are reasons for it. One who attains to wholeness through a single facet of his life not only negates all other facets of his own life, he also becomes instrumental in negating those aspects in the lives of many other multidimensional people.

On the other hand, one who attains to wholeness, to the absolute, through all aspects of his life, proves helpful even to all kinds of one-dimensional seekers in their journey to the supreme from their own aspect. In short, while Mahavira and Buddha can be of help only to a few, Krishna's help will be available to many. For example, we cannot think how a painter or sculptor or a poet can attain to the supreme through the path of Mahavira. Mahavira is one-dimensional not only for himself; all others who will try to understand him and experiment with his discipline will have to negate all other facets of their lives as ways to attainment. We cannot conceive how a dancer can attain to the supreme in Mahavira's terms, but in Krishna's terms he can. A dancer, if he so chooses, can drop all other aspects and keep to dancing, and by going deeper and deeper into it can attain to the same state Mahavira attains through meditation. This is possible in terms of Krishna.

Krishna makes every side, every facet of his life divine; with him every direction of life becomes sacred. It is not so with Mahavira: one particular direction in which he journeys becomes sacred, while all other directions remain profane. And in fact because his one direction becomes sacred all other directions are bound to remain profane; these are automatically condemned; doomed to live in the shade of profanity. And this is applicable not only to Mahavira, but also to Rama, Buddha, Christ, Mohammed—all those who adhere to one exclusive direction in life's quest.

Krishna is the sole being about whom it can be said that he made every path, every facet of life sacred and holy. He made it possible for every kind of seeker to attain to the supreme from any direction that comes naturally to him. In this sense he is multidimensional, not only for himself but for others too. With a flute on his lips one can dance his way to God; playing a flute he can touch that depth where *samadhi*, or ecstasy happens. But to Mahavira and Buddha with a flute there is no way. It is not possible on the paths of Mahavira and Buddha that a flute can achieve the majestic heights of meditation and *samadhi*. It is impossible. To Mahavira, Meera can never attain to the highest; she is attached to Krishna, she loves Krishna. And according to Mahavira, attachment can never lead you to God, only non-attachment can. But going with Krishna, both the attached and non-attached can reach the same destination.

That is why I say that Krishna's wholeness is incomparable; it is rare.

Secondly, you want to know if none of the Jaina *tirthankaras* attained to wholeness. No, they all had attained to it, but only to one-dimensional wholeness. And it was because of this that Jaina ideology could not achieve widespread popularity. It was inherent in the very nature of Jainism. Twenty-five centuries have passed, and there are only three and a half million Jainas, a very poor figure.

It is ironic that the message of a person of the stature of Mahavira—and he was not alone, he carried with him an immense heritage bequeathed by twenty-three *tirthankaras*—could reach only three and a half million people. If only three dozen persons had been influenced by Mahavira in his lifetime, they alone through procreation would have, in the course of twenty-five hundred years, reached this figure. What is the cause? The cause is obvious. It is their one-dimensional approach. They lack the multi-dimensional wholeness of Krishna. Their appeal is limited to a few; it is ineffectual in reaching the rest of mankind. People with inclinations different from the single dimension that Jainism represents remain wholly unaffected; they don't find themselves in tune with it.

It is ironic that even this handful of Jainas don't treat Mahavira the way he should be treated. It is all right to worship Krishna, but it is repugnant to

Mahavira's teachings. And the Jainas are worshipping Mahavira. Worship is okay with Krishna but not with Mahavira. It means Mahavira will not agree with the minds of even those few who are born into the Jaina community. The reason is that the dimension of Mahavira is very exclusive; it accords with few. So being born in the Jaina community one continues to be a Jaina, but takes on many things that don't belong to Mahavira's dimension. Devotion has entered Jainism, and along with it have come worship and prayer and other rituals. They have nothing to do with Mahavira; they are alien to his genius. In fact, devotion and worship are an outrage against Mahavira; there is no place for them in the life of Mahavira. But the Jainas have their own difficulty; they cannot feel gratified without worship and prayer. So they go on incorporating all these things into the religion of Mahavira.

Here I would like to say that all those who have attained to one-dimensional wholeness are bound to be unjustly treated by their followers; they cannot escape it. But you cannot misbehave in this way with those who have attained to multidimensional wholeness; whatever you do they will accept it. While all types of people can walk with Krishna, only a particular type can go with Mahavira.

This is the reason I have said that all the twenty-four *tirthankaras* of the Jainas are travelers on the same path; their direction is the same and their spiritual discipline is the same. And I don't say that they don't arrive at the goal, they do arrive. It is not that ultimately they don't achieve what Krishna achieves; they achieve exactly that which Krishna achieves.

It does not matter whether a river reaches the ocean in hundreds of streams or in a single stream. On reaching the ocean all journeys end and all the rivers become one with the ocean. Yet there is a difference between the two rivers—one has a single stream and another has many. While a river with many streams can water a very large area of the earth, the river with a single stream cannot—only a few trees and plants can be benefited by it. This difference has to be understood, it cannot be denied.

This is what I would like to say in regard to multidimensional wholeness.

And you ask: What is *samyama*, the discipline of balance in life, without repression?

In terms of renunciation *samyama* generally means repression. By and large, every seeker on the path of renunciation understands *samyama* in the sense of repression. For this reason the Jaina scriptures have even a term like body-repression; they believe that even the physical body has to be suppressed and repressed. It is unfortunate that *samyama* has become synonymous with repression.

But in Krishna's terms, *samyama* can never mean repression. How can Krishna say that *samyama* can be achieved through repression? For Krishna *samyama* has an absolutely different meaning.

Words sometimes put us in great difficulty. Words are the same, whether they come from Krishna's mouth or from Mahavira's, but their meanings change from mouth to mouth. This word *samyama* is one such word which has different meanings with different people. Mahavira means one thing when he uses this word, and Krishna means just the opposite when he uses the same word. While the word comes from the dictionary, its meaning comes from the person who uses it.

The meaning of a word does not, as is usually believed, come from the dictionary. Of course, people who have no individuality of their own depend on the dictionary for the meanings of words. People with individuality invest words with their own meanings. So what Krishna means by *samyama* can be known only in his context. Similarly Mahavira's meaning of *samyama* will have to be known from his context. Its meaning does not lie in the word itself, it lies in Krishna and Mahavira or whoever uses it.

Looking at Krishna's life no one can say that *samyama* means repression. If there has been a single person on this earth who can be called utterly unrepressed, uninhibited and free it is Krishna. So *samyama* for Krishna cannot have anything to do with repression. And as far as I am concerned, *samyama* and repression are antonyms, opposites.

This Sanskrit word *samyama* is really extraordinary. To me it means balance, equilibrium, to be just in the middle. When the scales are equalized so that neither side outweighs the other, it is *samyam*. In this sense a renunciate does not have *samyama*, balance any more than one who indulges in worldly pleasures. Both are unbalanced; they are wanting in *samyama*. Both are extremists: the indulgent holds to one extreme of life; the renunciate holds to the other extreme. *Samyama* means to be equidistant from the two extremes, to be just in the middle. Krishna stands for that middle state where there is neither renunciation nor indulgence. Or you can say *samyama* is indulgence with an element of renunciation in it, or it is renunciation with an element of indulgence; it is striking a balance between indulgence and renunciation. Really *samyama* is neither indulgence nor renunciation; it is a state where you don't tilt the scales to either side. He alone is *samyami* who maintains equidistance from either extreme.

There is a man who is mad after wealth. Day in and day out he is running after amassing money. Day in and day out he goes on adding to his bank balance. Money has become the be-all and end-all of his life—his demigod. This person has gone to one extreme of life. There is another person who has turned his back on wealth; he is running away from wealth. He renounces wealth and does not even look back lest it attract him and entrap him again. This person has gone to the other extreme. Both have lost balance, both lack *samyama*. Renunciation of wealth is the goal of one and acquisition of wealth is the goal of another.

Then who is *samyami*, the balanced person? In Krishna's terms a person like Janaka is *samyami*. Negation of the extremes is *samyama*; to be exactly in the middle is equilibrium. Too much fasting and too much eating go against *samyama*; right eating goes with *samyama*. Fasting amounts to tilting the balance on the side of hunger; overeating amounts to tilting the balance on the side of indulgence. The balance lies in eating just the right amount of food—neither less nor more. By *samyama* Krishna means balance, equilibrium, equipoise. Any movement deviating from the center, even a slight deviation from the middle to one side or another destroys the equilibrium; on either side there is the death of *samyama*.

And one can deviate from *samyama* in only two ways: one way is indulgence and the other is renunciation. Either you get attached to a thing, you cling to it, or you get repelled by it. Have you watched a wall clock with a pendulum? Its pendulum is constantly swinging from one side to the other; it never stops in the middle. It swings from the left side to the right and back; it does not stop at the center. Another significant thing about the pendulum is that when it is moving toward the right, it only seems so; in reality it is gathering momentum to move toward the left. And when it is moving toward the left, it is really gathering momentum to move toward the right.

We are exactly like this pendulum. When one is fasting he is in fact, preparing himself for feasting, and similarly when he is feasting he is preparing to go on a fast. One who is running after attachments and addictions will soon get tired and will pursue renunciation and asceticism. Both extremes are joined together; they are two sides of the same thing.

Only when the pendulum stops in the middle, swinging in neither direction, it is balanced. And it is such a pendulum that can symbolize *samyama*. So long as one pursues indulgence or asceticism, he is unbalanced, he is an *asamyami*. One can be called a rightist kind of *asamyami* and the other a leftist kind.

To be steadied in the middle is *samyama* in terms of Krishna. It can have no other meaning as far as Krishna is concerned. To be balanced is *samyama*.

Let us look at *samyama* in the context of real life. In the context of real life, in the sense of the interiority of life, a person of *samyama* has two connotations. Such a person is neither an ascetic nor a hedonist—or he is both. Such a person is a renunciate and a hedonist together. His indulgence is blended with renunciation and his renunciation mixed with indulgence.

But none of the old traditions of renunciation will agree with this definition of *samyama*. To these traditions *samyama* means aversion to enjoyment and *asamyama*, imbalance, means addiction to enjoyments. One who gives up his attachments and takes to asceticism is a *samyami* in the eyes of the traditionalists.

Krishna is neither a renunciate nor a hedonist. If we have to place him somewhere, he will be midway between Charvaka and Mahavira. In indulgence he will equal Charvaka, and in renunciation he will not lag behind Mahavira. If we can have a blending of Charvaka and Mahavira, it will be Krishna.

So in terms of Krishna, all such words as *samyama* and *asamyama* will undergo a transformation. The words will be the same, but their meanings will be radically different. The meanings will stem from Krishna's own being.

The second part of your question is: *What is Krishna's sadhana or*

> *spiritual discipline? What is his way
> of worship?*

There is nothing like *sadhana* or spiritual discipline in the life of Krishna. There cannot be. The basic element of spiritual discipline is effort; without effort *sadhana* is not possible. And the second inescapable element of *sadhana* is ego; without the ego, the "I", spiritual discipline falls apart. Who will discipline himself? Effort implies a doer; there has to be somebody to make the effort. Effort ceases if there is no doer.

If we go into the matter deeply we will know that *sadhana* is an invention of the godless people, people who don't accept God. Those who deny God and accept only the soul believe in *sadhana* or spiritual discipline. They believe the soul has to make efforts to uncover itself, to be itself.

Upasana, devotion, is the way of a very different kind of people, who say there is no soul, only God is. Ordinarily we think that *sadhana* and *upasana*—discipline and worship—go together, but it is not so. Theists believe in devotion and worship; they don't believe in effort. They say all one has to do is to get closer and closer to God.

The word *upasana* is beautiful; it means to sit near God, to get close to one's object of worship. And the worshipper disappears; his ego evaporates in the very process of getting close to God. There is nothing more to be done. The theists believe that it is really one's ego that separates him from God; ego is the gulf between the seeker and the sought. The greater the ego, the greater is the distance between the two. Ego is the measure of distance between the seeker and God. To the extent this ego melts and evaporates, one gets closer and closer to God. And the day the ego disappears completely, the day the seeker ceases to be, his *upasana* is complete and he is God himself.

It is like ice turns into water, and water in turn evaporates and disappears into the sky. Does ice have to make efforts to become water? If it makes efforts, it will only become more hardened as ice. Efforts will make ice more and more crystallized, solid. So if a seeker resorts to *sadhana* or spiritual discipline, it will only strengthen his ego, harden it and solidify it.

So *sadhana* ultimately leads to the soul, while *upasana*, devotion leads to God. One who disciplines himself will end with the soul; he cannot go beyond it. He will say that he has ultimately found himself, his soul. On the other hand the devotee will say that he has lost himself and found God. So the *sadhaka* and the *upasaka*, the man of discipline and the devotee, are contrary to each other; they are not the same. While an *upasaka* will melt and evaporate like water, a *sadhaka* will be strengthened and crystallized as a soul.

In Krishna's life there is no element of discipline; there is actually no place whatsoever for *sadhana*. It is *upasana* or devotion which has meaning for Krishna.

The whole journey of *upasana* is opposed to effort and discipline; it enters a different dimension altogether. For an *upasaka* it is a mistake to think that one finds himself. The self is the only barrier, the only falsehood. To be is the only bondage. And therefore not to be, or to be nothing, is the only freedom. While a *sadhaka* says, "I want to be free," an *upasaka* says, "I want to be free from the 'I', the self." A *sadhaka* says, "I want freedom," but his "I" remains intact. To an *upasaka*, freedom means a state of "non-I" or complete egolessness. Not freedom of the "I" but freedom *from* the "I" is the highest state for an *upasaka*. So *sadhana* has no place in the vocabulary of Krishna; *upasana* has.

Therefore I will go into *upasana* in depth. To understand it, it is necessary first to know that it has nothing to do with efforts or discipline. Unless we know it clearly, we will continue to confuse the two. And remember that very few people want to take the path of devotion and worship. Most people would like to be *sadhakas*, doers. A *sadhaka* has nothing to lose, he has only to gain something—his soul. And an *upasaka* has everything to lose, he has to lose himself totally, he has nothing to gain. Losing is his only gain, and nothing else. So very few people want to take this path. That is why even the lovers of Krishna turn into *sadhakas*. They too talk in terms of *sadhana* and discipline, because they love to be doers. The ego loves the words: strive, achieve, arrive; it is always after achievement.

Upasana is arduous, devotion is hard. Nothing is more difficult than evaporating and disappearing into nothingness. One would, for sure, want to know why he should die and disappear into nothingness, what he is going to gain by dying as an entity. A *sadhaka*, in spite of his lofty words, will always think in terms of gain and loss. Even his liberation is nothing more than a means to his happiness; his freedom is *his* freedom. So it is not surprising that a *sadhaka* is a selfish person in the deeper sense of the word. In this sense he cannot rise above the self. But an *upasaka*, a devotee will rise above self and will know the ultimate, where the self is no more.

What is this *upasana*? What is its meaning and significance? What is its way? Before you try to understand this question of *upasana*, it is essential that you drop the idea of *sadhana* altogether. Forget it; it has no place whatsoever. Only then you can know what *upasana* is.

As I said, the word *upasana* means to sit near someone, to sit close to someone. But what is the distance, the remoteness that has to be overcome in order to be near? There is physical distance, distance in space. You are sitting there and I am sitting here, and there is a distance between you and me. This is physical distance. We move closer to each other and the physical distance disappears. If we sit together taking each other's hands, the distance will disappear completely.

There is another kind of distance which is spiritual, inner, which has nothing to do with physical distance. Two persons can be together holding each others' hands and yet they may be hundreds of miles away from each other spiritually. And maybe, two other persons are physically separated from each other by hundreds of miles, yet they are intimately together in spirit. So there are two kinds of distances: one is physical and the other is psychological, spiritual. *Upasana* is a way of ending the inner distance, the psychological separateness between the seeker and the sought.

It is ironic that even a devotee is anxious to remove the physical distance that seems to separate him from his beloved. He says, "I am restless for you; don't torture me any more. I have made the bed for you; don't delay your arrival any longer." But the difficulty is that the inner distance remains even when the physical distance has been eliminated. To come close to one's beloved is altogether an inner phenomenon. A devotee can be with God, who is invisible, and there is no physical distance between the two. *Upasana* is a way of uniting the devotee with the divine. But how is this inner distance created?

We know how the outer distance is created. If I walk away from you in another direction, a physical distance will immediately come to exist between you and me. And if I walk back to you the distance will be gone. But how does the inner distance come into being? There is no way to walk in the inner space as we do on the outside. This inner space is created by becoming; the more solid my ego the greater is the distance between my becoming and being. And as the ego melts and evaporates the inner distance is destroyed in the same measure. And when my ego evaporates completely and I am no more, I am all emptiness, then the inner distance between me and God disappears altogether.

So *upasana*, devotion, means that the devotee becomes an emptiness, a nothingness, a non-being. To know the truth that "I am not" is to be a devotee, is to be with God. And conversely, to know that "I am" and to cling to this ego is to go far away from God. The declaration that "I am" makes for the separation and distance between the seeker and the sought.

Rumi has written a beautiful song. It is the song of the Sufis, who know what devotion is. Sufis are among those few people on this earth who know what *upasana* is. If any one can understand Krishna fully it is the Sufis. Although they are Mohammedans, yet it makes no difference. This song belongs to Jalaluddin Rumi.

A lover knocks at the door of his beloved. A voice from inside queries, "Who are you?"

The lover says, "I am; don't you know me?" And then no voice comes from inside; there is utter silence. The lover goes on knocking and shouting, "Don't you recognize my voice? I am your lover. Open the door without delay."

Then a small voice is heard coming from inside the house, "As long as you are, love's door will remain closed. This door never opens for one who says, 'I am.' So go back and return here only when your 'I' is no more."

The lover goes away disappointed. Many summers and winters, springs and falls come and go. Even years pass. Then one day the lover reappears and knocks at the same door. He then hears the same question coming from the inner sanctuary of the house: "Who are you?" And the lover answers, "Now only thou art." And the door opens.

Rumi's song ends here.

I think Rumi could not get inside the spirit of devotion fully; he fails to reach to the height of Krishna. He walks with him, but does not go the whole length. If I have to write this song, I would have the beloved say again to the lover, "As long as 'thou' remains 'I' will be here—maybe in hiding. So go back again and return here after you are finished with 'thou' too."

The awareness of "thou" cannot exist without "I". Whether one uses "I" or not, does not make a difference. As long as "thou" exists for me, I exist. Maybe my "I" hides itself in the dark recesses of the unconscious, but it is there. Because who will say "thou" if the "I" is not there? So it does not make any difference if one says, "Only thou art"; it is like Tweedledum and Tweedledee. If I am going to write this poem I would have the beloved say, "As long as 'thou' is, 'I' cannot be erased. So go back and get rid of 'thou' as you got rid of 'I'."

But do you think the lover will return after losing both "I" and "thou"? He will not. And then my poem will be in real difficulty, because then it cannot be completed. The lover will not return— Who will come? And to whom? Then he will never come again, because the inner distance, in which coming and going happens, is gone. In fact, the distance is made by the awareness of "I" and "thou"; with the cessation of "I" and "thou" distance is completely obliterated. So on coming to its end my song will be in real trouble. Maybe, for this very reason Rumi concluded his song the way it is. One cannot take it any further, because nothing remains to be said after it. The song has to be concluded there. There is no one who will go, and there is no one who will receive him. Who will go to whom? And for what?

As long as one comes and goes, there is distance. And when "I" and "thou" disappear, distances disappear. And with the disappearance of distances the meeting happens, merging happens.

A devotee need not go anywhere. The meeting happens wherever he is. It is not a question of going anywhere; one has to die as a self and one comes close to the supreme.

> *Questioner: Please tell us something about Martin Buber.*

Martin Buber's whole thinking is concerned with the relationship, with the intimacy between "I" and "thou". Martin Buber is one of the most profound thinkers of our age. But remember, profundity is not all; whatever the depth it is only the other end of the superficial, the shallow. Real depth comes when one is neither shallow nor deep, when both shallowness and depth disappear. Martin Buber has come upon something very profound: he says that life's truth lies in the interrelationship between "I" and "thou".

An atheist, a materialist, believes that only matter is; there is nothing other than matter. His world does not consist of "I" and "thou", it consists of "I" and "it". There is no place for "thou", because for "thou" it is necessary that another person possess a soul. So an atheist's world is confined to the relationship between "I" and "it". That is why it is such a complex world, where on the one hand he calls himself "I" and as such invests himself with a soul, he deprives others of this I-ness and reduces them into things, into "its". A materialist reduces every man and everything into matter. If I believe there is no soul or spirit, then for me you are nothing more than matter. How then can I call you "thou"? Because only an alive man, alive with a soul, can be addressed as "thou".

Therefore Martin Buber says a theist's world is comprised of "I" and "thou" and not "I" and "it". It is a theist's world only when my "I" addresses the world as "thou". This is how Buber thinks.

But I will not say so. I will say that even a theist is, in his depth, nothing more than an atheist, because he divides the world into "I" and "thou". Or you can say that Buber's world is the world of a dualistic theist. But it is not true, because dualistic theism has no meaning. In a sense, an atheist is non-dualist because he says that only matter is. And so is a spiritualist who says that only one is, and it is spirit. And I think it is easier to attain to oneness, non-dualism from the hypothesis that there is only one; it is very difficult to come to monism from the hypothesis that there are two—"I" and "thou".

In this sense, a dualist like Buber may find himself in a more difficult situation than an atheist. A materialist is a non-dualist, a monist, and if someday he comes to know that there is no matter, that only spirit is, only consciousness is, then he will have no difficulty in being transformed. Even as an atheist he accepts the oneness of existence; he does not accept the dualistic interpretation. But a dualist's problem is more difficult. He believes that existence is dual; it is matter and soul together. And as such it would be extremely difficult for him to attain to non-dualism, to the oneness of all existence.

Buber is a dualist. He says that the world is comprised of "I" and "thou". His dualism is human, because he cancels "it", and gives it the status of "thou" with a soul. But it remains a dualistic approach nonetheless. There can be only a relationship between "I" and "thou"; there cannot be a unity, a oneness between them. However deep and intimate the relationship, there is always some distance between "I" and "thou". If I am related with you—even if the relationship is really intimate—the very fact of relatedness divides me from you; we are not one but two.

And remember, a relationship is a double-edged sword which cuts both ways; it unites and divides at the same time. If you and I are related, it means we are divided as well. The point of meeting is also the point of parting. A bridge joins the two banks of a river and divides them too. In fact, whatever joins two persons or things is bound to divide them; it is inescapable, there is no way to avoid it. Two persons can relate with each other, but they cannot be one; relationship is not unity.

Even in a love relationship, the division between the lovers remains. And as long as there is a division, a separateness, love cannot be fulfilled. That is why all lovers are dissatisfied, discontented. There are two kinds of discontent in love. You are discontented if you don't find your lover, and you are discontented even if you find one.

When you find someone you love and who loves you, you realize that in spite of the meeting, a distance remains and nothing can be done to mitigate the pain of this separateness. In spite of everything you do to do away with this separateness, this distance from your lover, it continues to torment you. So very often a person who does not find his love is not as miserable as one who finds it. One who does not find can still hope to find, but the one who has found is robbed of all hope—his discontent and despair are much deeper. In fact, no meeting can be real, because two make a meeting, and as long as there are two entities, unity or oneness is impossible.

Martin Buber speaks of a deep relationship between "I" and "thou", and it is very humanistic. And in a world which is becoming increasingly materialistic in every way, this concept of Martin Buber's seems very religious. But I don't take it as such; I say it is not at all religious. I think Buber is just attempting a compromise; if "I" and "thou" cannot unite they can at least maintain some relationship. Religion stands for the non-dual, indivisible and integrated oneness of existence.

This is the difference between love and devotion, *upasana*. Love is relationship, it is dualistic; devotion is non-dual, non-relationship. Non-relationship does not mean that two persons have separated; it simply means that they have ceased to be two, they have become one. To be one is *upasana*, devotion. Devotion is a higher state of love—really the highest state. Unless two lovers become divine, godly, they cannot achieve a real unity. Really, two humans cannot unite, because their being human is the obstruction. A man and woman can at best be related with each other; they cannot be united and one. Only divine elements can meet and merge into each other, because now nothing can divide them. The truth is since they have dissolved themselves as separate entities, the question of unity or separation does not now arise. There is really nothing to unite or divide them; nothing is separate from them.

Martin Buber's concept can lead you to love; Krishna can take you to devotion. And devotion is something utterly different, it is rare. In devotion both "I" and "thou" disappear, and what remains after this disappearance is inexpressible; it cannot be put into words. When "I" and "thou" disappear there is infinity, which is nameless. Whatever names you use for it—spirit, matter, "I" and "thou"—they are all going to be wrong. That is why all the great devotees chose to remain silent, they refused to name it, they simply said, "It is nameless." They said, "It is without beginning and without end, it has neither form nor name." They said, "It cannot be expressed in words." And so they remained silent.

Great devotees became silent; they did not make a statement about the highest truth, because all statements land you in the mire of duality. Man has no such word that is not likely to lead to dualism. All words are loaded with dualistic meanings; the moment you use a word you divide existence into two opposites. As soon as you say a word you divide existence into two.

It is as if you pass a ray of the sun through a prism and it divides into seven colors. The prism of language divides every truth into two parts, and a truth divided turns into a lie. It is for this reason that great devotees kept silent. They danced, they sang, they played the flute, they made gestures, but they did not say a word. They said through their gestures, dance, laughter, what that truth is. They have raised their hands toward the heavens to say what it is like. They have said it with their silence; they have said it with their whole being. But they did not use words.

I am reminded of a story:

During the days of the mutiny, a British soldier stuck a bayonet in the chest of a sannyasin. The sannyasin happened to pass through a military cantonment, and he was in silence. He had been in silence for long; for thirty years he had not uttered a word. The day he went into silence someone had asked him why. The sannyasin said, "That which can be said is not worth saying, and that which is worth saying cannot be said. So there is no way except to become silent." And he had been silent for thirty years.

It was the time of the mutiny when Indian soldiers of the British army had revolted against their alien masters. The British officers were alarmed, so when they saw a naked sannyasin passing through their military camp, they captured him on the suspicion he was a spy. When they interrogated him he kept silent, and this strengthened their suspicion. The suspicion would perhaps have been cleared if the sannyasin had responded to their queries, but he simply smiled when they asked him who he was. So their suspicion of his being a spy was confirmed, and they stuck a bayonet in his chest. This man, who had been silent for thirty years, broke into a loud laughter and uttered a great maxim of the Upanishad: "*Tatvamasi Shvetketu!*" With this quote from the Upanishad he said to the British soldier who struck him with a bayonet: "You want to know who I am? What I am, you are."

Truth cannot be said in words; at the most it can be indicated with indications and signs, with gestures and hints. Or like Kabir one can say it with paradoxes, self-contradictory statements. Kabir's language has been described as *sandhyabhasha*, which literally means the twilight language. Twilight is a space where it is neither day nor night, where one can neither say a clear yes nor a clear no, where one can neither accept nor deny, where one is neither a theist nor an atheist, where everything is fluid, vague and mystical. It is for this reason that up to now no one has been able to discover a clear-cut meaning in Kabir's sayings. Krishna's sayings belong to this same category. Whosoever has attempted to express the truth in words, his language has invariably turned into the twilight language. They cannot be assertive, they have to say yes and no together. Or they will accept or deny the opposites together. And that is what makes their statements illogical and inconsistent.

It is for this reason that people who came to know the space where "I" and "thou" disappear, where all opposites cease to be and duality disappears, have decided to remain silent.

> *Questioner: Sartre says, "Existence precedes essence," and you say, "Essence precedes existence." Please explain the actual relationship between the two statements. Please also say*

something about the confusion in which we find ourselves with regard to the distinction between devotion and discipline, because here in Manali we are participating in a camp meant for spiritual discipline.

It is part of my work to put you into confusion. You will know the meaning of this camp only when all distinctions between devotion and discipline disappear.

Sartre and other existentialists believe that existence precedes essence, but it is a very odd statement. Perhaps never before had such a concept been put forth. Down the ages the contrary belief has been held. Almost every thought-system, every philosophy believes that essence precedes existence. So it is good to understand it in depth.

All schools of philosophy that were born before Sartre and other existentialists believe that the seed precedes the tree. And it seems natural and logical. But Sartre says the tree precedes the seed. By and large, every thought-system says that essence precedes existence; without essence or soul, existence is not possible. But Sartre asserts that existence comes first and essence later. He believes that in the absence of existence essence cannot be manifested.

Let us now go into this question in the context of Krishna.

In fact, all philosophical quarrels are childish. Even the biggest philosophical battles have been fought over a problem which can be summed up in a child's question: "Which comes first, the chicken or the egg?" It is really around this small question that all the great battles between philosophers have taken place. But those who know will say the chicken and egg are not two. Those who raise this question are stupid, and those answering it are even more stupid.

What is an egg but a chicken in the making? And what is a chicken but an egg fulfilled, come to its fullness? Egg and chicken hide each other in themselves. The question of who precedes whom is meaningful if egg and chicken are two separate things. The truth is that they are the same. Or we can say that they are the two ways of looking at the same thing. Or they are two different phases, two states of the manifestation of the same thing.

Similarly, seed and tree are not separate. Neither are light and dark. Nor are birth and death. They are two ways of looking at the same thing. Maybe, because we don't know how to see a thing rightly, we see it in fragments. For example, there is a big room inside a house and the house is locked. Someone wants to have a look at the room and so he drills a hole through a wall. Now he peers into the room from side to side. At first a chair will come into view, then another chair, and so on and so forth. He cannot have a full view of the room all at once. And he can very well ask, "Which comes first and which afterward?" No arguments can settle this question. But if the person manages to enter the room he can see the whole room together, and then he will not ask what comes first.

There is a laboratory in Oxford University which has to its credit some of the greatest explorations and researches done in the present century. And I think this laboratory is performing the most significant job for our future. It is known as the De La Warr Laboratory. There a miracle happened when a bud was exposed to a camera, and it turned out in print to be the picture of the full flower into which the bud was eventually going to bloom.

The film used in the camera had such high sensitivity, the highest ever, that it captured the hidden potential of the bud in the form of a fully-blossomed flower. It was simply incredible how a camera photographing a bud brought out the picture of the flower that the bud was going to be in the future. At the moment of photographing it was only a bud, and no one knew what kind of flower it was going to make. Maybe the flower was already present, physically present at some mysterious level of existence which we cannot see with our physical eyes—but the extra-sensitive film used in the camera succeeded in seeing it.

It was a breathtaking event, and even the scientists working at De La Warr were dazed and left puzzled about how the magic worked. They thought that perhaps at some unseen level of existence the bud and the flower were in existence simultaneously. The scientists thought perhaps through some technical error the film had been exposed earlier, when it had taken in the picture of a flower. Or, maybe some chemical mishap has brought about this inexplicable result.

So the scientists decided to wait until the bud turned into a full flower. But when it happened they were amazed to see that it was exactly the same flower whose picture the camera had captured earlier when it was only a bud. They now knew there was no chemical or technical error involved. A photographic miracle—say a scientific miracle—had really taken place.

This small incident happening within the small confines of the De La Warr Laboratory is packed with tremendous significance for the future. We can now say that at some unseen level of their existence the egg and chicken happen simultaneously, but we fail to see it with our gross eyes. It is something in our way of looking at things that the egg is seen first and the chicken afterwards. If we have the eyes of a Krishna, it is not difficult to see them simultaneously. But the way we are, we will say it is something impossible; it defies our reason and logic.

But in the past twenty-five years science has been compelled to accept many things that defeat our logic.

I would like to cite another case from the scientific lab, so that you don't go with the impression that I am saying something unscientific.

Only some fifty years ago no one could have imagined that it was the case. Soon after man succeeded in splitting the atom and discovering the electron, science found itself in deep water. The behavior of the electron put scientists in great difficulty; how to describe it? Never before had science been faced with such a dilemma; everything was going very well, as science should go. Everything was clear-cut, defined and logical. But with the discovery of the electron science was confronted with a tricky problem: how to define the electron. On being photographed sometimes the electron appeared as a particle and sometimes it appeared as a wave. And there is a great difference between a particle and a wave. If they called the electron a particle it could not be a wave, and if they called it a wave it could not be a particle. Therefore they had to coin a new word in English to define the electron. This new word is "quanta". This word is not found in any other languages of the world, because they have not yet reached that depth in science. Quanta means that which is both a particle and a wave simultaneously.

But quanta is a mysterious phenomenon; it is both a particle and wave, an egg and chicken together. With quanta science has entered a new phase of its journey.

So I don't agree with Sartre, nor do I agree with those who say essence precedes existence. I don't accept either position. I see the whole thing in a different perspective. To me, existence and essence are two ways of looking at the same thing. Because of our limited perception, we divide the same thing into fragments. In fact, essence is existence and existence is essence. They are not two separate phenomena. So it is wrong to say that essence has existence or that God has existence, because then it means God and existence are separate. No, if we understand it rightly we should say: God is existence.

It is utterly wrong to say that God exists. We say a flower exists because tomorrow this flower will cease to exist. But will God ever cease to exist? If so then he is not God. One who will never cease to exist cannot be said to have an existence. We can say that we exist, because we will certainly cease to exist sometime in the future. But it is an error of language to say that God exists, because he is ever and ever and ever. It is utterly wrong to say God exists; the right way to say it is: God is existence.

But language always puts us into difficulty; it is in the very nature of language. In fact, even the phrase "God is existence" is erroneous, because the word "is" between God and existence creates a schism and confusion. It means on one side is God and on the other is existence and the two are related by the word "is". This word really divides God into two—he and existence—which is again wrong. So even the word "is" has to go, and we had better say God means is-ness, God means being, God means existence. The word "is" is also a repetition; it is repetition to say God is. "Is" means God; is-ness is God or God is is-ness. That which is, is God. But language has its own limitations; it is created for the dualistic world.

This is the reason that one who knows wants to keep away from the trap of words and remains completely silent. The moment he says something, he at once separates himself from what he says; what he says becomes an object. But, in fact, he who says and what he says are one. Under the circumstances, there is no better way than to keep quiet.

Someone goes to a Zen sage and requests him to say something about God. The sage laughs and sways. The man says, "Why do you laugh and sway?

Why don't you answer my question? I have traveled a long way just to ask this question." The sage now begins to dance, and the visitor is puzzled. He says, "Are you crazy? I want an answer to my question."

The sage says, "I am answering your question, but you don't listen."

The questioner is annoyed and says, "It seems you are going to make me as crazy as you are. You have not said a word yet."

Now the sage remarks, "If I say something, it is going to be wrong. Whatever I will say will be untrue. If you cannot understand my silence it is better you go somewhere else where truth is spoken in words. But when the ultimate truth is said in words it becomes false. One can speak so long as he is journeying to the temple of truth; the moment he enters its innermost sanctuary all words, all languages fail. At the ultimate point one has no other way than to become silent."

Wittgenstein, one of the most profound thinkers of this age, wrote a small maxim toward the last days of his life. And what he said in this maxim is extraordinary: "That which cannot be said must not be said." Had Wittgenstein been alive I would have said to him, "But this much has to be said about that which cannot be said: that it must not be said. What you say is also a statement about the inexpressible, and whether you say much or little makes no difference."

Wittgenstein had written in his first book, *Tractatus*, that whatever can be said can only be said through language. This statement of his is correct to some extent. What is said through gestures will have to be included in this statement, because gestures are a kind of language. A dumb person raises his hand to his mouth to say that he is hungry; it is the language of the dumb. There is a maxim in Hindi which says, "God is the dumb man's candy." A dumb person can very well enjoy the flavor of candy, but he cannot

communicate it to others. This means to say that
God can only be expressed through gestures—the language of the dumb. In whatever way you express it,
whether you do it through silence or a dance or a
smile, it all amounts to saying something. But it is
true that despite everything we do to say that which
is, it remains unsaid and unsayable.

What Lao Tzu says in this context is much
more profound than Wittgenstein's maxim. He says,
"Truth cannot be said, and that which is said is not
truth." This much can be said. Therefore those who
know often become silent.

> Questioner: You often say that when
> "I" becomes whole it turns into "non-
> I" or "all". But what you said a little
> while ago contradicts this statement.
> It seems you are just shifting the em-
> phasis from one word to another. Is
> there a difference between the whole
> "I" and the "non-I"?

There is no difference. The whole "I" means this
much: that now there is no "thou", all thou's have
become assimilated by the "I". And when "thou" and
"I" become one there is no sense in calling it "I" or
"thou". So whether we say whole "I" or "non-I", they
are two ways of saying the same thing. When "I"
becomes whole it is empty, it is a zero experience; or
when "I" becomes empty it becomes whole. Whatever
way you say it makes no difference. The ultimate truth
can be said both ways—positively and negatively; it
includes both yes and no, and everything too. It is all
right if you say nothing about it; it is also fine if you
speak endlessly about it. After all that is said and
unsaid, truth remains beyond it; truth is always the
beyond. But in silence truth is complete, whole.

When we look at truth, what is, from a particular viewpoint, we are in difficulty. And we are all used to looking at truth from some viewpoint; we look at it through the screen of our ideas and concepts, our emotions and feelings. And as long as we have our thoughts and concepts and viewpoints, the truth that we see is bound to be fragmentary and incomplete. It is okay if we are aware that our perception of truth is partial and fragmentary, but the difficulty is that every viewpoint claims to be complete. And when a fragmentary vision claims to be the whole, when it lays claim to being a complete philosophy, it gives rise to great confusion and illusion. There is no such danger if a viewpoint is aware that it is simply a viewpoint. Complete perception of truth is possible only when all points and angles of viewing disappear, when one is nowhere or everywhere, when one is free of all ideas and concepts, of all words and images, of all associations. Then only knowing happens, truth happens.

And there are two ways—only two ways—of saying the truth. One way is positive and the other is negative. There is no third way of saying it. Buddha uses the negative way when he says truth is utter emptiness; it is absolute nothingness, it is *nirvana*. On the other hand Shankara uses the positive way, he calls it the supreme, the *Brahman*, the whole. The irony is that while Buddha and Shankara seem to be contradicting each other, they are saying the same thing: of course, their words, their metaphors, their ways of saying it are different. While Shankara loves the positive way, Buddha chooses the negative one.

If you ask me, I will say *Brahman* is another name for *nirvana*, and *nirvana* is another name for *Brahman*. And language comes to its end when both Shankara and Buddha meet. It is really there that truth begins, that truth is.

Questioner: You have said that while sadhana or spiritual discipline leads to the whole "I", upasana or devotion leads to "no-I", and that they are different things. But then you have also said that devotion and discipline are one and the same thing. Please explain.

No, I did not say that *sadhana* leads to the whole "I"; I only said that *sadhana* takes you in the direction of I or self. If spiritual discipline can take you to the whole "I" then there is no difference between *sadhana* and *upasana*. But the truth is that you cannot achieve the whole "I" through efforts, and that is why a moment comes in the life of a *sadhaka*, a traveler on the path of effort, when he is called upon to drop his self, to give up his "I".

Efforts can, at the most, lead you to the soul, which is an incomplete attainment. To complete it, to attain the supreme, the *sadhaka* will have to take a jump and give up the soul too. The devotee makes this leap with his very first step. You cannot come to the supreme through efforts. When all efforts cease, the ultimate truth comes into being. The devotee is in a much better position; he begins with the dropping of the "I", and after you have dropped your "I" there is nothing more to be dropped. What the *sadhaka* attains in the end, the *upasaka* attains at the very start.

And in my vision it is wise that what has to be dropped in the end should be dropped right at the beginning. Why cling to it unnecessarily? Why go through a long and tortuous and useless struggle? Why carry a heavy load on your head from the foot of a hill to its peak, when you are aware that it has to be dropped just before setting foot on the peak? It would be sheer stupidity and waste of energy and time. No one can climb the height of a mountain with a heavy load. Sooner or later it has to be dropped, but we say we will carry it as far as we can. The *upasaka* is more intelligent, he drops his "I" at the very start of the journey. And the miracle happens that with the dropping of the "I" the journey is complete. This is the difference between a doer and a devotee. However, there is no difference between them when they have arrived.

It is significant that while the journey of a doer is hard and painful, that of the devotee is joyful and easy. The doer's attachment to his "I" will continue to impede his progress at every step, and can even force him to leave the journey unfinished. The devotee has to face this problem only once—when he begins his journey. And if he can tackle it rightly he will be finished with it forever. He has another difficulty which comes when he compares himself with the doer. He can be tempted to think that if one can reach the summit with his "I", why should he drop it right at the start? He can be confused.

But it is a matter of inclination, type and choice that one person takes to devotion and another to discipline and effort. And while it is true that while the devotee's difficulty comes at the start and that of the doer comes at the end, the goal is the same.

But remember, the world of Krishna is the world of the devotee, the *upasaka*.

Questioner: Meditation seems to be central to the campaign of spiritual regeneration that you have been carrying on for the last seven or eight years. So please explain the difference between meditation and devotion and whether it is meditation and spiritual discipline that is central to your teaching, or devotion.

To me there is no difference whatsoever. To me words make no difference. The real thing is truth. And it is truth that I teach through meditation, and it is truth again that I teach through devotion and prayer. Even if I speak of spiritual discipline, I teach the same truth. As far as I am concerned it makes no difference. But it does make a difference in the context of Krishna. And it also makes a difference for Mahavira. Devotion is not relevant to Mahavira; he will never accept *upasana* as his way. Both Mahavira and Buddha adhere to spiritual discipline, *sadhana*, efforts. Their whole emphasis is on discipline. Of course, Christ is for devotion, and so is Krishna; Mohammed too. Devotion is their way. But as far as I am concerned I accept all of them together. I have no difficulty whatsoever.

So many times you will come to think that I contradict myself from day to day, that I am inconsistent. And it is true. I can sail through any of the different winds; they present no difficulty for me. At present I am speaking about Krishna, so I am selling *upasana* to you. Last year I was selling *sadhana* when I spoke about Mahavira. Next year I will be selling something else if I am going to speak about Christ. As I see truth, these differences don't make a difference. But when I am speaking about Krishna it would be wrong and unjust on my part to commit him to spiritual discipline. Krishna and *sadhana* don't go together.

Similarly I cannot impose dancing on Mahavira; he is utterly blissful with his silence and aloneness, as Krishna is with his flute. To me, the bliss of both Mahavira and Krishna, is the same. But I maintain it is not the same to them; Mahavira will not consent to dance, nor will Krishna agree to stand alone in the nude. Meditation and dancing can suit with me, but I have no right to make Mahavira dance and Krishna meditate with his eyes closed under a tree. Krishna has always danced in the shade of a tree; he has never meditated.

There is no record to say that Krishna ever meditated. And you cannot think that Mahavira danced even before he took up spiritual discipline.

So when I am speaking about Krishna I must bring devotion into focus and explain it. To me, devotion is a path for a particular type of people—the emotive ones. And discipline is a path for another type of people—the active ones. I see the relevance of every path and I know that they have their own advantages and disadvantages, as I explained a little while ago. And it will be very useful if you understand them rightly so you can choose your own paths correctly. You have to decide whether you follow the path of devotion or of discipline. I am finished with traveling; I have nowhere to go. And it does not matter to me whether one takes me as a devotee, as a doer or as neither.

It is for your sake that I am going to put devotion and discipline as two separate and distinct paths and explain their significance and their pitfalls. First you have to know what type of person you are; then choose your path in accordance with your type. This is very important to those who are going to be travelers on the spiritual path. There is no problem for those who think they have already arrived—wherever they are. And if someday you realize that you have nowhere to go, wherever you are you are in truth, then neither devotion nor discipline will have any meaning for you. Then you will simply laugh and say all talk of paths and techniques is sheer madness, there is nowhere to go; wherever you are you are in godliness, in truth. Truth is everywhere, and only truth is.

A Zen monk lives outside a cave and does nothing but sleep, day and night. A road passes by his hut and leads to an important place of pilgrimage in the mountains. Pilgrims passing by his hut are often surprised to see the monk lying about lazily and doing nothing. Once in a while they ask him, "Why are you lying here? Why don't you go on pilgrimage?"

The monk says to them, "I am already there where you are coming from or going to." And then he turns his back on them. He has never gone on a pilgrimage, nor is he likely to go ever. The pilgrims think him to be a madman, but he tells them again and again, "I am already there where you are going; I need not go anywhere or do anything."

For such a person neither devotion nor discipline has any meaning. But for you they are very meaningful. As far as I am concerned, from time to time I am going to speak about them, about their usefulness and even about their uselessness. But there is no contradiction in what I say if you understand me rightly. There is really no contradiction.

> *Questioner: There is yet another contradiction. You said that while Krishna was born enlightened, Mahavira attained to enlightenment through efforts. But in the course of your discourses on Mahavira in Kashmir last year, you said that Mahavira had completed all his spiritual discipline in his past lives, and in his last life as Mahavira he had nothing more to do than give expression to his experiences of enlightenment. If it is so, then Mahavira was also born enlightened. Please comment.*

No, I did not say that. I said that all of Mahavira's achievements came through discipline, through efforts. Whether he completed them in his last life or many lives before is not at all important. What is important is that he achieved everything through efforts, a long journey of efforts. Krishna did not have to do anything in any of his lives—past or present.

Questioner: Did he come to wholeness straightaway?

To us it seems difficult to understand how one can come straightaway to wholeness. We think one must pass through a criss-crossing of roads before he arrives. Again, this is the same question that pilgrims asked of the Zen monk lying near a cave. The monk says he does not have to do a thing, because he is already there where one should be. The pilgrims wonder how one could arrive without traveling, it seems impossible. They all had to walk long distances before they reached the place of pilgrimage, but the sage says to them, "If you cannot attain to truth right here, how can you attain to it by going to the mountain top? Truth is everywhere. It is here and now. This is not something that one needs any traveling to arrive at." But there are some types who cannot arrive without making a long journey. Even if they have to come home they will not do so without knocking at the doors of many other houses. They will enquire from others about directions to their own house.

Whether one chooses effort or effortlessness depends on what type of person he is. There is certainly a difference of type between Mahavira and Krishna. Mahavira will not choose to arrive without making a long journey. He will refuse to attain anything if it comes without effort. This needs to be understood. If someone tells Mahavira that he can achieve enlightenment without effort he will refuse it. He will say it is outright theft if you grab something without making any effort to achieve it, without striving and struggling for it, without earning it with the sweat of your brow. Before you have a thing, Mahavira will insist you must pay for it, deserve it. Mahavira will, as I understand him, reject even *moksha*, liberation, if it comes to him as a gift. He will search for it, struggle for it, he will earn it. He will accept *moksha* only when he is worthy of it.

Krishna will say just the opposite. He will say what is achieved through long search and struggle is not worth having. That which can be found can be lost too. He will say, "I will accept only that which comes uninvited, without efforts. I will be content with that which is, the true. And truth is not a thing that one can find."

This is a difference in approach to life that comes with individuals and their types. There is nothing superior or inferior about it. As individuals, Krishna and Mahavira are basically different from each other.

What is found through long search and striving has significance for Mahavira. This is the reason he and his whole tradition are known by that strange name *shraman*, which simply means one who toils. Mahavira believes the price of freedom is hard work, and what is had effortlessly is sheer thievery. According to him, if God is found without effort, it cannot be the real God; there must be some deception about it. And Mahavira's sense of self-respect will not allow him to accept anything that comes as a gift, he will earn it with the sweat of his brow. That is why a term like God's grace has no place in Mahavira's philosophy. On the other hand, it is replete with words like efforts, struggle, hard work, discipline, and *sadhana*. This is as it should be. His whole tradition is based on hard work.

There are two cultural traditions in India, running parallel to each other. One is known as *shraman sanskriti* or toil-oriented culture, and the other is called *brahmin sanskriti* or God-oriented culture. The *brahmanic* tradition believes man is God, he does not have to become it, while the *shraman* tradition believes that man has to earn godliness, he is not it. And there are only two types of people in the world— *brahmins* or *shramans*—conforming to one of these traditions. And the ratio of *brahmins* is very small; even the *brahmins* are not that *brahmin*. The vast majority consists of *shramans*, doers who believe in efforts. To them everything must come the hard way. It needs tremendous courage, patience, and trust to believe that one can find without effort, that one can attain without attaining, that one can arrive without stepping out of one's house. Our ordinary mind says that if you want to find something, you will have to make adequate efforts for it, nothing is had without a price. Our ordinary arithmetic believes that efforts and achievements have to be in equal proportions.

Once in a great while a few *brahmins* have walked this earth; they can be counted on fingers. The rest of us are *shramans*, whether we accept it or not. That is why despite great differences between Buddha and Mahavira, their traditions became known by the common name of *shraman*. In this respect Buddhists are not different from the Jainas, they are the same.

Krishna is a *brahmin*—a rare thing. He says, "I am already the supreme being."

And remember, I am not saying that one is right and another is wrong. To me both *shraman* and *brahmin* are right, there is no difficulty about it. They represent two different types of minds, two different ways of thinking, two different kinds of journeying. That is the only difference.

Questioner: One last question, if you permit. How is it that Krishna, in all his past lives, has never been ignorant and imperfect?

Not only Krishna, even Mahavira had never been ignorant and imperfect in any of his past lives. It is another thing that Mahavira came to know of it only in his last life. Krishna had always known it; he knew it eternally. Even you are not ignorant and imperfect. Each one of us is all-knowing and each one of us is whole—just we are not aware of it. It is all a matter of remembering, of being aware that we are it. The difference lies in awareness, not in being.

For example, the sun is high up in the sky, but all of us here go into deep sleep. The sun will be very much there, but then we will not be aware of it. Then one of us wakes up and knows that the sun is shining on him. The sun will be shedding light equally on all those who remain asleep, but they will not be aware of it. And when they awaken will they be right in saying the sun rose with their awakening? No, what would be right is for them to say the sun was already there, but they woke up to it later. No one—neither Mahavira, nor Krishna nor you—is without light and knowledge. Each one of us is whole as he is. It is all a matter of remembering it, waking up to it.

Throughout his existence, in all of his lives, Krishna has been aware that he is whole. So the question of his striving for it does not arise. At a particular level of his existence, say in his last life, Mahavira comes to know through efforts and discipline, that he is not ignorant and imperfect, but knowing and whole. And when he is awakened he also comes to know that this has always been the case, he has always been aware and whole. And what difference does it make if someone comes to know of it a few lives earlier or later?

But it makes a difference for those of us who live in time; we are always concerned about time—who comes first and who comes last. But in eternity no one is the first and no one is the last. In existence, time is without beginning and without end. So the question of one's awakening to reality sooner or later does not arise. This question has relevance only for those of us who believe time begins and ends. If time has no beginning, then what does it matter if someone awakens two days before me? If time is without end, then what does it matter if I attain to reality two days after someone else?

The measurement of time in seconds, days and years is imaginary; man has invented it. It is conceptual, but not a fact. It is utilitarian, but not real. The truth is that time itself is a concept, not a reality. Reality is eternal and immeasurable. And enlightenment, awakening, or whatever you call it happens beyond time, in timelessness.

It will seem strange to you when I say that the moment of Mahavira's attainment is the same as the moment of Krishna's. You will say it is incredible, yet it is a fact. But to understand it we will have to go more deeply into the question of time.

Let us understand it in this way. On a piece of paper I draw a circle with a center. Then I draw a number of lines running from the circumference to the center. Right at the circumference there is a distance, a gap between any two lines, but this gap goes on shrinking as the lines proceed towards the center. And as they reach the center this gap disappears altogether. While there is clearly a gap at the circumference, there is none at the center.

It is the same with time. At the circumference of time there is a gap between Mahavira and Krishna, between Krishna and me, between me and you, but there is no gap whatsoever when we all arrive at the center. All distance disappears at the center. But since we all live on time's circumference, and we have no knowledge of its center, we find it difficult to understand that Mahavira and Krishna arrive there together and at the same time.

I will explain it in yet another way. Think of a bullock-cart on the move; its wheel revolves but the axle remains unmoving. The truth is that the wheel moves with the support of the axle; without the axle the wheel cannot move. So a moving wheel is dependent on an unmoving axle. Even when the wheel has revolved a million times, the axle will be stationary. The wonder is that the wheel and axle are joined together, and yet one moves and the other is unmoving. Remove the axle and the wheel will become useless. And the two together make for the cart and its movement. Is it not strange? And how is it possible? It is possible because while the wheel is the circumference, the axle is the hub, the center.

In the same way time, or history forms the circumference while truth, or divinity forms the center.

The moment of arrival, whether Krishna's or Mahavira's or anyone else's, is always the same, because it happens beyond time. At that timeless center no one can say who came when. But those who live in time, which is the circumference, certainly have their different times of arrival and departure. All distances belong to time and space. At the center where eternity abides, all distances disappear.

> Questioner: It is a prayer, a request, and not a question. We have now only five days left. So I would suggest that you should devote mornings to

*answering our questions and evenings
to your independent discourses on
Krishna and his Geeta.*

No, it would not be proper. I will say what I have to
say; you need not worry about it. Whatever questions
you ask, I will say only that which I have to say.
Questions don't make any difference.

THIRTEENTH DISCOURSE
EVENING, OCTOBER 1, 1970
MANALI, INDIA

KRISHNA GOES TO THE WEST

Questioner: You have said one can encounter Krishna's soul any time, because it is everlasting, nothing in existence dies. If so, what should one do to make it possible? And tell us if one can attain to full devotion through concentration on Krishna's icon and chanting his name and hymns of his praise.

othing in existence perishes, nor does anything new come into being. Forms change, appearances change, but the deepest mysteries of life remain ever the same. Individuals come and go, waves in the ocean rise and disappear, but that which is hidden in the individual, in the wave is eternal.

We have to look at Krishna in two different ways, and then we can look at ourselves the same way. We exist at two levels—one at the level of waves and another at the level of the ocean. As waves we are individual human beings, and as the ocean we are the supreme being.

Krishna's physical form, his voice, his music are like the waves. His soul, hidden inside the body is like the ocean. Waves come and go, but the ocean is everlasting. While the forms of existence change, its soul, the spirit which abides in its *elan vital* is deathless, eternal. The spirit was there even when Krishna was not born and it is there when he is no more. It was there before your birth and it will be there even after your death. Krishna was like a wave that arose from the ocean, danced for a while with the winds, and disappeared again in the same ocean.

All of us are like Krishna, but there is a small difference. When Krishna is dancing as a wave he is aware that he belongs to the ocean, he is the ocean itself. But as far as we are concerned we know ourselves only as waves; we forget that we are the ocean. This is the difference between us and Krishna. And since we know ourselves only as waves, we fail to understand the oceanic form of Krishna.

Krishna's physical body, his picture and statue can be used to come in contact with his soul. But it is just a play that belongs to the world of appearances. And to understand it we have to approach it from two or three sides.

Even today we can make contact with the oceanic form of Krishna—his soul. In the same way we can come in contact with the souls of Mahavira and Buddha. And to contact the essential Krishna we can make use of his physical form as a medium, an instrument.

When statues of men like Krishna were first made, they were not meant for worship. In fact, these statues came in the wake of an esoteric science which has become almost extinct. Before leaving their physical forms, the awakened ones had given a promise and a technique to their lovers, their disciples, that they could contact their oceanic life by meditating on unconscious mind that whenever you repeat the process he will go into sleep, and then his unconscious mind will begin to operate on him.

The power of our unconscious mind is enormous; what we cannot do in our conscious state we can do with the help of the unconscious mind. Man's unconscious mind is much more sensitive than his conscious. What we cannot hear in the conscious state becomes audible to the unconscious. In deep hypnotic sleep you can see things you can never see while awake. It is not the talisman, but the post-hypnotic suggestion associated with it that works.

If a person like Krishna, Buddha or Christ is about to leave this world and some of his close lovers or disciples who have been in intimate contact with him, who have imbibed his vibes, request some techniques to contact him after his departure, the master in his compassion can give them such a technique. He can ask them to go into a state of meditation and then tell them that whenever they will meditate on a particular form of his—through a statue or a picture—they will immediately contact him even after his death. This is the esoteric science for which statues of Krishna, Buddha and others like them were first made.

These statues and symbols were specially given to chosen disciples in a meditative state. So your ordinary statues are not going to work, nor can ordinary seekers come in contact with them through these statues. To establish contact with Krishna one will need to have a special symbol and an inner suggestion given to him in his meditative state.

Before persons like Buddha, Mahavira and Krishna, depart from this earth, they leave such techniques and instructions with their most trusted group of disciples; those who are worthy of it. This generation of disciples takes full advantage of this special transmission. And if this generation passes it on to a second generation of disciples, it can work their statues. It was for this purpose that their statues were first made.

To explain this esoteric science I would like you to know something about hypnosis. You must have watched a magician demonstrating his magical plays by the wayside. One of these plays is like this. He makes a boy, who happens to be his assistant, lie down on the ground, and covers him with a piece of thick cloth. Then he puts a talisman on his chest which sends the boy into hypnotic sleep. He then asks him many strange questions, and to the amazement of the spectators the sleeping boy answers them. The magician then moves to one of the spectators and asks him to whisper his name into his ear. The spectator whispers his name so that even the person next to him can hardly hear it, but the sleeping boy immediately relays his name to the whole gathering. The magician moves to another spectator who happens to have currency in his pocket. He asks the boy to tell the note's number, and he shouts out the exact number. This casts a spell on the gathering, and then the magician tells them it is the power of the talisman that works through his sleeping aide. And he sells a few talismans—which are his only source of earning.

The magician uses hypnosis here, but he lies when he says that it is the power of the talisman. So when you take the talisman home and try it you meet with disappointment. The talisman is absolutely useless, except that it brings the magician some money. The magic really lies in hypnosis. In this case, it is post-hypnosis.

There is a simple technique for post-hypnosis. You put a person into hypnotic sleep through suggestions, and it is a very simple thing to do. After he goes into sleep—which is different from ordinary sleep—you ask him to look closely at the talisman and then tell him that whenever this talisman is put on his chest while he is lying down, he will go into sleep. This suggestion will sink so deep in the person's with them as well. But with the passage of time usually the science, the technique is lost and only statues and their rituals remain in the hands of succeeding generations. Then it turns into a dead and fossilized tradition without any significance.

Now whatever you do sitting before a statue of Krishna, nothing is going to happen. Now no rituals are worthwhile; they are a sheer waste of time and energy. It is as if you buy a talisman from a street magician and it does not work, because you don't have the necessary technique—the post-hypnotic suggestion—with you.

As I said, a statue, an icon works as an esoteric bridge between the disciple and his departed master's soul, his spirit. In the same way an awakened master's name can be used as an esoteric bridge, provided the name is received in a meditative state. Now any number of gurus are going about whispering name-bearing mantras into their disciples' ears, which is of absolutely no use. It is not a matter of whispering a name in one's ear; that is just stupid. If a competent master transmits a symbolic word to his disciple, who is in a meditative state, the word becomes alive with esoteric energy. And when the disciple remembers it rightly, chants it, his whole consciousness is transformed. Such words are called *beej shabda* or seed words, and they are packed with something subtle, sublime.

If Krishna's name is really your seed word, it means that it has been sown in the innermost depth of your psyche when you were in a meditative state and that the necessary suggestions have been associated with it. Remember, a seed is always sown in such a way—it lies underground for a while and then alone it sprouts and grows into a tree, which is always above the ground. Such words are pregnant with immense possibilities. Because of such a seed word Ramakrishna was often put into any number of troubles. It became difficult for him to pass through a street without going through such troubles.

Once he was going somewhere and on the way someone greeted him with the words, "Jai Rama"—meaning victory to Rama—and he immediately fell down and passed into *samadhi*, the highest state of meditation. At another time he visited a temple where devotees were chanting the name of Rama, and he again sank into deep *samadhi*. Rama's name was like a seed word for him; it was enough to transform his consciousness.

Since it will be difficult for you to understand the case of Ramakrishna, I will explain it to you in your own framework. There are situations which work like seed words for many people. Hearing some bad news, someone becomes worried and immediately puts his hand on his forehead. If you prevent him from taking his hand to his head, he will become restless. Another person sits up in a particular posture the moment he is faced with a serious problem. He will be in chaos if you prevent him from sitting in that posture.

Dr. Harisingh Gaud, a renowned lawyer of his time, has mentioned an extraordinary episode in his memoirs. He was once arguing a case before the Privy Council in London. He had a strange habit: whenever he was faced with a complex and difficult point of law and he needed some inspiration to help argue his case rightly, his hand almost instinctively reached for the top button of his coat and turned it right and left, and soon he got on very nicely. Those who had worked with him in the legal profession knew that as soon as Dr. Gaud started turning his coat button his argument took on a new and powerful thrust. Then he was unbeatable. It was a big case, and the lawyer on the opposite side was smarting under the power of Dr. Gaud's arguments. So he bribed Gaud's chauffeur, asking him to remove the top button of his master's coat before he came to the court the following day.

The next day Dr. Gaud was going to conclude his case. When he was proceeding before the court with his argument, a moment came when his hand automatically moved to his coat button. He was shocked to find the button was missing. Dr. Gaud could not proceed any further, he just collapsed into his chair. He later wrote in his diary that for the first time in his life, to his chagrin, his brain stopped functioning and he found himself in a vacuum. He then requested the court to adjourn the hearing until the following day on the plea that he had no energy left to proceed further.

It seems strange that a little button had so much power over the mind of a mighty lawyer. This is what psychological association does. If a mind is used to being activated by the touch of a button, it is bound to fail if the button is not available to it. This syndrome is known as conditioned reflex in psychology.

In this same way a name, or a seed word, or a mantra can be used. Like Dr. Gaud's button— which for him was not just an ordinary coat button but a powerful lever to turn his mind on and off—a name can be used to transform your consciousness. But an empty word won't do; it has to be charged with a master's energy; it must be a seed word. A seed word is one that is implanted in the innermost depth of your unconscious in such a way that its very remembrance can bring about a mutation in you.

The names of men like Krishna and Buddha and many other words and mantras have been used for this purpose. But now people are repeating them meaninglessly. You repeat "Rama, Rama" a thousand times and it doesn't work. If it were a seed word it would work at the first chanting. And it is not necessary that only names like Rama and Krishna can be used; any word can be transformed into a seed word and implanted in the depth of your unconscious. But unless a word or a mantra is charged with meditative energy, it won't work as a transforming factor in your life. The difficulty is that very often the basic know-how is lost and we are left with empty words and superficial rituals. Day in and day out someone is chanting "Rama, Rama", and another is chanting "Krishna, Krishna" and nothing happens. Do what you can till the end of time, nothing will happen.

You also want to know what *kirtan*, or singing hymns of praise to Krishna can do to enhance devotion. It can do a lot if we do it rightly. The way we are doing the second stage of Dynamic Meditation can be used for singing or dancing as well. It has been used in the past by those who knew its real meaning. Those who don't know the real meaning just dance and shout—which is a waste of time. If *kirtan* can be done in the way of the second stage of the Dynamic Meditation, it can be of tremendous help.

If you can dance with abandon, you will begin to see yourself and your body as separate from each other. Soon you will cease to be a dancer; instead you will become a watcher, a witness. When your body will be dancing totally, a moment will come when you will suddenly find that you are completely separate from the dance.

In the past many devices were designed to bring about this separation between a seeker and his body, and singing and dancing was one such device. You can dance in such a way and with such abandon that a moment comes when you break away from dancing and clearly see yourself standing separate from the dance. Although your body will continue to dance, you will be quite separate from it as a spectator watching the dance. It will seem as if the axle has separated itself from the wheel which continues to keep moving—as if the axle has come to know that it is an axle and that which is moving is the wheel, although separate from it.

Dancing can be seen in the same way as a wheel. If the wheel moves with speed, a moment comes when it is seen distinctly separate from the axle. It is interesting that when the wheel is unmoving you cannot see it as separate from the axle, but when it moves you can clearly see them as two separate entities. You can know by contrast which is moving and which is not.

Let someone dance and let him bring all his energy to it, and soon he will find there is someone inside him who is not dancing, who is utterly steady and still. That is his axle, his center. That which is dancing is his circumference, his body, and he himself is the center. If one can be a witness in this great moment then *kirtan* has great significance. But if he continues to dance without witnessing it, he will only waste his time and energy.

Techniques and devices come into being and then they are lost. And they are lost for the simple reason that man as he is tends to forget the essential and hold on to the non-essential, the shadow. The truth is that while the essential remains hidden and invisible like the roots of a tree, the non-essential, the trunk of the tree is visible. The non-essential is like our clothes, and the essential is like our soul. And we are liable to forget that which is subtle and invisible and remember the gross, the visible. It is for this reason when someone comes to me to know if *kirtan* can be useful, I emphatically deny it and ask him not to indulge in it. I know that now it is a dead tradition, a corpse without soul, as if the axle has disappeared and only the wheel remains.

Questioner: Do you think Chaitanya's singing and dancing was nothing more than a way of intoxication?

No, Chaitanya achieved the highest through singing and dancing. He achieved through dancing exactly what Mahavira and Buddha achieved through meditation, through stillness.

There are two ways to come to the axle, the center, the supreme. One of the ways lies in your being so steady and still—just at a standstill—that there is not a trace of trembling in you and you arrive at the center. The other way is just the contrary: you get into such terrific motion that the wheel runs at top speed and the axle becomes visible and knowable. And this second way is easier than the first.

It is easy to know the axle if the wheel is in motion. While Mahavira comes to know it through stillness, through meditation, Krishna knows it through dancing. And Chaitanya surpasses even Krishna in dancing; his dance is magnificent, incomparable. Perhaps no other person on this earth danced as much as Chaitanya. In this connection it is good to bear in mind that man has both a circumference and a center, and while his circumference—the body—is always moving and changing, his center—his soul—is still and quiet, it is eternal. And the question of questions is how to come to this unchanging, eternal center.

The second stage of the meditation that we are having here in the camp schedule, is a device and an attempt to bring about that stillness and silence through motion and restlessness. I am not using *kirtan* because the word *kirtan* has become too much loaded and obsolete in this sense; it has lost its original meaning. Words like money lose their value through too much use—too much wear and tear—and they go out of usage, and a time comes when they have to be replaced by new words. That is why you will often find it difficult to understand me because I am doing the same thing, I am minting new devices for the old ones which have become out-of-date. It is in the very nature of things: they are born, they grow into youth and have vigor and vitality, and then they grow old and die. The old coins are so worn out that one cannot say if they are coins or junk. Therefore, every time we have to begin from the beginning, and we do so with the awareness that again these new coins too will wear out through long usage and become antiquated, and again someone will have to declare them trash and mint anew.

Ironically we have to fight with the very things for which we live; we condemn the old coins and manufacture new ones in their place so the great work they are meant for gets going as ever. We oppose and fight old and worn out devices and fashion new ones in their place so that the dead ones go out of use and new ones take their place, and their great work comes alive once again. But through long association you get so attached to the old ones that it feels very painful to give them up. And then the fear of the new comes in your way of accepting the new devices, new techniques—you become resistant to them.

This is what happens with religion every now and then. Religion that is alive and dynamic at the time of its birth grows old and dies, but we refuse to part with them, we carry their dead bodies on our backs and get crushed under their dead weight. But whether you like it or not they have to be buried or cremated and a new alive religion has to take their place and keep the wheel moving.

Kirtan, singing and dancing can play a great and unique role in spiritual growth. But the difficulty is that if I ask you to use it you will take it to be the same old *kirtan* that you are familiar with, and your mind will think that you already know it. And this is what makes me wary; what your mind thinks is right can never be right, because mind itself is wrong. Therefore I cannot support the *kirtan* that you know and do; if it was right you need not have come here. You are not right; with all your singing and dancing in the old way you have not reached anywhere. So say goodbye and forget it.

When I speak about *kirtan* I mean the *kirtan* in its pristine form, which was used to separate you from your body and settle you at your center. I speak about the significance of names and statues in the same sense. I have nothing to do with statues that adorn your temples and houses; I am consigning them to the dustbin. They are no longer of any use. This does not mean they never had any significance. They had, but it is gone. The truth is that because they originally had great significance we continue to carry them thousands of years after they have lost their meaning. The fact that man persists with them long after they have ceased to be useful shows that the memory of their past significance lies buried deep in the recesses of his unconscious. Otherwise it would not have been possible for us to live under their dead weight for so long.

If you treasure some trash, it simply means you once had a glimpse of a diamond hidden behind it. If a wrong custom perpetuates itself, it means sometime in the past it embodied some truth which now is no more. That is why many outdated names and mantras and statues are still in vogue.

> *Questioner: To Chaitanya Maha-prabhu the world and God were both separate and together; it is called* achintya bhedabhedavad, *i.e. the principle of unthinkable difference and unity together. Does this principle fit with your principle of the axle and the wheel?*

It is going to fit for sure. Among the lovers of Krishna, Chaitanya's name is the most outstanding.

In the term *achintya bhedabhedavad*, the word *achintya*—which means the unthinkable—is precious. Those who know through thought will say that either matter and spirit are separate or they are one and the same. Chaitanya says they are both one and separate. For example, the wave is both one with and separate from the ocean at the same time. And he is right. The wave is separate from the ocean, and so we call it by a different name—the wave. And it is virtually one with the ocean, because it cannot be without it, it comes from it. Therefore the wave is both separate and inseparable from the ocean.

But all this is within the realm of thinking; one can mentally think out that the wave and ocean are different and the same together. But Chaitanya adds another word to it, another dimension—that is *achintya* or unthinkable. And this word is very significant. He says that if you come to know through thinking that the world and God, matter and spirit are both separate and inseparable, this realization is worth nothing. Then it is nothing more than an idea, a concept, a theory. But when a seeker comes to it without thinking, without word, when he realizes it in a state of no-mind, beyond thought, then it is his experience. Then it is worthwhile; it is real, and great.

It is good to go into this question of thinking and that which is beyond thinking. What we know through thought is known only in words and concepts. And what we know by living it, by experiencing it, is a realization beyond words. This is what Chaitanya means by calling it the unthinkable; it is beyond mind, beyond word and thought.

Someone wants to know what love is and he reads huge scriptures on love. Perhaps on no other topic has so much been written as pundits have written on love. There is a huge amount of literature on love in the form of poetry and epics and philosophical treatises. He will become knowledgeable about love, he can write great treatises on love, yet in reality he will not actually know what love is.

There is another person who has not read a word about love, but has experienced it, lived it. What is the difference between this man and the one who has gone through a huge pile of literature on love? This man knows love through experiencing; the other man knows it through words and concepts. Experiencing is always unthinkable, it does not happen through thinking; in fact, it happens before thinking. Experience precedes thought, and thought follows experience. Experience comes first and thought follows it by way of its expression.

That is why Chaitanya says that unity and separateness of the world and God is beyond thought.

When Chaitanya says this is unthinkable, he means much more than what meets the eye. Meera will say it is unthinkable, but she was never given to serious thinking—she was through and through a woman of feelings. But as far as Chaitanya is concerned, he was a great logician, renowned for his sharp mind and brilliant logic. He had scaled the highest peaks of thinking. Pundits were afraid of entering into argument with him. He was incomparable as a debater; he had won laurel after laurel in philosophical discussions.

Such a rational intellect, who had indulged in hair-splitting interpretations of words and concepts throughout his life, was one day found singing and dancing through the streets of Navadeep. Meera, on the other hand, had never indulged in pedantry and scriptures; she had nothing to do with logic. She was a loving woman; love was in her blood and bones. So it was no wonder when she walked through the streets of Merta with a tanpoora in her hands, dancing and singing hymns of love. It was just natural. But Chaitanya was her opposite; he was not a man of love, and he turned to love and devotion—which was a miracle. This one-hundred-and-eighty-degree turn in his life demonstrates the victory of love over logic. He had defeated all his contemporaries with his logic, but when he came to himself he found it to be a self-defeating discipline. He came to a point where the mind lost and life and love won. Beyond this point one can only go with life and love.

That is why I said that among people who walked the path of Krishna, Chaitanya is simply extraordinary, incomparable. When I say so I am aware of Meera, who loves Krishna tremendously. But she does not come near Chaitanya. It is unthinkable how a tremendously logical mind like Chaitanya could come down from his ivory tower, take a drum in his hands, and dance and sing in the market place. Can you think of Bertrand Russell dancing through the streets of London? Chaitanya was like Russell—out and out intellectual. And for this reason his statement becomes immensely significant. He makes his statement that reality is unthinkable not with words, but with a drum in his hands—dancing and singing through the streets of his town, where he was held in great respect for his superb scholarship. It is in this way that he renounces mind, renounces thinking and declares that, "Reality is beyond thought, it is unthinkable."

Chaitanya's case demonstrates that they alone can transcend thinking who first enter into the very depth of thinking and explore it through and through. Then they are bound to come to a point where thinking ends and the unthinkable begins. This last frontier of mind is where a statement like this is born. That is why Chaitanya's statement has gathered immense significance; it comes after he crosses the last frontier of mentation. Meera never walked on that path; she came to love straight-away. She cannot have the profundity of Chaitanya.

Questioner: Today a movement by the name of Krishna Consciousness is getting popular in America, England and other countries of the West where things like kirtan are becoming fashionable. Is it a new variety of entertainment or a fad? Or do you think that the ground is being prepared for Krishna's birth in the West?

This event has deeper implications.

The movement for Krishna Consciousness is growing fast in America and Europe. Like the villages of Bengal of Chaitanya's days, the streets of New York and London today are resounding with God's songs. And this is not accidental.

The whole of the West today has collectively reached a point where Chaitanya had once reached individually. It is the same last frontier of mind and intellect, where Chaitanya absolutely tired of thinking and realized that it leads nowhere. In the same way the West is now tired of thinking. From Socrates to Bertrand Russell, the West has long tried to find truth through thinking. It was a great and unique adventure to search for reality through reason and logic, and the West has consecrated all its energy to this quest. The West has always refused to accept that truth is beyond the boundary of intellect and reason, that reality is illogical and unthinkable. It has trusted only mind and intellect.

For twenty-five hundred years the West has traveled the path of intellect with dedication, and yet failed to have a glimpse of reality. Many times its great minds felt reality was within reach, but it continued to elude them. Each time they had only ideas and concepts in their hand, not truth. And now the whole of the West feels fed up with mentation.

Today the collective consciousness of the West is exactly where Chaitanya had found himself individually a few centuries ago. It is now on the brink of an explosion, a transformation which is every day coming closer. The first flowers of spring have already blossomed and new winds are blowing. Cracks have appeared in the old order and the young generation is rebelling against old ways and decaying values—against tradition itself. And they are now turning their ears to the music and message of that which is unthinkable—the mysterious.

And if the West has to go in the direction of the mysterious, Krishna is going to be its hero. He is the best representative of the truth that is beyond mind and its logic, that is mysterious. Mahavira and Buddha cannot serve that purpose. Mahavira is very logical; even when he speaks about the mysterious he uses the language of logic and reason; he sticks to the process of consistent and logical thinking. As far as Buddha is concerned, he persistently refuses to speak about the mysterious whenever he is asked about it. He just says it is inexplicable. He goes only as far as logic, not beyond.

The mental stress and tension the West is suffering from today is the direct result of too much thinking. The anxiety and anguish of the West comes from thinking stretched to its ultimate; it is suffering under the crushing weight of the mind. Consequently the younger generation is in revolt. And it is natural that when a whole generation rebels it does so in many different ways. On their journey to the unthinkable, some are singing "Hare Krishna, Hare Rama" and many others are taking drugs like LSD and mescaline. The same people are now traveling across India and wandering through the Himalayan mountains. In the search of the *achintya*, the unthinkable, they will go to Japan and squat in its Zen monasteries. The quest is the same all over.

In its search for the mysterious, it seems the western world will be coming increasingly close to Krishna. LSD cannot take them far; travels to India and Japan are not going to last long. Eventually they will have to discover their own consciousness, their own soul; they cannot live long on credit. That is why their boys and girls are restless—chanting "Hare Krishna" in the streets of New York, London and Berlin.

It is remarkable that when young men and young women of the West dance and do *kirtan*, they do it with an abandon and joy that cannot be found anywhere in India today. Go round this country where *kirtan* has been in vogue for centuries and you will nowhere come across that enthusiasm and joy among people who do *kirtan* here. For us it is a well-traveled road, a routine. For us the *kirtan* is now a worn out coin; we know it is worthless. For the westerners it is a new coin which is valuable. When a group passes through the streets of London singing and dancing, even the traffic police watch them in amazement. They think their youth are going crazy. No one in India will think like that; here it is an accepted ritual.

But remember, real religion is run by mad people, it is not the job of the so-called wise. Whenever and wherever a breakthrough happens it always happens with the help of those who are called crazy by their contemporaries. Now singing and dancing is not thought to be strange in India. It was considered strange when Chaitanya danced through the towns and villages of Bengal; people thought he had gone out of his mind. But tradition sucks down everything that comes its way and puts it in its closet. Even madness is tamed by tradition.

The West is on the brink of an explosion, a breakthrough, a revolution. That is why when young people in the West move through the streets dancing and singing, there is a newness and simplicity, beauty and charm in their performance. Certainly it is a preparation, but not for Krishna's birth; it is a preparation for the birth of Krishna consciousness in the West.

Krishna consciousness has nothing to do with Krishna. It is a symbolic term which means that now a consciousness is dawning in the West which will make them give up work and embrace celebration as their way of life. It is just symbolic. Work has become meaningless. The West has done plenty of hard work and hard thinking; it has done everything that man is capable of doing, and now it is tired, utterly tired of all that. Either the West will have to die or it will enter into Krishna consciousness. These are the two choices before the West. And since death is not possible, because nothing really dies, Krishna consciousness is inescapable.

Christ has ceased to be relevant for the West, and the reason is again tradition. For the West, Christ symbolizes tradition and Krishna represents anti-tradition. Christ is an imposition on them and Krishna is their free choice. And then Christ is very serious, and the West is fed up with seriousness. Too much seriousness turns into a disease ultimately. So the West is trying hard to get rid of its seriousness; the cross has proved much too heavy on its soul. Jesus hanging on the cross seems dreadful, and the West in its heart feels disturbed, uneasy with it. So the cross is being taken down and the flute ushered in. And what can be a better substitute for the cross than the flute?

For these reasons Krishna's appeal to the West is growing, and it will continue to grow. Every day it is going to come nearer and nearer to Krishna.

There are some other reasons for Krishna's incursion into the West. Only an affluent society can gather around Krishna; a poor society cannot afford him. A society steeped in poverty and misery cannot have that leisure and ease so necessary to dance and play a flute. The society in which Krishna was born was highly prosperous in its own way. There was no lack of food, clothes and other necessities of life; milk and yogurt and butter were available in abundance— so much that when Krishna wanted to play pranks with his numerous girlfriends, who were milkmaids, he went on breaking their containers full of milk and yogurt.

Judging by the standard of living of his time, Krishna's society was at the peak of affluence. People were happy, they had plenty of leisure; a whole family lived well on the earnings of one of its members. It is only in such a society that flute and raas and celebration take center stage. The West today is at that height of affluence which the world has never known before. It is not surprising that Krishna has such a great pull on the western mind.

Ironically, Krishna no longer has any appeal for the present day India, ravaged by poverty, squalor and disease. She will have to wait long to deserve him. At the moment Christ has more attraction for this country. It is natural that a country hanging on the cross should think of Christ as the right person to alleviate their pain and suffering. That is why a striking and unexpected event is taking place: Jesus' influence in India is growing every day, while it is declining in the West. And it is not enough just to say that Christian missionaries are proselytizing Indians through devious and questionable means. What is equally true is that the Christian symbol of the cross comes closest to the agonized mind of this country. It is because of this affinity between the two that the missionaries are succeeding here in their efforts.

On the other hand the golden statues of Rama and Krishna, symbolizing royalty and richness are becoming out of tune with the poverty-stricken people of this country. The day is not far off when the poor of India will not only mount an assault on the rich but also on the statues of Krishna and Rama. It is just possible, because they can no longer put up with their glittering gold. And they are going to fall in love with Christ on the cross, symbolizing their pain and misery. The possibility of India turning to Christ and of the West turning to Krishna is growing every day.

For the western mind the cross has lost its significance, because people there are no longer in suffering and pain; they have everything they ever longed for. The truth is that now their only pain is that which stems from affluence. Their affluence is frightening; they don't know what to do with it. Now for certain a singing and dancing religion is going to be very close to the western heart. So it is not surprising that youth in the West are chanting Krishna's name with great enthusiasm.

> *Questioner: At the moment the leadership of the Krishna Consciousness movement in the West has passed into the hands of that irrationalist poet Allen Ginsberg; so far the intelligentsia does not seem to have been impressed by it. You said that the society in which Krishna was born was prosperous, but the Geeta and the Bhagwad mention Krishna's friend, Sudama, who was the very picture of poverty. Krishna says in the Geeta that among sacrifices he represents japa or chanting and that chanting will be the path for the Kali-yuga, the dark age, in which we are living. Please comment.*

No, I did not say that no one was poor in Krishna's time, or that no one is poor in the present-day West. There are poor people in the West, but their society as a whole is affluent. In the same way, although poor men like Sudama existed in Krishna's time, his society was very prosperous. A poor society is one thing; the existence of a handful of poor people in a rich society is different. The Indian society today is definitely poor, although there are Tatas and Birlas among us. The presence of Tatas and Birlas does not make the society affluent. Similarly, in spite of the Sudamas, Krishna's society was prosperous and rich.

The question is whether a society on the whole is rich or poor. There are rich people even in an utterly poor society like India's, and similarly there are poor people in the very affluent society of America. The society of Krishna's time was rich; good things of life were available to the vast majority of people. The same is true in today's American society. And only an affluent society can afford celebration; a poor society cannot.

As a society sinks into poverty it ceases to be celebrative, to be joyous. Not that there are no festivals in a poor society, but those festivals are lackluster, as good as dead. When the Festival of Lights— *Diwali*—comes here, the poor have to borrow money to celebrate it. They save their worn out clothes for *Holi*—the Festival of Colors. Is this the way to celebrate a festival like *Holi*? In the past, people came out in their best clothes to be smeared with all kinds of colors; now they go through it as if it is a kind of compulsory ritual. The festival of *Holi* was born when Indian society was at the peak of prosperity; now it is only dragging its feet somehow. In the past people were pleased when someone poured colors on their clothes; now in the same situation they are saddened, because they cannot afford enough clothes.

The West now can well afford a festival like *Holi*. They have already adopted Krishna's dance; sooner or later they are going to adopt *Holi* as well. It does not need an astrologer to predict it. They have everything—money, clothes, colors and leisure—which is necessary to celebrate such a festival as *Holi*. And unlike us they will celebrate with enthusiasm and joy. They will really rejoice.

When a society on the whole is affluent, even its poor are not that poor; they are better off than the rich people of a poor society. Today even the poorest of America does not cling to money in the way the richest of India does. Living in a sea of poverty, even the rich people of this country share the psychology of the poor. Their clinging to money is pathetic.

I have heard that on a fine morning a beggar appeared at the doors of a house. He was young and healthy and his body was robust and beautiful. The housewife was pleasantly surprised to see such a beggar, he was rare, and she gave him food and clothes with an open heart. Then she said to the beggar, "How is it that you are a beggar? You don't seem to be born poor."

The beggar said, "It seems you are also going the same way. I gave away my wealth in the same way you gave me food and clothes a little while ago. You will not take long to join me in the street."

Clinging to money is characteristic of a poor society; even its rich people suffer from this malady. And clinging disappears in a rich society; even its poor can afford to spend and enjoy what little they have. They are not afraid, they know they can make money when they need it.

It is in this sense that I said Krishna consciousness happens in an affluent society, and the West is really an affluent society.

The questioner also wants to know why the revolt, the breakthrough in the West is being led by people like Ginsberg, who are irrationalists. It is true that all the young rebels of the West, whether they are existentialists, the Beatles, the beatniks, or the hippies or the yippies, are irrationalists who represent a revolt against the excessive rationalism of their older generations. It is also true that the intellectuals of the West are yet uninfluenced by these offbeat movements. In fact, irrationalists appear only in a society that goes to the extreme of rationalism. The West has really reached the zenith of rationalism. Hence the reaction; it was inevitable.

When a society feels stifled and strangled by too much logic and rationalism, it inevitably turns to mysticism. When materialism begins to crush a people's sensitivity they turn to God and religion. And don't think that Ginsberg, Sartre, Camus, and others who speak about the absurd, the illogical are like illiterate and ignorant villagers. They are great intellectuals of irrationalism. Their irrationalism, their turning to the unthinkable is not comparable to the ways of the believers, the faithful. It is a one-hundred-and-eighty-degree turn, like Chaitanya who after stretching thinking to its extremity, found that it was unthinkable.

So if Ginsberg's statements and his poetry are illogical and irrational, it has nonetheless a system of its own. Nietzsche has said somewhere, "I am mad, but my madness has its own logic. I am not an ordinary madman; my madness has a method." This irrationalism is deliberate. It stands on its own ground, which cannot be the ground of logic. It is a candid, ingenuous refutation of rationalism. Certainly it will not base its assault upon logic; if it does, it will only support rationalism. No, it opposes rationalism through an irrational lifestyle.

Somewhere Ginsberg is reading his poetry to a small gathering of poets. His poetry is meaningless; there is no consistency between one concept and another. All its similies and metaphors are just inane. Its symbolism is utterly unconventional; it has nothing to do with poetic tradition. It is really a great adventure; there is no greater adventure than to be inconsistent and unconventional. He alone can have the courage to be inconsistent who is aware of his innate consistency, his inner integrity, whose inner-most being is consistent and clear. He knows that howsoever inconsistent his statements may be, they are not going to affect the integrity and consistency of his being.

People lacking in spiritual consistency and in-nate harmony weigh every word before they make a statement, because they are afraid that if two of their statements contradict each other their inner con-tradictions will be exposed. One can afford to be in-consistent only when one is consistent in his being.

This Ginsberg is reading a poem which is full of inconsistencies and contradictions. It is an act of rare courage. Someone from among his listeners rises up in his seat and says, "You seem to be an audacious person, but to be audacious in poetry is nothing. Do you have the courage to act with audacity?"

And Ginsberg looks up at the questioner, takes off his clothes and stands naked before his listen-ers saying, "This is the last part of my poetry." Then he says to the man who has interrupted him, "Now please take off your clothes and bare yourself."

The man says, "How can I? I cannot be naked."

The whole audience is in a state of shock. No one had thought that poetry reading would end like this, that its last part would come in the form of the nude poet. When they asked him why he did this he said, "It just happened; there was nothing deliberate about it. The man provoked me to act audaciously, and I couldn't think of anything else. So I just con-cluded my poetry reading this way."

This is a spontaneous act; it is not at all delib-erate. And it is wholly illogical; it has nothing to do with Ginsberg's poetry. No Kalidas, no Keats, no Rabindranath could do it; they are poets tied to trad-ition. We cannot think of Kalidas, or Keats, or Ta-gore baring himself the way Ginsberg does. Ginsberg could do it because he rejects logic, he refuses to confine life into the prison of syllogisms. He does not want to reduce life to petty mathematical calculations. He wants to live and live in freedom, and with abandon.

A man like Ginsberg cannot be compared with a gullible villager. He represents the climactic point of a profound rationalist tradition. When a rationalist tradition reaches its climax and begins to die, people like Ginsberg come to the fore to repudiate the rational. I think Krishna too, represents the peak point of India's great rationalist tradition. This country had once scaled the highest peaks of rationalist intelligence and thinking. We had indulged in hair-splitting analysis and interpretation of words and concepts. We have with us books that cannot be translated into any other languages of the world, because no other language possesses such refined and subtle words as we have. We have such words that only one of them can cover a whole page of a book, because we use so many adjectives, prefixes and suffixes to qualify and refine them.

Krishna comes at the pinnacle of a rationalist, intellectual culture that had left no stones unturned. We had thought everything that could be thought. From the *Vedas* and *Upanishads* we had traveled to *Vedant* where knowledge ends. *Vedant* itself means the end of knowledge. Giants like Patanjali, Kapil, Kanad, Brihaspati and Vyas had thought so much that a time came when we felt tired of thinking. Then comes Krishna as the culmination, and he says, "Let us now live, we have done enough of thinking."

In this context it is good to know that Chaitanya happened in Bengal exactly at a similar time. Bengal reached the zenith of dialectics and reasoning in the form of the *Navya Nyaya*, the new dialectics. Navadip, the town in which Chaitanya was born, was the greatest center of learning and logic. It

was called the *Kashi* of the logicians. All logical learning of India found its apex in Navadip, and it became
known as *Navya Nyaya*, which represents the Everest
of dialectical reasoning. The West has yet to reach
that peak. Western logic is old; it is not new. It does
not go beyond Aristotle. Navadip took logic beyond
Aristotle and carried it to its last frontier.

It was enough to say anywhere in the India of
those days that such-and-such a scholar comes from
Navadip—nobody dared enter into a debate with
him. He was supposed to be invincible as a dialecti-
cian; nobody could think of defeating him in
polemics. Students from all over India went to
Navadip to learn logic. Scholars of logic went there
to debate with their counterparts, and if once someone won a debate he immediately became famous all
over the country; he was acclaimed as the greatest
pundit—the scholar laureate of India. Often enough
it happened that someone who went to Navadip to
debate got defeated at the hands of some scholar and
became his disciple. It was impossible to defeat
Navadip; the whole town was full of logicians; every
home was the home of a scholar. If someone defeated
one scholar there was another round the corner ready
to challenge him. The town was a beehive of scholars.

Chaitanya was born in Navadip, and was
himself a towering scholar of logic. He was the top
logician of the Navadip of his time, held in great
respect by all. The same Chaitanya one day said goodbye to scholarship and went dancing and singing
ecstatically through the streets of Navadip, saying
that everything is unthinkable. When such a person
says something it is bound to have tremendous significance. Chaitanya too represents the climactic point
of a great tradition. After exploring and analyzing
every nook and corner of thinking and intellectual
understanding, after going to the very roots of words,
concepts and their meanings, he renounces knowledge and returns to his basic ignorance and declares

he is now going to sing and dance like a madman. He said that he would not argue any more, not search truth through logic, he would simply live and live with abandon.

Life begins where logic ends.

> Questioner: You explained to us Chaitanya and his principle of the unthinkable togetherness and separateness. You spoke about Ginsberg and his irrationality. Earlier you dealt with the significance of words becoming mantras and also with the changing of names. You have also said that words give rise to dualism. But Krishna says with authority that one who utters "Aum" and meditates on God with awareness at the time of his death attains to moksha, the highest state of being. It means that there is a word—"Aum"—that can lead to non-dualism. How do you look at "Aum"? Is it rational or irrational? And what difficulties came in your way of giving "Aum" a place in your Dynamic Meditation?

Words are not the truth. Not even the word truth is truth.

Truth is found in a state of wordlessness, in utter silence. Even if one has to express truth, words cannot do it. Truth is best expressed through silence. Silence, not word, is the language of truth. As I said this morning, silence is the voice of truth.

If it is so then a question arises how a word, as I say, can serve as a seed and a basis for spiritual discipline. There is no contradiction in the two statements; in fact, they are just different dimensions of approaching the same thing. I said this morning that words are not the truth, but if those surrounded by untruth want to attain to truth they will have to take the help of untruth; there is no other way. Of course, if they can make a leap, they can go straightaway from word to silence. But in case they lack the courage to make a leap, they will have to get rid of words gradually, step by step.

When one is given a seed word, it means with the help of this single word he has to drop all other words which infest his mind. If one does not have the courage to drop all words together, once and for all, he is asked to hold on to a seed word, and to get rid of all other words with its help. But ultimately he will have to get rid of the seed word as well. The seed word cannot take him to the truth, but it can certainly take him to the gate of the temple of truth. At the gate you will have to leave this word, just as you leave your shoes there. You cannot take it into the temple's inner sanctuary. Even the seed word will impede your entrance into the temple, because however tiny, it is after all a part of noise. All words are noisy, and a seed word is no exception.

Even those who stress the importance of seed words say that in the final stage of their practice the seekers themselves disappear; this is the measure of their fulfillment. From *japa* or chanting one has to go to *ajapa* or no-chanting—wordless chanting. A moment comes in their discipline when even *japa* drops and *ajapa*, silence, enters. It is the same whether you drop words at the very first or the last moment. All words have to go, so that silence happens. Silence is the ultimate; there is nothing higher than silence. A courageous person will give up all words together, but one who cannot should for the time being hold on to a seed word, dropping all others. But in the end even this last word will have to go.

As far as I am concerned, I am in favor of a complete jump from word to silence. As far as possible a seeker should avoid getting involved in things like *japa*, because they are likely to turn into an impediment in the last stage. It really happened with Ramakrishna, and it would be good to understand it.

Ramakrishna's spiritual journey begins with remembrance—the chanting of the Mother's name. He has been worshipping God in the form of divine Mother Kali, and a moment comes while chanting the Mother's name when he reaches the final stage of the journey—the name has to be dropped. Beyond this stage there is no way to go on with the name; now he can enter the *sanctum sanctorium* all alone. Mother Kali serves him well traveling the path, but when he reaches the temple itself, Ramakrishna must face the problem of parting with the Mother. It becomes the biggest problem of his spiritual life. For years he has given all his love and devotion to Kali; he has grown with her, he has danced and laughed and cried with her, so much that she has entered into his blood and bones, has become his very heartbeat. And when he is asked to drop her altogether, he finds himself in a terrible dilemma.

At this stage, Ramakrishna is under the guidance of a non-dualist yogi named Totapuri, who insists that he give up the name, part with the Mother. According to Totapuri, a name, a seed word, a symbol has no meaning whatsoever for a seeker who wants to attain the non-dualist state, the one, the absolute. Ramakrishna closes his eyes again and again and tells Totapuri that he cannot give up Kali; he can easily give himself up but he cannot part with his Mother. His Master persuades him to try again and again—because if he gives himself up and not the Mother, he will be left on the doorstep of the temple—the Mother will be inside it. It will do him no good. If one is to attain to the non-dualist state, nothing short of absolute aloneness will do. Two are not allowed to enter its inner sanctum—the passage is utterly narrow. Ramakrishna tries again and again for three days, but fails and declares his helplessness.

Totapuri now threatens to leave Ramakrishna, he is not going to waste his efforts on him. Ramakrishna begs for another opportunity; he is aware of his thirst for the unknown, the ultimate reality. His life cannot be fulfilled without knowing it.

Totapuri comes to Ramakrishna the next day and brings with him a sharp-edged glass. Ramakrishna sits before him with closed eyes and his Master says, "With this glass I am going to make a cut on your forehead exactly above the seat of the third eye, the *ajnachakra*. The moment you feel the pain of it you take up a sword and cut your mother in two."

Ramakrishna is startled. He protests, "What do you say? How can I behead my Mother with a sword? It is impossible. I can behead myself if you ask me to do so, but how can I raise a sword at Mother? And then where am I going to find a sword?"

Then Totapuri says to Ramakrishna, "You are crazy. You have to find a sword from the same source where you discovered the Mother who is not. If your imagination, your will can materialize a non-existent Mother, it can also materialize a sword. It is not that difficult. I know you are skilled in this art. It needs an imaginary sword, a false sword to kill a false Mother. She was never real."

Ramakrishna is still hesitant, but he knows Totapuri will leave him if he does not listen to his instructions. He is aware that this Master does not believe in gradual progress, he stands for a headlong leap, for sudden enlightenment. He closes his eyes again, but he still feels reluctant. Then Totapuri says reproachfully, "Shame on you!" and cuts his forehead with the edge of the glass.

As soon as Ramakrishna feels the hurt he gathers courage to take up a sword and behead the Mother. And as soon as the Mother's image vanishes, he enters the state of *samadhi*—the supreme state. And on his return from this state he exclaims, "The last barrier is down."

The seed word, the mantra is going to be the last barrier for all those who use it as their spiritual discipline. And like Ramakrishna, one day they will have to take up swords to finish it too. And it is going to be a painful process. That is why I don't recommend it, because I am aware that both you and I will have to work hard at the end. It is better to be finished with it from the beginning.

You also want to know if *aum* is a word or something else. You quote Krishna as saying, "If someone can remember me in my *aum* form and live in *aum* at the time of his death, he will attain to the ultimate, the eternal."

This *aum* is an extraordinary word, a rare word. It is extraordinary just because it has no meaning whatsoever. Every word has some meaning, this *aum* has none. For this reason this word cannot be translated into any other language of the world, there is no way. If it had a meaning, it would be easy to find an equivalent word with the same meaning in any language, but being meaningless this *aum* is beyond translation. This is perhaps the only word on earth which has no meaning whatsoever.

People who discovered *aum* were in search of something which could be a bridge, a link between the word and silence. While the word has a meaning, silence is neither meaningful nor meaningless; it is beyond both, it is the beyond. Really *aum* came as a bridge between the word and silence. It is constituted with the help of three basic sound forms: a, u, and m. A, u, and m are the basic sounds of the science of phonetics: all other letters of the alphabet are their extensions and combinations. And the same a, u, and m constitute the word *aum*, although it was not written as a word; it remains a distinct and distinguished symbol. *Aum* in its original form is available in Sanskrit, where it is a pictorial representation of *aum*; it is neither a word nor a letter. *Aum* is not a word but a picture. And it represents the space where the finite world of the word—of sound—ends, and the infinite world of silence begins. It forms the frontier, the borderline between the word and the wordless; there is no word beyond *aum*.

Therefore, Krishna says if someone can think of him in his *aum* form—which is beyond word and meaning—at the moment of his death, he will attain to reality, to truth. Because *aum* is at the boundary line of the world and the beyond, one who can remember it at the time of his departure from the world is destined to be carried to the beyond.

India's genius has packed this word *aum* with far-reaching meanings and immense significance. *Aum* became tremendously meaningful—so much so that it has no more any meaning. And its significance is limitless, infinite.

But *aum* is not meant to be uttered and chanted; it has to be really heard and experienced. When you go deep into meditation, when all words disappear, the sound of *aum* will begin to vibrate. You don't have to say it; if you say it you can have the illusion while meditating that you are hearing it. Then you will miss the authentic *aum*. For this reason I have not included *aum* in the Dynamic Meditation. If you chant it during meditation you can miss the real music of *aum*, which is very subtle.

This real *aum* is heard when all words disappear, all noises cease. When mind and intellect, thought and word all come to an end and silence begins, then an extraordinarily subtle vibration remains, which this country has interpreted as *aum*. It can be interpreted in other ways too, but they all will be our interpretations. It is like you are traveling in a railway coach and you hear whatever you want to hear in the rattling noise of the moving wheels of the train. The wheels are not making noise for you, nor do they have any message for you, but you hear whatever you want to hear. It is all your projection, your construction imposed on the sound of the wheels.

When the immense emptiness comes into being, it has its own sound, its own music. It is called the sound of the cosmic silence, it is called the *anahat*, the unstruck, the uncaused sound. It is not caused by anything. It is the *aum*. When you clap your hands, the sound of clapping is created by striking one hand against the other. This sound is caused; so is the sound of a drum which you beat with your hands. But meditation is a journey into silence; when all sounds disappear, when there is no duality, when you are utterly alone, then the causeless sound comes into being. India's sages have called it *aum*.

Variants of *aum* are found in other lands and languages. Christians use a word "amen" which is a variation of *aum*. Mohammedans also say *"Amin"* which is the same. Every invocation of the Upanishads begins with *aum* and ends with *"Aum Shantih, Shantih, Shantih."* A Mohammedan ends his prayer with the word *Amin*. This *amin* is also meaningless; it is the same sound of cosmic silence.

The English language has three words: omniscient, omnipresent and omnipotent—all of which are constituted with the word *aum*. Philologists may not be aware that omniscient means that one who has known the *aum*, omnipresent means the one who is present in the *aum*, and omnipotent means the one who has become as powerful as the *aum*.

The *aum* has been found in many forms all the world over. It is available in both the ancient sources of religion—Hinduism and Judaism. If there is anything common between Hinduism and Jainism it is the *aum*. *Aum* occupies the same exalted place in Buddhism as in Jainism. It is the one universal word. *Amin* and *aum* are words that are not manmade; they have been heard in the depth of meditation. It is difficult to say which of the two, *amin* and *aum*, is the more authentic, but one thing is certain that they are one and the same. It is the ultimate sound. When all caused sounds disappear the uncaused *aum* comes into being. It is the cosmic sound.

Zen sages ask their disciples to go and find out the sound of one hand clapping. The sound of one hand clapping is something unheard of! This is Zen's own way of saying the same thing—the *anahat*, the unstruck sound. So Zen Masters direct seekers to go in search of one hand clapping—which really means the uncaused sound. Clapping with two hands make for sound, and one hand clapping is *aum* or *amin*.

Knowingly I did not give *aum* a place in our meditations. It is deliberate, because if you utter *aum* it is caused by you, it cannot be the uncaused *aum*. I wait for that real *aum* which will appear when you completely disappear. This *aum* will arise from your inmost depths, but it will not be caused by you. And Krishna is right in saying that if one comes to know *aum* rightly and lives *aum* with awareness till his last breath, he will attain to the ultimate. But this is not the *aum* that you will utter with your mouth; it will be a waste of efforts if you keep chanting *aum* at the time of your death. Then you will not even die peacefully.

The real *aum* is an explosion; it emerges from the depths of your innermost being. And it happens.

Let us now sit for meditation. And I hope you will now begin your journey to the real *aum*.

Don't talk, and sit at some distance from one another. Stop talking altogether, and leave some space between you and the other persons sitting next to you . . . Those who are just spectators should leave the compound and watch, if they want to, from the outside. Spectators should not remain inside the enclosure. Please move out.

I want you to sit at some distance from one another so that if someone falls down on the ground in the course of his meditation, he does not disturb his neighbors. There is enough space here, so you need not be miserly. Please spread out all over the place. Friends may fall down, and many are going to fall down, so make room for them. And don't think others will move, other's don't move. Each one of you has to move and make room for others.

Spectators are requested not to talk; they should remain completely silent so they don't cause any disturbance in meditation.

Before you begin please understand a few things rightly. You have to meditate in a sitting posture. This will be very useful and good.

For the first ten minutes we will breathe deeply. After ten minutes deep breathing your body will begin to shake; then allow it to shake freely. Someone will feel like shouting and screaming, another will feel like crying. Allow yourself to yell and cry without inhibition. After ten minutes, begin to ask yourself, "Who am I?" "Who am I?" This will continue for another ten minutes—with the difference that you will do so sitting. If someone falls in the meantime, he should not worry about it, he should just fall down.

Inside the compound no one will keep his eyes open.

Now, fold your two palms together and utter this pledge, this resolve. "I resolve with God as my witness that I will bring all my energy to meditation."

"I resolve, with God as my witness, that I will bring all my energy to meditation."

"I resolve, with God as my witness, that I will bring all my energy to meditation."

Now, constantly remember your resolve, and remember that God remembers it.

For ten minutes breathe deeply. Deep breathing will stimulate and arouse a great deal of energy, a lot more than when you breathe standing . . . With the stroke of breaths the energy is bound to rise . . . and it will run through your body . . . electricity will run through the whole length of your body . . . Breathe with energy . . . Don't withhold yourselves. If the body shakes let it shake, let it tremble.

Breathe deeply and energetically. Energy is beginning to rise, let it. Breathe deeply and let energy rise. It is going well, very well. Let each one of you do his best, no one should lag behind . . . Energy is rising, allow it. Let the body do what it wants to do, but keep sitting.

Deep breathing, more deep breathing, still more deep breathing. Cooperate with your rising energy. Don't withhold yourselves. Breathe deeply.

Breathe deeply, breathe deeply, breathe very deeply. It is going well. More and more friends are being energized. Let your energy rise freely, don't hinder it. Let go of you. Hit your energy with deep breathing, deeper and deeper breathing.

Be blissful, be filled with joy and bliss . . . Breathe deeply and joyously . . . Breathe deeply and be blissful. Breathe deeply, more deeply, still more deeply. And rejoice.

Your bodies are getting electrified. Cooperate with your bodies . . . Breathe deeply and joyously. Be filled with bliss and breathe . . . breathe deeply.

Intensify breathing and bring greater and greater joy . . . Be joyous and breathe more deeply, still more deeply. Bring all your energy to breathing . . . Don't withhold. Be totally into it. Then we will enter the second stage. There are four minutes to go; put all your strength into it.

It is gaining momentum; cooperate with it fully. Exert your best. Sometimes one misses it just by a fraction of an inch; so bring all your energy into deep breathing. And breathe joyously, blissfully.

There are three minutes to go . . . Go ahead and ahead. Bring all your strength together and breathe deeply and joyously. Go inside your being, enter your interiority, and breathe deeply.

Energy is rising. Let go of you. Your bodies will shake and dance. Keep sitting and dance if you feel like dancing. You will feel as if you are not your body. Let it shake, let it tremble, let it dance. Don't hinder . . . Don't withhold . . . Breathe deeply and more deeply . . . Everything is going well . . . Keep breathing deeply. Let the body shake.

It is getting into the right momentum, bring all your energy with great joy and bliss. Only two minutes are left, breathe deeply . . . Breathe deeply and more deeply . . . When I say one, two, three, then put all your energy, every bit of your energy into it. Be filled with joy . . . Rejoice . . . breathe deeply and let the body shake.

Let go of yourselves.

FOURTEENTH DISCOURSE
MORNING, OCTOBER 2, 1970
MANALI, INDIA

ACTION, INACTION AND NON-ACTION

Questioner: You say that on Krishna's path self-remembering is enough; it does not leave room for any other spiritual discipline. But since you also speak about disciplining the seven bodies, can you give us a brief sketch of Krishna's discipline in the context of the seven bodies?

here is no place in Krishna's philosophy for any spiritual discipline, so the question of disciplining the seven bodies does not arise. The path of discipline is quite different from that of devotion. While discipline is gradual, consisting of stages, devotion is integral and one—without any stages. Discipline divides man into different bodies and works in stages; devotion does not do anything like this. For the sake of making the spiritual journey in stages, those who believe in discipline have divided the human body into seven parts. Each part is used as a stepping stone to another. But devotion does not believe in dividing man; it accepts him as one piece—a whole and indivisible entity. Devotion absorbs the devotee wholly and totally into its bosom.

Spiritual discipline has a variety of divisions and subdivisions. One discipline divides man into seven bodies, another divides him into seven *chakras* or centers. Different disciplines have different ways of dividing and subdividing. But devotion rejects all divisions straightaway, and accepts man in his totality. And it is the total man who is called upon to remember himself. Devotion knows only one thing, remembrance. And you cannot remember a thing piece by piece; either you remember it whole or you don't. One cannot remember himself so that he is part God and part man; if he remembers he remembers totally. The process of remembering is sudden and total; it cannot be piecemeal and gradual. It happens in one sweep, a leap. Remembrance is an explosion.

Discipline has a sequence; devotion has none. For example, you need to recall some name that you have long forgotten. You need it badly, but you cannot remember it. The name has been so familiar to you that you wonder . . . You are simultaneously aware that you know the name and yet you cannot recall it. You are in a state of perplexity, confusion. You know that you know it—and yet you fail to remember it. You have completely forgotten it for the moment. The very word forgetfulness means you forget something you know. You are aware of it at some deeper level of your unconsciousness, yet it fails to communicate with your conscious mind. So you have to build a bridge between these two parts of your mind. What do you do?

You try different ways to recall this once-very-familiar name that you need so urgently. You strain your mind, you scratch your head, you close your eyes and twitch your brows, and yet it goes on eluding you. Nothing works. The more you strain yourself the more difficult it becomes to find it. The more you try, the more tense you become; this tenseness becomes another barrier between you and your mind. A tense mind goes into pieces; a quiet mind collects itself and becomes whole again. Your difficulty is that the more you strain your mind to remember the name, the more you become incapable of doing it. A part of the mind is trying hard to recall it, and another part is simultaneously worrying and cursing itself for its incapacity to do it. Two suggestions, contrary to each other, are being fed into your mind simultaneously, and they are enough to incapacitate it, to paralyze it. They also undermine your self-confidence.

Then some friend comes along and you tell him about your difficulty. He tells you to drop it, and engages you in some conversation which has nothing to do with the name you are trying to remember. You take two cigarettes out of your pocket, and you and your friend begin to smoke, talking about trivia. In the meantime you forget your worry about the name. And the wonder of wonder happens: the whole name suddenly pops up and you have it once again.

What has happened? How is it that you remember it suddenly in a state of relaxation? The reason is simple. As soon as you gave up straining yourself for the name, the tension caused by the opposing pulls on the mind just disappeared and you entered into a state of relaxation. Before, your mind was split into two parts—one which possessed the name and the other which wanted to recall it—and they were fighting with each other. This tension disappeared when your mind was withdrawn from the search for the name and engaged in conversation with your friend. The cigarette added to your relaxation, and the name surfaced. What you had failed to remember with effort came so effortlessly. And when it came it came whole.

I have said this as an illustration: this is how our ordinary memory works. Memory is one of the functions of mind which is divided into two parts.

One part is called the conscious mind and the other the unconscious, and curiously enough both the conscious and the unconscious have a hand in the way one's memory functions. We use the conscious mind in our workaday world—it serves us twenty-four hours of the day. The unconscious mind is used sparingly; it is used whenever we need it. The conscious is the lighted part of the mind, while the unconscious is submerged in the dark. The memory I was speaking about is lying hidden in the unconscious mind, whose conscious part is trying to remember it. The conscious part of the mind is fighting with its unconscious part, and so long as this fight continues you cannot recall a thing. Remembering is possible only when the fight stops and the two conflicting parts of the mind are put together. Then that which was standing on the doorstep of the unconscious, which made you certain that you knew it, emerges into the conscious and you have it.

Remembering the divine, or what we call self-remembering goes even deeper than the unconscious. It is not buried in the unconscious; it is beyond it. There is yet another part of the mind which is called the collective unconscious.

Let us try to understand it in another way. As I said, the conscious is the superficial part of the mind which is lighted, and below it lies the unconscious buried in the dark. Then below the unconscious lies the collective unconscious, and at the bottom lies the cosmic unconscious—which is the mind of the entire universe, which is the total mind, the universal mind. Remembrance of God or self-remembering happens at the level of the cosmic mind, which is the ultimate in consciousness. God or self is known when we become completely integrated—not only with our unconscious and collective minds, but also with the cosmic consciousness, which is of the highest. To be in contact with the cosmic mind is what we call the contact high.

I will explain it in yet another way. When you meditate here at the camp and go deep into meditation, you first come in contact with your individual unconscious mind. Then some of you begin to scream and cry and some others dance and whirl and sing. All these activities arise from your individual unconscious. And by the end of the first stage of this meditation you cease to be individuals; you all become a collectivity. Now you are not individual entities separate from each other, you are a collective whole. This is the moment when you go deep in meditation and touch those levels of the mind which are part of the collective mind. Then you don't feel that you are dancing—it feels that dance is going on and you are just a part of it. Then it does not seem that you are laughing; it seems the cosmic laughter is happening and you are just a participant in it. Then you don't feel that you are, it feels that only existence is and everything in existence is dancing: stars are dancing, mountains are dancing, birds are dancing, every particle under the sun is dancing. Then your dance becomes a small but integral part of the universal dance. This experience is coming from your contact with the collective unconscious.

Just below the collective unconscious lies the world of the cosmic unconscious. You arrive there via the collective unconscious; and once you are connected with the cosmic unconscious your awareness undergoes a complete mutation. Then you cease to feel that you are a part of the whole, rather you know that you and the whole are one—you are not a part of the total but you are totality itself. And then you suddenly remember who you are; this remembrance shoots up like an arrow from the depths of the cosmic unconscious and fills your conscious mind. Then you also know, and know simultaneously, that this awareness that you are the *Brahman*, the ultimate, the supreme is nothing new—it has always been with you, buried deep in your cosmic unconscious.

I divided the process of remembering into four parts just to make it easier for you to understand. Krishna would never consent to this division, nor do I. In fact remembering, or consciousness, is nowhere fragmented; it is an integrated whole. The conscious and the unconscious are extensions of the same intelligence which is one and indivisible.

In our innermost depth we are aware that we are God, we are divine. We do not have to become divine, we have only to discover our divinity. It is really a matter of recognition. The seer of the Upanishad says in his prayer "O Sun, please uncover the truth that is covered with gold." It simply means that truth is veiled and it has to be unveiled. Divinity is not to be achieved, but unveiled and recognized. What is it that veils it?

It is our own forgetfulness, our unconsciousness which covers the truth.

In fact, we make do with a very tiny part of our mind; a major part of it remains unused. It is like a person owns a big palace but lives in its porch. And he has become so accustomed to the porch that he has forgotten altogether that he owns a large palace, which is just behind. Really there can be no porch without a house; the porch is only the entrance to the house. But we have forgotten the large house that our mind is, and we spend our whole life in the porch— our conscious mind is nothing more than a porch. It is not that the conscious ever gets completely disconnected from the larger mind, but we never enter and explore it so we get psychologically isolated from it. But deep down we know it is there.

Entry into the depths of the unconscious does not take place in stages; it always happens in a leap. Of course we can discuss and understand the unconscious in terms of parts.

Those who follow the path of spiritual discipline do so piece by piece. Krishna's path, however, does not accept discipline. He says over and over again that we are already divine, but since we have forgotten it we have only to remember it again. That is why the Upanishads repeatedly say it is just a matter of remembering. We have to remember who we are. It is not that we have lost our godliness, we have only forgotten it. It is not that godliness is our future, which we have to become. It is sheer forgetfulness.

And that makes a great difference, because spiritual discipline believes that we have lost something which we have to regain. Or it thinks we have to become something which we are not. Or it is presumed that we have to use discipline to get rid of many wrong things that we have acquired through wrong living. But in the process of remembering we have neither to regain something nor to become something; we have only to remember that which we have forgotten. We are what we are, and it is divine. Nothing has to be added or subtracted. Only a screen of forgetfulness, oblivion, divides us from our real being, our divinity.

Devotion is the foundation of Krishna's teaching, and remembering is basic to devotion. But the devotee has forgotten remembering altogether, and instead has taken to chanting; he goes on chanting the name of Rama. The Sanskrit word *smaran*, for remembering, has been corrupted, it has become *sumiran* and *surati*, and these other words have taken different connotations. Chanting Rama's name will not make you remember that you are Rama or God. Even if someone constantly repeats, "I am God, I am God," it will not be of any use. Remembering has nothing to do with chanting or repetition of names. But constant repetition of God's name can create an illusion. You will begin to believe that you are God. This belief will be illusory, because it remains confined to the conscious mind while the unconscious remains absolutely untouched by it. Then what is the process, the way of remembering? What is its technique?

As I see, remembering comes through relaxation, silence and emptiness. You don't have to do a thing to remember, because activity will hinder rather than help you to remember. Just sit quietly without doing a thing; just be still and empty. Through action one can achieve something one does not have. By doing something you can become something that you are not. If you want to become an engineer you will have to do something to become it. Or you will have to act if you want to possess a car. But remembering is an entirely different dimension. To remember something you have forgotten, you have to sit still and quiet and do nothing. Doing will only obstruct remembering. In its deeper meaning, remembering is total inaction. That is why Krishna lays so much emphasis on *akarma* or inaction. Inaction is his key word. Inaction in depth is his message.

As I said earlier, even if you want to remember a friend's name you cannot succeed as long as you make efforts to remember. You will never remember it as long as you go on straining your mind. Memory comes alive only when you give up efforts and become totally inactive. Similarly if you become totally inactive—inactive in depth—the memory buried in the cosmic unconscious will spring like an arrow from there and shoot up to your conscious mind. It is as if a flower seed buried in the soil has sprouted and sent its shoots up in the form of a plant in your garden. And when the meteor of remembering, awareness arising from the cosmic unconscious, reaches and illumines your conscious mind, you know who you are.

So inaction is the key to remembering, as remembering is the key to devotion. On the other hand, action is central to spiritual discipline; it is only through action that you can discipline yourself and achieve your goal. And inaction is the door to devotion.

It would be good to properly understand Krishna's principle of inaction. Unfortunately it has not been rightly understood so far; all those who have interpreted Krishna up to now seem to have no right understanding of inaction. Most of them have interpreted inaction as renunciation. They always said, "Renounce the world, renounce your family, renounce everything!" But renunciation is an act; you have to do something to renounce the world or the family. The interpreters went on telling people to give up everything—their professions, families and even love—and escape to mountains and monasteries. But renunciation is as much an act as indulgence is; Krishna was really misunderstood. Inaction was thought to be just renunciation and escapism. For this reason, India has a centuries-long tradition of renunciation and escape from life.

And all this has happened in the name of Krishna. No one has ever bothered to see that Krishna himself is not a renunciate, he never left his world, his family and his worldly responsibilities. Sometimes I wonder how such a long tradition can be so blind; all along it has refused to see the stark fact that the man who applauds inaction so much is himself deeply engaged in action throughout his life. He loves, he marries, he has children. He fights war and negotiates peace. He does many other things. So by no stretch of imagination can Krishna's inaction be interpreted as renunciation and escape.

In this context Krishna uses three words: *akarma, karma* and *vikarma,* meaning inaction, action and non-action. What is action? According to Krishna, mere doing is not action. If it is true—if any kind of doing is action, then one could never enter into inaction. Then the inaction of Krishna's definition will be impossible. For Krishna, action is that which you do as a doer, as an ego. Really action for Krishna is an egocentric act, an act in which the doer is always present. A doing with a doer, in which one thinks himself as a doer, is action. As long as I remain a doer, whatever I do is action. Even if I take sannyas it is an act, an action. Even renunciation becomes an action if a doer is present in the act.

Inaction is just the opposite kind of action; it is action without a doer. Inaction does not mean absence of action, but it certainly means absence of the doer. An egoless action is inaction. If I do a thing without the egoistic sense that I am the doer, that I am the center of this action, it is inaction. Inaction is not laziness as is generally understood; it is very much action, but without a doer at its center. This thing has to be clearly understood. If the center, the ego, the I, the doer, ceases and only action remains, it is inaction. With the cessation of the doer every action becomes inaction. Action without a doer is inaction. It is action through inaction.

Krishna's every action is egoless, and therefore it is inaction. Even when he is doing something, he is really in inaction.

Between action and inaction there is *akarma* or non-action, which means a special kind of action. Inaction is egoless action; action is egoist action and non-action is a special kind of action. This thing which is midway between action and inaction, which Krishna calls non-action, needs to be understood rightly.

What does Krishna mean by non-action? Where there is neither a doer nor a doing, yet things happen, there is non-action. For example, we breathe, which we are not required to do by our own effort. There is neither a doer nor a doing so far as acts like breathing are concerned. Similarly the blood circulates through the body, the food is digested, and the heart beats. How can you categorize such acts? They come in the category of non-action, which means action happening without a doer and without a sense of volitional doing. An ordinary person lives in action, a sannyasin lives in inaction, and God lives in non-action. As far as God's action is concerned there is neither a doer nor any doing of the kind we know. There things just happen; it is just happening.

There are a few things in man's life too that just happen. And these are non-actions. In fact, these actions are divine operations. Do you think it is you who breathe? Then you are mistaken. If you were the master of this action known as breathing, then you would never die really. Then you can continue to breathe even when death knocks at your door. But can you say you are not going to stop breathing? Or try it otherwise—stop breathing for a little while and you will know you cannot stop it either. Your breath will refuse to obey you, it will soon resume its breathing. In breathing you are neither the doer nor the doing itself. Many things of life are like breathing; they just happen.

If someone understands rightly what non-action is, and comes to know its mystery, he will soon enter into a state of inaction which is acting without a center, an ego. Then he knows that every significant thing in life happens on its own; it is utterly stupid to try to be a doer. And he is a wise man. He alone is a sage.

I have heard . . . A person boarded a train and took a seat, but the bag he carried with him remained sitting on his head. His fellow travelers were surprised and asked him why he was still keeping his bag on his head. The man said he did not want to add to the burden of the train which was already overloaded. The fellow travelers were amused, and one of them said to him, "You seem to be a crazy person. Even if you carry the load on your head it is going to be a load on the train. Why carry an unnecessary burden on your head? Isn't it stupid?"

The man burst into laughter and said, "I had thought you were householders, but you all seem to be sannyasins." This man was a real sannyasin. He said, "I carry the bag on my head in order to conform to the ways of the world. I wonder why you laugh at me? I see all of you carrying the burden of the world on your heads, although you know that like this train it is God who bears all our burdens. I just wanted to conform to your ways." And then the man not only put the bag down on the train, but seated himself on it saying, "This is the right way a sannyasin should sit. He is not a doer; everything just happens."

One who understands the beauty of non-action enters the state of inaction which is acting without ego. As we are, we are all doers, and all our doings are egocentric. We live in action. But if we understand what non-action is we will begin to live in inaction. Then inaction will be at the center of our being and action at its periphery.

Inaction is foundational to Krishna's devotion or *upasana* or whatever you wish to call it. You don't have to do a thing; you have only to allow that which is happening. You have to die to your doer, to your ego.

And the moment the doer disappears, remembering happens. This doer is the steel wall that separates you from your authentic being and makes you forget it. As long as this wall remains you cannot know who you are. Chanting Rama's name or repeating the mantra "I am God" will not help, because it is the doer in you who chants and repeats the name, the mantra. As long as you exist as an ego, you can do what you will, nothing will happen. So let the doer go, let the ego disappear. But how will the doer go?

Just try to understand what non-action is. Continue to act, but try to understand what non-action is. Continue to do what you do, and try to understand life. The very understanding of life and its ways will tell you nothing is in your hands. Neither you decide to be born nor do you decide to die. Neither you breathe of your own volition, nor you have a hand in the circulation of your blood through the body. You were not consulted before your birth nor will you be consulted when your time arrives to depart from this world. Do you have a say in when you grow from childhood to youth to old age?

Existence was very much here when you were not, and it will continue to be here after you will be gone. You will make no difference whatsoever so far as existence is concerned. Stars will continue to shine as brightly as ever. Flowers will bloom as they have always bloomed. Streams will continue to flow and birds continue to sing. We are like lines drawn on the surface of the water: no sooner they are drawn than they disappear. Then why carry this utterly unnecessary burden of "I" on our heads and suffer endlessly? If the whole of existence can go without me, why cannot I go without me?

To understand the deeper meaning of non-action is wisdom. To understand non-action is to understand everything. And then every action becomes inaction, then you do without being a doer, then you act through inaction. Non-action is the gate to wisdom; it is alchemical. Passing through ordinary action, if one encounters non-action with understanding, he will soon come upon inaction, which in its turn leads to remembering. Remembering happens only in inaction. Remembering that comes with effort is false; it is another form of action. Remembering that comes on its own, effortlessly, is real; it comes straight from the cosmos. That is why we say that the *Vedas* are divine revelations. Whenever something comes from the beyond—whoever may be its medium —it is divine revelation. The Bible is as much divine knowledge as the Vedas are. That is why Jesus says again and again that his father in heaven speaks through him. And Krishna says, "I am not, only God is; I am God. And it is I who am making the Mahabharat happen; it is all my play."

Krishna says to Arjuna, "You need not be afraid of killing, because all those you are going to kill have already been killed by me. They are already dead, you have only to give them the news of it through your arrows. And what I am saying is not my words, they are coming straight from the cosmos, from the beyond. From the depths of the beyond comes this information that what you see as life before you is only an appearance, it has already become extinct, it is no more alive. It is just a matter of moments when those standing across the battle lines will be dead. You are only an instrument in the hands of existence, nothing more. So don't think that you are going to kill them. If you think you are the doer then you are bound to be afraid. With the doer comes fear, anxiety and anguish. Every suffering, every sorrow, arises from the ego, the doer, which is a false entity. You are utterly mistaken if you think you are the doer; you are merely an instrument in the hands of the divine. Let it do what it wants to be done through you, and let go of yourself."

Therefore, while concluding the ⸱Geeta, Krishna says to Arjuna, "Give up everything, give up all religions, all sense of the doer and doing, give up your ego and be established in inaction."

Inaction is the technique of remembering.

Questioner: We are grateful to you for your superb exposition of action, inaction and non-action. You had explained to the foreign disciples of Mahesh Yogi when they met you in Kashmir last year about the significance of inaction in achieving self-knowledge, and we have now no confusion about it. But some confusion surely arises from Krishna's exposition of inaction in the Geeta. He emphasizes the importance of inaction, but it seems to be confusing, because it has more than one meaning. He says that a yogi is one who, having acted does not think he has acted, and a sannyasin is one who does not act and yet action happens. There is yet another side to this question which seems important. Shankaracharya says in his commentaries on the Geeta, that a wise man does not need to act, because action belongs to the doer. And you say that we don't have to act, because action happens on its own. But what will happen to Arjuna's individuality if he consents to be just an instrument in the hands of existence?

Krishna says that when one acts as if he does not act at all, it is yoga. Yoga means action through inaction. To become a non-doer is yoga. The other thing he says is that when one does not do a thing and yet knows he has done everything, it is sannyas. This is another side of the same coin. Doing nothing, everything is done.

Sannyas and yoga are two sides of the same coin. Of course, they are two opposite sides of the coin, but they are inseparable. It is difficult to say where the one side ends and the other begins. It is true that the one side is the opposite of the other, but they are so inextricably joined that one cannot be without the other. In fact, there cannot be a coin with only one side, it has to have two sides—one opposite to the other. They really complement each other; they are not at all contradictory. Its front and back together make up a coin.

There is no contradiction whatsoever in the two statements of Krishna, and there is no room for confusion either. If you look at a wise man from his front side he will look a yogi, and the same wise man will look a sannyasin if you view him from the rear. And Krishna's definition of the two sides is absolutely right. He defines a wise man, who is both yogi and sannyasin, as one who is actively inactive and inactively active. And remember, these two sides are simultaneously present in one who knows the truth; it is not possible to separate one of his sides from the other. One who acts through inaction can also be non-acting through action. These are two sides of the same coin. And there can be no coin with a single side; up to now it has not been minted anywhere. It is a different thing that we look at it from a single side. It depends on us. Krishna looks at it from both sides.

Krishna is trying to explain truth from all of its sides. He says to Arjuna, "If you are interested in yoga then you should know what yoga is. Yoga means that one can attain to inaction through action. And if you are not interested in yoga, if you do not want to take part in the war, in bloody fighting, if you want to renounce the world and take sannyas, then you know from me what sannyas is. Sannyas means one does not do a thing and yet everything is done. A sannyasin is established in the center of inaction and allows nature to take its course. He gives non-action—which is a kind of action—a free hand."

Krishna is just trying to rope Arjuna in from every possible side. That's all. For this very reason his statements appear many times to be contradictory. I find myself exactly in the same space in relation to you. I am trying to surround you from every possible direction. If you refuse to move in one direction, I immediately try to persuade you to move in another direction, so you consent to go along with me from wherever you can. And the beauty is that once you get going from anywhere you will come across the same space in which you first refused to move. Krishna is trying to persuade Arjuna in every way. If Arjuna wants to follow the yogic path, Krishna says okay, because he knows yoga is one side of the same coin with sannyas as its other side. Take a coin from any side, front or back, you will have the whole coin in your hand.

There is a beautiful Taoist story which will help you to understand this point very easily. Sages in the line of Lao Tzu have gifted us with some of the most extraordinary stories of the world. They are rare.

A sage lives in a forest. He has raised a number of pets—all monkeys. One morning a seeker comes with a question like the one you have just now put to me. He says to the Taoist sage that his statements are often contradictory and they only confuse him. The sage grins and says to the visitor, "Just wait and see what happens." And he calls his monkeys to his side and tells them, "Listen, I am going to make some changes in your menu." The monkeys look surprised. For so long they were being given four breads in the morning and three in the evening. The sage says, "From now on you will receive three breads in the morning and four in the evening."

Hearing about this change the monkeys became wild with rage. They fret and fume and even threaten to revolt against the proposed change. They insist on the old system being continued. But the sage is equally insistent on his proposal. So his pets prepare themselves to attack and harm their Master. The sage grins again and says to them, "Wait another minute. You will continue to have four breads in the morning as ever." It calms down the monkeys instantly.

The Taoist sage now turns his face to his visitor and says, "Do you get it? The monkeys were to receive seven breads in all, even after the slight change I had proposed. But they refused to accept three breads in place of four in the morning. Does it make a difference if they receive four in the morning or in the evening? Yet they are happy to know that no change is being made."

This is how Krishna tries to hem in a reluctant Arjuna. He now tells him to accept three breads and Arjuna refuses vehemently. Then he tells him to take four breads instead of three. He is to receive only seven breads in all, but Krishna leaves the distribution of breads between the morning and evening meals in Arjuna's hands. It is for this reason that the *Geeta* runs into eighteen long chapters. Time and again Krishna changes his offers. Now he persuades him to take up devotion, and if Arjuna does not agree he persuades him to take up yoga. He gives him a wide range of choices from yoga to knowledge to action to devotion. But in every case the total number of breads remains seven. And it is towards the end of the *Geeta* that Arjuna comes to know the truth, that in every case the number of breads is the same and Krishna is not going to budge from this fixed number.

Now I come to the other part of the question. Shankara's definition of action is a partisan's definition. He makes a choice that agrees with him. He is against action; he believes that action binds. He says action is ignorance, it stems from ignorance. To attain to knowledge, to know the truth there is no way but to renounce action. He interprets Krishna's nonaction as renunciation of action. For him, action belongs to the world of the doers, the worldly people, and a seeker has to run away from the relationships that action entails. His emphasis is on renunciation of the world of action.

It is true that for one established in wisdom there is no action, he does not do a thing. But Shankara's interpretation is partial and wrong. There is no action for a wise man because he has ceased to be a doer, an ego. Krishna's emphasis is on the absence of the doer, not on the absence of action itself. Shankara changes the emphasis from the non-doer to non-doing. And his emphasis on inaction is wrong.

There are two sides of action—one is the doer and the other the deed. Krishna wants to emphasize that the doer should go and only doing remain. We cannot do away with action. Never mind the doer, the ignorant worldly person—even God cannot do without action. This universe is his work, his handicraft. Without God working on it this universe would not survive for a split second. How does the universe keep going? The energy behind it keeps it going. So let alone the wise, even God cannot give up action. Krishna's whole emphasis is on the cessation of the doer. But an escapist sannyasin, one who runs away from the world emphasizes inaction.

This is the reason Shankara has to declare the world to be *maya*, an illusion. He means to say that the world is not real, not the work of God; it is an illusion, it does not really exist. It is difficult for Shankara to accept the world as real. If all these suns and stars, mountains and rivers, trees and flowers, animals and insects, are His handiwork then He is also a workman, and not a renunciate. Then why ask human beings alone to take sannyas? And Shankara is a sannyasin; he does not want to get embroiled in the validity of action.

In fact, logic has its own difficulty. If you get hold of a particular line of argument, then you have to pursue it to its logical end. And it has its corollaries which cannot be bypassed. Logic is a hard taskmaster; once you get involved in it you have to follow it to its end. Having once accepted that action is ignorance and bondage and that there is no action for a wise man, Shankara has no choice but to declare the world an illusion, a dream. Because there is an immense world of action all around us; it is action and action all down the road. So to escape it Shankara calls it *maya*, an appearance which is not real. He says the world is magic, magical. It is like a magician sows a mango seed and instantly it grows into a mango tree with branches and foliage. In fact it only appears to be there; there is neither seed nor tree, it is just a hypnotic trick. But the irony is that even if the tree is a magical phenomenon for the spectators, it is real work for the magician. It is through his concrete action that the tree takes on an appearance. After all, hypnotizing the spectators is an act in itself.

This is the dilemma in which Shankara finds himself by denying action. To deny action he denies the whole world and calls it *maya*—a dream. But how to explain the illusion? Even if it is an illusion of our own making, it is God who allows us to create and see it as such. How can it be there without his implicit consent? Maybe the world is false, but what about our perception of it? Perception should be real. And perception in itself is action. What does he say about it?

Shankara is an accomplished logician, and he works hard to make his point. He asserts that action is false and there is no action for a wise man. His difficulty is that rather than denying the doer he is out to deny action itself. But don't go away with the impression that I mean that Shankara has not known the truth; I am not saying that. Shankara has known the truth. The moment you deny action, you have denied the doer in the same stroke. Without action there cannot be an actor; it is just unthinkable. It is action that creates the actor, although the latter is false, the actor is an illusion.

So Shankara's logic is absurd, but his experience of truth is not wrong. He arrived at the temple of truth through a long and devious path. He had to wander long around the temple, but ultimately he made it. And he arrived at the goal for a very different reason. If someone denies action totally, even if the denial is an imagination, then there is no room for the doer to be. The doer depends for his existence on the idea of action; deny action and the doer disappears.

Shankara arrived at truth, although he began his journey from altogether the wrong place. He did not touch the place that belongs to Krishna.

Krishna says let the doer go first, and the moment he goes action is bound to go. Action and the actor, as generally understood, are two ends of the same string. But I am willing to choose Krishna against Shankara, and there is a reason for my preference. In the ultimate analysis Shankara's whole interpretation of the *Geeta* turns out to be escapist; he becomes the leader of all escapists. But the irony is that all his escapist sannyasins have to depend on those people who don't escape, who remain in the world. If the whole world agrees with Shankara's philosophy, it will not last a day longer. Then there is no way for it but to die. That is why the world is not going to accept Shankara's definition. No matter how hard Shankara tries to prove action as illusory, it remains action even as an illusion. Even Shankara goes out to beg from the same world of illusion; he accepts alms from the same world. He goes into the world to explain his philosophy of *maya* and tries to convince it that it is not.

Shankara's opponents mock him saying, "If everything is illusory then why do you go about explaining your philosophy to a world that does not exist in reality? Why do you preach? And to whom? Why do you go to a place whose existence is illusory? and what about your begging bowl, your begging, your hunger and your thirst? Are they real?"

I am going to tell you a beautiful story.

Once a Buddhist monk who believes that the world is false, an illusion, visits a king's court. With the help of cogent and irrefutable arguments he proves before the court that the world is unreal. Logic has a great advantage; it cannot establish what truth is, but it can easily prove falsehood. Logic cannot say what is, but it can very well say what is not. Logic is like a sword which can kill something but cannot revive it; it can destroy but it cannot create. Logic is as destructive as a sword, but it cannot construct anything. So the Buddhist monk concludes his arguments with an air of triumph proclaiming that the world is not real.

But the king is not going to be defeated by arguments. He says, "Maybe every thing is false, but I have something in my possession which cannot be false. And I am soon going to confront you with this reality." The king has a mad elephant among his animals and he immediately sends for it. The roads of the town are cleared, and the mad elephant let loose on the defenseless monk. The king and his courtiers go to the roof of the palace to watch the play from there. The elephant rushes at the monk with fury, and the monk starts running away in panic. He yells and screams, "O King, please save me from being killed by this mad elephant!" But the king and his courtiers and the whole town are enjoying the fun. After a long chase the monk collapses and the elephant grabs him and is about to kill him when the king's men suddenly appear on the scene and rescue him from the elephant's deadly clutches.

The next day the monk is called to the court, and the king asks of him, "How about the elephant? Is it false?"

The monk promptly says, "Yes; the elephant is illusory."

"And what about your screams?" the king asked.

The monk says again, "They were illusory too." When the king looks puzzled the monk says, "You are deluded about the whole thing. The elephant was unreal, its attack on me was unreal. I was unreal and my screams were unreal. My prayers were unreal and you too, to whom they were addressed were unreal."

This monk is incorrigible; he defeats even a mad elephant. But he is consistent; he says, "If everything is false, how can my escape from the elephant and my screams and prayers be true?" You cannot argue with a person who believes the whole existence is unreal.

Shankara's opponents made fun of him, but it made no difference for him. He said to them, "Even your perception of me and my going about arguing with people is illusory. There is no one who argues, and there is no one who listens to these arguments. Even your taunts are unreal." How can you argue with a person like Shankara?

No matter how powerfully Shankara supports his belief that the world is *maya*, even *maya* has its existence. He cannot deny *maya*, or can he? We dream in our sleep; this dream is unreal, but dreaming itself is not unreal. You cannot deny the existence of the state of dreaming as part of man's consciousness. A beggar dreams that he is a king, which is not a fact, but his dreaming is a fact. I take a rope for a snake, which is false, but what about my deluded perception itself? Even as delusion it is very much there. Granted that there is no snake, but what about the rope? The rope exists. And even if you deny the perception as real, you cannot deny the one who perceives.

We cannot deny existence totally. In the ultimate analysis it is there. Descartes is right when he says that we can negate everything, but we cannot negate the one who negates. We can negate everything, but how can we negate Shankara? Shankara is. Shankara has to survive in order for his negation to survive. Therefore Shankara's interpretation is partial and incomplete. He emphasizes one side of the coin and is unaware of its other side. His denial of the other side is wrong; a coin has to have two sides.

It is true, however, that Shankara is less confusing that Krishna. For this reason he created a large following, and a self-confident following at that.

Krishna could not do that. The truth is that in India, Shankara alone has the largest group of followers—all self-confident, assertive sannyasins. It is so because Shankara's approach is simplistic, he speaks about only one side of the coin without worrying that another side exists as well. Presentation of both sides together is difficult, so subtle and complex that it needs great intelligence to understand it. That explains why most of Shankara's sannyasins are stupid. It is true that sannyas in India came with Shankara, but it is also true that it is lackluster and stupid at the same time.

It takes great intelligence to stand alongside Krishna. Such an intelligence refuses to be confused by contradictions, because contradictions are inherent in life. Most of us get confused and bogged down by contradictions. Because Shankara denies all contradictions, his commentary on the *Geeta* has achieved immense popularity in this country. He was the first man who eliminated all contradictions, all confusions from the *Geeta*, and presented a simplistic and monotonous interpretation of Krishna's superb philosophy. But I say that no one has done so much injustice to Krishna as Shankara has, although it is just possible that if he had not commented on it the *Geeta* would have been lost to the world. It is because of Shankara's commentary that the *Geeta* became known throughout the world.

But this is what it is.

Questioner: It is said that Shankara's mayic world, illusory world, really means a changing world, not a false one. What do you say?

You can put any meanings you like, but for Shankara, it is its very changeability, its ever-changing character that makes the world unreal. That which is changing, which is not everlasting, he says is false. That which was one thing yesterday, is another thing today and will turn into something else tomorrow, is false. Change is at the root of Shankara's definition of *maya*, of illusion. He says reality is that which is immutable and eternal. What is unchanging and unchangeable is truth, what is everlasting is truth.

Eternity is Shankara's word for the truth, and changeability is his word for the world. That which does not remain the same even for a moment is false. If a thing was one thing a moment ago, turns into another thing this moment, and is going to be something else the next moment, it means that it was not that which it was, it is not that which it is, and it will not be that which it will be. That which is not is false. And truth is that which ever was, is and will remain the same. In Shankara's definition, change is synonymous with untruth and the unchanging is synonymous with truth.

But in my vision, as also in the vision of Krishna, change is as much true as the unchanging. For Krishna, both the changing and the unchanging worlds are real. The reason is that the unchanging cannot be without the changing world. The wheel of change revokes on an axle that is itself still and unmoving. The changing wheel and the unchanging axle are interdependent; one cannot be without the other. The moving and the unmoving are like two wheels of the same chariot. Krishna absorbs all contradictions in himself; he rejects none—neither the moving nor the unmoving. For him motion and rest are inextricably linked; you reject one and the other is rejected at the same time. If we understand Krishna rightly, then we have to accept that for the truth to be, untruth is essential and inescapable. Truth and untruth are as inescapably interconnected as light and darkness, life and death, health and sickness. The opposites are not really opposites, they are complementaries. They are two sides of the same thing. But our difficulty is we take them not only to be opposites, but enemies to each other.

People often ask me about the source of untruth, but they never ask about the source of truth. If truth comes from nowhere, why cannot untruth come from the same source? Those who debate over the ultimate knowledge always ask, "Who is the author of falsehood?" But they never raise the question, "Who is the mother of truth?" And if truth can happen without a mother, why should untruth have any difficulty? In fact, in this regard, untruth is in a better position than truth, because untruth means that which is not. It does not need any source, any *gangotri*.

No, it is wrong to ask about the source of truth and untruth; they exist simultaneously, together. The question of their source does not arise. The day you were born your death too was born. Death is not going to come to you in some future, it always walks in step with you. Death is another side of birth, but it may take you about seventy years to see this other side. It is your incapacity that doesn't allow you to see the two simultaneously. But they are there together. Similarly truth and untruth are together. It is wrong to speak in terms of their coming and going; they are. Truth is, untruth is. Existence is, and non-existence is.

Shankara emphasizes one side of the coin, and for this reason we have to look into the other side too. Then only the coin is complete.

Shankara says that which is observed is *maya*, false. Buddha says just the opposite, and Buddha's philosophy finds its culmination in Nagarjuna. Nagarjuna says that the one who observes is false, the observer is false. If the world is false in the eyes of Shankara, the soul is false in the eyes of Nagarjuna. This giant among the Buddhist thinkers says that between the observer and the observed the former is much more basic, and this basic element itself is false. All that is false flows from this basic falsehood.

When I close my eyes, the world becomes invisible, but then I begin to dream with eyes closed. I am the basic lie; even when the world is absent I can create another world by dreaming. The most amusing thing is I can create dreams within dreams. Sometimes you too might have dreamed that you are dreaming. It is really a miracle that one dreams that he is dreaming. Like the magician's boxes within boxes you have dreams within dreams. You can dream that you are watching a movie about your own life and you go into sleep and start dreaming. There is no difficulty about creating such a dream. Therefore Nagarjuna says it is no use trying to prove the world to be false; the false is really within you; you are false. Nagarjuna asserts that the self is false.

In fact, the true and the false go hand in hand. If someone asserts that only truth is, then he will have to assign a place to untruth and say, "It is here." In the same way one who asserts that only the untruth is, has to say where truth is. Krishna is not that assertive, he hesitates. And Krishna's hesitation is deep. People who don't hesitate are often superficial, shallow. Hesitation arises from the depths of one's being; hesitation is very significant. You are fortunate if you are gifted with a grain of hesitancy. Your hesitation will show that you have begun looking at life in its totality. Then you will not say that this is true and that is false. Then you will not say that only the truth is, or only the untruth is. Then you will know the true and the false are two aspects of the same thing, two notes of the same song. Then you will know existence and non-existence are two different notes of the same flute. We can well imagine the problem of a person who sees life in its totality, because his statements are bound to be hesitant and hazy, paradoxical and confusing.

It is for this reason that Krishna's statements confuse you. It shows Krishna's perception is most profound.

Questioner: Is it a kind of compromise on the part of Shankara when he says that maya *is inexpressible?*

Shankara has no choice but to compromise. Whoever insists on an incomplete truth meets with this fate; he has to compromise at one level or another. The other side of reality which he goes on denying will assert itself, because it is very much there. He will have to accept it in one form or another. He will call it *maya* that is indescribable; he will call it utilitarian truth or the truth that is transient. It does not matter what he calls it, he will have to accept it because it is there. Shankara cannot say that he will not speak about *maya*. Why should he speak about a thing that does not exist? But he speaks. And then he has to compromise in one way or another.

Only a man like Krishna can be uncompromising, he need not compromise. He is uncompromising because he accepts both sides of truth together; he does not deny either of them. One who denies something is forced to compromise at some deeper level with what he denies, because it is. He who accepts life in its totality need not compromise at all. Or you can say he has already made his peace, his compromise.

Questioner: Now you say that hesitation is good. Earlier you said that indecisiveness is destructive and that one must know clearly where he stands. Please explain.

I only said that hesitation is good; I did not say to be always in a state of hesitation is good. Those who feel hesitant strive to go beyond it; those who don't are stuck there.

Hesitancy is the transitional stage—the beginning of the journey. It is only after one hesitates that he goes beyond it. And there are two ways to transcend it. If you accept one side of the truth, your hesitation will disappear. You can agree with Shankara or Nagarjuna, and you will cease to hesitate. You will be out of trouble, you will be certain. But this way of getting rid of hesitation is costly; you have to part with your intelligence. Stupid people never hesitate; so if you lose your intelligence then you will overcome hesitation. But this is certainly not the right way.

You have to go beyond your hesitancy intelligently. That is, you don't escape it, rather you face it and transcend it. Hesitation has to be transcended at the point where both sides of truth are seen as one and inseparable. This is a rational way of dealing with hesitancy. The other way is irrational, stupid, when you choose one side and reject the other. Then you go below hesitation, not beyond it. This is the way of the insane, who is also unhesitating, certain. There is a trans-rational state, above reason, when you see the two sides as together and inseparable. Then all contradictions disappear, opposites go and you come to oneness, unity and integrity.

That is why I say that hesitation is a blessing. It takes you from stupidity to intelligence. He is fortunate who hesitates, because it opens the door to that which is beyond intelligence.

Questioner: You say that Shankara's commentary on the Geeta is incomplete. There are dozens of commentaries on the Geeta. Can you say if

> *any one of them is complete? Do you think Lokmanya Tilak's interpretation is complete? At least it does not take an escapist view of life; it is activist and moralistic. Or are you trying to synthesize Tilak's activism with Shankara's supra-moralism?*

Not one commentary on Krishna is complete. It is not possible, unless someone like Krishna himself comments on him.

Every interpretation of Krishna is incomplete and partial. There are many sides to a single thing, and Krishna is a man of infinite dimensions. So every commentator chooses from them according to what appeals to him. Shankara establishes that sannyas and inaction form the cornerstones of the *Geeta*. From the same *Geeta*, Tilak chooses *karmayoga*, the discipline of action, and he brings all his arguments to prove that action is *Geeta's* central message. Now Shankara and Tilak are polar opposites.

A thousand years have passed since Shankara commented on the *Geeta*, and in the course of time his escapist philosophy has enfeebled India to her very roots, weakened her in many ways. By its nature, escapism is enervating. Shankara's teachings sapped this country's vitality and dynamism. A thousand years' experiences were enough to turn the pendulum in the opposite direction. It became urgent that someone comment on the *Geeta* saying that it stands for dynamism and action. So Tilak comes forward with a statement which is at the other extreme of Shankara. While Shankara had chosen inaction and renunciation, Tilak chose activism and action.

So Tilak's commentary is as incomplete as Shankara's.

There are any number of commentaries on the *Geeta*. They are not in dozens, but in hundreds, and the number increases every day. However, not one of them has done justice to Krishna's philosophy. And the reason is that not one commentator has shown the courage to be super-rational. Each of them has tried to be rational and logical.

In fact, a commentator cannot be other than rational. If he transcends the rational he will not write a commentary on the *Geeta*, he will instead create the *Geeta* itself. When one attains to the super-rational state a *Geeta* is born through him. Then commentary becomes unnecessary. A commentary means that you don't understand something in the *Geeta* and I explain it to you by way of interpreting it. It is an attempt at interpreting something. And when you explain something you have to keep within the bounds of logic and reason.

The moment something transcends reason it turns into a *Geeta*, not a commentary on it.

> Questioner: What is it that you are saying right now?

One thing is certain, it is not a commentary.

> Questioner: And what is the other thing?

I leave that to you. Should not something be left to you?

> Questioner: A part of my question remains unanswered. Do you think the Geeta will be complete if Shankara's supra-moralism and Tilak's activism are made into one piece? Because the supra-morality that you

> *speak about is echoed by Shankara,*
> *not Tilak; the latter is out and out a*
> *moralist. On the other hand Tilak,*
> *not Shankara echoes your positivism,*
> *your dynamism. Shankara is for*
> *renunciation.*

It is true. Shankara is a supra-moralist.

A moralist is action-oriented; he says do this and don't do that. Shankara says every action is illusory; whether you practice asceticism or indulge in stealing makes no difference. In sleep now you dream you are a robber, and then you dream you are a saint; it does not make any difference in your waking state. On waking you say both robber and saint are dream stuff, they are meaningless. For this reason nothing is moral or immoral for Shankara. There is no way to choose between morality and immorality, just as there is no way to choose between two dreams. Choice is possible only between two realities. Because the world is an illusion to Shankara there is no place for morality in his philosophy. Shankara's vision is supra-moralistic; it transcends morality. The principle of inaction is bound to go beyond morality.

When Shankara's commentaries on Indian philosophy were translated into the languages of the West, they were thought to be supporting immorality. Thinkers of the West said that Shankara's vision upheld immorality. If such a view that nothing is right or wrong—that all actions, like dreams, are the same—gains ground, then people will go off the track; they will simply sink into the mire of sin and degradation. And it is not surprising if the West reacts in this manner. Western people have lived down the centuries, have been brought up on the food of Judaic philosophy, which has ceaselessly harangued them to "Do this and don't do that." Their whole religion and culture are based on the Ten Commandments, which clearly enunciate what one should do and should not do. So it is no wonder that they reacted sharply to Shankara's thinking and called it immoral.

Certainly Shankara's thinking is not *im-moralist*, because immorality is a choice against morality. Shankara stands for choicelessness, and for this reason he is supra-moralistic. He does not ask you to be moral or immoral, a saint or a thief; he does not ask you to become anything. He is against becoming; he is for being what you are. In fact, he is for non-being. This is really a trans-moral vision.

Tilak, on the other hand, is a moralist. He believes there is a choice between a good action and a bad one, between what one should do and one should not. According to him religion consists of shoulds and should-nots. He really is for action. For this reason he does not call the world unreal. It is real. The visible world is true for Tilak; it is not *maya* or illusion. In the midst of this reality we have to decide what is right and what is not right. And religion simply means choice of the right, virtuous, good. It is true that Tilak holds a wholly contrary viewpoint to that of Shankara.

You ask whether it will make the thing complete if we combine Shankara's supra-moralism with the activism of Tilak. No, it will not be complete that way. And there are reasons for it.

The basic reason is we cannot make something whole by putting together its parts. It is like we break up a person's body into pieces and then put the parts together to make a whole person again. It is simply impossible. If the person is whole then his parts will function in unison, but separate parts put together cannot make a person whole again. Parts put together don't make a whole; it is a different thing, however, that a whole consists of many parts.

My vision of Krishna takes in both Shankara and Tilak, but just a mixture of their viewpoints will not make a complete philosophy of Krishna. There is yet another reason why a blending of Shankara and Tilak will not make a complete Krishna. There are a thousand views about Krishna; Shankara and Tilak represent only two. Even a combination of all the thousand views cannot make a complete Krishna.

Putting different parts together is a mechanical process, it cannot be organic. We can break up a machine into its parts and remake it by putting the parts together again. But we cannot do the same with a live, organic body. Please bear in mind this fundamental difference between organic unity and mechanical togetherness. While a mechanical combination is equal to the totality of parts, an organic unity is much more than the sum total of its parts.

For example, if we make a list of all the ingredients that make up a human body—like iron, copper, sodium, aluminum, phosphorus and the rest of it, they will be worth four to five rupees, not more. Nine-tenths of a human body is water, which does not cost anything at the moment. And the rest of these things are available in the market. If however, you put them all together in the right proportions they cannot create a live human body. They cannot. A live body is much more than the sum total of its parts, although it cannot be without these parts.

An organic unity exists in Krishna's philosophy of life, although it has a thousand different parts. And every part has been interpreted differently by different persons. Ramanuja says one thing, Shankara says another, and Nimbark says something else. Even Tilak, Arvind, Gandhi and Vinoba speak in different voices. And if you collect all these different views on Krishna, they cannot re-create the organic unity that Krishna is. There is no difficulty in putting them together, but you will not find Krishna in this amalgam. And it is also true that if Krishna is present, then all these parts plus something much more will be there.

Leave aside a blend of Shankara and Tilak—even if you blend all the commentaries on Krishna, it will not do. It will be a mechanical, dead unity. It will be nothing more than an arithmetical addition.

What I have been saying here is not a commentary on Krishna; I am not interpreting him. I have nothing to do with commentary. Therefore I am not afraid of contradictions; they are there. Contradictions exist in Krishna himself, and I cannot do a thing about it. So I am not commenting, I am just unveiling Krishna before you. I am not trying to impose myself on him, I am only unraveling him exactly as he is: right and wrong, moral and immoral, rational, irrational and transrational. As Krishna himself is choiceless, neither do I pick and choose anything from his life. I am presenting him to you exactly as he is.

I am aware I am going to be in difficulty on this score. It is going to be the same difficulty that Krishna had created for himself. For thousands of years people have been struggling to interpret and understand what Krishna said in the *Geeta*. In the same way, what I am saying now will need to be interpreted and you will all strain yourselves to understand it. I am unveiling Krishna in his entirety without caring for the inconsistencies and contradictions inherent in his life and teachings. I don't care if one of my statements about him is going to clash with another statement that I may make subsequently. I will go on revealing his life and philosophy as it authentically is. I want to give you Krishna whole and in one piece.

So what I am saying to you is not a commentary.

Questioner: Do you become Krishna himself when you speak about him?

One needs to become something which he is not. The question simply does not arise here. Becoming is needless; I am it.

> Questioner: Shree Arvind has written a commentary on the Geeta in which he talks about the relationship between the creation and its perception. From one point of view it is reality that is important, and from another its perception is important. In his concept of the supramental he believes that divine consciousness is going to descend on this earth, but this concept of his seems to be dualistic. What do you say? And do you think that Raman Maharshi's concept of Ajatvad, of unborn reality, is closer to you and to Chaitanya's concept of achintya bhedabhedvad, or unthinkable dualistic non-dualism? And can you shed some light on the episode of Arvind seeing Krishna's visions?

All Arvind's talk of supraconsciousness and the supramental is within the confines of the rational mind. He never goes beyond reason. Even when he speaks about the transcendence of reason, he uses rationalistic concepts. Arvind is a rationalist. Everything he says and the words and concepts he uses to say it belong to the grammar of rationalism. There is a great consistency in the statements of Arvind which is not there in statements from supra-rationalism. You cannot find the same logical consistency in the statements of mystics. A mystic speaks in terms of contradictions and paradoxes. He says one word and soon contradicts it by another word that follows it. A mystic is self-contradictory. Arvind never contradicts himself.

Arvind is a great system-maker, and a system-maker can never be a supra-rational. A system is made with the help of reason. Supra-rational people are always unsystematic; they don't have a system. System is integral to logic; that which is illogical cannot follow a methodology or order. The unthinkable cannot be systematized. All the thinkers of this century who have crossed the threshhold of reason are fragmentary in their statements; none of them followed a logical order. Wittgenstein, Husserl, Heidegger, Marlo Ponti and the rest of them, have made fragmentary statements. J. Krishnamurti belongs to the same category which denies system, order. Their statements are atomic, and they contradict themselves.

Arvind's case is very different. The truth is, after Shankara there has been no greater system-builder in India than Arvind. But this is what makes for the weakness and poverty of his philosophy. He is very skilled in playing with words, concepts and theories. But the irony is that the reality of life is far beyond words, concepts and doctrines. His trouble is that he was wholly educated in the West where he learned Aristotelian logic, Darwinian theory of evolution and the scientific way of thinking. His mind is wholly western; no one in India today is more western in his way of thinking than Arvind. And ironically he chose to interpret the eastern philosophy, with the result that he reduced the whole thing into a system.

The East has no logical system. All its profound insights transcend logic and thought; they cannot be achieved through thinking. Eastern experiences go beyond the known, the knower and knowledge itself; they all belong to the unknown and the unknowable— what we call mystery. And Arvind applies his western mind to interpret the transmental experiences and insights of the East. He divides them into categories and makes a system out of them, which no other eastern person could have done.

So while Arvind always talks of the unthinkable he uses the instrument of thought and the thinkable throughout. Consequently his unthinkable is nothing but a bundle of words. If Arvind had the experience of the unthinkable he could not have categorized it, because it defies all categories. One who really knows the unthinkable cannot live with categories and concepts.

Curiously enough, Arvind creates concepts out of things that have never been conceptualized. His concept of the supramental is a case in point. But he goes on fabricating categories and concepts and fitting them into logic and reason. And he does it without any inhibitions.

The other part of your question is relevant in this context. In a sense, no religious thinking subscribes to the concept of evolution.

In this respect, we can divide the religions of the world into two groups. One group believes in the theory of creation with a beginning and an end, and the other believes in an existence that has no beginning and no end. Hinduism, Christianity, and Mohammedanism believe in creation; they believe that God created the universe. The other group of religions like Jainism and Buddhism, deny the theory of creation; according to them, that which is, is beginningless. It was never created.

All those who believe in creation cannot accept the theory of evolution. If they accept it, it would mean God created an incomplete world which developed gradually to its present state. But how can a perfect God create an imperfect world? Evolution means that the world grows gradually, and creation means that the whole world comes into being altogether.

It is significant that originally the word *shristhi*, meaning creation, belonged to the Hindus, and *prakriti*, meaning pre-creation, belonged to the Jainas and

Buddhists and Sankhyaites. In the course of time, however, they got mixed up. But the Hindus cannot accept the word *prakriti*, which means that which is is there from the time before creation, that which is uncreated, which is eternal. Creation means something which was not always there and which was created and which can be terminated.

The concept of the pre-created, the uncreated, of *prakriti*, belongs to an altogether different school which does not believe in creation. Sankhyaites, Jainas, and Buddhists don't have the concept of a creator because when nothing is created, the question of a creator does not arise. So God disappeared, he has no place in their philosophies. God is needed only in the form of a creator, and so those who rejected creation also rejected God. God as creator belongs only to those who accept the idea of creation.

Arvind brought with him the idea of evolution from the West. When Arvind was a student in England, Darwin's ideas were sweeping across Europe. Evidently he was very much influenced by them. After his return to India he studied eastern philosophy, and studied it deeply. I deliberately use the word "studied" to say that he did not know the truth on his own, his knowledge was merely intellectual. Although he possessed a sharp intellect, his direct experience of truth was very dim. Consequently he produced a crossbreed of eastern mysticism and western rationalism, which is an anomaly. India's psyche is not much concerned with the study of nature, matter and their evolution; it is basically concerned with the understanding of mind and spirit. The meeting of the western thought of evolution with the eastern understanding of the psyche gave rise to a strange idea of psychic evolution, which became Arvind's lifework. Like nature, he thought consciousness evolves too.

Arvind added something new to the idea of evolution which is his own, and for this very reason it is utterly wrong. Very often original ideas are wrong, because they happen to be the finding of a single person. It is true that traditional beliefs, in the course of time, degenerate into fossils, but they have a validity of their own because millions of people go out to find them. This new idea which built Arvind's reputation concerns the descent of divine consciousness.

Down the centuries we have believed that man has to rise and ascend to God; it is always an upward journey, an ascent. Arvind thinks otherwise: he thinks that God will descend and meet man.

In a way this is also like the two sides of a coin. The truth happens to be exactly in the middle. That truth is that both man and God move towards each other and meet somewhere midway. This meeting always happens somewhere midway, but the old idea emphasized man's efforts—and not without reason. As far as God is concerned, he is always available to man providing man wants to meet him. That much is certain, and therefore God can be left out of this consideration. But it is not certain that man will make a move to meet God. So it mostly depends on man and his journey towards God, his efforts. God's journey towards man can be taken for granted. Too much emphasis on God moving toward man is likely to weaken man's efforts.

Arvind starts from the wrong end when he says that God is going to descend on us. But he has great appeal to people who are not interested in doing anything on their own. They took enthusiastically to Arvind's idea of the descent of the supramental energy and they rushed to Pondicherry. In recent years more Indians have gone to Pondicherry than anywhere else. There, God could be had for a song. They need not move a finger, because God on his own was on his way to them. There could not be a cheaper bargain than this. And when God descends he will descend on one and all; he will not make any distinctions. Many people believe that Arvind alone, sitting in seclusion at Pondicherry, will work for it and divine energy will be available to all, like the river Ganges was available when it was brought to earth by Bhagirath. Arvind is to be another Bhagirath, and at a much higher level. It has put a premium on man's greed and led to a lot of illusions.

I think that is a very wrong idea. It is true God descends, but he descends only on those who ascend to him. A great deal depends on the individual and his efforts. Divine energy descends on those who prepare themselves for it, who deserve it. And there is no reason for God to be collectively available to one and all. In fact, God is always available, but only to those who aspire and strive for him. And it is always the individual, not a collective or a society, who walks the path to God. And he has to go all alone. And if God is going to descend on all, why do you think he will exclude animals, trees and rocks?

The experiment that is in process at Pondicherry is utterly meaningless; there has not been a more meaningless experiment in man's history. It is a waste of effort, but it goes on because it is very comforting to our greed.

In this context, the questioner has remembered Raman who is just the opposite of Arvind. While Arvind is a great scholar, Raman has nothing to do with scholarship. Arvind is very knowledgeable, he is well-informed; Raman is utterly unscholarly, you cannot come across a more unscholarly man than him. While Arvind seems to be all-knowing, Raman is preparing for the non-knowing state, he does not seem to know a thing. That is why man's highest potentiality is actualized in Raman, and Arvind has missed it. Arvind remains just knowledgeable; Raman really knows the truth. Raman attained to self-knowledge, not knowledge. So his statements are straight and simple, free from the jargon of scriptures and scholarship. Raman is poor in language and logic, but his richness of experience, of being, is immense; as such he is incomparable.

Raman is not a system-maker like Arvind. His statements are atomic; they are just like sutras, aphorisms. He does not have much to say, and he says only that which he knows. Even his words are not enough to say what he really knows. Raman's whole teaching can be collected on a postcard, not even a full page will be needed. And if you want to make a collection of Arvind's writings, they will fill a whole library. And it is not that Arvind has said all that he wanted to say. He will have to be born again and again to say it all, he had too much to say. This does not mean that he did not bother to attain real knowing because he had already so much to say. No, this was not the difficulty.

Buddha had much to say and he said it. Buddha was like Raman so far as his experience of truth was concerned, and he was like Arvind in general knowledge. Mahavira has said little; he spent most of his time in silence. His statements are few and far between; they are telegraphic. In his statements Mahavira resembles Raman. *Digambaras*, one of the two Jaina sects, don't have any collection of his teachings, while the *Shwetambaras* have a few scriptures which were compiled five hundred years after Mahavira's death.

> Questioner: You compare Raman
> with Buddha who happened in the
> distant past. Why not compare him
> with Krishnamurti who is so close by?

The question of being close or distant does not arise. Krishnamurti is exactly like Raman. I compare Arvind with Raman and Buddha for a special reason. In the experience of truth, Krishnamurti is very much like Raman, but he lags behind Arvind in knowledgeability. Of course, he is more articulate and logical than Raman. And there is a great difference between Krishnamurti and Arvind in so far as the use of logic and reason is concerned.

Arvind uses logic to reinforce his arguments; Krishnamurti uses logic to destroy logic; he makes full use of reason in order to lead you beyond reason. But he is not much knowledgeable. That is why I chose Buddha as an example; he compares well with Arvind in knowledge and with Raman in self-knowledge. As far as Krishnamurti is concerned, he is like Raman in transcendental experience, but he is not scholarly like Arvind.

There is yet another difference between Raman and Krishnamurti. While Raman's statements are very brief, Krishnamurti's statements are voluminous. But in spite of their large volume, Krishnamurti's teachings can be condensed in a brief statement. For forty years Krishnamurti has been repeating the same thing over and over again. His statements can be condensed to a postcard. But because he uses reason in his statements, they grow in volume. Raman is precise and brief; he avoids volume. You can say that the statements of both Krishnamurti and Raman are atomic, but while Krishnamurti embellishes them with arguments, Raman does not. Raman speaks, like the seers of the Upanishads, in aphorisms. The Upanishads just proclaim: the *Brahman*, the supreme is; they don't bother to advance any argument in their support. They make bare statements that, "It is so" and "It is not so." Raman can be compared with the Upanishadic *rishis*.

> Questioner: Please tell us something about Raman's ajatvad or the principle of no-birth.

According to Raman and people like him, that which is has no beginning, it was never born, it is unborn. The same thing has always been said in another way: that which is will never die, it is deathless, it is immortal. There are hundreds of statements which proclaim the immortality of *Brahman*, the ultimate, who is without beginning and without end. Only that which is never born can be immortal, that which is beginningless. This is Raman's way of describing the eternal.

Do you know when you were born? You don't. Yes, there are records of your birth which others have kept, and through them that you came to know that you were born on a certain date, month and year. This is just information received from others. Apart from this information you have no way to know that you were born. There is no intrinsic, inbuilt source of information within you which can tell you about it; you have no evidence whatsoever to support the fact of your birth. The truth of your innermost being is eternal, so the question of its birth does not arise. In fact, you were never born; you are as eternal as eternity.

You say you will die someday, but how do you know it? Do you know what death is? Do you have any experience of death? No, you will say you have seen others die, and so you infer that you too will die someday. But suppose we arrange things, and it is quite possible, that a certain person is not allowed to see any other person die. Can he know on his own that he is ever going to die? He cannot. So it is just your conjecture, based on external evidence, that you will die in some future. There is no internal evidence, no intrinsic source of knowledge within you which can sustain your conjecture that you will die. That is why a strange thing happens, that in spite of so many deaths taking place all around, no one really believes that he is going to die; he believes while others will die he is going to live. Your innermost being knows no birth and no death; it is eternal. You only know that you are.

Raman asks you not to guess, but find out for yourself if there is really birth and death. You have no inner evidence in support of birth and death; the only dependable evidence available within you says, "I am."

I too, say to you there is every evidence that makes you know, "I am." And if you go still deeper you will know, "I am not." Then you will know only a state of "am-ness" within you.

FIFTEENTH DISCOURSE
EVENING, OCTOBER 2, 1970
MANALI, INDIA

LIFE AFTER DEATH AND REBIRTH

Questioner: A part of our previous question remains unanswered: it is about Shree Arvind seeing visions of Krishna. You had once said at Ahmedabad that such visions are mostly nothing more than mental projections. Is it a mental projection or a real mystical experience in the case of Arvind?

There is another question: If Arjuna is just an instrument in the hands of existence, what about his individuality?

isions of Krishna, or of Buddha, Mahavira or Christ are seen in two different ways. One is what we call a mental projection—what you see is nothing but your dreams, your desires, your imaginations taking a visual form, a shape in front of your eyes. There is nothing real in front of you; it is all imagination. The mind is quite capable of it; it can project an image of your dreams and desires, and you can think it is real. As you dream in sleep, so you can dream in the waking state. This is how a Hindu sees visions of Krishna or Rama, a Christian sees visions of Christ or Mary. It is just mental, imaginary, hallucinatory. The other way is real, but it does not bring you face to face with Krishna or his image; it makes you encounter and experience what may be called the Krishna-consciousness. In an experience like this there is no image whatsoever of Krishna or Christ, there is only a state of heightened awareness, a contact-high.

As I said yesterday, there are two forms of Krishna: one is his oceanic form and the other is his wave form. While his oceanic form represents the universal consciousness or superconsciousness, his wave form represents Krishna the man who happened some five thousand years ago.

Now an image, an icon of his wave form—Krishna the man—can be used to come in contact with his oceanic form, with Krishna-consciousness. But when you will really come in contact with Krishna-consciousness, this image, this symbol of Krishna will disappear and only the superconsciousness will remain with you. While it is true that his statue can be used for connecting with Krishna's superconsciousness, if someone sees only visions of Krishna and does not experience his consciousness, then it is merely a case of mental projection and nothing else.

The experience of Krishna-consciousness does not happen by way of visions and images. It is pure consciousness without any shape or form. We associate Krishna's name with it because a person loves Krishna and comes to this consciousness with the help of his image. Another person can come to it with the help of Buddha's image, and he can call it Buddha-consciousness. It can be called Christ-consciousness if someone attains it through the image of Christ.

Names don't matter; the real thing is the oceanic consciousness, which is without name and form.

Arvind's experience of Krishna-visions is concerned with Krishna's image, his physical form. He says that Krishna appeared before him in physical form. This is simply a case of mental projection. Of course such an experience is pleasant and gratifying, but it is nonetheless a projection of our mind. It is an extension of desire; it is exactly dreamstuff. It is our mind's creation.

We can begin with the mind, but we have to go beyond the mind. The journey begins with the mind, and ends with the no-mind, cessation of the mind. It is significant to know that the mind is the world of words, forms and images; words, forms and images constitute the mind. And where forms and images disappear the mind disappears on its own. There is no way for the mind to exist without words, forms and images. The mind cannot exist in emptiness, in void; it lives on the determined, the concrete. The moment the concrete world comes to an end, the mind itself comes to an end. Krishna-consciousness is attained only when the mind ceases to be; it is a state of no-mind.

Whoever says he has encountered Krishna in his physical form is a victim of mental projection; he is projecting his own mental images on the vast screen of universal consciousness and viewing them as objective reality. It is like a movie projector projects fast moving pictures on an empty screen; there is really nothing on the screen except shadows. Such visions are not a spiritual experience, they are wholly psychic. They are, however, very gratifying; a Krishna devotee is bound to be overjoyed to see visions of one he has been desiring to see all his life. But remember, it is only a kind of happiness, not bliss. Nor can you call it an experience of truth.

I don't mean to say that Arvind's experience is not real, but he describes it in the way of a scholar, an intellectual. And this makes the experience appear to be one of mental projection. It is not difficult to distinguish a real experience, an experience of the oceanic consciousness from the one that is projected or imagined. An oceanic experience is everlasting; once it comes it comes forever, and it wipes out all other experiences from your mind. It really wipes out the mind itself. One blessed with such an experience sees the divine everywhere—in trees and rocks, in streams and rivers, in mountains and stars. But so far as projected visions are concerned, they appear and disappear, they never last. They are transient, momentary. Being an intellectual, Arvind is not able to portray it rightly; for a man of intellect such a task becomes difficult.

But there is another side of Arvind which is poetic. He is not only an intellectual but also a great poet. As a poet he is not less than Rabindranath Tagore. If he failed to receive the Nobel Prize, it was not because he did not deserve it, but because his poetry is much too complex and difficult to understand. His *Savitri* ranks among the great epics of the world; there are hardly ten great epics of the stature of *Savitri*. And unlike the scholar, the poet in Arvind is quite capable of seeing Krishna's visions. Ironically, Arvind has expressed this experience strictly in terms of logic and reason, which is of course natural. And his account of the experience does not have the flavor of the transconscious.

We use words in two ways. In one way the word is kept within the confines of its known meaning; it conveys only that which is conveyed by its meaning. It fails to go beyond its own limitations. In the other way, the word used communicates much more than its given meaning. The word itself may be small, but its meaning is vast; the meaning is larger than the word itself. Arvind's way is quite different; while he uses big words, he fails to communicate any great meaning through them. He is known for his long words and lengthy sentences. That is why he always ends up as a philosopher.

When words really take off, when they transcend their given meaning, they enter a world of mystery, they become a vehicle for the transcendental experience. Such words are pregnant with tremendous meaning; they are like fingers pointing to the moon. Arvind's words are not that pregnant, they don't have an arrow directed toward the beyond. His words never transcend their given meaning. And there are reasons for it.

As I said this morning, Arvind was educated in the West at a time when, like Darwin in science, Hegel was the most dominant influence in philosophy. And Hegel is also known for the pompous language replete with big words and complex phrases in his treatises. Going through Hegel's works one has a sense of profundity about them in the beginning. We tend to think that what we don't understand must be very profound. But it is not necessarily so, although it is true that profound things are difficult to understand. So many people use obscure words and elaborate phrases to create an impression of depth on their listeners and readers.

Hegel is a case in point: his language is very complex, devious and bombastic—full of lengthy, explanatory statements enclosed within brackets. But as scholarship gained maturity in Europe, Hegel's reputation declined in the same measure, and people came to know that he knew much less than he pretended. Arvind's way of expression is Hegelian, and like Hegel he is also a systematizer. He too has not much to say, and so he has to say it in a great many words, and long and involved sentences at that.

Expression has to have a logical and rational buildup. But if it says something which goes beyond it then it means the person saying it has known that which lies beyond words. But if he exhausts himself in his words, which say nothing more than what they mean, then it is clear he is only a knowledgeable person. Going through all of Arvind's works you are left with a feeling that they are wordy; there is nothing experiential about them. If someone who knows something of the beyond keeps silent, even his silence will be eloquent. But in the absence of such an experience, even a million words will prove to be a wastage. When you say something, you have to say it logically, but if your "something" is experiential it will leave its flavor, its perfume in your every word and metaphor. Not only that, your words will also say that they could not say what they really wanted to say. As far as Arvind is concerned, it seems he has said much more than was worth saying.

In this context I recall a significant event from the life of Rabindranath, which will help you to understand the thing better. The great poet is on his deathbed, and an intimate friend has come to say farewell. The friend says, "You sang all you wanted to sing, you said all you wanted to say; not only that, you did all you wanted to do. I believe now you can leave this world in perfect peace and contentment, with a feeling of utter gratefulness to God."

Rabindranath opened his eyes and said, "You have got it all wrong. Right now I have been saying to God, 'How ironical it is that when I have put together all the musical instruments and am ready to sing, I am called upon to leave the world.' I have yet to sing my song. What people think to be my song is only preparation for the real song I was going to begin, but alas! I have yet to say what I wanted to say."

Arvind cannot say the same thing. He has said all that he wanted to say, and said them very methodically. And I say that as a mystic Rabindranath is head and shoulders above Arvind.

You also want to know what will happen to Arjuna's individuality if he is only an instrument in the hands of existence. If everything happens exactly as it has to happen, if everything is pre-determined, then what is the meaning and responsibility of an individual person? Isn't he just a cog in the machine?

It is a significant question, so try to listen carefully to what I am going to say here. You will come upon some basic truths of life if you understand this thing rightly.

Certainly one's individuality will be destroyed if he is forced to be an instrument in the hands of another. But if someone becomes an instrument on his own accord, just the contrary will happen, his individuality will achieve its ultimate flowering. There is great difference between these two states. If someone forcibly turns you into a means and uses you as such, you are bound to lose your soul. But your soul will be fulfilled if you surrender on your own and become an instrument in the hands of existence. Please understand this difference—it is very subtle and great. For instance, if you come and overpower me and fetter my hands and feet, I become your slave. But what will happen if I, on my own, willingly volunteer myself to be your slave? Then I become the master of slavery—its architect.

I would like to relate a story from the life of the Greek sage, Diogenes. I love to relate this story again and again; it is really beautiful.

Diogenes is passing through a forest. He is naked, walking fearlessly like a lion walks. Some people who are engaged in slave-trade happen to see Diogenes. They are tempted by his powerful physique. It is really splendid, as splendid as that of Mahavira. It is no wonder that both Mahavira and Diogenes discard clothes and live naked; they have such beautiful bodies that they alone can afford to go naked. Although the slave-traders are eight in number, they are very afraid of Diogenes who looks so powerful. It would be difficult for them to overpower and capture him.

In fact, one who wants to overpower another person is essentially a weak and fear-stricken person.

Only a fearful person wants to frighten and dominate others just to assuage his own fear. A really fearless person never tries to dominate others. He loves everybody's freedom as much as he loves his own. A fearful man is always afraid that if he does not dominate others, others will dominate him. This is the psychology of all wars. That's why Machiavelli says in his book *The Prince*, that to be on the offensive is the best defense.

So the traders are afraid of Diogenes, but their greed is equally strong. A slave like Diogenes would fetch a fabulous price in the slaves' market. After much discussion among themselves, they decide to make an attempt. Prepared for a good fight, they surround him from all sides, but Diogenes confounds them in a strange way. They would not have been surprised if he had resisted them. They were well-prepared for it. But instead they find Diogenes standing quietly and serenely in his place with not a trace of fear or agitation on his face. He folds hands and giggles, saying, "What do you want? What is your intention?"

The merchants are embarrassed and hesitatingly tell him that they wanted to capture and enslave him. Diogenes laughs and says, "Why make such a fuss about it? You are fools; you should have just asked me and I would have agreed. I have been watching you anxiously discussing and preparing an elaborate plan which is all useless. Where are the handcuffs? Take them out of your bags. And here are my hands." Saying this he stretches his two hands to them. His captors are amazed, and their confusion is worse. They have never seen such a man, shouting at them, "Where are the handcuffs? Take them out of your bags!" And he speaks as if he is the master and they are his slaves.

With great hesitation and fear they take out a pair of handcuffs and put them on Diogenes' hands, saying, "It is something incredible. The way you have put yourself in our hands is unbelievable. You baffle us."

What Diogenes says to them is significant. He says, "I have learned the secret of freedom, which is to become a slave on my own. Now no one can rob me of my freedom. You have no way to enslave me."

Then they chain him and with one end of the chain in their hands, they march him to the slave market. Diogenes then says, "Why carry a heavy chain in your hands unnecessarily? Don't you see I am going with you on my own accord? Take off the chains so we walk with ease, and take care that you don't run away before we reach the marketplace. And rest assured, I am not going to escape." The merchants soon remove the chains, because they know in their heart of hearts what kind of man he is. He has voluntarily surrendered himself to them. There is no use putting fetters on one who has given his hands for handcuffing without their asking.

Diogenes walks at their head as if a king is marching with his retinue. There is not a trace of fear on his face, while his captors look like his captives. He looks so charismatic that wherever he goes all eyes are turned on him. Pointing to his captors, Diogenes tells the spectators, "What are you looking for? They are all my slaves. And although they are not in chains yet, they cannot run away from me. They are so bound to me." The merchants are really crestfallen.

At long last they arrive at the marketplace where slaves are bought and sold. The leader of the gang approaches the market manager saying, "We have a strange man to sell, and sell as soon as possible. Otherwise all of us will be in trouble. He tells everyone that he is the master and we are all his slaves, because we are so bound to him that we cannot run away from him. And it is true, we cannot leave him, because he is going to fetch a fabulous price for us."

Diogenes immediately mounts the dock meant for slaves to be auctioned and stands there with the dignity of a king. Then the manager shouts, "Here is a great slave for sale; whosoever has enough money should bid for him."

Diogenes first shouts at the manager, "Shut up, if you don't know how to sell a master." Then he says to the bidders, "Here is a master for sale; whosoever can afford a master should bid for him."

If you are forced against your will to be an instrument, if it is not your own choice, then you are certainly a slave and your individuality is killed. But Krishna does not ask Arjuna to be such a slavish instrument; he only wants him to understand the reality and to flow with the stream of existence. It is foolish to fight with the river of life and try to swim upstream. He says to Arjuna, "Leave yourself in the hands of life, of existence, and you will be fulfilled." If someone surrenders himself to existence, to truth, to the whole, and surrenders with full understanding and joy, then his individuality, instead of being crippled, attains to full flowering and fruition. Then he is his own master. And there is no better way of proclaiming one's mastery than the way of surrender.

Try to understand this thing very clearly. There is no better way of proclaiming one's mastery over himself than the way of surrender. If I surrender it means that I am my own master; no slave surrenders, he is just overpowered and captured. By surrendering, Arjuna does not become a cog in a machine; he really becomes a man with a soul, he becomes godly. For the first time, his individuality attains full flowering, and it happens effortlessly and naturally.

> Questioner: We would like to return to Arvind seeing visions of Krishna, which you think to be a case of mental projection. In this connection we

> *recall what you once said about the*
> *Tibetan lamas, that on a particular*
> *day of each year some competent*
> *lamas gather together and establish*
> *contact with Buddha. On another oc-*
> *casion you had said something about*
> *Gandhi and on being further ques-*
> *tioned you said that you had your fact*
> *from Gandhi himself. And we have*
> *heard that till recently there were*
> *lamas in Tibet who traveled astrally*
> *from one place to another where they*
> *again appeared in their physical*
> *bodies. Will you please shed some*
> *more light on this matter?*

In this context a few things have to be understood first.

It is true that on a particular full moon night, which is known as Buddha's full moon night, five hundred lamas gather at one of the summits of the Himalayas—the same Himalayas where we are gathered at this moment—and see visions of Buddha. The number of lamas who gather there never exceeds five hundred; it is fixed for good. It is only on the death of one of them that another lama is admitted in his place. But there is a basic difference between this and Arvind seeing visions of Krishna. In the case of his visions of Krishna, it is Arvind who takes the initiative and makes efforts to see them. The lamas don't have to do anything; Buddha himself appears before them according to a promise he had given to his disciples in his lifetime. The lamas have only to be present there at the appointed time. And this dif-ference between the two events should be clearly understood.

Buddha has left behind him a promise that at a particular time of Buddha's full moon night of each year and at a particular spot in the Himalayas, he would appear for his chosen disciples. At this promised moment Buddha's oceanic body takes the form of a wave body, seen by five hundred lamas together. But the lamas have no part in it except that they present themselves on the said occasion. This is one difference between this encounter, this darshan, and the one that Arvind has.

Secondly, while Arvind is alone at the time of Krishna's appearance, there are altogether five hundred lamas to witness Buddha's appearance. An event of mental projection is always personal, you cannot make another person an associate with you. If you ask Arvind or any other person who sees such visions, for that matter, to allow you to share his experience, he will just say no, it is not possible. But when five hundred people see visions of Buddha together, it cannot be a case of psychic projection. Not only that, all the people present compare notes and accept something as real only when each of its accounts tallies with another. As far as Arvind is concerned, he is his own witness. And then while Arvind comes to it after long efforts, the lamas make no efforts whatsoever. It is just the fulfillment of a promise made by another person in another time.

Questioner: Can it be a case of collective auto-suggestion?

No, it is not possible. And there are reasons for it.

Anybody and everybody cannot be admitted into this council of five hundred lamas. There are very strict criteria governing one's admission into this group. Only those are admitted into it who fully succeed in knowing their unconscious minds, because unless they are masters of their unconscious they are not immune from individual or collective hypnosis. Hypnosis works upon one's unconscious mind and therefore when one becomes fully aware of his unconscious he cannot be hypnotized any more. There is no way to hypnotize a person who has burned all the trash of his unconscious and illumined his whole psyche. Now there is no such area in his mind where suggestions can be planted so that they eventually become projected visions and images. That is why the lamas have very strict rules regarding the admission of every new member. Only on the death of a sitting member a new one is chosen to fill his place, and the way he is selected is very unusual.

There are strange and very difficult rules that govern the selection of a person for lamahood. Not only his present life is investigated, even his past lives are looked into. To deserve this place, he has to have a long record of sustained spiritual practice. For example, the present Dalai Lama carries with him the soul of the previous Dalai Lama he has been selected to succeed. When the lama dies he leaves behind him a coded message saying that he will take his next birth with certain specific signs and the child that conforms to those signs should be selected as his successor. It is an arduous and complicated process. The whole country is informed by beat of the drums that if a child with specific signs is born in any family, the family concerned should inform the lamasery concerned about his birth.

Similarly when the Dalai Lama dies, he leaves certain clues to find his successor. These clues are a well-guarded secret, and thousands of children born after his death are interviewed to find out who is the incarnation of the late Dalai Lama. And the child who answers all the queries and signs is selected as the succeeding Dalai Lama.

Before they select a lama to fill the vacancy in the five hundred member council, they put him to a lot of tests to ascertain that he has known his unconscious, and that he cannot be hypnotized any more. So the question of collective hypnosis does not arise. And remember, when these five hundred lamas gather together for visions of Buddha, they stand in utter silence, not even a word is whispered around. It is an event altogether different from Arvind's experience.

Thirdly, it is quite possible to establish contact with souls who have left their bodies but have not attained to their oceanic existence. If someone dies without being enlightened he will continue to live in his subtle body; he will not be one with his oceanic form. And it is possible, with the help of certain techniques, to come in contact with such souls living in their subtle forms. There is no difficulty about it.

Krishna's soul cannot be available in his subtle body. He has transcended all his seven bodies and become one with the universal existence, therefore you cannot come in contact with him in the way you come in contact with ordinary souls that hang around their old world. For instance, Gandhi is a soul with a subtle body, and he can easily be contacted. There are rules and techniques for establishing contact with them. Many times such souls make efforts on their own to contact their friends and relatives. But they scare us, because we don't want to come in contact even with the souls of those dear to us. They now belong to an alien world unknown to us. Even if the spirit of one who was in his lifetime dearest to your heart appears at your door, you will scream with fright and run away from him. You will shout for help, because you were acquainted only with his physical body; his astral body is alien to you.

So it is easy to establish contact with a soul that is bodiless and is hungering for a new body. It is not a matter of mental projection on the part of one who wishes to come in contact with such a soul who has everything except the gross body. Very simple devices are available with which you can connect with such a spirit if you want to. For instance, so many of us are sitting here discussing Krishna and his philosophy. Do you think there are only as many persons here as are visible to our eyes? No, there are many more who are invisibly present here, and they can be contacted right now, if you wish. What you need is a willingness on your part to come in contact with them and certain receptivity toward it.

You can make an experiment as I suggest. Three of you can go into a room, close it from inside and sit quietly with your eyes closed and hands folded in the way of *namaskar*—salutation. Then say prayerfully that if there are any souls in this room, they should contact you all in the way you suggest—say by knocking at the door. And soon you will hear a knock at the door where there is no one with a body. You can suggest to the invisible soul present in the room to answer your questions through a paperweight lying on the table before you, and you will see that within three to four days the spirit will begin to answer your questions through the medium of the paperweight.

Then you can carry the experiment further; it is not that difficult. There are any number of bodiless spirits hanging around you everywhere and always, who are willing to communicate with you, but they have no way to do so, because we are aware of only one way of communication and that is through our physical bodies. And there is no bridge whatsoever between us and the bodiless souls. But there are simple devices, which form a part of occultism, to come in contact with them.

You also want to know if man's soul can leave his physical body, travel astrally and then return to his body again. It is quite possible that you leave your body, go out of it, travel astrally and then return to your body as you like. The physical body is only an abode and you can go out of it if you know the right techniques to do it. There is a special discipline, a

whole science about it. Sometimes it happens acci-
dently without any efforts on your part. In moments
of deep meditation you will find that you are out of
your physical body and watching it from a distance.
There is a whole occult science, and we can go into
it separately at some different time.

> Questioner: Is there a way, apart
> from occultism, to know intellectually
> about the soul and its rebirth? In
> other words, can the existence of the
> soul and the fact of rebirth be proved
> philosophically without the help of a
> practical discipline? How is it that a
> bodiless spirit knows all about its pre-
> vious life? Is it that only a soul that
> leaves its body with awareness comes
> to remember its past life?

Ordinarily when a person dies, it is only his physical
body that dies; he and his mind do not die with the
body. Ordinarily the mind of the dying person goes
with him, and for a little while after death he retains
all his memory of his previous life. It is like what
happens with our dreams. After you wake up from
sleep you remember your dreams for a little while.
Slowly the memory of dreams begins to fade and by
noontime it fades away completely. And by the evening you cannot say even a word about them.

Although you dream in your sleep, in your
unconscious state, yet on waking you can clearly recall a few fragments of your dreams, particularly the
latter part of your last dream. It happens because in
the latter part of your sleep you begin to wake up and
you are only half asleep. You can remember the
dreams fully or partly that visit you in your half-asleep

and half-waking state. But even this memory does not last long; as hours pass it disappears. In the same way a man's bodiless soul remembers its previous life, its friends and relatives for a little while after his death. And this memory is rather painful, because he cannot relate with them any more.

It is for this reason that we do a few things soon after someone close to us meets his death, so that he is relieved of the memories of his past associations and attachments. Now it is not good to carry them, because they are very painful. Hindus cremate the dead bodies of their relatives soon after their death; they try not to delay if it is avoidable. And it is significant. Cremation destroys all identity and attachment of the dead with their bodies, because they remember their past only through the medium of their dead bodies. The dead body serves as a bridge between the released soul and his past life. So cremation is in the interest of the departed souls.

When somebody dies suddenly or in an accident, he doesn't know he is dead. For a little while he feels stunned and bewildered to see that he is separated from his body, maybe, something has gone wrong somewhere. It happens because inside the body nothing really dies except that the soul leaves the body. Not a few, but the majority of souls feel utterly confused and confounded soon after their death. No one can figure out why his family members are weeping and crying, why there is so much grief all around, because he feels as much alive as before, except that his body is a little separate from him. It is the body that gives him a sense of continuity, because it is the medium of all his associations with the past. Only meditative people, those who have experienced deep meditation can escape being puzzled and bewildered, because they know that they are separate from their bodies.

Soon after cremation or burial of a dead body the soul is gradually freed from its past memories and associations. It is like we gradually forget our dreams. It is on the reckoning of time taken by different kinds of souls that we have different death rites for our dead. Some people, particularly children, take only three days to forget their past associations. Most others take thirteen days; so some communities in the East have thirteen-day long death rites. There are a few souls— souls with very powerful memories—who take a year's time for this purpose. Because of them, some of our death rites are spread over a full year. Three to thirteen days are the general rule, and very few souls survive without bodies for a full year; most of them are reborn with new bodies within a short time.

A person who dies with awareness, who remains fully conscious and aware at the time of his death, does not die really; he knows he is deathless. He is not dying, he is leaving his old body like we discard old clothes. And a person who attains to such a state of deep awareness is rare; he is free of all attachments and psychological memories. He has neither friends nor foes; he is free of all cravings and desires. He is a class by himself; dying with awareness he will be born with awareness, unencumbered by his past.

Just as one remembers his past for a while after death, so he does after his new birth too. A newborn child carries with him for a brief time the memories of his previous life as a spirit. But by and by this memory fades away and by the time he learns speaking it is completely lost. It is rare that a child remembers his past life even after he is articulate and able to communicate with others. He is called a freak of nature. He must have been a man of rare memory in his past existence.

In this context you also want to know if apart from going into it by way of mystical experiences there is any philosophical support for reincarnation. It is only through logic that philosophical evidence in support of reincarnation can be built. But logic suffers from an inherent weakness: it can be used as powerfully both for and against a proposition. If one wants to describe logic rightly, and those who know it well have said so, logic is like a lawyer or a prostitute who goes with anyone who pays the fee.

There are those who have proved logically and philosophically that reincarnation is a fact, and there are also those who have disproved and blasted this theory with the help of the same weapons of logic and philosophy. Logic is a kind of sophistry; it is like a lawyer who supports the case of anyone who pays his price. He has no viewpoint of his own, but he brings forth his whole reasoning skill to support his client's case. That is why logic is never able to establish anything—although it seems to be convincing at face value—because the contrary point can be made as skillfully with the help of logic. There is no difficulty about it. Logic is a double-edged sword which cuts both ways—for and against a proposition.

For this reason philosophy can never prove or disprove the theory of reincarnation. Although philosophy can say a lot, it can go on saying for thousands of years, it will never succeed in its endeavors. It is like a barren woman who looks to be complete, but cannot give birth to a child.

Logic has another side to it which is interesting. You use logic to establish something that you already believe to be true and right. Logic is just a means used to support your assumptions, your presuppositions.

There is a well known professor in an Indian university who is conducting research on rebirth. Only recently he came with a friend of mine to see me. At the very start of his conversation he asserted that he was going to prove the theory of rebirth scientifically. I said to him it seemed his mind was already made up in favor of rebirth and that he was looking for scientific evidence to support it. But it was utterly unscientific to accept something before one had fully investigated it from all sides. If someone wants to be scientific, he should say that he wants to enquire whether the theory of reincarnation is true or not. If he is going to prove rebirth, it means that he already believes it to be a fact and not a fiction.

As far as this person is concerned, the matter is already a proven fact for him and he has only to produce some cogent arguments in its support. And arguments can easily be collected and produced; it is not that difficult. If you want to prove the theory of rebirth you can find any number of arguments in its favor. This world is so vast and complex and paradoxical that you can gather all kinds of arguments and evidence for or against anything that you choose to support or demolish.

Philosophy will never be able to prove or disprove rebirth. So if you make a slight shift in your question, you should ask whether science can shed some light on this very ancient debate. Philosophy has failed, and failed utterly. It has been debating this question for five thousand years and nothing has been solved. There are people who believe in rebirth and there are equal numbers who don't believe in it. And no side has been able to convince the other side of the validity of its standpoint.

It is ironical that you can convince only one who is already convinced; you cannot convince the unconvinced. This is logic's impotence, which it fails to see. You can easily convince a Hindu of the truth of rebirth, because it is part of his belief system. But you will know how impotent logic is when you try to convince a Mohammedan of the truth of this theory. You can easily convince a Christian that there is no rebirth, but you cannot convince a Hindu that it is a fiction. Logic is a skill which works well for those who use it to prove something which they believe to be true. Therefore it is not a right question to ask if rebirth can be proved philosophically. The right question is: Is there a way to approach the question of rebirth scientifically?

Science is pure enquiry; it is objective and impartial. While philosophy and logic have their standpoints for or against a belief, a proposition, science has none. A scientific mind means that it is open and impartial; it wants to find the truth, it is open to both the alternatives, both sides of a thing; it is not closed. Science does not depend on belief. It wants to investigate into the truth or otherwise of a hypothesis. Science is the only discipline prepared to re-examine its own findings and conclusions. Science is prepared for any possibility that an objective enquiry and investigation can lead to.

Science has only recently begun to take interest in matters like reincarnation. It is only fifty years since psychic societies came into being in America and Europe, and they have done some good work in this direction. A handful of intelligent people with a scientific bent have interested themselves is psychic research. They are not mystics, who have said for a long time that things like life-after-death and rebirth are facts which they have known from experience but cannot prove with arguments. The mystics say anyone can know these things if he goes through a certain meditative discipline, but they cannot make you know what it is. It is like I have a headache and I know what it is, but I cannot make you know it. You will know it only when your own head starts aching. I can do nothing to communicate my headache experience to you.

For the last fifty years men like Oliver Lodge, Broad, and Rhine have explored some new frontiers of the human mind. They are all men of scientific persuasion, they don't have any beliefs and prejudices of their own. They have done some real work on life-after-death and reincarnation. Their findings are authentic, and they go a long way in support of reincarnation. Now there are scientific techniques to contact bodiless souls, and they have been contacted, and every care has been taken to eliminate the chances of deception and fraud in the use of these techniques. In the past there have been any number of cases of fraudulent seances to communicate with the dead. But if even a single case of authentic necromancy succeeds, it is enough. And many such experiments to contact bodiless spirits have been successful in establishing that souls change their bodies, that they are born again and again.

A number of people who had devoted their lives to necromancy before leaving their bodies, had promised to their psychic societies that they would communicate with them after death, in a specific manner. And some of them did succeed in their efforts. They communicated some very valuable information regarding the life-after-death phenomenon to their societies, and this information goes a long way in the support of rebirth.

A great deal of research has been conducted in the fields of telepathy and clairvoyance, and they have yielded good results. Without the help of any technical aids, I can communicate with a person who is thousands of miles away from here, which means that astral communication, communication without the help of any physical instruments is possible.

> Questioner: It may be a communication on the mental level, not on the level of the soul.

I am just now going to explain it. Even if it is a mental communication, it is certainly different from the physical one. And once science gets to know something different from the physical body, it will not be long before it comes to know of the soul. The whole quarrel is centered on the question of whether there is something in man which is different from his body. And if it is settled that there is something different from the body, half the journey is over. This is how science works. Let science begin with the mind, and gradually it will come to the super-mind, the soul. Science never accepts that mind is something higher than the physical body.

There is a man known as Ted, whose mind has taken the scientific world by surprise. And the psychic societies have learned a great deal from his experiences, which are simply extraordinary. For instance, I am now here and Ted is in New York. He does not know me, nor has he heard about me, nor seen a photograph of me. But he can create my image in his eyes just by concentrating his thought on me. If someone asks him to work on me, he will close his eyes and meditate on me for a full thirty minutes. And in thirty minutes' time he will create my image in his eyes and this image can be captured by a camera. And it will be my photograph, although a little fainter than the one taken directly here. Ted has produced thousands of such photographs and they have all been verified and found to be true.

What does it mean?

It means that Ted's eyes are capable of seeing me from such a long distance. They can not only see me but also capture my likeness exactly as your eyes do when you are looking at me here face to face. Scientists put Ted to all kinds of tests and he always proved authentic.

Now that we have entered the space age, and space travel is coming into vogue, scientists are getting interested in telepathy in a big way. We have already reached the moon, and are attempting to go to Mars. Incursions into distant points in space are underway, and some of these incursions will take years to be completed. Traveling to Mars alone is going to take a full year, and it is full of incomprehensible hazards. In case there is any mechanical failure, we will never know what happened to our astronauts. They, with their knowledge of space, will be lost to us forever. That is why both Russia and America, the most advanced countries engaged in space explorations, have become deeply interested in telepathy. This is to provide an alternative channel of communication to the astronauts in the event of failure of the normal channels they have at their disposal. They cannot wholly depend on their mechanical instruments; some cases of their failure have already occurred. It is believed that an astronaut skilled in telepathy can communicate with us in case his mechanical instruments fail him. We can afford such failures on the earth, but when it is a matter of space travel, we must have some alternative arrangements so that we keep track of our valuable astronauts and their great work. So now telepathy has a place in the scientific laboratories of America and Russia.

There is now a unique man in Russia, whose name is Fiodev. He has succeeded in sending telepathic messages to people who are at a distance of a thousand miles from his laboratory in Moscow. If someone is sitting in a park of a town a thousand miles away from Moscow, and Fiodev directs a message to him telepathically, the person will get the message intact.

Science is now searching for something which is more than just physical. It is coming closer to the mystics who say that man is not only his body, he is something incorporeal, spiritual too. And once it is settled that there is something spiritual, there will be no difficulty in coming to the truth of reincarnation. So science is going to accomplish what philosophy has failed to do. The mystic, of course, has known it, but he has no way to explain it. Science can do the explaining too.

Scientific enquiry into rebirth is quite possible.

> *Questioner: To find out if there is something like a soul in man, scientists have carried out experiments by placing a dying man in a glass casket. Please say something about this experiment.*

There have been many experiments like this, but none of them have yielded results. Scientists think—and naturally they think in terms of matter—that if there is something other than matter in man, then with the passing away of his life or soul there should be some reduction in his body weight. But is it imperative that the element that goes out of one's body at death have weight? It can be weightless as well. Or it can have so little weight that it cannot be measured by any instruments available to us at the moment.

For example, sun rays have a little weight, but there is no way to measure them. If all the sun rays spread over a square mile area are collected together, they will weigh roughly ten grams. But it is so difficult to work it out. Similarly, even if our souls have weight, it cannot be measured. So all glass casket experiments— they were carried out at many places—proved futile.

Apart from taking the weight of a dead body, the glass casket experiment had yet another objective to achieve. It was thought the soul of a dying person—if he has one—after leaving his body will break out of the sealed casket and thus leave some holes or cracks in the casket. But nothing of the kind happened; like sunshine a soul can pass through a wall of glass without breaking it. If x-rays can pass through a thick wall of bones and steel, why cannot a human soul pass through a glass casket? Logically speaking there is no difficulty.

And weight is a relative thing. What we call weight is really the pressure of gravitation on something. If your body weight is one hundred twenty pounds here, and you are flown to the moon, your weight will not remain the same; it will be eight times less than it is here. Your hundred twenty pounds will be reduced to a mere fifteen pounds. The gravitational pull of the moon is eight times less than that of the earth. For this reason, if you can jump five feet high here, you can jump forty feet high on the surface of the moon. In other words, weight is nothing but the gravitational pull of the earth, and it is possible the earth cannot pull a human soul to itself. Maybe, the law of gravitation does not apply to souls, and therefore souls have no weight whatsoever. If we can build a space which is free from gravitation, then everything in that space will be without weight.

The first and the most frightening experience of those who first landed on the moon was one of weightlessness. As soon as man passes beyond the earth's gravitational field, which extends up to two hundred miles in space, he becomes absolutely weightless. Every astronaut in a spacecraft hurtling through space has to keep himself tied to his seat, otherwise he will fly like a balloon to the roof of the spacecraft.

So the weight of a thing is relative to many things. And it is just possible that a soul has no weight. For this reason, experiments carried out in Paris and elsewhere were doomed to fail. In my view, the pull of gravitation applies to a thing only in proportion to the density of its matter; the less density the less weight. As far as the soul is concerned, it is the end part of density, it is all rarity, and therefore the law of gravitation ceases to operate on it. The soul is wholly outside the jurisdiction of this law. And as long as we continue to enquire into the question of soul with the tools of matter, science will go on denying its existence. We need altogether new tools of investigation to discover the law of the soul. The psychic societies and pioneers of parapsychology like Rhine and Meyer and Lodge, whom I spoke about a little while ago, are engaged in devising such new tools in place of the established tools of physical science, and perhaps with their help science will confirm the insights of the mystics which they cannot prove with any evidence.

> Questioner: You said that Arjuna was surrendered to Krishna, and yet he was a free individual. What have you to say about Vivekananda who was similarly surrendered to Ramakrishna? Why could he not be enlightened?

There are reasons for it.

The relationship between Ramakrishna and Vivekananda is basically one of the master and the disciple; it is not the same relationship between Krishna and Arjuna. Secondly, Krishna is not trying to prepare Arjuna in a way so that he can take his message to the world at large; all his teachings are meant for Arjuna's growth and are exclusively addressed to him. On the other hand Ramakrishna wants Vivekananda to be his messenger to the whole world.

Krishna is not aware that his dialogues with Arjuna are going to turn into the *Bhagwad Geeta*. It is incidental that they turned out that way. It is Krishna's spontaneous discussions with Arjuna while the two of them were standing on the battlegrounds of Kurukshetra. He does not know that his sayings are going to be so significant that they will be discussed for centuries upon centuries to come. They are meant for Arjuna alone, for his spiritual transformation. They are very intimate conversations meant exclusively for a close friend. My own experience says that every significant and momentous word of wisdom came into being by way of an intimate dialogue. A writer can never touch that depth which a speaker does. All that is of the highest in the world of wisdom has been spoken, not written.

As I said this morning, all of Arvind's words have been written by him, he did not speak anything. On the contrary, Krishna and Christ, Buddha and Mahavira, Raman and Krishnamurti, said everything by word of mouth. Speech is personal; it is between one person and another; there is an element of intimacy about it. Writing, except when one writes a letter, is impersonal; it is addressed to an unknown and abstract audience. Krishna is in direct communication with Arjuna; it is an intimate dialogue between two friends. There is no third person between them.

Ramakrishna's case is very different, and there are reasons for it.

Ramakrishna had attained to super-consciousness, to *samadhi*, he had experienced the truth, but his difficulty was that he lacked the ability to communicate to others that which he knew. He was in search of someone who could serve as his medium and take his message to the world at large. He knew the truth, but he could not communicate it. He was uneducated; he had hardly gone through two grades in an elementary Bengali school.

This simple villager had a great treasure with him, but he did not know how to share it with the world. He was not articulate; he was utterly lacking in language. His sayings that are available to us are highly edited, because it is said that being an uneducated country man, his original utterances were natural but coarse and uncouth, replete with four-letter words. Those who prepared an anthology of his sayings deleted everything they thought was coarse and vulgar, and almost remade it. I don't think they did a right thing; they should have made an authentic report. It should be exactly as he had said it. It is true that he freely used invectives, but what is wrong with invectives? They should have been there. But his disciples decided to present their Master, who was known as a *paramhansa*—one who had attained the state of absolute innocence—as a sophisticated teacher, and so they did a lot of pruning of his statements.

However, Ramakrishna was in need of someone who could be his mouthpiece. So when Vivekananda came to him, he decided to use him as his instrument. There is a small incident in the lives of Ramakrishna and Vivekananda which sheds light on their relationship, and I would like to relate it here.

Vivekananda once said to Ramakrishna that he wanted to have the experience of superconsciousness or *samadhi*. Ramakrishna explained to him the necessary techniques and guided him through its discipline. Ramakrishna was a Master of such great attainment that his very presence could trigger a process of *samadhi* in Vivekananda. He was so dynamic that just a touch of his hand sent Vivekananda into deep *samadhi*. Do you know what Vivekananda did after his first experience of the superconscious?

There was a man in Ramakrishna's ashram; he was known as Kaloo. He had come from some rural area of Bengal, and lived in a small hut close to the temple of Dakshineshwar. He was a very plain, simple and innocent person. A temple remains a temple only so long as simple and innocent people like Kaloo live in its premises. The day clever and cunning people enter and reside there, its beauty, its divinity, its glory, is destroyed.

Kaloo had collected a huge number of statues of gods and goddesses—wherever he found them he brought them to his room and installed them on an altar. They were so many that they occupied every inch of space available in his small room, so much that he himself had to sleep under the open sky. This is the way of God: he occupies all the space of one who comes close to him, he soon ousts him from his own house. Kaloo had no time for anything else; from the morning through the evening he kept worshipping them.

Vivekananda, who was educated with a strong rationalist background, did not like this orthodoxy of Kaloo; he often advised him to throw his crude statues of gods and goddesses into the Ganges and get rid of them. Vivekananda believed that God was formless and omnipresent, and it was foolish to worship him through the medium of statues and their rituals. He often said to Kaloo that he was wasting his time and energy in fruitless rituals. But Kaloo laughed saying, "Maybe you are right, but let me first worship them, they must be waiting for me. If others are wasting their time in other things, let me waste my time with my gods and goddesses. They are so nice and beautiful."

When Vivekananda achieved his first *samadhi*, it flooded him with a strange and powerful energy. A thought arose in his mind that if in this moment of ecstasy he sent a telepathic message to Kaloo to throw away his many useless gods and goddesses, he would not resist it. The moment Vivekananda thought like this, Kaloo sitting in his room got the message and he obeyed it without a question in his heart. He made a bundle of all his gods and goddesses, put them on his back and left for the bank of the Ganges to drown them into its holy water.

Vivekananda had only thought of it and it began to work—even before it was properly sent in the form of a message to Kaloo. That is why wise men say that such an energy, such a power should not be used, otherwise it will harm the seeker and impede his progress. They strictly prohibit its use: a seeker should just allow it to rise and watch it. That is enough use of it. But Vivekananda did otherwise, and he soon succeeded with poor Kaloo, whom he had so long failed to persuade in spite of all his cogent and logical arguments. What he could not achieve directly, he achieved through the backdoor when a tremendous meditative power became available to him.

Kaloo was busy with his gods when Vivekananda had thought of him, and suddenly and unknowingly he stopped his worship, put all the statues in a bag and moved to the Ganges. Ramakrishna was sitting on the roofed porch of his house, which faced the Ganges, and his eyes fell on Kaloo. He called to him and asked, "What is the matter, Kaloo?"

Pointing to his bag, Kaloo said, "They are no good; I am going to consign them to the Ganges."

Ramakrishna scolded him saying, "Go back to your room and put them all in their places. I know who is speaking through you. I am going to take that rascal to task."

Ramakrishna rushed to Vivekananda, shook his body and said, "This is your last *samadhi*; you are not going to have any more of it. I am going to keep the key to your *samadhi* with me, which will be returned to you only three days before your death."

Vivekananda was shocked and he burst into tears, crying, "Pray, don't deprive me of my *samadhi*!"

But Ramakrishna said firmly, "You have a great work to do; you are going to be my instrument and my messenger to the world. If you enter *samadhi* you will not be able to come back, and the great work will suffer. What I have known has to reach to every nook and corner of the earth. Don't be selfish; give up your attachments, and don't hanker for your *samadhi*. You have to build a huge temple sheltering millions of thirsty seekers from all over the world. That's why I am taking away the key to your *samadhi*."

This key remained with Ramakrishna. And Vivekananda had it back as promised, three days before his death. It was only three days before he left this world that he had his second *samadhi*.

But let me tell you that if someone else holds the key to your *samadhi*, it means it is only a psychic, a deep psychological *samadhi*, and not a full experience of the absolute. A *samadhi*, a superconsciousness that depends on another is not real and ultimate; it does not transcend the mind. The *samadhi* that made Kaloo think of parting with his statues cannot be said to be deeply spiritual; it is mental. Of course, Vivekananda had transcended his body, but he had yet to get to the soul, and Ramakrishna had to stop him there, because he thought if Vivekananda went deeper into it he would not be able to fulfill the assigned work.

It is through Vivekananda that the world came to know of Ramakrishna. But Vivekananda had to sacrifice much. However, such a sacrifice is worth it, and it is very meaningful. Ramakrishna had to deliberately stop his further progress, because he thought if Vivekananda transcended the psychic state of *samadhi*, he could not be made into an instrument. Ramakrishna was not like Buddha who had both wisdom and the skill to express it; Ramakrishna has attained to the same wisdom as Buddha had, but he was not articulate. So he had to depend on Vivekananda for its transmission to the world.

It is true that Vivekananda was an instrument in the hands of his Master, but this is not the case with Arjuna. Krishna is not trying to make him into an instrument. He is just pouring his wisdom on Arjuna standing at Kurukshetra.

Now, we will sit for meditation.

SIXTEENTH DISCOURSE
MORNING, OCTOBER 3, 1970
MANALI, INDIA

ATHEISM, THEISM AND REALITY

Questioner: Arvind had seen visions of Krishna and been in contact with Yogi Lele. Is it that a final judgment on the experiments conducted at Pondicherry will be made by future generations? What do you think of Alice Bailey who claims to receive messages? Where do the messages come from? And how? Do you too have such esoteric contacts with some masters?

rvind sees visions of Krishna inside a prison, in the walls of the prison, in the prisoners' faces and in himself. But who is the one who knows that he sees visions of Krishna? If there is a knower then it is surely his own mental projection. If someone says he sees Krishna, it means the one who sees is not Krishna; he is bound to be different from Krishna.

The oceanic, universal form of Krishna is something entirely different from Krishna the man who happened some five thousand years ago. But his universal form, which is universal superconsciousness, is eternal. And one who encounters the universal consciousness ceases to be an ego; he disappears as he is and turns into that universal intelligence itself. You can call it by the name of Krishna, Christ, or Buddha, or whatever you like. Names don't matter; the choice of name depends on the cultural background of the one who encounters it. And once someone comes in contact with this supreme intelligence—provided it is real, not imaginary—he is lost in it forever. Come what may, he cannot stage a comeback to his old life of misery and pain. Once someone really comes to this ultimate intelligence, he can never be deprived of it.

The irony is that Arvind's whole spiritual life begins after this incident of his prison days when he is said to have seen visions of Krishna. It is after his release from the prison that he meets Yogi Lele, who is referred to in your question, and learns meditation from him. It is unbelievable that a person who has yet to learn meditation can come in contact with the universal form of Krishna. If one has already attained to Krishna consciousness, he does not need to learn meditation. For what? And does such a man need a master or a guru?

And the kind of meditation that Arvind learned from Yogi Lele is nothing special; it is an ordinary technique of meditation which does not have much depth. And he practiced it for only three days; perhaps this was his first and last meditation. And we know on Lele's authority that Arvind did not make any headway, any progress.

Arvind sat for meditation only three days, when Lele gave him the simple technique of witnessing, watching his thoughts. Lele asked him to watch his thoughts as if he is watching a beehive swarming with bees within and without. Arvind was frightened to see the swarm of his teeming thoughts, but Lele persuaded him to watch patiently. If someone watches his thoughts he will find that by and by their movement slows down and then disappears. But Arvind did not pursue this technique beyond three days and thought it was enough. And this was the greatest mistake of his life.

Witnessing is the beginning of meditation; attainment of unity with the non-dual, with the supreme intelligence is its culmination. Witnessing is a means to the ultimate unity. One has to go beyond witnessing; even the witness should cease to be. Because as long as someone is a witness and there is something to be witnessed, as long as the observer and the observed are separate, duality will remain. A moment of meditation comes when both the observer and the observed disappear, and only pure consciousness remains. It is difficult to say who is the subject and who is the object, where the knower and the known melt and disappear into each other. As long as there is the slightest separation between the witness and the witnessed, know well that you have yet to transcend the mind.

That is why I say Arvind's experience is not real. That which comes and goes can never be real; it is sheer imagination, a dream, a projection.

Then what is a true experience of reality? One that is everlasting and indestructible is a real experience; all else is a mind game. Arvind did not go beyond witnessing, he just stopped at that. And then he severed his relationship with Lele who had so far taught only the rudiments of meditation. And this man had something of meditation in him; he was capable of leading Arvind further.

Arvind's second meeting with Lele happened at a time when he himself had become a master. And his behavior during their second meeting was marked by a lack of respect and gratefulness towards Lele. Arvind tried to show that what Lele had taught him was of no consequence and might as well be forgotten.

Arvind is not alone. This situation has happened many times when seekers have stopped with

their very first experience of meditation. The very
early experiences of meditation are so blissful, so
exhilarating and exciting, that a seeker comes to believe he has achieved all there is to be achieved. The
most formidable obstacles in the spiritual path do not
come in the form of the seeker's attachments to his
family and possessions; they invariably come in the
form of his first experiences of meditation itself. The
dangers that a seeker faces are more internal than
external. These experiences are so delightful, so blissful that one wants to cling to them forever. Not only
Arvind, but thousands of people have mistaken the
stopover for the destination. If a *caravanserai* gives a
traveler such comforts and happiness that he has
never known before, it is not surprising if he quits his
journey and makes a home of the *caravanserai*.

There is plenty of evidence that Arvind's
meditation never went an inch beyond what he had
learned from Lele. For the rest of his life he taught
his disciples and others the same rudiments of meditation that Lele had taught him in those first three
days. Whoever went to him for guidance in meditation received Lele's wine in Arvind's bottle. There
was nothing of his own, except that he, being an
accomplished intellectual and a master of words,
explained them in a sophisticated way and elaborated
them into thousands of pages. I have scanned all his
writings to see if he has said anything more than what
he had borrowed from Lele, and I say he does not add
anything worthwhile to Lele's teachings. Lele was a
simple man and said what he had to say simply. Arvind, on the other hand, is a complex man who can
turn even a simple idea into a complicated treatise.
But all he taught was simple witnessing.

And I believe Arvind lost even that which he
had learned from Lele, and got involved in useless
sophistry. You will be amazed to know what Lele later
said to Arvind: "You are a fallen man. You have lost
whatever meditation you had achieved and now you

are engaged in a jugglery of words—which is what doctrinaire discussion is—and it has nothing to do with real experiencing."

This statement of Lele's is very revealing, but Arvind's followers do not mention it in their discussions and deliberations about their master. It comes from the person who gave Arvind his first lessons in meditation, and perhaps the last too. And therefore it says a lot about him.

When Lele met Arvind for the second time, he advised him not to get entangled in writing philosophical treatises. He had yet to know truth, about which he had started writing volumes. But Arvind paid no attention to Lele; he just brushed him aside. So it is natural that his followers ignore Lele's comments about their master.

I said a little while ago that because original ideas are discovered by individuals they are likely to go haywire. This does not mean they invariably go wrong, but the chances of their going wrong cannot be minimized. I also said that the contrary is the case with traditional ideas and beliefs. It is true that with the passage of time such ideas and concepts become fossilized and dead, but there is every possibility that even these stinking fossils hide in themselves some great truths. Otherwise it would be impossible for a people to carry on with dead and stinking fossils of belief for centuries upon centuries. Undoubtedly a diamond lies buried in them, but we fail to see it. For this reason people cling to traditional beliefs with such tenacity that we are baffled.

I would like to explain another thing which is very relevant here. Arvind says that his concept of the supramental has its source in the *Vedas*—which is simply a travesty of truth. Down the centuries a very corrupt practice, an immoral act, has been perpetrated by persons who would least be expected to take part in it. Whenever someone has discovered something new and original he has not had the courage to claim it as his own. Why? First, because this country knows that new ideas carry with them the possibility of being wrong. So it became a tradition to find corroboration and support for every new idea from old and respectable scriptures. Everyone who came upon something new had to claim its origin in the *Vedas*, the *Upanishads*, the *Brahmasutra*. And for this reason right interpretations of these scriptures became difficult. Everyone indiscriminately imposes his own ideas and interpretations on these helpless scriptures. This is no different than a new business using the "good will" of old and established firms.

Evidently no one cared to know what the *Vedas* or the *Upanishads* really had to say; everyone imposed his own interpretations on them with impunity. So Shankara interprets the *Upanishads* in one way and Nimbarka interprets just the contrary way. So Dayananda interprets the *Vedas* to conform to his own ideas, and Arvind does it quite differently to suit his beliefs, which are different from Dayananda's. They have made a mess of these great scriptures; they have virtually debauched and defiled them. The *Vedas*, the *Upanishads* and the *Brahmasutra* have suffered terribly down the ages at the hands of their interpreters. The same has been the fate of the *Geeta*. Whoever wants to have his say claims the support of these scriptures, and does everything in his power to impose his meanings on them.

In my view this is nothing but intellectual prostitution, and it has existed in India for thousands of years. Because no one had the courage to say his thing, on his own authority, they had to take shelter in the *Vedas*, the *Upanishads*, and the *Geeta*. And this dishonest practice stemmed from a lack of self-confidence on the part of the great minds of India. Honesty demands that if Arvind has stumbled upon a truth, he should say it on his own regardless of what the *Vedas* say. Even if all the scriptures say the opposite, he should fearlessly state his own vision. But if he is not certain of his own ideas, he has no way but to seek the support of the *Vedas*, the *Upanishads* and the *Geeta*. Then he will have to use them as his soldiers to win the battle of debates.

Please bear in mind that the seers of the *Vedas* and the *Upanishads* do not seek any such support for themselves; they say on their own whatever they have to say. Their statements are straight, bold and emphatic. The author of the *Brahmasutra* does not quote authorities to support his viewpoint; he says positively this is his vision of truth. But after the *Vedas*, *Upanishads* and the *Brahmasutra*, the intellectual standard of India began to decline and it makes a long, sad story spanning thousands of years. Since then no one dared say his thing on his own authority as the seers of old had. Then everyone sought the support of the trinity of the *Upanishads*, the *Brahmasutra* and the *Geeta*. Straightforward and honest utterances became rare. And Arvind is the last link in that long chain of India's intellectual decline.

For this reason, I say Raman and Krishnamurti are much more honest; they don't seek support from the *Vedas* or anything else. Honesty means that when you err you take the responsibility, instead of passing it on to others, to the *Vedas*. Honesty means that when you find some right thing, some truth, you say it even if the whole world is against it. Only then will posterity be in a position to judge if there is substance in what you have known. But until recently, utter confusion has prevailed in the world of philosophical ideas and concepts.

In my view, India's philosophy has failed to follow the honest course of development of its counterpart in the West. If Socrates says something, he says it on his own authority; he does not try to prop himself up by the weight of his predecessors. Similarly, if Kant and Wittgenstein say something, they do so on their own; they don't claim the authority of

Socrates or anyone else. Western philosophy is much more honest than ours. And it is out of this honest way of thinking that science was born in the West. Science is the child of that honesty. In fact, science cannot come out of dishonest thinking; it is impossible. India could not create science because we have been victims of a deep-rooted intellectual dishonesty; here it is difficult to decide who says what. Everybody is quoting scriptures, everybody is citing authorities; everybody is mimicking the voice of everybody else.

Arvind's excessive dependence on the *Vedas* comes from his inferiority complex. It does not reflect his profundity; it only says he is not certain if what he says is true, so he is seeking authoritative support for his shaky ideas.

And the mind of India has been deeply influenced by the *Vedas*, the *Upanishads* and the *Geeta*. India's mind has been heavily conditioned by Mahavira and Buddha. The Indian mind is a prisoner of tradition; we accept anyone who says something on the authority of the *Vedas* or the *Dhammapada*. We don't care about scrutinizing him independently and finding out if what he says is genuine. We blindly accept anything and everything that is said under the cover of the *Vedas*.

But the question is: Why take cover behind the *Vedas*? Does truth need a cover? If I find some truth I will say it in plain words. And I will also say that if the *Vedas* see it the same way as I see, they are right, and if they don't, they are wrong. My perception of truth is self-evident; it is enough unto itself. I am not going to be right or wrong on the authority of the *Vedas*. For me, the *Vedas* have to be right or wrong on my authority.

If someone comes and tells me that what I say is different from what Mahavira says, I will tell him Mahavira is wrong. I cannot even be certain whether or not Mahavira really said it, but I am very certain about what I am saying. Even if the whole world says the way I see it is wrong, I will say that the whole world is wrong—just because I see it differently. I can be a witness to my own perception, I cannot be a witness to the perception of others.

But it is a very simple and convenient way of putting oneself in the right place. If you encounter truth directly, on your own, and say it exactly as you see it, history will take thousands of years to judge if you have found something real. But if you take cover behind the *Vedas*, you receive cheap and immediate recognition. Because you say the same thing the *Vedas* say, you become right on the authority of the most ancient of scriptures. It is a very simple trick and a very dirty trick at that.

I would like to explain it with the help of a story.

A French countess was known for her demanding nature and extravagant lifestyle. Once she visited China, brought home an ashtray from there, and she decided to have her living room painted in the color of the ashtray. She invited the country's greatest painters for this grand job. But no one could match the paint for the walls exactly to the color of the ashtray, which contained a special Chinese pigment available nowhere in France. So all her efforts failed. Any number of renowned painters came and went away defeated. Then came a painter who said he would do the job on the condition that no one should enter the room for the month during which he would be painting it. The countess agreed to his condition, and the man began his work in earnest.

For a whole month the painter came every day in the morning, closed the living room from inside and worked there till evening. After the month was over, he invited the countess to visit her living room, and she was immensely pleased to see her desire fulfilled: the room had exactly the color of the ashtray. And the painter happily went home with a million francs in his pocket.

Later the painter wrote in his autobiography that he first painted the walls of the countess' living room and then repainted the ashtray in the same color. And the job was done.

Arvind and Dayananda and the rest of the tribe first paint the walls and then they paint the ashtray in the same color. First they create their own doctrines and then they impose those doctrines on the *Vedas* and claim their infallibility.

All the ancient languages like Sanskrit, Arabic, Latin, and Greek, were meant for poetry, not for science. And such languages have both their advantages and disadvantages. Their advantage is that their words have more than one meaning; their words are pliant and tender. And this is their disadvantage too. Because their words have more than one meaning, it becomes difficult to uncover the meanings with which they were first used.

But they are most suitable for poetry; they lend tenderness and color, depth and richness to poetry. That is why poetry casts its spell on so many different types of people, who all discover their own meanings reflected in them. But these languages are not suitable for science, which needs definitive words with absolutely precise meanings. In science "a" should accurately mean a, and nothing else.

None of the ancient languages is scientific; and science did not develop in them. For the exact sciences, which require absolute or qualitative precision, an altogether different kind of language is needed, and scientists are busy creating it.

You will be surprised to know that physics, which is the most advanced of the sciences now, has gradually given up the use of words and instead begun to express itself through arithmetical formulas like H_2O. Mathematical formulas are much more exact than ordinary words with more than one meaning. So to understand Einstein it is necessary to be well acquainted with higher mathematics. It is not enough to know a language if you want to understand advanced physics; proficiency in mathematics is essential. So scientific language is taking the form of mathematics. And men like Einstein think the language of science in the future will consist more of signs and symbols than of words and phrases; otherwise it cannot be exact and precise.

Not only in India but all the world over, languages in the past had only one form—their verse. Most ancient scriptures were composed in verse form. It is amazing that even books on ancient Indian medicine were written in verse. And there is a reason for it. In the past, all knowledge had to be communicated orally from the teacher to the taught, and from one generation to another—writing came much later. For this kind of communication, verse became essential; verse could be easily committed to memory. Prose could not be memorized so easily. That is why the *Upanishads*, the *Geeta* and the *Koran* were composed in verse form, to keep the oral tradition going for thousands of years. But this tradition is also responsible for a lot of confusion about the meanings of words and phrases. And so everyone was free to interpret the *Vedas* the way he liked.

As I see it, the work they are carrying out at Pondicherry is the most sterile work ever undertaken in the field of spiritualism. We need not leave it for the future to decide whether it has any value or not. It can be decided here and now.

If someone is heating a bucket of water over a burning furnace, it can be said now and here that the water is going to turn into steam. We need not leave this decision to be made by future generations. And if the person is trying to heat water by placing the bucket on a slab of ice, we can immediately say that this water will never turn into steam. We need not wait for the future to decide what is what. Spiritualism is a whole science; it is not something pseudo like astrology and palmistry. And spiritualism has its own laws and rules. Therefore if someone puts the cart before the horse in the name of spiritualism, I will immediately tell him he is doing something foolish. And if the future has anything to decide, it will be whether what I say or what Arvind says is right.

All growth in this world happens at the level of the individual. The journey of consciousness and its progress begins with individuals, while its attainment, its culmination is cosmic. The source of all consciousness is universal, but its expression is always individual. The cosmos is like the ocean and the individual is like a wave. Consciousness is always seen in the form of individuals. You are an individual consciousness at the moment, and when you will lose your identity as individual consciousness, you will attain to universal consciousness. But then your experience of universal consciousness cannot become everybody's experience; it will remain yours.

There is an old controversy that needs to be rightly understood in this context. When for the first time someone said that there is one soul permeating each and every being, those who believed in the existence of individual souls countered it by saying, "In that event all persons should die when one person dies, and all people should be happy when any one of them feels happy." And there is some force in their argument. If the same consciousness, like electricity, abides in all of us and there is no separation between one and another, then how can you remain happy if I am unhappy? How can you live if I am dead? It is on the basis of this argument that they believed in the multiplicity of souls.

But I don't think their argument is entirely right. It is true that electricity is the same all over, but that does not mean that the destruction of one light bulb should lead to the destruction of all bulbs in a town. Electricity is regulated with the help of transformers and switches, wires and bulbs, and every bulb is attached to a switch of its own. So it is not necessary that with the extinction of one bulb or its switch all bulbs or switches will become inoperative.

The ocean is one and waves are many, arising from the same ocean. But you cannot say that with the disappearance of one wave all other waves will disappear. Maybe, when one wave is dying many other waves are being born. There is no difficulty in it whatsoever.

Looking at it another way, one can imagine that the universal, the supreme consciousness or God will descend on us and he will descend on all of us without discriminating between you and me. This is Arvind's fantasy—I deliberately call it a fantasy. It is pleasant, but it is a fantasy nonetheless. Many fantasies are pleasurable, but they don't become true just because they are pleasurable. It is exceedingly pleasant to fantasize that God will descend on us, but if I am determined to remain ignorant it is not in the power of Arvind or God himself to dispel my ignorance. He must allow me this much freedom: I can remain ignorant if I choose. And the day my freedom will be gone, to remain ignorant or whatever I choose to be, God and the descent of God's light to the earth will have no meaning. Then even wisdom will turn into a bondage, an imposition. So although Arvind's idea of the supramental appears to be pleasant, in reality it is frightful. And I don't agree with him. Human history does not testify to it.

History says it is always individual consciousness that ascends to divine consciousness and merges into it. Of course, when individual consciousness is ready for ascent and merger with the divine, the divine moves halfway to meet it. This is another way of saying the same thing, but it is always the individual who has to take the initiative. After they have met and merged into each other, it is difficult to say whether the drop merged into the ocean or the ocean merged into the drop. But up till now there is no evidence to say that the ocean on its own descended on some drop which was not prepared for it.

It is always the river which flows to the ocean and not vice versa. Arvind desires that from now on the ocean should flow to the river. But I am afraid if the situation arises, the river will refuse to accept the ocean. It is the river's responsibility and its prerogative too, that it should travel to the ocean and merge into it. The ocean never denies this merger; it is so vast the merger does not make any difference. Even if all the rivers go and merge into it—and they do—it makes no difference whatsoever. But if the ocean comes to a river, it will simply destroy it.

It is always an individual person who says that he has attained to divine consciousness; God never says that he has become one with an individual person. And I am certain man will resist any such efforts on God's part, because it will be a trespass on his freedom. And freedom is of the highest.

I am not prepared to accept that cosmic consciousness is ever going to descend on man, as Arvind thinks. The experience of all mankind will testify to what I say, and therefore I can speak for the future.

Arvind is no more on the earth, and nothing like the descent of the supramental happened in his lifetime. Arvind made many such stupid statements. For example, he declared that he was physically immortal, he would not die. And his blind followers believed that their master would eternally live in his physical body. They believed it in the same way they still believe that divine consciousness is going to descend on them. They argued, "How can he die who is the recipient of divine consciousness?"

It is strange how Arvind came to believe that the descent of divine consciousness will not only include one's spirit but also his physical form. He believed that with the descend of the divine, every atom of his body will become divine. How can such a body ever perish? So logically Arvind seems to be right.

Many people have spoken about immortality in the context of man's soul, but Arvind is the first person on this earth who talked in terms of physical immortality.

One who stakes his claim on physical immortality has an advantage. You cannot prove him wrong as long as he is alive, and there is no point in proving after he is gone. As long as Arvind was alive his claim was valid. And now that he is no more, there are none who will listen to your accusation that he was wrong. It is not surprising that for twenty-four hours after he died, the lady of Pondicherry ashram, known as the Mother, refused to believe that Arvind was dead. She believed he had entered a deep state of *samadhi*. For three days she refused to cremate his body in the hope that it might revive. She also believed that a yogi's dead body does not decompose, and Arvind was a yogi. But after three days when Arvind's dead body began to stink, his disciples hurriedly cremated it. They had to hurry through the whole thing because they did not want the country to know that their master's dead body had decomposed. Then India would refuse to accept Arvind as a great yogi.

The irony is, some people of the Pondicherry ashram still believe that Arvind will return to life, because he is physically immortal. It is foolish to think so, but India's mind is stuffed with such rubbish. All kinds of beliefs and superstitions have made this country their home. Now this belief that a yogi's dead body should not decompose is utterly stupid; nonetheless it should be examined.

I don't accept that a yogi's dead body does not deteriorate and disintegrate. It does and it should. And if a yogi's body is immune to decomposition there is no reason why it should not be immune to death itself. In fact, degeneration, deterioration of a body is the beginning of its death. What is old age but a deterioration of one's body? And a yogi is no exception to the law of life. When a yogi's body obeys all other rules of life—it grows from youth to old age and dies—why should it defy only one rule: that it cannot decompose after death? It will decompose as any other body does. It is inevitable!

If one is a yogi, his soul, not his body will achieve enlightenment. And the soul is present in every body, whether he is a yogi or not. Of course a yogi becomes aware of it; he comes to know that he is a soul. But this knowledge does not alter the chemistry of matter—which is his body—in any basic way. Even a yogi falls sick, but because of such beliefs we have to invent stories about our great ones.

Mahavira died of dysentery. He suffered from this disease for a full six months before his death. So the Jainas had to fabricate a story to explain away the whole thing. How can they accept that a great yogi like Mahavira, who had undergone so many fasts, should suffer from a disease like dysentery? His stomach should have immunity from such a disease. Jaina scriptures say that in a period of twelve years' time Mahavira took food for only three hundred and sixty-five days. For months at a stretch, he could go without food. How could a disease overcome him? In my view he was an ideal case for dysentery, because he had tortured his stomach so much. But all those who believed that he was a great yogi could not reconcile with this disease overtaking him. I have no such difficulty; to me a great yogi remains a great yogi whether he suffers from dysentery or not.

But the Jainas had to invent a story that Mahavira's dysentery was not an ordinary dysentery. They said that Goshalak had tried to inflict this disease on him through a special esoteric device, a mantra, and Mahavira had taken and absorbed it out of his great compassion. It is like stories going around the country that such and such yogis were sick because in their compassion they took upon themselves the diseases of their devotees. It is funny that we don't allow our yogis even to get sick on their own. These are stupidities that have pursued us down the ages.

Arvind was dead and his body decomposed and all talk of physical immortality became meaningless. I say they were meaningless even before his death. Physical immortality has never happened on this earth, and there are reasons for it. As Buddha says, whatever is put together is bound to fall apart, because every such togetherness is transitory. If I throw a rock it is bound to fall to the ground. It is my hand's energy that makes it move and when that energy is spent the rock falls to the ground. There is no rock in the world which is going to stay in space forever after it is thrown by me or anyone else. Distance can be extended, but the fall is certain.

One who is born is destined to die. One can be physically immortal only if one does not come to the earth through a regular process of birth, who materializes in physical form from nowhere without seeking the medium of a mother's womb. It is amusing that while you accept birth, which is one end of life, you deny death, the other end. Both ends are together; whoever is born will die. No mortal parents can give birth to a child with an immortal body. They will have to obey the laws of life which make birth inseparable from death. It is such a simple arithmetic. But one can argue that you cannot say Arvind is wrong as long as he is alive.

But I can say without waiting for his death. These laws of life are so simple, clear and self-evident, that Arvind's imaginations, his speculations, cannot make a difference for them. The irony is now he is dead; there is no way to argue with him.

And you say that Pondicherry's work in this regard will be judged by the coming generations. But what will happen to those of the present generation who are engaged in this act of crass stupidity at Pondicherry? Should we allow them to make fools of themselves in the meantime? Granted that the future generations will judge, but should we allow the present generations to perish? No, it cannot be left to the future. All those who are chasing this mirage at Pondicherry are very good people; they have to be cared for. And so we have to warn them against their folly and ask them to reconsider what they are doing. God never descends to us; we have to ascend to God. It is different; when one reaches him he has the feeling that God has descended on him. But this feeling is different from Arvind's theory.

There is a question about Alice Bailey, who claims that some Master K. has been sending messages to her from Tibetan mountains. This is quite possible, and Alice Bailey may be right.

In fact, there are bodiless souls in the universe who are very compassionate and loving to us and who try to help us even from their ethereal existence. And they do send messages if they come across some suitable medium.

Alice Bailey is not the first person on this earth to have received such messages. Many people like Madame Blavatsky, Annie Besant, Colonel Olcott and Leadbeater have worked as mediums for such bodiless souls in the past. And by contacting such souls who have attained higher states of spiritual growth many things can be known and communicated.

The Theosophists carried out a great experiment of this kind in relation to J. Krishnamurti. Many efforts were made to put Krishnamurti in contact with souls in search of right mediums. Krishnamurti's earliest books, At the Feet of the Master and Life of Alcyone belong to the period when he was in contact with Tibetan Masters. That is why Krishnamurti disowns their authorship. He did not write them in his conscious state; they were really communicated to him by Tibetan Masters. At the Feet of the Master is an extraordinary book, but it is not written by Krishnamurti; he was only a medium who received it in the form of messages.

Alice Bailey claims to be such a medium who receives messages from bodiless souls. Western psychologists will not accept Bailey's claim, because they have no way to verify it. Western psychology has absolutely no knowledge of anything beyond the life available to us on this planet. When I say western psychology, I mean the conventional psychology being taught at Oxford, Cambridge and Harvard, not the parapsychological sciences that have been developing in the West for some time. Conventional psychology is not at all aware that man can live in a bodiless state, and that bodiless souls can communicate with us. But such souls have always existed and they do communicate with us.

There is an episode in Mahavira's life: Mahavira is standing on the outskirts of a forest, alone and silent. A cowherd comes to him and asks him to take care of his cows for a while, because he has to go to his village on some urgent business. Since Mahavira is in silence, he cannot say yes or no, but the cowherd takes his silence as his consent and hurries away to his village.

On his return he is shocked to find that all his cows have disappeared, while Mahavira is standing there as before. The cowherd believes his cows have been stolen with the connivance of this man who is now pretending to be deaf by not answering his questions. He curses Mahavira and beats him mercilessly; he even sticks an iron rod into his ears, telling him, "You are pretending deafness—so have it for good." Mahavira does not say a word; he remains standing motionless and silent.

Legend has it that Indra, king of the gods, comes to Mahavira and offers protection but Mahavira declines the offer. This Indra is not a person, he is one of the bodiless souls who is grieved to see an innocent and defenseless person like Mahavira being tortured. But Mahavira emphatically says "no" to Indra. It is amusing that the one who does not say a word to the cowherd torturing him, says "no" to Indra. In fact this dialogue between Indra and Mahavira takes place at some inner level where Mahavira has received Indra's message psychically. If he spoke to Indra, he could have also talked to the cowherd and explained his situation. But he maintains his vow of silence in spite of all the tortures he is subjected to. His vow of silence is for twelve years. Evidently he does not have to refuse Indra verbally—it is an inner dialogue, that can be carried without words and language. There are such channels of esoteric communication where neither words nor sense organs are needed.

Mahavira's followers have been in difficulty explaining this episode. But it is quite possible. There are bodiless souls who can communicate with us astrally and without words.

Mahavira is reported to have said to Indra, "No, if I agree to be protected by you I will lose my freedom. Leave me undefended so my freedom remains intact. Your help will surely bind me to you, and I don't want bondage even in return for my protection." Mahavira means to say that the cowherd will not do him as much harm as Indra's protection because it will bind him with the king of gods. Tortures inflicted on him by a keeper of cows will not bind him in any way, but the security provided by Indra certainly will. He would not like to give up his freedom at any cost.

Another legend says when Gautam Siddhartha first attained to Buddhahood, gods came to greet him. Buddha did not say a word for seven days after his enlightenment—as if he had lost his voice. It happens often when one attains to the supreme knowledge; he loses his speech.

It is easy to speak in a state of ignorance. When one does not know the truth he has no sense of responsibility for what he says; he can say anything he likes. There is no difficulty in speaking about something we don't know, because we are not afraid of being wrong. But when one comes to truth, he becomes speechless, because truth cannot be said.

So when Buddha became Buddha, he kept absolutely silent for seven days, and it is said the gods became disturbed and implored him to resume speaking. It would be calamitous for mankind, the gods thought, if Buddha did not share his priceless wisdom with those who needed it. It is after millenia that a man like him is born on this planet. "Pray, speak for the sake of the suffering humanity," the gods begged him.

These gods are bodiless souls, not persons. They are highly evolved souls, aware that what Buddha has achieved is rare. And fortunately for the world he is in a human body, so he is in a position to communicate with the world. The gods cannot communicate, they lack bodies. Gods also know what Buddha has known, and they are anxious to communicate it to the world, but they are helpless. Here is a person who has known the ultimate truth and is still in his body and in the world. And it is only rarely that a member of the human race stumbles upon the ultimate truth. Therefore these bodiless souls insist that Buddha must speak, and speak without any further delay. And with great difficulty they succeed in persuading Buddha to speak, and they rejoice at their success.

But these astral souls are not going to use Buddha as their medium. It is not that Buddha will convey their message to the world. Buddha has his own message, his own speech.

What Alice Bailey says is right. But it is difficult for her to assert that what she says is right, because she is only a medium, the messages belong to somebody else. A medium can say only this much; the messages are received at the level of his inner space. But he cannot claim that whatever he receives is right, that it is not his own mind game, a trick of his unconscious. A medium cannot assert that he is not a victim of self-deception, because countless people are deceived by their own unconscious into believing that they are mediums of great souls or gods. It is really hard for a medium to assert his authenticity, and the psychologists can easily corner Alice Bailey.

And lastly you want to know if I am in contact with any such masters.

No, I don't believe in borrowing knowledge. I am not in contact with any of these masters; I stand wholly on my own. What I am saying, right or wrong, is my thing, and I am wholly responsible for it. I have nothing to do with any bodiless masters. And if I accept someone as my master, then there is every danger of my becoming somebody's master in turn. I don't indulge in such games. I am no one's disciple, nor do I want to be anyone's master. Therefore I say only that which I know, and I am not interested in the masters. If I speak about them it is only in passing, and by way of reference. I have nothing to do with their authenticity or otherwise.

All I want to say in this context is that there are both good and evil souls; good souls are known as gods and evil souls as ghosts. In the West these gods are known as masters: the word "master" has become a synonym for god in the current use in the West. These gods have always sent messages, and they continue to do so. Similarly, even evil souls send messages; they are also looking out for suitable mediums. If ever you are in a frame of mind that suits the evil souls, they will not fail to utilize you.

Many times people do things they would not do on their own. They become just instruments in the hands of evil spirits. So when a murderer swears before a judge that he committed the crime in spite of himself, he is not necessarily lying. It is possible. There are spirits that use people to commit heinous crimes on their behalf. There are buildings all over the world haunted by evil spirits, and if you go to live in them you will be compelled to commit murders at their behest. Feuds and vendettas are carried on not only from one generation to another, but also from one life to another.

A young man was brought to me recently. The house he has been living in was bought three years ago. And ever since, a process of deterioration in his personality set in and by and by he became a different man altogether. Before coming to this house this young man was known for being very gentle and meek; now he is arrogant and haughty, irritable and violent—ready to fight at the slightest provocation. This metamorphosis, this mutation in his personality took place the very day he entered the new house. If it had happened gradually over time his parents would not have been so frightened. And even more intriguing was that as soon as he was taken from the new house for a while he was his old self again. He was okay when he was brought to me. The young man himself said that in my presence he was feeling fine but the moment he entered that house everything turned upside down.

I put the young man under hypnosis and questioned him for a while. A harrowing story emerged from the session and it stretches over a period of eleven hundred years.

This new house where the young man lives is a haunted house. The spirit which haunts it happened to be the owner of the land on which the present house stands. And for these eleven hundred years this spirit has been continuously engaged in getting members of a particular family murdered. He has, up to now, thirty-five murders to his credit, spread over many generations. The spirit said that he would not leave this young man until he committed a murder for him.

Eleven centuries ago, members of the family that happen to be targets of the ghost's vendetta had murdered him on this very farm. Since then his ghost has been continuously camping here busy avenging his own death. And the ghost takes every care to trace the members of the family as they are born and reborn and gets them killed through such mediums as this young man.

Evil souls send their own messages and do their own things. Many times you are made to do things, good or bad. You think you did them. No, you are made to do these things by bodiless souls that lurk around everywhere. Sometimes you are amazed at your own performance. Never mind others, you yourself refuse to believe that you could do such a great thing. In fact some bodiless soul is behind it; he is getting it done through you.

There is nothing wrong in Bailey's statement, but she cannot prove its authenticity. No one can. Not even Madame Blavatsky could do it with the large volume of such messages she had received.

In this context I will explain further an event which I mentioned a little while ago. I said that a great experiment was being carried out with Krishnamurti and it failed. The venture was such that any number of godly souls got themselves involved in it in a concerted way. They were trying to see to it that a consciousness of the height of Buddha, Mahavira or Krishna enters the person of Krishnamurti. In fact, such a consciousness was already waiting for an opportunity like this. A promise given by Buddha before he left his physical body was close to its time of fulfillment. Buddha had said that after twenty-five hundred years, he would visit this earth once again in the name of Maitreya.

So Buddha's own soul, his own incarnation, has been waiting to come here in the form of Maitreya. But a suitable body, a right medium for his incarnation was not available. Theosophy's whole planning and efforts for a hundred years were consecrated in the search of a medium for Maitreya's incarnation. So they worked on four or five persons, but they failed in every case. They spent most of their attention and energy on Krishnamurti, but they could not succeed. Why?

The most important reason for the failure of this great effort was the effort itself; the theosophists really overdid it. All those who were involved in this venture concentrated their efforts on Krishnamurti and pressured him so much that his individuality revolted against them. Krishnamurti reacted and said a big No.

Forty years have passed since, but Krishnamurti has not been able to go beyond his reaction against the theosophists and all others who were after him. He continues to speak against them—who are now no more in this world. Whatever he says is tinged with the bitterness the old experience has left in him. Deep down the wound remains unhealed.

It was really a mistake to have selected Krishnamurti as a medium for Maitreya's incarnation. No doubt he was a very suitable soul, but he was much too evolved for being a medium for another soul—however high it may be. He could not be persuaded to be a medium. A weaker soul than Krishnamurti's should have been chosen. In fact, the theosophists had also worked on some weaker souls, but they were much too weak to be a vehicle for Maitreya. This was their dilemma: a superior soul like Krishnamurti's did not consent to be the vehicle, and inferior souls lacked in the requisite qualities. As long as Krishnamurti was in his teens he conformed to their wishes and demands, but as he grew in age and awareness, he began to resist their efforts and ultimately walked out of their court.

Thus a great venture failed, Maitreya's soul is still wandering, and it is difficult to say how long it will take to find a suitable vehicle for his incarnation. Those who are suitable as mediums don't agree to be vehicles for others. They are mature enough to be on their own. And those who agree are not that worthy. So the possibility of his incarnation is diminishing as time passes by. And there seems to be no more any organized efforts being made in this direction. Maybe some accidental planning will work, as it has in the past. Nobody had to be persuaded for the soul born first as Gautam Siddhartha, who later transformed himself into Buddha, the awakened one. He found an appropriate womb and became embodied. Similarly Mahavira came to this world through another womb. But then wombs of such superior quality are becoming rarer and rarer.

> Questioner: It takes at least four hours to go through the whole of the Geeta consisting of eighteen chapters and seven hundred and one shlokas —couplets. Does it mean that the battle of the Mahabharat was adjourned for this length of time when the dialogue between Krishna and Arjuna was going on?

That's right! Please sit down.

> Questioner: The other day you said that a soul is reborn within a year of its leaving its former body, and just now you said that a certain ghost lived in the bodiless state for eleven hundred years. Please explain the contradiction.

Yes, there are a few people who have extraordinary memory. People with ordinary memory don't take much time for being born. But those of extraordinary memory, who are few and far between, do take time.

Curzon, a former British viceroy of India, has mentioned an event in his memoirs.

A man of extraordinary memory was once brought to his court from Rajasthan. Even the word "extraordinary" does not rightly describe his memory; it was really incredible. The man did not know any language other than his mother tongue—Rajasthani. Thirty persons speaking thirty different languages were called to the Viceroy House in Delhi to test this man's memory. Each one of them was asked to formulate a sentence in his own language and keep it in his mind.

The Rajasthani man, a villager who knew no other language than his own, went to each of the thirty persons, one after another. Each of them uttered the first word of his sentence, which was followed by the sound of a gong. Then the villager went to the second man who in his turn said the first word of his sentence. Likewise all the thirty gave him the first word of the sentences they had in their minds, and each word was followed by the gong.

Then he returned to the first man who now gave him the second word of his sentence which was again followed by the sound of the gong. In this way he received the second words from the rest of them. This is how he collected all the thirty sentences belonging to thirty different languages interspersed by the sound of the gong. At the end, the man from Rajasthan correctly repeated each sentence of each language separately before the whole gathering.

When such a person as this Rajasthani villager dies and becomes a ghost he can remember things not only for eleven hundred years but for eleven hundred thousand years. It is a special kind of memory.

The other question is equally significant. It takes four hours to go through the whole of the *Geeta*. So it is a relevant question: how was such a lengthy dialogue possible in the midst of two inimical armies standing on the battlefield—ready to begin a decisive war like the Mahabharat? It does not seem probable. How could they have suspended fighting for four long hours? Someone must have raised the question: were they there to fight or to listen to a four-hour spiritual discourse? The question deserves consideration.

A historian, would say the dialogue of the Geeta in its original form must have been a brief one, which was elaborated in the course of time. And if we put this question to one who is an authority on the Geeta, he will say the Geeta is an interpolation; it looks completely out of context in relation to the war of the Mahabharat. It seems the Mahabharat in its original text did have the Geeta as one of its parts, and was extended later by some ingenuous poet. It does not fit in where it is found in the Mahabharat. Certainly a war is no occasion for such a long spiritual discourse.

But I don't accept the theory that the Geeta is an interpolation, nor do I believe it to be a later elaboration of a brief dialogue. I would like to explain it with the help of an anecdote from the life of Vivekananda.

When Vivekananda visited Germany, he was the guest of Duschen, a great scholar of Indology. He was as great an authority as Max Müller, and in many respects Duschen possessed deeper insights than Müller. He was the first western scholar who understood the Upanishads and the Geeta, and his translations of the Upanishads became well-known. It was Duschen's translation of the Upanishads that thrilled Schopenhauer so much that he put the book on his head and went dancing in the streets of his town.

Schopenhauer said the Upanishad was not a book to be read but a song to be sung, a dance to be danced. And Schopenhauer was not an ordinary man, he was a renowned philosopher known for his very serious and sad temperament. He was a pessimist and a total stranger to things like music and dance. He believed that life is essentially painful, and happiness is just a bait to lure us into suffering. The same person burst into a dance when he first read Duschen's translation of the *Upanishads*. Vivekananda was Duschen's guest.

On a fine morning, Duschen was in his study going through a book in the German language. He had been with this book for some days and had been able to read only half of it. Vivekananda entered Duschen's study to say hello, and Duschen mentioned the book he was reading saying it was a great book. When Vivekananda said he would like to have the book for an hour, Vivekananda knew little of German so his host said that he would not be able to understand it. Vivekananda then quipped, "Is it guaranteed that one who knows German well will understand it?" Duschen agreed that it is not. Vivekananda added, "Then the contrary can also be true: that one knowing less of German will understand it. However, you lend me the book."

Duschen asked, "How can you finish reading this book in just two days' time that you are going to spend with me? I have been with this book for fifteen days and have hardly been able to read half of it." His guest said with a grin, "I am Vivekananda, not Duschen." And Vivekananda took the book and left the study.

Vivekananda returned to Duschen's study just after an hour, carrying the book in his hand. When Duschen enquired if he had read the book, Vivekananda said, "I have not only read it, but understood it." Duschen was amazed, but he did not leave Vivekananda before putting him to test if he had really understood the book.

He asked some searching questions from the chapters he himself had read, and he was dumbfounded to see that Vivekananda had gotten it so well. He exclaimed, "Vivekananda! It is incredible! How did you work this miracle?" His guest said with a smile, "There are ways and ways of reading—ordinary ways as well as extraordinary ways."

Most of us are familiar with the ordinary way of reading, and it is enough if we can read and understand even a dozen books in a lifetime. But there are different ways of reading. There are people who take a book in their hands, close their eyes and then throw them away. They are finished with their reading. This is called the psychic way of reading something.

As I understand it, Krishna does not speak to Arjuna through words; he communicates with him at the psychic level. It is such a wordless, silent communication between two persons that a third person standing close by will never know it. No other people present at Kurukshetra could hear it; otherwise a crowd would have gathered round Arjuna's chariot. At least the Pandava brothers were sure to join them. Even the Kauravas would not have resisted the temptation to listen to this unique dialogue. If a spoken dialogue between Krishna and Arjuna had taken place, lasting for four long hours, anything—including fighting—could have happened. But nothing of the kind occurred. No, it was an inner communion between the two, a psychic communication.

It is significant that while no one present on the battlefield has any inkling of this dialogue, Sanjaya, who is far away from the battlefield, hears and relates it to Kaurava's blind father Dhritarashtra. Sitting in his home, Dhritarashtra anxiously asks Sanjaya, "On the field of Kurukshetra my people and the sons of Pandu have gathered together, eager for battle. What are they doing?" They are miles from the battlefield and yet Sanjaya makes a verbatim report to Dhritarashtra. He tells him that when the two armies are arrayed and eager for fight, Arjuna feels depressed and confused and desists from fighting. And

Krishna persuades him to come out of his despondency to fight as a warrior should fight. How does Sanjaya know this from such a distance?

This is a telepathic communication. Sanjaya is in telepathic contact with Kurukshetra and everything happening there. Otherwise he has no way to know and relate the goings-on at the battlefield. So first of all the dialogue happens between two persons at the psychic level and it is again at the psychic level that Sanjaya hears it and relates it in words to Dhritarashtra. Dhritarashtra is the first person to receive the *Geeta*, and then the whole world receives it. That is how it found its way to the whole world and a place in the epic of the Mahabharat. Transcribed into words it now takes four hours to go through the whole text. But it is just possible the whole thing happened within four moments. Maybe, it happened beyond time.

> *Questioner: According to the history of Jainism, the twenty-second Jaina tirthankara, Neminath, was Krishna's cousin. After going through a spell of severe ascetic discipline Neminath became renowned as a Hindu seer by the name of Ghor Angiras, and he is said to have served as a link between Krishna and esoteric knowledge. What do you say about it? Is such a relationship between Neminath and Krishna possible? You said that Krishna's coming into being depended on very inner reasons. What are those inner reasons in the context of esoteric knowledge?*

It is true that Neminath is Krishna's cousin, and the story comes from a time when Hindus and Jainas were not two separate traditions. It is after Mahavira, the last Jaina *tirthankara*, that Jainas separated from the Hindus. Neminath is the twenty-second Jaina *tirthankara*, and he is Krishna's cousin. But there is no esoteric connection between the two. And there is a reason for it.

Neminath belongs to the long tradition of Jaina *tirthankaras* who were all devoted to the pursuit of one-dimensional spiritual discipline. Perhaps no other tradition has done so much in the dimension of sacrifice and renunciation as the Jainas have done. In this respect Jainas have the longest history, adorned by a galaxy of extraordinary people. It is rare in the whole history of mankind.

The first Jaina *tirthankara*, Rishabhadeva, is a contemporary of the *Rigveda*. Maybe he even preceded this most ancient of the *Vedas*, because the *Rigveda* mentions Rishabhadeva with a respect not usually given to contemporaries. The terms used in the Rigveda to describe Rishabhadeva are so respectful that it suggests the first Jaina *tirthankara* has already an established reputation when the *Rigveda* is being created. Man has yet to be so civilized that he will be respectful to his contemporaries.

However, it is certain that Rishabhadeva is contemporary with the *Rigveda*, because this scripture mentions him with great respect. And there is a gap of thousands of years between the *Rigveda* and Mahavira, the last Jaina *tirthankara*. History has not been able to ascertain the time that passed between the *Vedas* and Mahavira. Western historians could not put this gap at more than one and a half thousand years. They were so hemmed in by the belief enshrined in the Christian Bible, that the world was created only four thousand years before Jesus. This means our universe is only six thousand years old, so the western historians have to compress the whole human history into this brief span of time. Evidently Hindus and Jainas also cannot be allowed to transgress this limit. So, those who think along western lines say that the distance in time between the *Vedas* and Mahavira cannot be more than fifteen hundred years. But this is not true.

Now Christianity itself is having to revise its calculation of time. Skeletons of human bodies have been found which are hundreds of thousands of years old. But strange are the ways of superstitious minds; they defy all proofs that go contrary to their old dogmas and beliefs. Do you know what a Christian theologian said when confronted with the fact of the discovery of these thousands of years-old human skeletons? He said that God is omnipotent, he is capable of doing anything, so when he created the world he planted these hoary skeletons in its soil.

But science now accepts that the universe is very ancient. So according to Tilak's calculations, the *Vedas* are at least ninety thousand years old. This much can be said without fear of contradiction, that they are much more ancient than the western historians believe. For thousands of years, the *Vedas* existed in oral tradition, and now they have existed in the written form for so many thousands of years. And the oral tradition is longer than the written one. The first Jaina *tirthankara* is mentioned in the *Rigveda*. And as far as their last *tirthankara* is concerned, he happened twenty-five hundred years ago, according to all historical evidences.

This long tradition of twenty-four Jaina *tirthankaras* is the oldest and greatest heritage in the dimension of renunciation. It has no parallel in the whole history of man. And there is no possibility that any other religion is going to surpass it in any future, because gradually the dimension of renunciation is itself dying. So it seems plausible to believe that there will be no more *tirthankaras* after the twenty-fourth, because renunciation has altogether lost its relevance for the future. However, it had immense relevance in the past.

Scriptures say that Neminath is the twenty-second Jaina *tirthankara* and he is Krishna's cousin. Scriptures also mention Krishna's meetings with Neminath. Whenever Neminath happens to visit his town Krishna goes to pay his respects to him. It is significant that when Neminath comes, Krishna pays him a visit; Neminath never goes to visit Krishna. A renunciate is not expected to pay his respects to a non-renunciate; it is very difficult. A renunciate becomes harsh, he tears himself away from all relationships and attachments. So while Neminath remains Krishna's cousin from Krishna's side, Krishna is no one to Neminath. He never goes to Krishna to ask, "How are you?" He has renounced the world. In the dimension of *vairagya* or non-attachment, one has to drop all associations and their ensuing attachments and become absolutely alone. No one is his friend and no one is his enemy. So the question of Krishna being linked with him in some esoteric venture simply does not arise.

Moreover, Neminath is not in a position to help Krishna spiritually, because he is one-dimensional. On the contrary, Krishna can very well help his cousin, because he is multidimensional. Krishna knows many things Neminath does not know, and he can know on his own what Neminath knows. Krishna is total; he covers the whole of life. Neminath is partial: he lives, and lives fully, but only in one particular dimension of life. Therefore, although Neminath is a very significant figure in Krishna's time, he does not leave his imprint on history.

A renunciate cannot impress history, he cannot leave any spectacular footprints on the sands of time. What more can history say about him than that he renounced everything? On the other hand, Krishna's influence on India was far-reaching and profound. The truth is that with Krishna, India touched a height she never touched again. Under his leadership, the Mahabharat was the greatest war that India had ever made. Ever since, Indians have fought only petty wars and skirmishes. A unique war like the Mahabharat could be possible only under Krishna's leadership.

Generally we believe that war destroys a people. Since India did not fight any great war after the Mahabharat, she should be the most advanced and affluent country in the world today. But the fact is just the opposite: today she is one of the poorest and most backward countries. And the countries that have passed through great wars are at the pinnacle of prosperity and advancement. Wars don't destroy a people, rather they awaken their sleeping energy and rouse their heroism. It is only in moments of war when a community touches the highest peaks of its being. It is only in moments of challenge that a people becomes fully alive and awake. After the Mahabharat we have never had another such great moment to fully come into our own.

It is true that countries involved in the Second World War suffered heavily. Destruction of life and wealth was colossal. But this is only a half truth. Japan suffered terribly in the last war, but just in twenty years' time, Japan has emerged as one of the most prosperous countries of the world. Japan's recovery and growth is spectacular and unprecedented; she had never reached this height before. The same is true of Germany, which went through the worst of death and destruction. Not one, but two wars visited her in the lifetime of a single generation.

Is it not amazing that twenty years after her defeat in the First World War Germany was again ready for the Second World War? And no one can say that in another ten years' time she will not be ready for the Third World War. It is ironic that we emphasize only the destructive side of war and overlook its creative possibilities. War awakens our slumbering consciousness. In facing the challenges of war our energies come alive, active and creative. In fact, with destruction comes creativity; they go hand in hand in life.

That is why Krishna, who lives a sensuous and colorful life, who plays the flute and loves singing and dancing, also accepts the challenges of a great war and becomes its instrument. And he delivers a spiritual sermon like the *Geeta* on the battleground. For him there is no contradiction between a flute and a missile and a *Geeta*.

People like Neminath don't leave their mark on history. It is interesting that of the twenty-four Jaina *tirthankaras* only two, the first and the twenty-third, are mentioned in Hindu scriptures. About the twenty-second *tirthankara*, it is guessed that the person named as Ghor Angiras is no other than Neminath. Even Mahavira is not mentioned in Hindu scriptures. All the *tirthankaras* were charismatic and renowned, but they could not leave their mark on history. In fact sacrifice, renunciation means severance of all ties with history; it means departure from the world of events, doings and non-doings. Renunciation is the journey into a space where nothing is made and unmade, where utter emptiness reigns.

There are things that Neminath can learn from Krishna, but he will not. And it is not necessary for him to learn from Krishna. Neminath has a great treasure of his own. He has the heritage of twenty-one *tirthankaras*, the essence of great spiritual experiences. He has enough provisions for his journey; he need not look for help from other quarters. So the two cousins exchange pleasantries when they meet; there is no relationship of give and take between them. Sometimes Krishna goes to listen when Neminath is speaking to people. This reflects Krishna's greatness, and his eagerness to learn. And only Krishna is capable of this humility. One who is interested in every aspect of life, who loves the whole of it can go anywhere to learn, can accept anyone as his teacher. But Krishna is equally well-equipped, sufficient unto himself. There is no reason to think that Neminath can make his inner life any richer.

> *Questioner: Did Krishna have to pass through atheism in order to attain to the highest in theism?*

One who is a profound theist is a profound atheist too. It is skin-deep theists who fight with skin-deep atheists. Fight always happens on the surface; there is no fight at the deepest levels of life. Foolish theists quarrel with foolish atheists; an understanding and wise theist does not bother about fighting with atheists. Similarly an understanding atheist does not quarrel with the theists.

Understanding, from whatever source it comes, unites. It always leads to the *adwait*—the one without the other. What does a theist say? He says God is. But when theism deepens, there is no God but me, I myself become God. A stupid theist, who does not know what theism really is, says God is there somewhere in the heavens. A wise theist says God is here. An atheist claims there is no God. If he is a man of deep understanding he means the same as the theist means. He says, "There is no other God than that which is: what is, is." And he calls it *prakriti*, the pre-created, or nature.

There is a saying of Nietzsche's which is significant in this context. Nietzsche is a profound atheist; as an atheist he is as profound as any theist can be as a theist. Nietzsche says, "If there is God I won't be able to tolerate him, because then, where will I stand? What will happen to me?" He means to say if God is, he as a man will be reduced to nothing. Then he has no ground to stand on, and he could not tolerate it. He says, "If God has to be, why not me?

Why can't I be that God?" Nietzsche is an atheist, and he says there is no God but existence. That which is, is God. Why think in terms of any additional God? Even a profound theist says the same thing: that which is, is God; there is no other God.

I have never differentiated between penetrating theism and penetrating atheism. In reality, while the theist uses positive terms in his description of reality, the atheist uses negative terms. There is that much difference. That is why positive theists think Buddha and Mahavira to be atheists. But neither Buddha nor Mahavira will agree with this description.

To superficial theists, both *sankhya* and yoga seem to be atheistic, but they are not. They are not atheistic in the sense they are thought to be. Their fault—if it is a fault—is that they use negative terms. Similarly persons like Krishnamurti look like atheists to superficial theists because they too use the negative language. But the difficulty is that there are only two ways of voicing reality the positive and the negative. The theist is using the positive when he says, "That which is, is God." And the atheist is using the negative when he says, "That which is, is not God."

There have been people who use both positive and negative together when they explain reality. The seers of the *Upanishads* have their own special term: *neti-neti*, which means it is neither this nor that, and that which is cannot be said. According to them both the theist and atheist say half-truths; they want to say the whole, which cannot be said. In fact, truth is inexpressible. And therefore they remain silent after saying *neti-neti*.

Krishna need not pass through any kind of atheism, because he is not interested in superficial theism. Krishna knows and accepts reality at a depth where names don't matter. Call it God, call it *prakriti* or nature, call it non-God, or whatever you like, it makes no difference. What is, is. The trees will continue to grow as ever, the flowers will continue to blossom. The stars will continue to move, life will continue to appear and disappear, waves will continue to rise and fall. Whether God is or not is a debate only fools participate in. That which is, is utterly unconcerned about it all.

I was camping in a village where two old men came to visit me. One of them was a Jaina, the other a Hindu *brahmin*. They were old friends and neighbors, and their debate was just as old. In fact, all debates are old because there is no end to them. Men come and go, but debates go on. Both friends had passed their sixties. The Jaina said to me, "We come to you with a question which has been troubling us for the last fifty years. I don't believe in God, whereas this gentleman believes in God. What do you say?"

I said to them, "You two have monopolized the whole debate between you. What is there for a third person like me to say? Since you have divided the thing between you on a fifty-fifty basis, where do I come in?" Then I asked them, "You have argued for the last half century; why couldn't you come to a decision?"

The *brahmin* friend said, "I hold on to my arguments because I like them, and my friend holds on to his because he likes them. And neither of us has been able to convince the other."

I said, "You have carried on this debate for fifty years, but do you know how long mankind has been debating over it? From time immemorial man has been arguing over it. Up to now, however, no theist has been able to convert an atheist to his point of view. Similarly no atheist has convinced a theist. And the dispute goes on unabated. It shows that each side has a half truth with it; that is they cling to it so tenaciously. If you have one end of reality in your hands, how can you believe there is another end to it?"

I told them, "I can be of help to you only if I completely keep out of the dispute. If I get involved, all I can do is to take up one of the two positions that you hold, but it will make no difference whatsoever. So I say to you, give up arguing and try to see the other side of the coin, if there is some truth in what the other person says. You don't insist on your own truth. I concede that there is some truth in what you say. From now on try to see the other side of reality. Give up believing that what the other says is all wrong; try to find out if there is some truth with him. That will be much more helpful."

Then I asked the Hindu gentleman, "What will you do if it is proved with certainty that God is?"

He answered, "There is nothing to be done." His Jaina friend said the same thing when I confronted him with the question: What will you do if it is proved that God is not?

I said to both, "Then why are you entangled in this useless controversy? You breathe when God is and you breathe when he is not. You love when God is, and you love when he is not. God does not expel you from the world even if you don't believe in him; he accepts you. And he does not seat you on a king's throne if you believe in him; he does not care for you more than he cares for others. Then of what value is this debate?"

No, we are victims of a linguistic error in regard to the question of God and no-God, theism and atheism. Most of what we call philosophy is nothing more than offshoots of philological errors. And when we accept these philological errors as truth, we are in a mess. Suppose there is a dumb person who is a believer and another dumb person is a non-believer. How will they argue their viewpoints? What will they do to say what and why they hold their beliefs?

Think of a day when all languages, all forms of speech suddenly disappear from the earth for twenty-four hours. What will happen to our philosophical debates? If only your languages—not your religions and beliefs—are taken away from you, what will you do to assert your convictions? In the absence of language, will you be a Hindu or a Mohammedan or a Christian? Will you then be a believer or a non-believer? But surely you will be there even without your languages, your beliefs and non-beliefs. And I say this: you who will be without any ideas and beliefs and dogmas will be a truly religious person.

I would like to close my talk with an anecdote. Mark Twain is the author of this joke.

Once the people of this world decided to carry out an experiment. They hit upon the idea that if all the people of the world agree on a time to shout with one voice, the noise will reach the moon. And if there are people living on the moon, they will hear our shout. And if they make a similar effort we can hear their answering shout from the moon. Man has always been fascinated by the moon, and his desire to relate with that planet is as old as the earth. That is why every child on coming into the world begins to ask for the moon. So a decision was taken and a time appointed when all the inhabitants would speak together to the moon in one voice. They were sure their call would reach the moon, and if the moon is also inhabited by people like us, they will answer in the same way.

"Hoo-Hoo" was chosen as the form of their shout.

The appointed time came. With a tremendous sense of anticipation the people all over the earth gathered on housetops, on raised platforms, on hills and mountains. But as the clock struck twelve, strangely enough an immense silence descended on the earth. Not even a whisper was heard. The reason was that everyone, being anxious to hear that rare and united "Hoo-Hoo" of all mankind, decided on his part to keep silent. He thought a single person's non-participation would not make any difference when the whole world was going to speak with one voice.

Why should one miss such an opportunity? Consequently, the silence that prevailed on the earth in that particular moment was unprecedented. Never before had the world experienced such a moment of penetrating silence.

If ever you come upon such utter silence, when words, concepts, and languages disappear from your mind, you will know the truth, the reality, or whatever you call it. It is only in utter silence that reality comes into being.

One half of truth lies with the theists and the other half with the atheists. And a half-truth is worse than a lie—it is always so. It is so because you can easily give up a lie, but it is tremendously difficult to give up a half truth. A half truth looks like truth itself. How can you give it up? And remember truth is indivisible; it can never be fragmented. And if you have a half truth with you, you can make it into a great doctrine. But a doctrine can be refuted; there is no way to refute and dismantle truth. Neither the theist is right nor the atheist; they cling to fragmentary truths and fight for them endlessly.

Krishna accepts the whole, the total. So it would be wrong to call him a theist, and it would be equally wrong to call him an atheist. And it is difficult to put any label on him without being wrong.

SEVENTEENTH DISCOURSE
EVENING OCTOBER 3, 1970
MANALI, INDIA

DON'T IMITATE, JUST BE YOURSELF

Questioner: As your discourse gathers momentum we are carried away with it, we give up resisting it, rather we try to flow with you. But our difficulty is that your energy is so powerful that we cannot keep pace with you. In the book named The Way of the White Cloud it is said, "Sometimes I take away the man, the subject, but do not take away the circumstances, that is object. Sometimes I take away the circumstances, but do not take away the man. Sometimes I take away both the man and the circumstances. And sometimes I take away neither the man nor the circumstances." You spoke about Shree Arvind this morning. I agree with you to a large extent, but I have *some reservations in regard to your interpretation of Arvind seeing visions of Krishna. Then you say it is meaningless to quote scriptures like the Vedas and the Upanishads in support of what one has to say, because it reflects one's inferiority complex. But Krishna thinks differently. He says to Arjuna, "I teach you the knowledge, the wisdom that is available to me from anadikal or time infinite." Krishna asserts that the wisdom he brings to this earth belongs to infinity. But Buddha claims that his wisdom is founded on personal experience, although his concept of nirvana or ultimate freedom is the same as is formulated by the first Upanishad and the Bhagwad Geeta. And Dr. Radhakrishnan says that Buddha's teachings are nothing but extensions of Upanishadic principles. Under the circumstances, it is difficult to vouch for one's authenticity. We find ourselves in difficulty in regard to your style, the way you speak. It seems you overwhelm us with your logic, but when you come to facts things become easier for us. When I came here I had a feeling that coming in contact with Rajneesh, the ice of my ego will melt and disappear. And it is true that my ego has diminished to a large extent. Please comment.*

ruth is beginningless.

The *Upanishad's* word *anadi* does not mean old, it means beginningless. *Anadi* means that which has no beginning, the beginningless. It does not mean ancient as you seem to think. However old and ancient a thing may be, it has a beginning, but truth has no beginning. And that which becomes old cannot be truth, because truth is now, in this moment.

Truth is neither new nor old. What is called a new truth is going to become old in the future. What is now called old was new sometime in the past, and what is new today will grow old tomorrow. It is in the nature of things that everything new becomes old. Truth is neither of the two; truth is eternal. Or you can say that which is eternal is truth. So *anadi* means the eternal, not old and ancient.

When Krishna says, "I teach the truth that is *anadi*," it does not mean that he is talking about some old and ancient truth. Krishna means to say that which is, is truth. He says, "I teach you the eternal truth." Those who knew it in the past—if they really knew it—knew the truth that is eternal. And those who know it today—if they really know it—know the same eternal truth. And those who will know it in the future, if they really know, it will be the same truth that is without beginning and without end. Only falsehood can be old and new; truth cannot be new or old.

Of course, there are two ways of saying the truth.

When Buddha speaks about truth he does not refer to all those who have known truth in the past, there is no need. When he knows truth on his own, he need not produce witnesses in his support; that would make no difference whatsoever. What he knows he knows; witnesses are not going to add anything to it. Even a thousand names of people who have known truth will not add one iota to the measure of Buddha's truth, nor will they add to the glory and grandeur of truth itself. That is why Buddha says it directly as he has known it.

And Buddha does so deliberately; there is a good reason why he does not mention the names of the old seers. In Buddha's time these authoritative names were being misused and they carried a danger with them. Remember, whenever Buddha said something he always asked his listeners not to accept it just because somebody else knows and says it. He always warned his listeners against authority. Throughout his life, Buddha insisted that unless someone knows truth on his own, he should not accept it as true on the authority of others—including Buddha.

Buddha is speaking to seekers; his listeners are all seekers of truth. They are very different from Krishna's solitary listener, Arjuna. It is essential for a master to ask his disciples, the seekers of truth not to accept anything, not to believe just because he says it. If they believe something as true, they cannot go on the quest for truth. And if Buddha cites authorities in his support he is laying a precedent for coming generations to cite him as an authority. So he steers clear of all previous authorities and says plainly, "I say to you what I have known, but don't accept it until you know it for yourselves."

But Krishna speaks to an altogether different kind of person; his listener is not a seeker of truth, he is not on an adventure to find truth. Arjuna is quite different from the disciples of Buddha. Arjuna is not seeking truth, he is confused and deluded. The situation of imminent war has overcome him with weakness and fear. So Krishna is not interested in unveiling and exposing truth to its roots—he only tells him what truth is.

Arjuna has not come to him for truth; he wants Krishna to dispel his confusion and fear. Therefore Krishna says that what he is saying has been said

by many others in the past. If Arjuna happened to be
a seeker, Krishna would certainly ask him to prepare
himself for an encounter with truth. But Arjuna wants
only to understand what reality is; he is not prepared
to go in search of truth. He is not in an ashram or a
monastery to learn truth from a master; he is preparing
to wage a war. And being confronted with the special
conditions of the Mahabharat he is frightened and
depressed. So Krishna, in order to dispel his despondency and bolster his morale, tells him that what he
is saying has the support of many wise men of the
past, that it is the eternal wisdom.

This kind of teaching has relevance and
meaning for Arjuna. If Arjuna had come to him on
his own with a desire to find truth, it would have
been altogether different. But this is not the case.
That is why Krishna explains to him the long tradition of truth so that Arjuna can grasp it properly.

There is yet another reason for Krishna's taking this approach.

If a person goes to Buddha, he goes as a disciple, as one surrendered to him. Arjuna is Krishna's
friend, he is not surrendered to him. Much depends
on particular situations and relationships. While
Buddha's disciples accept what he says, his own wife
refuses to take him at his word. When Buddha returns
home after twelve years—during which time he is
widely known as the Buddha, the awakened one, and
people from all over have come to his feet in search
of the truth he has known and proclaimed—his wife
Yashodhara, on meeting him, refuses to accept him
as Buddha. She takes him to be the same person who
had left his home stealthily in the dead of night
twelve years ago. And she resumes the argument from
that very point. She is as angry as she was the following morning when she had come to know how her
husband had deserted her, and she vehemently accuses Buddha of betraying her.

Buddha's wife has her own characteristics. If Buddha tells her straight off that he is now a Buddha, she would say, "Don't talk nonsense, I know who you are. Nobody is a Buddha." If Buddha has to communicate with his wife he will do it very differently, because she is altogether different from his devotees and other seekers. There is a sweet story related with this episode.

When Buddha initiated Ananda into sannyas, because he was his elder cousin, Ananda exacted three promises from him. At the time of initiation he said to Buddha, "Before I become your disciple, I would like to have a few assurances from you. Since I am your elder cousin brother, I am your senior and am in a position to command you to do certain things. Once I become your disciple, your junior, I will lose that status; then you will be in a position to command me and I will do your bidding. Right now you are my younger cousin brother, so give me three promises." Buddha asked him what his desires were.

Ananda said, "Firstly, I will always be with you from morning to morning; you will never send me away from you on an errand. Secondly, if I bring any visitors to you—even at odd hours of the night—you will never say no to them. And you will answer every question I will put to you at any time and place. And thirdly, I will attend, if I want to, even your very private and confidential discussions with your visitors." Being the younger brother, Buddha not only accepted Ananda's conditions, he honored them throughout his life. He never felt any difficulty about it.

But when he returned to his home town after twelve years and was going to visit his wife, Yashodhara, these promises given to Ananda years ago came in the way. Ananda, as usual, wanted to be with him during his meeting with his wife, but for the first time Buddha felt embarrassed. He said to Ananda, "Just think, I am going to visit her after twelve long years. And for her I am not Buddha, but the same old

Gautam Siddhartha, her husband who left her in the dead of night without informing her. And you know she is a proud woman and she will take offense if you come with me; she will think it is a strategy to prevent her from expressing all her bottled-up resentment and frustration, sorrow and suffering. I am aware of my promise, but I beg of you not to insist on it for once."

This is a very sensitive and delicate moment and Buddha's response to it is so human and beautiful. When Ananda reminds him that he has transcended all associations and attachments—no one is now a wife or a son to him—Buddha tells him, "This is quite true, Ananda, as far as I am concerned. But for Yashodhara I am her husband, and it is not in my hands to undo it."

Ananda keeps out of Buddha's way. When Buddha meets Yashodhara the expected happens. She bursts out crying; all the pent-up anger and pain and agony she has silently suffered for twelve years comes out in a torrent. Her outburst is quite justifiable. Buddha listens to her very silently. When she quiets down and wipes away her tears, Buddha says to her very gently, "Yashodhara, look at me attentively. I am not the same person who had left you twelve years back. I don't come back to you as your husband, the husband is no more. I am altogether different. You talked so long to the departed one; now you can talk to me."

The relationship between Krishna and Arjuna is radically different; they are friends. They have played and gossiped together as intimate pals. If Krishna tells him only this much, "I speak about the truth that I have known," Arjuna will retort, "I know you and your truth." So he has to say, "What I say is the same truth that has been said by many other seers. Don't take it amiss because it comes to you from a friend. What I say is really significant."

The *Geeta* is the product of a particular situation; and this has to be borne in mind, otherwise there is much room for misunderstanding. Buddha's situation is different from Krishna's. He can afford to say, "What I say is truth; I am not concerned with what others say about it. And I also urge you not to accept it on my authority. You need to come to it on your own." And it is not an egoist's statement. An egoist would insist on being accepted as an authority. Buddha is simply stating his individual experience to stimulate the thirst for truth in his listeners. He tells them again not to take it as a belief, but go on their own search for truth. But he is also clear that what he says is his own experience. This is simply a statement of fact.

We are aware that what Buddha says has been said by others too. We know that the *Vedas* and *Upanishads* have already said what Buddha says. But why doesn't Buddha say so? There are reasons for it, and the reasons are inherent in the conditions of Buddha's time. By the time of Buddha, the tradition of the *Vedas* and *Upanishads* had completely degenerated and decayed; it was really corrupt and rotten. To say a word in favor of these old scriptures was tantamount to providing support to a decadent and rotting tradition. Knowing well that the *Vedas* and the *Upanishads* contained the same truth, Buddha could not take their support. Because it was with their support that a monster of falsehoods, superstitions and crass hypocrisy was stalking the land, mercilessly exploiting and oppressing the people. That is why he kept quiet about them.

It is not that Buddha is not aware that the *Vedas* and *Upanishads* contain the truth. But it often happens in history that when a new Buddha comes he has to fight and uproot many old truths, because being old they get so badly mixed up with falsehoods that to support them would automatically strengthen those lies.

Krishna did not have to face such a situation. In his time the tradition of the *Vedas* and the *Upanishads* was very much alive. It was really at the height of its glory, absolutely unpolluted and pure. For this very reason we say Krishna's *Geeta* is the quintessence of the *Vedas* and the *Upanishads*. In fact, we can say Krishna himself is the embodiment of the great culture which had come out of these scriptures. Krishna reflects all that is essential and basic to that culture; he comes at a time when the *Vedic* civilization was at its zenith. Buddha comes when it had touched its nadir. It was the same culture, but Buddha had to witness its utter decadence and degradation, when the *brahmins* had ceased to be knowers of truth and instead were busy exploiting people in the name of God and religion. Every conceivable filth and ugliness, corruption and depravity had entered this culture, which now had nothing to do with religion.

Krishna represents the summit of *Upanishadic* teachings. In his times the *Upanishads* have touched the pinnacle of attainment and splendor. The light of knowledge emanating from them is spreading in all directions, and their perfume is everywhere in the air. The *Upanishads* are not a dead thing, they are fully alive and youthful and their music can be heard even in the bushes and shrubs of the land. So when Krishna talks about them, he is not talking about something old and dead; he is talking about something which is in the prime of its youth.

But by the time Buddha comes, twenty-five hundred years after Krishna, the whole tradition is dying and rotting, only its corpse is lying before him. Clearly, Buddha cannot invoke their support. It is not out of any arrogance that he declares his truth on his own.

At the same time there is nothing egoistic about Krishna when he seeks the support of the old seers and their sayings.

Questioner: Krishna, in chapter ten of the Geeta *describes himself to be the Ganges among the rivers, the spring among the seasons, the lion among the beasts, the garuda or eagle among the birds, the eirawat among the elephants, the kamdhenu among the cows, vasuki among the snakes, and so on. Does it mean that he is trying to declare himself to be the best and the greatest in all creation? Does it also mean that he refuses to represent all that is lowly and base? Why does he exclude the meanest of us all? And where does the meanest belong?*

It is a significant question. And there are two beautiful aspects to it.

Firstly, Krishna declares himself to be the best among all things—of all the seasons he is the spring, of all the cows he is the *kamdhenu,* of all the elephants he is the *eirawat.* And secondly—and this is more significant—he finds his peers even among the lowliest of creatures like cows and horses. Both things should be taken together. While he declares himself to be the best among different classes of creatures, he does not distinguish between one class and another. Even when he claims to be the *eirawat* among elephants, he remains nonetheless an elephant. Even when he claims to be the best among the cows he remains a cow. Similarly he is quite at home among snakes and reptiles. He does not exclude the meanest categories as you think. He chooses to be the best even among the meanest creatures of this universe. And there is a reason. But why does he declare himself to be the best and the greatest among us all?

On the surface it seems to us to be an egoistic declaration, because we are so much involved with our egos that everything we see appears egoistic. But if we go deep into it we will know what a great message is enshrined in Krishna's declaration. When he says that he is the *eirawat* among the elephants, he means to say every elephant is destined to be an *eirawat*, and if one fails to be *eirawat* he fails to actualize his best and highest potential. Similarly every season has the potential to grow into a spring, and if one fails to attain to the highest in its nature, it fails its nature. And if a cow fails to be the *kamdhenu*, it means she has gone astray from her nature. In all these declarations, Krishna says only one thing: that he is the culmination, the perfection of nature in everything. Whoever and whatever attains to the sublime reflects godliness. This is the central message of this declaration. Please understand its deeper significance.

It is not that an elephant who does not become the *eirawat* is not a Krishna, he too is a Krishna, but a backward Krishna; he has failed to be the *eirawat* which is his potential. Krishna says he reflects the innate potentiality of each being come to its completion, that each being can grow into Krishnahood, godhood. Krishna symbolizes the actualized form at its best, the highest of each one's possibility. Every being, every thing is capable of attaining to Krishnahood. And if one fails to realize himself fully, it simply means that he has betrayed his innate nature, he has deviated from it. There is not even a trace of egoism in Krishna's declaration. This is his way of saying that one cannot attain to godliness unless he becomes like the lion among animals, like the spring among the seasons, like the Ganges among the rivers. One comes to God only when one attains to one's own fullest flowering, not otherwise.

By way of these illustrations Krishna persuades Arjuna that if he flowers to the maximum as a warrior—which is his innate nature—he will become a Krishna in his own right. Had Krishna been born two thousand years later he would have said, "I am Arjuna among the warrior."

When Krishna declares his being, he is not claiming greatness. To claim greatness he need not compare himself with beasts and birds, snakes and reptiles. Claims to greatness can be made directly, but Krishna really does not claim any greatness for himself. He is speaking about a law of growth, a universal law which is that when you draw out the best in you, when you actualize your highest potential you become God.

One of the Sanskrit names of God is *Ishwar*, which is derived from *aishwarya*, meaning affluence. It means when you attain to the peak of affluence as a being, you become God. But we never pay attention to this aspect of godliness, which is affluence in every respect. So to be the lion among the animals, the *kamdhenu* among the cows, and the spring among the seasons is to attain to godliness, to God. When there is no difference whatsoever between your potentiality and actuality, you become God. When the highest possibility of your life is actualized you attain to Godhood.

If there is a distance between your potential and actual states of being, it means you are yet on the way to your destiny. And godliness is everybody's destiny; it is really everyone's birthright. When that which is hidden in you becomes manifest, you are God. Right now you are part hidden and part manifest, you are on the way to flowering. You have yet to burst into a full spring, you have yet to become God. If Krishna happens to visit our garden here and says that he is the most blossomed one among all the flowers of this garden, what does he mean by it? He means to say that other flowers have the potential to achieve this flowering, and they are on the way to it.

It is right that Krishna does not relate himself with flowers yet hidden in their buds or in their seeds.

He connects himself only with those that have fully flowered. And there is a reason for it. He is speaking to Arjuna who is depressed and confused, and he is not only trying to revive him but also to inspire him to blossom fully as a warrior, to actualize his potential as a warrior. Then alone, Krishna says, can he attain to God, to the utmost peak.

Here Krishna is having to play a double role. Because Arjuna is his friend, he cannot be too hard with him. He has to speak as a friend but all the time he is aware that he has to help Arjuna to come to the same flowering of being which he embodies in himself. Therefore, from time to time he gives glimpses of his own flowering, of his own fullness, so that these glimpses gently seep into Arjuna's awareness.

Krishna will be of no use to Arjuna if he remains only his friend, but if he reveals his godliness indiscriminately, Arjuna may be so frightened that he runs away. So all the time he has to strike a balance between the two roles he is playing. While he continues to be Arjuna's friend he also declares his godliness from time to time. Whenever he finds Arjuna is relaxed, he declares his godliness. And when Arjuna is assailed with doubt and confusion he returns to his friendly approach. His task is very delicate, and very few Buddhas have had to deal with such a situation as Krishna faces in the war of the Mahabharat.

Buddha does not have to deal with such a delicate situation. He knows his people clearly; he knows who is who and what they want. His people have come to sit at his feet to learn truth from him, so communication with them is easy and straight. Mahavira too, has no such difficulties with his listeners. Krishna's difficulty with Arjuna is real; he has to play a double role.

It is really difficult to teach a friend, to be his teacher. It is difficult even to be an advisor to an intimate friend. If you try he will say, "Shut up, don't show off your wisdom." Arjuna can say to Krishna,

"Keep your sage advices to yourself, I know how much you know, since we have grown together from childhood." Arjuna can run away in such a situation. So Krishna on the one hand placates him with phrases like "O great warrior," and on the other he tells him, "You are an ignoramus, you don't know the reality."

If you bear in mind this aspect of the *Geeta*, you will have no difficulty understanding it.

> *Questioner: There are two sides to the life of every great man. While one side is personal and private, the other is open, public. These few days that you have been talking to us about Krishna, we have been helped to understand some features of his life which are such that if we try to imitate him today we will at once be ostracized by the society. We cannot play pranks with our girlfriends in the streets; we cannot run away with their clothes while they are bathing in a swimming pool; we cannot dance with our Radhas as Krishna dances with his Radha who is his girlfriend, not his wife—even if we are deep in love with them. But another side of Krishna's life is aboveboard. His sayings have tremendous relevance for all times—past, present and future. And it is in this context that we request you to shed light on his philosophy of life, on his discipline of work,*

*knowledge and non-attachment, and
his art of living, so that we can emulate him in our day to day life.*

Don't think that only in the present it is difficult to
play the role of Krishna; it was difficult in Krishna's
own times. Otherwise there would have been not only
one, but any number of Krishnas. And if it seems
difficult for you today to become Krishna-like, know
that it would have been as difficult in Krishna's time
if you were his contemporaries. And for Krishna it
would be as easy to be a Krishna today—if he were
born again—as it was in his own days. But this illusion stems from our idea and habit of following and
imitating others in every way. In fact, imitation is the
beginning of all our problems.

You could never have imitated Krishna if you
lived in his days, nor can you imitate him now. It is
impossible. And if you do, you are right in saying that
you will end up in a mess.

I have been talking on Krishna's life and
philosophy not so that you will make him your ideal
and imitate him. Nothing is farther from me than the
idea of imitation. If we can understand Krishna's life,
it will help us to understand our own life in its right
perspective. If we fully unfold and understand Krishna's
life, which is vast and multidimensional, it will enable
us to unfold our own life and know it. But you will
never understand Krishna if you think in terms of
imitating him.

If we imitate someone or other, we will never
understand him because of that. And we will never
understand our own life. In fact, the reason we want
to imitate someone is that we don't want to take the
trouble of understanding ourselves. It is convenient
to live in somebody else's shadow and imitate him; it
is a way to escape the arduous task of understanding
ourselves. Understanding begins when someone ceases

to imitate others, to be like others, when he wants to know directly who he is and what he can be.

The life of one who has achieved his full unfoldment helps to understand one's own life. It doesn't mean that one becomes like him, becomes his carbon copy. To become like others is neither possible nor desirable. Everyone is different and will remain different.

If you think in terms of imitation when we are discussing Krishna—and it seems from your question that you do think in such terms—then you will never understand Krishna. Never mind Krishna, you will never understand yourselves.

Secondly I would like to emphasize that although Krishna's philosophy, his vision of truth is significant and useful, it is not to be imitated, followed. When I ask you not to imitate his life which is so rich and dynamic, how can I ask you to imitate his ideas and thoughts, even his truth expressed in words? No, you have only to understand them, not follow and imitate them.

Of course as you understand Krishna your own understanding and intelligence will grow and deepen; it will enrich you in your own way. No ideas, no thoughts, no principles will help you; only understanding will. Understanding is the key, the master key.

It is unfortunate that imitation has become the hallmark of our life; we imitate from the cradle to the grave. We imitate others' ways of living; we imitate their ideas and thoughts. We are nothing more than imitators in every aspect of life.

Before I go into Krishna's philosophy, it is necessary to warn you against imitation and following. Don't follow anyone, not even Krishna. I say so not because it is not possible today to play pranks on your girlfriends or to run away with their clothes or to dance with them in the streets. Everything is possible, there is no difficulty in it. And if dancing with girlfriends is difficult today, it was difficult in

Krishna's time too. Playing a flute was as difficult then as it is now. There is no basic difference between old and new times; the differences are minor. So it is not because of changed times that I ask you not to imitate. Imitation itself is wrong, utterly wrong, and it is always wrong. Imitation is suicidal. If you want to kill yourself, then only is imitation okay.

Krishna never imitates anyone. Buddha does not follow others. Can you name a person whom Krishna or Buddha or Christ ever imitated? It is ironic that we imitate those who never imitated others. It is so absurd. So the first thing to know about men like Krishna is that they never follow and imitate others, howsoever great the others may be. Persons like Krishna, Buddha, and Christ, are the exquisite flowerings of individuality; they are not carbon copies of others.

But we all try to imitate others. And imitation is dangerous. Playing the flute or loving a Radha is not so dangerous. Even today one does not refrain from falling in love with somebody else's wife. It happens almost every day. The husband is afraid of his wife, the wife is afraid of her husband, and yet extramarital relations happen everywhere. And it is nothing new, it has always been so. As long as husbands and wives are there, their fear of each other will be there. And to be without husbands and wives is equally frightening. Man as he is is in fear, and this fear permeates his whole life.

Let us first understand this fear, and then we will go into the matter of truth and reality. You are not afraid of imitating Krishna because of public opinion. Fear of imitation is more basic, and I would like to go into it before I take up your question on philosophy and truth. I did not go into Krishna's personal life on my own, but because you had asked questions about it. And as you have raised the question of the fear of imitating Krishna, I will deal with it first and then take up the rest of the question.

The basic fear of imitation is quite different. Imitation in itself is unnatural and ugly and wrong. In this whole world no two persons are alike, the same; they cannot be. Each person is different, unique and incomparable. There is no way to compare you with any other person in the whole world. You are like you; you are you. Never a person like you has happened in the long past of mankind, and never one like you is going to happen again in the future. God is a creator; he is creativity itself; he is always original, and whatever he creates is original. He never makes a carbon copy; he has no use for carbon papers in the whole process of creation. He never repeats; you can't accuse him of repetition. And therefore, if you deny your individuality and try to follow and be like somebody else, you are violating the fundamental law of life. Imitation is a crime against God. He made you an individual and you are trying to be somebody's copy. He gave you individuality, and you are trying to impose somebody else's personality on yourself, an alien personality. This is the basic fear and fundamental problem of our life.

Up to now all religions of the world have taught imitation. Parents and teachers all over the world exhort young men and women from their early childhood to be like others; they never ask them to be like themselves, to be themselves. They insist to you, "Be like Krishna, Christ or Buddha, but never commit the mistake of being like yourself." Why? How is it that all educational institutions in the world teach you to be imitators and they never ask you to be yourself?

There are good reasons for it. The most important reason is that if everyone becomes himself, he will be a free individual, a rebel—not a conformist, a camp follower. He will be a danger to the institutions of parents, teachers, priests, managers of society, and to society itself. Every society is afraid of non-conformists and rebels. It honors the conformists, the yes-sayers. That is why everybody, from the president down to the parents pressures children, with one voice, to be followers, imitators. Otherwise they can't be certain who will turn into what.

There is no danger if you become like Rama, because everything about Rama is known, what he does and what he does not do. He is predictable. And if you become another Rama you will be as predictable, and society will know what you are going to do. And if you deviate from the outlined path they will declare you an outlaw and punish you.

If everyone is allowed to be himself, then it will be difficult to say what is right and what is wrong, what is virtue and what is sin. Therefore the society wants you to fit into its well-defined patterns and clear-cut molds. It does not care if by this effort your individuality is destroyed, your life is ruined, and your soul is impoverished. Its sole concern is to turn men into machines so that the status quo is maintained at any cost.

It seems man lives for society, society does not exist for man. The individual has no importance; he is just a cog in the social machine. It seems education is not meant for man; on the contrary, man is meant for education, for being educated the way the society wants. It seems tenets and doctrines are not made to serve man; on the contrary, man is born in the service of tenets and doctrines. It seems religion is not for man; man is for religion. It is ironic that man is not an end unto himself, he is just a means. And things that are meant to be means have become ends unto themselves. This is the danger. This is the curse of imitation, that man has been reduced into a thing, a non-entity.

Imitation is destructive, it kills the individual. And this danger is inner, spiritual; it is not circumstantial. It is a kind of slow poisoning. Whether you imitate Krishna or Buddha, it makes no difference; all imitation is suicidal.

There is no mold, no pattern, no type into which man can be fitted. Every person is a unique and different individual, and he is meant to be himself. This is his freedom, his birthright.

So when I am speaking to you about Krishna, let no one think even mistakenly that I want you to be like Krishna. I am against all following, all imitation, all comparisons. Every suffering that comes to man from external sources is secondary; the suffering that imitation and following brings in its wake is real and colossal. You cannot become like Krishna without being dead. And it is only dead people who are afraid—afraid of everything. You are afraid of being beaten by the public if you dance and sing like Krishna. This is the fear of the dead, the imitator. A man who is fully alive is himself; he does not imitate. The more one is alive the more he is himself. And an alive man, a real individual is not afraid of society; on the contrary, the society is afraid of him. And that is why the society condemns him.

It is amusing that every society slanders and condemns the free individual, who is the only alive person—but this is not the whole story. The free individual is condemned in the beginning and worshipped in the end. It has always been the case. If a fully alive man remains alive to the end, he is destined to be condemned first and worshipped and adored later. And a really free person is not afraid of condemnation, ostracism, even crucifixion.

Krishna is one of those rare beings in man's history who choose to be themselves. He is not concerned about what you say about him. Do you think he was accepted as Bhagwan or God in his own times? No, he was accused and condemned in every way. And even today you will not spare him unless you shut your eyes to many episodes of his life.

Do you know how Jesus was crucified? He was condemned as a disreputable and dangerous person. When he was hanged he was not alone: he was placed between two thieves who were going to suffer the same fate. This was a declaration that Jesus was no better than the criminals. It is interesting that not only the people of Jerusalem—who had gathered in thousands to witness his crucifixion—had ridiculed him. Even one of the thieves on the cross made a joke at Jesus' expense. He is reported to have said, "Since you and I are going to die together, we are kith and kin. So please save a place for me too in your father's kingdom when I reach there." Even a thief mocks Jesus and his kingdom of God. Not only his persecutors, not only the public of Jerusalem—even a criminal who was going to be hanged for theft thought Jesus was a good-for-nothing vagabond. He thought himself better because while he had done something to deserve punishment Jesus was going to be hanged for nothing.

The society in which Krishna or Christ, Mahavira or Buddha are born does not accept them as Bhagwans, incarnations and messiahs. At first it condemns them, calls them names, mocks them, persecutes them. But they are brave people and cannot be intimidated. They bear the insults and humiliations with a smile of compassion on their faces. So how long can you go on? You will feel embarrassed, conquered by their love, their forbearance and compassion. And you begin to honor and worship them. But they take your worship with the same detachment and equanimity with which they take your insults and curses, because really nothing affects them—neither fame nor infamy. And then the society hails them as God-incarnates.

I attach importance to a discussion of Krishna's life not because I want you to emulate him, but because he is the most beautiful and rare example of a multidimensional person. And if his treasures are laid before you they will help you uncover your own hidden treasures. This much importance Krishna has for me, nothing more. And remember, Krishna's treasures are Krishna's, and your treasures will be your own. And no one can say your treasures will not be even richer than Krishna's. I want to remind you again that what happened to Krishna can happen to each one of you, and this awareness is enough. This whole discussion is just meant for this remembrance, that you all are heirs to godliness.

You want to know about Krishna's philosophy of life. This desire for a life philosophy stems from the same source; you want something ready-made, an ideology, a doctrine, a tenet which you can impose conveniently on yourself and be finished with it. I will take up his philosophy tomorrow, but for a different purpose. I want you just to understand your own life with its help. I don't want you to accept and follow Krishna's views and ideas. People like Krishna look at life with extraordinary eyes; their perception is rare. It penetrates the innermost depth of life, and it will be a great gift if for a while we can look at life through the eyes of Krishna. That will go a long way to change and deepen our own perception, our own perspective of life.

You are here in Manali, in the Himalayas, surrounded by beautiful hills and majestic mountains. But you can see only that much beauty in these mountains as your eyes, your perception, your perspective are capable of. Nicholas Roerich, the renowned painter, happened to live here for a long time. If you go and see his paintings, they will give you quite a different perspective of the same mountains; you will see them with the eyes of Roerich. He came to these mountains from distant Russia at a time when there were no roads as there are today to connect the Himalayas with the rest of the world. And once he saw the Himalayas he made them his lifelong home; he never left again. These very mountains before you now had possessed Roerich, enchanted him.

You have been in the Himalayas for some time, and I don't think you look at these mountains any more. You might have seen them for a little while the first day you arrived and you were finished with them. They are now nothing more than mountains.

But Nicholas Roerich spent his lifetime watching and painting the same Himalayas. The eternal and inexhaustible beauty of these mountains continued to enchant him till his last day; he never felt sated. He dedicated his life to painting them, yet his thirst and passion and love for them remained undiminished. He looked at them from hundreds of angles—during the day and night; morning, noon and evening; summer and winter; spring, rains and autumn; sun and moon and stars—and in all their myriad colors and moods. He was busy painting them even at the time of his death. So these mountains will look very different if you see them through the eyes of Roerich. They will tell you a different story if you get acquainted with the works of this man.

I don't say that you should see these mountains the way Roerich saw them. No, I don't say that. And it is impossible for you to see them as this great painter has. But for sure, after knowing him and his works your perspective will change and deepen; you will know these mountains better.

Many people have loved, but the love of Farhad and Majnu was extraordinary; it was as great as the Himalayas. And it is better to read their story, to be acquainted with their lives; it will be so rewarding. Our love is utterly poor and fleeting; it begins and ends almost simultaneously. And once it is gone it becomes difficult to recall if it ever happened. No sooner the river of our ordinary love appears than it disappears and leaves us high and dry. But there are a few people who continue to love and love passionately till the last breath of their lives. Their love is immense and immeasurable. And it will do you good if you come to know these great lovers; it will help you to understand you own love and the problems of love. Maybe knowing them you become aware of the hidden sources of your own love. It is there in every being, but we smother it and kill it.

I don't say that you should imitate Majnu and become like him. No, it is neither possible nor desirable, and an imitation Majnu can only be a caricature. You can have your cut in the pattern of Majnu's, you can dress like him and wander like a madman shouting, "Laila, Laila." But that has nothing to do with Majnu. You can act, but you cannot know his essential love. Acting is stupid.

But it is possible that the love of Majnu and Farhad will kindle the lamp of your own love, which is as good as extinguished. Maybe his love's power will catch fire inside you and you will become alive and aware of the source of your own love, which is as inexhaustible. It is in this sense I ask you to know them.

Many people compose poems and lyrics, but the lyrics of Kalidas, Shakespeare, or Rabindranath have something special, something unearthly about them. Listening to Kalidas or Rabindranath you come upon something you have never known before. Perhaps for the first time you glimpse your hidden possibilities.

From tomorrow morning I will speak about Krishna's philosophy, but I hope you will not make it into your belief and doctrine. I don't want you to become doctrinaire. Krishna is utterly undoctrinaire. So keep a distance from all theories, doctrines and dogmas. We are trying to understand Krishna for an altogether different purpose. When a glorious and resplendent person like him—who has attained to the fullest flowering of his being—looks at this universe of ours with the eyes of a seer and says something about it, his words have an extraordinary significance for us. His verdict about our world carries tremendous weight, and it is good to be acquainted with it.

It is useful to know what a man of such clarity and enlightenment has to say about man and his mind and the ways of his fulfillment. This knowledge, this information he brings us can touch some inner chord of our being and set us on a voyage of exploration. And there is only one worthwhile quest in life, and that is to know who I am or who you are. Then you will not turn into a Krishna-ite, but a traveler on the path to become yourself. And then you will also know that the man who asks Arjuna to die in pursuit of his self-nature is not going to impose any doctrines on you.

So I invite you to bring your questions on Krishna's philosophy from tomorrow onward, and I will go into them all. It is so convenient for me to speak in response to your questions. Then I don't need to strain my mind; it comes out naturally and flowing like a stream. Otherwise I find it hard to say a thing. My difficulty is that words and ideas are with me only as long as I am speaking to you. When I am not speaking my mind is utterly empty and silent, and resumption of speech becomes so difficult in such a state.

When you ask a question, it serves me as a peg to hang my ideas on. Ordinarily, speaking has become really difficult for me; I have to strain hard to say something. It is becoming increasingly difficult to speak on my own; it puts a great strain on me. Lately many friends have expressed a desire that I should speak independently, without the assistance of your questions. That will be really too much. It will not be long when I will cease to speak independently. Without your questions I don't know what I should say; words and ideas have left me. But when you bring a question there is no way for me but to respond to it, and so I become articulate. In the absence of your questions I have nothing to say on my own. On my own I am utterly silent. If I speak I speak for you. So bring your questions tomorrow and we will discuss them.

Now we will sit for meditation.

EIGHTEENTH DISCOURSE
MORNING, OCTOBER 4, 1970
MANALI, INDIA

NON-ATTACHMENT IS NOT AVERSION

Questioner: Krishna says that by giving up desiring and attachment, which he calls niskamta and anasakti respectively, one is released from bondage and he attains to the supreme. But it is so difficult for ordinary men and women to be free of desiring and attachment. Please explain the significance of desirelessness and non-attachment and ways to achieve them.

n the first place try to understand the meaning of the word *anasakti* or non-attachment. It is unfortunately one of the most misunderstood words.

Non-attachment is generally taken to mean aversion, but it is not aversion. Aversion is a kind of attachment—the opposite of attachment. Someone is attached to sex and someone else is attached to its opposite—*brahma-*

charya or celibacy. Someone is attached to wealth; he is running after wealth, and someone else is attached to renunciation of wealth; he is running away from wealth. One person is obsessed with the idea of looking handsome; another person is obsessed with the idea of looking ugly. But those who are averse to sex, money or good looks appear to be non-attached because their attachments are negative.

Attachment has two faces, positive and negative. You can fancy a thing so much that you madly run after it, you cling to it—this is positive attachment. And you can be so much repelled by a thing that you want to escape it, to run away from it; then it is negative attachment. Negative attachment is as much attachment as positive attachment.

Non-attachment is altogether different; it is freedom from both the positive and the negative kinds of attachment. Non-attachment means one is neither attached to something nor averse to it. Non-attachment is transcendence of both attachment and aversion.

In the world of spiritualism there are many words like non-attachment, which have been badly distorted and misconstrued. *Veetrag* is one such word which means transcendence of attachment, but it has become synonymous with aversion. When someone goes beyond both attachment and aversion, he achieves the state of *veetrag* or transcendence. This word *veetrag* belongs to the tradition of Mahavira, while *anasakti* belongs to the tradition of Krishna, and they are synonymous. But there is a difference in the approach of the two.

While Mahavira attains to the state of *veetrag* by renouncing both attachment and aversion, Krishna attains to the state of *anasakti* by accepting both positive and negative attachments. And these are the only possible ways. While their ends remain the same, their means are different. While Mahavira insists on renunciation of attachment, Krishna emphasizes its acceptance. So in a deeper sense *veetrag* is negative and *anasakti* is positive.

A non-attached mind, according to Krishna, is one who accepts everything unconditionally. The interesting thing is that if you accept something totally it does not leave a mark, a scar on your mind; your mind remains unscathed and undisturbed. But when you cling strongly to a thing it leaves a mark on your mind. And when you are strongly averse to something, you detest and deny it, then also it leaves a mark on your mind.

But when you neither cling to a thing nor run away from it, when you become receptive to everything — good or bad, beautiful or ugly, pleasant or painful—when you become like a mirror reflecting everything that comes before it, then your mind remains unscathed and unmarked. And such a mind is a non-attached mind; it is established in non-attachment.

You want to know how an ordinary person can achieve non-attachment. In fact, everyone is ordinary until he attains to non-attachment. So the question how an ordinary person can become non-attached does not arise. As long as one is attached or averse to something he remains an ordinary person. Extraordinariness comes with non-attachment, not before. It is not that ordinary people come to non-attachment in one way and extraordinary ones come to it in another way. Only one who has transcended both attachment and aversion is extraordinary. So the right question to ask is: How can one attain to non-attachment?

Before we go into the question of non-attachment, let us understand the matter of attachment itself. How is it that one ceases to be non-attached and becomes attached to persons, things and ideas?

According to Krishna, non-attachment is embedded in the very nature of a human being, in his very being. Non-attachment is our basic nature, our original face. So the real question is how one deviates from his nature. We don't have to practice non-attachment, we don't have to do something to come to it. We have only to know how we have gone astray from our nature. This is our basic question.

Someone came to me the other day and said, "I want to find God." I asked him when and how he had lost his God. His answer was that he had never lost him.

Then I asked him, "How can you search for a thing that you have not lost? Search implies that you lost something and now you are trying to recover it. Therefore," I said to him, "it is not a question of finding God. You would have to find God if you had really lost him. So first you have to know if you have lost him. And if you come to know on your own that you never lost him, the search is complete."

Non-attachment is our self-nature; we are born with it. So it is strange that in life, we all become victims of attachment and aversion. Non-attachment is our very nature. If attachment is our nature, we cannot manage to be averse to anything. If aversion was our nature, we could not fall prey to attachment. For example, a branch of a tree sways westward with the westerly wind and eastward with the easterly wind. How is it that the branch sways with the winds? Because it is neither in the east nor in the west; it is just in the middle.

Let us take another example: when we boil water it becomes hot, and when we cool it it becomes cold, because water in itself is neither hot nor cold. If water was intrinsically hot it could never become cold; it could never be heated if it was basically cold. Water's own nature transcends both hot and cold, so we can easily heat or cool it as we like.

If attachment is our self-nature, there is no way to be repelled by anything. But we are easily repelled. If clinging was our self-nature we could not give up anything, but we do give things up. In the same way if renunciation was our self-nature, we could not cling to a thing, but we cling like leeches. It simply means that neither attachment nor aversion is intrinsic to our self-nature. Therefore we move in both directions—we now become attached and then averse to something. Because our innate nature transcends both these states of mind, we can move conveniently into them.

Let us take yet another example. We can open and shut our eyes whenever we like, because basically our eyes are neither open nor shut. If to be open was the very nature of the eyes, we could never close them. And if they were inherently closed we could never open them. Eyes can be both opened and closed at will because their self-nature transcends both states, they are beyond them. Opening and closing is external to them; really it happens because of the eyelids. In the same way our consciousness is essentially non-attached; it is only its eyelids, its coverings that get attached or repelled by something.

So the first thing to understand is that non-attachment is our self-nature; we are born with it. It is our original face.

Secondly, we have to understand that it is only our self-nature that we can attain to; we can never attain to that which is alien to our self-nature. Really we can achieve only that which we already are at some deeper level of our beings. A seed grows into a flower because it is already a flower in its depth. A rock cannot grow into a flower, because never mind its depth, not even its surface has anything to do with a flower. If you sow a rock in the soil like a seed, it will ever remain a rock; it can never turn into a flower. On the surface both rock and seed look alike, but if you sow them together the seed will turn into a flower, while the rock will remain always the same. So we can say that a seed becomes a flower because it is inherently a flower.

It is one of the fundamental laws of life that we can become only that which we already are at the center of our being; what is hidden at the center becomes manifest at the circumference.

Therefore non-attachment is our self-nature —not attachment or aversion. That is why sometimes we get attached to a thing and then are repelled by it.

And we can return to non-attachment because it is our essential nature: that is to say, the seed can grow into a flower.

It is not that non-attachment is the nature of a few; it is everybody's nature. Wherever consciousness is, it is always beyond attachment and rejection. Our highest intelligence transcends both clinging and aversion. It is a different matter that in its behavior, consciousness attaches itself to something or rejects something else. But that is its behavioral side; it is like the eyelids open and close whenever they have to.

If I am left exclusively with my consciousness, will I be attached or detached in that moment? I will be neither. Attachment and aversion invariably happen in relationship with others. If I say Mr. X is attached, you will immediately ask, "To whom?" or "To what?" How can one be attached without the other? In the same way, if I say that Mr. Y is averse, you will soon ask, "To what?" or "From what?" Because aversion too, is possible only in relation to someone or something. Both clinging and rejection reflect our relationships; they belong to our behavioral side. In ourselves we are neither.

It is very important to understand the behavioral side of self-nature. And since it is a question of behavior, I can be attached to a person today and can reject him tomorrow. Because it is behavioral, if I am averse to someone today I can be attached to him tomorrow. And the irony is that I can be both attached and averse to someone or something at the same time. It is quite possible I can be simultaneously attached to one aspect of his personality and averse to another. We are often in conflicting relationships with the same persons or things — attached and averse together. But one thing is certain: attachment and aversion belong to our behavior, not our self-nature. Behavior means that one enters into some relationship—with another person or thing or thought—but the other is essential. Behavior is not possible without the other. It is impossible when you are alone.

Self-nature means that which is all alone. Aloneness is the intrinsic quality of self-nature. Self-nature is aloneness. If I am left utterly alone, away from men and things, from ideas and images; if I am in total aloneness, will I be attached or averse in that state? No, both attachment and aversion are utterly irrelevant to aloneness, because they are reflections of relationship. Once I am out of all relationships I am all alone—unattached and untouched.

I am explaining it at length so that you rightly understand the meaning and significance of non-attachment, its context and associated words. And once you understand them rightly you will not have much difficulty in coming to non-attachment.

Both attachment and aversion are relationships in which the other is needed, the other is essential. Without the other these words are meaningless. And because of this "other", both attachment and aversion turn into bondages, slavery. In both cases we are dependent on others. So a person of attachment is a slave, and a person of aversion is a slave of the opposite kind. Take away the vault of one who clings to wealth and he will die. Put a vault in the room of one who is averse to wealth and he will not be able to sleep.

Someone who is addicted to sex cannot live without a woman or a man. But put one who is an avowed celibate with a beautiful woman or a man, and he will be in a mess. Both types of people are in bondage, they are dependent on the other. It does not matter whether the other exists or not; he may be imaginary, but the other has become an inseparable part of their being. They cannot think of themselves without the other. The greedy cannot think of himself without money, and the renunciate cannot think of himself in association with money. But the other is present at the center of both.

If you understand this behavioral aspect of non-attachment, then you will know that changes in behavior don't make much difference. It often happens that a person of attachments reacts and turns his back on everything he clings to. Similarly a renunciate turns into a worldly man again and begins to run after money, position, and prestige. People of considerable success in the world come to me and say they are in a mess and want to get rid of it. Renunciates also come to me and say it seems they made a mistake by leaving the world. Who knows? There may be something really worthwhile which they are missing.

A monk is always thinking that the people of the world are having a good time, while really they are wasting their lives. And worldly people think they are missing some higher experiences of life the monks and recluses are having. In fact, only their situations are different. Psychologically the householder and the monk are both in the same boat. Psychologically they are heavily dependent on others, they are in shackles. And such people cannot know freedom, truth, bliss. Really the "other" is the bondage.

Usually a renunciate thinks that he has given up the other, but he is not aware that he is mistaken to think so. He is still bound with the other; he is now in another kind of relationship with the other, a relationship of escape. What he leaves behind pursues him. Although he is no longer running after it, he is afraid of it. Because he has escaped from it, he is worried lest it overcome him again. And where can you run away from the other?

The other is everywhere. The other is everywhere except one place, and that is your innermost being, the center of your being. If you leave your home, the ashram or the monastery will take its place. And you will be attached to it the way you were attached to your home. If you leave your wife or husband or children, then the master and the disciples will take their places and you will again be attached to them. You can leave a palace for a hut, but a hut is as much a house as a palace. You can give up costly clothes and take to a loincloth, but a loincloth is as binding as a king's robe is. Even if you go naked, you will become attached to your nudity.

The other is all over. In this world you cannot run away from the other, because the world is the other, and wherever you go the world will be with you. You cannot run away from the world. Wherever you go, the other will be there, so you cannot run away from the other. Of course, the other will take on new forms, but it will be there. By changing appearances you cannot change reality.

Except one space, the space of love, the other is everywhere. At the deepest core of love there is no other—not because the other cannot enter there, but because at your deepest core even you disappear. At the deepest center of one's being even the self, the "I", disappears; so there is no way for the "other" to be there.

Now I tell you that as long as you are, you cannot escape the other. Earlier I said that as long as you are in the world you cannot escape the other, he is everywhere. Now I tell you the other side of the same truth: that as long as you exist, as "I", as ego, the other will be there. Even if you close your eyes and the world disappears, the other will not disappear. Now the other will exist behind your closed eyes, in your desires and longings, in your dreams and imaginations, but he will be there. As long as you are, the other is inescapably with you.

In fact, *svabhava* or self-nature is a state where the self, the "I", the ego, ceases to be. Self-nature is also one of those unlucky words that have been greatly misunderstood. By self-nature we generally mean the sense or feeling of the self. But where *svabhava* or self-nature begins, the self disappears. There is no relationship whatsoever between self-nature and self. Self-nature is that which was there when I was not in this world, and it will be there when I will be gone from here.

Whether I am here or I am not, self-nature is always in existence. That which is eternal is self-nature. Self-nature is that which is and will be even when I disappear, when my "I" disappears absolutely. The association of the word "self" with nature creates all the confusion; it gives rise to a feeling that it has something to do with the self.

Svabhava means: the nature, the primordial nature, the original face, the *prakriti,* that which is, even without me. When you are asleep there is no self, but self-nature is. In deep sleep, which in Sanskrit is called *susupti*, there is no self but self-nature is. When someone is lying in a state of coma, there is no self, but self-nature is. There is this much difference between *susupti* and *samadhi*, deep sleep and superconsciousness: in *susupti* the self disappears because of unconsciousness, in *samadhi* it disappears because of wakefulness, awareness, enlightenment.

Therefore, as long as the world exists the other will exist; as long as I exist, the other will exist. But we can look at this phenomenon in a different way. As long as I am, all that I see is the world. The world is a subjective reality which I see from the lens of my self, my "I", and therefore it is the other. The world is the other. So if the "I" ceases, the other will cease too. Then there is no one who can be attached and no one with whom one can be attached; there is no one who can be averse and no one to whom one can be averse. Then I am nowhere and everywhere and in everything.

Anasakti or non-attachment is our innate nature. But how to come to it?

The greatest mistake one commits in this regard is that he embraces aversion as a means to come to non-attachment. Remember, attachment is not as harmful as aversion is, because the face of attachment is clear-cut and simple, it can easily be recognized. No one can mistake attachment for non-attachment. It is impossible. How can you say that clinging to money is non-attachment? But the face of aversion is very deceptive, it is masked. And that is why it poses the greatest danger for one who is trying to attain to non-attachment.

There is every possibility one can mistake aversion for non-attachment, and think that by rejecting men and things he has attained to non-attachment. Aversion is a false coin, it can easily adopt the name of non-attachment. It is therefore essential to beware of aversion, which is no better than attachment. Aversion is attachment standing on its head, and to know this is to beware of it.

Secondly, as I said, wherever you go the other will be there, because the world is the other. I also said there is only one space where the other is not, and it is the center of one's being. So let us move in that direction; let us move into that space, which is entering into the innermost core of our being. Let us descend into that shrine of aloneness and solitude. There is no one in that solitude, not even you; it is a space of absolute silence. What does it mean? Does it mean that if I shut my eyes to the world I will enter the space of my aloneness and solitude?

Every day we close our eyes, but we are never alone. As soon as we close our eyes we begin to see the same images we had seen with open eyes. Thoughts and imaginations, dreams and daydreams surround us from all sides. The world is again with us.

Although it is imaginary it is nonetheless the same world. We use our eyes like a movie camera; what we see with our eyes is imprinted on our mind's film, and we then watch it inside with closed eyes. All our thoughts and images are concerned with the other. And unless they are dropped, unless this inner world of thoughts and dreams goes, we cannot be free from the other, we cannot be alone.

This inner world of thoughts and dreams and images can be dropped, it is not that difficult. It is there because we want it to be there; it exists with our cooperation. And it will disappear the moment we withdraw our cooperation. It is because we relish and enjoy our world of thoughts and images—we find it pleasurable—that it is alive and flourishing. Not only our enjoyment of it, even our aversion to it helps to keep it going.

I repeat: not only our addiction to this world, even our aversion is equally responsible. Not only do we think of our friends and loved ones, we also think of our adversaries and enemies whom we hate. And it is ironic that those we hate haunt us much more than those we enjoy and love. But when we neither identify ourselves with something nor condemn it, when we are neither interested in remembering something nor in forgetting it, then the thing drops and disappears on its own; we don't have to do anything. It becomes irrelevant and meaningless, and so it removes itself from the screen of the mind.

If you watch the movie which is your mind like a spectator, a witness, without identifying with it, without condemning it, with total disinterest, then you will find the whole movie dropping away. Before long, it disappears. And by and by the witnessing consciousness alone remains, without any object before it. This objectless awareness is alone; it is aloneness. And one who attains to this aloneness attains to non-attachment. The very experiencing of this consciousness, empty and alone, is non-attachment.

The behavior of a man of non-attachment will be radically different from others, and this behavior is called *anasakti yoga* or the discipline of non-attachment. He accepts everything—like a mirror—without attachment or dislike. Now he knows for himself what self-nature is, what non-attachment is.

He knows that self-nature and non-attachment are inseparably together, and he also knows that attachment and aversion are just behavioral. Having known and understood it in depth, he is not going to behave the same as he had behaved before. His behavior with the outside world will be radically different, because for him the world has ceased to be what it was before. His consciousness has undergone a mutation. It is no more like the film of a camera; now it is like a mirror, and he will use it as a mirror.

A mirror reflects everything that appears before it, but unlike the camera it does not retain impressions when the object has moved away from it. A man of such consciousness will relate with people and things, but he will not enter into relationships involving attachment and aversion. He will mix in society, but his aloneness will remain inviolate and untouched. He will love, but his love will be like lines drawn on the surface of water. Even if he goes to fight, he will fight as though in a play which leaves no marks on the player after he is finished with it. His mirror of consciousness will reflect both love and war, but in itself it will remain unaffected by either. Whatever he will do, his consciousness will be still and steady like the center of the cyclone. His behavior will be just an acting. He will no more remain a doer; he will be an actor on the stage of life.

If Krishna is anything, he is an actor—a superb actor at that. There has never been a greater and more skilled actor in the whole history of mankind. He is incomparable even as an actor—he who turned the whole world into a stage. While all other actors perform their skill on petty stages, Krishna uses the whole earth for his stage.

If a wooden stage can be used why not the whole earth? It does not make much difference; the world can be turned into a *leela*, a theatrical performance—which it really is—and we all can play our roles as actors and performers. An actor weeps and laughs, but tears and laughter don't bind him; he remains untouched by them. When he loves he does not love, when he fights he does not fight; he is never involved in his roles as worldly people are. He plays a friend and a foe without being involved in friendship and enmity.

The life of one who treats everything as play-acting becomes a triangle, a complete triangle. Ordinarily our life is only two points of this triangle, while the third is submerged in darkness. While the two points of attachment and aversion are functioning and visible, the angle of non-attachment is shrouded in darkness. A person of non-attachment brings this third side into light, and the triangle becomes complete. While he acts around the points of attachment and aversion, he remains centered at the third—the point of non-attachment. In his behavior he appears to be attached or averse to people and things, but it is only appearance, acting, it is not real. In reality, he exists at the third point, and to be on this third point is called *anasakti* or non-attachment.

In fact, all the three points of the triangle exist in each of us but we are ordinarily aware of only two—one of attachment and the other of aversion. The third point, that of non-attachment, remains unknown to us. And the two points of attachment and aversion are like the frying pan and the fire: move from one to the other, do what you can, there is no escape from suffering, pain and misery. One comes to the third point of the triangle when after long suffering, he turns in and discovers his self-nature, his center, the center of the cyclone.

When all the darkness of the mind, of the unconscious is dispelled, the third point of the triangle becomes visible. And one who achieves this third point of non-attachment achieves Krishnahood or Buddhahood, of Jinahood or godliness, or whatever you want to call it. He achieves everything that is worth achieving. Once he knows that he can remain non-attached in every situation, he can afford to play the roles of attachment and dislike.

Someone has written a book called *Games People Play*. In this long book he has described all the games that people play, but he has missed the very basic game of life. What is this basic game of life? To play the game of attachment and aversion and yet remain non-attached is the ultimate game. But because very few people have played this game, the author of the book missed it.

By turning inward one attains to non-attachment. And turning in is possible only if you become a witness—a watcher on the hill. Begin witnessing from any point of life and you will reach your innermost depth. And the moment you arrive at your center, you are non-attached, you are like a lotus in water. The lotus is born in water, lives in water and yet remains untouched by it.

Questioner: You have explained to us beautifully the meaning and significance of non-attachment. Besides non-attachment, Krishna has talked about two other things in the Geeta: one is sannyas or inaction, and the other is action without attachment to results. Please explain the relationship between non-attachment, sannyas, and action without desire for results.

The yoga of non-attachment is foundational, and it is the third point of the triangle, the basic point of life from which arise the two other points of the triangle.

The two other points are: first, action through inaction; and second, inaction through action. One can be called sannyas—inaction, and the other can be called action without desire for results.

Desireless action means action through inaction. If you do something without any motive, without a sense of compulsion to do it and without desire for successful results, it is desireless action. If what you do is undone or it does not bear fruits and you accept it without regret or pain, it is desireless action.

I would like to go into this question in depth. Desireless action is sannyas if the sannyasin has a sense of involvement and responsibility even in inaction, when he is not doing a thing.

It will be a little difficult to understand: a sense of involvement in inaction, when one is not doing a thing. For example, there is a sannyasin who does nothing to earn his living. So he comes to your house for alms and you share with him your food, which you have stolen from somewhere. If he is a true sannyasin he will say that he is party to theft; he is a thief too. If he is a pseudo sannyasin, he will say that he has nothing to do with the theft of the food, he is not concerned with what you do or don't do. But an honest sannyasin will admit that although he did not steal food directly yet he is responsible for your action of theft.

But suppose he does not even beg, he does nothing—what is his position in regard to action? I think if there is a true sannyasin on this earth and if a war is going on in Vietnam—as it is in fact happening, where people are being mercilessly slaughtered— he will share the responsibility for the Vietnam War. Although he is thousands of miles away, he actually has nothing to do with what is going on in Vietnam, still he will take the responsibility on himself.

A sannyasin, a true sannyasin is aware that wherever there is consciousness embodied on this wide earth, he is inextricably linked with it. It cannot be without him, he is present everywhere. And therefore he is responsible for everything—good or evil—that happens anywhere.

For example, I am now in this village as a visitor, and a Hindu-Muslim riot breaks out here. I am neither a Hindu nor a Muslim; I am a sannyasin. So where do I stand in relation to the riot? If I am really a sannyasin I will say, and say truly that, "I am responsible for it; I must have done something to engender it. Maybe I have done nothing to cause it. I am only a silent spectator, yet I cannot run away from the responsibility."

A sannyasin is one who, not doing a thing, knows that he is party to whatever is happening around the earth just because he is a part of the universal life. He has to be utterly responsible for all that mankind does or does not do. He is also aware that whatever he does or does not do—even his inaction—is going to be of great consequence.

If Hindus and Muslims were fighting somewhere and I silently escaped from the scene of the riot, I cannot say that I had nothing to do with it. I could have done something to avert the riot, but I did not. My abstention from action in this case was action enough, and I should hold myself responsible for not averting the bloodshed.

What is generally taken to be sannyas is not real sannyas; it is simple aversion. The sannyas of Krishna's concept is a much different and more difficult affair. Krishna's sannyas is exactly the state of a non-attached person. He lives with this awareness, that he is fully responsible for his inaction—which is action through inaction—just because he exists as a part of cosmic consciousness. He knows that ultimately all consciousness is united and one.

You have seen waves in the ocean; they seem to be constantly moving towards the shore. But you will be surprised to know they never move to the shore; they are virtually stationary. You will say it is unbelievable; you have seen with your own eyes how they travel a mile-long distance to come to the shores. You might have even played with waves that come rolling over the ocean.

But those who know the ocean will say that no wave moves; it only appears to be moving. The fact is that one wave gives rise to another and another and the process goes on ad infinitum. It is not that a wave rising at a mile's distance from the shore moves toward the shore; really it dies as soon as it rises, but it gives rise to another wave which in its turn gives rise to another. What really happens is that when a wave rises it depresses the water on either side, which causes another wave to rise. Thus one wave causes thousands of waves to rise. They don't move even a millimeter, but they appear to be moving because they are so contiguous and continuous.

Now suppose a child is drowned in a wave near the seashore, can you hold a distant wave responsible for his drowning? It will deny responsibility on the grounds that it never moved to the shore; there was a mile's distance between the wave and the drowned child. But Krishna thinks that if the distant wave is a sannyasin, it will own the responsibility for the child's death, because it is an integral part of the ocean. Whether the distant wave visited the shore or not, it is as much responsible as the wave that drowned the child. The ocean is one and indivisible.

A right kind of sannyasin takes responsibility for everything that happens anywhere in this wide world, even though he has no direct hand in any of it. This is a very difficult role to play. Not to be a doer when one is doing something is not that difficult, although this and the other thing are two sides of the same coin. We have lost sight of this side of sannyas, which has as much involvement in inaction. To do without being a doer, and to be a doer when one is not doing a thing are two sides of the coin of sannyas.

But unfortunately we have a very limited concept of sannyas: to us a sannyasin is one who leaves the world and shuts himself up in a mountain cave or a monastery and ceases to have any relation with the world. Such a sannyasin says now he is not at all responsible for what happens in the world. But this is a very sectarian and mistaken view of sannyas. This world is like waves rising on the surface of the ocean where no wave can say that it is not responsible for what happens to the rest of the waves.

Life is very complex; it is vast and deep. It is like an ocean of consciousness which is constantly creating waves. If I say a word here and now, do you think it will die soon after it is uttered? No, I may not be here tomorrow, but this single word uttered by me will continue to affect the world till the end of time. And if I don't say a word, if I remain silent, then my silence too will continue to affect the world endlessly. Who will be responsible for it when I am gone?

Perhaps the wave that gave rise to the wave which drowned the child in the ocean is no more in existence, and we will not hold it responsible for the child's death. But Krishna will definitely hold that wave responsible; he will never let it go blameless. Krishna will say that both our being and non-being have a hand in creating this great web of life on earth, and in no way can we escape involvement and responsibility. In fact, every wave is a member of every other wave and is responsible for every other wave.

So know well that a true sannyasin is one who is as much responsible for his non-doing as one who is responsible for his doing. Even in his inaction he is aware that he is doing. And he is not at all a sannyasin who says he is not responsible for what others do.

There are hundreds of thousands of sannyasins in India; never has there been any dirth of *sadhus* and sannyasins, monks and mendicants in this country. And this country has suffered political slavery for hundreds of years. Now these renunciates from the world can say, "We have nothing to do with the politics and political slavery of India; we own no responsibility for her social and political degradation." Their argument seems to be plausible, but it is erroneous.

And I say this attitude of theirs definitely had a hand in India's downfall and long political slavery. They cannot run away from this responsibility. At least an authentic sannyasin will never run away from responsibility. He is not only responsible for himself, but also for all others. He shares in the vices and virtues of the meanest of us all. Because we are not separate, we are not islands; we are one indivisible continent where everybody is a member of everybody else.

So one can remain a doer even when one does not do a thing. And it is very significant.

If I can remain a doer in non-doing, I will attain to non-attachment. Now there is no difference between my action and that of others; I cannot escape responsibility. If I abstain from stealing, it will not make a difference, because theft will continue in the rest of the world. And even if I steal it is not going to make a difference. If I am responsible for everything that happens anywhere in this wide world, if all vice and virtue, hate and love, war and peace, are mine, then there is no sense in owning this and disowning that.

If all hands are mine, then what difference does it make if I disown the two hands that hang on the sides of my body? If all eyes are mine, then it makes no difference if I am personally blinded. And if all homes are my homes, then there is no sense in my running away from the one that is called mine.

Sannyas affirms that every one is inseparably involved in this vast world of action and we cannot run away from it. Therefore it is good to know, and know on our own, that we do even when we don't do anything, we are responsible even for our inaction.

The other side of the coin, according to Krishna, is to know I am not doing even when I am doing something. Ordinarily this side seems simple, but knowing the side of our total involvement in the whole pattern of action, you cannot say it is that simple. It is really difficult. Someone says glibly that he can do things as if he is acting, but it is easier said than done. The truth is that even professional actors often forget they are actors; they become doers. They become so involved in acting that they think they are the very roles they are expected to play. They become so conditioned by long acting that they forget altogether their reality, they begin to identify themselves with their roles. They become what they are long accustomed to act.

This identification of an actor with his role, which is a kind of delusion, needs to be understood carefully. When even an actor is deluded into believing that he is the person whose part he is playing, how can the very person whose role is being played by the actor believe that he is acting a role? When someone playing the role of Rama in Ramaleela—Rama's play—sheds real tears when his wife Sita is stolen, it is difficult to think that the real Rama would not shed real tears. When even spectators in a drama begin to weep, it is quite possible the actor cries really. For the time being he forgets that he is only playing Rama's role. So when actors become victims of deluded identification it is really difficult for us in real life to conduct ourselves as if we are actors on the stage.

To take life as playacting is arduous, but not impossible. If we carefully watch the way we live, if we closely observe our daily life, it will not take long to know that we are really acting. You are passing on the street and someone asks, "How are you?" and you promptly say, "I am fine," and you never think what you are saying. Next time when it happens and you say, "I am fine," pause for a moment and think carefully if you are really fine. And you will know that what you said was nothing more than acting, it was not your reality. Someone meets you in a club and you say to him, "Good morning, I am so happy to see you." Stop then and there and look back to see if you were really happy to see him. If you carefully watch your day-to-day life you will soon come to know that it is all acting.

Whenever you do something and think yourself to be a doer—and such moments are many—reflect inside if what you have done is real. You say to your loved one, "I love you with all my being; I cannot live without you." Look back and examine yourself: "Is it true that I cannot live without my lover?" How many people have really died for the sake of love? And you will know clearly how you act in your day-to-day life. Watch every step of your life, every single thing that you do, every word that you say, and you will realize that it is different from playacting.

I love to tell the stories of Mulla Nasruddin.

He falls in love with a king's wife. He spends a night with her and at the break of dawn he is preparing to take leave of his beloved. With great feeling he says to her, "You are the most beautiful and loving woman I have ever met; I cannot live without you." Hearing this the queen begins to shed tears of happiness. Nasruddin then turns back and says, "But I have said the same thing to many women in the past. I say I cannot live without them and I go on living. And I am going to live so that I have occasions in life to say it to other women too. And I have also spoken the same cliché to many women: 'You are the most beautiful woman on this earth.'"

This shocks the queen; she is now grievously hurt and angry. Then the Mulla says, "I was just playing a joke; really I cannot live without you." And the queen is pleased once again.

This man Nasruddin knows that life is a play and nothing more, and he can go through life as an actor, treating the world as a play. But it is not that easy for his beloved to know; she has taken it very seriously.

It is not that you will miss anything if you take life as a play. The truth is that it will add to the quality of your life; it will make for its richness and excellence. Therefore Krishna says, "Yoga brings excellence to your action." In fact, when life becomes a play, all its pinpricks and hurts go, all its thorns disappear and we are left with its flowers in our hands. If life is a play, why should anyone burn himself in the hellfire of hate and anger? Then only a madman will enact anger and hate in his life; all sensible people will enact only affection and love. If you have to dream, why dream that you are a beggar? Then everyone will dream they are kings.

If I explore my doings with attention I will find that I am playing roles all along the road of life. I am acting the role of a father and a son, a mother and a daughter, a wife and a husband, a friend and a foe. You really need to observe and examine all your actions minutely and see if they are different from acting. And you will soon laugh at yourself. Maybe you are crying and watching your tears, and soon you begin to laugh inside. Maybe you are one thing on the outside and quite its opposite within. And by and by your life will turn into a play.

A Zen monk was dying. He called a few of his friends and said, "Countless people have died; I am going to die too. But I want to die in some novel manner. It is time we should change the ways of dying. Enough is enough. Please help me."

His friends laughed saying, "What are you talking about? Is dying a joke?"

The monk queried, "Have you heard that anyone died walking? That he kept walking and died?" His friends shook their heads. But an old man among them said, "I have read in some story book about a monk who has died walking. And the dying monk had observed before his death that only a saint could die in this manner."

The dying monk said, "Then it is not a novel way; someone has already used it. Can you say if someone died standing?" One of his friends said that he had heard about such a case. Then the monk said, "One dies the way one lives. It is possible someone died standing. But have you heard if someone died in the headstand posture of yoga?" His friends said laughing, "We have neither heard nor can we think that someone can die standing on his head. It is impossible."

The monk leaped at the suggestion, stood in the headstand posture and died.

Dying in this way he created a problem for the whole monastery. How to take down his dead body was the problem. People were also scared by the very sight of such a death. It was really an unheard of way, a dangerous way of dying. They were not even sure that he was really dead. They examined him in every way and found that his breathing, his pulse, his heartbeat, had stopped. Yet they could not decide how to handle his corpse. Never before had they faced such a situation, nor heard of it. This monk was known for his unconventional ways, he had been a troublemaker all his life, and the way he chose to die created the greatest trouble ever.

So they conferred among themselves at length. Not even the intimate friends of the dead monk had a workable suggestion to offer. Then the oldest among them, the one who had read about someone dying while walking, said that the elder sister of the dead monk—who was a nun—lived in a neighboring monastery. She could be of some help to them, because she knows her brother well and whenever he made any trouble in the past she was called to discipline him.

His sister was a ninety-year-old woman living in a nearby village. When she came, she tapped her brother's dead body with her staff saying, "Can't you give up being naughty even when you are going to die? Is this the way to die? Die properly!"

Immediately the monk stood on his legs and said to his sister, "Please don't be angry; now I will die properly. It does not make any difference to me." And he lay on the ground and died.

His sister picked up her staff and left for her monastery. She did not even look back on her dead brother or his friends.

This man, who can die playfully, knows that life is a play. He can live playfully and die playfully. And he also knows what action without a motive, without being attached to its fruits is. When one turns his work into play, his whole life becomes a play. Then he can take everything, including death, as a play. But it is possible only when you know the real actor within you. You don't have to act; you are already acting, and you have only to know the truth of it.

Krishna does not tell you to become an actor, or to practice acting. If you practice you will remain a doer, and you will become serious about every role. Krishna says you have only to know the reality of your life. As far as he is concerned, he knows for himself that it is nothing different from acting. And once you know it for yourself you will cease to be a doer in life. Then your life will turn into a play, and that is what sannyas is.

Krishna speaks of two kinds of action: one is action without attachment, and another is inaction with a sense of involvement in action. These are the two ways of sannyas and action, and it depends on you which way you choose for yourself. Someone can choose doing and yet remain a non-doer, and another can opt for non-doing and yet remain a doer.

These are really two types of people in the world, and you have to know your own type. As I see it, a male mind will choose doing and yet remain a non-doer, and a female mind will choose non-doing and yet remain a doer. There is a basic difference between the two minds—male and female minds. While the male mind is active, the feminine is passive. If a woman has to do something she will do it as if she is not doing. And to the contrary a man, even when he is inactive, seems to be active and aggressive.

These are two broad divisions of the mind— the male mind and the female mind. I call them broad divisions because not all men are aggressive nor are all women passive. There are men with feminine minds and women with male minds. Even if a woman wants to do a thing, she does it as if she is doing nothing. If she loves a man she does not express her love to him directly. She hides it in every way, she turns her love into a non-doing. A man on the other hand, will show off his love even if he is not really loving to a woman.

Remember, I am not talking about man and woman; I am talking about the male mind and the female mind. You will come across a few men who love passively, and similarly a few women who love aggressively. Krishna's division approximates this division of masculine and feminine mind.

As far as sannyas is concerned it is one and indivisible, but you can approach it in two ways. A person with a feminine mind, one who can surrender and wait, will approach sannyas by way of inaction. Non-doing will be his pattern, his way, but he will know that non-doing is his doing; he remains a doer even in his non-doing.

For example, when a woman comes to love a man she does not take the initiative. For this reason some men feel deceived, being unaware of the ways of feminine love. But the woman knows that she has set the ball of love rolling in her own way. Waiting is the way of her initiative; she waits. Feminine love is not articulate, while masculine love is. That is why a woman is hurt if the man she loves does not respond to her silent love in an articulate manner. If a man begins to love a woman without expressing his love in words, the woman will never come to like him. The woman will never really know that he loves her unless he expresses his love in an aggressive manner.

This is the dialectics of male and female love. While the woman on her part remains passive, waiting and expectant, she wants her lover to be aggressive and articulate in his love. Unless a man is assertive and aggressive in his love, the woman won't believe he truly loves her. That is why a quiet and peaceful man, rich in goodness but lacking in aggressiveness, fails to satisfy a woman. But a woman feels at home with even a mean man if his love is aggressive and articulate. On the other hand, a man is averse to a woman who is assertive and aggressive.

Krishna has made this division of action and inaction in accord with the two types of human mind—the male mind and the female mind. The male mind will choose action without being a doer, and the female mind will adopt inaction and yet remain a doer. Those are two sides of the same coin.

> Questioner: There is a problem with action without attachment and what you call the inaction of sannyas: it kills incentive to work. It is like our public sector in industries; while there is enough room for incentive in the private sector, there is very little in the public one. Please explain.

It is possible, if people don't choose rightly between action and inaction, don't choose according to their types.

As I said, there are two types of minds—male and female. If a person of feminine mind—who can be a doer without doing—becomes a sannyasin, he will turn sannyas into inaction. Action without being a doer is not his way. But if a male mind takes sannyas, then action will be his way, and he will know in his depth that he is not a doer, action just happens. If such a mind chooses inaction he will lose incentive and will become dull and lethargic. The problem always arises because of the wrong choice.

Therefore it is very important that everyone should know his type rightly. If someone's choice of action or inaction does not accord with his basic type, he will certainly have difficulties; his life will become dull and lackluster. Only if you don't commit the mistake of choosing the wrong thing for yourself, only if you choose rightly will your action gain vigor and vitality. It will be expansive and rich. There is only one thing that undermines the action of a male mind, and it is the idea of being a doer. If the doer disappears, leaving action free and on its own, then there is no end to its dynamism; you cannot even imagine how explosive it can become. The action of one who has ceased to be a doer gathers its full momentum; it becomes total. The great amount of energy that was spent in being a doer will now be exclusively available to action, making it dynamic and total.

Similarly if a person with a feminine mind, who is not meant for action as we know it, fully accepts his or her inaction, then this inaction will generate in its own way such immense action that you cannot even imagine. Because then his or her whole energy will be together and total. And this summation of energy is explosive. But the ways of a feminine mind will be totally different from those of the masculine mind.

But most of us err on this score; we often choose the opposite. And it is not without its reasons.

In all our life the opposite attracts; man attracts woman and woman attracts man. Always the opposite is attractive. Life is a play of attraction of the opposites; yin attracts yang and vice-versa. This is the way of nature, of biology. Even spiritualism is not unaffected by this rule, although it is a different journey altogether. Spiritualism is a pilgrimage to self-nature, to being oneself. You don't have to seek through spiritualism that which attracts you, that which is your opposite. On the contrary, you seek that which you are; you seek your own pristine nature, your original face.

But ordinarily your life is a search for the opposites.

I have heard . . . It happened once that the inhabitants of a small island in the sea became lazy and lethargic and ceased all activity. All farms and cottage industries became idle. Men and women ate whatever came to their hands and idled away their time doing nothing. The sage, the spiritual head of the island became worried; people even stopped going to him. He went about shouting that they had become idlers, but no one was prepared to listen to him. Even listening to his wise advice was heavy on them. Slowly life on the island began to shrink and wither away; it came to a standstill, which made the sage really anxious. But he could not figure out any way to help his people.

Ultimately the sage went to a very old man of the island and consulted him about the problem. The old man said, "Now there is only one way to resolve the issue: we have to segregate our women from their men. We should send all our women to a neighboring island, leaving all the men here."

The sage asked, "What will it do?"

The old man answered, "Soon the menfolk will be busy building boats and the women will begin preparations to receive their men. It is now imperative to separate them, to separate the opposites; otherwise they will never return to active life."

And the magic worked.

In youth everyone is so active, and as he grows old all activity begins to ebb. Why? Just for the reason that the youth is packed with feminine and masculine energy, so young men and women become busy building boats and preparing for adventures. With the advent of old age, the fire of life dims considerably. By this time men and women come to know all about each other, and so the pull of the opposites withers away. Too much familiarity breeds indifference.

As it is the natural law of life that the opposite attracts, so it is the natural law of spiritualism that self-nature attracts, not the opposite. Here the similar, the same attracts. Because of this, we find ourselves in trouble when we apply the ordinary law of the world to spiritual discipline. For this very reason, countries where spiritualism grows become lazy and inactive. India is the living example. We wrongly applied the law of matter in choosing our spiritual discipline. People with male minds took paths meant for feminine minds, and those with feminine minds took the opposite paths. The one who was meant to be a Meera turned into a Mahavira and another meant to be a Mahavira turned into a Meera. Naturally we made a mess of everything. It was bound to be so.

Therefore, I envision a scientific discipline for the spiritualism of the future whose basic law will clearly say: no law of biology applies to spiritualism. In biology the opposite attracts; in spiritualism self-nature is the magnet. Spiritualism is not comprised of the attraction of opposites; it is actually one's immersion in self-nature. In the spiritual journey I don't have to reach the other; I have to reach myself.

But our lifelong habits come in the way.

I have heard . . . When electricity became available, Sigmund Freud had his house electrified. Soon after this he had a visitor from the countryside who had never seen electricity; he was only familiar with lanterns and lamps as instruments of light.

After the night's supper, Freud put his guest in one of the bedrooms and took leave of him for the night. But his guest was immediately faced with a serious problem—it was a problem caused by electricity.

Since the light in the room was so bright, the man could not sleep. How to extinguish the light was the problem. Because the bulb hung high from the ceiling of the room, he fetched a ladder from somewhere, climbed it and began to try to blow out the light. But he failed, and failed miserably. How can one extinguish an electric light with the breath? He was in a quandary. He looked all around the room, he examined the bulb from every side again and again to find a hole through which he could blow it out. But nothing helped. He felt embarrassed to go to Freud and tell him he did not know how to extinguish the light in his room.

And thus he kept turning and tossing in his bed till his host came to say good morning to him. When Freud asked him why he did not put out the light he said, "Now that you have asked I should tell you of my struggle with your lighting device. I could not get a wink of sleep the whole night as the lamp stubbornly refused to be blown out."

Freud pushed a button saying, "You are a fool; it is so easy."

Now this man had no idea of light controlled by a distant switch. And we cannot blame him for that.

All our life's experience can be summed up in two words; attraction of the opposites. So even when we enter the world of spiritualism—which is a different dimension altogether—we carry our old ways with us. We try to blow out the electric light with our breath, and we never think of the switch. This error is centuries old and enduring. For this reason all spiritually advanced communities have become lethargic. Contrarily, sex-oriented communities are active and aggressive, and they are on the march to progress and prosperity. Every dynamic civilization in the world happens to be sex-oriented, and every passive and peaceful civilization is spiritual.

It has been so up to now, but it is not necessary that it should always be the case.

It is true that sex energy is the basic drive to action and dynamism. Wherever sex is freed from its fetters there will be an explosion of action and activity. If we look at nature we will find all activity arises from sex. If flowers bloom in the spring and birds build nests and the air is filled with scent and song, know that sex is behind all these lively activities. The bird is building a nest only to lay its eggs. The cuckoo is calling not to please you, but to invite and entice its sex partner. These are all biological activities.

Man too, is familiar only with biological activity. For this reason buildings in permissive societies, where sex is free, begin to touch the skies; they are nothing but extensions of the birds' nests. Permissive societies are humming with song, music and orchestra; they are full of colors and gay costumes. The same calls of the cuckoo and the dance of the peacocks! There is not much difference between the two.

Against this, countries that turn their backs on biological activities and take a different road, and yet by force of habit continue to follow the rule of opposites, become inert and sad and dull. Their houses turn into huts, their songs die and their colors fade out. Their whole life becomes flat and drab, poor and miserable.

As I see, both biology and spiritualism have their own laws. And a right kind of culture, a complete culture can come into being only if both biology and spiritualism are allowed to grow in their own ways. A right kind of culture will not suppress sex. It will accord it its due place in life; it will accept and enjoy sex without inhibition and guilt, it will celebrate sex. Such a culture will be expansive and it will generate immense activity. In the same way spiritualism, if allowed to grow on the basis of its natural laws—if seekers choose their disciplines rightly, in accord with their types—will lead to explosive action in the field of religion.

Krishna is in full accord with his own type; he does not deviate from his self-nature. So is Buddha. And Mahavira too. For this reason Krishna's life is crammed with action of a particular style. Not that Buddha lacks in action; his life is filled with a different kind of action. Mahavira keeps moving from one village to another for a full forty years. It is true that he does not take part in war, but he engages himself in a higher kind of war waged on a different level. Buddha does not play a flute, but his discourses resound with a note that is higher than that of the flute. It does not make a difference because Buddha is fully established in his own self-nature. He has found his authentic being at its highest. Krishna has discovered his own sublime reality, his truth, and he is complete and contented.

So far as men like Krishna, Buddha and Mahavira are concerned, they have found their true types, their authentic self-nature. But their followers often err in discovering their own authentic types: they become confused. To find one's intrinsic nature is of the highest in spiritualism. And I repeat Krishna's words: "It is better to perish in one's self-nature than to accept another's, which is perilous."

Questioner: How can one know his own distinctive type?

It is not that difficult to know one's type. One way is to remember this simple maxim: that which attracts you is not your type; it is the opposite of your own nature, because the opposite attracts. So beware of the opposite, reflect for a while on it and know that it is not your cup of tea. It seems paradoxical, and difficult too, to understand that what repels you is your type. How does a man know he is a man? Another man does not attract him, while a woman does. How does a woman know she is a woman? She wants to be with a man, not a woman. A woman repels another woman; it is difficult to keep two women together. So take it for a rule: you are not what attracts you; you are its opposite. You are really that which repels you.

It is really arduous to figure out this paradox, but life is paradoxical. It is difficult to believe that what you detest and condemn, what you want to avoid, to keep at arm's length, is invariably your own thing. It is within you. If someone is always in opposition to sex, then know that his unconscious is reeking with sex and sexuality. It is really complex. But if you care to understand it deeply, it is not that difficult. If someone condemns money, his very condemnation says that he craves money with his whole being. Similarly he is a worldly man who is trying to run away from the world. I mean to say that it is always your opposite that seems inviting to you. So beware of it and know that it is not your type.

Questioner: What if I am attracted now by one thing and then by another?

Then know that you are confused, nothing more.

Questioner: If two men share a common addiction they become friends.

You say if two men are addicted to the same thing they become friends. In this context a few things have to be understood.

It is possible two persons of the same type become friends if they share a common addiction, but such a friendship is not real, it is propped up by addiction. Remove the prop of addiction and the friendship will go down the drain. Two alcoholics become friends because they drink together, attend a common club, play common games. But it is alcohol that unites them. Remove the bottle and they will turn their backs on each other.

True friendship is always without a cause. Love is causeless. If there is a cause, it is just association, not friendship. And there is a great difference between association and friendship.

If two persons are traveling by a common route, they can come together and become friendly to each other—but it is not friendship. Reaching their destination they will part company. Friendship based on a common addiction is like friendship between fellow travelers. It is friendship in name only.

The truth is that friendship always happens between persons of opposite orientations. The opposite attracts, is the rule. The more opposite two persons are, the deeper their friendship. In fact, opposites are not really opposites, they are complementary to each other. Because of it you will rarely find two equally intelligent persons making friends; if they do they will only quarrel and wrangle over every conceivable issue. An intelligent person will find a stupid partner to join him in friendship, so they complement each other.

Two powerful persons will not make friends; not even two persons having the same skills. You will rarely come across two poets or two painters as intimate friends. If two poets become friends, the cause of friendship will be something other than poetry. Maybe they drink together or gamble together, but then it is association and not friendship.

Psychologists believe if there is intimate friendship between two men, deep down it is a homosexual relationship. Similarly they think any such intimacy between two women to be homosexual. You will find it difficult to agree with the psychologists, but there is some element of truth in what they say. It has been observed that more or less everyone misses the intimate friendship of his early years for the rest of his life, because there is a phase of homosexual relationship in everyone's life in his adolescence. Before they get interested in the opposite sex boys get interested in boys and girls in girls. In fact, before they attain sexual maturity there is not much difference between a boy and a girl as far as sex is concerned. So boys become interested in boys and girls in girls. For this reason friendships struck in the early years are so enduring.

After they attain sexual maturity, boys and girls who are psychologically natural and normal begin to take interest in the opposite sex. Then they become what psychologists call heterosexual. Old relationships are forgotten and new intimacies with the opposite sex begin to build up. Of course, about twenty to thirty percent of young men and women remain fixed at their adolescence, which means their psychological age is stuck at fourteen years. It means they are not growing psychologically; they are stunted and sick and need psychotherapy.

If a young woman of twenty-five continues to be interested in members of her own sex, if she refuses to take interest in some young men, there is certainly something wrong with her psyche and she needs treatment. It does not mean that now they will not enter into friendship with any members of their own sex;

they will—but it will be a kind of association, it cannot be real friendship. Two men or women will be friends if they are members of the same club—say the Rotary Club, or if they subscribe to the same political ideology—say communism, or they are disciples of the same guru. But these relationships can never have the depth and intimacy of the early years.

The opposite has great attraction. Look at it from some different angles. Often lovers of good clothes are attracted by a naked fakir; lovers of delicious dishes become disciples of a master who is known for fasting. It is ironic that the followers of a renunciate saint comprise those who are known for their indulgence. It is deserving of serious consideration that while Mahavira, the founder of Jainism remained naked, most of the Jainas chose to sell clothes—and they have been selling clothes down the centuries. For sure, people who loved good clothes were attracted by the nude Mahavira and they became his followers. It is surprising but true that Mahavira renounced a kingdom and became a beggar, and the Jainas are the richest community in India.

This is not accidental; there is a sound reason behind it. When Mahavira renounced his kingdom and wealth—he really gave away every bit of his possessions to the poor before he left for the forest—it was the wealthy class, chasing wealth that was most impressed by Mahavira's sacrifice. While they clung to every penny like leeches, there was Mahavira who threw away a whole kingdom. He became God in their eyes. Mahavira attracted them because of their attachment to wealth.

A renunciate would not be influenced by Mahavira. He would say, "There is nothing great in parting with trash; wealth is trash." But those who took trash for diamonds bowed down to Mahavira and worshipped him. Even one who cannot give up a thing cherishes a desire to give up; renunciation becomes his ideal, his dream. He knows in his heart of hearts that clinging is painful and he dreams of the day when he will be capable of renunciation. So a renunciate becomes his polestar; he worships him as his God. This is how renunciates are surrounded by those who are steeped in indulgence.

The opposite works like a magnet, it is magnetic. And it works on its own as every scientific law does. If we understand this law rightly we can divide the whole world into different magnetic fields of consciousness, as the physicists do in regard to matter and energy. Then we will know how consciousness is attracted, drawn and formed and then it disappears. Very strange things happen in the world of consciousness which are not apparent.

So whenever you are attracted to someone, know well that he is not your type—he is your opposite, your complementary. He can never help you in your spiritual journey. He can however be helpful in your worldly life, and he can also help you in a way to know your type.

Remember, spiritualism is a search of the self, of self-nature. You have to know who you are. And once you know who you are, you will attain to inaction without quitting action. You will attain to truth without leaving the world. The world will remain as it is, but you will undergo a mutation. Everything will remain the same, but you will not remain the same, you will be transformed. And the day you are transformed, everything is transformed for you because what you see is your world. Your perception creates your world.

Questioner: Krishna says to Arjuna, "If you fight, treating equally victory and defeat, gain and loss, pleasure and pain, no sin will attach to you, *and you will go to heaven." Does it mean that if one fights without attachment then violence ceases to be violence?*

A few things need to be understood in the context of this question.

The first thing Krishna says is that violence is a lie which does not exist; violence is an illusion, it is not real. Nobody can be killed really. Krishna says, *"Na hanyate hanyamane sharire:* nobody is killed when his body is killed." And so far as the body is concerned, it is already dead; so it is wrong to say that the body dies.

In the first place Krishna says that violence is impossible, it is a misnomer. But it does not mean that one should freely indulge in violence. While violence itself is not real, violent mind is real. It is true, you can desire to kill someone, although he cannot be killed. This is a different thing—that one cannot be killed—but if you desire to kill him then this desire is real, and this desire is sinful. Violence is not a sin, but the will to violence, a violent mind is certainly a sin. If you want to kill someone, it is enough of a sin. It is a different thing that you cannot kill, but your desire to kill is in itself sinful.

In the same way it is a virtue if you desire to save someone. Whether he will be saved or not is a different matter, but the fact that you want to save him is enough unto itself; this desire is virtuous. For example, someone is dying, he is a terminal case, and you are trying to save him. He is going to die tomorrow, but you have already earned merit by trying to save him.

The desire to hurt others is sinful, and the desire to help others is virtuous.

But Krishna soars still higher; he says one can transcend both violence and non-violence, vice and virtue, pleasure and pain, and then there is nothing—neither violence nor non-violence, neither vice nor virture. They all are illusory.

If one goes beyond the dialectics of violence and non-violence, pain and pleasure, if he knows for himself they are illusory, then in the very knowing all his violent thoughts and feelings will drop, he will be free of them. When you realize that no one is killed, then why will you think of killing? When you know that no one is saved, you will not be bothered with the problem. And if, in the light of truth, you know your mind with all its urges and emotions, you will attain to heaven. Then it is not a question of going to heaven in some future time, you are already in heaven.

When one attains to a state where pleasure and pain, gain and loss, victory and defeat are all alike, when one transcends all dualities and divisions, when one realizes the integrity and oneness of life then he is in heaven. Because this state of equanimity and evenness itself is heaven.

According to Krishna, this *samatvabuddhi*, this balance and steadiness, equanimity and evenness of intelligence is called yoga.

Krishna says there are two kinds of illusions. One is that you think that someone can be killed, and the other that you can kill him. Similarly it is an illusion to think that someone can be saved and that you can save him. When you are released from the first illusion that someone can be killed or saved, then the second illusion that you sin by killing and earn merit by saving will drop by itself.

The idea of vice and virtue is part of the same ignorance which makes you believe that life and death is a reality. If life and death is an illusion, then what is, is. Then vice and virtue are equally illusory. And to know what is illusory, to know the false as false, is knowledge. It is wisdom. And one established in wisdom does not do a thing on his part, he allows everything within and without to happen on its own. It is a state of total acceptance.

Krishna says this much to Arjuna: "See and accept that which is, and don't interfere with the ways of existence. Don't swim upstream in the river of life; just float with it. If you do so you are in heaven."

NINETEENTH DISCOURSE
MORNING, OCTOBER 4, 1970
MANALI, INDIA

RITUALS, FIRE AND KNOWLEDGE

Questioner: Yajnas or rituals have an important place in spiritual discipline, and there are many forms of yajnas or sacrificial rituals mentioned in the scriptures. But the Geeta attaches special importance to japa-yajna and jnana-yajna—the rituals of chanting and knowledge. Talking about the significance of japa or chanting, you mentioned ajapa or wordless chanting. So please explain to us the significance of japa-yajna, jnana-yajna and ajapa as envisioned by the Geeta.

ituals have an important place in human life; what we call life is ninety percent ritual. Human mind is such that it takes recourse to many seemingly unnecessary activities so that the harshness of life's journey is mitigated.

In the course of man's long history thousands of such rituals—I would like to call them plays—have been developed. If they are taken playfully they add juice to life, they become occasions for celebration. And if we take them too seriously they become pathological, an aberration.

It was a D-day in the whole life of the human race when fire was discovered for the first time. It is the greatest discovery ever made throughout man's history. We do not know the name of the person who first discovered fire; whoever he was, he made the greatest revolution in man's life. Since then man has discovered many other things. There has been a galaxy of great names like Copernicus, Galileo, Kepler, Einstein, Max Planck—but none of them reaches the height of that unknown person who first discovered fire. Even the splitting of the atom and landing on the moon are not that important.

Now the same fire is such a common and ordinary thing in our day-to-day life—we have captured it in a tiny matchstick—that we cannot comprehend its pristine glory; but it was not so ordinary in the distant past. We are indebted to fire for most of the growth and progress our civilization and culture have achieved down the ages. Human civilization today is essentially the product of fire. None of the great inventions of history would have been possible without this igniting spark called fire. Fire is foundational to everything in our life.

Evidently when it was first discovered, we celebrated the occasion by dancing around it in utter ecstasy. This celebration, now turned into a ritual, was so natural and spontaneous—as if it had exploded on us from nowhere. There was no other way to express our gratefulness to existence except by dancing and celebrating. And we said fire was God, because it occupied such a central place in man's life.

Every religion in ancient times grew around fire or the sun. The night was frightening; it was full of darkness and danger and man was terribly afraid of wild animals and snakes and reptiles. And the day was comforting, full of light and warmth. One could look around and take care of himself against any danger. So darkness looked inimical and the sun seemed friendly. With darkness there was danger and death. With light there was hope; fear disappeared and everything was relatively safe. So human beings worshipped the sun as God. When fire was discovered, it heralded man's victory over darkness, and so he began to love fire more than anything—including the sun. Naturally many beautiful things like song and dance, love and festivity grew around fire.

You know when Yuri Gagarin returned from his voyage into space—he was the first man to enter outer space—the whole world joined to celebrate the event. Overnight Gagarin became world renowned; his name reached the farthest corners of the earth. Hundreds of thousands of newborn babies all over the world were named after him. It takes a lifetime to attain to the fame which this first astronaut achieved in no time, because he orbited the earth. It was a great event, an epochal event. Wherever Gagarin went, people went mad to receive him; wherever he went, millions thronged to see him. Hundreds of people lost their lives in stampedes caused by his visit. Why this madness?

The advent of the new fills man's heart with delight and joy, and he always celebrates the occasion with great fanfare. As we celebrate the birth of a child with song, music and feasting, so we welcome everything new and rejoice over it. That is how it should be. It will be a sad day when we cease to rejoice over the new; it will mean the death of all that is meaningful and vital in our life.

I say all this to explain to you how *yajna* came into being and how it became so significant in our life. *Yajna* was our way of celebrating the discovery of fire; we danced around it with abandon and offered to it every good thing we had.

Our ancestors who initiated these sacrificial rituals did not have much to give. They had wheat and they made an offering of it to the fire. They had *somras*, the best wine of their times, and they offered it to the fire. They sacrificed even their best cows to greet this god who had come to transform their life so radically. And everything was so impromptu and spontaneous. It was an outpouring of a simple, innocent and unsophisticated heart-mind that our people had then. They were a rural people—cities had yet to come into being—who lacked sophistication.

By the time of Krishna and the *Geeta* civilization had made great strides—thanks to fire. And so fire became a household thing, the extraordinary became ordinary. Now it seemed meaningless to dance around fire and make sacrificial offerings to it. In the meantime thousands of people had opposed it. Fire was no longer taken as the greatest blessing that it was when it was first discovered. So Krishna grafted a new word onto the old stem of *yajna* and called it *jnan-yajna* or the ritual of knowledge. A new word, *jnan* or knowledge was added to the old word, *yajna* or ritual.

Vinoba Bhave is now doing the same thing, he has started a *bhoodan yajna*, popularly known as the Land-gift Movement. The ancient word *yajna* has been yoked to a socio-political concept known as *bhoodan* or land-gift.

The society in which Krishna was born was a highly developed and sophisticated society. Now dancing around fire looked so primitive and backward. So Krishna thought of igniting the fire of knowledge, which is the last luxury of a society that comes to the pinnacle of material prosperity. But he used an old word, because a word to be a word has to be old. Krishna said, "If we want to dance we will dance around the fire of knowledge. If we have to offer something to the sacrificial fire we will offer ourselves in place of grains and wines and cows."

Jnan-yajna or sacrificial ritual of knowledge stands for a special spiritual path, and every traveler on this path burns his ego, his "I-ness" in the fire of the knowledge of reality. Ordinary fire burns everything that is gross, but it cannot burn subtler elements like thoughts of arrogance, pride and ego. Only the fire of knowing can destroy it.

It is interesting to know that down the centuries the symbol of fire remains alive. And it is not without reason.

The most important reason was that in the life of the primitive man there was nothing like fire which by its nature moved upward. Water moves downward: pour it anywhere and it will find a downward path to flow. But no matter what you do, the flame will always rise upward. Even if you turn a burning torch upside down, its flames will keep going up. So fire became the symbol of ascension—upward journey; its flame reflects man's highest aspiration to reach the unknown.

Fire was the first thing in the knowledge of man that rebelled against the law of gravitation. The earth seems to have no power over fire. So those who danced around fire and rejoiced over its blessings also nursed a hope and prayer that a day might come in their life when they would go on the upward journey to the highest, the ultimate in existence.

Like water, human mind as we know it is inclined to move downward. There is some similarity between man's mind and water. Pour a container full of water on the hilltop and it will soon find its way down to the lowest lake in the valley. Such is man's mind. Therefore the seers who first exalted the fire and danced around it in joyous homage declared their aspiration to become like fire and ascend to the heavens. Their prayer said, "We want to turn our spirit into a flame so that even if it is put in an abyss it will continue to move upward and reach the zenith." So the ritual of the sacrificial fire was symbolic and significant.

There is another attribute of fire which is still deeper and more meaningful; it is that first it burns its fuel and then burns itself. As soon as the fuel turns into ashes the fire is extinguished. This aspect of fire is deeply representative of knowledge, which first burns the dross of ignorance and then burns itself. It means to say that after one's ignorance is dispelled, the ego, the knower himself disappears. The *Upanishad* says, "While the ignorant wander in darkness the knowledgeable wander in blinding darkness." For sure, this has been said to ridicule the pundits and scholars who subsist on borrowed knowledge. One who attains to true knowledge, what is called wisdom, disappears as an ego, and so there is no way for him to wander in darkness. True knowledge first destroys ignorance and then it destroys the knower too, who ceases to be an ego, an entity. It is like fire, that after burning the fuel extinguishes itself.

So those who came to know the truth realized that knowledge is like fire. It burns ignorance like fuel, and then burns the knower as an ego, who disappears into emptiness. Therefore, he alone can embark on a journey to knowledge who is prepared to become an utter emptiness, nothingness.

There is yet another attribute of fire which is still more relevant to the knowledge of truth. As the fire's flame rises upward it is visible only to an extent and then disappears into the vast space; it becomes invisible. The same is the case with the knowledge of truth; it is related with its knower only to a small extent and then it disappears into that which is unknowable. The visible part of reality is very tiny in comparison with its invisible part which is immense and infinite.

For all these reasons fire became a very useful and powerful symbol of knowledge, and Krishna ushered in *jnan-yajna*. Worship of knowledge is like worship of fire.

If you rightly understand the significance of fire as a symbol, you will know that worship of knowledge is eternal. While all other rituals that came into being with the discovery of fire have died because they were products of circumstances, the pursuit of knowledge remains with us forever. Knowledge is not bound with circumstances; it is eternal. So for the first time Krishna freed *yajna* from the fetters of time and events and yoked it to the eternal. From now on in the future, *yajna* or rituals will be in vogue in the way Krishna refashioned it; its meaning and purpose will be derived from Krishna alone. The pre-Krishna chapter of *yajna* is closed forever. It is now outdated and dead. If someone still talks of the *yajna* of the pre-Krishna days, he is only trying to perpetuate a dead and meaningless ritual. Now it is not possible to dance around fire in the old way, because fire is no more an event, it is an everyday affair.

Krishna talks about another kind of *yajna* which is *japa-yajna* or the ritual of chanting. The secret of *japa* is the same as that of knowledge. *Japa* at first burns all your thoughts, and then it burns itself— the thought of *japa* or chanting. And what remains is knowns as *ajapa*—wordless chanting. For this reason it is called *yajna*, because it works like fire.

Your mind is stuffed with thoughts, all kinds of junk. So you use a word for chanting, and with the help of this chanting you banish from your mind all other thoughts—except the one thought which is your word for chanting. However, when all other thoughts disappear, then this last thought—the thought of chanting—becomes unnecessary and it drops on its own. It is followed by a state of utter silence which is called *ajapa* or wordless chanting or non-chanting. So *ajapa* too, is a kind of fire which first burns the fuel and then burns itself.

But there is a danger with chanting just as with knowledge. In fact, there is danger with every kind of spiritual discipline. There is no path from which one is not going to deviate. Every path leading to a destination has its bypaths of deviation, and you can use them to deviate from your journey. The truth is that we use paths more to digress from them than to reach.

For example, Krishna talks about the path of knowledge. For most people knowledge is scholarship, information, concepts, ideas, doctrines. If someone mistakes knowledgeability for knowledge he is on a wrong path, he is going astray. Now he cannot attain to truth, to knowledge, even if he crams his head full of all the scriptures there are in the world. And remember, ignorance is not as harmful as false knowledge. False knowledge is harmful, pernicious. It is lifeless, it lacks fire altogether. Pseudo knowledge is like ashes left after the fire has been extinguished. You can collect ashes in tons, but they are not going to change you. So if someone mistakes scholarship for knowledge he is already off the track.

It is the same with *japa* or chanting. If someone thinks he will reach through chanting he is mistaken. No one has ever found God or truth by chanting the name of Rama or Ave Maria. Chanting is like a thorn—one uses it to take out another thorn sticking in his flesh and then throws away the two together. Both thorns are equally useless. If he leaves the second thorn in the place of the first, thinking it is something valuable, then he will continue to suffer. And he is for sure a stupid person. But there is no dearth of such stupid people in the world.

Buddha had a beautiful story he loved to tell again and again. A group of eight persons—perhaps they were all pundits and priests—crossed a big river in a country boat. Reaching the other bank they conferred among themselves as to what they should do with the boat which had helped them to cross the river. One—perhaps the most knowledgeable among them—suggested that they were indebted to the boat for having done such a great job for them, and so they should carry it on their heads to repay the debt. Everyone agreed with him and they lifted the boat to their heads and carried it to the next village they were scheduled to visit.

The people of the village were amazed to find their guests carrying a big boat on their heads. They said, "What are you doing? A boat is meant to carry us; we are not meant to carry the boat on our heads. Why did you not leave it in the river?"

The visitors said, "It seems you are all very ungrateful people. We know what gratefulness is. This boat helped us cross the river, now we are repaying our debt to it. It is going to stay on our heads forever."

Buddha says many people turn means into ends and cling to them for the rest of their lives. A boat is useful for crossing a river; we are not supposed to carry it on our heads after it has served our purpose.

Japa can be used with the awareness that it is a means which helps one to be free of his thoughts. But if someone takes *japa* to be an end in itself, of course he will be free of other thoughts but he will be a prisoner of this *japa* which is as good as a thought. His mind will remain as burdened and tense as ever. There is no difference between a mind teeming with thoughts and another filled with the chanting of Rama or Ave Maria. They are equally tense and restless. It is possible a thought-filled mind can achieve something worthwhile in the workaday world; a few of his thoughts may be found useful. But as far as the chanting-filled mind is concerned, it is completely a waste. But this man will say what helped to free him from wasteful thoughts is something valuable, and he is not going to part with it. This man is carrying a boat on his head.

To give *japa* the place of a *yajna* or sacrificial ritual has a deep secret, it is meaningful. When Krishna calls it a *yajna*, a sacrificial ritual, he means to say that *japa* is also like fire, which first burns its fuel and then burns itself. And it is meaningful only when it burns itself.

So we can use a word, a mantra, a seed word, as a means to cast away other words from our minds. But ultimately we have to throw away the mantra itself. If we get attached to the mantra, if we cling to it, then it will cease to be *japa*; it will turn instead into a kind of hypnotic trap, you will be a prisoner of its hypnosis. If you become obsessed with *japa*, you will go berserk. There are people who get so fixated with *japa* that they begin to derive an infantile kind of gratification from it, and then they can never be able to part with it. Then it becomes pathological.

Japa has to be used with awareness. If you are a witness while chanting a name or a mantra, if you know that while chanting goes on at the mental level, you remain a witness to it, then you are making a right use of *japa*. And it is only then that some day you will be able to go beyond it. And then *japa* becomes a *yajna*, a fire which first burns its fuel and then burns itself. And when you are empty, utterly empty, silent, you attain to meditation, you attain to *samadhi* or superconsciousness.

For this reason Krishna gives both knowledge and *japa* the status of *yajna*, because *yajna* happens around fire. And fire is immensely significant. If you understand the significance of fire, you will understand what *jnan-yajna* or *japa-yajna* is. The truth is: one who is ready to burn his ego, his "I", who is ready to totally efface himself, is ready for *yajna*. He alone is deserving of *yajna* who is capable of making an offering of himself into the fire of knowledge. And then all other *yajnas* fade into insignificance before this great *yajna*, which I call the *yajna* of life.

> Questioner: Krishna says a man of
> wisdom, who gives up attachment to
> the fruit of action, is released from
> the bondage of birth and death and
> becomes one with the ultimate. How
> is it that Krishna believes that life is
> a bondage? You don't believe so, you
> say this very life is freedom, this very
> world the nirvana. Please explain.

Krishna says a wise man gives up attachment to the
fruits of action and attains to freedom from the bondage of birth and death. The whole thing needs to be
understood in depth.

Firstly, Krishna does not talk about one's release from action itself, he emphasizes release from
attachment to the fruits of action. He does not ask
you to give up action and become inactive; he only
urges you not to do something with a motive, with
an eye on the results of the action. There is a meaningful difference between action and the fruit of action. It is in the interest of action itself, to make
action real and total, that all wise men urge you to
give up your desire for its result. Action without attachment to its fruit is what forms the heart of
Krishna's teaching.

I would like to go deeply into this important
matter of action without attachment to its fruits, because it is really arduous. Ordinarily, if you give up
your desire for the fruit of action, you will give up
action itself. If someone tells you to do something,
but not to expect any result from it, you will say, "It
is sheer madness to suggest such a thing. Why should
anyone do something if he does not want to achieve
a result? Everyone works with a motive to achieve
something, be it bread, or money, or fame. If there
is no motive to work, why should one work at all?"

This phrase "freedom from attachment to the fruit of action" has put many interpreters of Krishna in difficulty. These interpreters were themselves at a loss to understand or accept Krishna's emphasis on renunciation of the fruits of action. So they found a clever way to circumvent the real meaning of Krishna's teaching and bring in "the fruit of action" by the back door. They said one who relinquishes attachment to the result of one's labor attains to *moksha*, liberation. So the fruit of action was back in the form of liberation

What is after all this "fruit of action"? We often say, "If you do this you will achieve that," or "If you do this you will not achieve that." This is what we mean by the term "fruiit of action." It is the same if you say that one attains to liberation if he gives up his attachment to the fruit of action. In my view, however, these interpreters have been very unjust to Krishna. They have betrayed him.

When Krishna says "A wise man, who gives up attachment to the fruit of action is released from the bondage of birth and death," he is not providing an incentive to desireless action. An action with an incentive can never be desireless, because what is incentive but a desire for result? Krishna's "release from bondage" is a consequence which follows desireless action as its shadow.

Krishna does not say that those who want to be free from the bondage of birth should give up attachment to the fruit of their action. If he says so, he is providing a motive, he is contradicting himself. No, he only says that freedom or liberation is a consequence of desireless action, not its motive. One who desires liberation or freedom can never come to it, because desiring is the barrier. So the question is: How to work without attachment to result?

To understand this thing rightly, it is first necessary to know that there are two kinds of action in our life. One of these is what we do today in order to achieve something tomorrow as a result. Such an action is future-oriented; future is leading you into action. Just as an animal is dragged by a rope tied to its neck, so our future is dragging us into action. I do something with an eye on the future when my action of today will yield some result for me. While action takes place in the present, its fruit lies in the future. And the future is unknown and uncertain. Future means that which is not in existence, which is only a hope, a dream, an expectation. In that hope we are being dragged like cattle by our future.

The Sanskrit word for animal is *pashu*, which is meaningful. *Pashu* is derived from *pash* which means bondage. Hence *pashu* is one who is a captive, a slave. In that sense we are all animals, because we are captives of the future, we live in future hopes. The reins of our life are in the hands of the future. Man always lives today in the hope of tomorrow. And likewise he will live tomorrow in the hope of the day after, because when tomorrow comes, it will come as today. So he never lives really, he goes on postponing living for the future.

And he will never live as long as he lives on hope for the future. His whole life will pass away unlived and unfulfilled. At the time of his death he will say with great remorse, "All my life I only desired to live, but I could not really live." And his greatest sorrow at the time of death will be that the future is no more, there is no hope of achieving results in the future. If there was a future and a hope beyond death, he would have no regrets. That is why a dying man wants to know if there is life after death. In reality he wants to know if there is any chance of reaping a harvest of hopes in the future, because it was only hopes that he had sown in the soil of his life.

He had wasted all his todays in the hope of a tomorrow that never came. And on the last day of his life he faces a cul-de-sac beyond which there is no tomorrow, and no hope of any fruits of action. That is the despair of a future-oriented life.

There is another kind of action which is not future-oriented, which is not done with a motive to achieve some future result, which is not based on any ideas and patterns. Such an action is natural and spontaneous; it arises from the depths of our being. It springs from what I am, not from what I want to become. You are passing down a street when you come across an umbrella dropped unaware by a person walking ahead of you. You pick up the umbrella and hand it to the owner without any fuss. You don't look around for a press reporter or a photographer to report to the public your great act of selfless service to a fellow traveler. You don't even expect a "thank you" from the person concerned, nor hope for any results in the future. This is what I call a natural and spontaneous act.

But if the owner of the umbrella goes his way without thanking you, and if you feel even slightly hurt thinking how ungrateful the man is, then your action is no more natural and spontaneous, it is not without motive. Maybe you were not aware of your expectation of a thank you when you picked up the umbrella and handed it to him, but it was very much there in your unconscious. An expectation even of a thank you destroys the spontaneity and purity of action; it is no more free of attachment to its fruits. Then it is a contaminated act, contaminated with the desire for result.

If action is total in itself, if it is self-fulfilling, a love's labor—if it has no other expectation outside of it, then it is what Krishna and I call action without attachment to its fruits. This action is complete in itself like a circle; it has no expectations for the future. It is an end unto itself. In that case you will feel thankful to the other person—say the man with the umbrella—for giving you an opportunity to act totally, to do something without desire for results.

A future-oriented mind is full of desires for achieving results in the future, and its action is always fragmentary and partial. But when there is no such desire for results, when the action is without any motive, such an action fills you with tremendous joy and bliss. In my vision action without attachment to its fruits is so complete, so total, that there is nothing beyond it. It is its own fruit, it is its own end result. It is fulfilling in the moment. Such an action is its own reward, there is nothing outside of it.

Jesus is passing through a village and he comes across a field full of lilies. He stops near it and says to his disciples, "Do you see these lilies?" The disciples look at the flowers, but they really do not look because looking through eyes alone is not enough, one has to look with his whole being. So Jesus says again, "Do you see these flowers?"

The disciples say to him, "What is there to see? They are lilies as other lilies are. They are nothing different." Jesus then tells them, "It seems you are not looking, look again. How beautiful they are! King Solomon in all his grandeur and glory is not that beautiful."

The disciples are surprised to hear their Master compare the lilies with King Solomon, who happened to be the wealthiest king of their times. There was, they thought, no point in comparing an ordinary flower with the wealthiest king of the world. So noticing their confusion and bewilderment, Jesus again says, "Look at them again and look with attention. They are ordinary flowers, but they are so beautiful that they outshine even King Solomon with all his grandeur and glory."

One of the disciples asks why they are so beautiful. Jesus says, "These lilies are blossoming here and now; they live and act in the moment. They don't do anything out of hope for the future, whereas Solomon lives for the future and in the future. And this tension between the present and the future makes everything tense, sick and ugly. These flowers have no idea of tomorrrow; they are fulfilled in the moment. This small piece of land on which they are growing is enough for them, they don't crave a larger field. The wind that is passing through them, making them sway, is everything for them. The sun that is shedding light on them is more than everything they desire. These bees humming around them give them the joy of the world.

"They are contented in being what they are; just being is enough, and they don't want to become anything else. Not that another moment will not come for them. It will come, and it will come of its own accord. And when it comes they will welcome it and live it as totally as they are living this existing moment. Not that the lilies will not bear fruit, they will, but it will be another action complete in itself and it will arise from their existential moment. That is why they are so beautiful."

We believe everything happens according to our desires and expectations. We are like that crazy woman of a fable I love to tell again and again.

This crazy old woman had lived her whole life in a certain village, but one fine morning she left the village in anger, cursing the inhabitants with foul words. When the people enquired why she was leaving the village she said, "I go because of the torments that you have inflicted on me so long. But you will know what my going means to you from tomorrow. You will learn the lesson of your life."

The villagers were surprised at the threat the old woman made. They asked, "What is that lesson you are going to teach us?"

She said, "I am taking with me my cock at whose crowing the sun rose here every morning. Now the sun will rise in another village where I am going."

And the story says when the old woman reached another village and her cock crowed and the sun rose, she said to herself, "The idiots of that village must be weeping bitter tears, because the sun is now rising here, and they are in the dark forever."

The old woman's logic is flawless. Her cock crowed and the sun rose in the village where she had lived before. And when she went to another village and the sun rose with her cock's crow, there was no doubt left in her mind that sunrise depended on her cock's crow. But no cocks become victims of such illusions, only their masters. Cocks know they crow when the sun rises, but their masters think otherwise.

This fable reflects human mind.

The future comes on its own; it is already on the way. We cannot stop it from coming; we cannot prevent tomorrow from becoming today. Let man do his work and do it completely; that is enough. There is nothing beyond or outside of the act. We need not worry about tomorrow, which will come for itself.

The act must be total; this is the whole of Krishna's teaching. By total action he means, once you have done your thing you are finished with it; there is nothing more to be done about it. And if something remains to be done, even if you have to wait in expectancy for its result, then the act is not total. Your act is complete in itself when you don't look forward to some reward, some recognition or even appreciation.

For this reason Krishna says, "Leave the fruits of labor to God." By God he does not mean there is some accountant-cum-controller general sitting somewhere in the heavens who will take care of it on your behalf. Leaving it to God means: please do your work and leave it at that, leave it to existence.

Existence is like a mountain which echoes every sound that is uttered around it. It is like someone telling us, sitting here among the hills, to make a sound and leave it to the hills to echo it. We don't have to wait prayerfully for the echo, it will come on its own.

If one worries about what the echo is going to be, he will not be able to create a sound properly. And then it is possible the hills won't echo it. To produce an echo a proper sound, a sound of a particular volume is needed. This is how the desire for a result, the tension caused by desire and expectation does not allow you to do your work rightly.

People who are anxious for results often miss the moment of action itself, because the moment of action is now and here, while the result lies in some future. So those whose eyes are set on the future are bound to miss the present. If you are concerned with the result, if the result is what is important to you, then the action itself becomes meaningless. Then you don't love your work, you love only the result. Then you don't give your whole heart and mind to action— you do it reluctantly, haphazardly.

If your attention is focused on the future— and you are where your attention is—then you cannot be totally in the present. And action lies in the present. And that which is done inattentively cannot be deep and total; it cannot be blissful.

Krishna's vision of action without attachment to results is clear. He tells you to be totally in the present, in the moment. He tells you not to divide yourself between the present and the future. Not even a fraction of your attention should be passed on to the future. Then only you can act wholly and joyously, and then only will your action be total.

Desire for results is a distraction from action, so give up your attachment to results and be totally in action.

Leave future to the future, to existence, and be totally in what you are doing now and here. Then you will also be total in the future when that future comes. Otherwise your habit of being fragmentary will pursue you throughout. Be whole in the now and you will be whole in the future, you will always be whole. And this wholeness, not your desire, will bear fruit.

So you can trustfully leave the matter of fruit in the hands of God or existence or whatsoever you like to call it.

I would like to explain it in a different way. Unless we make action our joy, unless we love what we do, unless we do something for the love of it, we cannot be free of our attachment to the future, to the result. And unless our action flows from our being, our blissfulness, like a stream flows from its source, we cannot be totally into it; we will always be pulled by the future.

Do you think a stream is flowing towards some future? Do you think a river is running to the sea? You are mistaken if you think so. It is another matter that the river reaches the ocean—but it is certainly not flowing for the sake of the ocean. A river flows for the love of flowing, it is really its abundant energy that is flowing. And this energy, this force, this strength of a river comes from its source, its original source.

The Ganges flows with the strength of the Gangotri; it is the Gangotri flowing through the Ganges. Of course she reaches the sea, but it is just a by-product, it is inconsequential. In her whole journey the Ganges has nothing to do with the ocean; she is not even aware that she is going to the ocean. It is her own abundant energy that makes her flow and dance and sing and celebrate.

The Ganges dances not only when she reaches the shore of the ocean, she dances on every shore, on every bank. She dances through hills and valleys, through green forests and dry deserts, through cities and villages, through happiness and misery, through human beings and animals. She dances and rejoices wherever she happens to be. And if she reaches the ocean it is just a consequence which she had neither desired nor expected. It is the culmination of her life's journey; it is existence's echo, its answer to her.

Life is a play of energy; like a river it moves with its own energy. Krishna says man should live so that his action stems from his own energy, from its innermost source. In my view there is only one difference between a householder and a sannyasin: a householder lives for tomorrow, he is future-oriented; a sannyasin lives and flowers now and here. He derives his strength from his today. For him today, now is enough unto itself. And when a sannyasin's tomorrow comes, it will come in the form of his today, and he will live it the way he lives his today.

There is a significant episode in the life of Mohammed. Mohammed is a rare kind of sannyasin, and I would like to see many more sannyasins like him in the world.

Every day his lovers bring all kinds of gifts for him. Someone brings sweets, another brings clothes, and another money. Mohammed shares everything with his visitors and others, and if something is left over by the evening he asks his wife to distribute it among the needy.

By the evening Mohammed again becomes a pauper, a fakir. When sometimes his wife suggests that something should be saved for tomorrow, Mohammed says, "Tomorrow will come as today, and it will care for itself." If his wife still grumbles he says to her, "Do you think I am an atheist that I should care for tomorrow? Caring for tomorrow is what I call atheism. Worrying for tomorow means I don't trust existence, who has provided everything for today. I trust existence will provide for our tomorrow too. Worrying about tomorrow is lack of trust in existence, in the cosmic energy. And after all, what can we do? What worth is our own effort?"

Mohammed insists that his wife give away everything that is left over saying, "With trust in our hearts we will wait for tomorrow. I am a theist, and if I save for tomorrow God will say, 'Mohammed, don't you have even this much trust in me?'"

This is the way Mohammed lives all through his life. Then he becomes critically ill, and one evening his physicians declare that he is not going to survive the coming night. So his wife, thinking she should save something for any emergency that may arise that night, saves five dinars and hides the money under her pillow.

As midnight comes Mohammed becomes restless, tossing and turning in his bed. He is surprised at this strange kind of suffering. At last he uncovers his face and tells his wife, "It seems tonight Mohammed is no more a pauper; you seem to have saved something for this night."

His wife was surprised and asked, "How could you know it?"

Mohammed answers, "Looking at your face tonight I can see you are not calm and peaceful as you always are. For sure there is some money in the house. Those who are worried become acquisitive and acquisitive people become worried. It is a vicious circle. So take out what you have saved and distribute it so that I can die in peace. Remember, this is my last night. I don't want to spoil it and appear before God with a guilty conscience."

His wife hurriedly takes out the five dinars from under her pillow, and says to Mohammed, "But there is no one out there to receive this money, it is midnight."

Mohammed says, "Just call out and someone will come."

And someone, a beggar really appears at the door. Mohammed says to his wife, "Just see, if someone comes to take in the dead of night, someone else can come to give as well." With these words he drew the shawl over his face and sank into eternal sleep. This was his last act—to cover his face with the shawl.

It seems the five dinars were blocking Mohammed's passage to eternity. They were too much load on the heart of a true sannyasin like him.

If each day, each moment, each act is complete, it will be followed by a complete tomorrow. Tomorrow always comes, but if you complete your today your tomorrow will be new and fresh, not old and stale. It will not be frustrating.

But if you leave your today incomplete with expectations for tomorrow, it will frustrate you and your expectations, and you will be miserable on top of it.

The future will never conform to your expectations, because the future is immense and your hopes and desires are petty, trivial. The immense, the infinite cannot be controlled and manipulated by the trivial. A drop cannot decide the course of a river— the river goes its own way irrespective of what the drop wants.

But if a drop has its own desires and expectations, if it wants to go upstream, or go right or left, then it will suffer and suffer immeasurably. This is man's misery; it is hopes and dreams that turn into his frustration and despair.

One who lives each moment totally knows no anxiety and no frustration; he is contented and blissful and fulfilled.

Let each of your actions, no matter whether you are peeling a potato or composing a poem, be complete in itself. Leave the result to God. If you do so, Krishna says, you will be released from the bondage that comes in the form of birth. Krishna does not say that birth is a bondage. He only says that one who is full of expectations, who is attached to the fruits of action is always in need of tomorrow, future, future life.

One who lives in desires, in hopes and expectations anxiously seeks a new birth after his death; he cannot escape rebirth. And for such a person birth becomes a bondage; it can never become his freedom. Because such a person is not really interested in life and living, he is interested in his expectations, in the results he expects from it. For him birth is just an opportunity for achieving some results.

And for such a person death is going to be very painful, because death will put an end to all the desires and demands he lived for. Naturally when he is born again he will find his birth to be his bondage. Birth is bondage for one who does not know the life that is freedom. In fact desiring is bondage, craving and attachment to result is bondage.

To live and know life totally is freedom. And for one who knows this life there is no birth and death. He is released from both birth and death. Krishna has said only the half truth; it is a half-truth to say that one is released from the fetters of birth. To complete it, I say he is released from death as well. He is released from both birth and death.

This does not mean that birth and death are bondage. In ignorance, for an ignorant person birth and death appear to be bondage; they bind him. For a wise man, one who knows the truth, birth and death cease to be, he is in freedom. In fact, bondage and freedom are states of mind. While the ignorant mind experiences bondage, the mind of the wise is free. Krishna does not condemn birth as such, but the way we are, birth feels like imprisonment to us.

We are a strange people, who turn even love into a bondage. I receive any number of weddng invitations from time to time. Someone's daughter is going to be married; another friend's son is being married. They invariably write in their invitation letters that their daughter or son is going to be "bound with the fetters of love." We turn even love, which is utter freedom, into shackles.

Love is freedom, so the right way to say it is that someone is going to be set free in love. But we say and do the opposite, we turn love into an imprisonment. Not that love is imprisonment, but we make it into one. The way we are, even death looks like captivity to us. The way we are, we turn life itself into a concentration camp.

On the other hand, he who lives in the present, in the moment, who lives without expectations and attachments and does his work without hope for reward or fear of punishment, whose action is like inaction and whose inaction is like action, who turns his whole life into a play—he turns even bondage into freedom. For such a person, action is freedom, love is freedom, living is freedom, life is freedom, and even death is freedom. For him everything is freedom.

It all depends on the way we are; we carry both our slavery and freedom within us. If one begins to live without desire for the fruits of action, if he becomes responsible to himself and to existence, if he trusts life, then life for him will cease to be a bondage— it will be a blessing, a benediction. Such a person attains to a life of freedom; he is free while he is living in this world. Such a life is possible here and now. And it depends on us.

I have heard that a rebel sage—a sage is always a rebel—was thrown into prison for his irrepressible love of freedom. He was going around the country singing songs of rebellion. He was a Sufi sage and his captor was a Caliph who was both the religious and temporal head of Mohammedanism. The sage was put in shackles from his neck downward, but he continued to sing his songs of freedom.

One day the Caliph came to see him and enquired if he had any troubles. The sage asked, "What troubles? I am a royal guest, your guest; what troubles can I have? I am utterly happy. I live in a hut and you have put me in a palace. Thank you!"

The Caliph was amazed. He asked, "Are you joking?"

The Sufi said, "I say so because I have turned life itself into a joke."

Then the Caliph came with a down-to-earth question: "Are the chains on your hands and feet heavy and painful?"

The Sufi looked at his chains and said, "These chains are far away from me; there is a great distance between me and these chains. You may be under the illusion that you have imprisoned me, but you can only imprison my body, you cannot imprison my freedom. You cannot turn freedom into prison because I know how to turn prison into freedom."

It all depends on us, on how we see things. Seeing is foundational. The Sufi told the Caliph, "There is a great distance between me and the chains on me. You cannot imprison my freedom."

Mansoor, another Sufi rebel, was executed. And the manner of his execution was very cruel and brutal. One by one, his limbs, even his eyes were severed from his body. Hundreds of thousands of people had gathered to witness the event. As his hands and feet were being cut off, Mansoor was laughing and his laughter went on getting louder as his body shrunk in size. Someone from among the spectators shouted, "Are you crazy, Mansoor? Is this a time to laugh?"

Mansoor said, "I am really laughing at you, because you think you are killing me. You are badly mistaken, you are really killing someone else. Don't forget that Mansoor is laughing when you are killing him in such an inhuman manner. How could it be possible? Let alone killing him, you cannot even touch Mansoor. The one you are killing is not Mansoor. Mansoor is the one who is laughing."

These words of Mansoor infuriated his executioners, his enemies, and they said to him haughtily, "Now we want to see how you laugh!" and they cut his tongue. Then Mansoor's eyes began laughing. Someone among the spectators mocked at the executioners. "Even after you have removed his tongue his eyes are laughing." And the executioners gouged out his two eyes. But then Mansoor's face, every fiber of his being was laughing. Spectators told them, "You cannot stop his laugh; see, his whole being is laughing." They had spared nothing, not a single part of his body, and yet he was laughing.

Our life becomes what we are psychologically and spiritually; our death becomes what we are in our mind and spirit. If we are free, our birth, our life, our death, everything becomes free. And similarly if we are in bondage, then everything we do or don't do binds us. Then action binds, love binds, life binds, even death binds. Then even God binds.

In fact, we are our own makers.

> Questioner: You have said that a man is sixty percent male and forty percent female, and a woman is sixty percent female and forty percent male. In case the ratio is altered and equalized, do you think male and female energies will neutralize and sterilize each other? And how is it God has been called Ardhanarishwara, half man and half woman?

I did not say that the proportion of male and female energy is fixed at sixty and forty percent. It can vary; it can be seventy and thirty, even ninety and ten. But in case it is fifty-fifity, it makes a man or woman asexual. Then he or she is out of the dialectics of sex, then he or she is neutral or impotent.

It is significant that in Sanskrit the word *Brahman* or the supreme energy or God, is categorized as neuter gender. Is *Brahman* male or female? No, it is neutral. What has been called omnipotent has been indicated in language as without gender. How can the supreme be male or female? That would make *Brahman* partial. No, the ultimate being is impartial. This impartiality is possible only if the proportion of male and female energy is fifty-fifty.

The concept of *ardhanarishwara* is the symbol of *Brahman*, the supreme, because the proportion of male and female in *Brahman* is fifty-fifty. *Brahman* is both man and woman, or it is neither. If God were all male, then there would be no way for the female species to be. And if God were all female, then there would not be a male species on the earth. It is both together and therefore it is capable of creating both the species—male and female.

And as long as we are man and woman, we are two separate fragments of God, broken away from him. That is why man and woman attract each other; this mutual attraction stems from their desire to be united and one. Separately they are half and incomplete. And everything incomplete strives to complete itself; that is the way of life.

Not only our concept of *ardhanarishwara* is unique, even the statue of *ardhanarishwara* that we have created is rare in the known history of mankind. There are many beautiful statues around the world. But the *ardhanarishwara* depicts a great psychological truth—it is simply incomparable. This statue, this ancient symbol is a blend of male and female energies, because the statue is half male and half female. One of its sides is feminine and the other is masculine, or you can say it is a blending or the combination of the two. It can also be said to be beyond the two.

As I said, God is the median, the golden mean. Jesus has used a weird phrase, "eunuchs of God" to point to the same phenomenon. He says those who want to find God should become eunuchs of God, which really sounds outlandish. But Jesus is right; those who want to find God should become like God: neither male nor female. And if you look attentively at men like Buddha and Krishna, who reflect godliness on this earth at its highest, you will find that they too are neither male nor female. Seen in their full glory and grandeur they are both or neither, or a blending of the two. In a way they reflect the transcendental sex, they have gone beyond the duality of the sexes.

As far as we are concerned, we are dual—both male and female in different proportions.

You want to know why some people are born eunuchs who are neither men nor women, people who may be called a third sex. The reason is the same. If the child in its embryonic form in the mother's womb has both male and female elements in equal proportion, then he cannot grow into one sex clearly. Then the two equal elements will neutralize each other and the person will be a eunuch.

From time to time cases of sex-change have been reported. Usually their news is suppressed. It has happened that a young man slowly changed into a young woman and vice versa. It was thought to be accidental, a freak of nature. But now medical science knows how it happens, and is virtually in a position even to effect such changes clinically.

In the recent past a very sensational case came before a court of law in London. The case was that a young man and young woman were duly married as husband and wife. After they lived as husband and wife for a few years, the woman's sex underwent a change and she became a man. The crux of the complaint was that the woman was never a woman, she was a man and that she deceived the young man by disguising her true sex.

The judges were in real difficulty to come to a correct judgment. The wife pleaded that she was always a woman and that the change came later. At the time of the hearing of this case even medical science was not clear about the matter. In the course of the last twenty-five or thirty years many cases of sex change have come to light and physicians accept that it is possible. And science is busy exploring this area with the help of such cases.

If the difference between one's male and female elements is very small or marginal—say it is fifty-one to forty-nine, then a change of sex can take place any time. It is just a question of chemical changes taking place in one's physiology. And with the discovery of hormones and synthetic hormones, the day is not far off when medical science will bring about this change clinically.

Now it is not necessary that a man or woman should suffer the boredom of being man or woman for good. He or she can have a change any time they want. It is just a matter of manipulating the quantity of certain body chemicals and hormones. Soon we will see that a man turns into a woman and a woman into man if they choose to. In fact, there is not much difference between man and woman; the difference is rather quantitative.

The concept of God as *ardhanarishwara* says that the primeval source of creation is neither male nor female or it is both. But I don't say that a eunuch or an impotent person is nearer God as a result. I don't say so.

It is true, God is both man and woman, but this man or woman is not impotent. This difference has to be kept in mind: while God is both male and female, the eunuch is neither; he is a negation of both. While God is the presence, the affirmation of yin and yang, the eunuch is their absence, their negation. Therefore the statue of *ardhanarishwara* is part male and part female. If it were a eunuch we could have depicted it as such. God represents positivity; the eunuch is utter negativity. The eunuch has no individuality and for this reason there is no end to his misery. Jesus does not say that we should become eunuchs to attain to God, all he means to say is that we should neither remain men nor women, and then we will be both together.

Questioner: Why do Jaina scriptures say that there is no liberation for women?

This question will change the context of our discussion and therefore I would deal with it briefly and then we will sit for meditation.

You ask why the Jaina scriptures say that women cannot attain to freedom. The reason is that Jaina scriptures are the handiwork of the male mind. The truth is, the whole of Jaina discipline is male-oriented, it is aggressive. Therefore Jaina scriptures cannot think how women, who represent passive energy can attain to liberation. But devotees of Krishna think otherwise. If you ask one of them about it he will immediately say women alone can attain to it, no one except them can. The male mind is simply incapable of reaching God, according to Krishna's philosophy. Even male devotees of Krishna turn into feminine minds so they can fall in love with Krishna.

There is a beautiful anecdote in the life of Meera, the renowned devotee of Krishna. When she went to Vrindavan, Krishna's birthplace, she was prevented from entering the temple on the grounds that she was a woman and women were not allowed in that temple. She was told the chief priest of the temple was under a vow not to look upon a woman— he had never seen a woman since he had taken charge of the temple. Meera strongly protested, and what she said is significant. She said, "As far as I know there is only one man in all the universe and he is Krishna. How can there be another man in the form of the priest of this temple? I wonder how he continues to be a man and a Krishna devotee too!"

When this message from Meera was conveyed to the chief priest he was taken aback, speechless, and he rushed to the temple gate where Meera was being held. He threw the gates of the temple wide open and asked her forgiveness. He said to Meera, "I am grateful to you for reminding me of my relationship with my Lord."

Krishna stands for the feminine mind, the trusting mind, the surrendering mind.

But Mahavira represents the male mind, the aggressive mind, the conquering mind. Therefore he cannot think women as women can achieve liberation. So the Jaina tradition believes that a woman seeker will have to be born as a man before she attains to complete freedom. If there were only one spiritual path in the world, the path of Mahavira, then there would be no way for any woman to seek God. It is exclusively meant for the male mind, the aggresive mind.

Similarly a male mind can have no way with Krishna; his is the path of love and trust and surrender.

These are the two psychological archetypes in the world, and everything depends on these archetypes.

I will take up the rest of the question tomorrow.

TWENTIETH DISCOURSE
MORNING, OCTOBER 5, 1970
MANALI, INDIA

BASE YOUR RULE ON THE RULE

Questioner: What is the subtle dif-
ference, if any, between Mahavira's
transcendence of attachment, Christ's
holy indifference, Buddha's indiffer-
ence and Krishna's non-attachment?
And in what way are they the same?

 here is a good deal of similarity be-
tween Christ's concept of neutrality,
Buddha's idea of indifference, Mahavira's transcendence of attachment,
and Krishna's non-attachment. These
are the ways of looking at and meet-
ing the world. But there are some basic differences
too. While their end-points are similar, their approaches are very different. While their ultimate goal
is the same, they differ much in the ways and means
they use to achieve their ends.

There is deep similarity between what Christ
calls neutrality or non-alignment with the world at

large, and what Buddha calls indifference to it. As the world is, with all its strange goings-on, its contradictions and conflicts, its struggles and trials, a seeker on the spiritual path will do well to keep a distance from it. But remember, neutrality can never be blissful; deep down it makes one sad and dull and drab. Therefore Jesus looks sad; even if he attains to some bliss he comes to it by way of his sadness. And his whole path is dull and dreary; he cannot walk it singing and dancing. Neutrality is bound to turn into sadness; Jesus cannot help it.

If I don't choose life, if I reject it completely, if I say I take neither this nor that, then I will soon stop flowing, I will stagnate. If a river refuses to move in any of the directions—east, west, north or south— it will cease to flow, it will stagnate. It will turn into a closed pool.

It is true that a stagnant pool of water too will reach the ocean, but not in the way the river reaches it. It will first have to turn into vapor and then into clouds and then descend on the ocean in the form of rains. It will not have the joys of a river, pushing its way to the ocean singing, dancing, celebrating.

A pool of dead water, a pond, dries up under the scorching sun, becomes vapor, clouds, and then reaches the ocean through a detour. It is deprived of the delight, beauty and ecstasy a river has. Such a pool of water is nothing more than a pond of listlessness and boredom.

Jesus is like a wandering cloud—somber and sad—not like a river, rejoicing, exulting, singing.

There is something common to the lifestyles of Jesus and Buddha, but the difference between them is as great. Buddha is very different from Jesus. While Jesus' neutrality looks sad, Buddha's indifference is silent, peaceful and quiet. Buddha is never sad, he is quiet, serene and silent. If he lacks the dance of Krishna, and the secret bliss of Mahavira, he is also free of the sadness of Jesus; he is utterly settled in his peace, his silence.

Buddha is not neutral like Jesus; he has attained to indifference, which is much different from neutrality. He has come to know that everything in life, as we know it, is meaningless, so nothing now is going to disturb his peace. Every alternative, every choice in life is the same for him. So his stillness, his peace, his calm is total.

Jesus is only neutral; every choice, every alternative is not the same for him. Jesus will say this is right and that is wrong; although he is non-aligned with the opposites, he is not that choiceless. Buddha has attained to absolute choicelessness. For him nothing is good or bad, right or wrong, black or white. For him summer and winter, day and night, pleasure and pain, laughter and tears are the same. For him, choosing is wrong and only choicelessness is right.

Jesus, in spite of his neutrality, his "holy indifference," takes a whip in his hand and drives away the money-changers from the temple of Jerusalem. He overturns their boards and whips them. In the great synagogue of the Jews, the priests indulge in usury when people come from all over the country for the annual festival. Their rates of interest are exhorbitant, and so it is a way of exploiting the poor and the helpless. It is a way of draining the wealth and labor of the people, while it makes the temple of Jerusalem, the richest establishment in the country. So Jesus upturns their tables and beats them.

Jesus is indifferent, yet he chooses. He advocates neutrality in worldly matters, but if there is something wrong he immediately stands up against it. He is not choiceless.

We cannot imagine Buddha with a whip in his hands; he is utterly choiceless. And because of his choicelessness he has attained to a silence that is profound and immense. So silence has become central to Buddha's life and teaching.

Look at a statue of Buddha, silence surrounds it, peace permeates it, serenity emanates from it. Silence has become embodied in Buddha; peace has come home with him. Nothing can disturb his peace, his silence. Even the pond is disturbed by the passing breeze, by the rays of the sun which turn it into vapor and carry it to the sea. Buddha is so still that he has no desire whatsoever to move to the ocean of eternity; he says the ocean will have to come to him if it wants. Even to think of the ocean is now a strain for him.

For this reason Buddha refuses to answer questions about the transcendental. Is there God? What is liberation? What happens after death? Questions like these Buddha never entertains; he gently laughs them aside saying, "Don't ask such questions that have to do with the distant future; they will distract you from the immediate present, which is of the highest. The thought of the distant future will give rise to the desire to travel to it, and to reach it. And this desire will create restlessness. I am utterly contented with what I am, where I am. I have nowhere to go; I have nothing to choose and find."

So Buddha is not only indifferent to this world, he is also indifferent to the other world of God and *nirvana*. Jesus is indifferent to this world, but he is not indifferent to the other, to God. He has for sure chosen God against the world.

But Buddha says, "Even to find God you will have to pass through the swamp of hopes and fears, attachments and jealousies. Why should a river yearn to reach the sea? What is she going to achieve if she finds the sea? There is not much difference between the two except that there is a lot more water in the sea than in the river." Buddha then says, "Whatever I am, I am; I am utterly contented, I am in perfect peace." So his indifference has no objective, no goal whatsoever to achieve. Look at Buddha's face, his eyes; there is not a trace of agitation in them. They are as silent as silence itself. It is like a still lake where not even a ripple rises.

Naturally Buddha's peace is negative; it can have neither Krishna's outspoken bliss nor Mahavira's subtle joy. It is true that a man of such tremendous silence, who has no desires whatsoever—not even the desire to find the ultimate—will attain to bliss without asking. But this bliss will be his inner treasure, this lamp of bliss will shine in his interiority, while his whole external milieu will be one of utter peace and silence. His halo will reflect only harmony, stillness and order. Bliss will form his base and peace will make his summit.

One cannot think of Buddha and movement together; he is so relaxed and rested. Looking at his statue you cannot imagine that this man has ever risen from his seat and walked a few steps or said a word. Buddha is a statue of stillness. In him all movements, all activities, all commotions, all strivings have come to a standstill. He is peace itself.

Buddha represents cessation of all tensions, of all desires, including the desire for liberation. If someone says to him he wants to find freedom, Buddha will say, "Are you crazy? Where is freedom?" If someone says he wants to discover his self, his soul, Buddha will say, "There is nothing like a soul." In fact, Buddha will say, "So long as there is the desire to find something, you can never find. Desiring takes you nowhere except to sorrow and suffering. Cease seeking and you will find."

But Buddha does not say in words that "You will find"; he keeps silent on this point. He is aware that the moment he talks about finding freedom or something, you will begin to desire it and run after it. So he negates everything—God, soul, freedom, peace—everything. So long as there is something positive before you, you will want to find it and so long as you strive to find something you cannot find it. It is paradoxical, but it is true. It is only in utter

stillness, in absolute silence, in total emptiness—
where all movement ceases—that truth, *nirvana*, or
whatever you call it, comes into being.

Desiring, which is *tanaha* in Buddha's language, keeps you running and restless. So desiring is
the problem of problems for Buddha. And indifference, *upeksha*, is the solution, the key that releases
you from the bondage of desiring. So Buddha says
over and over, "Don't choose, don't seek, don't run,
don't make something into a goal, because there is
nothing like a goal, a destination. Everything is now
and here."

Jesus has a goal, a destination. This is why,
while he talks of holy indifference toward the world,
he cannot be indifferent to God. Indifference to God
cannot be holy in the eyes of Jesus, he will call it
unholy indifference.

Buddha is indifferent to everything; his indifference is complete. If you ask him how it is that
there is nothing to find—neither the world, nor God,
nor soul, he will say, "What we see before our eyes is
not real, it is only a collage, an assemblage, something
put together. It is something like a chariot which is
nothing but a collection of four wheels and back seats,
rods and ropes, and a horse that carries it. If you
remove all the parts one by one and put them aside,
the chariot will simply disappear.

"Like the chariot you are a collage, the whole
world is a collage, a collection, a composition of
things, sights and sounds. And when the collage falls
apart, then all that remains in its place is nothingness,
emptiness. This nothingness, this emptiness is the
reality, the truth which is worth attaining." Buddha
calls it *nirvana*—the ultimate state of extinction, nothingness, which cannot be put into words. So
Buddha does not say it in words, he says it with his
being, his interiority, his silence.

For this reason only men and women of deep
intelligence and understanding can walk with

Buddha. Those who are greedy and goal-oriented, who are out to achieve something—either gold or God—will simply run away from him. They will say, "This man Buddha is no good, he has nothing to give but peace. And what use is peace? We want heaven, we seek God, we yearn for *moksha*." And Buddha will simply laugh at them, because he knows that what they call God or soul or *moksha* is attained only in the immensity of peace, of silence.

So one cannot make God into a goal. That is why Buddha consistently denies God, because if he accepts, you will immediately turn this into a goal, into an object of desire. And one who runs after a goal cannot be peaceful, he cannot be silent. So you can understand why Buddha insists on indifference; it is only indifference that can lead you into peace, into the silence where all journeying ends.

Mahavira's transcendence of attachment accords with Buddha's indifference to some extent, because he too stands for indifference toward the world. In the same way Mahavira agrees with Jesus to an extent because he, like Jesus, stands for liberation. Mahavira is not choiceless in regard to the goal of freedom. Mahavira will argue that without liberation, peace is irrelevant; without freedom there is no difference between peace and lack of peace. Then restlessness is as good as peace and silence.

Mahavira says that someone gives up a thing so he can gain something else in its place. If there is nothing to be gained the question of renunciation does not arise. So Mahavira is not indifferent to *moksha* or freedom. His transcendence of attachment is a means to help you go beyond the contradictions and conflicts of the world; so it is only an instrument of achievement.

Buddha's indifference is total. It has no goals to achieve, it is not goal-oriented. Or you can say Buddha's indifference is a means to non-achievement, where you lose and go on losing till there is nothing but utter emptiness before you. And this emptiness is what reality or truth is in the eyes of Buddha. So in a sense Buddha's sannyas, his renunciation is complete, because it seeks nothing, not even God or *nirvana*.

Mahavira's sannyas is not that complete, because it has freedom as its goal. Mahavira thinks sannyas is irrelevant without a goal—the goal of freedom. Mahavira's reasoning is very scientific; he believes in causality, the law of cause and effect. According to him everything in this world is subject to the law of cause and effect. So he will not agree with Buddha that one should attain to peace for nothing, because there is a reason why one loses his peace and then seeks it once again.

Mahavira will not consent to Krishna's choiceless acceptance of that which is. If one accepts everything as it is, he cannot attain to his self, his soul, his individuality. Then one will simply vegetate and disintegrate. According to Mahavira, discrimination is essential to the attainment of the self, of individuality.

To be oneself one must know how to discriminate between good and bad, right and wrong, virtue and vice. Discrimination is wisdom, which teaches you not only to know the black from the white, but also to choose one against the other. He says both attachment and aversion are wrong, and one who drops them attains to the state of *veetrag*, which is transcendence of attachment and aversion. And this transcendence is the door to *moksha* or liberation.

Therefore Mahavira is not only peaceful, but blissful too. The light of liberation not only illuminates his interiority, it also surrounds his exteriority. If you put Mahavira and Buddha together, you will notice that while Buddha's silence seems to be passive, Mahavira's silence is positive and dynamic. Together with peace a kind of blissfulness radiates around Mahavira.

But if you put Mahavira and Krishna together Mahavira's bliss will look a shade paler than Krishna's. While Mahavira's bliss looks quiet and self-contained, Krishna's is eloquent and aggressive. Krishna can dance; you cannot think of Mahavira dancing. To discover his dance one will have to look deep into his stillness, silence and bliss; it is engrained in every breath, every fiber of his being. But he cannot dance as Krishna dances; his dance is embedded in his being; it is hidden, indirect. So while Mahavira's transcendence outwardly radiates his bliss, Buddha's indifference reflects only silence and nothing else.

And this indifference is well reflected in their statues. Mahavira's statue reflects extroversion; bliss emanates from it. Buddha's statue reflects introversion; he seems to have completely withdrawn himself from the without. Nothing seems to be going out from him. Buddha's being looks as if it is a non-being.

Mahavira on the other hand seems to have come to his fullness; his being is complete. That is why he denies the existence of God, but cannot deny the existence of the soul. He says there is no God; God cannot be, because he himself is God. There cannot be yet another God, two Gods. Therefore he declares the self, the soul is God; each one of us is God.

There is no God other than us. In utter ecstasy Mahavira declares that he is God, there is no one above him. He contends that if there be another God, a superlord over him, then he can never be free. Then there is no way for anyone to be free in this world; then freedom is a myth.

If there is God, a governing principle, running the whole show, then there is no meaning whatsoever in freedom; then freedom is dependent on God. And a dependent freedom is a contradiction in terms. If someday God decides to withdraw one's freedom and send him back into the world, he can't do a thing. Freedom, which is the highest value, can only exist if there is no God; freedom and God cannot go together. Therefore Mahavira emphatically denies God and declares the supremacy, the sovereignty of every soul. According to Mahavira, the soul itself is God. So his bliss is clear and expressive, which is a reflection of his transcendence.

Mahavira is in agreement with Buddha so far as choicelessness is concerned; there can be no choice between attachment and aversion. But he does not accept the other part of Buddha's thesis—that there is no choice between even the world and *moksha*, freedom. Mahavira clearly chooses freedom against the world. And in this respect he is in accord with Jesus; he is closer to Jesus' neutrality. But since his God lives in some heaven, Jesus can be happy only after his death, when he will meet him in heaven. Mahavira has no God outside himself; he has found the highest, the supreme being within himself, and he is blissful now and here. So it sounds reasonable that while Jesus is sad, Mahavira is not.

Krishna's *anasakti*, non-attachment, in its turn has some similarity with Mahavira's transcendence, Buddha's indifference and Jesus' neutrality, but it has some basic differences too. It would not be wrong to say that Krishna's *anasakti* is transcendence, indifference and neutrality rolled into one, plus something more.

Krishna's non-attachment is different from Buddha's *upeksha*, or indifference. Krishna says indifference is a kind of attachment, inverted attachment. If I meet you in passing and don't look at you, it will be indifference on my part. But if looking at you is attachment then non-looking is equally attachment—attachment in reverse gear.

And furthermore, Krishna asks, "How can anyone be indifferent? Indifferent to what? If the whole world is nothing but the manifestation of God, then one is indifferent to God himself." And then

Krishna raises another question: "How can one who is indifferent be free of ego? To be attached or to be indifferent one needs ego. If I am attached to God and indifferent to the world, it is my ego which is operating in both cases." So Krishna does not use a condemnatory term like indifference.

Similarly Krishna is against neutrality. How can we be neutral about anything when God is not neutral? He is utterly involved in everything that there is. Neutrality in life is unnatural and impossible, according to Krishna. We are in the midst of life, we are life. It is life and nothing but life all over. Then how can we afford to keep ourselves aloof from life and be neutral about it? The Sanskrit word for neutrality is *tatasthata*, which means to leave the mainstream and stand on the bank. But so far as life is concerned, it is mainstream all over without any banks; how can we stand on the non-existent bank of life? Wherever we are, we are in the mainstream of life, we are in the thick of life. So to be on the bank, to be neutral is an impossibility. Krishna cannot be neutral and he cannot be indifferent.

Krishna does not accept Mahavira's concept of transcendence of attachment or aversion. He says if attachment and aversion are wrong then there is no reason for them to exist, but they do exist.

Looking at it in another way, we can say there are two forces in the world: one is the force of good or God, and the other is the force of evil or the devil. This is how Zoroastrians and Christians and Mohammedans all believe in the existence of both God and the devil. They think that if there is evil in the world then it has to be segregated from God, who represents goodness and goodness alone. God can never be the source of evil; he represents light, he cannot be the source of darkness. Neither Zarathustra nor Jesus nor Mohammed could think of God being associated with evil in any way. So they had to find a separate place for the devil, and they assigned an independent role to him.

Krishna strongly contends this assumption. He asks: if there is evil and it is separate, is it so with the consent of God or without his consent? Does evil, in order to be, need the support of God, or not? If there is an independent authority of evil, called the devil, it means it is an authority parallel to the authority of God. Then there are two independent and sovereign authorities in the universe, and there is no question of good or ever winning over evil or evil being defeated by good. Why should an independent and all-powerful devil ever yield? In that case there are really two Gods, independent of each other.

The concept of there being two independent Gods or parallel authorities in the universe is not only ridiculous but impossible. Krishna rejects this concept outright. He says there is only one sovereign force, one primal energy in the universe, and everything that is arises from this single primeval source. It is the same energy that brings forth a healthy fruit and a diseased fruit on the branches of a tree. It is not necessary to have separate sources of energy or power for the two—the healthy fruit and the sick one.

It is the same mind that gives rise to both good and evil, virtue and vice; two separate minds are not required. Both good and evil are different transformations of one and the same energy. Day and night, light and darkness are emanations of the same force. Therefore Krishna is against denial, renunciation of any of the dualities. He is all for acceptance, total acceptance of both. Life, as it is, has to be accepted and lived choicelessly and totally. That is what Krishna's *anasakti* or non-attachment means.

Krishna's *anasakti* does not mean choice of one against the other. It does not mean that you choose to be attached to virtue against vice, or to be attached to vice against virture. No, neither attachment nor aversion—no choice whatsoever. He stands for acceptance of life as it is, total acceptance. He stands for surrender to life as it is, and this surrender has to be total. *Anasakti* means that I am not at all separate, I am one with the whole existence. And if existence and I are one, who will choose whom? I am like a wave in the ocean and I just float with it.

However, Krishna's *anasakti* has some similarity with Buddha's indifference, Mahavira's transcendence and Christ's holy indifference. Krishna can have the peace of Buddha because he has nothing more to achieve, he has achieved everything there is. He can attain to Mahavira's transcendence, because his bliss like Mahavira's is illimitable. He can, like Christ, declare the immanence of God—not because there is someone sitting on a throne somewhere, but because whatever there is in the universe is God, godly; there is nothing other than God.

Krishna's non-attachment is absolute surrender of the ego, total cessation of the "I".

It is just to know that I am not, only God is. And once I know that what is, is, there is no way but to accept it in its totality. Then there is nothing to be done or undone, altered or modified. Krishna sees himself as a wave in the ocean; he has no choice whatsoever. Then the question of attachment or aversion does not arise. If you understand it rightly, Krishna's *anasakti* is not a state of mind, it is really cessation of all states of mind, of mind itself. It is to be one with existence, with the whole.

Through this royal road of unity with the whole, Krishna arrives exactly where Mahavira, Buddha and Jesus arrive through their narrow paths and bypaths. They have chosen narrow short-cuts or footpaths for themselves, while Krishna goes for the highway. Both the footpath and highway take you to your destination, and they have their own advantages and disadvantages. And it depends on what we choose.

There are people who love to walk on unkempt footpaths which are narrow and lonely, which very few people choose to traverse, which are rough and hard and which present challenges at every step, on every crossing. It is like going through a dense forest where paths are difficult to find and follow. There are others who don't like narrow and deserted pathways, who don't want to go as lonely travelers, who enjoy going pleasantly with large groups of fellow-travelers, who want to share their happiness with others. Such people will naturally choose highways, great thoroughfares which have been used by hundreds of thousands of people.

Wayfarers on narrow and unknown paths can very well walk sadly if they like, but travelers on highways cannot afford to be sad. If they are sad they will be pushed out of the highways, they will be cast away. One has to go singing and dancing through highways where thousands and thousands move together; one can't go his own way there.

Travelers on footpaths can walk quietly, but one cannot escape the noise and tumult of the multitude if he chooses a highway for his journey. He will have to face the high winds of restlessness and uneasiness, which will in the long run usher him into peace and quietness. Those who choose to move off the beaten paths can have the joy of being alone and individual, but those on the highways have to share in the pleasures and pains of all others. There is this much difference between the two.

Krishna is a multidimensional, a multi-splendored person, and the highway is his choice.

The truth is, there is no one path, and no ready-made path to God. There are as many paths as there are people in the world. No two persons are alike, or in the same state of being. So each one of us will have to begin his journey just where he is and find his way to God all alone. Everyone will have to go his own way, in his individual way. Of course, all

roads lead to the same destination, which is one and
only one. Whether you follow the path of neutrality
or indifference or transcendence or bliss, the goal remains the same.

While paths and roads are many, the goal is
the same. And everyone should choose the way that
is in tune with his lifestyle or type. Instead of debating
endlessly on what is a right path or a wrong path,
which is a waste of time and energy, one should carefully choose the path that accords with his individuality, his self-nature. That is all.

> *Questioner: You explained to us
> Krishna's choicelessness. The Geeta,
> however, says that one who departs
> from this world when the sun is on
> his northward path attains to libera-
> tion. But what about the one who
> dies when the sun is on his southward
> path? And how does Krishna's
> sthitaprajna, one who is settled in
> his intelligence, compare with his
> devotee who is on the path of love?
> Krishna defines sthitaprajna as one
> who remains unperturbed and steady
> in the midst of both happiness and
> pain. But this state can also lead to
> utter insensitivity. And will you call
> it human if somebody does not take
> pleasure as pleasure and pain as pain?*

This statement of Krishna's is very profound and
meaningful. He says *sthitaprajna* is one who remains
unperturbed and steady in the midst of both happiness
and misery. And your question is equally relevant:

that if someone does not feel happy in happiness and miserable in misery will it not destroy his sensitivity?

There are two ways of remaining unperturbed in the midst of happiness and suffering. One way is to kill your sensitivity. Then you will cease to be happy in happiness and miserable in misery. If your tongue is burned you will cease to taste both the sweet and sour. If your eyes are blinded you will know neither light nor darkness. A deaf person is insensitive to every kind of sound—pleasant and unpleasant. Insensitivity is the simplest way of achieving evenness of mind in both pleasure and pain.

And it is not surprising that by and large Krishna's followers have chosen the way of insensitivity. Most of those who are known as sannyasins, renunciates or recluses, do nothing but systematically destroy their sensitivity so they become dead to the experience of pleasure and pain, happiness and misery. But this is a travesty of what Krishna really means.

Krishna's meaning is very different. He says a *sthitaprajna* remains unperturbed in pleasure and pain—he does not say he is insensitive to them. He means to say that a wise man goes beyond happiness and sorrow, he transcends them—not by killing his sensitivity but by attaining to a higher state of consciousness, to superconsciousness. An unconscious person, one under the influence of drugs, is insensitive to pain and pleasure but he cannot be said to have transcended them. He has rather fallen below the normal state of consciousness. In that way every dead person is insensitive. Transcendence is entirely different.

And I interpret this aphorism of Krishna's very differently. In my view, Krishna's way of transcending happiness and sorrow is different and unique. If someone experiences happiness fully, if he is utterly sensitive to pleasure, if he lives it so totally that nothing remains to be lived, he will soon transcend it.

Then he will be unperturbed and steady in every situation of pleasure and happiness.

Similarly if someone experiences pain and misery totally, if he goes into it with all his being, without trying to escape it in the least, he too will go beyond pain; he will never again be disturbed by suffering. Krishna does not ask you to kill your sensitivity; on the contrary, he wants you to heighten your sensitivity to its utmost, so it becomes total. Krishna stands for sensitivity, and total sensitivity at that.

Let us understand it in another way. What do I mean by total sensitivity? For example, someone insults me and I am pained. If I know, if I think that I am in pain, it means that I am not fully in pain. I am yet keeping some distance from pain. In that case I say I am in pain, I don't say I am pained. Even when I say that I am pained, I am not totally in pain, I am still keeping a distance from my pain. I never say that I am pain itself. And unless I know and say it truly, the distance between pain and me will remain. The truth is that when I am pained, I am not separate from pain, I am pain itself. The distance that I keep from pain is my way of resisting it, escaping it, not meeting it totally.

This thing needs to be understood in depth. We divide everything in life, and this is not a right thing to do. Life is really indivisible. When I say to someone "I love you," the statement is linguistically correct, but existentially it is all wrong. When I am in love with someone I really become love itself in respect to that person. Then I am wholly love; no part of me remains outside of love. Even if there is a fragment in me that knows or says I am in love, it means I am not totally in love. And if I am partially in love I am not in love at all.

Love cannot be fragmentary, partial; either I love or I don't. Fragmented love is not love; fragmented happiness is not happiness. But the way we are, we divide everything into fragments. And that is our problem, that is our misery. When one says he is happy, know well that he has ceased to be happy. Happiness might have visited him without his knowing, and he might have been really happy in that split second. But the moment he comes to know he is happy is the moment when happiness has left him. Who is the one who knows he is happy? It is certainly the unhappy part of his being which knows and recognizes happiness. To know happiness some unhappiness is always needed.

If one is integrated and total in himself, then there will be no one to know or say that he is happy or unhappy. Then he will not be happy, he will be happiness itself. Then he will not be unhappy, he will be unhappiness itself. Then and only then his sensitivity will be alive and total. Then sensitivity will be at its highest, at its peak.

In such a state of total sensitivity, every fiber of my being, my total being will be happy or unhappy, loving or hating, quiet or restless. Then there will be no one to be disturbed about it, or even to know it. If I am totally in happiness or unhappiness, if I am happiness or unhappiness itself, then I don't evaluate it or compare it. I don't identify myself with it or condemn it, I don't cling to it or resist it. Then I don't even name it.

When sensitivity is total, the question of being agitated or disturbed does not arise. Then there is no reason why I should not be settled in my intelligence, steadied in my wisdom.

A friend visited me the other day and said that he was very worried about his addiction to smoking. I told him, "It seems you have divided yourself into two parts, one of which is addicted to smoking and the other addicted to worrying. Otherwise how is it possible that you smoke and worry together? You either smoke or worry. But since you smoke and worry together, it is obvious there are two 'yous', two selves in you—one of whom goes on smoking and another who keeps repenting it, condemning it, cursing it. And the problem is, the one that smokes will continue to smoke till the end of life and the other part of you will continue to repent all along the line. The repenter will go on taking vows and pledges again and again to quit smoking, and the smoker will go on breaking those vows and pledges with impunity one after another."

So I said to him, "You should do only one thing: either smoke without repenting, or repent without smoking. If you do both things together you will always be in hell. If you smoke, become a total smoker, don't be a partial one. Be totally involved in smoking without sparing an iota of your being. Don't allow even a small fragment of your being to stand aloof like a judge condeming smoking or justifying it."

And then I said, "If you can become integrated and whole in smoking, then a day will come when the whole man in you can quit smoking, and quit it effortlessly and completely. The one who smokes totally can quit smoking as totally. He will never live perpetually in conflict whether to smoke or not to smoke; to be or not to be. And he will enjoy both smoking and non-smoking."

A fragmented person is neither here nor there. He is neither fish, flesh nor good red herring; he is perpetually in conflict, in misery, in hell. He is miserable when he smokes, because his other part condemns him as a sinner. And when he quits smoking, the smoker in him asserts, saying he is missing a great pleasure and luxury. There is no need for this man's misery; he is disturbed, restless and miserable in every condition. Whatever he does he cannot escape conflict, restlessness and misery. He can never be unperturbed and steady.

He alone can be unperturbed and steady who is integrated and total. Because then there is no part of him left to be disturbed and unsteady. One who is complete, who is total, who becomes one with any and every situation that comes his way, such a person ceases to be a witness; he transcends witnessing. Witnessing is a means, not an end. Krishna is not a witness, although he exhorts Arjuna to be a witness. Krishna is total, he has arrived. Now there is no alienation between the subject and the object, between the observer and the observed. Now there is only observing, a process of observation. And this observation is total.

The witness, the observer, divides the world into subject and object, into the witness and the witnessed. Therefore as long as there is a witness, duality will continue. Witnessing is the last frontier of the dual world, after which the non-dual begins. But one cannot reach the non-dual without being a witness. To be a witness means that I now give up dividing the world into many. Instead I will divide it into two—the witness and the witnessed. And when I have reduced the many fragments of the world to two, it will not be difficult to come to the complete unity of existence when duality will disappear, when the observer and the observed will become one and the same. If one succeeds in becoming a witness he will soon have glimpses of the one without the other, when there is neither the witness nor the witnessed, but only witnessing.

For example, if I love someone there is one who loves and another who is loved. But if love is real, then moments will come when both the lover and the loved one will disappear, and only the energy of love will abide between the two, connecting them. There will be moments when lovers disappear and only love remains. These are the moments of *adwait*, the non-dual, moments of unity—the one without the other.

In the same way there are moments of unity in witnessing too, when subject and object disappear and only the witnessing consciousness remains, like

an ocean of energy bridging two formless entities—
the witness and the witnessed—like two distant sea-
shores. The near shore is called the "I" and the distant
shore the "thou"; one is the observer and the other
the observed. Such moments will come and go.

And when this state achieves its fullness it
will abide forever, and then even witnessing will disappear. Then one is settled in intelligence, steadied
in wisdom; one is whole. He is the awakened one.

Krishna is not a witness. Of course he asks
Arjuna to become a witness, but he is all the time
aware that witnessing is only a means, a transitory
phase. So he also talks of moments when even witnessing will cease to be. Krishna explains both to
Arjuna—the means and the end, the path and the
goal. And when he speaks about being unperturbed
and steady, he does not speak about the means but
the end, the goal itself—although most interpreters
of the Geeta think that he is talking about the means,
the witness. They think if someone remains a witness
in happiness and pain without experiencing it, without indulging it, he will attain to the state that is
unperturbed and steady.

But in my view, this is a wrong approach. If
someone only witnesses without living it, this witnessing will become a kind of tension, disturbance,
restlessness for him. Then he will always be on the
defensive, trying to protect himself from happiness
and pain.

To be undisturbed, to be relaxed and peaceful, it is essential that one is not at all conscious of
happiness and pain. If one is conscious it means a
kind of disturbance is happening, a kind of agitation
is alive and there is a separation between the two—
the observer and the observed. This consciousness,
this separation is subtle, but it is there. So long as one
continues to know this is happiness and that is pain,
he is not integrated and whole. And he is not settled

and steady in himself; he has not attained to equilibrium and peace and wisdom. He is not a *sthitaprajna*.

To me, the state of unperturbed and steady intelligence and the way to it are altogether different. My approach is one of total involvement in the experiencing of pleasure and pain, love and hate, or whatever it is. I don't want you to be a distant watcher, a mere spectator. I want you to be an actor, fully involved in your role, in your acting; I want you to be totally one with it.

All duality, every division between the actor and the act, between the experiencer and the experienced, the observer and the observed, has to disappear. I say that if a river drowns you it is because you are separate from the river. If you become one with the river, if you become the river itself, then the question of being drowned by the river does not arise. Then how can the river drown you? Who will drown? And by whom? And who will shout for help? Then you are one with the moment—totally one. If you can be totally one with the moment at hand you will have learned the art of being one with another moment that is on its way. Then you will be one with every coming moment.

And then a miracle will happen; both pleasure and pain will chasten you, enrich you, add to your beauty and grandeur. Then both happiness and misery will be your friends and they will have equal share in making you. And when your time to leave this world will come, you will thank both in tremendous gratefulness.

The truth is that it is not only light that creates you, darkness has an equal hand in your creation. Not only happiness enriches you, pain and suffering have an equal share in building your richness. Not only life is a moment of rejoicing and celebration, death also is a great moment of bliss and festivity.

It is possible only if you can live each moment totally, if you can squeeze out every drop of juice the moment possesses. Then you will not be able to say that happiness is friendly and pain is inimical. No, then you will gratefully accept that happiness and misery are like your own two legs on which you walk, and that now they are together available to you. Then you will realize how you have tried impossibly all your life to walk on one leg alone—the leg of happiness.

It is interesting to know that when you raise your right leg you are wholly with your right leg, and when you raise your left leg you are completely with the left leg. In the same way you have to be whole when you speak, and you have to be whole when you are silent.

Disorder begins when we choose. And when the chooser is separate the world of choices is unending. Therefore witnessing is not a very lofty stage of being, it is just in the middle. It is, however, a higher thing than the doer, because a doer cannot take a jump into the non-dual—the one without the other.

Witnessing is like a jumping board from where a plunge into the river of oneness becomes possible. But in one respect the doer and the witness are alike: they are holding on to the river's bank, neither of them is in the river yet. It is true that while the doer is away from the river, the witness is at a point close to it from where he can easily take a jump. But as long as they are out of the river, they are on the same land, in the same trap—the trap of duality. Only after a leap into the river can you be out of duality, you can be one with the one.

When Krishna talks about an unperturbed and steady state, he really talks about *adwait*, the non-dual state, where there is no one to be disturbed. So I hold that Krishna's vision does not violate sensitivity; on the contrary, it is the attainment of total sensitivity.

So far as Krishna's reference in the *Geeta* to the northward and southward movement of the sun is concerned, I think it has been grossly misconstrued always. It has nothing to do with the sun who makes our days and moves northward and southward the year round, and who presides over our solar system. It is not that one dying during the sun's northward movement attains to liberation and another dying during his southward trip misses it. The whole thing has nothing to do with our planet and the sun; it is a different matter altogether. It is really a symbolic statement, a metaphor.

Like the sun on the outside, there is an inner sun, a sun of consciousness inside us which has its own ways and spheres of movement. And as we divide our earth into northern and southern hemispheres, so we divide our inner sky into similar hemispheres. Inside us too there is a movement of the sun, or light or truth or whatever you call it, and a network of centers which can compare with the stellar system on the outside.

If in this inner world a particular space is lighted at the time of one's death, he attains to liberation, otherwise not. This subject is important, but needs to be explained at length, so it is better to take it up another time. For the present, it is enough to know that Krishna's reference to the sun's movement in the Geeta is not concerned with the outer sun.

Each one of us, in our interiority, is a miniature universe with our own inner suns and moons and stars and their movements. It has its own spatial movement of light or consciousness or truth or whatever you call it. The Geeta says that if someone dies when his inner sun is on its northward movement he is freed from the cycle of birth and death. It is like we say that water turns into vapor when it is heated to one hundred degrees temperature. Short of a hundred degrees—even at ninety-nine degrees—water remains water.

To understand it we will have to go into the whole matter of inner bodies and their centers. So I leave it here for the present.

> *Questioner: A comparative study of*
> *a* sthitaprajna, *one settled in his in-*
> *telligence, and a devotee, remains to*
> *be made by you.*

You want to understand how a *sthitaprajna* compares
with a devotee, a *bhakta*. A *sthitaprajna* is one who
has ceased to be a devotee and becomes Bhagwan,
God himself. And a devotee is one who is on his way
to becoming God. So while a devotee is one who is
on the path, a *sthitaprajna* is one who has already
arrived. In other words, devotion is the path and
steadied intelligence or wisdom is the destination.
One who has arrived at the goal is called a *sthitaprajna*,
and a traveler to this goal is called a devotee.

As such there are many similarities between
an awakened man, a wise man and a devotee, because
the path and the goal are inescapably united. A goal,
a destination is nothing other than completion of the
path; when the path ends the goal arrives. There is a
lot in common between a devotee and a man of settled
intelligence, because one who is on the path is also
on his way to the goal; there is just a small distance
between the two.

It is only a matter of some distance, some
time, which a devotee has to cover so he becomes a
sthitaprajna. It is always the traveler who arrives at the
goal; so the difference is one of journey and destination. The devotee is journeying; the *sthitaprajna*, the
wise man has arrived. The aspirations and expectations of a devotee turn into the achievement of the
enlightened, the awakened one—the traveler turned
sthitaprajna, wise man. They are inextricably linked
with each other.

The last stage of a devotee's journey is the
stage of his disappearance as a devotee and his
emergence as God. And so long as a devotee does not
become God himself, he will be thirsty, he will be

discontented. Even if a meeting between them takes place and they are in the embrace of each other, the devotee is not going to be satiated and satisfied.

No matter how intimate an embrace is, a subtle separation remains between two lovers. Even if I squeeze you tightly in my embrace, a distance, a separation will be there. This distance can disappear only when two lovers disappear as egos and merge into each other and become totally one. Otherwise every distance is a distance, whether it is a distance of an inch or of a million miles. Even if you reduce the distance to a thousandth part of an inch, it remains a distance nonetheless.

So a devotee cannot be satisfied even if he remains locked in God's embrace. He can be fulfilled only when he disappears as a devotee and becomes God himself.

This is the sorrow and pain of every lover. No matter how close and intimate he is with his loved one, he remains discontented and unhappy. His problem is that unless he becomes one with his beloved— not only physically but spiritually, at the level of love, of being—there is no way for him to be satisfied and happy. And this is really, really difficult. To be one at the level of love and being is one of the hardest things to achieve.

This is not going to happen even if two lovers remain tied to each other like faggots for the fire. And the irony is, the nearer they are to each other, the greater their disillusionment and misery. When there was a distance between them they had hoped for the heavenly happiness and joy that would come when they became close to each other. But when they are really close, even closest to each other, they feel disillusioned, almost cheated by their own hopes.

Nothing is lacking in their relationship, in their intimacy and trust, yet the hoped-for happiness remains a distant dream. Then the lovers begin to fret and fume at each other, they begin to suspect each other. Each of them thinks that while he is doing his best, the other has his reservations, or is deceiving him. Now they are besieged by worries and anxieties that they never had before. But the real reason is that unless lovers become totally one, they can never be content and happy.

For this reason I say the lovers of today are devotees of tomorrow; they have no way but to turn to devotion. When they know for themselves that it is impossible to be one with an embodied person, they will turn to God, who is bodiless, because it is quite possible to be really one with him. So sooner or later every lover is going to turn into a devotee, and every word of love is going to turn into a prayer.

This is how it should be. Otherwise there is no escape from the torture and misery of love. A lover who refuses to be a devotee is bound to be in everlasting anguish. Ironically, while his longings are those of a devotee, he is trying to fulfill them through ordinary love. His aspirations are running in one direction and his efforts in another, and so frustration is inevitable. He so longs to be one with another that nothing should come in between them, not even the thought of "I" and "thou". But he has chosen a wrong medium for the fulfillment of his longings.

No two persons can come so close to each other that the thought of "I" and "thou" cannot come in between them. It is impossible. Only two non-persons, non-egos, can achieve this unity and oneness. And since God is a non-person, a devotee can be one with him the day he ceases to be a person, an ego. As long as a devotee remains a separate entity, fusion with God is impossible.

God is not an entity as a devotee is; God's being is like non-being, his presence is like an absence. This aspect of God is significant, and needs to be understood rightly.

We always ask, all devotees have asked why God does not manifest himself. We forget that if he becomes manifest, meeting with him in the sense of fusion, unity, oneness, will be impossible. Such fusion is possible only with the unmanifest. Devotees have always said to God, "Where are you hiding? Why don't you manifest yourself?" This is an utterly wrong question. If he really becomes manifest, then a great wall will rise up between the seeker and the sought, and oneness will be simply impossible.

Because he is unmanifest, a merger with God is possible. Because he is invisible and infinite like the sky, the devotee can drown himself in his being, which is as good as non-being. He is visible nowhere, and so he is everywhere. If he becomes visible, union will be impossible.

Eckhart, a seer of extraordinary vision, has expressed his thanks to God in a strange way. He says to God, "Your compassion is infinite that you are so invisible no one can see you, no one can find and meet you. One reaches for you everywhere and you are nowhere to be found. And this is your singular compassion for man, because this way you teach him a lesson. The lesson is that unless a person becomes as invisible as you are, unless he becomes a non-being, an absence like you, union with you is impossible." God is formless, and so when a devotee becomes as formless, when he becomes a non-entity, an absence, he becomes one with the ultimate.

If there is any obstruction in the way of meeting and merging, it is from the side of the devotee, not from God.

A *sthitaprajna* is a devotee who has disappeared, who has become nothing. Now he does not even cry for God, because there is no one who will cry. Now he does not pray, because who will pray to whom? Or we can say, in the words of Kabir, that whatever he does now is worship, whatever he says is prayer. We can say it both ways: he is nothingness and he is all. A *sthitaprajna* is a man who has become God-like.

A devotee is one who has set himself on God's path, who is a pilgrim, but he yet remains a man; all his hopes and aspirations are those of a man. Meera's songs are a case in point. She cries for God, she dances for God. Her songs are superb in the sense that they are so human. Her cries are the cries of a lover, a devotee. She says, "I have made a beautiful bed for you, please come and grace it. I have opened the door and I have been waiting long for you." These are all human feelings. So a devotee is one who is yet human aspiring to be God, to melt in him, be lost in him.

A *sthitaprajna*, one steadied in his intelligence, has ceased to be a man, an ego. He has ceased to be a pilgrim; he has stopped all movements. He is not going anywhere. Now the question of going anywhere does not arise; he is where he is. Now he knows God is everywhere and only God is. He knows God is eternal, he is eternity itself. But unless we become as invisible as he is, unless we become nobodies, we cannot find him. Jesus says, "He who saved himself will be lost; he who loses himself will be saved." The *sthitaprajna* has lost himself, and he is saved, he has arrived.

A devotee is only an aspirant, a seeker. So he is yet an ego, his ego is intact. By and by, his ego will be burnt in the fire of experience and understanding. Kabir says, "As I wandered around searching for God I lost myself." This is the miracle of the spiritual search: the day one loses himself the search is complete. As soon as the seeker disappears, God, the sought, appears.

In fact, the seeker is the sought. Lao Tzu's words in this context are of tremendous significance. He says, "Seek and you will not find. Do not seek and you will find, because Tao is here and now." One really misses God or truth or whatever you call it, just because he seeks him. How can you seek something which is here and now? Seeking means that what you seek is not here, it is there, somewhere else. Because of seeking you drift away from reality.

Someone goes to Kashi, another goes to Mecca, some others go to Gaya, Jerusalem and Kailas; one can even come to Manali. But they are all deviating, drifting away from reality or truth, which is here and now. But so long as a seeker goes on seeking and searching, he also goes on losing himself. And the day he is dead tired, the day he loses himself completely and falls down to the ground, he finds he is in reality. It does not matter whether he falls down in Manali or Mecca, in Kashi or Jerusalem, in Girnar or Gaya—wherever he falls he finds him present. God is ever-present, he is present everywhere, but our own presence prevents us from meeting him. The moment the seeker becomes absent, God or truth is present. God is always present, he is eternally present.

The devotee is one who is present, who is an ego. The *sthitaprajna* is not, he is absent as an ego, a self.

It has to be clearly understood: so long as the devotee is present, God is absent. For this reason the devotee creates a substitute God, a proxy God. He makes a statue of God, or he builds a temple of God; this is proxy. But this is not going to help, because it is the devotee's own creation, it is his own projection. Soon he will be fed up and disillusioned with such games. How can a God of his own making satisfy him? He will realize the unreality of the whole game; he will throw away the statue, the proxy, and he will now seek for the real.

But reality comes into being only when I die as an ego, when I am not. Reality has a single condition: that I should disappear. My being is the wall; my non-being is the door.

This is the difference between a *sthitaprajna* and a devotee. While a devotee is a wall, the *sthitaprajna* has become a door. In fact we are all walls, but a devotee is a wall with a difference. While we are comfortably settled in our position as walls, the devotee has begun to move away from the wall to the door.

> Questioner: Please explain fully Krishna's revolutionary concept of sex. What was the secret of his tremendous sex appeal for women that thousands of them were mad after him and felt satiated and fulfilled by him? Besides, you said that fullness of love leads to cessation of sex. If so, how is it then possible for one to enter into sex after achieving fullness of love and the highest state of samadhi or ecstasy?

We have already gone into the matter at length, and so I will answer this question only briefly.

Krishna's attraction for thousands of women can be compared to a stream of water that leaves the mountains and rushes to the plains and settles in some lake. You never ask why water from the mountains rushes down to the lake. If you ask, the answer will be: because a lake is a lake and it is the way of water to collect in a lake. Water leaves the high mountains and collects in lowly lakes because mountains cannot hold it—the lake can. It is in the nature of water to seek hollows and lakes where it can reside restfully.

Similarly it is in woman's nature to seek man; she can feel at home only by being with man. And it is in man's nature to seek woman; he can feel at home only by being with woman. It is his or her nature, as everything else in life has its own nature. As fire burns, water flows downward, so man seeks woman and woman seeks man.

In fact, they don't seek the other, they seek their own completion, their own fulfillment. To put it rightly, man is the one who seeks himself in woman and woman is the one who seeks herself in man. In themselves man and woman are incomplete and discontented. And unless they meet and merge into each other, they can never be complete and content. For this reason they constantly seek each other, and they feel frustrated when this search is frustrated; they have to go through untold pain and suffering. When this search is thwarted for any reason, it amounts to a violation of nature. And it causes both man and woman severe anxiety, misery and anguish.

The fundamental reason for Krishna's tremendous appeal for woman is that he is a complete man, a total man. The more complete a man, the greater his appeal for woman. In the same way the more complete a woman, the greater her attraction for man. Completion of manhood has found its full expression in Krishna.

As a complete man Mahavira is not less than Krishna; he is as complete as Krishna. But Mahavira's whole discipline consists in going beyond the law of physical nature, transcending the world of yin and yang. It is strange that in spite of this, there are thirty thousand nuns and only ten thousand monks among his disciples—three women for one man. It simply means Mahavira has great attraction for women. The ratio of women and men among his renunciates is three to one.

It is significant that one whose whole discipline aims at transcendence of sex, who negates his own male nature and refuses to accept the femininity of woman, who treats the whole matter of sex as mundane, as unspiritual, who puts the spiritual quest far beyond these worldly pursuits should continue to attract women in such a big way. The irony is that women are prohibited from touching Mahavira or even sitting in his close proximity, and yet they are so mad after him.

By the way, I should say this aspect of Mahavira's life and teaching has never been looked at in this way. It should be. Let alone his thirty thousand female disciples, if we probe deep into the psyche of his ten thousand male disciples, we will find an element of femininity in their nature. It cannot be otherwise. It is not necessary that every man has a male mind and every woman a female mind.

The mind is not always in harmony with the body, or it is in much less harmony than we think. It has often been seen that while one has a male body, his mind has a feminine inclination. If ever it is possible to investigate the minds of Mahavira's monks, then we will know they were predominantly feminine in nature. It is bound to be so. Mahavira—or anyone for that matter—who is the epitome of masculinity, cannot attract you unless there is a strong woman inside you. Attraction is like two-way traffic. Mahavira's attraction does only half the job, the other half comes from the one who is attracted.

In this respect Krishna's position is uncommon and rare. Krishna has not renounced the world or anything; he accepts life in its totality. It is not that women can be near him only as nuns and ascetics or can only watch him from a distance. No, they can freely dance and sing with Krishna; they can make *maharaas*, a prodigious dance with him in the center. So it is not at all surprising that thousands of women have gathered round him. It is so natural, so simple.

So is Buddha a complete man. There is an extraordinary story associated with his life. When after his enlightenment he turns the wheel of *Dhamma*, he declares that he will not initiate women into his commune, his *sangha*. He does so because the danger inherent in admitting women is obvious. The danger is that around a luminous man like Buddha, women can flock like moths and they can overwhelm the *sangha* merely with the weight of their numbers.

It is not necessary that women will come to him just for spiritual growth. Buddha's charisma, his masculine attraction will have a big hand in drawing them to him. It is not that the large number of *gopis*, cowmaids, who surround Krishna are there for God-realization; Krishna is enough of an attraction for them. To be with such a complete man is a bliss in itself. For them he is nothing less than God. And because Krishna is choiceless, he is not in the least concerned why they come to him; he accepts them unconditionally. But Buddha is not that choiceless; he has his constraints and conditions for admitting anyone into his fold.

So Buddha stubbornly refuses women admission in his commune, and he resists every pressure brought to bear upon him on behalf of women who strongly protest his decision. It is only after intense pleadings and pressure from the women that Buddha yields to their demand to be initiated into his fold. It is understandable why Buddha long remains unyielding to their numerous entreaties for being initiated. He knows that ninety-nine women out of a hundred will come to him not for Buddhahood but for Buddha himself. It is so obvious, that Buddha goes on resisting till a woman comes and finally disarms him. This woman is rare, as rare as Buddha, and the story is beautiful.

One morning a woman named Krisha Gautami comes to Buddha and says to him, "Why are we women being deprived of Buddhahood? You are not coming to this world once again to redeem us. What is our crime? Is it a crime to be born as women? And remember, all the guilt, all the responsibility for depriving women of this gift of Buddhahood will lie singly at your door." This Krisha Gautami is the hundredth woman—the one who comes for Buddhahood, not for Buddha. And so Buddha has to yield to Krisha Gautami. She leaves Buddha defenseless.

She says to him in very clear words, "I come to you, not for you, but for the rarest gift of Buddhahood that you bring to this earth. It happens once in millennia. Why should it be the sole preservation of men alone? Why should women be deprived of this blessing just because they are women? This is the most unkind and harshest of punishments that you can inflict on them; in a way you are punishing womanhood. And it seems you too are partial, you too pick and choose; it seems not even a Buddha is choiceless."

Buddha yields to Krisha Gautami; he initiates her as his first woman disciple. And then the gate is thrown wide open for women. And the story of Mahavira repeats itself: women disciples come to predominate over men disciples in the same ratio of three to one.

Even today more women visit temples and *buddha-viharas* and *gurudwaras* than men do. Unless statues of women Buddhas and incarnations and *tirthankaras* adorn these temples, men will continue to keep away from them, because ninety-nine always go for natural reasons; only the hundredth goes there for the trans-natural reason.

With Krishna the matter of men and women is as simple as two and two make four. Krishna has no difficulty whatsoever with women; he accepts them as naturally as anything. Krishna takes life and everything about life playfully and in its totality. He accepts a woman being a woman just as he accepts himself being a man. The truth is that Krishna has never said a word of disrespect for woman, even inadvertently.

Jesus can be found guilty of being disrespectful to women; so can Mahavira and Buddha, because they are trying to eliminate their male nature and go beyond it. They have nothing to do with women. Mahavira, Buddha, and Jesus want to wipe out the sexual part, the biological part of their beings, and so they are aware if they allow women to be around them the women will come in their way. Surrounded by women, their male nature will begin to assert itself, because women provide nourishment to manhood.

Curiously enough, women gather round Mahavira, Buddha and Jesus, who are not favorably inclined to them. Jesus is withdrawn and sad and is said to have never laughed. But those who take down his dead body from the cross are all women, not men. The most beautiful woman of her times, Mary Magdalene, is one of them. All his male disciples have escaped. Only three women are there to take care of his dead body. And Jesus never said a word of respect for women.

And Mahavira says that woman cannot achieve *moksha* or liberation unless she is reborn as a man. Buddha refuses to initiate them into his religion. And when Krisha Gautami persuades him to admit them in his *sangha* he makes a strange statement. He says, "My religion was going to last five thousand years, but now that women have entered it will last only five hundred years."

Questioner: There is truth in this statement.

This is not the question. This is not the question at all. There is a relative truth in this statement; it is true from the side of Buddha. It is true from his side, because his path—or for that matter, Mahavira's path—is not meant for women. Women don't have much scope on Buddha's path, which is male-oriented. Nonetheless women rush to them because they are so charismatic. So Buddha's statement is relatively true in the context of his path, but it is not an absolute truth.

There is no difficulty for women in achieving *moksha*; they can achieve it as much as men can, but certainly their path will be different. They cannot make it on the path of the Jaina *tirthankara*. It is like there are two pathways for going to a mountain, one of which is straight, steep and short with a sign on the entrance: Not For Women. And another is long, circular and flat with a sign at the beginning: For Women. This much is the difference.

So the statement that women cannot achieve liberation is true in the context of Mahavira's path or Buddha's for that matter. If some woman insists on treading these male-oriented paths, she will surely have to wait for another incarnation as a man.

Mahavira's path is particularly steep and precipitous and hard, and there are good reasons for it. One important reason is that you have to go it alone, there is neither God nor any companion to lean on in times of difficulty. And the psychological make-up of a woman is such that she needs someone's shoulder —even a false shoulder—to lean on when in difficulty. She has a sense of assurance when a shoulder is available to lean on, a hand to hold. This is the way she is.

But man's way is different; he loves to be on his own. Dependence on others is alien to his nature; it fills him with self-pity. When a woman puts her hand in the hand of a man she feels assurance, strength, and dignity. Left alone she pities herself and feels forlorn and miserable.

> *Questioner: Gandhi used to walk leaning on two women—one on each side.*

It is a different thing altogether, and I would like to discuss it later. This particular aspect of Gandhi, walking with feminine support, deserves special consideration. He is perhaps the first man to do so. No man in the past had walked leaning on the shoulders of women.

> *Questioner: Was it because he was old?*

No, not because he was old. Even when he was not old he walked that way. This gesture of Gandhi's is symbolic and significant. In this country where woman has always been leaning on man, where she is taken to be the weaker sex, where she is treated as a second-class citizen in society, Gandhi is the first person to go against this long-established tradition.

Gandhi, by leaning on the shoulders of two women, declares that the woman is not the weaker sex, she is as strong as man and man can equally lean on her shoulders. It is a step against an old tradition; it is a protest. It is nothing more than a protest.

However, Gandhi does not look right when he walks leaning on women, nor do the two women feel good about it. They must be feeling awkward, heavy and crushed under Gandhi's weight—physical and psychological. In fact, it looks unnatural and ugly, because it goes contrary to the nature of both man and woman.

Gandhi does not seem to have a right understanding of their nature and relationship. He is just opposing an old tradition—but this is a different thing. It also shows how poor is Gandhi's understanding of male and female minds.

I don't think Gandhi's remedy has done any good for the community of women. He turned any number of women into men, which has done them immense harm. Woman cannot be made into man;

she has her own way of being. Leaning comes naturally to her. What is significant when she leans on a
man is that not only she feels honored but the man
feels equally honored. It is a matter of give and take:
by leaning on man she makes man lean on her. He
is a very poor and miserable man on whom no woman
has ever leaned.

So as far as Mahavira, Buddha and Jesus are
concerned, the negation of biology forms part of their
spiritual discipline. But Krishna's vision is altogether
different. He accepts the whole of life without discrimination; biology or sex is as much acceptable to
him as soul or God. Body, mind and soul are equally
welcome; one is no less significant than the other;
nothing is denied.

In Krishna's eyes he who denies, who says no,
is more or less an atheist. In fact, to deny, to say no
is atheism. Denial is the way of the atheist; it makes
no difference whether he denies matter or God, body
or soul, hunger or sex. He who denies sex or the body
is as much an atheist as one who denies the soul.
Similarly, acceptance, yes-saying is the way of theism.

So in my view, neither Mahavira nor Buddha
nor Jesus is as complete a theist as Krishna is; he is
really a total yes-sayer. There is not an ounce of denial
or condemnation of anything in Krishna's life. Total
acceptance is his way. Whatever is, has a place in
existence. Krishna's trust in existence is indomitable,
invincible. And it is rare too.

It is not accidental that thousands and
thousands of women surround Krishna. And there is
no reason for this other than what I have just mentioned. If they gather round Mahavira they have to
keep a formal distance from him, they have to observe
some formality, certain conventions with him. They
cannot hug him; it would be considered highly impolite and improper. Neither Mahavira will tolerate it
nor will the women concerned feel happy about it.
They may even feel humiliated.

Questioner: Why can't Mahavira tolerate it?

Mahavira will not tolerate it in the sense that he will not accept it, he will not respond to it, he will remain unmoving like a rock. He will refuse a woman's hug with his whole being. He will not say in words, "Don't touch me," but the woman will know it; she will feel as if she is hugging a piece of rock.

A woman will not feel humiliation if you ask her not to touch you, but she will really feel hurt if you don't respond to her hug. Not that Mahavira has any disrespect for women, but the way he is he cannot do otherwise, he cannot take hugs and embraces from women. Therefore women have to keep a respectful distance from him; they can never be on intimate terms with him. There is a limit, a boundary line beyond which they cannot come near him.

It is entirely different with Krishna; even if a woman wants to keep a distance from him she cannot. He is so open, so receptive, so accepting, and so charismatic that no woman can resist him. Once a woman goes to him she will be pulled by him, she will soon be as close to him as is physically possible. Krishna is like an open invitation of love; he is like a clarion call of friendship, intimacy and love. He is, in this respect, the antithesis of Mahavira who, as I said, will be as still as a rock if someone goes to embrace him.

Emerson has said about Henry Thoreau that if someone shook hands with him he had the feeling that he had a dried-up stem of a tree in his hands. In response to someone's hand he just extended his hand without a word or warmth or feeling, as if it was a dead hand. He was so stoical, indifferent to emotions of joy and grief. Henry Thoreau can well be paired off with Mahavira.

Krishna is the opposite of Thoreau; even if you are at a distance from Krishna, you will feel he is touching you, calling you, he is on the verge of embracing you. His whole being is so sweet, so inviting, so magnetic, so musical, that it is no wonder thousands of women become his *gopis*, girlfriends. It is utterly natural in his context. And it is all spontaneous.

You further ask if it is possible for Krishna to enter into sex, if he can make love. Nothing is impossible for Krishna. For us sex is a problem, not for Krishna. It is strange that we ask if Krishna has a sex life; we never ask if flowers have sex. We never ask if birds and animals indulge in sexual intercourse. The whole world is immersed in sex; it is all a play of sex abounding. The whole of existence is engrossed in love-making. And we never ask why.

But when it comes to man we raise our eyebrows immediately, and we ask how can Krishna have sex? For man as he is, tense and anxious, full of condemnation for life, drowned in self-pity, even an act like sex—which is utterly inbuilt and natural and simple—has become a most tangled problem. He has made such a simple, innocent gift of existence into a hornets' nest. He has made sex a prisoner of principles and doctrines.

What is the meaning of the sex act or sexual intercourse? It simply means coming together of two bodies in as intimate contact with each other as nature has ordained. Sex is two bodies coming together in biological intimacy with each other in the way nature wants it to be. It is nothing more or less. Sex is the ultimate intimacy between two beings, male and female, at the level of nature. Beyond it nature has no reach. Beyond it the jurisdiction of God begins.

Krishna gives nature all its due; he accepts the biological intimacy provided by nature as gracefully as he accepts unity with God or the soul. He says nature belongs to God, it is all within God. For Krishna, sex is not at all a problem; it is a simple fact of life.

We find it so difficult to understand how one can take sex so simply, innocently. For us it has ceased to be a fact of life; we have made it into a seemingly intractable problem of life. Thank God we have not yet done so with many other simple things of life, but who knows the way we are, if we will not do it tomorrow?

Tomorrow we can say that to open one's eyes is a sin. And then we will ask if Krishna opens his eyes too. Tomorrow we can turn even such a simple thing as the opening and closing of eyelids into a philosophical problem, a matter of theology and doctrinaire debate. Then we will endlessly ask what to do or not to do with our eyes, just as now we ask about sex.

In my view Krishna's life is utterly uninhibited, unconstrained, unlimited; he does not admit constraints and limitations. And that is his beauty and grandeur, his uniqueness. For him all constraints, all limitations are bondage; for him real freedom is freedom from constraints and limitations. Unconstraint is his freedom.

But Krishna's meaning of unconstraint is different from ours. By unconstraint we mean violation of constraints; for Krishna it is just absence of constraints, limitations. If you bear this in mind, you will have no difficulty in understanding Krishna's life in the context of sex, or anything for that matter. Sex is not a problem for him as it is for us; we keep thinking and re-thinking endlessly about it. For him sex is just biological. If sex happens it happens; if it does not, it does not.

So far as we are concerned, sex has become much more psychological, cerebral, than biological; it is much more in our minds than it is in its own right place—the sex center.

Psychologists say that modern man has sex on the brain. Krishna does not have to think about sex; we do. We think when we enter into sex and we think even when we don't. Krishna does not have to think and come to a decision about it, it is not at all a matter of mentation for him. If a moment of love arrives which calls for sex, Krishna is available to it. It is just a happening. If it does not happen, Krishna does not crave for or care about it. For him sex is just sex; he neither justifies it nor condemns it.

Justification or condemnation is our education, our opinion, our prejudice. It has nothing to do with the fact of sex, which is pure biology. That which is, is; it is neither good nor bad. And Krishna accepts that which is and even that which is not.

I repeat: Krishna's meaning of acceptance is not the same as ours. When we accept something we do so against our denial of it; we do so by suppressing our denial. The denial is there but we suppress the denying part of our mind and somehow manage to accept it. This acceptance is fragmentary, it is done reluctantly. It is acceptance with reservations, with some ulterior motive. For us it is never unconditional and total acceptance. When Krishna accepts he just accepts, there is not a trace of denial in it.

For this very reason it has been tremendously difficult to understand Krishna. It is easy to understand Mahavira, Buddha, Jesus and Mohammed, but Krishna is one person in the whole world who is the most difficult to understand. That is why we have done Krishna the greatest injustice, and we have done it with impunity.

Most of our ideas, concepts, and thoughts come from Mahavira, Buddha, Jesus and Mohammed. All our moral tenets and dogmas, all our values of good and evil, virtue and vice—all our ideals and high-sounding principles—have been determined by men like Manu, Mohammed and Confucius. So it is easy to understand them, because we are, in the world of thoughts, their creatures. Krishna has no hand in creating us that way. The truth is that Krishna refuses to circumscribe life with ideas and ideals, doctrines and dogmas, because life is larger than all ideas and ideals put together. Life is illimitable, infinite. Ideas are for life; life is not for them. Life is the ultimate value. So Krishna says that which is, is right.

Because of this, Krishna has been widely misunderstood. Even if we try to understand him, we see him through the eyes of Manu and Moses, Christ and Confucius. And all these people are conventional. They have their constraints and limitations, while Krishna is utterly unconventional, without any constraints and limitations.

Krishna does not accept any limitations on himself. He says, "If you want to understand me, remove all kinds of glasses from your eyes, and see me with your bare eyes." It is very arduous to see something with bare eyes, with clarity, to see something as it is without judging it. But as long as you see Krishna through the eyes of others you are bound to find fault with him. But these faults will come from your glasses, not from Krishna. Put aside your prejudices and Krishna is the most simple and natural, innocent and authentic person ever. Then his life is an open book; he has really nothing to hide. He is naturalness embodied; he is innocence personified.

It can be asked why there has been no woman yet as natural and innocent as Krishna. At least one should be there who, like Krishna, could attract thousands of men toward her. There has been none so far. Why?

It is not enough to say that women have been suppressed down the ages, that they have been denied liberty and freedom in a male-dominated world. In this context this argument is irrelevant and absurd. Everyone can have as much freedom as he or she needs; otherwise he or she will refuse to live. So the reason why there has not been a single woman as natural as Krishna—and there is no likelihood of her coming into being for another thousand or more years—is quite different. The reason is that the whole biological make-up of woman is intrinsically monogamous; she is dependent on one man psychologically, emotionally.

Questioner: Like Cleopatra?

No, I will take it later. Woman is by nature monogamous; she can lean on a single person for her whole life. Her mind is made that way. I don't say that she will always be so; it is not necessary.

On the other hand man is polygamous by nature; he cannot remain tied to one woman. Living with one woman, a man is invariably bored; living with one man a woman is not so bored. A woman longs to live with a man she loves for life after life; she often prays for the same man to be her life-partner in her life after death.

The institution of monogamy—togetherness of one man and one woman—is woman's gift to society, not man's. She has always insisted that a man or woman should have only one spouse. And this insistence is justifiable both on biological and psychological grounds. It is always woman who has to depend on, to lean on man, and she cannot be dependent on many men. That would create uncertainty and unreliability.

For instance, a creeper can lean on one tree alone, it cannot lean on many. But a tree can accommodate more than one creeper, and it will be the richer for it. Similarly many women can lean on one man, and he will be the richer for it.

As I said, the reason for a woman's preference for depending on one man and not more is both psychological and biological, but on well-grounded reasoning it can be said that it is more biological than psychological. Woman alone has to bear and rear children and will need someone to care for them and for their future. And if there is more than one person in this position there will be confusion and difficulties. That is why I say that it will take a thousand or more years for women to get rid of the idea of monogamy.

With the growth of scientific knowledge it is quite possible in the future when woman will not be required to carry children in her womb; soon laboratories will take over this job from the mother. And the day woman is free of child-bearing she can be as natural and spontaneous as Krishna is.

This matter of being natural and spontaneous is crucial to humanity and its future. This is the only way for us to free ourselves from the age-old clutches of gnawing anxiety and anguish. Most of our stress and strain stems from our struggle against our own nature. All our anxieties and miseries arise from our fight with ourselves. Ever since man has gone against himself he has been perpetually in pain and misery, anxiety and anguish. And the tragedy is that while we can easily fight with ourselves, we can never win against ourselves. In fighting with ourselves we can only be defeated and destroyed.

Once in a long while, someone, a Mahavira, a Gorakh, wins in a fight with himself. It is rare. But in emulation of this rare person, millions fight with themselves only to end up in defeat and despair.

In my vision, one in a million can succeed on the path of Mahavira, but unfortunately a vast majority of seekers choose this path. On the other hand while ninety-nine out of a hundred can succeed on Krishna's path, rarely one takes to it. As I said, the paths of Mahavira, Buddha and Jesus are narrow and hard, because one has to go the whole way fighting with himself. So one in a million succeeds. On the other hand, Krishna's highway is wide and easy, but very few choose it.

It seems man has by and by lost his capacity for being natural; to be unnatural has become natural for him. It seems he has forgotten altogether what it is to be healthy and whole. So a thorough re-thinking on his part is the need of the hour. And as I see it such a re-thinking is already on its way.

After Freud, Krishna is going to be more and more relevant for our future. For the first time—because of Freud—man has come to realize the utter importance of naturalness and spontaneity in life. Now a social milieu is coming into being in which acceptance of a simple and natural being will be easier. Man as he is will be accepted and allowed to grow the way he is.

Up to now, almost every culture has rejected man as he is and insisted on the creation of an imaginary ideal man—man as he should be. The ideal has been all-important and man has all along been urged to struggle to reach that ideal, that utopia.

Freud is the forerunner of a worldwide intellectual awakening, an upsurge, a renaissance, a cultural revolution which has come to realize that man has utterly failed in his efforts to reach utopia and that he has suffered immeasurably in its pursuit. If once in a while someone reaches utopia, he is the exception, not the rule. And the exception proves the rule. So for the first time after Freud, honest thinking is being done which seeks to understand man as he is. What we have to really understand is that which is, not that which should be. What is, not what should be is the crux.

For instance, every wife wants that her husband should not be interested in any other woman. This desire, which is natural for a woman, runs counter to the male nature which is basically polygamous. The problem is that if social laws and conventions are laid in obedience to the male nature, women will suffer, and if they are laid to conform to feminine nature, men will be unhappy. And the core of the problem is that neither can be happy if one of them is miserable. But until now, we have followed this zigzag course alternately and as a result the whole of mankind has perpetually been in misery and anguish.

So the only way out is that both man and woman try to understand and know each other as they basically are. When a husband gets interested in some woman, let the wife understand that this is in the nature of man, and she need not suffer on this score. Similarly when a wife is depressed and unhappy about her husband taking interest in other women, let the husband understand her with love and sympathy instead of flying into a rage over it. If we want to create a humanity free from anxiety and anguish, there is no way but to go into and understand the basic nature of man and woman to its very roots.

And if we have to change our nature, its roots will need to be changed—moral teachings and moralist discipline will never go deeper than the surface of the problem. The woman will continue to be jealous as long as she is economically dependent on man. She will be jealous so long as she has to bear the burden of children alone, so long as she remains a second-class citizen, an inferior human being.

When the society gives her a place of equality with man, when she is economically on her own, when she does not suffer from the biological handicap of bearing and rearing children alone, she will not take a day longer to drop jealousy. And then she too will take interest in other men besides her husband. Then she will not insist on monogamy.

It was not possible in the past, but now that man's understanding of himself has grown, a transformation of both the individual and the group is quite feasible. All of our old order was based on the needs of man, not on the understanding of his nature. We made laws according to the needs of our society, not according to needs of human nature. But after Freud, a revolution is taking place in man's mind, and I believe the return of Krishna is in the offing.

And Krishna will return through the door of Freud, who has prepared the ground. But a lot more remains to be done; Freud is only the beginning. The ball has been set rolling however. In the coming future, more and more people will be inspired by Krishna's life and philosophy. His way of life, his affirmation of life, his naturalness and spontaneity, his openness and authenticity are going to have increasing impact on our life and time.

I think we have failed to create a healthy world following Mahavira, Buddha, Jesus and Confucius. So a venturesome experiment to pattern the world after Krishna will be worthwhile. And I think it will be much better than the one we have created so far. In the past we did everything to make the exception into a rule, and we failed miserably. It is time we base our rule on the rule itself.

I repeat: Base your rule on the rule.

TWENTY-FIRST DISCOURSE
EVENING, OCTOBER 5, 1970
MANALI, INDIA

CHOOSE THE FLUTE OR PERISH

Questioner: Speaking in the context of Krishna and Jesus, you observed, "The civilization that began with the cross had to end up in an atomic war, and therefore the modern civilization is faced with a choice between the cross and the flute." But the question is that the civilization that began with the flute also ended up in a war—the war of Mahabharat. Please explain the anomaly.

he cross is the symbol of death. It is okay as an emblem of the grave, but it is dangerous to accept it as a symbol of life. But many so-called religious people have treated human life and body as no more than a grave, and it is going to result in a disaster.

A man bearing a crucifix on his breast declares that life is not acceptable to him; he is worshipping death really. For him life is a curse, not a blessing. Christianity—I don't mean Jesus—believes that man is born in sin, that life is the original sin. According to them, what we think of as life is not God's gift, but a form of punishment inflicted on man.

This kind of thinking is essentially masochistic, pessimistic, morbid. Standing near a rosebush a pessimist takes note of every thorn, but he ignores the flowers altogether. Looking at day and night, a pessimist sees two dark nights sandwiching a short day instead of seeing two bright days enclosing a brief dark night. Such a mind gathers together all the hurt and pain of life and completely forgets its delights and pleasures.

In fact, paying too much attention to the miseries of life is the sign of a diseased mind, a neurotic and deranged mind. Of course a philosophy of life that affirms and emphasizes sorrow and suffering is bound to be negative and nihilistic. And this is what the cross represents.

Had he not been crucified, Jesus would have never made such a powerful impact on the world. In all probability the world would have forgotten him. His crucifixion became the foundation of Christianity.

Today nearly a billion people all over the world are within the fold of Christianity. I don't take this to be the triumph of Christ, it is undoubtedly the victory of the cross. Jesus hanging on the cross became a great attraction for our miserable and diseased minds. Our lives are virtually on the cross; we are ridden with anxiety, sorrow and suffering. We are a people who collect only hurt and pain, as some people collect used stamps. We all have our stockpiles of miseries; we don't have any remembrance of having any happy moments in life.

Krishna is absolutely the opposite type of individual, and his flute as a symbol is just the opposite of the cross. There is no sense in putting a flute on a grave; it needs throbbing lips and supple fingers to play it. It needs a singing and dancing heart, a soul brimming with joy and bliss to hold it. And I think it is time man makes a clear choice between the cross of Jesus and the flute of Krishna.

It is not that life is without its hurts and pains; it cannot be. But if a person brings his focus only to the hurt and pain and goes on accumulating them, he will soon cease to meet with any happy moments in life. It is not that there is no happiness in life; it has its fair share of happiness too. And if someone trains his attention on happiness alone and goes on gathering it, he will eventually cease to come across painful moments in life.

Life consists of both pleasure and pain, happiness and misery. And it depends on us what we choose to see and take. My own understanding is that if someone sees rightly and loves rose flowers, then soon the thorns on the rosebush will disappear from his sight. Eyes attuned to the beauty and fragrance of the flower don't take notice of the thorns. Not that the thorns disappear from the bush; they become part and parcel of the grandeur of the roses, and one sees them as something protecting the roses. They are really to protect the flowers, not to hurt anyone.

But if someone sees only thorns he will miss the flowers. He will say, "How can there be any flowers in the midst of so many piercing thorns and thistles?" He cannot even think of flowers where thorns abound. For him thorns become the truth and flowers disappear like dreams. But for a lover of flowers, thorns become illusory and flowers the truth.

It depends on man, what he chooses; he is free to choose. There is a saying of Sartre's which is strange but close to truth. He says, "Man is condemned to be free." It seems freedom is an imposition on us, inflicted on us. It seems we can choose everything except freedom—because we are free to choose or not to choose it. Never had anyone described freedom as something inflicted on man.

Man is free, and this freedom affirms his being God. But he can choose anything—even not being God. Similarly, he is free to choose pain and misery. Life will be pure suffering for one who makes suffering his choice. We become that which we choose to become. In fact, we see what we want to see; we find what we want to find; we receive what we ask for. So if you seek suffering you are going to have it, without fail.

The irony is that if someone opts for suffering he does not suffer alone, he makes many others suffer with him. And this is where immorality comes into being. Unhappiness is a contagious disease: a single unhappy person can be the cause of the unhappiness of thousands. It is impossible that an unhappy man can make another happy. How can he give happiness to another when he refuses to take it for himself? Remember, we can share with others only that which we have, not what we don't have.

One who has turned his life into a bundle of hurts and wounds is going to be the cause of much suffering in the lives of many people around him. Since suffering has become his life's breath, wherever he goes he will carry the germs of suffering with him. So an unhappy man does not suffer alone; he shares his sorrow with everybody he comes in contact with. Walking or sitting, speaking or silent, active or inactive, he emits and transmits the vibes of unhappiness like nuclear fallout all around him. An unhappy person really adds to the unhappiness of the whole world.

Remember, when you choose unhappiness, you are not choosing it for yourself alone, but for the whole world as such.

As I said, it is man's preference for pain and suffering which the cross symbolizes. And that has led him to the doorstep of war—a war that is going to be a total war. For the first time, mankind is on the brink of committing global suicide. But he has asked for it by opting for misery.

We know very well that sometimes individuals driven up the wall commit suicide in despair. But for the first time a situation for collective suicide has arisen, when the whole of mankind has become so miserable that it is going to commit global hara-kiri.

It seems war has become our way of life, and the mounting number of wars are nothing but our mounting steps to collective death and destruction. And this destruction is the cumulative effect of mankind's choice of suffering. Really, war is of our own choosing; it does not descend out of the blue.

And when we court suffering religiously, when we accept it as something religious, then nothing remains to be chosen irreligiously. When we turn sorrow into a religion, then there is nothing like irreligion on the earth. Sorrow is really enshrined when it is made part of religion.

A whole milieu of unhappiness and misery was created around the cross. I don't say it was created around Jesus, because Jesus is not necessarily connected with the cross; he could very well do without the cross. The fact is, that Christianity was created not by Jesus, but by the people who crucified him.

I always say Christianity was not founded by Jesus; its real founders were those Jewish theologians and priests who crucified him. Christianity comes from the cross, not Christ. Poor Jesus was simply hanged on the cross—so he is secondary. First comes the cross in relation to the religion founded after his name. In fact, it should be called "crossianity," not Christianity. It is the cross that occupies the place of honor in the hearts and minds of people whose life is every day on the cross.

Man as he is, is in suffering; he is perpetually on the cross. It is not much different whether it is the cross of the family or of relationships, of friendships or of enmities, of religions or of nationalities. For man, life is a cross that he has to carry on his shoulders from the cradle to the grave. For him, life is really a curse, a sin, not a blessing. And the cross became increasingly important to him, and he clung to it. In fact, Christianity is a worldwide conglomeration of all such pessimistic and miserable people.

It is relevant to note that the last two world wars were mostly fought by Christian countries. A few non-Christian countries that were involved in these wars were dragged into them by their imperialist masters, who were all Christians.

Japan was the only non-Christian country that willingly joined the war as an aggressor. But Japan has ceased to be an eastern country except geographically; it is now virtually a part of the western world. And Japan has a long tradition of suicide which in Japanese is called *hara-kiri*. A Japanese kills himself on very small excuses; his wife has died, or he has committed an act of misdemeanor and he thinks he is finished with life. Then there is no way for him but to end his life—as if there is no hope of his redemption.

According to this thinking, a tree should commit hara-kiri when its flowers wither—who knows if new flowers will open the next morning? The Japanese don't have even this much hope and patience in their hearts. So the last two world wars were fought by peoples who have been traditionally associated with the cross and the custom of hara-kiri.

If the Third World War happens, it will spell the destruction of mankind; it will be a case of collective crucifixion of the human race. So what began with the crucifixion of a single individual is going to end in the collective crucifixion—the crucifixion of the entire race of *homo sapiens*. I don't say that Jesus is responsible for it; the responsibility belongs to those who hanged him on the cross.

I also don't say that people rallied round the cross because they were influenced by Jesus; the contrary is the truth. They came to Jesus because they were influenced by the cross. But it is undeniably true that a civilization based on crossianism, on sado-masochism, was destined to lead mankind to self-destruction. Actually there is no sense in accepting the cross and worshipping it. Even if life bears a cross, it is in our hands to replace the cross with a flower.

In my view, Krishna's flute is exactly the opposite of the cross. And it is important to know that while it is others who hang Jesus on the cross, they really impose it on him; Krishna chooses the flute for himself. It is necessary to bear in mind that while the flute is intrinsic to Krishna and his life—it symbolizes him—the cross is extrinsic to Christ; it does not represent him. It is others, the Jewish priests and the Roman governor, who force the cross on Christ.

Krishna plays the flute for the love of it. Nobody has forced it on him; he has chosen it for himself. I see Krishna's flute symbolizing life's benediction and man's gratefulness to life for this blessing. Krishna has made his choice for happiness, for bliss. In fact, when life is so good and great, Krishna cannot but choose to be happy, and he says it with the flute.

And just as an unhappy person does not suffer alone, he makes many others unhappy, similarly a happy person becomes the source of happiness for countless numbers of people. So when Krishna plays his flute, its melody, its bliss, does not remain confined to him, it gladdens all those whose hearts come to hear it. And it is as it should be.

If you happen to pass by a cross with Jesus hanging on it, you will immediately be depressed and sad. On the other hand, seeing Krishna dancing in ecstacy on the banks of the river Yamuna will fill your heart with delight and joy. Pleasure and pain, happiness and unhappiness are contagious; they are communicable from one to another; they spread and escalate like wildfire.

So the one who decides to be unhappy is condemning the whole world to be unhappy; he might as well say he has decided to punish the whole earth by choosing to be unhappy. And the person who decides to be happy is going to bless the whole to be happy; he is going to add to the song and music of life all over this planet. Therefore a happy person is a religious person; and an unhappy person is utterly irreligious.

I call the man religious who brings happiness to himself and to others. For me, nothing except happiness, blissfulness, is a religious quality. In this sense Krishna is truly a religious person, whose whole being exudes nothing but happiness and bliss. And such a person can bless the whole of mankind; he is a living blessing to the world.

But you ask why did the war of the Mahabharat happen in a civilization that had accepted the flute as its symbol? I say, this happened in spite of Krishna's flute. Krishna is not the cause of the Mahabharat. There is no relationship whatsoever between the flute and war. But there exists a logical relationship between the cross and war.

The Mahabharat took place in spite of Krishna and his flute. It simply means we are so attached to sorrow, so steeped in misery that even Krishna's flute fails to bring a ray of hope and joy to our hearts. The flute continued to play, and we plunged into the vortex of war. The flute could not change our sado-masochistic minds; Krishna's flute could not become our flute too.

It is interesting to know how difficult it is for someone to share in another's happiness. It is so easy to share in another's sorrow. You can easily cry with someone crying, but it is so hard to laugh with someone laughing. You can easily sympathize with one whose house has been burned down, but it is arduous to participate in the joys of one who has built himself a beautiful new house. And it is not without some fundamental reasons.

It is easy to come close to Jesus' cross, because it strikes a note of empathy in our hearts, which are already filled with pain and misery. On the other hand, Krishna's flute will fill our hearts with envy and we will escape from him. Krishna's bliss will bring up envy in us; it will not find an empathic response from our hearts.

Conversely, the cross will not make us jealous; it will certainly bring up our empathy. The happiness of another creates jealousy, and jealousy turns into misery. So to participate in another's happiness is really arduous.

It needs extraordinary intelligence to participate in another's happiness. To share in the joys of another, to make them one's own is a rare quality; it is of the highest. But to share in another's sorrow is not that difficult. It is so because we are ourselves burdened with sorrow and suffering; we are already in misery. So we have no difficulty in identifying ourselves with the suffering of others. But if someone is happy we fail to connect with him for the simple reason that we don't know what happiness is, we are only unhappy in ourselves.

I repeat, the Mahabharat happens in spite of the flute. It is interesting to note that after the advent of the cross it takes two thousand years for war to grow to its present dimensions of a massive war enveloping the whole earth, but the Mahabharat takes place even when Krishna is playing his flute.

The truth is that the flute and its message is not rightly understood and appreciated. It fails to make an impression on the sado-masochistic minds of the people.

Another thing worth considering in this context is that Krishna participates personally in the war. You cannot think of Jesus joining a war of any kind. If someone suggests to him to do so, he will say, "Have you gone mad? Don't you know what I teach?" Jesus has said, "The prophets of the past have said that if someone gouges out your one eye you should take out his both, but I tell you if someone slaps you on the right cheek, turn to him the other one too. And I tell you if someone takes your shirt, let him have your coat as well. And if someone asks you to carry his bag one mile, go with him two miles—maybe out of shyness he does not ask for more than a mile." Now this person cannot be goaded into fighting a war.

It looks somewhat paradoxical and complex that while Jesus refuses even to resist evil, Krishna feels no compunction in leading a destructive war like the Mahabharat. But the reason is obvious. For Jesus, life is so miserable and meaningless that it is not worth fighting for. For Krishna, on the other hand, life is so blissful that even a war can be risked for it.

I would like to go into this matter rather deeply, because it is significant for us and our times.

For Jesus, life as it is is so utterly miserable and meaningless that a slap or two on the cheek will not add to its pile of miseries. It can be said that his cup of suffering is so full that any more suffering will not make a difference. So he turns his other cheek to you so you don't have to take the trouble of turning it yourself. He is already so miserable that you cannot make him any more miserable.

For this reason, Jesus cannot be persuaded to take part in war. He alone can agree to fight who declares that life is a blessing and not a curse, that life is bliss and not suffering. He will stake everything to defend the joy and bliss of life. He will do anything for the sake of life.

Not only Jesus, even Mahavira and Buddha will not say yes to war. Only Krishna is capable of doing it. If there is any other person in the world of spiritualism and religion who can come near Krishna in this respect, it is Mohammed. At some level, at some depth Mohammed is closer to Krishna than others, although he cannot be fully with Krishna.

Whosoever feels that there is something precious and worthwhile in life which needs to be preserved, to be fought for—he will join hands with

Krishna. For those who think otherwise, who see nothing in life worth preserving, the question simply does not arise.

But remember, Krishna is not a warmonger. He is not a hawk, as some pacifists would like to call him. He is a supporter of life, he stands by life, and he will fight for it if need be. If the great values of life—without which life would cease to be life—are in peril, Krishna will not hesitate to defend them with missiles. Not that he relishes violence or war, but if it becomes unavoidable he will not shirk the responsibility.

That is why, from the beginning, he does everything to avoid the Mahabharat. He leaves no stone unturned to avert war and save life and peace. But when all his efforts for peace fail, he realizes that the recalcitrant forces of death and destruction— forces that are against righteousness and religion—are not amenable to an honorable peace. He readies himself to fight on behalf of life and religion.

As I see it, life and religion are not two different things for Krishna. And therefore he can fight as naturally as he can dance. It is remarkable that a man like Krishna, even when he goes to the battlefield, is happy and joyful; he never loses his bliss. And men like Jesus are sad even as they keep a distance from the battlefield. Krishna can be blissful even on the battlefield, because war comes to him as part of life; it cannot be segregated from life.

As I said earlier, Krishna does not divide life into black and white, good and evil, as the moralists and monks do. He does not subscribe to the view that war is purely evil. He says that nothing is good or evil under all circumstances. There are occasions when poison can work like nectar and nectar can work like poison. There are moments when blessings turn into curses and curses into blessings.

Nothing is certain for all time and space, under all circumstances. The same thing can be good in one time and bad in another; it is really determined by the moment at hand. Nothing can be predetermined and prejudged. If someone does so, he is in for troubles in life, because life is a flux where everything changes from moment to moment. So Krishna lives in the moment; nothing is predetermined for him.

For long, Krishna does his best to avert war, but when he finds that it is inescapable he accepts it without hesitation. He does not want that one should go to war with a heavy heart, he does not believe in doing anything reluctantly in fact. If war becomes inescapable he will go to it with all his heart and mind.

With all his heart he tries to avert it, and when he fails, he goes to war whole-heartedly. In the beginning of war, as you know, he has no mind to take any active part in it. He tells Arjuna that he will not use his particular weapon—*sudarshan*—on the battlefield, he will only work as Arjuna's charioteer. But then a moment comes when he takes the *sudarshan* in his hand and becomes an active participant in the war.

As I said, Krishna lives in the moment; he lives moment to moment. In fact, every blissful person lives in the moment; that is, he lives in a timeless space.

But those who choose unhappiness and are pessimistic and miserable cannot afford to live in the moment; they live in time, they have a time-continuum. They have a long span of time—not chronological but psychological—which extends both to the past and the future. And it is this time-continuum that makes for their abiding misery and anguish. They carry with them the heavy load of all the miseries of the dead past—which is no more, and all the imaginable miseries of the endless future—which is yet to come. So of course they feel crushed under the dead weight of their psychological pain and agony.

On the other hand, a man of bliss does not accept the existence of any other time except the present, the living moment. He has no past and no future; for him the whole of existence is squeezed into the moment, in the now. For him the moment is eternity itself, and he journeys from one moment through another. He dies totally to the past—which is not. And he does not take into account the future—which is yet to come. For him both past and future are non-existential. Such a person is fully responsible to this moment. To be open to the living moment is his way of life, his joy, his bliss.

A masochist, a seeker of pain and misery, is utterly blind to the present, to the moment. He is closed in himself, like a cocoon; he is not responsive to that which is. If you take him to a rosebush and say to him, "Hey, man! Look at these blossoms, how enchanting they are!" he will say, "What worth is this beauty which is going to wither away by the evening?" Speak to him about the splendor of youth and his reaction will be, "It is nothing; soon it will pass into old age and to the grave." About happiness he will say, "It is nothing more than a mirage, an illusion; the more you chase it, the more distant it becomes. I am not going to be deceived by it." His mind is always set on time, the future; he never lives in the moment.

A hedonist, on the other hand, lives totally in the moment. He is finished with his past, and so he does not think of the future either, which is psychologically nothing but a projection of the past. Coming to a garden in bloom, the blissful person will be totally with the riot of colors, he will dance and sing with the dancing flowers. And he will tell the pessimist, "Why should I worry about the evening which is not yet here, when even these flowers which are going to wither away are not the least concerned about it? Look at them, how festive they are!"

And the wonder of wonders is that when the evening comes, the man of bliss celebrates the withering of the flowers with the same enthusiasm with which he had celebrated their blossoming in the morning. Who says that only blooming flowers are enchanting? The withering ones are as beautiful to look at! They are as beautiful as they were in the morning, but our sorrow-filled eyes fail to perceive that beauty.

Who says only sunrise is beautiful? Sunset is not a whit less beautiful. Who says only children are beautiful and not the old people? Old age has its own beauty, its own grace. When a person like Ravindranath or Walt Whitman, really grows into old age, his beauty is immeasurable.

Looking at Walt Whitman in his old age, one feels to have come across a beauty that cannot be surpassed. In fact, if childhood has a beauty of its own, youth and old age each have some distinctive beauty which is no less fascinating. When one's hair becomes snow-white, when one is about to complete his life's journey, when one is loose and relaxed, he radiates a beauty and grace that you find in the sunset. But a pessimist cannot know it.

I repeat: a Krishna lives in the moment. The journey of bliss is the journey of the moment. It is really wrong to call it a journey, because you cannot travel in the moment; you can only drown in it. You can travel in time, but in the moment you can only sink deeper and deeper.

The way of the moment is vertical, it is not horizontal. The moment has only depth, and no length at all; whereas time has only length, and no depth at all. Therefore one who sinks into the moment transcends time, he goes beyond time. One who reaches the timeless, achieves the eternal. So Krishna is in the moment and eternity together. The moment is eternity itself.

But one who lives in time can never know the eternal, because time is a series, a continuity; it stretches from the dead past to an unborn and unknown future. Time is tension; time is anxiety and misery. One who lives in time does not live really, because all the time he is either brooding over his past, which is gone forever, or he is worrying about a future which is yet to be born. When it is morning he is thinking of the evening; when he is alive he is worrying about death. The moment he meets a loved one, he begins to grieve over the separation that is going to happen in some future.

Krishna is accused of breaking promises he makes from time to time. A moment comes in the battle of Mahabharat when he takes up arms, his *sudarshan chakra*, although he had given his word that he would not take an active part in the fighting, he would only act as Arjuna's charioteer.

In answer to the charge, Krishna would say, "The one who made the promise is no more, nor is the moment which had brought forth the promise." He will ask, "Where is the Ganges that was there at the time my promise was being made? Where are the flowers that had bloomed at that moment? Where are those clouds that had glided through the sky when I had given the assurance in question? Everything has changed, everything has moved away since then. How can you bind me with that moment which too is gone? I am now existing in the moment that is before me, and I am responding to it totally."

Krishna does not apologize for the so-called breach of promise, nor does he regret it. He never repents; he never recants. He is true to the moment.

What do I mean when I say he is true to the moment? He is so utterly true to the existing moment that even if it confronts him with an unthought-of eventuality he goes into it without flinching and as totally as ever.

Of course, he will seem, at times, to be somewhat unfaithful to us, to the conventional society, because he does not keep his promises. That is the difficulty with a person like Krishna who is true to existence. Such a person cannot be as true to the society he lives in—because while the society lives in time, he lives in the timeless, in eternity. The society has a past and a future to care for, while Krishna has none. He is free, absolutely free.

A young man came to Rinzai, a celebrated Zen sage who lived in the mountains. The young man said to Rinzai, "I am in search of truth, and it is this search that has brought me to you from a long distance."

Rinzai said to him, "Leave aside this matter of truth for the present. I want to know something else from you since you are coming from Peking. Can you say what is the price of rice in Peking?"

The youth was flabbergasted to hear such a question from a great Master like Rinzai, who supposedly had nothing to do with such mundane matters as the price of rice in Peking. He had made a long and arduous journey in search of the highest. He had never imagined that a great sage like Rinzai would talk about such a petty thing in place of truth.

So the young man said to Rinzai, "Excuse me, sir, for my impertinence. But I say it so you don't ask any more questions like the one before me. I don't carry any past with me, I leave behind me the paths that I travel, burn the bridges that I cross, pull down the stairs that I climb. I die to the past totally, even to the minutes just gone by."

"Then sit down," said Rinzai patting the youth's back. "Now we will talk about truth. I brought up the question of the price of rice only to know if you yet carry your past with you. Had you remembered the price of rice in Peking when you left it, I would have flatly refused to talk about truth. One who clings to his past cannot come to truth, because truth is always now and here, it is in the moment. Truth has nothing to do with the past nor with the future. Truth is really timeless, and one who lives in the past can never be in the present. Truth and time don't walk together."

The Mahabharat happens in spite of Krishna. And yet Krishna becomes a participant in the war, because a partisan of bliss can become a partisan of war too. And Krishna believes that war is as much part of life as peace is. One cannot be without the other. And war will be with us as long as life exists on this earth. Maybe, the character of war will change, its structure and shape will vary, its plane, strategy, and style will be different, but war will continue.

It is impossible that war will ever disappear from the earth. It can only disappear from the earth if man himself disappears from here. Or it can disappear if man becomes perfect. Unless the human race as a whole reaches its perfection, or becomes extinct as a species, there is no way to abolish war. Man as he is cannot do without war. War has always been with us; it is with us now, and it is going to be with us in the future. Then what is the problem in regard to war?

Krishna's answer to this question is, war should be righteous, it should be waged for the highest values of life like freedom and truth.

In the same way, peace needs to be righteous. Remember, some kinds of peace can be unrighteous, irreligious, and war can be made to uphold religion and truth.

The pacifist thinks that peace is always righteous, and the warmonger thinks that war is right in every case. Krishna is neither a partisan of peace nor of war; he really has no "isms." He is not bound to any ideology, he is liquid like water. He is never stagnant, he is always moving with life. He is not solid and immobile like a rock; he is fluid like air. So he says, "Peace can be evil too."

For example, a pacifist who is religiously committed to peace is passing a street where someone is being robbed. He can say that he has nothing to do with others' feuds and strifes, and he refuses to interfere in the matter, going peacefully on his way. This peace is irreligious, because it is indirectly helping someone rob another person who may be innocent and helpless. It is not necessary that peace is right in every case. Men like Bertrand Russell think that peace is always right, it is inviolable. But he is only being dogmatic about peace.

Sometimes cowardice and impotence can take shelter behind the facade of peace. Krishna tells Arjuna again and again, "Give up faint-heartedness, O Arjuna. I had never thought that you could be as unmanly and impotent as your words reveal you to be. When war faces you, war that forces of unrighteousness have unleashed, it does not become you to talk like a coward. Where is your manliness, your skill?"

Peace is not necessarily righteous, nor is war unrighteous. It depends on the conditions that bring the forces of peace and war into play. But then you can say that warmongers are right in claiming that war is righteous. They can claim so, and nobody can prevent them. Life is very complex. But they will find it increasingly difficult to make such a claim if understanding grows among the people of what religion is.

Let me explain to you what religion and irreligion are according to Krishna. That which helps life grow, flower and dance ecstatically is religion. And that which impedes life's growth, which distorts and stifles life's flowering, which smothers life's joy and festivity is irreligion. Irreligion is what blocks and suffocates life; religion is what helps it to come to its fulfillment.

> *Questioner: Who has ever under-*
> *stood and imbibed Krishna rightly?*
> *What should one do to imbibe him?*
> *Can you give an outline of human*
> *civilization and culture patterned on*
> *Krishna's life and teachings?*

How can one imbibe another? How can one take after
Krishna or anyone else? And why? Is it incumbent on
me to imbibe another, become like another? I can
only imbibe and be myself, not Krishna.

Krishna does not pattern himself after
another. He imbibes himself and remains himself.
Why should another try to pattern himself after
Krishna, to be like him? It is enough that I imbibe
myself and am totally myself. No, to imbibe another,
to be like another, is the worst kind of corruption,
and it is the greatest injustice that someone can do
to himself.

The whole idea of imitation is mistaken and
wrong. I have my own soul which should come to its
full flowering. What will happen to it, to my own
soul if I imbibe another and copy him? It is true, I
can impose another's personality on myself, which
can overpower me, but what will happen to me, to
my own being? I owe a responsibility to myself, and
if I become like someone else I will be betraying
myself.

No, it is enough if one understands Krishna.
Trying to be like him is utterly uncalled for. Understanding is enough. And one should understand him,
not with a view to imbibe and imitate him, to be his
carbon-copy, but to understand himself and be himself.

You certainly have to know how a person like
Krishna is fulfilled and also know the laws of this
fulfillment. You certainly have to understand how
Krishna attains to his naturalness and spontaneity, so

that you can come to your own naturalness and spontaneity. Krishna's life can give you a cue, a clue to know yourself and come to yourself. If Krishna can flower, why not you? If Krishna's self-nature can blossom, why should you go on withering and wasting as you do? If Krishna can laugh and sing and dance, why should you continue to shed tears and be miserable?

It is not that you will dance the way Krishna dances. Your dance will be different, it will be your own; you will uncover your own innate dance. You don't have to copy Krishna's dance, you have only to know the law that helped him to find his dance and be fulfilled. Krishna's life can help you in self-discovery, which is of the highest. Self-discovery, and not assimilation or imitation, is what you have to seek. And Krishna's life can be of tremendous help in this adventure.

So the first thing to know is that no one can be your ideal, not even Krishna. And you need not follow and imitate another, Krishna included.

It is true that any number of people have wasted their lives following and imitating others. In reality, no one can wholly succeed in becoming like another; it is impossible. You can impose another's personality on yourself, wear his mask and look like him, but you cannot make your very soul into him. Do what you can, you cannot succeed; at best you can enact him, but it will not be more than acting. Being cannot be borrowed; it is always one's own. In spite of all efforts, you will remain what you innately are.

Imitation is dangerous in many ways. To imitate someone you have to suppress yourself, suppress your individuality, your self-nature. And this suppression can be so deep that you will lose all contact with yourself—which is the worst thing that can happen to any individual. Although you will yet survive at your innermost core as yourself, you will now be far removed from yourself. That is the problem.

Millions of people down the ages have tried to imitate Krishna, Buddha, Christ and others, but none has succeeded so far. Success is impossible. Five thousand years have passed since Krishna happened, but there has not been a second Krishna in all history. Twenty-five hundred years have passed after Buddha, and there has not yet been another Buddha. Nor has there been another Zarathustra, Jesus, or Mohammed.

Whosoever tries to imitate others is destined to court failure. It is really worse than failure, it is disaster, it is suicide. Even as suicide it is the worst kind. In ordinary suicide, as we know, only one's physical form is destroyed. In this suicide the very soul is sought to be destroyed. So all followers, all disciples, all imitators are suicidal.

Many people try to imitate Krishna, and in the process they not only injure themselves but they also injure Krishna. If you copy Krishna, you will, with all your efforts, make yourself a caricature of him. And this thing will not only distort you, but it will also distort Krishna's image. You will imitate him in your own way, and to that extent you will distort him, you will adulterate him.

So you are not only insulting and abusing yourself, but you are also insulting and abusing Krishna. So this imitation is really outrageous. All theologians, all priests—whether they follow Krishna or Christ—are guilty of this crime. And they all tell the same story—the story of man's failure to be himself, the story of man's attempts at suicide.

But we cannot say the same thing about Meera and Chaitanya. They are a class by themselves, and they are certainly no imitators. Through understanding Krishna's ways of expressing himself, his self-nature, Meera and Chaitanya express themselves as they are; they reveal their own distinctive self-natures. They don't impose Krishna on themselves, nor do they ape his lifestyle, his demeanor, his songs and dances. They sing their own songs; they dance their own dances.

So Meera remains Meera and Chaitanya remains Chaitanya. Of course they carry with them their love of Krishna, and as this love grows Chaitanya and Meera disappear as egos. As this love grows even Krishna disappears and only love remains. If you ask Chaitanya if he is Chaitanya or Krishna in that moment, he will say, "I really don't know who I am; I even don't know if I am." In this moment even the "I" disappears, and only an "am-ness" remains. This is pure existence. And this achievement of Chaitanya is the flowering and fruition of his own self-nature. There is nothing of imitation about it.

We are all prone to imitate others. And there is a good reason for it. Imitation is like ready-made garments: buy and wear garments. You don't have to do a thing, not even to wait for them. It suits our easygoing minds which want everything gratuitously.

To explore and find one's own innate being is arduous; to imitate Krishna is easy enough. It takes time to be oneself, but imitation comes in handy. Self-nature, self-fulfillment, has to be earned; borrowing is effortless, convenient.

But this pursuit of convenience is disastrous; it really lands one into the very vortex of sorrow and misery. So never commit the mistake of imitating others; it is utterly disastrous. It is calamitous.

I call him a religious person who goes on a voyage of self-discovery, who really discovers himself. In this adventure of self-discovery, understanding Krishna or Mahavira, Buddha or Jesus, can be helpful. Because in understanding others we lay the foundation of self-knowledge which is central to spiritualism. Instead of knowing oneself directly, it is easier to know through knowing others, because others provide you with a distance, a perspective to know.

Because there is a lack of distance between the knower and the known, direct self-knowledge is

really arduous. So in understanding oneself, the other
is helpful. But when you go to understand another—
Krishna, Buddha or Mahavira—remember, he is only
a means to self-understanding and self-discovery. He
is not your goal.

You might have observed on many occasions
that when somebody comes to consult you about a
complex problem of his own, you advise him so com-
petently. But when it comes to your own problem,
even a simple problem, you begin to shake in your
shoes.

What is the matter? You are considered to be
a very wise man by many who rush to you in their
hours of difficulty for your sage advice, and you have
the reputation of solving many of their problems. But
when you are yourself in a mess you rush to others—
perhaps to those very people you have helped—for
their advice. The reason is that you are so close to
your problem, you are so involved in it, that you can't
have the perspective to correctly figure it out.

It is comparatively easy to understand others,
and if we see others as a medium for self-understanding
then the lives of men like Krishna and Buddha are of
immense value. Then as we grow in self-understanding,
Krishna and Christ, Mahavira and Buddha will drop
by the wayside and we will be left with ourselves in
our utter purity.

This purity of the self, this virginity, this un-
spoiled innocence is what matters. And attainment
of this innocence, purity, is freedom. This ultimate
purity or aloneness is called *nirvana* or ultimate liberation. This primeval innocence is called Krishna-consciousness or God or what you will.

One who reaches this supreme state of being
with the help of Krishna will say that he has attained
to Krishna. This is a way of repaying an old debt that
he owes to Krishna; this is a way of expressing one's
gratitude to him. One who attains to this ultimate
state with the help of Buddha, will say that he has

attained Buddhahood. He is only expressing his gratitude to one whose life and teachings helped him in his arduous journey of self-discovery.

Ultimately, every seeker—whether he walks with Krishna or Christ—discovers himself. He cannot discover the other, because the other is not. The day I find myself, when I know who I am, the other, the "thou" ceases to be. But I will need some name to describe my experience, and certainly I will use one which helped me in coming to myself, in coming home.

One last thing, and then we will sit for meditation.

> Questioner: A part of the question yet remains to be answered. Please give us an outline of human civilization and culture patterned on Krishna's life and teaching.

It will need a lengthy answer. All these days, however, I have been doing the same thing—drawing an outline of human civilization reflecting Krishna's vision. Yet I would like to say a few things in this regard.

Human civilization, according to Krishna's vision, will be life-affirmative and natural in the first place. This is my vision too, that affirmation of life and nature should be the cornerstone of human civilization if it wants to be healthy and holistic. Such a civilization will be dedicated to the moment, to bliss and to celebration.

This civilization will refuse to be life-negative, renunciatory, masochistic and time-oriented. It will reject all fragmentation of life. Life will be accepted as a blessing, and there will be no division whatsoever, between life and God.

This civilization will declare that life is God, and there is no other God in opposition to life or separate from life. That life itself is God will be the overall faith of man. This man will declare: there is no creator other than creation; creativity itself is God.

This summing up will be clear to you if you take it in the context of the whole discussion we have had here for these ten days. During these days I said many things, some of which might have pleased you and some others which might have displeased you. But remember, both pleasant and unpleasant feelings come in the way of right understanding. Without trying to understand, we gullibly accept that which is pleasant and reject off-hand all that is unpleasant. I don't want you either to accept or to reject; all I want is that you should understand simply, effortlessly, and naturally.

I don't want that you should collect my words and take them home. That will not be worthwhile. What is worthwhile then? If in the course of listening to my words, some understanding, some wisdom has dawned on you—and if that understanding, that wisdom is really worthwhile, then it will go with you naturally, effortlessly.

It is like you visit a garden full of flowers and fragrance, and when you leave it, the garden is left behind but some of its fragrance goes with you— clinging in your nostrils, in your hair, in your clothes. So leave the flowers of words behind and take their essence, if you have gathered it, with you.

My words are as useless as all words are, but if in your encounter with them something has clicked in your being it is certainly of great significance.

My words, or any words for that matter, can have significance if you listen to them with an open mind, an unprejudiced and empty mind, without judging them, without identifying with them or condemning them. They can give rise to some understanding or wisdom in you if you listen without saying,

"This is right and that is wrong. That is what I believe too, and that is what is against my belief."

If you think that I am for Krishna and against Mahavira or whoever is your favorite, you will only earn unhappiness, and not understanding. But I will not be responsible for your sorrow; nor will Krishna or Mahavira. The responsibility will be entirely yours. Even if you happily think that I am in support of Krishna, who is your favored *avatara* or incarnation of God, you have missed me, you will remain as ignorant as you were when you came here.

I have nothing to do with Krishna: I am neither for him nor against him. I have unfolded his life and teachings exactly as I see them, and I am not concerned with what you think about it.

And remember, I live in the moment, I live moment to moment; I am not at all predictable or dependable. From what I say today one should not and cannot infer what I am going to say tomorrow. What I say today is exactly how I see it today. And what I will say tomorrow will be exactly how I see it tomorrow. And what you understand while listening to me today or any day is not important. But if this listening adds to your understanding, your intelligence, it has done its work. Understanding is important, all-important.

I hope these ten days have helped you grow in understanding, in clarity, and in some degree opened you to the sun of life and truth. I don't say by what name—Krishna or Buddha or Christ—you should call him when that sun of understanding comes to you.

I say this much: that if your mind is uncluttered and empty, if your heart is vulnerable and your perception is clear, there is no doubt whatsoever that the sun will rise and you will see light, you will be illumined. What you will call it will depend on you. The sun will not come saying, "I am so and so"; he is really without a name.

But remember, he alone has an open heart-mind who lives with understanding, who lives in understanding, who lives without ideas and ideals, concepts and beliefs, creeds, doctrines and dogmas. He alone is vulnerable to life and truth who is not a partisan of some belief-system like Hinduism, Catholicism or communism.

In fact, ideas and concepts, doctrines and dogmas are meant for those who have no intelligence and understanding of their own. They go to the market of ready-made ideologies and philosophies and buy them from theologians, priests and philosophers by mortgaging their own minds. Understanding is like a river—fluid and alive and flowing. All philosophies and theologies, all doctrines and dogmas are like stagnating pools of water, dead and stinking.

So if you have listened to me through the screen of your thoughts and beliefs—it makes no difference whether you are their partisans or enemies—you have not listened to me at all. Then you will never understand that which I have said.

The last thing that I have to say is this: I have nothing to do with Krishna; I have no relationship with him. I am not for him or against him; neither have I intention of converting you into his partisans or enemies. I have used Krishna exactly as a painter uses a canvas. The painter has nothing more to do with the canvas than to express himself through some colors daubed on it. I too had a few colors to spread on Krishna's canvas, and I am finished with it. Even Mahavira's or Buddha's canvas would have served my purpose.

And it is not necessary for me that I should use the same kind of colors on every canvas; nor am I committed to create the same kind of portraits on every canvas. I am free to express myself the way I am, and in the way I choose to express. If I am a real painter, I will create a different kind of painting, even a contradictory painting, each time I take paint and brush in my hands. He is only an imitator who repeats the same work again and again.

It is not necessary that you should cling rigidly to my statements. It is enough that you understand them and move ahead of them. You should leave the statements and live with their understanding, their essence.

If you do so you will not ever be in danger of clinging to my words. It will do me no harm if you cling to them, but it will certainly harm you immensely, because when one clings to some person or idea or thing, he immediately loses himself. And when one is free of all clingings and attachments, when one is utterly empty, he is immediately filled with himself, with the eternal, or God, or call it what you will.

It is with this hope that I talked to you these few days sitting in the lap of the Himalayas. I am grateful to you for having listened to me with such love, patience and peace, and I bow to God sitting inside each one of you.

A SPECIAL DISCOURSE
SEPTEMBER 28, 1970
MANALI, INDIA

September 28, 1970 was a memorable day.
At Manali in the Himalayas, Bhagwan Shree
Rajneesh initiated His first group of sannyasins.
This event was followed by this special evening
discourse, on the significance of Neo-Sannyas.

SANNYAS
IS
OF
THE
HIGHEST

o me, sannyas does not mean renunciation; it means a journey to joy and bliss. To me, sannyas is not any kind of negation; it is a positive attainment. But up to now, the world over, sannyas has been seen in a very negative sense, in the sense of giving up, of renouncing. I, for one, see sannyas as something positive and affirmative, something to be achieved, to be treasured.

It is true that when someone carrying base stones as his treasure comes upon a set of precious stones, he immediately drops the baser ones from his hands. He drops the baser stones only to make room for the newfound precious stones. It is not renunciation. It is just as you throw away the sweepings from your house to keep it neat and clean. And you don't call it renunciation, do you? You call it renunciation when you give up something you value, and you maintain an account of your renunciations. So far, sannyas has been seen in terms of such a reckoning of all that you give up—be it family or money or whatever.

I look at sannyas from an entirely different angle, the angle of positive achievement. Undoubtedly there is a fundamental difference between the two viewpoints. If sannyas, as I see it, is an acquisition, an achievement, then it cannot mean opposition to life, breaking away from life. In fact, sannyas is an attainment of the highest in life; it is life's finest fulfillment.

And if sannyas is a fulfillment, it cannot be sad and somber, it should be a thing of festivity and joy. Then sannyas cannot be a shrinking of life; rather, it should mean a life that is ever-expanding and deepening, a life abundant. Up to now we have called him a sannyasin who withdraws from the world, from everything, who breaks away from life and encloses himself in a cocoon. I, however, call him a sannyasin who does not run away from the world, who is not shrunken and enclosed, who relates with everything, who is open and expansive.

Sannyas has other implications too. A sannyas that withdraws from life turns into a bondage, into a prison; it cannot be freedom. And a sannyas that negates freedom is really not sannyas. Freedom, ultimate freedom is the very soul of sannyas. For me, sannyas has no limitations, no inhibitions, no rules and regulations. For me, sannyas does not accept any imposition, any regimentation, any discipline. For me, sannyas is the flowering of man's ultimate freedom, rooted in his intelligence, his wisdom.

I call him a sannyasin who has the courage to live in utter freedom, and who accepts no bondage, no organization, no discipline whatsoever. This freedom, however, does not mean license; it does not mean that a sannyasin becomes licentious. The truth is that it is always a man in bondage, a slave, who turns licentious. One who is independent and free can never be licentious; there is no way for him to be so.

That is how I am going to separate the sannyas of the future from the sannyas of the past. And I think that the institution of sannyas, as it has been up to now, is on its deathbed; it is as good as dead. It has no future whatsoever. But sannyas in its essence, has to be preserved. It is such a precious attainment of mankind that we cannot afford to lose it. Sannyas is that rarest of flowers that blooms once in a great while. But it is likely that it will wither away for want of proper caring. And it will certainly die if it remains tied to its old patterns.

Therefore, sannyas has to be invested with a new meaning, a new concept. Sannyas has to live; it is the most profound, the most precious treasure that mankind has. But how to save it, preserve it, is the question. I would like to share with you my vision on this score.

Firstly, it is a long time that sannyas has remained isolated from the world, and consequently it has been doubly harmed. A sannyasin living completely cut off from the world, living in utter isolation from the world, becomes poor, and his poverty is very deep and subtle, because the wealth of all our life's experiences lies in the world, not outside. All our experiences of pain and pleasure, attachment and detachment, hate and love, enmity and friendship, war and peace, come from the world itself. So when a man breaks away from the world, he becomes a hothouse plant, he ceases to be a flower that blooms under the sun and the open sky. By now, sannyas has become a hothouse plant. And such a sannyas cannot live any longer.

Sannyas cannot be grown in hothouses. To grow and blossom, the plant of sannyas needs an open sky. It needs the light of day and the darkness of night; it needs rains, winds and storms. It needs everything there is between the earth and the sky. A sannyasin needs to go through the whole gamut of challenges and dangers. By isolating him from the world we have harmed the sannyasin enormously, because his inner richness has diminished so much.

It is amusing that those who are ordinarily called good people don't have that richness of life their opposites have; they lack the richness of experience. For this reason, novelists think it is difficult to write a story around the life of a good person, that his life is flat and almost eventless. Curiously enough, a bad person makes a good story; he is a must for a story, even for history. What more can we say of a good man than this, that he has been good from the cradle to the grave?

Isolating him from the world, we deprive the sannyasin of experience; he remains very poor in experience. Of course, isolation gives him a sort of security, but it makes him poor and lackluster.

I want to unite the sannyasin with the world. I want sannyasins who work on farms and in factories, in offices and shops right in the marketplace. I don't want sannyasins who escape from the world; I don't want them to be renegades from life. I want them to live as sannyasins in the very thick of the world, to live with the crowd amid its din and bustle. Sannyas will have verve and vitality if the sannyasin remains a sannyasin in the very thick of the world.

In the past, if a woman wanted to be a sannyasin, she had to leave her husband, her children, her family; she had to run away from the life of the world. If a man wanted to take sannyas he had to leave his wife, his children, his family, his whole world, and escape to a monastery or a cave in the mountains. For me, such a sannyas has no meaning whatsoever. I hold that after taking sannyas, a man or woman should not run away from the world, but should remain where he or she is and let sannyas flower right there.

You can ask how someone will manage his sannyas living in the world. What will he do as a husband, as a father, as a shopkeeper, as a master, as a servant? As a sannyasin how will he manage his thousand and one relationships in the world?—because life is a web of relationships. In the past he just ran away from the world, where he was called upon to shoulder any number of responsibilities, and this escape made everything so easy and convenient for him. Sitting in a cave or a monastery, he had no responsibilities, no worries; he led a secluded and shrunken life. What kind of a sannyas will it be which is not required to renounce anything? Will sannyas without renunciation mean anything?

Recently an actor came to visit me. He is a new entrant into the film world. He asked for my autograph with a message for him. So I wrote in his book: "Act as if it is real life and live as if it is acting."

To me, the sannyasin is one who lives life like an actor. If someone wants to blossom in sannyas living in the thick of the world, he should cease to be a doer and become an actor, become a witness. He should live in the thick of life, play his role, and at the same time be a witness to it, but in no way should he be deeply involved in his role, be attached to it. He should cross the river in a way that his feet remain untouched by the water. It is, however, difficult to cross a river without letting the water touch your feet, but it is quite possible to live in the world without getting involved in it, without being tied to it.

In this connection it is necessary to understand what play-acting is. The miracle is that the more your life becomes play-acting, the more orderly, natural and carefree it becomes. If a woman, as a mother, learns a small truth, that although the child she is bringing up has been borne by her, yet he does not belong to her alone, that she has been no more than a passage for him to come into this world, that he really belongs to that unknown source from which he came, which will sustain him through his life and to which he will return in the end, then that mother will cease to be a doer; she will really become a play-actor and a witness.

Conduct an experiment sometime. Decide that for twenty-four hours you are going to do everything as acting. If someone insults you, you will not really be angry, you will only act as if you are angry. And likewise, if someone praises you, you will not really be flattered, you will only act as though you are flattered. An experiment like this, just for twenty-four hours, will bring astonishing results for you; it will open new doors to life and living for you. You will then realize to your surprise that you have gone through any amount of unnecessary pain and misery in life by being a doer; they could have easily been avoided if you had been an actor instead. When you go to bed after this experiment in play-acting, you will have a deep sleep such as you have never known. Once you cease to be a doer, all your tensions and anxieties will disappear. Your miseries will just evaporate, because all your miseries and agonies come from your being a doer in life.

I want to take sannyas to every hamlet and every home. Only then can sannyas survive. We need millions of sannyasins; just a handful won't do. And millions can take sannyas only if sannyas is positive and life-affirmative. We cannot have many sannyasins if you cut sannyas off from the world. Who will feed them? Who will provide them with clothes and shelter? Sannyas of the old kind, which was a haven for idlers and recluses, cannot produce the millions of sannyasins that we need. Those days are gone when society bore the brunt of a vast army of recluses. Moreover, sannyasins of the old kind have to be dependent on society, and as a result they became extremely poor physically and spiritually. Consequently, they cannot be as effective and influential as they should be. Sannyas on a massive scale is not possible if we cling to its old ways.

If sannyas has to be effective on a large scale throughout the world—which is so very necessary—and if sannyas has to be meaningful and blissful, then there is no choice but to allow a sannyas that will not be required to break away from society and grow in isolation. Now a sannyasin should remain wherever he is, acting his role in society and being a witness to it.

So I want to unite sannyas with the family, with the workshop and with the market. It will be a unique and beautiful world, if we can make one where a shopkeeper will be a sannyasin. Naturally, such a shopkeeper will find it difficult to resort to dishonest means in business. A shopkeeper who is just acting his role as shopkeeper, and who is also a witness to it, cannot afford to be dishonest. We will change the world radically if we have sannyasins as doctors, lawyers, clerks and office assistants.

A sannyasin living segregated from society is a poor sannyasin, and the society is poorer for him too, because he is one of its best products. When such a person leaves the society to become a sannyasin the society becomes lusterless.

A worldwide campaign for positive sannyas has therefore become urgent. It is very necessary to have sannyasins in every home, in every field and factory across the earth. A sannyasin should be a father or a mother, a wife or a husband; he will remain where he is as a sannyasin. Only his outlook on life will change; now life for him will be no more than a drama, a play. Life for him will be a celebration and not a task, a duty, a drag. And with celebration everything will change.

I have yet another kind of sannyas in my vision which I would like to share with you. It is the vision of short-term sannyas. I don't want a person to take a vow of lifelong sannyas. In fact, any kind of vow or commitment for the future is dangerous, because we are not the masters of the future. It is utterly wrong to think we are. We have to allow the future to take its course, and we should be ready to accept whatever it brings to us. One who has become a witness cannot decide for the future; only a doer does so. One who thinks that he is a doer can vow that he will remain a sannyasin for his whole life, but a real witness will say, "I don't know what tomorrow is going to be. I will accept it as it comes and be a witness to it too. I cannot decide for tomorrow."

In the past, sannyas was much handicapped by the concept of lifelong sannyas: once a sannyasin, always a sannyasin. We closed the gate of society forever once one entered sannyas. Maybe a person takes sannyas in a particular state of mind, and after some time, when he finds himself in a different state of mind, wants to return to the world—but he cannot do so because the house of sannyas has only an entrance, it has no exit at all. You can enter sannyas, but once in it you cannot leave. And this single rule has turned sannyas into a prison. Even heaven will turn into hell if there is no exit.

You can say that sannyas has no hard and fast rule like this. That is true, but the fact that society looks down upon one who leaves sannyas is a stronger prohibition than any rule. We have an ingenious device to prevent a sannyasin from going back to the world again. When someone takes sannyas we make a big event of it, give him a farewell with great fanfare, with a band and flowers and eulogies. The poor sannyasin does not know that this is a clever way to say goodbye to him forever. He is not aware that if ever he returns to society he will be received by the same people with sticks instead of flowers.

This is a very dangerous convention. Because of it, any number of people are prevented from participating in the great bliss that sannyas can bring them. It becomes too difficult for them to make a decision for lifelong sannyas, which is indeed a very hard decision. Besides, we don't have the right to commit ourselves to anything for our whole lives.

In my vision, short-term sannyas is the right way. You can leave it any time you like, because it is you who take it. It is your decision; no one else can decide for you. Sannyas is entirely a personal, individual choice; others don't matter in any way. I am free to take sannyas today and leave it tomorrow, provided I don't expect any reward for it from others in the form of their praise and acclamation.

We have made sannyas a very serious affair, and that is why only serious people—who are really sick people—take to it. It is now necessary to turn sannyas into a non-serious thing, a play. It should be entirely for your joy that you enter sannyas for a while and then leave it or remain in it forever. Others should have no say in the matter. If the vision of short-term sannyas becomes prevalent, if people are allowed to enter sannyas even for a few months from time to time, millions of people can enjoy this blessing. It will really be a great thing.

There was a Sufi *fakir* known for his wisdom. The king of his country came to visit him. The king said, "I am thirsty for God; I want to see God. Please help me."

The *fakir* asked him to visit him the next day, and the king came again. The *fakir* told him, "Now you have to live with me for a week. Take this begging bowl in your hand and go every day into the adjoining villages to beg alms from house to house. After begging, return to this place, where you will get your meals and a place to rest. And then on the eighth day we will discuss God."

The king was in a fix. He had to go begging in his own kingdom, from his own subjects, which seemed such an arduous and embarrassing task. So he asked for the *fakir*'s permission to go begging outside his kingdom, but the *fakir* refused him with a curt warning, "If you cannot go begging, it is better you return to your palace right now, and never come to me again to talk about God." After some hesitation the king ultimately decided to live with the *fakir* for a week. And for a week he was on the streets of his own city with a beggar's bowl in his hand, visiting the houses of his own subjects, asking for alms.

After seven days the *fakir* sent for him and said, "Now you can ask about God."

The king said, "I now have nothing to ask. I had never dreamed I would find God only after a week's begging." Then the *fakir* asked what had happened in the course of the begging. The king said, "Just a week's begging destroyed my ego; it is now nowhere. I had never thought that I would attain as a beggar what I had never had as a king."

The moment humility is born, the door to the divine opens.

It would be a great experience if someone takes sannyas for a month or two every year and then returns to his householder's world. This experience will enrich his life in a great way; it will go with him for the rest of his life. And if a person, in his sixty or seventy years' life, takes short-term sannyas—say twenty times—he will not need to be a sannyasin again; he will be a sannyasin as he is. Therefore I think that every man and woman should have the opportunity of sannyas in his or her life.

A few things more and then you can put your questions.

Up to now every kind of sannyasin in the world has belonged to some religion, to this or that religion. And this has done immense harm to both sannyas and religion. It is utterly absurd that a sannyasin should belong to some sectarian religion; a sannyasin at least should belong to religion alone, and not to this or that religion. He should not be a Christian, or a Hindu, or a Jaina; he should be a sannyasin of "religion", with no adjective attached to it. He should be the one who, in the words of Krishna, gives up all religions and takes shelter in the only religion there is. Religion, like truth, is one; it cannot be many. And it will be great if we can give birth to a sannyas that belongs to religion and not to religions, not to communal and sectarian religions. The sannyasin of true religion can be a guest everywhere, whether it is in a temple or a church or a mosque; none will be alien to him.

Another thing to bear in mind is the role of the Master, the guru, in sannyas. Up to now sannyas has been tethered to a Master who initiates someone into it. But sannyas is not something which anyone can give you as a gift; it has to be received directly from the divine. Who else but God can initiate you into sannyas? When someone comes and asks me to initiate him into sannyas, I tell him, "How can I initiate you into sannyas? Only God can initiate you. I can only be a witness to your being initiated. Get initiated by the divine, the supreme being, and I will bear witness that I was present when you were initiated into sannyas. My function is confined to being a witness, nothing more." A sannyas tied to the Master is bound to become sectarian. It cannot liberate you; instead it will put you in bondage. Such a sannyas is worthless.

There are going to be three categories of sannyasins. One of them will consist of those who will take short-term sannyas, say for two or three months. They will meditate and go through some kind of spiritual discipline at some secluded place and then return to their old lives. The second category will be of those who will take sannyas, but remain wherever they are. They will continue to be in their occupations as before, but they will now be actors and not doers, and they will also be witnesses to life and living.

And the third category will consist of sannya- sins who will go so deep into the bliss and ecstasy of sannyas that the question of their return to their old world will not arise. They will bear no such respon- sibilities as will make it necessary for them to be tied to their families; nobody will depend on them and no one will be hurt by their withdrawal from society. The last category of sannyasins will live in meditation and carry the message of meditation to those who are thirsty for it.

It seems to me that never before was the world in such dire need of meditation as it is today. And if we fail to make a large portion of mankind deeply involved in meditation, there is little hope for man's survival on this earth any longer; he will simply disap- pear from the earth. There is already so much neurosis and insanity in the world, there is so much political madness all around, that the hope for mankind re- maining alive grows dimmer and dimmer with the passing of each day. And the sands of time are running out fast. So it is urgent for millions of men and women all over the world to become meditative in the short time that we have; otherwise man, with all his civili- zation, is going to perish. Even if he survives physi- cally, all that is good and great in him will perish.

Therefore a very large band of young men and young women who have yet no responsibilities on their shoulders is needed. And we will include in this band those old people who have laid down their responsibilities and are free. This band of young and old together will first learn meditation, and then they will carry the torch of meditation to every nook and corner of the earth.

The meditation that I teach is so simple, so scientific, that if a hundred people take to it, seventy of them are going to make it. There is no condition that you are qualified to do it; that you do it is all that is needed. Besides, you are not required to owe allegiance to any religion, any scripture, or to have faith and belief as a pre-condition to meditation. As you are right now, you can join it and do it and go deeply into it. It is such a simple and scientific technique that you are not required to have faith in it. All that is required of you is that you take it as a hypothetical experiment, as you do a scientific experiment, to see how it works. And I assure you it works; you will make it.

I feel that meditation can be spread throughout the world as a chain-reaction. If a person decides to learn meditation himself and then, within a week of his learning it, initiates another person into it, we will cover the whole earth with meditation within ten years. No greater effort is needed. Then all the lofty things of life that man is heir to, but has lost, can be restored to him in ten years. And then there is no reason why Krishna should not play his flute amongst us once again, why Christ should not come again and again, why Buddha should not get enlightened under the bo-tree over and over again. Not that the same old Krishna or Buddha will be born again, but that in us we have the potentialities of that meditation which can flower into a Krishna, a Buddha, a Christ over and over again.

It is for this reason that I have decided to be a witness to your being initiated into sannyas. I will be a witness for friends who are ready to join one of the three categories of sannyasins that I have mentioned. I will not be their Master, but only a witness to their initiation into sannyas. In fact, sannyas will be a matter of a direct relationship between them and God.

There is going to be no ritual for initiation into sannyas, so that one does not have any difficulty in leaving it when he feels like it. And sannyas will not be a serious affair; so you need not be worried on this score. It should be such a simple and natural thing that if, one morning getting out of bed, a person feels like taking sannyas, he should not have to face any difficulty in the matter. There will be no difficulty, because it is not going to be a lifelong commitment. If the following morning he feels like quitting it, he can do so as easily. He is his sole judge and master; others have nothing to do with it.

I have explained to you how I envisage this neo-sannyas. Now you can ask a few questions that arise in your minds.

> *Questioner: What is the meaning of*
> *wearing orange clothes as a sannyasin?*

It is true that wearing a particular kind of clothes does not make one a sannyasin, but it is also true that sannyasins do wear some particular kind of clothes. Clothes don't make for sannyas, but that does not mean that a sannyasin cannot have his own clothes. He can. Clothes are not that important, but they are not that unimportant either.

What clothes you wear has meaning. And why you wear clothes has meaning too. Someone wears loose clothes and someone else prefers tight ones. There is not much of a difference between loose and tight clothes, but it does say something about the mental makeup of the people who wear them. Why does someone choose loose garments for himself while another chooses tight ones? If a person is quiet and peaceful he will go in for loose clothing, he won't like tight ones. On the other hand, tight clothing is preferred by one who is disturbed, hot-tempered and sexual. Loose clothes are not good for fighting. That is why soldiers all over the world have tight-fitting outfits; they cannot be given loose uniforms. The job of a soldier is such that he needs to be tight and smart. His clothes really should be so tight that he is always ready for action, that he feels he can jump out of his body whenever he is required to do so. But a monk, a meditator, a sannyasin, needs loose and light clothes.

Orange clothes have their own utility. Not that one cannot be a sannyasin without being in an ochre robe, but the ochre robe does have its due place in sannyas.

And those who discovered it, after long search and experiment, had a good many reasons to commend the ochre color for sannyas.

We will come to know the significance of different colors if we make some small experiments with them. Our difficulty is that we never make such experiments. Take seven glass bottles of different colors—there are seven colors in all—and fill them with water from the same river and leave them for a while under the sun. You will be amazed to find that the colors of the glass have affected the quality of the water, each in its own way. There are now seven kinds of water in those bottles. The water in the yellow bottle will deteriorate in no time, while the water in the red bottle will remain pure for a long time.

You can ask, "What does the color of a bottle do?" The color of the glass affects the rays of the sun in its own particular manner when they pass through it. While the yellow color accepts a particular kind of ray, the red one accepts another kind, and the water inside the bottles is affected by those rays in a big way. The rays of the sun serve as food and nourishment for the water.

Experiments and research conducted over thousands of years led to the discovery of ochre clothes for sannyas, and it has yielded rich results. Physicists know well the function of colors. They know that the color of your clothes keeps the same color away from it. We think just the opposite; we think that a piece of red cloth is red, but it is not so. For instance, when the rays of the sun, which have seven colors, fall on a particular object and the object appears to you as red, it means that the said object has absorbed all the colors of the sun except the red one; it has kept the red away. And that is why you see the object as red. And if some object appears to you to be blue, it means that the object has repelled the blue color. So when this blue of the rays of the sun reaches your eyes, you see the object as blue in color. So whatever color you have on your body, it will not allow the same kind of color to enter you.

Ochre was selected as the color of sannyas after a great deal of investigation and experiment. The color red arouses many kinds of sexuality in a human being, because it is very strong and vital. On entering a human body it provokes its sexuality. For this reason people living in hot countries are more sexual than others. The hotter a country's climate, the more sexual its people.

It is not accidental that a book on sexology like the *Kamasutra* was not written in a country with a cold climate. It is the same with *Tales of the Arabian Nights*; it is the product of a tropical climate. People living in tropical climates are more sexual because of the sun. Therefore people who were working on sannyas from many directions thought that sexuality could be calmed if the red color were kept away from sannyasins' bodies—hence ochre was selected.

You can ask why ochre was selected and not red. Pure red could well have been selected; it would have been more effective in calming sexuality. But there was a difficulty in choosing red, true out-and-out red; it would have totally prevented red from entering the body. But the body needs some amount of red rays to keep fit, so it would have been bad for the health to keep red totally away from the body.

There is yet another reason we did not opt for pure red. Even the sight of the pure red is harsh and harmful; we had to be wary that the color of sannyas should be such that it did not hurt others. Sannyas takes care of everybody and everything. You put a piece of red cloth in front of a bull and see how furious he becomes. The red hits the bull's eyes hard; he cannot take it.

You will be surprised to know that people who work on color psychology in the West have arrived at very strange conclusions. A lot of work on colors is in progress in the West; large scale research is underway. And they have found many new uses of colors. An owner of a department store in America had a study done on the colors on cans and containers of goods he sold. It was amazing to find that even the color influenced the sale of goods in a big way. A researcher kept constant watch on the customers—mostly women do the shopping—just to see how they were attracted to various colors. It was found that while the yellow attracted only twenty percent of the customers, red attracted eighty percent. The sale of the same article increased fourfold when the color of its container was changed from yellow to red. Red attracts women like anything, and it is not surprising that this color has been the most popular among women all over the world.

So the selection of ochre for sannyas is meaningful. Ochre is a shade of red; it is less bright, less offensive. While it retains all the advantages of red, it discards its disadvantages. It diminishes sexuality as much as red does; at the same time it does not harm you in the way red does.

There are many other advantages of the ochre, but it will not be possible to go into them all here. It would be a lengthy subject if we were to go into colors in detail. But a few things can be discussed.

Ochre is the color of the sunrise. When the sun is just emerging on the eastern horizon, when the first light of dawn begins to show itself, its color is exactly ochre. When you enter meditation, the first light that you see is ochre, and the ultimate light of meditation is blue. Meditation begins with ochre and ends with blue; it reaches its peak with blue. Ochre is the index of the beginning of meditation; a sannyasin encounters this color on entering meditation. So in the course of the whole day the color of his own clothes reminds him of meditation again and again. An association is established between the two, clothes and meditation. Ochre helps him in going into meditation, which is an integral part of the life of a sannyasin.

If you want to remember you have to buy a particular thing from the market you make a knot in your handkerchief or in any other part of your clothing so it reminds you in time. There is obviously no connection whatsoever between a knot and some thing to be purchased from the market, but when you reach the market the first thing that comes to mind is the knot, and in association with it, the thing to be bought. The knot becomes associated with it; it becomes a kind of conditioning.

Pavlov's experiment in this respect has become famous. He put a piece of bread before a dog and rang a bell at the same time. The sight of the bread immediately made the dog salivate. Pavlov continued this practice of putting the bread before the dog and ringing the bell for a full fifteen days, after which he stopped putting the bread but continued to ring the bell. But he found to his surprise that the dog still salivated just at the sound of the bell. What has happened to this dog? An association between the sound of the bell and the secretion of saliva has been established, and this association has created a conditioned reflex. Now the sound of the bell is enough to remind the dog of the bread that came with the bell.

We live our whole life in this way; we live like Pavlov's dog. All our behavior is nothing but a bunch of conditioned reflexes, and the irony is that most of our reflexes are wrong.

If, while he is walking, eating or taking a bath, his clothes repeatedly remind a sannyasin of the first color of the meditative experience, then the ochre color has served a great purpose. It is a kind of conditioning, a knot to remind him over and over again that meditation is his way. But this does not mean that one cannot be a sannyasin without the ochre robe. Sannyas is such a lofty thing that it cannot be confined to garments. But garments are not altogether useless; they are very meaningful.

I would like millions of people to be seen in ochre all over the world.

> Questioner: What is the difference between a seeker and a sannyasin? Can't one be a seeker without being a sannyasin?

One cannot be a seeker without being a sannyasin, because to be a seeker is the beginning of sannyas. A seeker is one who is seeking sannyas. What else can a seeker do except seek sannyas, except practice and perfect sannyas? He has to gradually transcend the pains and pleasures of the world and attain to bliss. He has to transcend the doer and attain to witnessing. He has to go beyond his ego and attain to emptiness. He has to transcend matter and be one with God. All these things are collectively known as sannyas.

Being a seeker means he is starting on a journey to sannyas. A seeker is a beginner on the path of sannyas, and a *siddha*, an adept, is one who has fulfilled his sannyas. The whole of seeking is directed towards sannyas. A seeker is one who is in search of sannyas.

But always remember what my sannyas means. It is a journey to positive achievement, to achievement of the immense, the infinite.

> *Questioner: What would be the*
> *daily routine, the discipline of your*
> *sannyasin?*

You ask what the daily routine of my sannyasin would be. It is not a question of *my* sannyasin. How can anyone be my sannyasin? He or she will be just a sannyasin. And what would be his routine, his schedule of daily life, his discipline?

If we try to impose a fixed daily routine on a sannyasin, it is bound to harm him instead of doing any good. Someone asked a Zen sage, "What is your everyday routine?"

The sage said, "When I am sleepy I sleep, and when I wake up I am awake. When I am hungry I eat and I don't eat when I am not hungry." And the sage is right. A sannyasin is one who does not impose something on himself, who takes life as it is and lives it very naturally, spontaneously, moment to moment.

We are a strange people. When we feel like sleeping we resist it, and when we cannot sleep we chant *mantras* and try to get to sleep somehow. We eat when we are not hungry, and we don't eat when we are hungry, because we have a fixed schedule of eating according to the clock. That is how we destroy the inner harmony of our body, and that is why we are in a mess.

A sannyasin will live in accord with the wisdom of the body. He will sleep when he feels sleepy, and he will wake up when his sleep is over. He will not wake up in what the Hindus call the *brahmamuhurta*, the divine hour, the hour before dawn. Whenever he wakes up will be his *brahmamuhurta*. He will say, "When God brings me out of sleep, I call it my *brahmamuhurta*." He will live naturally, easily, spontaneously.

That is why I cannot give you a routine, a discipline of living. You will be in trouble, you will suffer if I impose any discipline on you, because I will determine it the way it suits me, and my way of life can never be yours. If I tell you to wake up every morning at three o'clock, maybe waking up at three is blissful for me, but it will ruin your health.

Everybody's physical organism is unique and different, but we are not aware of it. People say that modern women are very lazy, that they keep sleeping and their husbands make the morning tea for them, but that is how it should be. The inner organism of woman is such that her body clock is always behind man's by two hours. If a man leaves his bed at five in the morning, a woman should leave hers at seven.

A lot of study and research has been done in this respect, and the findings are very surprising. It has been found that in the course of every twenty-four hours our body temperature goes down for two hours, and it usually happens in the latter part of the night. You might have noticed that nearabout four in the morning you usually feel cold. This cold is caused by the fall in your body temperature, and not by any change in the weather. And this period of the fall in temperature is different for everybody. For me it might occur between three and five and for another between five and seven. And it is in these two hours of low body temperature that one goes into deep sleep each day.

Over the last five years ten thousand people in America were put under observation while they were sleeping, and it was confirmed that this time of deep sleep is different for everybody. So your time of going to bed and leaving it cannot be determined in a collective way. It has to be left to each individual to find out from personal observation what time is most suitable for him to rest and sleep. And the criterion is that a good night's sleep should keep you fresh and energetic for the whole of the following day.

Even the duration of one's sleep has to be determined individually. For someone, five hours sleep can be sufficient, while another person might need seven hours sleep each day. And there are a few people who do with just three hours sleep and it goes well with them. But this person who completes his sleep in three hours can prove to be dangerous for others. He will think himself a pious person and call all those who sleep long hours idlers and good-for-nothings. He will sermonize that three o'clock is the best time to get out of bed, and say that those who don't conform to this rule will go to hell. Beware of such people!

There can be no hard and fast rule for things like this. We cannot have set laws about what to wear, about what to eat and how much to eat, about when to sleep and how long to sleep. We can discuss these things in a general manner, but it would not be proper to set rules about them. Everyone should find his own discipline, his own way of living; it should be entirely an individual decision. And this much freedom you must have, that you decide your own way of living. Others don't do it, but a sannyasin should. He should insist on this freedom to be the way he is, and to live in the way that is joyful and blissful for him. In this respect he has also to bear in mind that he does not live in a way that impinges on the freedom and happiness of others. And this is enough.

I repeat that we can broadly discuss the question of a daily routine and a discipline for a sannyasin, but we cannot lay down strict rules about them.

There is a person who is addicted to smoking. The whole world is against him, and yet he goes on smoking. Physicians tell him that smoking will ruin his health, and he says he knows it, yet he cannot quit. What is the matter with this person? Is it that he lacks something necessary for him and smoking provides it? An investigation on smoking done recently in Mexico came to a very strange finding. It says that people who are mad about smoking are those whose bodies lack nicotine. These people are seeking nicotine through tobacco, tea and coffee. But smoking is being condemned as something immoral. But what is immoral in taking some smoke in and out? It is of course senseless, but it is never immoral. He is not harming anyone except himself. It is an innocent stupidity and nothing more. Maybe it is his need; maybe he lacks something which he is fulfilling through smoking. He would be better to discover and know his problem.

Our knowledge of the human body is very poor. It is poor in spite of so much development in medical science. We have yet to understand the body fully, its needs, its problems. And because of this the body has to tackle its problems on its own. If it lacks nicotine it makes you smoke. And once you take to smoking you are in the clutches of habit and you become helpless. It is not that everyone smokes for lack of nicotine; nine out of ten smokers simply take to smoking out of imitation. And then it becomes a mechanical habit; they become prisoners of a habit.

However, no routine, no discipline can be imposed from the outside. It is not possible, nor is it desirable to prescribe a general code for the daily life of sannyasins, as to when they should leave their beds and what they should eat. Of course, some broad guidelines can be given. What is essential is that whatever a sannyasin does, he does it with awareness; whatever he does, he does it keeping his own good and the good of others in view. And whatever he does is right if it promotes his health, his peace and his happiness. And if, on the other hand, it harms his health and happiness, he should shun it.

In the matter of food, he should take care that his food is fresh, light and health-giving. He should avoid unnecessary violence in eating; he should not eat anything that is obtained by killing and maiming living beings. In brief, health should be your prime consideration in the selection of food.

Another important thing in respect to food is to learn and develop a sense of taste in eating. And it depends more on the art of eating than on the food itself. On the basis of such broad hints about food one should draw up his menu in accord with his own individuality.

Others can't give you a discipline; it is just absurd. In fact, everybody is the architect of his own destiny. Being initiated into sannyas means that a man chooses to be his own master, that he will make his own decisions, that it is his right to conduct himself in his own way. You can say that a sannyasin is liable to err if he makes his own decisions. Let him err; he will suffer for his mistakes. Why should you worry about it? If he does things rightly he will be happy, and if he does them wrongly he will suffer. It is wrong to take undue interest in what others do and how they do it. It is really immoral to interfere in another's life. Who are you to come in his way? One should come in another's way only if his mistakes begin to harm others; otherwise, he should not be interfered with. He can make mistakes and learn from his mistakes.

A sannyasin is one who lives with discrimination, with wisdom, who is always investigating what it is that brings happiness and what it is that causes pain, and who, through his own experiences, learns what is good for him. He is on a journey to his bliss; you need not worry about him.

Sometimes I am amazed to see that others become more worried than a sannyasin himself that he does not err. It is just silly. These self-appointed judges are always prying into the lives of sannyasins—whether they wake up in *brahmamuhurta* or not, whether they sleep in the daytime or not. But who are they? Why should they be after others?

But it is not without reason they do so. These are the ways to persecute and torture others; it is so pleasurable to them. They often say that they respect the unerring sannyasin, which is another way of dominating him. If the sannyasin wants to have their respect, he will have to obey their rules and live in the way they would like him to live. There is yet another danger to the sannyasin from these self-appointed judges. To earn their respect he will turn into a hypocrite; he will publicly show that he follows their rules of conduct while privately he will go on living outside those rules.

I am not going to allow a sannyasin to be a hypocrite. I hold hypocrisy as the worst sin ever. And the only way to save him from turning into a hypocrite is to abstain from imposing any discipline on him and to leave him free to live in the way that comes naturally to him; otherwise he is bound to be a hypocrite. This is how we have made hypocrites of all the old sannyasins the world over. And so they are in a mess. There is a class of monks in India who cannot take a bath, because people around them are always watching to see if they bathe themselves. They have thus forced them to remain covered with dirt and filth. In return they give them respect. So these monks have sacrificed cleanliness for the sake of respectability. But whenever they find an opportunity, whenever they are away from the watchful eyes of their followers, they hurriedly dip their towels in water and sponge their bodies. And then they suffer guilt and self-condemnation.

Recently a gentleman came to me and said, "I have heard that a certain Jaina nun, who often visits you, uses toothpaste. Is it not deplorable?"

I told him, "Have you gone mad? Whether a nun uses toothpaste or not is none of your concern. Do you sell toothpaste? What have you to do with it?"

In reply he said, "The use of the toothbrush is prohibited in our community."

"Then don't use it if your community does not permit it," I told him. This gentleman himself uses a toothbrush and toothpaste with impunity, but a nun of his community cannot. This is the price she has to pay for the respect she receives from the community.

I will ask my sannyasin, who I think is a true sannyasin, not to expect respectability from the society, because this expectation will create bondage for him. There are dishonest people all around and they will immediately entrap you and make you their prisoner. They will say, "Since we respect you, since we touch your feet, you will have to fulfill certain conditions of ours, you will have to obey our laws."

In fact, a sannyasin is one who says, "I don't care for your society, for your laws, for your conditions. Now I have started caring for myself, so you need not be concerned about me."

A sannyasin's own wisdom sheds light on his path.

> *Questioner: You said that sannyas is a blissful phenomenon; it is not renunciation. In my view, the first Shankaracharya was a sannyasin of bliss, and in that sense he can be taken for your sannyasin. Please explain. Also explain why you lay so much stress on play-acting. And can a businessman, who takes to your sannyas, play-act as a black marketeer? And lastly, why don't you use the ochre color for your clothes when you prescribe it for your sannyasins?*

You ask, "It is okay if a sannyasin play-acts as a businessman, but can he play-act in the same way as a black marketeer?

If he does, it would not be that harmful. He would have indulged in black marketing if he were not a sannyasin, so it would not be that harmful if he also play-acts as a black marketeer. But I think that a person who has the courage to take sannyas, and who is going to make a great experiment in his life, and who is ready to play-act as a businessman, will not play-act as a black marketeer. Because to indulge in black marketing one will have to be a doer; play-acting is not enough. The more evil you want to indulge in, the more of a doer you have to be, because evil is painful. To go into it, you will need to be involved in it, to be deeply committed to it. You cannot play-act stabbing a man with a knife, because another man's life will be at stake, and play-acting at real stabbing is meaningless.

If you understand the idea of play-acting you will know that even if a sannyasin indulges in black marketing he will not be harming anybody, because if he remains a black marketeer as a sannyasin, it means that he has been a black marketeer and would have remained one if he had not taken sannyas. Therefore you need not be unnecessarily concerned about it. The greater possibility is that one who is inspired with the thought of sannyas will not play-act as a black marketeer; he cannot. The wisdom of sannyas, its awareness, will guide him and his actions. He will play-act only at that which is worth doing, which is his responsibility and which he cannot shirk without putting those he is responsible for in great difficulty. He will not do more than that. Play-acting will be confined to that which is utterly necessary and which he must do. Unnecessary things will drop by themselves.

You also want to know why I don't wear ochre clothes. I don't use ochre knowingly. Firstly, it is so because in my case sannyas happened long before I knew the ochre robe was necessary for sannyas to happen. And it became meaningless after sannyas had already happened; there was no reason for me to use ochre clothes then. Secondly, if I wear ochre clothes and then I ask you to do so, that would mean I am anxious to impose my kind of clothes on you. I have, however, no wish to impose myself on anybody in any manner. I don't want you to imitate the way I live, the way I function. If I wear ochre clothes and then commend them to you, it would perhaps mean I am attached to them and therefore I admire them. But because I don't use them, it is obvious that I don't have any attachment to them and commend them purely for objective and scientific reasons. Since I don't use them I can be objective and impartial about them.

You say that it was out of bliss that Shankaracharya took sannyas. I don't accept this suggestion. Shankaracharya is very negative towards the world. His negativity is so deep that he is always trying to prove that the world is mere illusion. To assert over and over again that the world is false, that it is illusory, that it is not, evidently means he is in great difficulty with this world. It offends him so much he cannot do without denying it, without calling it dream stuff. Shankar's negativity is much too deep.

Of course, Shankar talks of bliss, but there is a fundamental difference between my bliss and his. He talks of a bliss which is attained after renouncing this world, which comes after shedding the illusion and attaining the supreme. But I talk of a bliss which is attained through the acceptance of all, of the whole, of this world and God together. I am for total acceptance of all that is. And there is no place for negativity in my vision; I am absolutely against renunciation. Shankar's bliss lies in the renunciation of the world; his bliss is limited. For me bliss is so immense, so infinite, that it includes the world and God and everything else in it. For me bliss never negates anything.

The last thing. When I said, "my sannyasin" it was not a slip of the tongue. My tongue is strange, it rarely slips. The first time one friend referred to someone as my sannyasin I asked him not to. But I said it for a reason: that a sannyasin cannot be mine or anybody else's. But when I use the term "my sannyasin" the second time, it was certainly not a slip of my tongue. No sannyasin belongs to me, but I can belong to all sannyasins whose witness I have consented to be. And I have a special relationship with the sannyasins of bliss I have been talking about. I don't expect them to be attached to me; I have no expectation from them that they should relate with me in any manner. But I do have a relationship with them, because I see in them the future of sannyas. It is only through the kind of sannyasin they are that there is hope for sannyas in the future.

> Questioner: You said that sannyas is a direct relationship between a sannyasin and God, and that you are just a witness to it. But then the question arises if your witnessing will not create a kind of distrust in sannyas. Please explain.

You are right when you ask: If sannyas is a matter between you and God, what is the use of my being witness to it?

There is no use if you really understand that sannyas is a matter between you and God, but the very fact that you have come to me says there is no relationship between you and God yet. At least you are not aware of it; otherwise you would not have wandered to this distant place.

Then I am going to be your witness.

> Questioner: Don't you think that initiation into sannyas will lead to the formation of a sect around you?

You think it will lead to the formation of a sect. No, it will not. To form a sect certain things are essential. To form a sect one needs a Master, a scripture, a doctrine and an adjective for the sect. Besides these, one also needs a blind, dogmatic belief that one's doctrine alone is right and everything else is utterly wrong. None of these things are here.

The sannyasin of my vision is not going to have any adjective like the rest of the sannyasins, who are either Hindus, Christians or Buddhists. And a sect cannot be formed without such an adjective; it is extremely difficult. I call a man a sannyasin who does not have a religion, who does not belong to any religion. And you cannot organize a sect without a religion. I call a man a sannyasin who has no scripture like the *Geeta* or the Bible, and who does not belong to a temple, church or *gurudwara*. And without them a sect becomes impossible.

It should be our great endeavor to see that no sect is born, because nothing has harmed religion as much as these sects have. Sects have done more harm to religion than irreligion itself. In fact, a genuine coin is always harmed by its counterfeits; nothing else can harm it so much. Similarly, if ever true religion is harmed, it is harmed only by pseudo religions. And a tremendous awareness is needed to avoid this danger.

A sect is not going to emerge in the wake of our efforts, because no one is my disciple and I am no one's guru or Master. And if I am offering to be a witness to some people taking sannyas, it is because, right now, they cannot connect with God directly. And I ask them to be on their own and not to disturb me any longer when they become directly connected with the supreme. I don't want unnecessary troubles; I have no axe to grind. It is great if you can relate with existence on your own; nothing is greater than this. Then the question of someone being a witness does not arise. And it is of the highest.

Questioner: Is there a special significance in changing one's name and wearing a mala given by you?

Yes, it has significance, great significance. The change of name has great significance for a sannyasin. It is an index, a symbol. Everything in our life is symbolic. You have a name; you are identified with this name. This name has become your symbol; it is identified with your individuality. Your name has an association with everything that you have been before yesterday. Changing the name of a sannyasin means we disconnect him from his old identity, from his old associations. We say to him, now you are not the same as you were before yesterday. Now you are starting on a new journey with a new name, a new identity.

Since ancient times they have had a small ceremony at the time of one's initiation into sannyas. It is a kind of cremation ceremony. Exactly as we bathe a dead body and shave its head before putting it on the pyre, a candidate for sannyas was bathed and shaved and then put on a pyre of wood. People stood around the pyre, like witnesses at his initiation, telling him, "Let all that you have been before now be burned in the fire, and what will emerge from this pyre will be an altogether new you. You are now reborn, you are now a *dwija*, a twice-born."

It was a ritual, a symbolic ritual. And because it was symbolic you can think there would be no harm if you did not go through this ritual. You can do without it provided you have a deep understanding of the thing. With deep understanding we need no rituals whatsoever. But where is that understanding?

The change of name is helpful in breaking your old identity. With the changed name you suddenly come to know that you are not the same person now. Every time, while you are on the road, somebody calls you by your new name, not by the old one, you will be startled to learn that you have ceased to have your old identity. Every day your identification with your old life will wither; every day a new man will come into being in his place. You will be reminded again and again that you are now on a new journey. The change of name is useful for this purpose.

Secondly, you want to know about the mala and its meaning. Nothing in this universe is meaningless. It is different if something loses its meaning through long usage. Everything wears out and becomes dirty after being in currency for a long time. The same has happened with the mala. But it is meaningful.

There are one hundred and eight beads in a mala. Do you know what this number stands for? There are one hundred and eight techniques of meditation, ways of meditation, and this mala will be with you to remind you of the hundred and eight possible paths to meditation. And if you and I continue to be related I am going to acquaint you with all the different techniques of meditation.

The hundred and eight beads of the mala represent all the techniques of meditation there are.

And when a witness like me gives this mala to an initiate into sannyas, he only tells him through this symbol that while he has explained only one path to the unknown to him, there are really many others, as many as one hundred and seven. So don't be in a hurry to say that people who are on paths other than yours are wrong. And always remember that there are countless paths, all of which lead to the divine.

At the bottom of the mala hangs a large bead which says that whatever path you follow you will reach, because all paths lead to the one, to the ultimate one. So all the beads, including the large one, are symbolic and meaningful.

When someone in our family marries a woman and brings her home as his wife, we change the name of the woman. Why? Just to break her identity with the past. She comes from another family where she was born and brought up, where she was educated and conditioned in their ways of life. Her whole past is associated with her name, so we change her name after she joins her new family. Thus a new journey of her life begins. Thus she is asked to forget her past, her old associations and conditionings and begin her life anew in a new family, a new environment, a new world. Now, around her new name a new crystallization will take place.

Whether it is a mala or a new name—there are many such things—they are very meaningful for the journey of sannyas. Unfortunately they have fallen in disrepute through long use, and that is why I speak against them over and over again. I criticize the uselessness to which they have been reduced. You cannot understand my difficulty in this matter. My difficulty is that I know how useful they are and how useless they have become. So I will continue to speak both for and against them. That is my difficulty and destiny, and I would like you to understand it.

I will continue to speak against many things, because they have been rendered useless. And yet through different ways I will do everything to resurrect them, because I, for one, know their basic significance, and their basic significance has to be saved. So both processes will go together. For this reason I will lose many of my friends, and many of them will turn into my enemies. But this will go on, and there is no way to stop it.

If some traditionalist will come to me and talk about the importance of the mala, I am going to simply decry it.

I have been amazed to see that I have criticized the mala in the presence of the top sannyasins of this country and none of them had a word to say in its favor. I expected them to say some good things about it, but they could not, although each of them had a mala around his neck and almost worshipped it. Since there is no one who can say something in its favor, I will have to do it myself. There is no other way.

BOOKS BY BHAGWAN SHREE RAJNEESH
PUBLISHED BY
RAJNEESH FOUNDATION
INTERNATIONAL

For a more complete descriptive catalog of the books published by Rajneesh Foundation International, contact:

> Rajneesh Foundation International
> P.O. Box 9
> Rajneeshpuram, Oregon 97741 USA
> (503) 489-3462

ACADEMY OF RAJNEESHISM TITLES

Rajneeshism	$3.00 pb
an introduction to Bhagwan Shree Rajneesh and His religion	
THE RAJNEESH BIBLE, Volume 1	6.95 pb
THE RAJNEESH BIBLE, Volume 2	6.95 pb
THE RAJNEESH BIBLE, Volume 3	6.95 pb
The Book	
an introduction to the teachings of Bhagwan Shree Rajneesh	
Series I from A-H	5.95 pb
Series II from I-Q	5.95 pb
Series III from P-Z	5.95 pb

BIOGRAPHIES

Books I have Loved	pb
Notes of a Madman	4.50 qp
Glimpses of a Golden Childhood	qp

cl - clothbound
qp - quality paperback
pb - paperback

PHOTOBIOGRAPHIES

The Sound of Running Water	100.00 cl
a photobiography of	
Bhagwan Shree Rajneesh	
and His work, 1974-1978	
This Very Place The Lotus Paradise	100.00 cl
a photobiography of	
Bhagwan Shree Rajneesh	
and His work, 1978-1984	

THE BAULS

The Beloved	
Volume 1	15.95 cl
Volume 2	15.95 cl

BUDDHA

The Book of the Books	
the Dhammapada	
Volume 1	15.95 qp
Volume 2	4.95 pb
Volume 3	4.95 pb
Volume 4	4.95 pb
The Diamond Sutra	19.50 cl
the Vajrachchedika Prajnaparamita Sutra	
The Discipline of Transcendence	
the Sutra of 42 Chapters	
Volume 1	16.50 cl
Volume 2	16.50 cl
Volume 3	16.50 cl
Volume 4	16.50 cl
The Heart Sutra	16.95 cl
the Prajnaparamita Hridayam Sutra	

BUDDHIST MASTERS

The Book of Wisdom	
Atisha's Seven Points of Mind Training	
Volume 1	9.95 qp
Volume 2	4.95 pb
The White Lotus	17.95 cl
the sayings of Bodhidharma	13.95 qp

EARLY DISCOURSES AND WRITINGS

A Cup of Tea	4.95 pb
letters to disciples	
From Sex to Superconsciousness	15.50 cl
And Now, and Here	
Volume 1	4.95 pb
Volume 2	4.95 pb
Beware of Socialism	3.95 pb
Krishna: The Man and His Philosophy	5.95 pb
The Long and the Short and the All	4.95 pb
The Perfect Way	3.95 pb
In Search of the Miraculous	
Volume 1	4.95 pb

HASSIDISM

The Art of Dying	14.95 cl
The True Sage	16.50 cl

INITIATION TALKS
between Master and disciple

Hammer On The Rock	22.50 cl
(December 10, 1975 - January 15, 1976)	
Above All Don't Wobble	21.95 cl
(January 16 - February 12, 1976)	
Nothing To Lose But Your Head	19.50 cl
(February 13 - March 12, 1976)	
Be Realistic: Plan For a Miracle	19.95 cl
(March 13 - April 6, 1976)	
Get Out of Your Own Way	18.95 cl
(April 7 - May 2, 1976)	
Beloved of My Heart	19.95 cl
(May 3 - 28, 1976)	

cl - clothbound
qp - quality paperback
pb - paperback

The Cypress in the Courtyard *(May 29 - June 27, 1976)*	18.95 cl
A Rose is a Rose is a Rose *(June 28 - July 27, 1976)*	18.95 cl
Dance Your Way to God *(July 28 - August 20, 1976)*	19.95 cl
The Passion for the Impossible *(August 21 - September 18, 1976)*	18.95 cl
The Great Nothing *(September 19 - October 11, 1976)*	18.95 cl
God is Not for Sale *(October 12 - November 7, 1976)*	18.95 cl
The Shadow of the Whip *(November 8 - December 3, 1976)*	18.95 cl
Blessed are the Ignorant *(December 4 - 31, 1976)*	19.50 cl
The Buddha Disease *(January 1977)*	21.50 cl
What Is, Is, What Ain't, Ain't *(February 1977)*	18.95 qp
The Zero Experience *(March 1977)*	21.50 cl
For Madmen Only (Price of Admission: Your Mind) *(April 1977)*	19.50 cl
This Is It *(May 1977)*	19.95 cl
The Further Shore *(June 1977)*	22.95 cl
Far Beyond the Stars *(July 1977)*	20.95 cl
The No Book (No Buddha, No Teaching, No Discipline) *(August 1977)*	26.95 cl
Don't Just Do Something, Sit There *(September 1977)*	25.50 cl

Only Losers Can Win in this Game *(October 1977)*	23.50 cl
The Open Secret *(November 1977)*	25.50 cl
The Open Door *(December 1977)*	18.95 qp
The Sun Behind the Sun Behind the Sun *(January 1978)*	21.95 cl
Believing the Impossible Before Breakfast *(February 1978)*	22.95 cl
Don't Bite My Finger, Look Where I'm Pointing *(March 1978)*	14.95 qp
Let Go! *(April 1978)*	22.95 cl
The 99 Names of Nothingness *(May 1978)*	18.95 qp
The Madman's Guide to Enlightenment *(June 1978)*	18.95 qp
Don't Look Before You Leap *(July 1978)*	4.95 pb
Hallelujah! *(August 1978)*	25.95 cl 18.95 qp
God's Got a Thing About You *(September 1978)*	4.95 pb
The Tongue-Tip Taste of Tao *(October 1978)*	26.95 cl
The Sacred Yes *(November 1978)*	4.95 pb
Turn On, Tune In and Drop the Lot *(December 1978)*	18.95 qp
Zorba the Buddha *(January 1979)*	21.95 qp

cl - clothbound
qp - quality paperback
pb - paperback

Won't You Join the Dance? *(February 1979)*	4.95 pb
You Ain't Seen Nothin' Yet *(March 1979)*	4.95 pb
The Shadow of the Bamboo *(April 1979)*	3.95 pb
Just Around the Corner *(May 1979)*	3.95 pb
Snap Your Fingers, Slap Your Face and Wake Up! *(June 1979)*	3.95 pb
The Rainbow Bridge *(July 1979)*	4.95 pb
Don't Let Yourself be Upset by the Sutra, Rather Upset the Sutra Yourself *(August, September, 1979)*	5.95 pb
The Sound of One Hand Clapping *(March 1981)*	22.50 qp

JESUS

Come Follow Me
the sayings of Jesus

Volume 1	12.95 cl
Volume 2	12.95 cl
Volume 3	12.95 cl
Volume 4	12.95 cl

I Say Unto You
the sayings of Jesus

Volume 1	19.50 cl
	4.95 pb
Volume 2	15.95 qp

The Mustard Seed *the gospel of Thomas*	5.95 pb

KABIR

The Divine Melody	16.50 cl
Ecstasy: The Forgotten Language	16.50 cl
The Fish in the Sea is Not Thirsty	22.95 cl

cl - clothbound
qp - quality paperback
pb - paperback

Until You Die	15.95 cl

The Wisdom of the Sands

Volume 1	19.95 cl
	15.95 qp
Volume 2	19.95 cl
	15.95 qp

TANTRA

The Book of the Secrets
Vigyana Bhairava Tantra

Volume 4	7.95 qp
Volume 5	4.95 pb

Tantra, Spirituality & Sex	3.95 pb

excerpts from The Book of the Secrets

Tantra: The Supreme Understanding	4.95 pb

Tilopa's Song of Mahamudra

The Tantra Vision
the Royal Song of Saraha

Volume 1	16.50 cl
Volume 2	16.50 cl

TAO

The Empty Boat	16.50 cl

the stories of Chuang Tzu

The Secret of Secrets
the Secret of the Golden Flower

Volume 1	16.95 qp
Volume 2	4.95 pb

Tao: The Golden Gate

Volume 1	4.95 pb
Volume 2	4.95 pb

Tao: The Pathless Path
the stories of Lieh Tzu

Volume 1	17.95 cl
	15.95 qp
Volume 2	17.95 cl
	15.95 qp

Tao: The Three Treasures
the Tao Te Ching of Lao Tzu

Volume 1	4.95 pb
Volume 2	15.95 cl
Volume 3	15.95 cl
Volume 4	15.95 cl

When The Shoe Fits   16.50 cl
the stories of Chuang Tzu

THE UPANISHADS

I Am That   5.95 pb
Isa Upanishad

The Ultimate Alchemy
Atma Pooja Upanishad

Volume 1	18.95 cl
Volume 2	18.95 cl

Vedanta: Seven Steps to Samadhi   16.50 cl
Akshya Upanishad

Philosophia Ultima   4.95 pb
Mandukya Upanishad

WESTERN MYSTICS

The Hidden Harmony   16.95 cl
the fragments of Heraclitus

The New Alchemy: To Turn You On   15.50 cl
Mabel Collins' Light on the Path

Philosophia Perennis
the Golden Verses of Pythagoras

Volume 1	19.95 cl
	15.95 qp
Volume 2	15.95 qp

Guida Spirituale   4.95 pb
the Desiderata

Theologia Mystica   4.95 pb
the treatise of St. Dionysius

cl - clothbound
qp - quality paperback
pb - paperback

YOGA

Yoga: The Alpha and the Omega
the Yoga Sutras of Patanjali

Volume 1	16.95 cl
Volume 2	16.95 cl
Volume 3	16.95 cl
Volume 4	16.95 cl
Volume 5	16.95 cl
Volume 6	16.95 cl
Volume 7	16.95 cl
Volume 8	16.95 cl
Volume 9	16.95 cl
Volume 10	16.95 cl

Yoga: The Science of the Soul
(Originally titled Yoga: The Alpha and the Omega)

Volume 1	4.95 pb
Volume 2	4.95 pb
Volume 3	4.95 pb

ZEN

Ah, This!	8.95 qp
Ancient Music in the Pines	15.50 cl
And the Flowers Showered	16.95 cl
	5.95 pb
Dang Dang Doko Dang	14.50 cl
The First Principle	17.95 cl
The Grass Grows By Itself	15.50 cl
	4.95 qp
Nirvana: the Last Nightmare	17.50 cl
No Water, No Moon	14.50 cl
	4.95 pb
Returning to the Source	15.95 cl
A Sudden Clash of Thunder	16.50 cl
The Sun Rises in the Evening	17.95 cl
Zen: The Path of Paradox	
Volume 1	16.95 cl
Volume 2	16.95 cl
Volume 3	16.95 cl

Zen: The Special Transmission   4.95 pb
Zen stories

ZEN MASTERS

Hsin Hsin Ming: The Book of Nothing   4.95 pb
Discourses on the faith-mind of Sosan

The Search   14.95 cl
the Ten Bulls of Zen

Take It Easy
poems of Ikkyu
Volume 1   21.95 cl
Volume 2   21.95 cl

This Very Body the Buddha   16.95 cl
Hakuin's Song of Meditation

cl - clothbound
qp - quality paperback
pb - paperback

Please make payment to:
Rajneesh Foundation International
P.O. Box 9
Rajneeshpuram, OR 97741 USA

BOOKS FROM OTHER PUBLISHERS

ENGLISH EDITIONS

UNITED KINGDOM

The Book of the Secrets (volume 1)
(Thames & Hudson)

Roots and Wings
(Routledge & Kegan Paul)

The Supreme Doctrine
(Routledge & Kegan Paul)

Tao: The Three Treasures (volume 1)
(Wildwood House)

UNITED STATES OF AMERICA

The Book of the Secrets (volumes 1-3)
(Harper & Row)

The Great Challenge
(Grove Press)

Hammer on the Rock
(Grove Press)

I Am The Gate
(Harper & Row)

Journey Toward the Heart (Original title:
Until You Die)
(Harper & Row)

Meditation: The Art of Ecstasy
(Harper & Row)

The Mustard Seed
(Harper & Row)

My Way: The Way of the White Clouds
(Grove Press)

The Psychology of the Esoteric
(Harper & Row)

Roots and Wings
(Routledge & Kegan Paul)

The Supreme Doctrine
(Routledge & Kegan Paul)

Words Like Fire (Original title:
Come Follow Me, volume 1)
(Harper & Row)

BOOKS ON BHAGWAN

The Awakened One: The Life and Work
of Bhagwan Shree Rajneesh
by Swami Satya Vedant
(Harper & Row)

FOREIGN LANGUAGE EDITIONS

DANISH

TRANSLATIONS

Hemmelighedernes Bog (volume 1)
(Borgens Forlag)

Hu-Meditation Og Kosmisk Orgasme
(Borgens Forlag)

DUTCH

TRANSLATIONS

Drink Mij
(Ankh-Hermes)

Het Boek Der Geheimen (volumes 1-5)
(Mirananda)

Geen Water, Geen Maan
(Mirananda)

Gezaaid In Goede Aarde
(Ankh-Hermes)

Ik Ben De Poort
(Ankh-Hermes)

Ik Ben De Zee Die Je Zoekt
(Ankh-Hermes)

Meditatie: De Kunst van Innerlijke Extase
(Mirananda)

Mijn Weg, De Weg van de Witte Wolk
(Arcanum)

Het Mosterdzaad (volumes 1 & 2)
(Mirananda)

Het Oranje Meditatieboek
(Ankh-Hermes)

Psychologie en Evolutie
(Ankh-Hermes)

Tantra: Het Allerhoogste Inzicht
(Ankh-Hermes)

Tantra, Spiritualiteit en Seks
(Ankh-Hermes)

De Tantra Visie (volume 1)
(Arcanum)

Tau
(Ankh-Hermes)

Totdat Je Sterft
(Ankh-Hermes)

De Verborgen Harmonie
(Mirananda)

Volg Mij
(Ankh-Hermes)

Zoeken naar de Stier
(Ankh-Hermes)

FRENCH
TRANSLATIONS

L'éveil à la Conscience Cosmique
(Dangles)

Je Suis La Porte
(EPI)

Le Livre Des Secrets (volume 1)
(Soleil Orange)

La Meditation Dynamique
(Dangles)

GERMAN
TRANSLATIONS

Auf der Suche
(Sambuddha Verlag)

Das Buch der Geheimnisse (volume 1)
(Heyne Taschenbuch)

Das Orangene Buch
(Sambuddha Verlag)

Der Freund
(Sannyas Verlag)

Sprung ins Unbekannte
(Sannyas Verlag)

Ekstase: Die vergessene Sprache
(Herzschlag Verlag, formerly Ki-Buch)

Esoterische Psychologie
(Sannyas Verlag)

Rebellion der Seele
(Sannyas Verlag)

Ich bin der Weg
(Rajneesh Verlag)

Intelligenz des Herzens
(Herzschlag Verlag, formerly Ki-Buch)

Jesus aber schwieg
(Sannyas Verlag)

Jesus M-der Menschensohn
(Sannyas Verlag)

Kein Wasser, Kein Mond
(Herzschlag Verlag, formerly Ki-Buch)

Komm und folge mir
(Sannyas Verlag Droemer Knaur)

Meditation: Die Kunst zu sich selbst zu finden
(Heyne Verlag)

Mein Weg: Der Weg der weissen Wolke
(Herzschlag Verlag, formerly Ki-Buch)

Mit Wurzeln und mit Flügeln
(Edition Lotus)

Nicht bevor du stirbst
(Edition Gyandip, Switzerland)

Die Schuhe auf dem Kopf
(Edition Lotus)

Das Klatschen der einen Hand
(Edition Gyandip, Switzerland)

Nirvana: Die Letzte Hürde auf dem Weg
(Rajneesh Foundation Europe)

Vorsicht Sozialismus
(Rajneesh Foundation Europe)

Spirituelle Entwicklung und Sexualität
(Fischer)

Vom Sex zum Kosmischen Bewusstsein
(New Age)

Yoga: Alpha und Omega
(Edition Gyandip, Switzerland)

Sprengt den Fels der Unbewusstheit
(Fischer)

Tantra: Die höchste Einsicht
(Sambuddha Verlag)

Tantra Religion und Sex
formerly published as
Tantrische Liebeskunst
(Sannyas Verlag)

Die Alchemie der Verwandlung
(Edition Lotus)

Die verborgene Harmonie
(Sannyas Verlag)

Was ist Meditation?
(Sannyas Verlag)

Die Gans ist raus!
(Rajneesh Foundation Europe)

Rajneeshismus - Bhagwan Shree Rajneesh und
seine Religion
*(Eine Einfuhrung
Rajneesh Foundation International, USA)*

GREEK

TRANSLATION

I Krifi Armonia (The Hidden Harmony)
(Emmanual Rassoulis)

HEBREW

TRANSLATION

Tantra: The Supreme Understanding
(Massada)

ITALIAN

TRANSLATIONS

L Armonia Nascosta (volumes 1 & 2)
(Re Nudo)

Dieci Storie Zen di Bhagwan Shree Rajneesh
(Né Acqua Né Luna)
(Il Fiore d'Oro)

La Dottrina Suprema
(Rizzoli)

Dimensioni Oltre il Conosciuto
(Mediterranee)

Estasi: Il Linguaggio Dimenticato
(Riza Libri)

Io Sono La Soglia
(Mediterranee)

Il Libro Arancione
(Mediterranee)

Il Libro dei Segreti
(Bompiani)

Meditazione Dinamica:
L'Arte dell'Estasi Interiore
(Mediterranee)

Nirvana: L'Ultimo Incubo
(Basaia)

La Nuova Alchimia
(Psiche)

Philosophia Perennis
(Ecig)

La Rivoluzione Interiore
(Mediterranee)

La Ricerca
(La Salamandra)

Il Seme della Ribellione (volumes 1-3)
(Rajneesh Foundation, Italy)

Tantra: La Comprensione Suprema
(Bompiani)

Tantra Spiritualita e Sesso
(Rajneesh Foundation Italy)

Tao: I Tre Tesori (volumes 1-3)
(Re Nudo)

Tecniche di Liberazione
(La Salamandra)

Semi di Saggezza
(SugarCo)

BOOKS ON BHAGWAN

Rajneeshismo
una introduzione a
  Bhagwan Shree Rajneesh a sua religione
  (Rajneesh Foundation International, USA)

JAPANESE

TRANSLATIONS

Dance Your Way to God
(Rajneesh Publications)

The Empty Boat (volumes 1 & 2)
(Rajneesh Publications)

From Sex to Superconsciousness
(Rajneesh Publications)

The Grass Grows by Itself
(Fumikura)

The Heart Sutra
(Merkmal)

Meditation: The Art of Ecstasy
(Merkmal)

The Mustard Seed
(Merkmal)

My Way: The Way of the White Clouds
(Rajneesh Publications)

The Orange Book
(Wholistic Therapy Institute)

The Search
(Merkmal)

The Beloved (volumes 1 & 2)
(Merkmal)

Tantra: The Supreme Understanding
(Merkmal)

Tao: The Three Treasures (volumes 1-4)
(Merkmal)

Until You Die
(Fumikura)

Rajneeshism
*an introduction to
    Bhagwan Shree Rajneesh and His religion
    (Rajneesh Foundation International, USA)*

PORTUGUESE (BRAZIL)

TRANSLATIONS

O Cipreste No Jardim
(Cultrix)

Dimensões Além do Conhecido
(Soma)

O Livro Dos Segredos (volume 1)
(Maha Lakshmi Editora)

Eu Sou A Porta
(Pensamento)

A Harmonia Oculta
(Pensamento)

Meditacão: A Arte Do Extase
(Cultrix)

Meu Caminho:
    O Comainho Das Nuvens Brancas
(Tao Livraria & Editora)

Nem Agua, Nem Lua
(Pensamento)

O Livro Orange
(Soma)

Palavras De Fogo
(Global/Ground)

A Psicologia Do Esotérico
(Tao Livraria & Editora)

A Semente De Mostarda (volumes 1 & 2)
(Tao Livraria & Editora)

Sufis: O Povo do Caminho
(Maha Laxshmi Editora)

Tantra: Sexo E Espiritualidade
(Agora)

Tantra: A Supreme Comprensao
(Cultrix)

Antes Que Voce Morra
(Maha Lakshmi Editora)

Extase: A Linguagem Esquecida
(Global)

Arte de Morrer
(Global)

SPANISH

TRANSLATIONS

Introducción al Mundo del Tantra
(Colección Tantra)

Meditación: El Arte del Extasis
(Colección Tantra)

Psicológia de lo Esotérico:
La Nueva Evolución del Hombre
(Cuatro Vientos Editorial)

¿Qué Es Meditación?
(Koan/Roselló Impresions)

Yo Soy La Puerta
(Editorial Diana)

Sòlo Un Cielo (volumes 1 & 2)
(Colección Tantra)

El Sutra del Corazon
(Sarvogeet)

Ven, Sigueme (volume 1)
(Sagaro)

SWEDISH

TRANSLATION

Den Väldiga Utmaningen
(Livskraft)

OVERSEAS DISTRIBUTORS

AUSTRALIA

RAJNEESH FOUNDATION OF AUSTRALIA
P.O. Box 11, Paddington, NSW 2010 Australia

CANADA

ASTRAL MUSE
5161 Ave. Du Parc, Montreal, Quebec H2V 4G3
Tel: (514) 270-4182

INDIA

RAJNEESHDHAM NEO-SANNYAS COMMUNE
17 Koregaon Park, Poona 411 001 India

AUM RAJNEESH MEDITATION CENTER
1st Floor, 31 Israil Mohalla, Near Satkar Hotel
Masjid Bunder Road, Bombay 400 009 India

RAJYOGA RAJNEESH MEDITATION CENTER
C-5/44 Safdarjang Development Area
Opp. ITT, Palam Rd., New Delhi 110 016 India

THE NETHERLANDS

VERENIGING DE STAD RAJNEESH
NEO-SANNYAS COMMUNE, I.O.
Prinsengracht 719, 1017 JW Amsterdam, Netherlands
Tel: 05207-1261

SWITZERLAND

KOTA RAJNEESH NEO-SANNYAS COMMUNE
Baumackerstrasse 42
CH 8050 Zürich, Switzerland
Tel: (01) 31-21 600

WEST GERMANY

RAJNEESH SERVICES GmbH
Lütticher Strasse 34
5000 Cologne 1 West Germany
Tel: 0221-519451-2

RAJNEESH MEDITATION CENTERS, ASHRAMS AND COMMUNES

There are many Rajneesh Meditation Centers throughout the world which can be contacted for information about the teachings of Bhagwan Shree Rajneesh in English and in foreign languages.

USA

RAJNEESH FOUNDATION INTERNATIONAL
P.O. Box 9, Rajneeshpuram, Oregon 97741.
Tel: (503) 489-3301

UTSAVA RAJNEESH MEDITATION CENTER
20062 Laguna Canyon Rd., Laguna Beach, CA 92651.
Tel: (714) 497-4877

AUSTRALIA

MESTO RAJNEESH NEO-SANNYAS COMMUNE
4A Ormond St., Paddington, N.S.W. 2021
Tel: (2) 336570

RAJNEESHGRAD NEO-SANNYAS COMMUNE
6 Collie Street, Fremantle 6160, W.A.
Tel: (9) 336-2422

BRAZIL

PURNAM RAJNEESH MEDITATION CENTER
Caixa Postal 1946, Porto Alegre, RS 90000.

UDGITI RAJNEESH MEDITATION CENTER
Rua Macaubal 7, Sumaré, SP 01256.
Tel: 62-9257

CANADA

SHANTI SADAN RAJNEESH MEDITATION CENTER
5161 Ave. du Parc, Montreal, Quebec H2V 4G3.
Tel: (514) 270-4182

EAST AFRICA

PREETAM RAJNEESH MEDITATION CENTER
Spring Valley Estate, P.O. Box 10256
Nairobi, Kenya. Tel: 582093, 29722

INDIA

RAJNEESHDHAM NEO-SANNYAS COMMUNE
17 Koregaon Park, Poona 411 001, MS.
Tel: 60953, 60954

RAJYOGA RAJNEESH MEDITATION CENTER
C5/44 Safdarjang Development Area,
Palam Road, New Delhi 110 016

JAPAN

SHANTIYUGA RAJNEESH SANNYAS ASHRAM
Sky Mansion 2F, 1-34-1 Ookayama, Meguro-ku. Tokyo 152.
Tel: (03) 724-9631

NETHERLANDS

DE STAD RAJNEESH NEO-SANNYAS COMMUNE
Prinsengracht 719, 1017 JW Amsterdam
Tel: (20) 766212/261674

SWITZERLAND

KOTA RAJNEESH NEO-SANNYAS COMMUNE
Baumackerstr. 42, 8050 Zurich. Tel: (01) 3121600

WEST GERMANY

BAILE RAJNEESH NEO-SANNYAS COMMUNE
Karolinenstr. 7-9, 2000 Hamburg 6.
Tel· (040) 432140

DÖRFCHEN RAJNEESH NEO-SANNYAS COMMUNE
Dahlmannstr. 9, 1000 Berlin 12.
Tel: (030) 32000710

RAJNEESH BYEN NEO-SANNYAS COMMUNE
Klenzestr. 41, 8000 Munich 5.
Tel: (89) 2609576

WIOSKA RAJNEESH NEO-SANNYAS COMMUNE
Lütticherstr. 33/35, 5000 Cologne 1.
Tel: (221) 574070

"Fall in tune with the
energy of the person . . .
fall in tune so deeply
that his unconscious,
her unconscious,
starts stirring your unconscious,
and in your unconscious,
things start arising
— visualizations.
Those visualizations
will be meaningful . . .
but remember
you are not predicting the future.
So you can use this
for making people
more alert and more meditative,
more responsible
for their lives . . ."

Bhagwan Shree Rajneesh
THE FURTHER SHORE

Rajneesh Neo-Tarot

A Totally new concept in Tarot — 60 luminous cards inspired by the living Master, Bhagwan Shree Rajneesh.

Each card represents one of life's major lessons. Based on stories from Zen, Sufi, Christian, Hindu, Tibetan Buddhist, Tantric, Hassidic and Greek religious traditions, given new meaning by the clarity and wisdom of Bhagwan Shree Rajneesh.

A booklet of instructions and stories giving the key to the meaning of each card is included.

1983 Rajneesh Foundation International

ISBN 0-88050-701-2

$14.95

Please make remittance payable to:
Rajneesh Foundation International
P.O. Box 9, Rajneeshpuram, OR 97741 USA

THE
RAJNEESH BIBLE
Volume I

BHAGWAN SHREE RAJNEESH

After 1,315 days of silence, Bhagwan Shree Rajneesh started to speak in an unprecedented discourse series—because "... the picture I have been painting my whole life needs a few touches here and there to complete it . . . I want to now speak spontaneously, directly, immediately, the simple truth that is mine . . ."

THIRTY COMPLETE DISCOURSES
FROM THE RAJNEESH BIBLE,
VOLUME I

ISBN: 0-88050-200-2 $6.95 paperback

THIS VERY PLACE THE LOTUS PARADISE

by
Bhagwan Shree Rajneesh

Covering the period March 1978-March 1984, this beautifully illustrated photo-biography provides an indepth account of the life and work of Bhagwan Shree Rajneesh and the world-wide community which has arisen around His vision. Many never-before-published color photographs and more than 500 original black and white photographs.

$100 clothbound 564 pages   ISBN 0-88050-705-5

Please make payment to:
Rajneesh Foundation International
P.O. Box 9
Rajneeshpuram, OR 97741 USA